Industrial Economics and Organization

Industrial Economics and Organization

A European Perspective

David Jacobson and Bernadette Andréosso-O'Callaghan

The McGraw-Hill Book Companies

London · New York · St Louis · San Francisco · Auckland · Bogotá · Caracas · Lisbon
Madrid · Mexico · Milan · Montreal · New Delhi · Panama · Paris · San Juan · São Paulo
Singapore · Sydney · Tokyo · Toronto

Published by

McGRAW-HILL Publishing Company

Shoppenhangers Road, Maidenhead, Berkshire SL6 2QL, England
Telephone 01628 23432
Facsimile 01628 770224

British Library Cataloguing in Publication Data
Jacobson, David
 Industrial economics and organisation: a European perspective
 1. Industrial organization (Economic theory)
 2. Microeconomics 3. Europe – Economic conditions – 1945–
 I. Title II. Andreosso-O'Callaghan, Bernadette

 ISBN 0 07 707889-6

Library of Congress Cataloging-in-Publication Data
Jacobson, David
 Industrial economics and organization: a European perspective/
David Jacobson and Bernadette Andréosso-O'Callaghan.
   p. cm.
 Includes bibliographical references.
 ISBN 0-07-707889-6 (pbk. : alk. paper)
 1. Industries – European Union countries. 2. Industrial policy – European Union countries.
3. Deregulation – European Union countries. 4. Industrial location – European Union countries.
5. Industrial organization – European Union countries. 6. Industrial organization (Economic theory)
I. Andréosso-O'Callaghan, Bernadette, II. Title.
HD2844.J33 1996
338.094–dc20
                    96-8430
                    CIP

Reprinted 1997

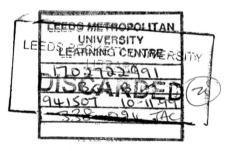

McGraw-Hill

A Division of The McGraw-Hill Companies

Typeset by Alden Bookset, Didcot, Oxon
Printed and bound in Great Britain at the University Press, Cambridge.

Printed on permanent paper in compliance with ISO Standard 9706

To
Yvonne, Daniel, Rebecca and Matthew
and
Frank, Aoife, Prisca and Peter

Contents

Acknowledgements

Very helpful comments were received from Professor Pierre Maillet, University of Lille, during the preparation of this book. We are indebted to Dr Patricia Conlon and Siun O'Keefe, University of Limerick, Department of Law, for providing information related to the legal aspects of the book. A number of colleagues at Dublin City University made suggestions which either improved the book, or would have improved the book if there had been time to act on them. In particular Dr Siobhain McGovern commented on Chapters 2, 3, 4 and 5, Billy Kelly on Chapters 4 and 6, and Professor Alastair Wood on part of Chapter 4. Other colleagues and friends who helped in various ways include Teresa Hogan, Ziene Mottiar, Rachel Hilliard, Deirdre Lavin, Breda Griffith, Professor Eunan O'Halpin, Phil Mulvaney, Sarah Ingle, Ciaran O'Hogartaigh, Gary Murphy, Anne Marie Rooney, Sheila Boughton, Dr Rory O'Donnell and Dr Jim Stewart in Dublin and Jack Hyams in London. Finally we are grateful to Marie Dineen, Mark Guilfoyle and Mary Dundon of the European Documentation Centre and the library of the University of Limerick, and Carmel O'Sullivan and Helen Fallon of the library of Dublin City University, for their valuable help.

1 Introduction

1.1 Scope and method of industrial economics in the European context

It is our purpose in this book to describe and analyse the theory and practice of what normally goes under the general heading of *industrial economics* (in Europe) or *industrial organization* (in the United States). We present both the traditional approaches and recent and alternative developments in the field. Many of these developments emanate from criticisms of the deterministic nature of the structure–conduct–performance (SCP) paradigm.

Many of the issues in this area of economics date back to Adam Smith in the eighteenth century. More recently, Cournot in the first half, and Marshall in the second half of the nineteenth century, from different parts of Europe, in different ways, laid foundations that, as we shall see, remain appropriate concerns in industrial economics today. In the twentieth century Chamberlin and Robinson, on either side of the Atlantic, influenced developments which led, among other things, to Bain's work on SCP. Thus, although in the United States, for example, industrial organization did not appear as a distinctive branch of economics until the 1930s, main concepts such as pricing strategies, and collusive and non-collusive behaviour, had already been formulated. (Edward Chamberlin and Edward Mason taught the first graduate courses in Industrial Organization in Harvard in 1936 (Grether, 1970).)

There have been two major traditional concerns of industrial economics. *First*, there has been a focus on the functioning of firms within various market structures. This includes the conduct or behaviour of firms, and their performance; the determinants and consequences of different market structures; and the relationship between behaviour and performance of firms, and the market structure within which firms operate. *Second*, both in separate chapters, and with frequent references throughout the texts, attention has been paid to the role governments play in influencing the organization of industry. These two areas remain central and our discussion of work on these and related issues forms a large part of this book.

In relation to *method*, the work of industrial economists was for many years subject to the predominant influence of the SCP paradigm. This was expressed in numerous econometric exercises testing relationships between aspects of S, C and P. Methodologically this approach was essentially *positive* rather than *normative*; it aimed to identify, for example, the extent to which various factors affected the conduct of firms. The conclusions were, however, often normative. In relation to structural determinants of firms' behaviour, for example, a positive finding that certain market structures are related to higher than average profits, led to the normative conclusion that where these structural characteristics prevailed, the state should intervene to prevent excessive profits. Such normative conclusions may not be appropriate, depending on one's political preferences. We do not avoid normative conclusions. However, we show as clearly as possible the reasons for these conclusions. More broadly we are aware of and, where appropriate, draw out the relationships between theory and policy (see the discussion on contestable markets in Chapter 2).

The SCP paradigm has itself changed and developed. The unidirectional causality sought in the early work has given way to acceptance of the possibility that structure, conduct and performance are interrelated in various ways. Even with these changes, however, much of the work in this tradition is less than satisfactory. The empirical work has had to become more complicated, but even the most sophisticated econometric tests have assisted little in explaining key features of how the industrial world operates and changes.

A major methodological response to these problems has been to focus on individual firms and their strategic behaviour as factors requiring explanation. At the same time, richer *theoretical depth* to industrial economics was demanded. *Game theory*, facilitating both a focus on firms' strategies, and a means of regenerating theoretical thinking, has become a cornerstone of modern industrial economics, and central to what has been called 'New Industrial Economics'. This book, without going into the mathematical complexities of game theory, provides an introduction, particularly to the use of the *payoff matrix* as a means of organizing thinking about strategic behaviour.

A recurrent theme in the book is the experience of European industry. What we mean by 'European industry' is the industry of the members of the European Union (EU).[1] Taking into account the January 1995 enlargement, the EU now has 15 members. Our data will in general include all the major countries within the Union and wherever possible will refer to all 15. We will also refer to, and where appropriate provide comparisons with, other countries in the continent of Europe, Asia and the United States.

1.2   Major concepts defined: firms, industries, industrial structure, industrial system

We will briefly define some of the key concepts. Of necessity, brief definitions involve simplification. In most cases the complexities of the concepts are drawn out in more detail later in the book.

The *firm* (enterprise, company or organization) is the basic decision-making entity. It converts inputs (capital, labour, raw materials, entrepreneurship) generally into marketable outputs. It may comprise many establishments and divisions.

An *industry* is the aggregation of units of production selling goods that are in some sense similar. The notion of industry is also often referred to as a branch of production. The *market* is the realm of interaction among all buyers and sellers.

Under *industrial structure* we study 'the relative importance of individual industries or groups of related industries within an economy and ... the pattern of transactions between these industries' (Devine *et al.*, 1985, p. 27). One way of describing this pattern of transactions between industries is by using an *input–output table*. This is a table that shows all the value and volume transactions as between industries, during a time period of one year. Table 1.1 is a hypothetical and simplified input–output table for a given economy. It represents only the inter-industry matrix (or matrix of intermediate consumptions). To complete the picture, the matrix of final demand and other transactions such as imports, taxes, wages, depreciation and profits would have to be included.

The inter-industry matrix facilitates a very detailed examination of industrial structure. It shows the sales of domestically produced goods and services by domestic industries to those same industries. For example, the first row of Table 1.1 shows all the sales of Industry 1 (i.e. Product 1) to the other domestic industries. The first column represents all inputs bought by

TABLE 1.1 **Hypothetical input–output table (Year *t*, ECUs million)**

	Industry 1	...	Industry j	...	Total
Product 1	30	...	50	...	600
Product 2	20	...	40	...	500
...	...	...	...	...	...
Product i	40	...	70	...	900
...	...	...	...	...	...
Total domestic flows	400	...	800	...	8000

Industry 1. This column informs us that Industry 1 has bought a total of ECUs 400 million worth of inputs, of which 20 million came from Industry 2, 40 million from Industry *i*, and 30 million from itself (retained). A similar matrix, showing the pattern of transactions as between industries at the EU level is computed by the Commission of the EU.

The notion of industrial structure needs to be distinguished from that of *market structure*. The traditional, neoclassical theory of market structures presents a range of types, from perfect competition to monopoly. The main elements of market structure are the number and size distribution (concentration) of firms, and the barriers to entry into the market. The method used in examining market structures has been primarily *comparative statics*. This is used to answer such questions as what difference it would make to increase the number of firms, or introduce taxes, or reduce costs. The difference is introduced as a difference between two time periods. It is introduced into the model and the implications—in terms, for example, of price and profit—identified. That firms will make more or less profit, or that consumers will have to pay higher or lower prices, are examples of the concerns of this type of analysis, rather than the process that firms, industries and markets will go through in adjusting to the change. While we present in some detail, and in various parts of the book, diagrams showing the comparative static methods in the neoclassical approach, elsewhere we focus on processes and emphasize *dynamic* perspectives. In relation to theories of the firm, for example, dynamic approaches such as the evolutionary theory are introduced.

Using the idea of *industrial*—or production—*system*, allows the industrial economist to adopt 'holistic' perspectives. What holistic refers to generally, is the notion that the whole is greater than the sum of the parts. Here what we are referring to is the view of the firm or a group of firms as a set of interconnected components; as an industrial system there is a pattern of interactions that is reproduced. At the level of the firm, the industrial system refers to the set of different stages of the transformation process as well as to the nature of the connections between these stages. In the case of a perfectly vertically integrated firm, the transformation process includes everything from the extraction of raw materials to the distribution of the final product on a market. However, very few firms are perfectly vertically integrated; it is referred to here to illustrate the notion of firm as industrial system. All firms are composed of a specific number of stages, and have forged specific connections between these stages. Some firms develop well-known, seminal production systems. The Ford system, for example, is characterized by standardization, large scale, extreme specialization of the productive functions, and large amounts of stocks and inventories; the Toyota production system is centred around the notion of 'Just in Time', with its connected stock minimization, information maximization, very high quality, and close integration between the productive functions.

At a wider—meso—level (meso = medium), industrial systems involve a number of firms. Various ways in which firms relate to one another—whether sharing technologies, supplying or buying goods or services, at arm's length or in alliances—and at various geographical removes, constitute different industrial systems. Among types of industrial systems at this wider level discussed in this book are *industrial districts, filières* and *clusters*.

Industrial structures, market structures and industrial systems are all discussed in Chapter 4. The discussion is both theoretical and empirical. The empirical focus is the EU, in which the standard industrial classification system is NACE (*Nomenclature des Activités de la Communauté Européenne*), the General Industrial Classification of Economic Activities. The NACE system classifies industries on the basis of the nature of goods and services produced and/or the nature of the production process employed.[2] Appendix 1.1 shows a taxonomy of industries based on the two-digit classification.

1.3 Approach of this book

In a number of respects, this book is different from other industrial economics texts. Our approach is to incorporate, as much as possible, the EU as a focus or theme. In order to achieve this aim, it is necessary to include explanations of the specifically EU-related complexities of many of the aspects of industry in Europe. To understand changes in *barriers to entry* in the EU, for example, one must have a clear idea of the nature and results of the recent developments towards the *Single European Market*. More generally, the use of a major group of highly integrated trading partners like the EU as a focus in an industrial economics textbook has necessitated the inclusion of a number of issues not usually found in books of this kind. Among these, the geographical, trade and legal dimensions of industrial economics stand out.

Another important difference between this and other texts, is its attention to a wide range of different theoretical approaches. A number of theories of the firm are described, for example. In general, where work elucidates a discussion, it is brought in, irrespective of its theoretical origins.

1.3.1 Geographic dimension: locational and regional aspects

The location of a firm is crucial to the organization of production, and yet very little attention has been paid to the geographical dimension in conventional texts on industrial economics or industrial organization. Locational aspects are essential to the understanding of firms' activities in the EU.

To explain—or even define—industries or markets in an area in which, although significantly diminished, international borders still exist, can be significantly different from a similar exercise in a homogeneous economy (like Japan) or even a federal state (like the United States). With the process of international economic integration, which started among the six founding members in the late 1950s, the national boundaries between member states have been lowered. The 1992 Programme on the Completion of the Internal Market, however, is proof that 30 years after the Rome Treaty these national barriers had not completely disappeared. In relation to most industries and markets, integration within the EU is still not total. The implications of this for both the location of firms, and the relevant product market, are important to economists studying firms or industries in the EU. In addition, there is the question of whether the lowering of barriers between member countries will encourage firms to locate in particular regions or sub-regions of the EU, or whether it will result in a more even distribution of industrial activity throughout the Union. If the former, then firms' location decisions will jeopardize the objective of convergence—the reduction of inequality and uneven development; if the latter, then firms' decisions will promote this objective.

Our aim of incorporating the spatial dimension is expressed in various parts of the book. We have included concepts like *location quotients*, *agglomeration effects*, *industrial districts*, *clusters* and *filières*; in discussion of EU action to prevent illegal pricing practices, the importance of regional issues is brought out; and throughout the text an effort is made to make the spatial aspects of firms' activities clear.

1.3.2 International trade, foreign investment and industrial organization

International trade theory has in recent years begun to acknowledge the importance of developments in industrial economic theory. Trade theory had for many years been based on assumptions of *perfect competition*; *imperfect competition*, *product differentiation* and *increasing returns* to scale, although central concerns of industrial economics, had been ignored, at least by neoclassical trade theorists. We have included a discussion of this development and of its significance to the understanding of developments in the EU, in both Chapters 4 and 5.

Localization, where a firm or group of firms concentrates their activities in a particular place, may appear to conflict with the phenomenon of *globalization*, which is related to the increasing significance of multinational enterprises (MNEs). However, they can and do co-exist. For example, MNEs, through their international trade, foreign investment and licensing activities can, while seeing their markets as global entities, still cause spatial concentration. Both the way MNEs perceive markets, and their production and distribution activities, impinge on economies in various ways. All these have spatial implications. We attempt, by our attention to such implications in this book, to draw a bridge across orthodox, spaceless industrial economics, modern approaches to firms and industries, and European economic integration.

1.3.3 Legal framework

The concept of the EU firm, even in 1995, does not convey a precise legal meaning. As part of our focus on the implications for firms of operating in the EU, we discuss this problem in Chapter 4 (Section 4.2). That this legal issue is worthy of discussion in a text on industrial economics is easy to show. The fact that the law in relation to the rights and obligations of different forms of enterprise is not identical across all member countries, means that additional information is required for firms wishing to operate in more than one member country. This extra information is costly, and constitutes a barrier to entry. Barriers to entry are a fundamental concern of industrial economics, and are the target of much of the effort in Europe to complete the Single Market. Attempts to harmonize the legal frameworks in which European firms operate, and to define a *Societas Europaea*, are discussed in Chapter 4.

1.3.4 Wide range of different theoretical approaches

Like most industrial economics texts, this book describes the origins and development of the SCP paradigm. It also, like most texts, provides critiques of this paradigm. Unlike most other texts, this book also includes a discussion of how debates around similar issues have taken place in a number of other radically different traditions, including the Marxian, Austrian and Schumpeterian traditions.

Neoclassical approaches are discussed throughout the text. We accept the usefulness of many of the applications of neoclassical economics, at least for pedagogical purposes. Most such applications in this text are diagrammatic. Where they are appropriate, we provide critiques of the neoclassical perspective.

Emerging into great prominence within industrial economics in the last 10 years is game theory. Rather than a theory, this is a tool used by economists from a number of different traditions. We use game theory as a means of representing problems in strategy throughout the text.

Different theories of the firm are introduced in Chapter 3. The discussion includes their sources, origins, applications and differences. A concept like *transaction costs*, which we show is the basis for a theory of the firm, is also useful in explaining government intervention. We use the concept for this purpose in Chapters 4 and 7.

There are other links between the discussion of theories of the firm and other parts of the book. For example, we show in Chapter 3 that economists working on the *evolutionary theory* of the firm are close to, and in some cases overlap with, those working on new approaches to technological change and innovation. This is drawn out further in the discussion of *national systems of innovation* in Chapter 5. Here, *institutional*, including cultural, aspects of the context within which firms operate are shown to be important.

1.4   Structure of the book

Chapter 2 reviews the standard SCP paradigm, highlights its limits, and goes on to describe the arguments of the critics of SCP. Following a discussion of the neoclassical theory of the firm, and problems with the assumption of profit maximization, Chapter 3 proceeds with outlines of other significant theories of the firm. It concludes with a discussion of the similarities and differences among these theories. The following three chapters cover, in turn, aspects of the structure, conduct and performance of firms and industries in theory, and in the EU in practice. In Chapter 4, traditional market structure types are described, including an extensive discussion of oligopoly theory. This includes a presentation of Cournot's original model as basic, and of the main developments since then as variations. The industrial structure of the EU is described and discussed in Section 4.2 of Chapter 4 which concludes with the theory and types of location of industry in the EU. Chapter 5 covers various types of behaviour of firms in theory and in the EU, including pricing, advertising, corporate integration and innovation. Chapter 6 deals with the performance of firms, countries and the EU. Finally Chapter 7 is devoted to elements of industrial policy; EU industrial policy is discussed in detail, and some comparisons and contrasts drawn with other industrial policies.

Notes

[1] It should be noted that the European Union—as defined in the Maastricht Treaty—is not completed. As argued by Church and Phinnemore (1994), the Maastricht Treaty on European Union does not clearly define the EU; the EU is an evolving structure, a process.

[2] This is arranged on the decimal system and is subdivided into divisions (one-digit code), classes (two-digit codes), groups (three-digit codes), sub-groups (four-digit codes), and items (five-digit codes).

Questions

1.1 What is industrial economics, and how would you differentiate it from microeconomics?

1.2 What is the difference between an industry and a market? Discuss in detail, giving examples.

1.3 Provide examples of three questions that might be answered using input–output tables.

1.4 Why might regional and spatial issues be important in industrial economics?

Appendix 1.1 European Industrial Classification System (NACE)

11 Extraction and briquetting of solid fuels
12 Coke ovens
13 Extraction of petroleum and natural gas
14 Mineral oil refining
15 Nuclear fuels industry
16 Production and distribution of electricity, gas, steam and hot water
17 Water supply
21 Extraction and preparation of metalliferous ores
22 Production and preliminary processing of metals
23 Extraction of minerals other than metalliferous and energy-producing minerals; peat extraction
24 Manufacture of non-metallic mineral products
25 Chemical industry
26 Man-made fibres industry
32 Mechanical engineering
33 Manufacture of office machinery and data-processing machinery
34 Electrical engineering
35 Manufacture of motor vehicles and motor vehicle parts and accessories
36 Manufacture of other means of transport
37 Instrument engineering
41/
42 Food, drink, and tobacco
43 Textile industry
44 Leather and leather goods (except footwear and clothing)
45 Footwear and clothing
46 Timber and wooden furniture industries
47 Manufacture of paper and paper products; printing and publishing
48 Processing of rubber and plastics
49 Other manufacturing industries
50 Building and civil engineering

2 Industrial organization

Until recently, most analyses of industries were conducted according to the linear relationship prevailing in the well-known paradigm of structure–conduct–performance (SCP). In the paradigm, the market structure of the industry determines the conduct of the firm which, in turn, determines the firm's performance. The conflicting results of the numerous tests carried out on the causal relationship underlying this paradigm, as well as the need to deepen the theoretical base of industrial economics, have paved the way to what has become known as the '*new industrial economics*' (see Norman and La Manna, 1992). (Note that in this book we use the terms 'industrial economics' and 'industrial organization' interchangeably.)

In this chapter we shall discuss the evolution of industrial economic theory, identifying the weaknesses which have given rise to change. The main changes will be emphasized, both in terms of the underlying theories and of the methodologies.

2.1 The SCP paradigm and its limits

2.1.1 The structuralists

Industrial organization emerged during the 1950s and 1960s essentially as an empirical study, centred on the SCP paradigm. According to this framework exogenous types of market structure (such as oligopoly) determine endogenous types of market behaviour (such as collusion) which in turn determine performance (such as high profitability). More specifically, a number of factors, including the numbers and sizes of buyers and sellers, degree of product differentiation and barriers to entry (see Chapter 4), together form the elements of market structure. Market structure determines conduct which is, broadly speaking, the policies and strategies of firms, including pricing behaviour, investment, research and development, and various types of strategic alliances with other firms. (Conduct of firms is treated in Chapter 5.) Conduct, in turn, determines performance, measured, for example, by profitability or efficiency (see Chapter 6).

This analytical framework was popularized by Bain (1958), who himself claimed his roots to be in the work of Mason (1939, 1949) and Clark (1940). Others (e.g. Hay and Morris, 1991) suggest that the theoretical basis for the work on structure, conduct and performance was laid by Chamberlin (1933). Chamberlin's (and, simultaneously, Robinson's 1933) development of a model of monopolistic competition involved an examination of the theoretical relationship between industrial structures on the one hand, and prices and profits on the other, and it was just this type of relationship that Bain and his followers attempted to test empirically. Monopolistic competition (as well as the other neoclassical models of market structure) will be discussed in some detail in Chapter 4. For the purposes of the present discussion it is sufficient to explain that what Chamberlin did was to define a market in which there was a fixed number of similar firms producing goods that were to some extent differentiated. Given assumptions, first, that the firms were all profit maximizers, and second, that firms could freely enter or leave this industry, the result was that, in the long run, i.e. relaxing the assumption that the number of firms is fixed, the price would settle at a point at which price was equal to the average cost of production. Average cost includes 'normal' profit, i.e. a return on capital just sufficient to keep the firms in the industry, so this would be a long-run 'equilibrium' in the sense that there would be no incentive for additional firms to enter or existing firms to leave the industry.

The advantage of the approach was that, if the direction of causality was, as assumed, from S to C to P, then for policy purposes all that had to be shown was the relationship between S and P. In Chamberlin's model, for example, all that had to be done about conduct was to impose the reasonable assumption that the firms would behave as profit maximizers. The result was that if there was monopolistic competition, long-run equilibrium would be where price was equal to average cost. In general, if it could be shown that certain industrial structures were associated with some firms earning excess (above normal) profits, then the government should intervene to prevent that type of industrial structure. This obviated the need for 'direct inquiry into the inherently more intractable, and largely unobservable, process of market conduct' (Cable, 1994).

A famous debate ensued between those supporting the Chamberlin model (who together constituted what came to be known as the *Harvard School*) and those who opposed it in favour of the original perfect competition model (the *Chicago School*). This debate left Bain and the other industrial economists, who saw a need to identify circumstances requiring government intervention, clearly associated with the Harvard School. The Chicago School was in general more antipathetic to government intervention.

Since the first wave of industrial economists accorded structure an influential or even determinant role, their view came to be known as a *structuralist* conception of industrial organization.

The causal relationships posited by the structuralists have been widely tested. Many of the results of this empirical work were contradictory. Even, for example, so basic an issue as the relationship between firm size and profit rates was apparently contentious. Relying upon the simple correlation between firm size (as a measure of market structure), and profit rates (as a measure of performance), Haines (1970) found that 'the firms that appear most frequently among the 10, 50, or 100 most profitable are small or medium-sized rather than large'. This went against the results of studies by Baumol (1967) and Hall and Weiss (1967), among others, which suggested that profitability is directly related to firm size. Somewhere between these two extremes, Marcus (1969) found that 'size of firm influences profitability in *some*, but not in all, industries'.

2.1.2 Critics

These controversies contributed to the dismantling of the simplified form of the SCP paradigm as the core of industrial economics, though at least in the 1960s, they generated a great deal of research and constituted a rich vein within which to develop and sharpen econometric techniques. The SCP model came under attack on a number of different fronts. We attempt here to identify four such critiques of SCP. They are not mutually exclusive, some having writers and ideas in common, others methods. Each is associated to varying extents with the traditional, neoclassical perspective:

1 The Chicago School criticized the model for being non-theoretical and for having diverged to too great an extent from the basic neoclassical price theory (Stigler, 1968; Davies and Lyons,

1988).[1] Even if their empirical work was based on more realistic assumptions, the Chicago School argued, Bain *et al.* came up with nothing more powerful in predictive ability than the traditional *perfect competition model*.[2] In another important difference, within the SCP paradigm high concentration (a small number of firms accounting for a large part of the market—see Chapter 4) was believed to lead to collusion, and hence to higher profits. Demsetz (1974) of the Chicago School, on the other hand, argued that where concentration was high, firms tended to be large; larger firms tended to be more efficient and it was this greater efficiency that led to higher profits. Clearly, if improved profitability was a result of collusion, intervention may be desirable, while if the reason for higher profits was greater efficiency, intervention would be counter-productive.

2 Even among those working within the SCP paradigm (e.g. Scherer, 1970), the linearity of the structuralist view came into question. The possibility was identified, for example, of behaviour and performance affecting market structure. In this partial reversal of the direction of causality, conduct such as product differentiation may exclude some firms and may thus alter market structure; advertising, for example, may be used to raise entry barriers (Comanor and Wilson, 1967). This 'anti-structuralist' view considered the paradigm as an iterative process. Scherer (1970), summarizing the work of others, introduced the notion of a simultaneous interdependence of the three elements of the triad. (For an excellent critique of the structuralist view, see Auerbach (1989, especially pp. 44–6). Auerbach's contention is that 'the behaviour of participants in a market (whether oligopolistic or otherwise) can never be determined exclusively by a set of market parameters which are exogenous to this behaviour' (p. 46).) According to Cable (1994), these problems of causality were damaging to the SCP framework, leading to disagreement over the interpretation of results of statistical research. The theoretical and empirical weaknesses reinforced one another. Nevertheless, the idea of examining industries, and, to some extent, of organizing theory, under the three headings continues to have a role. Without implication as to the direction of causality among them, structure, conduct and performance remain important elements in the present text, as they do in other well-known texts on industrial organization (IO) (see Scherer and Ross, 1990; Martin, 1994).

3 With roots going back to Cournot in the nineteenth century, more recent contributions in the field of IO have accorded behaviour or conduct the dominant role. Implications in terms of both market structure and performance are then derived (see, for example, Stiglitz and Mathewson (1986) and for a brief summary of work in this area, Davies and Lyons (1988, pp. 7–10)). Even more important than this, the methodologies used to posit the conduct and derive the implications, have changed. Economists like Spence (1977) and Dixit (1979) began to apply game theory to the analysis of the conduct of firms and this induced a transformation in the nature of the subject of industrial economics; it has become more theoretical. A great number of the articles on IO now published in British, American and European journals contain game theoretic models or methods (game theory is discussed in more detail in Section 2.2 of this chapter).

4 Also emerging from an older tradition, a number of economists have focused on firms and markets as alternative means of organizing production. Oliver Williamson (1985) has called this range of theories the *new institutional economics*. Coase's *transaction cost* theory expounded in 1937 and greatly extended by Williamson (1985), and *principal–agent* theory associated among others with Ross (1973), Stiglitz (1974) and Mirrlees (1976), are examples of this intensified interest in the 'nature of the firm'. (This is the title of Coase's 1937 article. These theories will be discussed in some detail in Chapter 3. See also, on the economics of organization and management, Milgrom and Roberts, 1992.) In an early example of this

attention to the implications of the structure of the firm, Williamson (1967) incorporated aspects of organization theory into an examination of management as a limitation on the growth of the firm. Arguing that the behaviour of government bureaucracies is in many respects similar to that of hierarchical firms, Williamson presented a model in which control loss in such firms constituted a limitation on their size. The question of diminishing returns to management, as we shall see in our discussion of theories of the firm in Chapter 3, continues to be a subject of debate in this literature.

While there are differences among them, the above four streams in industrial economics can in many respects be considered to be mainstream. The training, concerns and broad methodologies of the economists discussed under each of them, are all similar to those of the neoclassical tradition.[3] For example, they all use marginal analysis, they all attempt in various ways to model the behaviour of firms mathematically, and they all rely to a greater extent on deductive than inductive theorizing. While there have been debates and disagreements in the IO literature in these streams, there is a certain commonality of language among them.

In addition to the debates within the mainstream of IO, there have also been a number of critics writing from what Davies and Lyons (1988, pp. 10–19) call 'radical' perspectives. They emphasize three such approaches: Hayekian, Schumpeterian and Marxian. Aspects of the work of each of them continue to reverberate in IO.

Hayek and his followers (all part of the *Austrian school*) based an intensely anti-interventionist policy prescription on the belief that important economic information is held by individuals in an extremely disaggregated way (Hayek, 1949). The centralization of information which is necessary for governments to decide on whether and how to intervene is thus impossible. Competition, for the Austrian school, is a process of continual interaction between the entrepreneur and the environment; the distinction between perfect and imperfect competition as static structures determining the behaviour of firms is therefore inappropriate. Indeed, for Hayek, 'the economic problem of society is mainly one of rapid adaptation to changes in particular circumstances of time and place' (quoted in Williamson, 1985, p. 8). To remain in business firms must, in this view, constantly obtain information about market conditions and how they change.

Auerbach (1989, pp. 22–7) agrees with the necessity for viewing competition as a dynamic process, but points out that Hayek's 'categories are deeply rooted in the static utilitarian calculus of choice inherited from the earlier Austrian school of Menger and others'. There is, Auerbach argues (1989, p. 26), a contradiction between the dynamic conception of competition and the static theory of utility upon which Hayek bases his individualist philosophy of economics. Davies and Lyons (1988), too, while finding some validity in the Austrian notions of 'entrepreneurial alertness' (to replace the neoclassical 'optimization') and 'order in the competitive process' (to replace 'equilibrium'), nevertheless conclude that 'the Austrian creed [is] at odds with a more dispassionate and balanced view of government policy'.

Schumpeter[4] was a contemporary of Hayek's, and a fellow Austrian, though not of the Austrian school. His view was that incessant innovations by firms destroyed existing economic structures and created new ones. This is Schumpeter's famous notion of 'creative destruction' (Schumpeter, 1943, pp. 83–5). For Schumpeter, while there existed equilibrium positions, these were far less important over time than the massive shifts brought about by 'the new commodity, the new technology, the new source of supply, the new type of organization (the largest scale unit of control for instance)' (ibid.). If the investment required to create these shifts involved elements of collusion, monopoly and even government intervention, then, for Schumpeter such elements were acceptable. The Schumpeterian view is thus different both from the neoclassical insistence on the importance of perfect competition and the Austrian antipathy to government intervention.

The importance of large-scale and monopoly power for innovation in Schumpeter's later work is at odds with his earlier view, in *The Theory of Economic Development* (1934), that innovations were more likely to emanate from small, new firms. (This was first published in German in 1912. See Scherer (1992) for this comparison, for a review of Schumpeter's work and for the reaction to it over the last 50 years.) This distinction between the types of structures most conducive of innovation has continued to be debated, and although much of the literature 'supports a conclusion that Schumpeter overstated the advantages of large, monopolistic corporations as engines of technological change' (Scherer, 1992), a great deal of research on this and other aspects of Schumpeter's work continues to be done (see also Chapter 3). Irrespective of the size of the firm introducing the innovation, the innovative activity remains crucial for Schumpeter. Schumpeterian competition—as distinct from the price competition of standard neoclassical models—is the 'competition from the new commodity, the new technology, the new source of supply, the new type of organization' (Schumpeter, 1943, p. 84). These notions of change in the products, processes and organizations of production and distribution have deeply informed a rather heterogeneous group of post-SCP industrial economists including Auerbach (1989), Porter (1990), Best (1990) and Lazonick (1991) and, among those particularly interested in technological change, Nelson (1993), Lundvall (1992) and Dosi *et al.* (1988). (The work of many of these writers is associated with the evolutionary theory of the firm, to be discussed in Chapter 3. On technological change and innovation, see Chapter 5.)

Schumpeter, though politically a Tory, had a 'professional sympathy for socialism' (Stolper, 1994). He was greatly influenced by *Marx*, the third of Davies and Lyons's radicals. Much of Marx's work has relevance to IO, but we will concentrate here on his view of the determinants of the growth of the firm. For Marx, the accumulation of capital was crucial both to the existence of capitalism and to the growth of firms (individual capitals). Accumulation began historically with such developments as the enclosure movements, the great trading monopolies and colonies. From then on, competition forced capitalists to continue to accumulate: 'Competitors were constantly developing new and better methods of production. Only by accumulating new and better capital equipment could this challenge be met' (Hunt and Sherman, 1990, pp. 91–2).

Accumulation, according to Marx, would lead to a tendency for larger and larger firms to be concentrated in the hands of fewer and fewer capitalists, for three reasons. First, competition forces firms to adopt more and more capital-intensive means of production. As capital intensity ('organic composition of capital') increases, so does the minimum efficient scale. 'Large capitals, therefore, get the better of small ones' (Marx, 1972, p. 691). Second, small firms will concentrate in industries not yet dominated by larger firms. Here,

competition rages in direct proportion to the number and in inverse proportion to the magnitude of the competing capitals. It always ends in the overthrow of a number of the lesser capitalists, whose capitals to some extent pass into the hands of the conquerors... (Marx, 1972, p. 691)

Third, the credit system, developing concomitantly with capitalist production is, with competition, one of the two 'mightiest levels of concentration' (Marx, 1972, p. 691). Large, growing firms are a better credit risk than small ones, and therefore more likely to succeed in obtaining loans and other forms of credit.

Clearly there is much of interest in Marx for IO, and modern industrial economists have indeed paid attention to Marx.[5] Davies and Lyons (1988), referring to Marx's claim that natural monopolies 'do not prevent the equalisation of profits between industries', argue that this suggests that he 'deserves credit as an early contestability theorist!'. (Contestability theory is discussed in Section 2.2 of this chapter. It argues basically that in the absence of barriers to entry, firms in imperfectly competitive market structures will behave as if there is perfect competition.)

Cross-fertilization of ideas (and/or arriving at the same conclusions independently), is common between radical and mainstream economists, as well as among those in different groups within the mainstream of industrial economics. In an example of two groups arriving at the same conclusion from very different perspectives, the Chicago School and Hayek's Austrian School both profoundly oppose government intervention. Also showing links, albeit in a different way, some institutional economists draw explicitly on the radical economists. Douglass C. North, for example, in his attempt to develop a new theory of institutional change (1990), adopts much of Coase, and builds not only on Williamson, but also on Schumpeter and Marx. The most common recent instance of this type of interrelationship between different groups in IO is that of the adoption of game theory by neoclassical, SCP, new institutional and Marxist economists. By no means all of the economists in these different schools use, or believe it appropriate to use, game theory, however. (For a debate on game theory among Marxist economists, for example, see Mayer and Varoufakis, 1993/94). Following a brief introduction to the New IO, the basic techniques of game theory will be explained, together with a discussion of its advantages and disadvantages.

2.2 New industrial economics

Since the late 1970s, a wide range of mathematically more sophisticated, mainly game theoretic, models have been introduced into the mainstream of industrial economics. Largely displacing the traditional SCP approach, many of these models nevertheless continue to examine the types of issues underlying the SCP paradigm. For example, the debate over size of firm and profitability, and the related issues of concentration, market power and efficiency, still concern both theoreticians and empirical researchers. This debate, among other theoretical concerns, at first dominated the work in game theory. It is only in recent years that the wide number, range and complexity of the hypotheses generated by the game theoretic models have begun to be tested empirically.

According to Martin (1994, p. 221), most economists now accept Demsetz's (1974) compromise explanation for the conflicting empirical results of structure–performance relationships. This compromise is that where high profits for large firms, but low profits for small firms in highly concentrated industries are observed, the explanation could be both greater efficiency and greater market power of the large firms. Efficiency could arise from the lower unit costs of large-scale production (*returns to scale*), and market power could be expressed through collusion by the large firms to keep prices high, but not so high as to facilitate high profits for the small firms. The extent to which each of these—efficiency and market power—is present, varies from industry to industry and, as a result, empirical work on size and performance was, as we have seen, inconsistent. Recent studies attempting to avoid this problem have focused on single industries, or even single firms.

This narrowing of the focus of industrial economics, together with an increasing recognition of the importance of the *strategic behaviour*[6] of firms, has both encouraged and facilitated the application of game theory. Strategic behaviour is a fundamental element of conduct, and as such is a natural concern of those who, as we discussed above, have in recent times accorded conduct the key role in the SCP triad.

2.2.1 Game theory

Correctly speaking, game theory is not itself a theory of IO but a method that can be used to describe and test other theories. Basically, game theory is a mathematical modelling technique in which the players' moves (or decisions) are influenced by their expectations of the responses of the other player(s). (Gardner (1995, p. 4) defines a game as 'any rule-governed situation with a well-defined outcome, characterized by strategic interdependence'.) This is so close to the definition of oligopoly, that the application of game theory to IO, and particularly to strategies within oligopolies, was inevitable.

There is some disagreement over the roots of game theory as applied in IO. Some (e.g. Hyman, 1992, p. 373) credit von Neumann and Morgenstern (1944) with the original formulation, while others (e.g. Forges and Thisse, 1992) argue that 'game theory and industrial economics... have been very much intertwined from the outset', an outset that goes back to Cournot (1838). Recent work suggests that the models like those of Cournot were later incorporated into game theory, but that von Neumann and Morgenstern were the crucial progenitors: 'Had von Neumann and Morgenstern never met, it seems unlikely that game theory would have been developed' (Leonard, 1995). Whoever was originally responsible, it is clear that the modern use of game theory in IO builds on the work of a number of mathematicians and economists, including Cournot (1838), Bertrand (1883), Hotelling (1929), von Stackelberg (1934), Nash (1951) (Nash was among three Nobel prizewinners for economics in 1994) and Schelling (1960), as well as von Neumann and Morgenstern.

In game theory,[7] as in neoclassical economics in general, there is usually an equilibrium concept. In the neoclassical approach the equilibrium relates to the structure of a market, but in game theory it relates to the conduct of the firms. In the Cournot equilibrium, for example, the firms each choose a level of output which together constitute an equilibrium if, given the outputs chosen by its rivals, no firm can increase its profit by changing its output. In this case, output is the strategic decision variable. The Bertrand equilibrium is one in which price is the decision variable. (The original Cournot and Bertrand models are presented mathematically under the discussion of oligopoly in Chapter 4.) More generally, where a firm optimizes in this way, given the strategic choices of its rivals, the result is known as a Nash equilibrium. Thus a Nash equilibrium where output is the decision variable is a Cournot (or a Nash–Cournot) equilibrium, and where price is the decision variable it is a Bertrand (or Nash–Bertrand) equilibrium.

The basic tool of game theory is the *payoff matrix*. (The presentation of game theory in terms of equations and reaction curves is illustrated in the discussion of oligopoly in Chapter 4.) This shows the strategies available to the players, and the outcomes for each player, depending on the strategy chosen by rivals. Most common, both for analytical and heuristic purposes, are two-player games. The analogy in economics is the duopoly, that is, an industry in which there are only two firms. Figure 2.1 illustrates. In this industry there are two, and only two firms, and they are identical. Each has a choice of output, either 3 or 6 units. The cells of the matrix indicate the payoff in ECUs of profit. The choice of 3 units by Player A and 6 units by Player B will give Player A the payoff which is the first figure in brackets (−3, or a loss of 3 ECUs) and Player B the payoff which is the second figure (a profit of 33 ECUs).

The aim in game theory is to identify each player's best strategy, that is, the strategy that will maximize the player's payoff, taking the other player's strategy into account. If, for example,

Player B

	3 units	6 units
Player A		
3 units	(27, 27)	(−3, 33)
6 units	(33, −3)	(12, 12)

Figure 2.1   The payoff matrix

Player B chooses 3 units, Player A's best strategy would be 6 units (a profit of 33 ECUs for an output of 6 units is preferable to a profit of −3 ECUs for an output of 3 units). If Player B chooses 6 units, again Player A would choose 6 units. So, from Player A's point of view the two possible outcomes are the two bottom cells of the matrix (33, −3) or (12, 12). By analogy, from Player B's point of view the two possible outcomes are the two cells on the right side of the matrix (−3, 33)—if Player A chooses to produce 3 units—and (12, 12)—if Player A chooses to produce 6 units. The cell (12, 12) is one at which, if either player has chosen to produce 6 units, there is no incentive for the other to choose any other strategy. This is the Nash–Cournot equilibrium position in this game.

The same result would be arrived at by assuming, as is most commonly done in such situations, that the *maximum* strategy will be adopted. Here Player A will compare the worst possible payoffs in each of the choices facing it, and choose the best of these—thus maximizing the minimum payoff. In our example, if Player A chooses 3 units, the worst possible outcome is where Player B chooses 6 units, a payoff for Player A of −3 ECUs. If Player A chooses 6 units, 12 ECUs is the worst possible payoff. Because 12 ECUs is preferable to −3 ECUs, Player A will choose to produce 6 units. By analogy, Player B will also choose to produce 6 units, and although each firm, and the industry as a whole, could make greater profits if the 3-unit option had been chosen, by acting independently the firms will choose to produce 6 units. Acting independently is indeed the essence of non-co-operative games: the players cannot collude.

Where the results are such that, if collusion was possible then both firms could improve their payoffs (as in the example in Fig. 2.1), then this is known as the *prisoner's dilemma*. More formally, prisoner's dilemma is 'where the pursuit of self-interest leads to a Pareto-inefficient solution for the players' (Forges and Thisse, 1992). (Pareto-efficiency in this context is where there is no way of reallocating decisions to improve one player's situation without disimproving another player's situation.) There is a dominant strategy, the payoff of which is less than the best possible outcome. This situation is called prisoner's dilemma because its original application was to an example in which two people are charged with an offence (Fig. 2.2). If both confess, then each will get, say, three years in jail. If both hold out, they both go to jail for one year. If either confesses (and implicates the other), the confessor goes free and the other gets ten years. Both will confess because each will fear that holding out may result in a much longer sentence. It is also appropriate to call this situation prisoner's dilemma because, as Gardner (1995, p. 52) writes, 'The players are prisoners of their own strategies'.

Depending on the payoffs, and the assumptions about the behaviour of the firms, different results can be obtained. If, for example, the choice of 6 units by both players had given a payoff of (27, 27), the choice of 3 units by both players a payoff of (12, 12), with all other

Defendant B

		Confess	Hold out
Defendant A			
Confess		(3, 3)	(0, 10)
Hold out		(10, 0)	(1, 1)

Figure 2.2   The prisoner's dilemma

things the same, then the two players would still both choose 6 units, but this time it would given them both the best possible payoffs. Where a player chooses a strategy (6 units), irrespective of what the other firm does, then this is called a *dominant strategy*, and where, as in this case, both players have dominant strategies, it is an equilibrium of dominant strategies.[8]

The above are examples of variable sum games. Where the payoff to Player A is derived entirely from B, and vice versa, then it is called a *zero sum game*. An example of a zero sum game is where there is a duopoly with a fixed market size. An increase in the market share of either firm is at the cost of market share of its competitor, and the size of the increase of the share of Firm A is equal (and opposite) to the loss of the share of Firm B. This is illustrated in Fig. 2.3, in which the amounts in the cells are the share of the market that will go to Firm A. (A minus figure is the share that will go to Firm B.)

If this is the market for a transducer used in the electrical engineering industry and the total demand is known to be 2000 units a week, then Firm A adopting strategy a_1 and Firm B adopting strategy b_1 will result in A supplying an additional 200 units (10%), and B 200 fewer units, per week. The adoption of a maximin approach to choice of strategy will direct A to a_3, where the worst that can happen is no change, and it will direct B to b_2, where again the worst that can happen is no change. With A having chosen a_3, B has no incentive to change; b_1 will result in a decline in demand for its transducers of 40 units per week, and b_3 will mean a decline of 100 units per week. Similarly, B having chosen b_2, A has no incentive to change. This position, a_3 and b_2, is thus a Nash equilibrium.

We have so far dealt with variable and zero sum, two-player games, in which the two players are either identical or similar and in which each player only makes one move. Let us now relax

Firm B

	b_1	b_2	b_3
Firm A			
a_1	10%	−8%	−12%
a_2	18%	−15%	−4%
a_3	2%	0%	5%

Figure 2.3   Zero sum game

some of these conditions, beginning with the assumption that there is only one move. Returning to Fig. 2.1, we can ask whether the same result would occur if the game were to be repeated many times. Firm A and Firm B both know that each producing three units would be a better outcome for both, and both know how much the other is producing. If there is only one move, the fear that the other firm will choose six units drives both to choose three units. If the output in the payoff matrix is, say, monthly output, then, assuming demand is constant, the decision has to be made every month. The best strategy to adopt in such cases is the *Tit-for-Tat strategy* (Axelrod, 1984). This states that a player should co-operate on the first move, and therefore do whatever the other player did on the previous move. If both choose three units the first month, then both achieve higher profits than if they had both chosen six units. The next month Firm A might again choose three units but, hoping to make extra short-term profits, Firm B might choose six units. Firm A, if it adopts Tit-for-Tat, will, in the third month, choose six units. This will reduce B's third month profits, whether it chooses three or six. Eventually, both will realize that their long-term profit interests are best served by producing three units continually. A dynamic approach, allowing for learning effects, brings about a different (Pareto-efficient) result from the static, one-move approach.

Where a firm's behaviour is based on its expectations of the behaviour of its rival(s), then the rules governing the way it makes its decisions together constitute its *reaction function* (see *reaction curve* in Chapter 4). Modelling the situation in which one firm learns another firm's reaction function, is an example of a game where the firms are not, as in previous examples, similar. Here, one firm has a clear advantage over the other(s); there is *asymmetric rivalry*. This example, developed by Heinrich von Stackelberg and known as the *Stackelberg* model, results in the firm with the information about the likely reactions of the other firm(s) becoming the leader; it takes the lead in setting output. The Stackelberg leader incorporates the reaction function of the followers into its maximization behaviour. The follower(s) take the leader's output as given, and responds accordingly. The result is a Stackelberg equilibrium.

The mathematical presentation of basic game theory is not difficult, but as variations are introduced, so the models become more complex. The dynamic, multi-player games are beyond the appropriate confines of this book. In general, and as argued by Radner (1992), in particular in relation to the economics of management, 'game-theoretic treatments typically leave us with a serious multiplicity of equilibria, and hence with indeterminate predictions of behaviour'. Game theoretic models 'have helped us understand better the logical consequences of choices over some important strategy variables' according to Michael Porter, but, he continues 'they fail to capture the simultaneous choices over many variables that characterize most industries' (Porter, 1991). Game theoretic models are best used metaphorically, rather than literally (as argued by Saloner, 1991); they are useful in the illustration, in particular, of the theory of oligopoly, and will be used to do so in Chapter 4. The optimal use of game theory is in many cases the simple, stylized representation of industrial economic (and other) problems.

Among the most quoted recent such uses of game theory, is that of Krugman (1987a). In this example, Krugman illustrates the incorporation of industrial economics into international trade theory. He shows that there is a possible role for strategic trade policy where 'government policy can tilt the terms of oligopolistic competition to shift excess returns from foreign to domestic firms'. He assumes two countries, Europe and America, in each of which there is one firm that can produce a 150-seat passenger aircraft, the market for which is such that if either of the firms produces it, that firm will make a profit, but if both produce it, both will make a loss. With Airbus and Boeing as the two firms, Fig. 2.4 is a possible payoff matrix (slightly different from those used by Krugman). There is no obvious equilibrium in this case. A maximin strategy

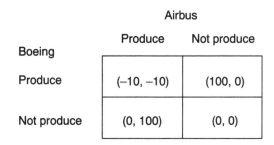

Figure 2.4 Possible payoff matrix for Airbus and Boeing

will result in neither firm producing $(0, 0)$, but if one firm can provide a clear, early indication of a commitment to produce, then this may deter the other firm from entering. This is known as a *pre-emptive strategy* (see Mansfield, 1993, pp. 449–50). The point of strategic trade policy is that if Europe's government can commit itself to paying Airbus a subsidy of, say, 15, prior to any commitment by Boeing to produce, then this will create a different payoff matrix, shown in Fig. 2.5. In this altered situation, if both firms adopt the maximin strategy, the outcome will be $(0, 115)$. A subsidy of 15 results in an increase in Airbus's profits from 0 to 115.

The example raises many questions, and does not necessarily prove the efficacy of strategic trade policy, but it does show the power of game theory to illustrate an argument. Krugman, in fact, seems to insist that his example does no more than this when he states, first, that in reality the government of Europe could not know what the response of Boeing (or, for that matter, the government of America) would be to its subsidy; second, that there is uncertainty in relation to the response of any economic policy; and third, that there is even greater uncertainty in relation to the effect of policy on oligopolistic competition. Krugman would clearly agree with Radner: economists, he writes, 'do not have reliable models of how oligopolists behave' (Krugman, 1987a).

2.2.2   Contestable market theory

Just as game theory attempts to inject theory into IO, so does the contestability school associated with the names Baumol, Panzar and Willig (1982). The notion of contestable markets is, in some respects, an example of (or an application of) the type of reasoning that is done in game theory. It is based on the argument that firms (call them Group A) will refrain from

Airbus

	Produce	Not produce
Boeing		
Produce	$(-10, 5)$	$(100, 0)$
Not produce	$(0, 115)$	$(0, 0)$

Figure 2.5 Pre-emptive strategy

behaving in certain ways because of their expectation that behaving in those ways will bring about responses on the part of other firms (Group B) that are undesirable to Group A.

The originators of the theory, focusing on perfectly free entry and exit, claimed that it was a new 'unifying framework' and it did, to some extent, provide a bridge between the criticisms brought to the linear SCP paradigm by the anti-structuralists, and the emerging views of the new wave of industrial economists. Baumol *et al.*, suggesting an alternative to the unrealistic notion of perfect competition, show that, under the condition of perfectly free entry, the threat of entry will drive prices down and guarantee efficiency, even in the limit case of one monopoly firm in the market. What is meant by perfectly free entry is that if a firm must purchase assets (e.g. plant and equipment) in order to enter the industry, then, if the firm subsequently wishes to leave the industry, those assets can be resold with no loss on the transaction. Another way of expressing this is to say that there are zero *sunk costs*. Thus if there are zero sunk costs, firms in the industry will refrain from raising prices above what the price would be if the industry were perfectly competitive. This result is independent of the structure of the industry. *Economies of scale and scope*[9] may limit the number of firms in the industry, but if there is perfect contestability the price will still be set in the market to be equal to the average cost of production. Contestability theory thus incorporated both the interest in structure of the SCP paradigm, and the notion of strategic behaviour in pricing—pricing in ways determined by expectations of the responses of competitors (or, in this case, potential competitors)—that is a fundamental element of game theory.

Martin (1993, pp. 297–325; 1994, p. 76), among others, is sceptical of the claims of the contestability theorists, and has pointed out first that other than the mathematical presentation, there is nothing new about the theory, and second that the theory has very limited application.[10] Nevertheless it has the merit of exploring the adjustment in the behaviour of firms to the threat represented by potential entrants into that market. An application to the airline industry, for example, while rejecting perfect contestability, identifies circumstances in which the threat of entry can have an impact on the performance of firms (Hurdle *et al.*, 1989).

The contestability theorists, in fact, used the airline industry as the prime example of a contestable market throughout the development of the theory during the early 1980s (see, for example, Bailey and Panzar, 1981; Baumol, Panzar and Willig, 1982; and Baumol and Willig, 1986). At first they treated the airline industry as perfectly contestable, based on the fact that, if it was deregulated, then airline companies could simply fly planes into airports to compete with existing companies flying the routes from that airport. The capital assets, it was argued, are perfectly mobile. There are no sunk costs because a decision to leave a particular route simply means flying the plane out and into another route. Investments in aircraft, Baumol, Panzar and Willig (1982, p. 7) asserted, did not involve sunk costs because they constituted 'capital on wings'. By 1986, they had accepted that the airline industry was not perfectly contestable. In particular, Baumol and Willig (1986, p. 24) identified three departures from perfect contestability that became clear in the aftermath of deregulation in America: the heavy sunk costs in the construction of airports, shortages in the availability of aircraft arising from technological change, and the lower costs facing newcomers because of the absence of the labour contracts prevalent among established carriers.

The argument that the American airline industry was perfectly contestable was at least part of the justification for its deregulation in that country. As early as 1978, for example, a proposed merger of two airline companies was passed by the Civil Aeronautics Board (CAB), despite the fact that it involved an increase in concentration which in previous merger cases had been declared unlawful by the American Supreme Court. The CAB justified this on the grounds that the Airline Deregulation Act of 1978 made possible the entry, even of small carriers, into the airline industry (this case is reported by Martin (1993, p. 320), quoting Bailey (1981, p. 181)). Contestability theory suggested that there may have been an increase in concentration, and therefore of the market power of the fewer, larger firms, but this would be offset by increased efficiency arising from the threat of entry of new competitors. In a careful study of the impact of mergers in the wake of deregulation, Kim and Singal (1993) show that while mergers between airlines resulted in both efficiency gains and increases in market power, 'On the whole, market power dominated efficiency gains, making the consumer worse off'. According to Martin (1993, pp. 324–5), despite the evidence, and the admission on the part of the contestability theorists themselves, that the theoretical basis for deregulation was unfounded, the contestability doctrine remains influential in Washington.

There is an echo of contestability theory in the attempts of the EU to define markets for the purposes of competition policy. As recently as 1988, for example in the *Eurofix-Bauco* v. *Hilti* case, the notion of *supply substitution* began to be introduced (see Chapter 4, Section 4.1.2). Supply substitution refers to the potential provision of additional supplies on the part of both incumbent firms and potential entrants, and was introduced in an attempt to assist in determining the likely level of concentration in an industry following a merger. On the basis of the American evidence, this consideration of potential entrants may not be appropriate, unless there are very low barriers to entry.

Rather than determining a strategy on the basis of what market structures actually are (structuralists' view), the contestability school assumes that firms adjust their strategy to what market structures could become. Firms, in this view, follow a sort of pre-emptive, or entry-deterring strategy. The primary weakness of the theory lies in its extreme assumption of perfectly free entry and exit. Hurdle *et al.* (1989), for example, in their examination of the circumstances in which the pricing of firms is influenced by potential entrants, show that this influence is only significant where potential entrants are not deterred by economies of scale or scope. While this discussion is pitched in terms of contestability, its real focus is the relation between structure and conduct. As such it can be argued to add little to what could have been done under the SCP paradigm. To the extent that it is not the threat of entry, but the actual entry of competitors that influences the prices set by incumbent firms, the discussion could as well be set in terms of a Bertrand, price-setting game. While contestability has had theoretical interest, it seems not to have fulfilled its promise. What the theory has added to industrial economics is an intensification of interest in the effects of both economies of scale and scope. These will be discussed in more detail in Chapter 3. As Martin (1994, p. 76) writes: 'The fundamental contributions of the theory of contestable markets seem likely to lie in the analysis of multiproduct firms, rather than the analysis of the determinants of market structure or performance.'

2.3 Conclusion

We have discussed in this chapter the origins and development of industrial economics, at least in terms of broad theoretical approaches. The SCP paradigm, in its simple, linear-determinist form was, as we showed, considered defective, and has been revised by some and replaced by others. Nevertheless, in terms of interest in the three elements—structure, conduct and performance—the SCP paradigm continues to have an influence throughout the discipline, and this book included. Indeed, aspects of each of the theories discussed will appear again in the following chapters of the book, but none has influenced the overall shape of the book more than SCP.

Other theories, or other aspects of theories, introduced here, and finding place in later chapters of the book, include game theory, whose roots in Cournot and Bertrand will be shown in detail in Chapter 4 under the discussion on oligopoly, and neoclassical theory, whose models of market structure are also discussed in Chapter 4.

The theories of the firm, to be discussed in Chapter 3, in many ways reflect a narrowing of focus of the broad theoretical approaches discussed in this chapter. Thus, for example, Schumpeterian perspectives on the nature of economic change become focused, in the evolutionary theory of the firm, on the important elements in the strategic behaviour of individual firms, in particular successful, innovative firms. The new institutional economists have already been shown to be interested in firms, as well as markets, and the theories of the firm—transaction cost and principal–agent—emerging from this tradition will also be explained in more detail in Chapter 3. The oldest, neoclassical, theory, and a recent, cooperative game theory, will be included in the chapter, and compared with the evolutionary and game theories.

Notes

[1] The neoclassical approaches will be discussed in more detail in Chapter 3. Suffice to say here that what is referred to is the set of assumptions including rational behaviour, profit maximization and free entry and exit from an industry, leading to an equilibrium market price and quantity. The methodology is deductive, involving assumptions which give rise to principles or hypotheses which may then be tested. At least some of the work in SCP was inductive, involving the examination of data in order to draw out patterns or hypotheses.

[2] Among the key assumptions of perfect competition are: a large number of firms, and of consumers, each too small to affect equilibrium price or quantity; homogeneous product; free entry or exit from the industry.

[3] Not all would agree with this. Williamson (1985), for example, clearly differentiates his own transaction cost perspective from neoclassical theory, on the basis, among others, that 'transaction cost economics... regards the business firm as a governance structure rather than a production function' (p. 18).

[4] This paragraph on Schumpeter is based, unless otherwise specified, on Davies and Lyons, 1988, pp. 14–16. It is interesting to note a contrast between the view of Schumpeter as a radical with the view, as expressed in Auerbach, 1989, p. 266, that his approach is 'paradoxically, congruent with the traditional practice in orthodox economics of pushing the question of technological change to one side'.

[5] See, among those who pay attention to Marx and modern Marxian economists, Davies and Lyons, 1988, pp. 16–19, Auerbach, 1989, and Williamson, 1985, pp. 231–238. Williamson, for example, devotes a chapter of his book (1985, Chapter 9) to an examination and critique of the Marxian notion that hierarchy is the organizational device by which bosses exploit workers.

[6] Strategic behaviour is where a firm acts in ways influenced by its expectation of how its competitors will respond to its actions. One type of strategic pricing behaviour, for example, is where a firm deliberately keeps the prices of its products below the profit maximization level in order to prevent the entry of competitors into the market. On the economics of strategic behaviour, see the special issue of *Strategic Management Journal,* **12** winter 1991.

[7] This paragraph draws on the explanation of Davies and Lyons (1988, p. 7). For a more complete description of game theory at a level equivalent to the present text, see Gardner (1995).

[8] Note that the Fig. 2.1 example of a prisoner's dilemma game is also an equilibrium of dominant strategies because if Player B chooses 3 units, Player A will choose 6 units, and if Player B chooses 6 units, Player A will choose 6 units. Note, too, that an equilibrium in dominant strategies is also a Nash equilibrium—i.e. given the choices of its rivals the choice of each firm is such that no other choice would give it higher profits—but all Nash equilibrium situations are not necessarily situations of equilibrium in dominant strategies.

[9] There are economies of scale when the average cost of producing the good declines the greater the number of units of the good produced; there are economies of scope when two or more goods, when produced together, cost less than when produced separately.

[10] For further critical appraisal of the assumption of ultra-free entry, see Shepherd (1990, pp. 282–5). The first large, international comparison of entry and exit of firms and market contestability has recently been published (Geroski and Schwalbach, 1991).

Questions

2.1 Who were the structuralists and why were they so called?

2.2 What were/are the Chicago and Harvard Schools and what are the differences between them?

2.3 Compare and contrast any two criticisms of the SCP paradigm.

2.4 What is game theory? Why is it not a theory?

2.5 Use a game theoretic model to answer the following question: should I look for a job after I graduate, or should I try to start my own business?

2.6 Explain why contestable market theory has been so vociferously criticized.

3 Theory of the firm

3.1 A review of the neoclassical theory of the firm

Parallel with the developments in IO, the theory of the firm has evolved from representing the firm as a purely profit maximizing automaton or 'black box', operating in a spaceless and timeless environment (neoclassical theory). While to some extent this view continues to prevail in introductory courses in microeconomics, a number of other perspectives are widely held.[1] The firm is now seen either as a more complex organization where control and ownership are distinct, and/or as a nexus of different activities, composed of diverse constituents. The roles of transactions, of technologies and of contracts have all been focused upon, with varying degrees of intensity by the different schools of thought.

In a recent article, Chandler (1992a, 1992b) referred to four 'established theories involving the firm'. These he named as the *neoclassical, principal–agent, transactions cost*, and *evolutionary theories*. In addition, particularly important in the context of the development of modern theories of the firm, there is the *managerial theory*. Finally, not 'established', but interesting as an example of the application of the new IO, is the *co-operative game theory* of the firm. All these will be discussed below.

3.1.1 Profit maximization as the objective of firms

The competitive equilibrium paradigm has been the dominant representation of the economic system since the writings of Adam Smith. According to this paradigm:

- On all markets, supply and demand are equated.
- This equilibrium is achieved by price adjustments.
- Individuals react primarily to price signals. The firm (or its owner-manager) takes the input prices as given.

With the work of economists like Walras, Marshall and Jevons, this developed during the second half of the nineteenth century into what became known as the neoclassical theory. They introduced the concept of *marginal analysis* and the mathematics with which to execute this analysis. Among the first such presentations was that of Walras, who in 1874 published a highly formalized version of the competitive equilibrium paradigm. Modern mathematical economists like Arrow and Debreu (1954) have built on this Walrasian vision.

Central to the neoclassical view of the firm is that the objective determining the behaviour of the firm is *maximization of profits*. Here we will briefly discuss the meaning, limits and alternatives to the profit maximization objective.

According to the neoclassical vision, the firm is an abstraction, an idealized form of business,[2] whose existence is solely explained by the purely economic motive of generating a profit. Generally, profit is generated through satisfying wants by producing a good or a service on a given market and at a given price. The firm's legal or organizational characteristics are insignificant. The only objective guiding its operations is the desire to maximize profit (or minimize costs).

The neoclassical firm is thus a profit-maximizing (or cost-minimizing) entity operating in an exogenously given environment which lies beyond its control. It is described by a *production function* which shows the relationship between inputs and outputs. *Costs* can be derived from the production function, as long as the prices of the inputs on the input (or factor) markets are known. *Revenues* can be derived from the demand schedule. The demand schedule shows the number of units of the good that the consumers are willing to buy at each different price per unit; the price actually paid multiplied by the number of units bought is the firm's revenue. The quantity the firm will produce is the profit-maximizing level of output. Profit is the difference between costs and revenues. The firm will continue to increase output as long as the last (*marginal*) unit produced adds to total profit. If the revenue obtained from selling the last unit produced (*marginal revenue*) is greater than the cost of producing the last unit (*marginal cost*), then output will continue to be increased. When the last unit no longer adds to profit— when marginal revenue (*MR*) equals marginal cost (*MC*)—then profit is maximized.

This formulaic approach to the behaviour of firms does not provide for much leeway in the decision-making process within the firm. As long as the assumptions hold—in terms, in particular, of the information that the firm is assumed to have—then, as a profit maximizer, it will behave in such a way as to set $MR = MC$.

3.1.2   Impediments to profit maximization[3]

Since the early 1930s, research both within and critical of neoclassical theory has cast doubts on the profit maximization principle. We will discuss in this section objections to the profit maximization principle under three main headings: that $MR = MC$ is not a conscious goal of decision makers in firms; that information, particularly about the future, is imperfect and this undermines a basic assumption of the theory; and that the organizational complexity of firms may impede the application of the profit maximization principle. The discussions under these headings are not mutually exclusive. For example, the lack of—or distortion in the transmission of—information is an aspect of the objections to profit maximization under both other headings, as well as constituting an objection in itself.

Decision makers do not aim for $MR = MC$

One of the first challenges to the neoclassical theory of the firm as a profit-maximizing centre was presented by Hall and Hitch (1939).[4] In their famous article, which rests to a large extent on earlier research, in particular on Chamberlin (1933) and Robinson (1933), the authors criticize the 'obscurity' surrounding the precise content of the terms 'marginal and average revenue', and raise questions about the nature of the demand curve assumed to be facing the firm. Their major criticism, however, focuses on that tenet of neoclassical theory according to which entrepreneurial behaviour will result in the equating of marginal cost with marginal revenue. Hall and Hitch's objection to this principle stems from the results of a questionnaire submitted to a small sample of manufacturing firms on how they decide the price to charge and the output to produce. The most striking finding of their research is that the firms interviewed appeared not to aim at profit maximization by equating MC and MR; instead, they applied what Hall and Hitch called a 'full-cost' principle.

The 'right' price, or the price that 'ought' to be charged, according to the interviewees, is 'based on full average cost (including a conventional allowance for profit)' (Hall and Hitch, 1939, p. 19). If maximum profits were reached as a result of the application of this 'full-cost' principle, it was only 'accidental'.

There are a number of orthodox defences against this objection to the $MR = MC$ principle. First, the conventional allowance for profit may itself be variable. Thus, as demand shifts downwards, lower profits will be accepted and price will be reduced. While not behaving precisely in accordance with profit maximization, the direction of response will be the same. Second, profit maximization may be accidental in the absence of perfect knowledge and data, but those decision makers with the best intuitive understanding, or who make the best guesses—that is, the managers of the successful firms in an industry—will get closest to $MR = MC$. Those that do not get near this level of profits will probably leave the industry. Even if the neoclassical profit maximization principle is not something that is consciously acted upon by decision makers in firms, the defence of orthodoxy suggests that it is still *ex ante* the best way of explaining the behaviour of surviving firms. (For a similar argument in defence of orthodoxy, see, for example, Machlup, 1946.)

Recent empirical research has, however, further substantiated the argument that firms do not profit- or value-maximize. 'The most marked examples entailed firm behavior with respect to taxes and takeovers' (Stiglitz, 1991). Many firms, 'perhaps most', do not minimize tax payments, and 'many studies have found that firms undertaking hostile takeovers experience no increase in share value' (Stiglitz, 1991).[5] Moreover, among such firms are major, long-surviving firms in key industries. This suggests that, even *ex ante*, profit maximization does not seem to be the best way of explaining at least some important aspects of firms' behaviour.

Information is imperfect

In the neoclassical paradigm, profit maximization is performed in the light of perfectly known cost and demand conditions. Imperfect information, and thus uncertainty, are irrelevant in this theory since markets are characterized by transparency, and since the equilibrium reached by the firm is the result of the interactions between variables defined in the present period of time. The firm operates in a timeless environment; the future is ignored.

When time is incorporated into the analysis of the firm, uncertainty as to the outcome of a given strategy arises. Decision makers cannot know precisely how interest rates and exchange rates will evolve in the next period, whether or to what extent demand will change, or how stable prices of raw materials will be. However, firms can improve on the static notion of profit maximization (and can reduce uncertainty) by systematically looking at the determinants of future streams of profits. Statistical and computer techniques in business and finance have become more sophisticated, particularly in relation to comparisons between different projects. As such techniques have improved, so they have been increasingly utilized in large companies, though there are still arguments in favour of 'satisficing and rule-of-thumb strategies'.[6] The following example illustrates how the common technique of net present value (*NPV*) may be applied in an attempt to estimate profit beyond the present. Long-run profit maximization implies maximizing the discounted present value of the firm's future stream of profits:

$$\mathrm{NPV} = \sum_{1=0}^{n} \frac{\Pi_i}{(1+r)^i} \qquad (3.1)$$

where n = time horizon (the highest value of i)

i = number of interest compounding periods (e.g. number of years)

r = discount rate

$\Pi = R - C$ = profit

$\Pi_i = R_i - C_i$ = profit in the ith year

R = revenue

C = costs.

In the future, revenue and costs may depend, among other things, on the following:

- *The actions of competitors* They may, for example, introduce substitute products that reduce the demand for the firm's product.
- *Changes in technology* Costs may be reduced by an improvement in technology, and/or increased by the need to introduce new machinery to achieve higher quality.
- *Changes in consumer tastes* Fashion may shift away from the firm's product, reducing demand.
- *Changes in the markets for inputs* Most typically, wage costs may rise.
- *Government policies* A change in monetary policy, for example, could change interest rates, and, consequently, the appropriate discount rate at which to calculate *NPV*.

Each possible project or strategy must be assessed on the basis of such combinations of future occurrences. The profits from each may have different *NPV*s, because of different time horizons and discount rates, as well as costs and revenues. To complicate matters further, the forecasts as to the future values of any of these variables may be made with different degrees of uncertainty. There are thus different possible combinations of factors influencing profit, and any particular choice of action or strategy may have different possible outcomes, with different degrees of likelihood.

Assume, for example, that a firm has three possible strategies, A, B and C. The best possible profit level of any of them is considered to be £100,000. Strategy A is assessed as having a 30 per cent chance, Strategy B a 20 per cent chance and Strategy C a 15 per cent chance of achieving this top profit level. Such assessment, though often subjective and imprecise, may actually be a factor in a firm's decision making and, with no other information, this firm will probably choose Strategy A. However, it is not just the probability of a high profit that determines the firm's choice of strategy. The probability distribution (and in particular its variance) may also be important. Thus, Strategy A, as well as having a 30 per cent chance of high profits, may also have a 30 per cent chance of bankrupting the firm, and a 40 per cent chance of average profit. This is shown, together with the probabilities of different outcomes of Strategies B and C, in Table 3.1.

While on the basis of the high profit column alone Strategy A is the best choice, when the average profit and bankruptcy probabilities are also known, there is no longer an obvious best choice of strategy. It depends on the attitudes of the firm's decision makers. *Risk averse* decision makers are more likely to go for Strategy C, while those more willing to take risks would choose Strategy A or B.

Attitudes to risk are variable, and may, like the length of time horizon, differ from firm to firm, from industry to industry, country to country, and period to period. In the UK during

TABLE 3.1   Probability distributions of different profit levels for Strategies A, B and C

Outcome	High profit	Average profit	Bankruptcy
Strategy A	0.3	0.4	0.3
Strategy B	0.2	0.6	0.2
Strategy C	0.15	0.7	0.15

the 1980s, for example, many firms responded to the increase in competitive pressures by cutting research and development (R&D) expenditures. These firms have either gone out of business or found alternative sources of new technology in the 1990s. For some of these firms, the reduction in R&D may have been necessary to safeguard short-term profit levels, but it jeopardized their long-term survival. In another example combining risk aversion, time horizon and R&D, Abegglen and Stalk (1985) contrast the firms in the Japanese with those in the American semiconductor industries. Debt-financed Japanese firms, they argue, in comparison with their American counterparts, have closer relations with their bankers, take more financial risks by borrowing more, distribute lower proportions and reinvest higher proportions of profits, spend more on R&D and market development, and, as a result, grow faster. 'Traditional financial institutions in the United States are uncomfortable with the aggressive financial policies of the Japanese; US shareholders are assumed to want high profits and dividends' (Abegglen and Stalk, 1985, p. 14).

While there have been changes in both the American and Japanese economies since the early 1980s, that differences did exist at that time is substantiated by a well-known survey of Japanese and American managers. The survey showed, among other things, that while American managers ranked return on investment as their primary goal, Japanese managers ranked improving products and introducing new products as theirs; the American managers ranked higher stock prices as second out of eight goals, the Japanese ranked it eighth (Scherer and Ross, 1990, p. 40). These differences reflect the different time horizons. The introduction of new products, for example, may reduce current profits, but the aim is to have a positive impact on future profits. The Japanese have taken more financial risks but, with their longer time horizon, have reduced competitive risks by investing in the future of their companies (Abegglen and Stalk, 1985, p. 14). Among the reason for the longer time horizon of the Japanese are: lower cost of capital arising from a higher Japanese propensity to save; life-time employment in the large Japanese firms;[7] close relations between firms and banks, and between buyers and suppliers; and culture.

A similar contrast to that between American and Japanese business behaviour could be drawn between British and German business behaviour. The British financial system is, like that of the United States, based more on capital market funding than on bank credit, and Germany, like Japan, is more credit-based than capital-market-based. As a result, the problem of 'diverse shareholders who take little interest in the development of the firm, except for the short term prices of their shares' (Christensen, 1992, p. 161), is likely to be more prevalent in the UK (and the USA) than in Germany (or Japan). The financial system is just one factor in the differences between the time horizons of firms and countries. Whatever the reason, it is clear that firms—even in the same industry—can and do attach different values to n in Eq. (3.1).

The choice of r (discount rate) is also important. The higher r, the lower the NPV. The higher n, the less certainty there can be about r. Arguably, firms will tend to choose as a discount rate the rates of interest they would have to pay on borrowed money, or the rates of interest they could obtain from a bank if they deposited the money instead of investing in projects (the *opportunity cost* of the investment). The greater the discount rate, the greater the opportunity cost of the investment and, in particular, the greater the opportunity cost of forgoing current income for the sake of some future return on the investment. Where interest rates are high, therefore, the immediate future will be more important to firms, and where they are low, the projection of calculations will be further into the future. If, as suggested above, there is a higher propensity to save in Japan and, therefore, lower rates of interest, time horizons will indeed be longer in Japan than in economies with higher rates of interest.

The differences between firms, industries or countries may not prevent—and may indeed encourage—attempts by firms to obtain more accurate and complete information. An important factor here is the cost of and expected returns from information. Arguably, if particular information is seen as potentially contributing to the profitability of the firms in an industry, the market for that information will be competitive. The more competitive this market is, the lower the net return from purchasing the information. The information *market structure*, like that of all other inputs into the production process, will be a factor in determining the value of information to the buyer.

This discussion may lead to the conclusion that attempts to increase the sophistication of analysis are misplaced. After all, no matter how sophisticated or precise the formulae, the information will be inaccurate. However, the increase in the sophistication of means of assessing potential profitability may itself have an impact on competition between firms, even if rules of thumb are as good as mathematically complicated formulae in terms of their accuracy in forecasting profit. One channel through which this influence on competition may occur is through business schools, where ability to handle mathematics and statistics has become increasingly important. The analytically inclined graduates of these schools may in general be better suited to the demands of managerial decision making in large firms (Auerbach, 1989, p. 112). On the basis of this argument, even without actually applying the techniques, the people who have successfully mastered them make better managers. The future may not be 'knowable' and profit maximization may therefore be impossible, but the development of techniques can, in this way, contribute to the success of large, complex firms.

Firms are organizationally complex

The complex structure and size of organizations form the basis of another objection to the focus on modern corporations as profit-maximizing entities. The production of most goods and services takes place in business organizations that are multi-plant operations structured into multiple divisions, such as the research and development, production, advertising, sales, and accounting–finance departments. As firms become larger, activities become increasingly separated, and so it becomes more difficult to ensure that information is communicated rapidly and accurately between them. Decisions that might be consistent with profit maximization are more difficult to enforce. Bureaucracy may set in. In addition, the separation of activities may breed diverse and conflicting objectives. There are at least two broad reasons for these conflicts of interest. The first is technological, the second cultural or psychological.

The *technological* reason arises from differences in the number of products that the various parts of the firm produce efficiently. Let us take, for example, a large software firm which also produces its own software manuals. The technology of software manual printing may require that in any one print run, 10,000 manuals have to be printed if the average cost of printing manuals is to be minimized. The distribution department may require no more than 1000 manuals in any one delivery from the printing department. There are techniques available to the firm to help decision makers to decide on how to solve this problem, such as including storage costs for manuals in the costs of production. However, there is a conflict of interest that arises from the nature of the technology in printing, a conflict that requires resolution.

The *cultural/psychological* reason arises from the established customs and practices of different disciplines' training, education and experience.[8] For example, in a given pharmaceutical company, the scientists of the research division may be convinced that they are about to make a breakthrough in relation to a new medicine they are developing. The accounting department may have already extended all the finances allocated for that particular project. The research division requests that additional finance be made available, and the accounting division refuses. The scientists in the research division optimistically perceive the possibility of a breakthrough; the accountants perceive their role as cost-containment, and the confining of expenditure to that which was planned.

Where there are such conflicts, efforts may be made to resolve them by the passing of decision making up the line to more senior management. But senior management may get messages distorted by the interests of the parties in conflict. Each will want management to be convinced of the immutability of its position, and will attempt to present it in such a way as to achieve that end. In addition, management itself may be more closely associated with one side than another. Managers with an accounting background may lean towards cost-constraining decisions, while those from an engineering, production, or scientific background may prefer process- or product-improving decisions.

There is a partial counter-argument to that which posits increasing organizational complexity as an impediment to profit maximization. Increasing complexity leads to an awareness of the need for more precise cost accounting. Auerbach (1989, p. 109) writes that 'interest in the problems of costing increased with the growing scale and complexity of business, the ever greater importance of overheads in total costs, and the need for a method for setting prices in heavy goods sectors such as engineering'. This is related to the discussion above of the impact of improved techniques on the training of managers. Both developments—in costing and in techniques for assisting in decision making—may improve information, but information remains imperfect.

Another partial counter-argument is that if we consider the value of the firm to be the *NPV* of the differences between all its future revenues and all its future costs then this can be used to assess the impact of decisions in different functional areas of firms. In the example of the software firm, a decision as to whether to improve the efficiency of manual printing by buying in larger machines, would be analysed for its impact on the value of the firm as a whole. While the printing department may reduce its printing costs, the distribution department would increase its storage costs.

Thus, various decisions in different departments of the firm can be appraised in terms of their effects on the value of the firm as expressed in [the *NPV* equation]. Therefore, the value maximization model is useful in describing the integrated nature of managerial decision making across the functional areas of business. (Hirschey and Pappas, 1993, p. 2)

While it is true that growth in size and complexity of firms drives them to find better ways of measuring their costs and of assessing and integrating the different functional decisions, this does not obviate the possibility of intra-firm conflict of interests (due in particular to the divorce between ownership and control, which is discussed in Section 3.2, below). As long as these exist, there will be incentives for misinformation to be generated.

Differences within firms, and between firms, industries and societies, thus all raise difficulties for the profit maximization theory: those within firms because they engender separate interests from those of the firm; those between firms because they suggest that there might be different types of profit-maximizing behaviour.

The decision about the appropriateness of assuming profit maximization to be the objective of firms is inconclusive. Under each of the three headings arguments both for and against have been put. For example, under the first heading, it was argued that firms may not consciously aim for $MR = MC$. However, some evidence suggests that *ex ante* those firms that succeed/survive may be those that have actually achieved this result. Other evidence suggests that even *ex ante* some aspects of the behaviour of long-surviving, successful firms are not profit maximizing. Generally, neoclassical theory continues to assume profit maximization as the objective of firms while other theories focus either on other objectives or on factors other than the goals or objectives of firms in their long-term survival and success. However, there are neoclassical elements in other theories of the firm, and many economists working on the nature and behaviour of firms use more than one approach to enhance their attempts to understand and explain firms.

3.2   Other theories of the firm

Among teachers of management theory the dissatisfaction in the 1930s with the simple conception of a firm as a mechanism which transforms atomistic inputs into marketable outputs resulted in alternative perspectives. A legal–economic view of the firm emerged, aimed at revealing key aspects of the internal structure of the corporate firm. One development of this view formed the basis of the managerial theory of the firm (Section 3.2.1). Other developments, based on the work of Coase, Williamson and others, are discussed in Sections 3.2.2–3.2.5.

3.2.1   Managerial theory

Throwing some light into the neoclassical black box, the managerial theory emphasized the complex nature of the modern corporate firm. In their pioneering work, Berle and Means (1932) described the diminishing influence of shareholders in the decision-making process of large corporations in the USA from the turn of the century. This left much of the decision making to the manager, whose objectives, it was suggested, could be different from those of the owners of the firm. If, in terms of its influence on managers' salaries, size of firm, for example, was more important than a firm's profitability, then growth could be a more important objective of firms than profit.

Other reasons why hired managers may be more preoccupied by sales or revenue maximization than by profit maximization include, according to Baumol (1967), the following:

1 If sales fail to rise, this is often equated with reduced market share and market power, and consequently, with increased vulnerability to the actions of competitors.
2 When asked about the way his or her company performs, an executive would typically reply in terms of what the firm's level of sales are.
3 The financial market and retail distributors are more responsive to a firm with rising sales.

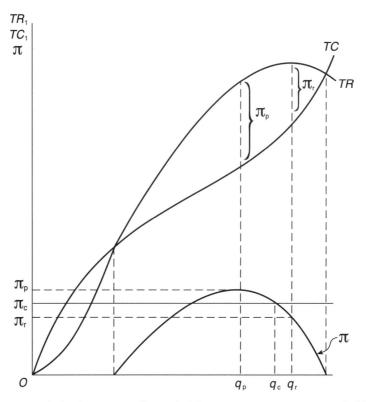

Figure 3.1   Revenue maximization: q_p, profit-maximizing output; q_r, revenue-maximizing output; q_c, revenue-maximizing output, subject to a minimum profit constraint, π_c

The model developed by Baumol attempts to reconcile the behavioural conflict between profit maximization and the maximization of the firm's sales (i.e. its total revenue). It assumes that the firm maximizes sales revenue subject to a minimum profit constraint. Figure 3.1 depicts the firm's total sales revenue (TR), total cost (TC) and total profits (π). The quantity q_p represents the output produced by a profit-maximizing firm, and q_r the output produced by a revenue-maximizing firm.

The revenue-maximizing level of output is the level at which the marginal revenue is zero (and the elasticity of demand is unity). The output q_c is that which is produced by the revenue-maximizing firm *when constrained by a minimum profit* π_c. The difference between the maximum possible level of profit and minimum constrained profit (i.e. between π_p and π_c) is called 'sacrificeable' by Baumol. In his view, these profits will be voluntarily given up by the firm in order to increase sales revenues. If the sacrificed profits are too apparent, they would tend to attract other firms acting in the same market, and would tend to create the ultimate threat of takeovers. This is why the sacrifice 'will be done quietly and only in way which *don't* look like sacrificing' (Shepherd, 1990, p. 251). In any event, the profit-maximizing output will generally be less than the revenue-maximizing output. The profit-constrained revenue-maximizing output may be greater than or less than the revenue-maximizing output. If $q_c < q_r$, then the firm will produce q_c. If $q_c > q_r$, then the firm will produce q_r. Baumol argues that the unconstrained equilibrium position never occurs in practice.

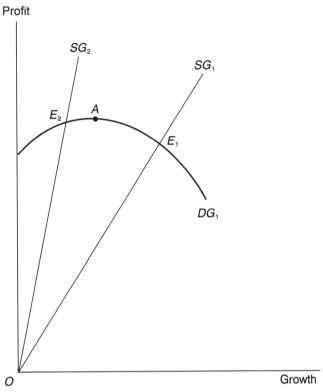

Figure 3.2 Growth maximization

The managerial theory of the firm was further developed by a number of writers, and in particular by Marris (1963, 1966), whose 1966 formulation has become 'the standard one for analysis of [the growth of] the managerially controlled firm' (Hay and Morris, 1991, p. 328). In this model, Marris formalized the hypothesis that managerial control would lead to growth as an objective, showing that shareholders were a less important constraint on such firms than financial markets. Marris's model is dynamic in the sense that it incorporates growth. Like Baumol's model, it assumes that managers will act to maximize their utilities rather than profits, but in contrast to Baumol, it assumes that this will be achieved through growth rather than sales (Fig. 3.2).

At its simplest, the model has two curves, one of supply growth (SG_1), and one of demand growth (DG_1). The axes are profit rate and growth rate, with growth arising through diversification into new products, rather than expansion of output. The supply growth is the maximum growth of supply that can be generated from each profit rate, given management's attitudes to growth and job security. Supply growth is directly and constantly related to profit, because a higher profit facilitates both more investment from retained earnings, and more funds to be raised in the capital market. Unlike in relation to demand growth, the positive relationship between supply growth and profit is possible at both low and high levels of profit (and growth).

The demand-growth curve shows the maximum profit rate consistent with each growth of demand. With demand growth, growth is seen as determining profits, rather than—as in supply growth—profit determining growth. Growth, which is diversification into new products, leads to an increase in the profit rate at low levels of growth because the first new products that the firm introduces will be the most profitable. As more and more new products are introduced (i.e. as the growth rate increases) so more has to be spent on R&D for the next lot of products and on advertising for the sale of the current new products. In addition, other costs will increase as a result of the need for more complex management of increasing numbers of products. So, at some point (A in Fig. 3.2), further growth will lead to a decline in the rate of profit.

In the Marris model, where the supply-growth and demand-growth relationships are satisfied, there will be a unique state of growth and profit equilibrium. The rate of growth of demand will match the rate at which investment in the firm provides the volume and range of products required to meet this demand. This occurs at the point of intersection between the two curves, at point E_1 in Fig. 3.2. Rather than at point A, where the profit rate would be maximized, management chooses to situate the firm at point E_1, where, under certain constraints, the growth rate is maximized.

To elaborate on the nature of these constraints, the model introduces the possibility of alternative supply-growth curves. Assume, for example, that rather than the rate of retention inherent in SG_1, management had chosen to retain a much lower proportion of profits for reinvestment. This would lead to a much steeper supply-growth curve, say SG_2. Along SG_2 each profit rate will result in a much lower level of growth than was the case along SG_1, and the equilibrium will be at E_2, at a lower growth rate than E_1.

In this model, what determines which retention rate is actually chosen? Management would prefer to be at a point like E_1, shareholders would prefer the firm to be at point A (though in the short term they presumably would not mind a high proportion of profits being redistributed in dividends). Ultimately, management's desire to keep their jobs, interacting with the financial markets, will determine where the equilibrium will be situated. If managers pursue growth in such a way as to borrow too much, fail to maintain appropriate levels of liquidity and/or retain too high a proportion of profits, then shareholders will begin to sell shares, share prices will decline and the company will become subject to takeover. Alternatively, it will become bankrupt. Either way the managers are likely to lose their jobs. So the relative weights of job security and desire for growth in the utility of management on the one hand, and the sensitivity of the financial market to the company's performance on the other hand, will determine the position of the supply-growth curve and, by implication, the equilibrium point. For example, the more expansionist the management, and the less sensitive the markets, the further to the right, beyond point A, will be the equilibrium.

There are other managerial theories of the firm and, as will be shown in Section 3.2.2, more recent theoretical developments arising from some of the basic principles of managerial theory. The three major principles around which general managerial theory came to be articulated during the 1960s are as follows:

1 In a firm, the ownership (by shareholders) is distinct from control (exercised by managers).
2 Because of this separation, it is possible to conceive of a divergence of interests between owners and controlling managers.
3 Firms operate in an environment that affords them an area of discretion in their behaviour.

Attempts to verify empirically the difference in motivation between owner-controlled (OC) and management-controlled (MC) firms have been inconclusive, primarily because of the variety of exogenous (outside-the-firm) factors facilitating the growth of the firm. Comparing two groups of firms (OCs and MCs) in order to identify the differences in motivation is possible only if these exogenous factors (such as growth-of-demand and growth-of-supply conditions) are identical (Hay and Morris, 1991, pp. 356–62).

Douma and Schreuder (1992, p. 80) suggest that the inconclusive results of empirical attempts to verify the difference in profitability between OC and MC firms may be because there are in fact no such differences. There are three mechanisms, they explain, that may act to prevent managers from enriching themselves at the expense of the shareholders: the *market for corporate control*, the *market for managerial labour*, and the *market for the company's products*.

1 Where there is a market for corporate control, a decline in the performance of a management team can result in its displacement by another management team. For example, if the company is quoted on the stock market, incompetence or other underperformance on the part of the managers will result in a decline in the company's share price. If this decline is perceived to have resulted from poor management, and therefore rectifiable by its replacement, the shares can be subject to purchase by individuals or institutions aiming to gain control of the firm. Having gained such control, they can then replace the management. Alternatively, existing shareholders, to prevent takeover, may themselves replace the management. The point is that where, as in this example, there is a market for corporate control, there is pressure on top managers who wish to hold their jobs, to keep the firm's performance near to what is perceived to be its potential by the market.

2 The market for managerial labour is one in which shareholders are the buyers, and managers the sellers of their managerial expertise. The better this market works, the less likely is a top manager to enrich him or herself at the expense of shareholders. To do so—and be caught—would damage the manager's reputation, and prevent him or her from getting a better job elsewhere. If there are relatively few top managerial jobs in comparison to the number of people seeking these jobs, arguably these people will attempt to get the best-paying, most prestigious of these jobs. Their desire for higher income will be expressed in their attempts to manage the firm as best they can, in the shareholders' interests.

3 Even if there is no market for corporate control, a competitive market for the company's products can ensure that managers act in the interests of the owners. Self-enrichment on the part of the manager will increase the company's costs, it will have to charge higher prices or reduce the quality of its products and this will result in a loss of market share. At the extreme, the company will be forced to go out of business, and the manager will lose his job. In this way a competitive product market can generate disincentives to inefficient management.

It is possible that all three of these mechanisms either do not operate, or do not operate efficiently in a particular industry. Even in their absence, there are ways of ensuring that the interests of managers (agents) are brought into line with those of the owners (principals) of a firm. We discuss this issue in Section 3.2.2.

3.2.2 Principal–agent theory[9]

At its simplest, principal–agent theory examines situations in which there are two main actors, a principal who is usually the owner of an asset, and the agent who makes decisions which affect the value of that asset, on behalf of the principal. As applied to the firm, the theory often identifies the owner of the firm as principal, and the manager as agent, but the principal could also be a manager, and an employee nominated by the manager to represent him in some aspect of the business could be the agent. In this case the asset, which the agent's decisions could enhance or diminish, is the manager's reputation.

To explain the relationship between principal–agent (or agency) theory, and other theories of the firm, we turn to Williamson's (1985, pp. 23–9) categorization of approaches in IO in terms of their views on contracts. There are two main such approaches or branches: monopoly, which views contracts as a means of obtaining or increasing monopoly power; and efficiency, which views contracts as a means of economizing. The early work on SCP and particularly on barriers to entry, for example, belongs on the monopoly branch of contracts. Both transaction cost and principal–agent theories belong on the efficiency branch (together with most of what Williamson calls the New Institutional Economics). Thus, in Williamson's perspective, agency theory is the theory that focuses on the design and improvement of contracts between principals and agents.

Among the major concerns of principal–agent theory is the relationship between ownership and control,[10] and in this respect it can be seen to have emerged from the managerial theory tradition. Indeed, in that it focuses on the contractual aspects of that relationship, and often adopts game-theoretic methods, principal–agent theory can be seen as a new IO version of a sub-set of managerial theory. Recent work in this area tends to be highly theoretical.[11]

Principal–agent theory sees the firm—as does neoclassical theory—as a legal entity with a production function, contracting with outsiders (including suppliers and customers) and insiders (including owners and managers). There is information asymmetry between principals and agents but, unlike in transaction cost theory (which usually assumes *bounded rationality*) there is often assumed to be *unbounded rationality*. We will discuss this in more detail below; in the context of the design of contracts between principals and agents, unbounded rationality refers to the ability of those designing the contract to take all possible, relevant, future events into consideration. The principal may know various things not known to the agent (in relation, for example, to the prospects of the firm), and vice versa (the agent may have a lower commitment to the firm than he leads the principal to believe), but if the obligations of both under the contract can be specified, taking into consideration the possibilities arising from private information, then there is unbounded rationality despite the information asymmetry.

The agency theorists' concerns—and in this they are different from neoclassical theorists— are with 'owners' and managers' problems of coping with asymmetric information, measurement of performance, and incentives' (Chandler, 1992b). The major difference between principal–agent and transaction cost theories is that the former focuses on the contract, the latter on the transaction. The problem for principal–agent theory is how to formulate a contract such that the *shareholders* (the *principal*) will have their interests advanced by the *manager* (the *agent*), despite the fact that the manager's interests may diverge from those of the shareholders. Or, to express it in terms closer to those of the theorists in this area, the problem 'is whether there exists any class of reward schedule for the agent (the manager) such as to yield a Pareto-efficient solution for any pair of utility functions both for the agent and the principal' (Aoki, 1984, p. 49).

Where objectives of the agent are different from those of the principal, and the principal cannot easily tell to what extent the agent is acting self-interestedly in ways diverging from the principal's interests, then the problem of *moral hazard* arises. The problem originated in the insurance industry, referring to the possibility that people with insurance will change their behaviour, resulting in larger claims on the insurance company than would have been made if they had continued to behave as they did before they had insurance. This change in behaviour may, moreover, be known to the insurer, but may not be fraudulent—or, at least, may not be provably fraudulent. In the context of relations between principals and agents, moral hazard refers to the possibility that, once there is a contract, the agent may behave differently from how he or she would have behaved had he or she not had the contract. It must, in addition, be difficult to determine whether this behaviour has conformed to the terms of the contract.[12] This arises particularly where the agent is a member of a team.

Principal–agent theorists have attempted, by specifying conditions such as that the manager's salary be equal to the expected value of his or her marginal product, to design contracts on the basis of which there will be an incentive for the manager to act in the shareholders' interests. However, the importance of the *team element* in managerial jobs discredits the notion of a manager's marginal product (Aoki, 1984, Ch. 2 and p. 50). This team element (raised, as we saw in Chapter 2, by Alchian and Demsetz, 1972) is also present at the production level. Doeringer and Piore (1971, p. 27; quoted by Aoki, 1984, p. 26) emphasized the importance of 'social cohesion and group pressure' in the establishment of work customs. The process whereby such routines are created, and their importance in the success or otherwise of firms, are central concerns of the evolutionary theory of the firm (Section 3.2.4). Principal–agent theory is more concerned with implications for *shirking*, that is, a reduction in effort by an agent who is part of a team. There may be a slight decline in total output as a result, but the cause will usually be unidentifiable. The shirking manager knows that his or her diminished effort is unobservable. Shirking is the moral hazard arising from the employment contract. What the principal can do, in the formulation of contracts, to offset shirking (and other types of management misbehaviour), is a key problem of principal–agent theory.

There are a number of ways of controlling moral hazard. Rather than attempting to calculate the value of each manager's marginal product, managers could each be paid a salary plus a bonus based on the performance of the company. The problem here is that if the utility of leisure is different for different managers, then again some may work more and others less at maximizing the long-run value of the firm. (On the other hand, where there is a great deal of cultural homogeneity, as can be argued to be the case in Japan, this salary plus bonus system seems to be effective.) Other examples of suggestions by principal–agent theorists for solving employment contract problems include the development of efficient ways of *monitoring* the performance of individual managers (or management teams), providing *incentive contracts* which reward agents only on the basis of results, bonding (where the agent makes a promise to pay the principal a sum of money if inappropriate behaviour by the agent is detected) and mandatory retirement payments. This last acts like a bond, in that there is a disincentive for the employee to misbehave because if he or she does misbehave he or she may be fired with the resultant loss of retirement payment.

It should be emphasized that, to the extent that managers want to keep their jobs, the three markets (for corporate control, managerial labour and the firm's products) can control moral hazard. In relation to the market for corporate control, for example, 'many observers have interpreted the hostile takeovers [of the 1980s] as a corrective response to managerial moral hazard: the takeovers, it is claimed, were intended to displace entrenched managers who were pursuing their own interests at the expense of the stockholders' (Milgrom and Roberts, 1992, p. 182).

The fact that the acquisition share prices were higher than they had been in the market prior to takeover, may be evidence of management misbehaviour or moral hazard. This would be so if the original market value of the shares had been the equivalent of the company's value (net present value of the future stream of profit that could reasonably be expected) under the original management, and the acquisition price was the company's value under the new management. It may, on the other hand, indicate an overestimation by the acquiring firm or individual of its/his or her capacity to improve the performance of the company. Milgrom and Roberts (1992, pp. 182–3) seem to conclude that the takeover premium was indicative of moral hazard when arguing that there is other evidence of management misbehaviour in the adoption during the 1980s by management of the *poison pill* defence against takeovers. The poison pill is a special security, which gives the holder the right to acquire shares at very low prices in the event of a hostile takeover. Poison pills were created by management, in some cases without shareholder approval.

If, as Stiglitz (1991) suggests, the acquiring firm in takeovers generally experiences no increase in its own share values, then it is more likely that there has in fact been an overestimation by the acquiring firm of its ability to improve the performance of the target company. This is indicative, in other words, of an overestimation of the moral hazard of the managerial employment contract in the acquired firm.

The most obvious solution to the problem of conflict of interest between the principal and agent is for the principal to become his or her own agent. Where there is team production, and the existence of a monitor can reduce shirking by enough to pay his or her own salary, then it may be appropriate for that monitor also to be the owner of the firm. If he or she is not the owner, then there could be a need to monitor the monitor, to ensure that he or she does not shirk. This leads to the conclusion that the existence of firms in which there is an owner and a group of people working as a team for that owner, is a consequence of the need to monitor team production, and the need for the monitor to be the owner—with, for example, the power to fire shirkers, to pay each of the members of the team in accordance with his or her view of their productivity, to keep the residual and to sell the firm.[13] We return to the question of the basis for the existence of firms in the next section, where transaction cost theory, among other things, takes exception to principal–agent theory's conclusion about the significance of the need for monitoring.

3.2.3 Transaction cost theory

Rights of ownership (or *property rights*) to a good or service must be able to be established before a market for that good or service can exist. In an as yet relatively clean-air world, for example, property rights over breathable air cannot be established and no market in this good exists. Transaction costs 'are those incurred in enforcing property rights, locating trading partners, and actually carrying out the transaction' (Hyman, 1992, p. 134). If property rights over a good cannot be established, then transaction cost theory is inappropriate. Work incorporating transaction cost theory has been applied to such issues as the absorption of risk in subcontracting by the Japanese car industry (Asanuma and Kikutani, 1992), problems in the transformation of institutions in the post-Communist period in Eastern Europe (Iwanek, 1992; Williamson, 1992) and the design of policies to encourage research and development (R&D) given the problems related to the low appropriability of the results of R&D (Itoh *et al.*, 1991).

Originally a rather narrow, minority-interest specialism within IO, the work of Coase and his followers has thus clearly become in recent years a major concern of the discipline. In the title of his speech on receipt of the 1991 Nobel Prize for Economics, Coase called this work 'The institutional structure of production' (1992). In this speech Coase was critical of the continuing tendency among some theorists of the firm to ignore the fact that 'the efficiency of the economic system depends to a very considerable extent on how these organizations [firms] conduct their affairs'. He was even more surprised at the 'neglect of the market or more specifically the institutional arrangements which govern the process of exchange'. He was pleased to acknowledge, however, that institutional factors are beginning to be introduced into mainstream economics (1992, p. 714).

What have Coase's contributions been, and how have they been developed in recent years? His seminal article on 'The nature of the firm' (1937) argued that it is due to the existence of transaction costs that firms exist. If it is through the market mechanism that prices determine how factors of production are to be combined to produce what goods, for what markets, then why are organizations necessary? Coase's answer is that where transactions between individuals would be too difficult, inefficient or expensive, such that an organization could co-ordinate them at a lower cost than if they were market transactions, then firms emerge to do this co-ordination and thereby, in a sense, obviate these transactions by *internalizing* them. In general, 'If the costs of making an exchange are greater than the gains which that exchange would bring, that exchange would not take place and the greater production that would flow from specialization would not be realized' (Coase, 1992, p. 716).

The internalization of transactions enables the exploitation of economies of scale or of scope.[14] The extent to which economies of scale can be exploited determines the size of a firm. Under what circumstances will transaction costs be lower when internalized than when left to be negotiated in an external market? This is among the questions asked by Williamson (1985), whose 'many significant insights' have given 'substance to Coase's suggestion that firms reduce transaction costs' (Alchian and Woodward, 1988, p. 65).

Williamson focuses on *bounded rationality* and *opportunism*, and *asset specificity*, in his study of economic organization. Bounded rationality refers to the imperfect ability to solve complex problems. In a game like chess, for example, each player has the same amount of information as the other (there is symmetry of information), but there are so many possibilities that even a brilliant player may not be able to make a fully rational decision. There is bounded rationality when there is imperfect ability to process the available information, and/or when the information itself is imperfect (i.e. there is uncertainty), both in relation to present and future events. Opportunism relates to how people will respond to conflicts, given the existence of bounded rationality. They will behave opportunistically if they act in their self interests by, for example, finding loopholes in contracts. If there was unbounded rationality, the potential opportunistic behaviour would be known, and avoided. Asset specificity refers to assets, involving non-trivial investment, that are specific (or idiosyncratic) to particular transactions (for example skills in an employer–employee contract). Williamson shows that different combinations of these three elements give rise to different contractual models (Williamson, 1985, p. 31).[15] (This attention to contracts, both in terms of the relations within and between firms, has been a central feature of Williamson's work on transaction cost analysis.)

To illustrate, if there was no opportunism, there would be no need for internalization. Without opportunism, Williamson (1985, p. 51) argues, 'there is no occasion to supplant market exchange by other modes of economic organization if promises to behave in a joint profit-maximizing way are self-enforcing and if sharing rules are agreed to at the outset'.

Without opportunism, the transaction would take place within the market, rather than within a hierarchy. But bounded rationality is a precondition for opportunism. So, opportunism and bounded rationality are likely to give rise to internalization. This, however, is still only part of Williamson's explanation for why and when internal governance will be preferable to market governance. The third element is asset specificity: 'Market contracting gives way to bilateral contracting, which in turn is supplanted by unified contracting (internal governance) as asset specificity deepens' (Williamson, 1985, p. 78). Asset specificity refers either to physical or to human elements in the transaction. For asset specificity, assets involved in the transaction are, by definition, not freely available for other uses. There are costs involved in applying them in any other than this particular transaction. This results in a need for continuity, so that those who have invested in the assets can derive revenues from them. In terms of an individual adapting skills for a particular firm, for example, once that has been done, this is no longer the kind of 'faceless contracting' characteristic of market transactions—the 'pairwise identity of the parties' now matters (Williamson, 1985, p. 62). The more specific the asset, the greater the need for continuity, the more likely it will be that internal governance will replace market governance.

There are importance differences between Coase and Williamson. Williamson himself (1985, p. 78) differentiates his theory from that of Coase as follows:

	Coase	Williamson
Factors favouring organization of production in the firm rather than in the market	Bounded rationality	Bounded rationality, opportunism and asset specificity

While they understand the determinants of transaction costs differently, however, both Coase and Williamson are agreed that minimization of transaction cost is the basis for the existence of firms. There is not unanimity on this issue. Alchian and Demsetz (1972) argued that *technological non-separability* is the main factor responsible for the existence of firms. This refers, for example, to essential co-operation among workers in order to load freight. The firm exists to monitor, measure and allocate the benefits of team performance. While this concept has been useful in emphasizing the network of relationships underlying—and created by—firms, it has not, in general, been as successful as transaction cost in the analysis of more complex organizations (Alchian, 1984; Williamson, 1985, p. 88). It should be added, however, that Demsetz (1988) has more recently argued that much of the work on transaction cost does not adequately take into account the role of the firm in the acquisition and use of knowledge. Loasby (1990) points out that 'Demsetz recognizes the need for patterns of organization which foster the development and use of knowledge, and of the embodiment of knowledge in people, in a way which suggests an unrecognized link with the evolutionary theory of the firm' (discussed in Section 3.1.5 below).

This particular inadequacy of Williamson's transaction cost approach is elaborated by Lazonick (1991, Ch. 6). Lazonick argues at length and convincingly that 'Williamson has viewed the organization as an economic institution that can *only adapt* to a given economic environment' (1991, p. 214). Williamson's is a theory of the *adaptive* firm, and not the *innovative* firm. Lazonick draws on the work of Schumpeter and, in particular, Chandler, to develop an alternative theory, that of the innovative organization. He shows that, although dismissed by Williamson, strategic behaviour of firms is extremely important. Strategic behaviour includes, for example, the development of an organization's resources, making them organization-specific assets, 'with unique productive capabilities' (Lazonick, 1991, p. 217). (Lazonick's ideas on the firm fit firmly into those of the evolutionary theory, discussed in Section 3.2.4.) So, while asset specificity is for Williamson an expression of market failure, for Lazonick it is an outcome of organizational success. In summary, Lazonick's (1991, p. 224) view is that: 'At best, Williamson's transaction cost perspective explains what some *established* business organizations do to *survive* in a capitalist economy. With his focus exclusively on the adaptive organization, his ... framework cannot explain how innovative organizations attain and sustain competitive advantage.'

Related to the transaction cost theory's difficulty in explaining the innovative organization, is the problem of the innovation itself. We will discuss the theory of technological change and innovation in detail in Chapter 5. Among other recent concerns in that theory is the notion of incremental change, not arising from any revolutionary, patentable invention or innovation. Such changes can often not be patented or, in other words, ownership rights cannot be established over them. By definition, therefore, they are not amenable to explanation by transaction cost analysis.

There are other criticisms of transaction cost theory, even of Coase's basic conception of transaction cost minimization as the fundamental reason for the existence of the firm. Best (1990, p. 112) shows that Coase relies on diminishing returns to management to explain the size of the firm. The firm will grow, according to Coase, until the point is 'reached where the costs of organizing an extra transaction within the firm are equal to the costs involved in carrying out the transaction in the open market' (quoted in Best, 1990, p. 112). This dependence on substitution at the margin is a failing of neoclassical theory, too, Best argues, and it is a failing because it does not take into consideration that the firm may continue to grow until the industry is monopolized, before the point of diminishing returns to management is reached. If this was possible, it would lead to the indeterminacy of both price and firm size. Best applauds Coase for 'dropping the assumption of perfect information about the future', and for showing that market co-ordination is not synonymous with efficiency, that 'under certain conditions planned coordination within a firm could be more efficient'. But 'Coase, like Marshall, was constrained from developing promising concepts for analysing business organization by ... the specter of inconsistency with the equilibrium theory of price' (Best, 1990, p. 112).

Another criticism of Coase is provided by Auerbach (1988, Ch. 6), who argues that Coase, among others, is wrong to assume that markets exist, and that then, as a response to market imperfections, firms are created. This assumption results in a 'failure to see the role of firms in the *making* of markets'. A market, according to Auerbach, is a behavioural relation. Without the participants (e.g. firms), there would not be a market (Auerbach, 1989, pp. 121–2).

Lazonick, Best and Auerbach, while criticizing other theories of the firm, have also developed their own theories, each of which is in some respects similar to the other, and all related closely to the evolutionary theory of the firm, to which we now turn.[16]

3.2.4 Evolutionary theory

This theory, while acknowledging Williamson's contribution and particularly his concern with firm-specific assets and skills, differs from him in relation to its basic unit of analysis. (See Chandler, 1992a, for a discussion of Williamson's contribution to Chandler's thinking.) For Williamson it is the transaction; for Chandler and other evolutionary theorists it is the firm itself 'and its specific physical and human assets' (Chandler, 1992b).[17] The features of the firm on which they focus are strategy, structure and core *organizational capabilities*. Broadly defined, organizational capabilities refer to a firm's spare managerial capacity arising from indivisibilities or different rates of growth of the various aspects of the firm, as well as the knowledge, skills and experience within the firm. The spare capacity can be in virtually any area of operation of the firm, including marketing, production, raw material procurement and finance (see Robertson and Langlois, 1995). Best (1990, p. 128)—drawing on Penrose (1959)—explains one aspect of the generation of spare capacity by arguing that 'each time a new system is in place and procedures become routinized, idle managerial resources appear'. *Organizational routines*—different at different levels in the organization—are thus the building blocks of organizational capabilities. There are learned routines in each of the various functional areas of the organization—including buying, production, distribution, marketing and R&D—and, even more importantly, in the co-ordination of these functions (Chandler, 1992b).[18] As Clark and Juma (1987, p. 59) put it, 'Routine is the genetic code of the firm; it carries the adaptive information required for competition and survival.'[19]

Robertson and Langlois (1994) clarify the relationship between capabilities and routines by pointing out that 'routines refer to what an organization actually does, while capabilities also include what it may do if its resources are reallocated. Thus a firm's routines are a subset of its capabilities that influence but do not fully determine what the firm is competent to achieve.'

It is important to note that the recently developed evolutionary theory of the firm is critical of that expounded by Alchian (1950), which was essentially a social Darwinist theory. According to this theory the internal workings of the firm are irrelevant, because the 'pressure to survive will in the long-term dictate the behaviour of firms' (Auerbach, 1988, p. 46). Those that do not follow what turns out to have been the correct course of action (pursuit of profit) will not survive. Alchian's theory ignored the patterns of behaviour, attitudes and motivations of firms or, to be more precise, he reduced all these to 'adaptive, imitative, and trial-and-error behaviour in search for profits' (Alchian, quoted in Clark and Juma, 1987, p. 52). The critique of Alchian's evolutionary theory is that it was concerned with outcomes rather than processes, it was static, ignoring the time dimension (Auerbach, 1988, p. 48) and that it made technical change 'exogenous to economic evolution', a response to but not affecting market conditions (Clark and Juma, 1987, p. 53). Alchian's was an extreme form of the structuralist view (Auerbach, 1988, p. 46).

In Chandler's recent articles (1992a, 1992b)[20] he applies the evolutionary theory of the firm to the empirical information in his book, *Scale and Scope* (1990). The theory, emphasizing 'the continuous learning that makes a firm's assets dynamic', provides an understanding of how and why certain firms have succeeded (Chandler, 1992b, p. 98). In the late nineteenth century, for example, Britain had all the comparative advantages necessary for domination of the world dye markets, including the scientific knowledge, the raw materials and large markets, yet by the turn of the century the German firms like Bayer, BASF and Hoechst had become the world leaders. The explanation is the investment in production, distribution and management undertaken by the German firms. This investment was designed for—and succeeded in—the exploitation of economies of scale and scope. They thereby achieved competitive advantage which offset the British comparative advantage.[21] Moreover, like other successful firms in other industries, they continued to lead by expanding into foreign markets and related industries, 'driven much less by the desire to reduce transaction, agency and other information costs and much more by a wish to utilize the competitive advantages created by the coordinated learned routines in production, distribution, marketing and improving existing products and processes' (Chandler, 1992b, p. 93).

'Economists,' Chandler writes, 'particularly those of the more traditional mainstream school, have not developed a theory of the evolution of the firm as a dynamic organization' (1990, p. 593). His work contributes to, and encourages others in the development of, such a theory.

Best (1990), for example, like Lazonick, draws on Schumpeter and, although critical of Chandler, formulates a theory of the firm which is consistent with the type of theoretical development that Chandler calls for. 'Schumpeterian competition' on which Best bases his theory, is very different from price competition. It focuses on competition from new commodities (which includes both new products and new versions of old products), new sources of supply, new technologies and new types of organization. The firms most likely to face such competition successfully, Best argues, are not the hierarchically organized firms on which Chandler concentrates, but what he calls 'entrepreneurial' firms (Best, 1990, p. 11). There are three main characteristics of such firms. Firstly, they act strategically, i.e. 'choosing the terrain on which to compete'. Secondly, they seek strategic advantage not through continuity and long production runs aimed at achieving cost minimization, but through continuous product, process and organizational innovation. Thirdly, they organize production not by repeating the same operation but by maintaining organizational flexibility at all levels, including the micro production level. 'They depend upon learning to maintain competitive advantage' (Best, 1990, p. 13).

Unlike Best, but also contributing to the evolutionary theory, Lazonick (1991, Ch. 3) writes of the 'innovative' firm as one which adopts a high fixed cost strategy of developmental investments. The formation of a new cost structure is an 'evolutionary process' which if successful gives the firm competitive advantage. The process involves innovation 'because it creates quality–cost outcomes that previously did not exist' (1991, p. 97).

One implication of the difference between the perspectives of Best and Lazonick is that the former—with an emphasis on organizational flexibility—underlines the advantages of small firms, while the latter—emphasizing the advantages of a high fixed cost strategy—suggests that large firms are more likely to succeed. This difference shows that among writers broadly within the evolutionary tradition—as within most others—there is not necessarily unanimity, even on basic questions about firms. Robertson and Langlois (1994), in focusing on inertia, uncover another difference among evolutionary theorists of the firm. They show that Nelson and Winter (1982) are aware of both the positive and negative aspects of routine: 'To the extent that these routines are efficient and difficult to come by, they are a most important asset, but they also induce inertia because they are difficult for the firm to change once in place.' Teece (1982), on the other hand, though he discusses the positive aspects of routines, 'neglects the negative side . . . and fails to note that the inflexibility, or inertia, induced by routines and the capabilities that they generate can raise to prohibitive levels the cost of adopting a new technology or entering new fields' (Robertson and Langlois, 1994).

Despite differences of emphasis among writers within the evolutionary school, there are unifying themes. They are all interested in change over the relatively long term—years and decades rather than weeks and months. They are all convinced of the importance of change within firms, not just in terms of products, but also in terms of processes of production and of decision making. They all focus also, to some extent, on industries as well as firms, their concern for what goes on within firms being related to their interest in the determinants of success of one firm or group of firms over another. Finally, as with many other theorists, evolutionary theorists adapt and use elements of other theories—and in particular managerial and transaction cost—in the development of their own views on the nature of firms and industries.

The ideas of the evolutionary theorists will be among those that inform our discussions of the conduct and behaviour of firms. It should be pointed out that, as a far more empirically based and inductive approach than many of the others discussed above, it is also more difficult to rigorously operationalize. As a result of this, research losses may be incurred, but there are also gains to be derived from the extent to which this approach is empirically and historically rooted. Schmalensee (1987) has written of the continued necessity for empirical studies as 'an important source of the general stylized facts needed to guide the construction of useful theoretical tools'. Chandler's work, and that of other evolutionary theorists, can be seen in this light.

3.2.5 Co-operative game theory

Not among established theories, but associated with principal–agent theory and, in some respects, each of the other established theories, Aoki has developed the co-operative game theory of the firm which sees the firm as a coalition of various parties (Aoki, 1984).

As argued by Aoki, the firm can serve 'as a nexus for co-operative relationships between the employees and the shareholders which makes possible the optimal redistribution of risk as well as the efficient collective use of skills, knowledge, and funds' (Aoki, 1984, p. 56).

Strongly opposed to the managerial conception where the objective of the firm is identified with the objective of one of its separate constituents, the idea of a 'nexus of co-operative relationships' provides a link between the various units forming the firm. The behaviour of the firm on the market emerges from this nexus; this behaviour is a co-operative game solution called the 'organizational equilibrium' (Aoki, 1984, p. 69).

This 'coalitional view' disregards, reluctantly, other potential players. Financial institutions, supplying capital to the firm, customers and suppliers, interacting closely with it, and other firms, in competition with it, are all potentially influential players. Although they all lie outside the boundaries of the firm itself—except in the case where some of the employees are also shareholders and customers of the firm—their actions do matter for the determination of the co-operative game solution. Aoki acknowledges, in particular among these outsiders, his omission of the role of the customers of the firm. More importantly, from the point of view of his analysis, he also acknowledges the omission of the '*Schumpeterian* entrepreneurial role' of the manager (Aoki, 1984, p. 196).

Non-cooperative game theory is, as we have seen, much more common in IO. It is, indeed, regarded as a 'characteristic feature' of what has come to be known as the 'new IO' (see Davies and Lyons, 1988, p. 7). Focusing on the strategies of rival firms, it is primarily concerned with the external environment of the firm, and less with its internal coalitional nature.

3.2.6 Summary and consolidation

We have briefly reviewed the major theories of the firm. Each has merits, and each has limitations. They are not necessarily mutually exclusive, in that some economists will use one theory for one application, and another for a different application. The managerial theory was the first to focus on the importance of the structure of the firm, leading to hypotheses on the determinants of the growth of firms. Principal–agent theory, on the basis of a similar view of the structure of firms, focuses on contracts and how they might encompass conflicts of interest to enhance the efficiency of firms. The organizational equilibrium theory also incorporates a notion of structure, but emphasizes the existence of co-operative relationships between the various components of firms. For each of these theories, it has been found to be very difficult to undertake empirical work to test or validate their hypotheses. Table 3.2 summarizes these conclusions.

One early weakness was the absence of a time dimension. Both technology and contract views of the firm have gone some way towards incorporating this dimension: the technology view as in the evolutionary theory with its emphasis on the gathering of capabilities; and the contract view as in the principal–agent theory with its emphasis on eventualities over different time frames. Again, rigorous empirical research is rare.

Chandler (1992a), as a business historian working within (and developing) the framework of evolutionary theory, is unusual among theorists of the firm in having an empirical basis for his

TABLE 3.2 Major theories of the firm

Theory of the firm	Point of focus
Neoclassical	Firm (black box)
Managerial	Firm (owners v. managers)
Transaction cost	Transaction (firm v. market)
Principal–agent	Contract (employer v. employees)
Evolutionary	Firm (organizational capability)
Co-operative game	Firm (organizational equilibrium)

views. Indeed, in his book on *Scale and Scope* (1990), he compared 'the fortunes of more than 600 enterprises—the 200 largest industrial firms at three points in time (First World War, 1929, and Second World War) in each of the three major industrial economies' (Chandler, 1992b).[22]

The significance of technological change (including organizational innovation) as a factor in the conduct (and structure) of firms and in the structure of markets, is accepted in much of the literature. The technological non-separability and transaction cost views both to some extent incorporate this, but it is more fully accounted for by the evolutionary theory.

Within his historical, empirical type of overview, Chandler incorporates the role of technology. He compares, for example, the role in the growth of firms of specific technologies and market situations with that of existing competitive advantages arising from learned routines in 'production, distribution and marketing, and improving existing products and processes'. Specific technologies and market situations were, he concludes, more important in the vertical integration of firms. The desire to exploit competitive advantages arising from the learned routines was more important in the growth into new markets (Chandler, 1992b). This includes expansion into markets in regions or countries new to the operations of the firm, which brings in the geographical dimension of industrial structure to which we turn in the last section of Chapter 4.

Both Best and Lazonick, in their contributions to the development of evolutionary theory, also explicitly incorporate technology and innovation, and this perspective leads them also to address locational issues. In Lazonick's words firms' strategies and structures 'take on a national character because the relevant business organizations do not develop and utilize resources in a political and cultural vacuum' (1991, p. 109). Best accepts even sub-national regional differences, as evidenced in his focus on small-firm *industrial districts* in Italy. These, too, will be addressed in the context of the locational aspects of industrial structure in Chapter 4. *National* and *regional systems of innovation* will also be considered in Chapter 5. First we turn to industrial structure in general.

Notes

[1] According to one recent reviewer of work in industrial organization, 'Neoclassical decision-theoretic analysis and competitive general equilibrium theory have been supplanted almost completely by non-cooperative game theory' (Porter, 1991).

[2] The firm is often said to be a 'black box' in the neoclassical view, suggesting that the internal structure of the firm is irrelevant.

[3] This section draws on George, Joll and Link (1992, pp. 29–38).

[4] According to the authors, a 'real' demand curve shows what actually happens when prices are altered. A hypothetical demand curve 'is based on some particular assumption regarding the behaviour of other firms'. An 'imaginary' demand curve 'shows what the entrepreneur believes will happen when price is altered' (Hall and Hitch, 1939, p. 14).

[5] See discussions on the Marris model, Section 3.2.1 below, and on principal-agent theory, Section 3.2.2 below, where it is suggested that among the goals of takeovers is the one of replacement of the existing management.

[6] Referring to March and Simon (1958), Stiglitz (1991) writes of the finding that because of imperfect information, managers would, in general, not act in such ways as to maximize shareholder value, and, in particular, the cost of obtaining and processing information encouraged the adoption of 'satisficing and rule-of-thumb strategies'.

[7] 'The corporate management decisions of Japanese firms are subject to the dual control (influence) of financial interests (ownership) and employees' interests rather than to unilateral control in the interests of ownership' (Aoki, 1990).

[8] Hofstede (1983) writes, in a different context, of culture as 'that part of our conditioning that we share with other members of our nation, region, or group but not with members of other nations, regions or groups'. The example that follows does not mean to suggest that optimism is necessarily an aspect of the culture of scientists, nor that dogmatic 'sticking to the plans' is necessarily an aspect of the culture of accountants. It aims merely to suggest that there are differences in such cultures and that they may cause conflicts of interest.

[9] This section draws in part on Milgrom and Roberts, 1992, Ch. 6. The reader is encouraged to read that chapter for more details, particularly on the relationship between moral hazard and performance incentives. For game theoretic perspectives on the relationship between principals and agents, see Gardner, 1995, Ch. 10.

[10] See, for example, the article on the 'separation of ownership and control' by Fama and Jensen (1983). Other important articles on principal–agent theory include Mirrlees (1976) and Fama (1980).

[11] See, for example, Maskin and Tirole, 1992, who analyse as a three-stage game the relationship between the principal and agent in which the principal has private information that directly affects the agent's payoff.

[12] An example of moral hazard in employment contracts arises in universities, where there are two differe:t groups of employees, those on short-term contracts, and those with tenure. Tenure is supported by many, and not only those who have tenure(!), as a feature of the independence of the academic, and the need to protect the academic against political pressure. Tenure may perform this function to some extent but it also enables those who have it, to change their behaviour and shirk various duties. The academic on short-term contract, it can be argued, works hard, prepares excellent lectures, volunteers for administrative duties, does above-average research and publishing. Then he or she obtains tenure, relaxes more, gives last year's lectures, avoids administration, and does less research and publishing. In practice there is, no doubt, moral hazard in tenure, but given that the best teachers, administrators and researchers in academia have tenure, academics certainly do not always, or even usually, change their behaviour in the way predicted by moral hazard.

[13] For a more detailed discussion on the issue of team production and the monitor as owner, see Holmstrom and Tirole (1989), or at a more introductory level, Douma and Schreuder (1992, Ch. 6).

[14] Economies of scale arise when the production cost per unit of a good decreases as the number of units produced increases. Economies of scope exist when the cost of producing good x and good y together is less than that of producing either of them separately. For a detailed study of the significance of scale and scope in the evolution of firms, see Chandler (1990).

[15] Different contractual models in this context refers primarily to internal governance and market governance or, in other words, hierarchy and market.

[16] These theories were developed more or less separately from one another—there is no reference in Auerbach (1989) to either Lazonick or Best, no reference in Best (1990) to either Auerbach or Lazonick, and no reference in Lazonick (1991) to Auerbach and only a brief mention (pp. 301–2) of Best's substantiation of some of Lazonick's basic arguments.

[17] See Nelson and Winter (1982), Nelson (1995) and Teece (1987). It should be noted that at least some writers using 'an evolutionary approach to economic change' focus as much on the process of innovation as on firms. Thus Clark and Juma (1987, p. 64) attempt 'to examine the co-evolution between technology and institutions'. Auerbach (1988), although he is clearly concerned with 'The Evolution of Giant Firms' (p. 149) and 'The Changing Pattern of Firm Organisation' (Ch. 8), focuses primarily on the 'competitive process' (Chs 4 and 9).

[18] This article also shows how evolutionary theory, drawing on transaction cost analysis but emphasizing the 'continuous learning that makes a firm's assets dynamic', clarifies the basis for the emergence and development of firms in some of the major industries of the world (Chandler, 1992b).

[19] Demsetz (1988) is interested in the preservation of commitments, which may be either efficiency enhancing or stultifying. As Loasby (1990) points out, this reinforces Demsetz's unrecognized link with the evolutionary theorists.

[20] The rest of this paragraph, unless otherwise specified, is based on these articles.

[21] The comparison between comparative and competitive advantages is also made by a number of other authors, including Teece (1987) and Porter (1990).

[22] According to Porter (1991) 'the most pressing need [in IO research] is for more evidence, including both well-formulated tests of behavioural theories and the more mundane documentation of empirical regularities'. It is just such documentation of empirical regularities—mundane or otherwise—at which Chandler excels.

Questions

3.1 What are the most important impediments to profit maximization: (i) for firms; and (ii) as an assumption on which to build theory?

3.2 If profit maximization has so many impediments, why do so many economists continue to assume it?

3.3 In Table 3.1, which strategy would you choose, and why?

3.4 In what respects are managerial theory and agency theory similar, and in what respects are they different?

3.5 According to Coase, what is the essence of the firm?

3.6 Why is the evolutionary theory of the firm so called?

4 Market structure and location of industry

4.1 Market structure

The contrast between the definition of market structure by those operating within the early SCP paradigm, and the more modern, strategically based definition of market structure, is indicative of the evolution of the SCP paradigm itself. According to Bain (1958), market structures are 'the characteristics of the organization of a market that seem to exercise an influence on the nature of competition and pricing within the market'. On the other hand, Koch (1980) sees market structures as 'the relatively permanent strategic elements of the environment of a firm that influence, *and are influenced by*, the conduct and performance of the firm in the market in which it operates' (Koch, 1980, p. 90). While Bain's definition identifies only a one-way causality, from the organization of the market to competition and pricing, Koch's definition envisages the structure influencing and being influenced by conduct and performance. Both definitions call for the clarification of the concept of a market.

4.1.1 Defining the market and the industry

Although the terms *industry* and *market* are often used interchangeably in economics, they actually refer to different types of economic institutions and activities. An industry is a firm or group of firms and a market is a nexus of interaction between buyers and sellers. (These terms are defined more comprehensively in the paragraphs below.) In general, in order to discuss either industries or markets, we need to find ways of demarcating between them. Two obvious ways of doing so are, first, in terms of the output or product of the industry (or market), and second, in terms of the spatial or geographic extent of the industry (or market).

The nature of the product

A *market* is normally defined as the locus of purchase by buyers and sale by suppliers of similar goods. More broadly, it is the institution within which the interaction between economic agents performing these two functions—buying and selling—establishes the price of the good. For the buyer, two goods x and y are 'similar' if the purchase of x brings the same level of utility as the purchase of y, and if x and y are deemed to satisfy the same need. In other words, x and y belong to the same market if they are highly *substitutable*. The degree of substitutability is computed with the help of the *cross elasticity of demand* (CED) between products. The CED between two products measures the responsiveness of quantity sold of one product to a change in the price of the other product. In other words, it is the degree to which the price change of product y will affect the quantity sold of product x, or:

$$\text{CED} = \frac{\% \text{ change in quantity of } x}{\% \text{ change in price of } y}$$

If, for example, a 30 per cent rise in the price of butter causes a 50 per cent increase in the quantity sold of a soya-based butter substitute, the cross elasticity of demand will be equal to 1.66, a relatively high value. The two goods will be close substitutes and will be classified in the same market, say the market for spreads.[1] The more narrowly defined the product market, the higher the CED would have to be for the two products to be in the same market. Two goods for which a change in the price of one has little or no effect on the quantity demanded of the other can clearly not be considered as part of the same market.

On the producer side, the market becomes the *industry*. In her *Economics of Imperfect Competition*, Joan Robinson (1933) attempted to provide a definition of the industry. She defined it in terms of a commodity, where a '*commodity* is a consumable good, arbitrarily demarcated from other kinds of goods but which may be regarded for practical purposes as homogeneous within itself'. She continued:

An *industry* is any group of firms producing a single commodity. In some cases where a commodity in the real world is bounded on all sides by a market gap between itself and its closest substitutes, the real-world firms producing this real-world commodity will conform to the definition of an industry sufficiently closely to make the discussion of industries in this technical sense of some interest. (Robinson, 1933, p. 17)

In some respects, the 'market gap' identified by Robinson is more difficult to detect today. Indeed, technical change, increased product differentiation and consumers' sophistication render industries' edges more blurred (particularly true for products incorporating new technologies). Nevertheless, we continue to examine industries in terms of relatively homogeneous products, such as the car industry, the computer industry or the clothing industry.

The geographical extent of the market

If the technical boundaries of an industry and of a market are difficult to draw, the geographical limits of a market for a manufactured good are just as difficult to identify. One possible way to solve the problem is to make a convention (rule of thumb) on how much is actually shipped in and out of a particular region at a particular time (Shepherd, 1990). For example, region r_i will be a geographically distinct market for soft drinks, if less than, say, 10 per cent of its local production is shipped out, and less than 10 per cent of its local consumption is shipped in. Other criteria have been suggested for the delimitation of regional and local markets: a low sales value per unit of weight, a high ratio of transportation cost per unit of sales over a standardized distance, or a short average shipment radius (Scherer and Ross, 1990). Although the intuitive meaning of the EU market for cars, as opposed to the Japanese one, is straightforward, the specification of intra-EU geographical limits of the market is a more arduous task. (A comprehensive analysis of the difficulties arising from the definition of the EU market may be found in Fishwick, 1986.)

4.1.2 Definition of the relevant EU market

The Commission of the EU and the Court of Justice have on many occasions attempted to draw the boundaries of the market within the EU. They have done so because of the necessity to deal with the problems of market domination, of concentration and mergers, and in general, of practices seen as endangering the smooth functioning of competition. These are all dealt with in the Competition Policy of the 1957 Treaty of Rome (mainly Articles 85 and 86) and by the 1989 Merger Control Regulation (see Chapter 7). Articles 85 and 86 did not specify what a market was. The only quantitative measurement can be found later in the preamble of the Merger Control Regulation where it is specified that concentration is unlikely to impede competition where 'the market share of the undertakings concerned does not exceed 25 per cent either in the Common Market or in a substantial part of it'.

According to the 1965 Memorandum of the Commission (CEC, 1965), market domination cannot be solely defined by quantitative elements of a given market structure, such as the market share held by the firm. Market domination is regarded first and foremost as putative economic power. A firm with a small market share, but with the ability to evict other competitors from a market can be said to hold such economic power. The non-reliance on conventional quantitative measures led inevitably to a loose definition of the market, within the geographical limits of the EC.

In fact, throughout the period since the establishment of the European Community, the Commission and the European Court of Justice have tried to avoid defining the relevant geographic and product market. In many of the cases dealt with under Competition Policy such definitions were unnecessary. As shown by Fishwick (1993), in one-third of all proposed concentrations (mergers and takeovers) examined under the Merger Control Regulation since its implementation, precise definitions of the market have been unnecessary because even with the narrowest definitions of the product and geographic market, the 25 per cent threshold limit was not reached. Only when it was considered essential, have the Commission and the Court of Justice attempted to define the market. This has led to a myriad of definitions of the relevant market, varying from case to case. 'The definition of the market and the degree of power necessary for a dominant position vary with the offense' (Fox, 1983, p. 368).[2] A case by case approach is inevitable since a firm's strategy can be regional, national or EU-wide.

Arguably, more precise benchmarks are required so that a generic definition of the market can be provided. Progress towards this end has recently been made (see Fishwick, 1993). The application of Articles 85, 86 and of the Merger Control Regulation requires different frameworks, but these variations have been built around the same theme. Under the three policy instruments, the relevant market is defined in terms of (i) product range and (ii) geographic area on the basis of the concept of demand substitution in the short term *and* supply substitution in the short term. *Supply substitution* refers to the potential provision of additional supplies on the part of both incumbent firms and potential entrants.

The inclusion of the notion of supply-side substitution is new; it was introduced for the first time in 1988, in the *Eurofix-Bauco* v. *Hilti and Tetra Pak II* cases which fell under Article 86 (see *Official Journal* (OJ) L 72, 18.3.1992, p. 1). The potential expansion of supply helps in determining the likely concentration level in the market.

Issues surrounding both product and geographic extents of markets and industries have been clarified by Kay's (1990a) concept of the *strategic market*, 'the smallest area within which it is possible to be a viable competitor'; the strategic *product* market is 'the minimum feasible product range'. The geographic dimension of the industry is different from that of the market when 'the location of production can be determined independently of the location of consumption'; a hairdressing salon must be within its market, and production and consumption occur at the same time and place, while the production of watches can take place where it is cheapest, even though the market is global. Beer is somewhere in between, not usually brewed on the premises where it is consumed but for consumption in Europe usually brewed in Europe (shipping it from Australia or the USA is too expensive). In terms of product or process, the 'scope of the industry is influenced by cross elasticities of supply'; we can think of the product/process boundaries of the industry in terms of 'the degree to which manufacturers can choose to substitute one line of production for another'.

It follows from Kay's analysis that although the method used is the same in each case, the market and industry can only be defined on a case by case basis. Applying this to the European Single Market, Kay points out that the strategic market for a good or service may or may not coincide with the aggregate market of the members of the EU; and that the geographic domain of the industry producing the good may be more or less than, or the same as that of the market.

The relevant product market in practice

In the *Aérospatiale-Alenia/De Havilland* case (CEC, 1991) the Commission repeated the definition of the product market based effectively on cross elasticity of demand: 'A relevant product market comprises in particular all those products which are regarded as interchangeable or substitutable by the consumer, by reason of the product characteristics, their prices and their intended use' (Commission Regulation No. 2367/90).

In its 21st Report on Competition Policy (1991), the Commission adds the time dimension, specifying the short-term nature of the definition of the product market: 'In order to belong to the same market, two products must compete to a sufficient degree... This competition must exist or be brought about in the near future and not only be based on a medium or long-term change in demand or supply' (CEC, 1991, p. 357).

In the *Lucas/Eaton* case examining the braking systems industry, the Commission took into account a period of one year when considering the supply substitution between different systems.

Determination of the relevant geographic market

The Commission has endeavoured to define local, national, regional, Community and world markets in the various product markets considered. The relevant geographic market was defined as the EU-wide market for bleach sulphate pulp in the *Woodpulp* case (1985). The allegation was that the Canadian, US, Finnish and Swedish firms were colluders fixing prices at above competition levels. The fact that there was price parity across the EC market, constituted evidence that there was an EC-wide market for this particular product (Fishwick, 1993). In the *Mannesmann/Boge* case,[3] the Commission similarly defined the relevant market (for shock absorbers) as the Union market.

In the *Nestlé–Perrier* case, the market was defined as France, among other factors because of the insignificance of imports—less than 2 per cent of the market. In Belgium, the fact that 51 per cent of consumption is met by imports and the 42 per cent of domestic production is exported, was evidence that Belgium is not a separate market. The relevant geographic market was similarly defined as national in the *Alcatel/Telettra* case (transmission equipment) and in the *Varta/Bosch* case (starter motors). In other instances, the market was, for various reasons, defined as local (retailing), and as international (*Aérospatiale-Alenia/De Havilland* and *Mannesmann/VDO* cases).

Statistics on regions and industries in the EU

Information exists that facilitates rough definitions of industries in terms both of their product and their spatial range. Eurostat, the statistical office of the European Union in Luxemburg, gathers and publishes data on a wide range of economic and social indicators in the EU by region and by industry. The regional data are provided on the basis of the Nomenclature of Statistical Territorial Units (NUTS). There are three different NUTS levels: NUTS 1, at which there are 71 regions in Europe (and an additional one for the French Overseas Departments); NUTS 2, at which there are 183 basic administrative units; and NUTS 3, at which there are 1044 subdivisions of basic administrative units. To illustrate, Spain has seven regions at the NUTS 1 level. Most of these (the exceptions are the smaller regions) break down into a number of basic administrative units at the NUTS 2 level; the NUTS 1 region Noroeste, for example, contains Galicia, Asturias and Cantabria at the NUTS 2 level. Each of the NUTS 2 units in turn is made up of different numbers of NUTS 3 units, depending on size.

The General Industrial Classification of Economic Activities, NACE, provides a system for classifying such economic variables as earnings and numbers employed. Like NUTS, these data are provided at different levels of disaggregation. For example, at the one-digit level, the code 3 refers to metal manufacture: mechanical, electrical and instrument engineering. This breaks down at the two-digit level into seven different categories of metal manufacture; the code 32 refers to mechanical engineering, 33 to office and data processing machinery, 34 to electrical engineering, etc. Each of these two-digit classes in turn subdivides into a number of three-digit groups; under 32, mechanical engineering, 321 refers to manufacture of agricultural machines and tractors, 322 to manufacture of machine tools, and so on.

Combining the NUTS and NACE data can facilitate researchers in answering questions about the relative importance of certain industries in certain countries, regions or units. Jacobson and Mack (1994), for example, use a location quotient methodology to compare Ireland with Denmark as peripheral regions in the EU.

A location quotient (LQ) is a simple measure of spatial concentration based upon either employment or income. Using the notation of Table 4.1:

$$LQ_p = \frac{e_{ip}/e_{op}}{E_{io}/E_{oo}}$$

In the example referred to, location quotients (LQs) were calculated for employment in Ireland and in Denmark as peripheral regions, with the EU as the total base. Each set of LQs—i.e. one set for Ireland and one for Denmark—contain as many LQs as there are NACE two-digit classes. The two sets were then compared with one another. The main finding of the research is that business services are more concentrated in Denmark than in Ireland.

Such research does not, however, answer questions about the relative importance of firms within industries. It is to a closer examination of market structures that we must turn for the focus on the relationships between firms and markets or industries.

TABLE 4.1   Location quotient notation

Employment in Industry i	*Total employment*
e_{ip} = a peripheral place	e_{op} = a peripheral place
E_{io} = total base	E_{oo} = total base

4.1.3   Determinants of market structure

Market structure refers to the way markets are organized. In general, this structure is the result of actions and interactions of individuals and institutions including firms, other business organizations and public bodies. The structure of the market is defined in terms of the number and size distribution of the competing firms. In the traditional model, there are three main elements of market structure:[4]

- The degree of seller (and buyer) concentration
- The degree of product differentiation within individual markets
- The conditions of entry and exit.

In simple competition models, large numbers of firms sell a standardized product on a determined market. However, a high level of price competition gives firms an incentive to differentiate their products. Product differentiation exists when products sold on the same market are no longer considered as perfect substitutes by buyers. Moreover, the greater the extent to which a firm has succeeded in differentiating its product, the greater the extent to which it has raised a barrier to entry into its market. Product differentiation can thus be regarded as an element of market structure but in many empirical studies it is also included as a barrier to entry.

Measurements of product differentiation have been attempted, based on the following assumption: in a given market, the degree of product differentiation is reflected in the advertising intensity. Since product differentiation can be a means of softening price competition, and can be included as such in the list of strategies available to firms, it will be referred to again in Chapter 5.[5] Our analysis here will focus on the two other elements of market structure, concentration and entry conditions.

Measures and definition of concentration

Concentration is a measure of the intensity of competition or of control. It provides information about the relative size of firms in a specific market. The relative size of firms can be measured through their market shares. The market share (MS_{ij}) of firm i (F_i) in a particular industry (I_j) is normally defined as the share of firm i's sales revenue in the total sales revenue of industry j, or:

$$MS_{ij} = \frac{F_i\text{'s sales revenue}}{I_j\text{'s sales revenue}}$$

Among other possible variables for the measurement of market shares are the output, turnover, value added, numbers employed and assets. There are various ways of summarizing the distribution of market shares of the firms in an industry using a single figure known as a concentration index. The most commonly used indices are:

- The n firm concentration
- The Herfindahl index (H)
- The Gini coefficient
- The entropy index
- The Lerner index.

The CRn or n firm concentration ratio   CRn refers to the cumulated market shares of the *n* leading firms in the industry. Normally, *n* is between 4 and 8, but the four-firm concentration ratio (CR4) is most widely used. CR4 measures the share of the market (or industry) held by the four largest firms. CRn is computed as:

$$\text{CR}n = \sum_{i=1}^{n} S_i$$

with $i = 1, 2, \ldots n$

where: the *i*th firm has rank *i* in descending order (i.e. where $i = 1$ that is the largest firm, where $i = 2$ that is the second largest, etc); S_i is the share of firm *i* in the market. This share can be defined on the basis of output, turnover, sales, numbers employed, shipments, etc.

A value close to zero would indicate that the largest *n* firms supply a small share of the market. Conversely, a value close to 1 denotes a high level of concentration. The concentration ratio is popular because of its limited data requirements. Information on size of markets and on shares of the largest firms is available in the EU.[6] In spite of its popularity, this ratio is flawed by its inability to inform us of the relative importance of firms within a particular industry. For example, let the four-firm concentration ratio be equal to 0.9 in two hypothetical industries A and B. The relative market shares of the four largest firms is given in Table 4.2. The same ratio represents two radically different distributions of firms.

The fact that CR4 for industry A is equal to CR4 for industry B suggests that concentration is the same in the two industries and yet, in industry A a dominant firm covers 80 per cent of the market, whereas industry B is characterized by equal sized firms. The four-firm concentration ratio does not reveal the extent to which one or more firms *within* the top four dominate a particular market. This criticism can be answered by providing other CRn ratios, such CR1, CR2, etc. However, this solution is only partial in that, ideally, the index should be a single figure.

The Herfindahl index (H)   The Herfindahl index, which is the second most widely used concentration index, is defined as the sum of the squares of the market shares of the *n* firms in the industry, i.e.:

$$H = \sum_{i=1}^{n} (S_i)^2$$

with $i = 1, 2, \ldots n$

where the *i*th firm and S_i are as defined for CR*i*. S_i, can, for example, be measured in terms of firm *i*'s sales on the market (Q_i) as a fraction of total sales (Q_t).

TABLE 4.2   **Market shares of the four largest firms in two industries**

	Firm 1	Firm 2	Firm 3	Firm 4
Industry A	0.80	0.05	0.03	0.02
Industry B	0.25	0.23	0.22	0.20

Industry A: CR4 = 0.90
Industry B: CR4 = 0.90

TABLE 4.3   The squares of the market shares of the 14 firms in each industry

	Firm 1	Firm 2	Firm 3	Firm 4	Firm 5	...	Firm 14
Industry A	0.6400	0.0025	0.0009	0.0004	0.0001	...	0.0001
Industry B	0.0625	0.0529	0.0484	0.0400	0.0001	...	0.0001

Industry A: $H = 0.6448$
Industry B: $H = 0.2048$

Defined in this way the H index would be:

$$H = \sum_{i=1}^{n} \left(\frac{Q_i}{Q_t} \right)^2$$

The H index combines information about the size of all firms in a market. It is a measure of dispersion and can vary between 0 and 1. The higher H, the higher the dispersion. If H is 0, this suggests that there is a large number of equal-sized firms in the particular industry, and that concentration is low. If H is close to 1, the market is dominated by one large firm.

Let us for the sake of illustration use the same data as in Table 4.2, assuming that in both Industry A and Industry B firms 5 to 14 account for equal shares of the remaining 10 per cent of the market (i.e. each accounts for 0.01, or 1 per cent, of the market). The Herfindahl index (sum of the cells in Table 4.3. for each industry) shows that Industry A is far more concentrated than Industry B. This is in contrast with CR4 and CR14 both of which are identical for the two industries.

The Gini coefficient   The Gini coefficient is a statistical measure based upon the Lorenz curve.[7] The Lorenz curve relates the percentage of total market value of any variable (shipments, value-added, numbers employed, etc.) to the percentage of firms in the market, cumulated from the smallest to the largest (Fig. 4.1).

The diagonal line OD represents the limit case of perfect equality in the distribution. It suggests that there is an even distribution of the market's value of sales among the firms in the market. The greater the deviation of the curve from the diagonal OD, the greater the inequality in firms' sizes. The Gini coefficient enables us to calculate the concentration area, which is situated between the diagonal and the Lorenz curve. It can be defined as the area A over the area $A + B$.

$$GC = S_A/(S_A + S_B)$$

If the Lorenz curve is the diagonal OD, then, in a sense, $S_A = 0$, and, $GC = 0$. It can be shown that at the other extreme, where there is complete inequality in the sizes of the firms (and $S_B = 0$), the Gini coefficient will tend towards 1.

A limitation of the Gini coefficient is that the same GC can correspond to different distributions of firm sizes in the market.

The entropy index   The entropy index (E) is equal to the sum of the shares weighted by their logarithm.

$$E = \sum_{i=1}^{n} S_i \cdot \log \frac{1}{S_i}$$

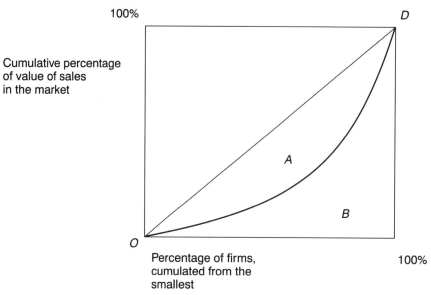

Figure 4.1 Lorenz curve for a hypothetical market x

Borrowed from the theory of information, the entropy index measures the degree of uncertainty associated with a particular market structure. If there is only one firm in the market, the index is 0, and the uncertainty for the monopolist in relation to whether it can keep a random customer is at a minimum. Conversely, when all market shares are equal, the uncertainty is maximum, and:

$$S_i = 1/n$$

In this case, $E = n \cdot 1/n \cdot \log n = \log n$.

In an industry comprising n equal sized firms, the entropy index is equal to $\log n$. The advantage of the entropy index over other measures of concentration is that, in the case where a distribution relates to groups of firms belonging to different size classes, to different industries, and/or to different countries, the index can be decomposed into several components; this facilitates the measurement of the entropy within different groups as well as between groups (See Jacquemin, 1979, p. 40).

The Lerner index The Lerner index (devised by Lerner, 1934) is in fact a measure of monopoly power. It is defined as follows:

$$L = (P - MC)/P$$

where P = price, and MC = marginal cost.

As will be shown in Section 4.1.4. below, in markets defined as perfectly competitive, no single firm can influence price; the demand curve is perfectly elastic. As a result, the price the firm will obtain for each unit sold, will be the same as the price obtained for all other units. In other words, price is equal to marginal revenue (MR). If, in accordance with neoclassical assumptions,

TABLE 4.4 Market shares of the top three firms in two industries

Year	Firm					
	A_1	A_2	A_3	B_1	B_2	B_3
1991	40	20	15	40	20	15
1992	30	15	30	40	20	15
1993	20	20	35	40	20	15
1994	25	25	25	40	20	15

the firms are profit maximizers, production will occur where $MR = MC$. In a perfectly competitive market, where $MR = P$, the Lerner index will be zero. The higher the index, the more concentration (or at least power to extract above normal profits) there is.[8]

Difficulties arising from indices of concentration

The various measures of market concentration incorporate, usually implicitly, the assumption that there is a clear correspondence between a firm and a market, and that firms operate within their national boundaries. In practice, neither condition is fulfilled.

Multi-plant and multi-product firms, for example, do not belong to precisely definable, single markets. It follows that an industry is not necessarily congruent with a market. In which industries should one classify groups such as Ferruzzi, and LVMH (Louis Vuitton Moët Hennessy)? Published accounts do not report in detail the results of the different divisions of a firm, which may be specialized in the production of different products. Concentration indices are thus not able to reveal the dominant positions hidden within conglomerates.

The second problem relates to the association between concentration and competition. The greater the level of concentration, the less competitive the market is considered to be. To illustrate the problem, let us assume two industries with identical concentration ratios, say Industry A and Industry B, in each of which the top three firms account for 75 per cent of the market. The three firms are, respectively, A_1, A_2 and A_3, and B_1, B_2 and B_3. From whatever measure of concentration we choose, with no other information we would conclude that the two industries have the same level of competition. However, if we further assume that Table 4.4. indicates changes in the positions of the three top firms over time, then, even though the concentration ratios remain the same, the level of competition can be seen to be different.

Such large changes in firms' share as those indicated for the leading firms of Industry A are very unlikely over a small number of years. In fact, there is some empirical evidence of an inverse relationship between changes in firms' market shares and levels of concentration (Caves and Porter, 1978). Nevertheless, the table does indicate the possibility of high *rankmobility*, where the rank of top firms changes frequently, together with constant concentration ratios. Whether through price or non-price competition, the table suggests that the firms in Industry A are vying far more intensely for market leadership than in Industry B.

The third problem refers to the omission of international trade from the data computed according to these methodologies, based on output, turnover, sales or employment figures. This omission is particularly disturbing in the case of highly open economies such as the Benelux countries, Ireland, Portugal and Greece, and also in the case of specific industries where import penetration is high (such as the Office Machinery and Data Processing Equipment industries) in the EU as a whole. In the case of an open economy, a domestically based concentration index may exaggerate the actual degree of concentration. We can use an example to demonstrate this.

Assume that in country A, one firm represents 90 per cent of the total domestic turnover, and $n - 1$ other firms make up the remaining 10 per cent of domestic output. The computation of the concentration ratio through any of the methods described above would suggest a high level of concentration; the four-firm concentration ratio, for example, would be close to 1. If however, we introduce international trade considerations, and assume that the n firms export a high percentage of their total turnover, and that a high percentage of domestic sales are accounted for by imports, then the real concentration ratio drops sharply. The dominant firm may account for far less than 90 per cent of domestic sales (depending on the relative proportions of the domestic firms' turnovers that are exported), and foreign firms may actually be dominant in country A's market.

In order to take into account the greater openness of international markets such as that of the EU market, and the increased phenomenon of intra-EU trade, an adjusted-for-trade concentration ratio can be used. It is defined as:

$$C_{ati} = [(Q_i - X_i)/Q_t - (X_t - M_t)] \cdot 100$$

where: C_{ati} is the concentration, for the top i firms, adjusted for trade
Q_i is the turnover of the top i firms
X_i is the exports of i firms
Q_t is the total domestic turnover
X_t is total domestic exports
M_t is total imports.

Using adjusted-for-trade concentration ratios is also necessary in the case of large and more diversified economies such as the UK. Including imports in the UK market's sales will have the effect of reducing UK concentration ratios (unless an importer is among the larger suppliers). Allowing for imports in general increases the degree of competition for the domestic market however, for, as Caves (1971) found, the intensity of collusion between domestic producers and importers is less than that among domestic producers alone. More imports/importers thus means less collusion and more competition among domestic suppliers. If imports represent an increasing large share of the total supply in a given market, we eventually reach a point where we must redefine the market as greater than the national market.

Conditions of entry

Entry in a particular market or industry may be difficult or impossible, depending on the height of barriers. Barriers are all types of obstacles erected at the market edge by incumbent firms, by the nature of the product or process, and/or by the government, which make entry difficult for potential entrants. The idea of barriers is an old one, the erection of barriers first having been observed in the 1894–1901 trust wave in the USA (see Bullock, 1901). Bain's (1956) taxonomy of entry barriers, included technology, economies of scale and product differentiation. Much work has been done in this area since then For example Shepherd (1990) identifies two broad categories of sources of entry barriers.[9]

First, he argues, there are exogenous conditions which are 'fundamental causes that cannot be altered'. They lie outside the leading firms' control and are related to the nature of the product. They comprise: capital requirements, economies of scale, product differentiation, absolute cost advantages, diversification, R&D intensity, high durability of the firm's specific capital which includes sunk costs, and vertical integration (Shepherd, 1990, p. 274). These are all of an economic nature. To this list we could add institutional barriers more or less outside firms' control, such as government regulation,[10] though some writers (e.g. Sapir, 1993) include regulatory barriers as a third type of barrier (in addition to exogenous and endogenous).

Second, there are endogenous conditions which emanate from the dominant firms. There are results of the strategic actions of the dominant firms. They include: retaliation and pre-emptive actions, the building up of excess capacity to bar entry, advertising and other selling expenses, patents, control over strategic resources and other strategies such as 'packing the product space' that leave no room for other potential branded products. These barriers reflect the degree of imperfection in the market. They can be used by the incumbent firms against both potential entrants and existing rivals.

While at first the classification into exogenous sources (given to the firm) and endogenous sources (created by the firm) of barriers seems neat, it can in practice be difficult to determine whether a barrier has an endogenous or exogenous source. For example, product differentiation (included in the exogenous category) is in fact intimately related to advertising which is directly determined by the firm's decisions (i.e. it is endogenous). R&D intensity (defined by Shepherd as exogenous) is a direct result of the strategy of acquiring a leading edge in technology developments and/or application (i.e. it is endogenous). Patents are also closely associated with R&D intensity.

A second criticism of this categorization of barriers relates to how fundamental and unalterable the exogenous conditions actually are. This depends on one's view of the firm. A dynamic perspective, such as that of the evolutionary theorists, would suggest that even the fundamental underlying technology (capital requirements, economies of scale, etc.) of the firm is variable.[11] To this criticism can be added the 'capture theory of regulation', according to which regulation is influenced by the firms in the industry being regulated, such that the design and operation of that regulation is primarily in the interests of that industry, rather than in those of the consumers of the industry's product, or of the public at large.

Many strategies implemented by firms are aimed either at deterring entrance or at neutralizing the actions of existing competitors. A more detailed examination of these strategies will be undertaken in Chapter 5, and barriers to entry in Europe are described in Section 4.2.2 of this chapter. In the next section, we concentrate on different types of market structures.

4.1.4 Market structures

In introductory neoclassical theory, concentration, product differentiation and barriers to entry are considered to be the main factors differentiating among four models of market structure. The two extremes are perfect competition and monopoly, where competition and the number of firms are greatest in perfect competition, and least in monopoly. The other two are monopolistic competition and oligopoly. Duopoly is a special form of oligopoly in which there are only two firms (see Fig. 4.2).

Markets in reality rarely conform to any one of these market structures. They are abstract models derived from sets of assumptions. The assumptions vary from large numbers of small firms producing a homogeneous product and no barriers to entry under perfect competition to a single firm under monopoly. The models enable us to examine how firms would behave (in

Perfect competition → Monopolistic competition → Oligopoly → Duopoly → Monopoly

Figure 4.2   Models of market structure

terms of a limited range of options) if operated within one of these abstract models. The 'firms' examined here are, in general, neoclassical firms.

Perfect competition

The perfect competition model is familiar from all introductory textbooks. Diagrammatically the model is based on the notion that the demand curve faced by the individual firm is perfectly elastic (i.e. horizontal). This follows from the assumption that there are many firms, each too small to influence price or quantity; the price is given for the individual firm. The level (price) at which this horizontal line is drawn is determined by the intersection of market demand and supply. The horizontal price/demand line facing the firm is also the marginal revenue. This is because the price received by the firm for each unit is the same, and that is also the price that will be received by the firm for each additional unit.

Like all profit-maximizing firms, the firm will produce a quantity determined by the inter-section of the marginal revenue (MR) and marginal cost (MC) curves. Where the demand curve is horizontal, $MR = MC$ also implies price $= MC$. If that price is such that profits are made above the normal amount already incorporated in the average cost (AC) curve,[12] then additional firms will enter the market. This follows from the assumption that there are no barriers to entry. (If the initial price was too low, there would be losses, and some firms would leave the industry. There are no barriers to exit.) The diagram for the firm is representative of that of any firm in the industry because, in view of the assumption of perfect flows of informa-tion, each firm will adopt the best methods of production and obtain inputs and factors of production at the best prices; they will all have the same cost curves. Referring to Fig. 4.3, if $p_1 > AC_1$, then the rectangle p_1AC_1BE represents above normal (or super normal) profits, and new firms will enter the industry. The market supply curve[13] will shift to the right from S_1, and will continue shifting in the short run until the intersection of market supply and demand (at the equilibrium price and quantity) is at a price equal to the minimum average cost (p_2). This is the long-run equilibrium position.

It can be argued that there are inherent contradictions in this model. On the one hand it follows from the two assumptions, that information flows perfectly among all suppliers, and that there is no product differentiation and that all firms are identical. However, in deriving the long-run equilibrium position, the model states that, if there are losses, then some firms ('leader' firms?) will leave. If, on the other hand, there are supernormal profits being made, then some firms not in the industry (leader firms) will enter. In the first case the market supply curve will shift to the left, and in the latter case the market supply curve will shift to the right. If there were no means of differentiating leader firms from other firms, then all firms would leave the industry if losses were being made and the industry would cease to exist, and all non-industry firms would enter if supernormal profits were being made. So, all firms are not identical.

In addition, once it is accepted that there are leader firms, then, if short-run supernormal profits are being made, they are more likely to be made by leader firms than others. These will then accumulate to supernormal profits and have capital to differentiate themselves from other

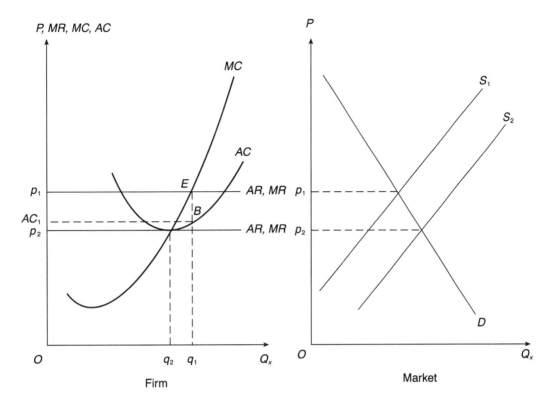

Figure 4.3   Perfect competition

firms. If they are quicker acting than other firms, they will stay ahead, differentiate their product, change their process or organization structure, and/or expand either internally or by taking over some of their competitors.[14] Some firms will, as a result, become larger than others and, perhaps, dominant firms in this industry.[15] The conditions underlying perfect competition are thus in some sense contradictory.

In practice, no firm would prefer a perfectly competitive market structure to one in which supernormal profits could be made. It follows that firms will constantly be trying to find ways of impeding the operation of perfect competition: differentiating their products, preventing information about their operations and products from leaking out, imposing barriers to the entry of new competitors, etc. As soon as one or more of the firms in the industry achieve any of these objectives, perfect competition breaks down.

That the perfect competition model is theoretically defective did not undermine its power and influence. After all, if the conditions were achieved, the price would be as low as possible and optimize the interests of the consumers; the greatest possible number of firms would be sustained by the market and the interests of the suppliers would be optimized;[16] even efficiency is optimized because production takes place at the lowest possible average cost per unit. It is this general optimality[17] that is the attraction of perfect competition. It provides a basis for ideological arguments against government intervention, against concentration (for example through mergers and acquisitions), and in favour of small firms. From the model there follow generalizations such as: the more firms in a market, the lower the profits of each firm; the lower the barriers to entry, the more competition; the more competition, the lower the price; and the lower the barriers to information flows, the more rapidly innovations will be diffused among the firms in the industry. Each of these has been empirically tested with mixed results. It is out of the theoretical critiques and empirical tests of perfect competition that other market structure models and, ultimately, much of industrial economics in general, has evolved.

Monopolistic competition

The perfect competition model was the main one in neoclassical theory all the way into the fourth decade of the twentieth century. Then, mainly because the behaviour of firms and markets was at odds with the model, efforts were made to develop models that were more consistent with this non-perfectly competitive behaviour. Koutsoyiannis (1979, p. 202) mentions three main empirical deviations from perfect competition: products were differentiated; firms advertised; and firms experienced declining average costs, and expanded output to exploit these returns to scale, but only up to a point—they apparently stopped growing even though an increase in output would result in even lower average costs. The attempt during this period to bring neoclassical economic theory into closer touch with reality culminated in the monopolistic competition model.

The monopolistic competition model, developed independently by Chamberlin (1933) and Robinson (1933), centres on the idea that under certain circumstances, even relatively small firms in markets with large numbers of firms can exercise a degree of monopoly power. The assumptions of the model of monopolistic competition are close to those of the perfect competition model, the main difference being that the product is not homogeneous (i.e. there is a degree of product differentiation). Another way of expressing this is to say that while in perfect competition the products of the different firms in the industry are *perfect* substitutes, in monopolistic competition they are *close* substitutes. Thus, in monopolistic competition there are a large number of buyers and sellers and there is freedom for firms to enter or exit the industry.

In the monopolistic competition model there is a single market, but differentiated products.[18] We may consider the market to be *segmented*, with each firm (or product) fitting into a different market segment. Firms differentiate the products they sell in a number of ways: quality, technical performance, durability, design, prompt service, etc. (see Chapter 5, Section 5.1.3). Product differentiation is perceived and enhanced through brand names and trade marks.

Chamberlin (1933) incorporated for the first time the notion of selling costs into the theory of the firm. The rationale for this inclusion is to account for the costs of advertising and other selling activities. The seller, Chamberlin wrote, 'may influence the volume of his sales by making expenditures, of which advertising may be taken as typical, which are directed specifically to that purpose. Such expenditures increase both the demand for his product, and his costs'. He went on to argue that this was one of the distinguishing characteristics of monopolistic competition because there can be no reason for a perfectly competitive firm to advertise; perfectly competitive firms can, after all, sell as much as they like without advertising (Chamberlin, 1962, p. 72).

We could not now agree with the view that advertising is, to use Chamberlin's words, 'peculiar' to monopolistic competition, as firms in both oligopoly and monopoly market structures can under certain circumstances derive benefits from advertising. However, Chamberlin's main point in this context was to differentiate between his new monopolistic competition model and the perfect competition which was the main theoretical model at the time.

Selling costs were defined by Chamberlin 'as costs incurred in order to alter the position and shape of the demand curve for a product ... Advertising of all varieties, salesmen's salaries and the expenses of sales departments, margins granted to dealers..., window displays, demonstrations of new goods, etc., are all costs of this type' (Chamberlin, 1962, p. 117).

Chamberlin assumed that the selling-costs curve is U-shaped, exhibiting economies and diseconomies of, for example, advertising. Beyond a certain level of output, the firm will have to spend more on advertising and other promotional strategies to keep and/or attract customers. Because of the product uniqueness, a firm can raise price without losing all of its sales. If it reduces its price, it will attract customers from other competitors. The demand curve facing the firm is thus downward sloping, as in the case of all other than the perfect competition model.[19] The uniqueness of the product may be a consequence of its style, the services offered by the firm, and/or the firm's particular selling strategy.

The model as presented in most modern textbooks is still more or less as first presented by Chamberlin and Robinson in 1933. Monopolistic competition is defined as a market structure characterized by a large number of sellers of differentiated products. They are assumed to compete both on the basis of price and quality, advertising and other non-price characteristics of the product. There is assumed to be free entry into and exit from the market.

Figure 4.4 shows the cost curves for an individual firm in a monopolistically competitive market structure. The firm faces a demand curve, D_1, which represents the part (or segment) of the market primarily interested in its product.[20] It will maximize its profits where $MR = MC$, that is where the marginal revenue curve (MR_1) and the margin cost curve (MC) intersect. This indicates that the firm should produce the quantity q_1, and, if it produces that quantity the demand curve D_1 indicates that it will be able to sell the product at a price of p_1 per unit. The cost per unit of producing (and selling)[21] q_1 of the product is AC_1. The price (which is also average revenue) is greater than the average cost, so the firm is making

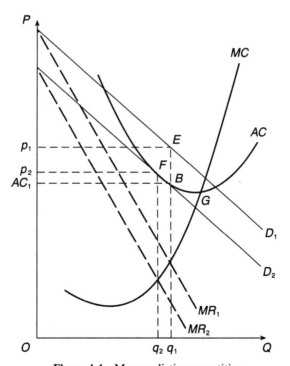

Figure 4.4 Monopolistic competition

supernormal profits. The total supernormal profits is the profit per unit ($p_1 AC_1$) multiplied by the quantity (q_1) represented by the rectangle $p_1 AC_1 BE$.

Because there are no barriers to entry, new firms, responding to the possibility of making supernormal profits in this market, will enter. The increase in the number of firms will reduce the demand facing each firm, and the demand curve for our individual firm will shift to the left. Eventually (i.e. in the long run), this model suggests, all supernormal profits will be eliminated. This occurs when the demand curve shifts to D_2, which is tangential to the average cost curve at a point F such that the line $q_2 F$ is also the profit-maximizing price. In the long run, the price (p_2) is equal to the average cost, so the firm will earn zero supernormal profits.

The point F must clearly be to the left and above the minimum point of the average cost curve, G. (Minimum average cost is also known as the minimum efficient scale, MES.) Thus, the monopolistically competitive firm operates at less than efficient output. The difference between the price and the minimum average cost is interpreted in welfare economics as the cost, accepted by consumers, of having a choice of product among a variety of similar products rather than, as in perfect competition, a single, homogeneous product.

It is the combination of price reduction and the entry of new firms that brings about equilibrium in this model. But the incorporation of selling costs, as distinct from production costs, makes the model interesting from a strategic point of view. These selling costs are in some sense discretionary: firms may increase or reduce them. Their function is to change the demand curve facing the firm, in the firm's favour. This means that there is a choice of strategy for the firm, as between reducing price and increasing, say, advertising. In Fig. 4.4, the firm has a choice between shifting its AC curve down and having the demand curve shift down and to the left (and, perhaps, becoming flatter), or shifting its AC curve upwards and having the demand curve shift up and to the right (and, perhaps, becoming steeper).

The monopolistic competition model allows for the three empirical contradictions of perfect competition mentioned above; it incorporates both product differentiation and advertising, and it shows the possibility of an equilibrium position on a downward sloping part of an average cost curve.

Hotels, laundry services, business services (e.g. legal and consultancy services), repair services, barber and beauty shops, all have product differentiation and operate to some extent like monopolistically competitive firms. In particular, there may be many sellers in the market, the product is differentiated and the firms advertise. However, entry is never free. The more differentiated the products are, and, for example, the stronger the brand loyalty that has been established by each firm for its product, the more difficult it will be for new firms to enter the market. This suggests that, as with perfect competition, there is a theoretical inconsistency in the model. Barriers to entry—particularly through collusion—are characteristic of oligopoly.

Another important difference between the monopolistic competition model and the oligopoly model in this context is that in the former, firms act independently and in the latter, firms are continuously aware of, and act in ways influenced by, the behaviour of their competitors. While strategic choices for the firm can be incorporated into the monopolistic competition model, these choices are not influenced by the possible responses of competitors. However, in the presence of differentiation among products that are close substitutes, firms are highly unlikely to ignore their competitors' possible responses to their actions. Once product differentiation is allowed for, therefore, the market structure is likely to become oligopolistic.

In terms of the empirical definition of monopolistic competition, a major difficulty is how high the cross elasticity of demand must be for the products in the industry to be close substitutes. This is an inevitably subjective issue, for two products considered by one person (or group of people) to be close substitutes may not be considered such at all by others.

From the perspective of our critiques of both the perfect competition and the monopolistic competition models, even structures at first consistent with the assumptions of the models are likely to evolve into oligopolies. For this reason, among others, oligopoly has become the most important focus of modern industrial organization. We will therefore examine oligopoly in some detail. First, however, we turn to the monopoly market structure.

Monopoly

In monopoly, the industry consists of a single firm that produces and sells a product with no close substitutes.[22] For the firm to remain a single firm in the industry, there must either be barriers to entry, or no supernormal profits. By definition, the demand curve facing the monopolist is the industry demand curve, and therefore, as for a firm in monopolistic competition, downward sloping.

Referring to Fig. 4.5, the monopoly firm will maximize profits where $MR = MC$, i.e. at quantity q_1. At this quantity it can charge the price the price p_1. (Once the firm has chosen the quantity to produce, the price will be determined by the market demand.) The cost per unit, if it produces q_1, is AC_1. The supernormal profits are $(p_1 - AC_1) \times q_1$, represented by the rectangle $p_1 AC_1 BE$. Supernormal profits in perfect competition are eliminated by a reduction in price resulting from the entry of new firms into the industry. If new firms are for whatever reason prevented from entering, then the monopoly firm can continue to earn supernormal profits. It may reduce costs in the long run by using different plant and equipment (shifting its AC curve downwards), but it is unlikely, except by coincidence, to produce at the bottom of its AC curve. Monopolies result in *allocative inefficiency*; social welfare would be enhanced if output was

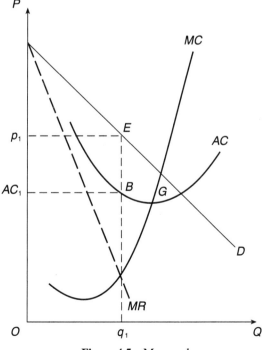

Figure 4.5   Monopoly

expanded up to the point where price (indicative of the marginal benefit to society), and marginal cost (the cost to society of the last unit produced) are equal.[23] The only beneficiary of the monopoly market structure is the monopoly firm itself.[24]

Allocative inefficiency explains the hostility to monopoly in virtually all European countries. Monopolies have been tolerated in the limit case where the minimum efficient scale is so large, in relation to demand, that only one firm can realize economies of scale. These are *natural monopolies*, monopolies that produce on the downward sloping parts of their average cost curves. (The diagram in Fig. 4.5 is that of a natural monopoly.) Many utilities, such as electricity, gas and water distribution, and local telephone services are natural monopolies. Only natural monopolies can make losses. Monopolies other than natural monopolies (where MR cuts MC to the right of minimum AC, i.e. to the right of point G in Fig. 4.5) by definition must be making supernormal profits.

Elsewhere in this chapter (Section 4.2.4) we discuss the ways in which monopolies have been regulated and deregulated in the EU. Among ways of reducing the supernormal profits of monopolies in theory, are (1) taxes, (2) price control and (3) removal of barriers of entry.

1 Taxes on profits simply reduce the after tax profits, and do not affect the profit-maximizing price or quantity. A sales tax will shift the MC curve upwards, quantity produced will go down and price will go up. The incidence of the tax will fall more on the monopoly than on the consumers. If it is a natural monopoly, production will take place even further from minimum average cost; if it is not a natural monopoly, the sales tax may bring production closer to minimum average cost.

2 The government (or monopoly regulating authority) can also reduce a monopoly's profits by imposing a maximum price. To be effective, this must be between the profit-maximizing price and the average cost at the profit-maximizing quantity; referring to Fig. 4.6, the maximum price must be between p_1 and AC_1. Let us assume the maximum price is set at p_m. The horizontal line from p_m to the demand curve D represents the price that the monopoly will charge for those quantities; it is the equivalent of a perfectly elastic demand curve, and, therefore, also a marginal revenue curve. The profit-maximizing quantity (where $MR = MC$, i.e. point H) is q_2. Supernormal profits will have been reduced from p_1AC_1BE to p_mAC_2JH. If the aim of the intervention is to move the monopoly towards allocative efficiency, then it will impose a maximum price such that $MC = P$, that is a maximum price through point K. This is known as *marginal cost pricing*. It is possible that where the MC curve cuts the demand, the monopoly is making losses. In this case the government can impose a maximum price where average cost cuts the demand curve (known as *average cost pricing*). This will leave the firm with just enough (normal) profits to keep it in the industry.

3 Where it is in the government's power to do so, it can remove barriers to entry. If new firms enter the industry, the entire market structure will change, either towards monopolistic competition or towards oligopoly. Note that this is not likely to be an effective way of dealing with natural monopolies because, as can be seen from Fig. 4.6, if one or two additional firms entered the industry, each producing, say, q_3, their average costs would be AC_3 and even if they made no supernormal profits the price would still have to be higher than the natural monopoly price to keep them in the industry. The average cost, even if below p_1, would still be far above the AC_1 of the natural monopoly, and therefore even further from the *MES*.

Public ownership is also sometimes suggested as a means of controlling monopolies (see Chang, 1994, p. 9). However, it is arguably not the ownership of a firm but the competition it

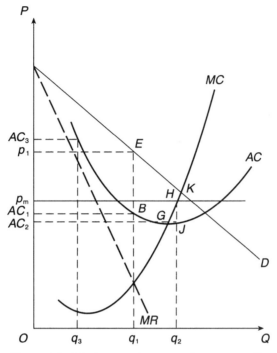

Figure 4.6   Maximum price to regulate monopolies

faces—and, in general, the incentive structure facing its decision makers—that determines its pricing and other strategies.

The analysis of monopoly can be extended to the cases of the multi-plant monopoly, the price discriminating monopolist and the bilateral monopolist. These are demonstrated in most microeconomics and managerial economics textbooks. They all provide examples of marginalist analysis. For a multi-plant monopolist in a single market, it can be shown that if MR is the marginal revenue derived from the market demand curve, and $MC_1, MC_2, \ldots, MC_n$ are the marginal costs of producing the good in each of the n plants, then $MR = MC_1 = MC_2 = \cdots = MC_n$ is the condition for profit maximization.[25] For a (single plant) monopolist able to sell into distinct markets, if $MR_1, MR_2, \ldots, MR_n$ are the marginal revenues in each of the n markets, then the profit will be maximized where $MC = MR_1 = MR_2 = \cdots = MR_n$.[26]

In view of the fact that the bilateral monopoly model takes us towards the bargaining models underlying much of modern oligopoly theory, we will demonstrate this in more detail. In the bilateral monopoly model there is a single seller (monopoly) and a single buyer (monopsony). Let us assume that the buyer is a firm that is the only firm requiring workers with a particular skill and the seller is a trade union that organizes all the workers with that skill. The firm could, for example, be the sole beer manufacturer in the economy (the monopsony buyer of brewing skills), and the trade union organizer of all brewers (the monopoly seller of brewing skills).

The firm's demand for labour, which is also the marginal revenue product of labour (MRP_L), is D_L. MRP_L is the extra revenue generated by employing an extra unit of labour (or marginal revenue times the marginal product of labour). S_L is the supply of labour and, from the firm's point of view, has a related marginal cost, MC_L. This is because to increase employment by an

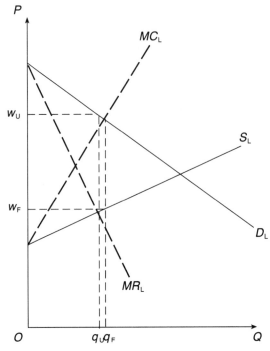

Figure 4.7   Bilateral monopoly

additional unit, the firm must raise the wage for all units (workers).[27] So, the firm will wish to employ workers up to q_F, where D_L and MC_L intersect. It can obtain this quantity at a price of w_F per unit and this is, therefore, the wage that the firm will offer.

From the union's point of view, the demand curve facing it, D_L, is the average wage. Moving down the demand curve, the union sees that the extra revenue arising from an increase in employment (MR_L) is less than the payment per unit of employment; extra workers must be offered much less if the wages offered to them brings the average of all wages down. The union will wish to offer for employment q_U of labour, where its supply curve (and marginal cost from its point of view) intersects the marginal revenue. For this quantity it will expect to receive w_U per unit.

This model has the advantage of a result which, like much that occurs in the competition among firms, is indeterminate. The union wishes to charge w_U per unit for q_U units of labour; the firm wishes to pay w_F per unit for q_F units of labour. They will have to bargain with one another. The end result is likely to be a wage between w_U and w_F, but exactly where it is impossible to say; it depends on many other factors. This type of indeterminacy, of results contingent upon such elements as relative power and strategic skill, is common in modern approaches to oligopoly, on which we focus in the next section.

Oligopoly

Oligopoly can be defined as a market structure in which firms behave in ways determined by their expectations of the responses of others. Unlike in other market structures, the oligopolistic firm is not assumed to be independent of others in the industry. Also unlike other definitions, that of oligopoly does not refer explicitly to numbers of firms, product differentiation or barriers to entry. This is because as oligopoly theory has developed, so it has incorporated a range of possibilities, of various combinations of these traditional determinants of market structure. Indeed, oligopoly has arguably become the main focus of modern industrial economics, its definition being based on behavioural, strategic factors rather than structural ones.

Characteristics of oligopoly can be found in a wide range of industries, including the mining industry, banking sector, car industry, air transport, inter-city bus lines, much wholesale trade and retail trade in so far as it is dominated by chains of supermarkets. Even small grocery stores could be part of an oligopoly, where, for example, there are three of them vying for market share in a small town. In general, firms within oligopolies have a greater degree of control over price than firms in perfect competition. How much control depends on the number and size distribution of firms, the intensity of competition and product differentiation.

Among the roots of the modern theory of oligopoly is the work, first published in 1838, of the French philosopher and mathematician *Augustin Cournot*. At that time, Cournot was overshadowed in France by the *laissez faire* principles—presented most prominently by Jean Baptiste Say—which became accepted almost as dogma.[28] It was not until the 1860s that economists—such as Walras—recognized the value of Cournot's work, and in particular his development of a mathematical approach to political economy.[29] It is both for this general contribution and for his specific work on duopoly that Cournot is most remembered today.

Cournot's duopoly (two-firm) model is a quantity-setting oligopoly in which each firm selects a quantity of output to maximize its own profit. He builds his model around the strategies of two firms, each of which owns a natural mineral water spring, of identical quality, and equidistant from the same market. Assuming that the two producers have the same cost structures, the price will be the same for each. Each firm does not have any influence on the quantity produced by its rival. Cournot's behavioural assumption is that each firm knows what its rival produces, takes the rival's output as given, and selects its own output so as to maximize its own profit. This assumption is a simplification in that it means that, should Firm 1 alter its output, its rival will not react. The *conjectural variation*—Firm 1's view of the extent to which its rival will change its output in response to Firm 1's output decisions—is thus zero.

In fact, since Firm 1 treats Firm 2's output as fixed, Firm 1 believes that it faces a residual demand curve; Firm 1's residual demand curve is obtained from the market demand curve by subtracting the output of Firm 2, i.e.:

$$q_1 = Q - q_2 \tag{4.1}$$

where Q denotes the total output in the market.

Using the notation:

$$p = f(Q)$$

or

$$p = f(q_1 + q_2)$$

to denote that price is a function of quantity, Firm 1's total revenue, R_1, will be:

$$R_1 = q_1 \cdot f(q_1 + q_2) \tag{4.2}$$

and Firm 2's total revenue will be:

$$R_2 = q_2 \cdot f(q_1 + q_2) \tag{4.3}$$

Equations (4.2) and (4.3) show that the rival's output is a variable taken into account in each firm's strategy, though this variable is fixed by the rival. In Cournot's own words: 'Firm 1 cannot directly exert an influence on the fixing of output $[q_2]$; the only thing the firm can do after $[q_2]$ has been fixed by Firm 2, is to choose for $[q_1]$ the value that suits him best, something he can achieve by modifying the price appropriately.'[30] Firm 1's revenue-maximizing (and profit-maximizing, if we ignore production costs) output will be determined as a function of q_2 under the condition:

$$\frac{d\{q_1 f(q_1 + q_2)\}}{dq_1} = 0 \tag{4.4}$$

Similarly, q_2 will be determined by:

$$\frac{d\{q_2 f(q_1 + q_2)\}}{dq_2} = 0 \tag{4.5}$$

The values of q_1, q_2 and p will be determined by the following system of equations, derived by differentiating Eqs (4.4) and (4.5):

$$f(q_1 + q_2) + q_1 \frac{df(q_1 + q_2)}{dq_1} = 0 \tag{4.6}$$

$$f(q_1 + q_2) + q_2 \frac{df(q_1 + q_2)}{dq_2} = 0 \tag{4.7}$$

Assuming, with Cournot, that Firm 1 believes that Firm 2 does not respond to Firm 1's actions, Eq. (4.6) can be written as:

$$f(q_1 + q_2) + q_1 \frac{df(q_1 + q_2)}{d(q_1 + q_2)} = 0 \tag{4.6a}$$

Similarly, if Firm 2 believes that Firm 1 does not respond to Firm 2's actions, Eq. (4.7) can be written as:

$$f(q_1 + q_2) + q_2 \frac{df(q_1 + q_2)}{d(q_1 + q_2)} = 0 \tag{4.7a}$$

It follows that, if both firms optimize under these conditions, $q_1 = q_2$, which indicates that both firms supply the same quantity (measured in Fig. 4.8 by the segments q_1 and q_2 respectively).[31] Adding Eq. (4.6a) to Eq. (4.7a), and substituting p for $f(Q)$, we get:

$$2p + Q \, dp/dQ = 0$$

or

$$2p \cdot dQ/dp + Q = 0 \tag{4.8}$$

i.e.

$$p = (-Q)/2(\mathrm{d}Q/\mathrm{d}p) \qquad (4.9)$$

Cournot goes on to say that if the two springs had been part of the same firm, or if the two producers had co-operated, p would have been determined by the equation:

$$p \cdot \mathrm{d}Q/\mathrm{d}p + Q = 0 \qquad (4.10)^{32}$$

i.e.

$$p = (-Q)/(\mathrm{d}Q/\mathrm{d}p) \qquad (4.11)$$

Clearly p in Eq. (4.11)—that for which total revenue in the industry is maximized—is greater than p in Eq. (4.9). *Through co-operation, price would be greater, and each firm would obtain a total revenue greater, than that derived from Eq. (4.8).* This illustrates the costs of non-co-operative (competitive) behaviour, and shows that, under these assumptions it would be in the interests of the two firms to co-operate.

Cournot rules out co-operation or collusive behaviour in practice, because:

Firm 1, having fixed its production level according to equation [4.10] and to the condition $[q_1 = q_2]$, the other [firm] will, with a *temporary benefit*, be in a position to bring its own production to a higher or lower level; however, Firm 2 will soon be punished for his wrongdoing, in that he will force the first firm to select a new production level that will have an unfavourable impact on Firm 2. These successive reactions, far from bringing the two producers closer to the original state [of equilibrium], will make them increasingly diverge from it. In other words, this state [Eq. (4.10)] will not be a situation of stable equilibrium; and, although it is the most favourable to the two producers, it cannot last unless there is a formal link. (authors' translation, Cournot, 1980, p. 62).[33]

Cournot generalizes his model to n producers. He shows that under the same circumstances as before, Eq. (4.8) would be replaced by

$$3p \cdot \mathrm{d}Q/\mathrm{d}p + Q = 0 \qquad (4.12)$$

in the case of triopoly, and

$$np \cdot \mathrm{d}Q/\mathrm{d}p + Q = 0 \qquad (4.13)$$

in the case of perfect competition (i.e. where n is a large number).

His conclusion is that 'the resulting value of p would diminish indefinitely through the indefinite increase in the number n' (authors' translation, Cournot, 1980, p. 63). Since the value of p reached by the monopolist (or by a co-operative duopoly) is always greater than the value of p derived from a non-co-operative duopoly, which in turn is always greater than the value of p obtained in a competitive framework, this implies that the total revenue of the monopolist is greater than the total revenue of the duopolist, which in turn is greater than that of the competitive firm.

Cournot shows that the introduction of cost functions does not change the conclusions as to the situations in which producers maximize profits. For the same value of p, or for the same total quantity produced, the costs of production will always be greater for rival firms than for the monopolist (see Cournot, 1980, p. 65).

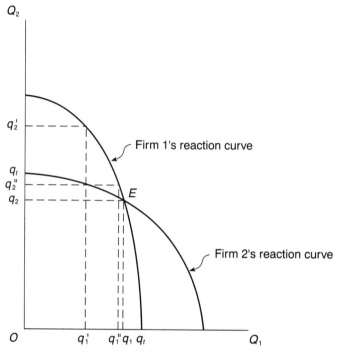

Figure 4.8   Reaction curves and Cournot duopoly equilibrium

Cournot's diagrammatic representation of duopoly is shown in Fig. 4.8. Each curve is a *reaction curve* showing a firm's profit-maximizing output, given the output of the other firm. If Firm 2 produces nothing, Firm 1 is a monopolist and maximizes profit (which is in this case equal to total revenue) by producing the monopoly output q_t. Point E represents for Cournot a point of stable equilibrium, at which q_1 and q_2 are produced by Firms 1 and 2 respectively. If, for any reason, either producer deviates from this position of stable equilibrium, a series of 'reactions' will bring him or her back to the equilibrium. The point of intersection of the two reaction curves is referred to, in the industrial economics literature, as a Cournot non-co-operative equilibrium point.

Cournot's major aim was to show (algebraically and graphically) the existence of a stable duopoly equilibrium. His explanation of the diagram was as follows. If Firm 1 decides to produce an output $q_1' < q_1$, its profit can be maximized only for a value of $Q_2 = q_2'$. In other words, Firm 1 produces q_1' in the expectation that Firm 2 will produce q_2'. However, Firm 1's production of q_1' leads Firm 2 to react by planning to produce q_2'' such that $q_2 < q_2'' < q_2'$. Firm 1 will react to Firm 2's production of q_2'' in turn by increasing his output to q_1''. Each reaction is of a smaller and smaller magnitude, up to the point where the stable equilibrium is reached.

Walras was later to call this repeated adjustment towards a convergent equilibrium the '*tâtonnement*' process. With all its limitations, Cournot's was the first attempt to describe dynamically the process whereby a static equilibrium is arrived at.

Criticism of Cournot has focused on three main issues: the nature of the relationship between the two variable q_1 and q_2; the ruling out of co-operative behaviour; and the fact that Cournot treats the duopolists as quantity-setters rather than as price-setters.

1 *Relationship between q_1 and q_2* In his famous short article published in 1883 in *Journal des Savants*, Joseph Bertrand criticized Cournot for treating the outputs q_1 and q_2 as two independent variables. According to Cournot, when q_1 changes as a result of the strategy of Firm 1, q_2 remains constant. In Bertrand's view, it is 'obvious' that under these circumstances q_2 will change. In that it led to the question of how responsive Firm 1 expects Firm 2 to be to Firm 1's actions, it was this criticism of Cournot by Bertrand that gave rise to the *conjectural variation* approach.

Pareto (1911, p. 606) later showed, in a critique of both Cournot and Bertrand, that the fact that q_1 and q_2 are treated as independent of one another does not imply Cournot's behavioral assumption according to which Firm 1 can act only on q_1 and Firm 2 only on q_2.[34] This undermines part of Bertrand's objection to Cournot, but leaves intact his criticism of Cournot's assumption that each duopolist acts in the belief that the other's output is fixed.[35]

2 *Co-operative behaviour* The second criticism relates to whether the firms will continue to compete in all respects. The question is whether it is possible that each duopolist, rather than maximizing its own profit only, will co-operate in some way with the other to maximize joint revenue. The fact that Cournot ruled out co-operative or collusive behaviour was strongly criticized by Bertrand (1883) who argued that it would be in the interests of the two firms 'to come together, or at least to fix a common price, so that they can derive a maximum possible revenue from the buyers; but this solution is rejected [by Cournot]'.[36]

3 *Price-setting oligopoly* Finally, probably the most fruitful criticism has been that Cournot neglected the price variable in the strategies of firms. The Cournot model is a quantity-setting model as opposed to a price-setting model. The price variable is treated as a result of duopoly behaviour, rather than as a strategy available to the firm. Bertrand's main contribution was his development of a price-setting alternative to the Cournot model.

Bertrand (1883) regarded price-setting oligopoly as a more acceptable alternative in practice. A firm exhibiting Bertrand behaviour selects a profit-maximizing price under the assumption that its rivals will maintain their prices at the current levels. His assumption is that, if Firm 2 does not react, the entire market can switch to Firm 1 in response to a slight reduction in price.

Note that if consumers respond to price changes only, then Bertrand's model does not allow for any product differentiation. Hence, if we assume that the products sold are standardized and that there is no inertia in behaviour, the Bertrand duopoly model leads to a competitive equilibrium, even if as few as two firms supply the entire market. To show that each firm will charge the same price—and that that price will allow only for normal profit—assume for example that the two duopolists are charging a price above marginal cost. If Firm 1 keeps its price at that level, Firm 2 can attract all the buyers if it charges a slightly lower price. Firm 1 will then react by cutting its price even further. The process will stop only when any further reduction in price would result in one of the firms leaving the industry.

Diagrammatically, *price reaction curves* can be drawn, showing the price that Firm 1 will set in order to maximize its profits, given the price set by Firm 2. This is shown in Fig. 4.9.

Price reaction curves are positively sloped, because the higher the price one firm charges for the good, the higher will be the price set by the other firm. Similarly, the lower the price set by one firm, the lower the price that will have to be set by the other firm if it wants to compete. When the good is homogeneous, the price reaction curves will intersect at E, at which point the price p_{c1} set by Firm 1 will be equal to the price p_{c2} set by Firm 2. This price, as explained

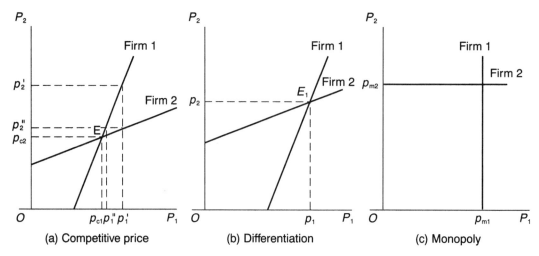

Figure 4.9   Price reaction curves and Bertrand duopoly equilibrium

above, will also be the competitive price (no supernormal profits). The process of adjustment is analogous to the Cournot case, except that each firm changes price—rather than quantity—in the convergence towards equilibrium. Thus if, for some reason, Firm 1 charges a price p_1' above p_{c1} (in the expectation that Firm 2 will charge p_2') Firm 2 will actually respond by charging p_2''; Firm 1 will then change its price to p_1'' and so on, until the equilibrium is reached at E. This is the result of the basic Bertrand model.

There are a large number of possible variations to Bertrand and Cournot. Here we will concentrate first on relaxing Bertrand's assumption of product homogeneity, and second on different reactions by firms in different circumstances. In a variation on both Cournot and Bertrand, we will examine, thirdly, the implications of relaxing the implicit assumption of symmetric information by allowing one firm to obtain information on the other's reaction function. In a fourth variation we will consider the possibility of a collusive oligopoly. Conjectural variation is the fifth and final variation in oligopoly theory that we will discuss. It involves—as do the second, third and fourth—departure from the implausible assumption that the oligopolist believes that rivals do not respond to his changes.

First variation, product differentiation   If there is a degree of differentiation between the products of Firms 1 and 2, then the second firm to enter the market will be able to set a price for its product above that of the first product. This is the basis for differentiation strategies, like advertising to establish brand loyalty. Each firm's price reaction curve will shift (Firm 2's upwards and Firm 1's to the right) because for each price that one firm charges, the other will be able to set a price above the price that would have been possible if the firms' products had been identical. With a degree of differentiation, if each firm is less reactive to a change in price by the other firm then the price reaction curve of Firm 1 may also be flatter, and that of Firm 2 steeper than if the good was homogeneous. The equilibrium, at E_1, will be at a price higher than the competitive price (see Fig. 4.9b).

If there is complete differentiation, so that each of the firms becomes a monopolist, the price will be still higher. Each firm can now ignore the price charged by the other. Firm 1's price reaction curve becomes vertical, and Firm 2's horizontal; Firm 1 sets the price at its profit-maximizing monopoly price (p_{m1}) irrespective of the price Firm 2 charges for its product, and

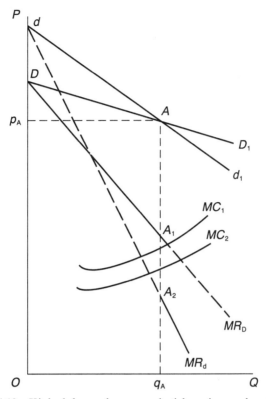

Figure 4.10   Kinked demand curve and sticky prices under oligopoly

Firm 2 similarly sets the price at p_{m2} irrespective of the price Firm 1 charges for its product (see Fig. 4.9c).

Second variation, differentiated reactions   Published in an article in 1939, Paul Sweezy's model formally introduced the kinked demand curve as a tool for the attempted determination of the equilibrium of an oligopoly with a standardized product.[37] Sweezy's major assumption is that a firm expects its competitor(s) to behave differently in their responses to price increases and decreases: a firm believes that its rival(s) will respond immediately to a price cut, but will be reluctant to match a price increase. Sweezy's behavioural assumption generates a kink (point A in Fig. 4.10) in the firm's perceived demand curve at a given price.

Let us assume the firm faces a demand curve, DD_1. At point A, the oligopolist considers the possible responses to an increase or decrease in price. His competitor(s), he believes, will not respond to an increase. If he increases price above p_A, by keeping their price at p_A his competitors will undercut his price, and force him out of business. If he decreases his price, they will have to respond by decreasing their price too, or else they will be undercut, and be forced out of business. Now, if DD_1 is the firm's demand curve under the assumption of *ceteris paribus* (i.e. all other things remain the same) and if those other things include the prices set by competitor(s), then above A the relevant demand curve is DA, but below A it is a steeper demand curve, Ad_1. If his reduction in price was not followed by a reduction in the price of competitor(s), DD_1 would be relevant throughout its length. When competitor(s)' response is also to cut price, then the quantity left for our firm is less than it would be if the response was to stay at p_A. So, instead of the greater quantities available along AD_1, he faces the lower quantities along Ad_1. The relevant demand curve is DAd_1. Raising his price leads to a much greater response on the part of his customers than a price reduction (DA is more price elastic than Ad_1).

Due to the kink in the oligopolist's demand curve, his MR curve will be discontinuous at the level of output corresponding to point A. The relevant marginal revenue curve for DA is DA_1 and the relevant marginal curve for Ad_1 is A_2MR_d. The marginal revenue of the demand curve DAd_1 is $DA_1A_2MR_d$. Any marginal cost curve that intersects the vertical section of the marginal revenue curve will result in the profit-maximizing price and quantity combination of p_A and q_A. Changes in cost conditions that shift the marginal cost up or down will not result in a price change, as long as the shift is between A_1 and A_2. This is the main result of the kinked demand curve model, namely that, under these conditions the price under oligopoly will tend to be 'sticky'.

The equilibrium point in the model is the original point on the demand curve. There is no explanation of how equilibrium in oligopoly comes about. Notice that, in drawing the diagram, we identified A as any point at which the oligopolist was located, and from which he was considering a move. All the model provides is a theoretical basis for the notion that price might be sticky in oligopolies.

Third variation, Stackelberg leadership In 1934, the German economist Heinrich von Stackelberg brought some refinement to oligopoly theory by developing the idea that the industry might contain a dominant firm that acts as the leader in setting quantities.

In the Stackelberg duopoly model, it is assumed that Firm 2 follows the Cournot behavioural assumption, whereas the other firm is a first mover. For the follower, the problem is simple: it observes Firm 1's output and tries to determine a profit-maximizing level of output. The leader takes Firm 2's behaviour into account; knowing Firm 2's reaction curve, the leader will pick the point on Firm 2's reaction curve where it (Firm 1) has the largest possible profit.

The price leadership model is the logical extension of the Stackelberg model. Suppose that Firm 1 is the price leader, and that Firm 2 follows and reacts to signals given by Firm 1. Suppose also that Firm 1 is aware of Firm 2's behaviour.

The market demand curve assumes, for the sake of simplicity, the linear form:

$$p = f(Q) = a - bQ$$

where $Q = q_1 + q_2$

Firm 2's reaction function is thus:

$$q_2 = \frac{a - c_2}{2b} - \tfrac{1}{2}q_1 \qquad (4.14)[38]$$

Either firm will see price as:

$$p = a - b(q_1 + q_2) \qquad (4.15)$$

Because Firm 1 knows Firm 2's reaction curve, it can substitute it into Eq. (4.15), so that, from Firm 1's point of view:

$$p = a - b\{q_1 + (a - c_2)/2b - \tfrac{1}{2}q_1\}$$
$$p = \tfrac{1}{2}(a - bq_1 + c_2) \qquad (4.16)$$

The dominant firm's profit is:

$$\pi_1 = pq_1 - c_1q_1$$

where c_1 is the average cost of producing q_1 (and marginal cost if average cost is constant). Substituting from Eq. (4.16),

$$\pi_1 = q_1(\tfrac{1}{2}a - \tfrac{1}{2}bq_1 + \tfrac{1}{2}c_2) - c_1q_1$$

Firm 1 will maximize its profit where:

$$\frac{d\pi_1}{dq_1} = \tfrac{1}{2}a - bq_1 = \tfrac{1}{2}c_2 - c_1 = 0$$

which gives:[39]

$$q_1 = \frac{(a + c_2 - 2c_1)}{2b}$$

Substituting this result into Firm 2's reaction function (4.14), we get:[40]

$$q_2 = \frac{a - c_2}{2b} - \frac{1}{2}\frac{(a + c_2 - 2c_1)}{2b}$$

The greater the leader's cost advantage (i.e. the smaller is c_1 in comparison to c_2) the greater will be q_1 and the smaller will be q_2, i.e. the greater will be Firm 1's share of the market.

If we assume that neither firm has a cost advantage over the other, then $c_1 = c_2$, and

$$q_1 = \frac{(a - c)}{2b}$$

$$q_2 = \frac{1}{2}\frac{(a - c)}{2b}$$

Even without a cost advantage, Firm 1 will supply twice as much as Firm 2. The total supply of the industry, in terms of number of units of output, is:

$$q_1 + q_2 = 3(a - c)/4b \tag{4.17}$$

and the price, in terms of monetary units, is:

$$p = a - b(q_1 + q_2) = (a + 3c)/4 \tag{4.18}$$

The leader's profit will also be twice that of the follower.[41]

These results can be compared with the Cournot solution. With linear demand,[42] the two reaction functions derived from each firm's profit-maximizing quantity (see Eq. (4.14)) are:

$$q_1 = \frac{a - c}{2b} - \tfrac{1}{2}q_2 \tag{4.19}$$

and

$$q_2 = \frac{a-c}{2b} - \tfrac{1}{2}q_1 \qquad\qquad (4.20)$$

Solving, we get equilibrium output:

$$q_1 = q_2 = (a-c)/3b \qquad\qquad (4.21)$$

Total output is:

$$q_1 + q_2 = 2(a-c)/3b \qquad\qquad (4.22)$$

and price is:

$$p = a - b(q_1 + q_2)$$
$$= (a + 2c)/3 \qquad\qquad (4.23)$$

We see that in the Stackelberg model of asymmetric rivalry, the quantity supplied by the industry, Eq. (4.17), is greater than in the Cournot symmetric duopoly, Eq. (4.22). Because the market demand is linear and downward sloping, it follows also that the Stackelberg price, Eq. (4.18), is less than the Cournot price, Eq. (4.23).

This result leads to the suggestion that the Stackelberg model is associated with higher levels of welfare (or less welfare loss) than the Cournot model. This suggestion is borne out in a study by Cable, Carruth and Dixit (1994). They find that differences in conduct (as reflected in the different variations on the basic oligopoly model) have a major impact on welfare loss. In particular, in this context, they rank models of duopoly, from greatest to least welfare loss, as follows: collusive duopoly, Cournot, Stackelberg and Bertrand models. Of those discussed in this section of the book, only the Bertrand model gives rise to less welfare loss than the Stackelberg model. A model with a dominant firm and a competitive fringe has even less welfare loss than the Bertrand model, but this finding, unlike the others in their study, is sensitive to product differentiation.[43]

Fourth variation, collusive duopoly   The behavioural assumptions that the oligopolist will make changes in output (Cournot) and price (Bertrand) in the belief that competitors will not react to those changes, is implausible. It was Chamberlin's (1933) view that when the number of firms became so small that they all recognized their interdependence, the monopoly quantity would be produced and sold at the monopoly price.[44]

Where two or more firms come to an agreement on the price at which their product is to be sold, and/or on the quantities to be produced, and/or on the spatial division of the market, then this is called *collusion*. Collusion can be overt—when it is usually called a *cartel*—or covert. Collusion of any kind among firms is illegal in most countries (see Chapter 7).

There is a simple, diagrammatic way of explaining the gains from and potential instability of collusion. We concentrate on the case of two firms with different cost structures. We assume that the firms produce a homogeneous product. In Fig. 4.11, the horizontal summation of the two MC curves gives the industry MC curve denoted by ΣMC. Given the market demand DD, the cartel maximizes its joint profit by producing the output at which ΣMC equals MR (point L) in Fig. 4.11(c). From point L, a horizontal line to the left identifies, at the intersection point

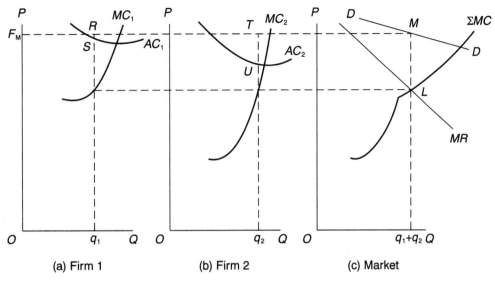

Figure 4.11 Collusive oligopoly

with MC_2, the quantity to be produced by Firm 2 (q_2) and at the intersection point with MC_1, the quantity to be produced by Firm 1 (q_1). By construction—ΣMC is the horizontal summation of MC_1 and MC_2—the quantity at L will equal $q_1 + q_2$. The price to be charged is the price that $q_1 + q_2$ can be sold at, identified at point M as p_M (monopoly price). Firm 1's profit will be $RS \times q_1$, Firm 2's profit $TU \times q_2$.

The neoclassical profit maximization condition, $MC_1 = MC_2 = MR$, is satisfied. The total profit of the two firms together will be greater through collusion than if they had competed. One of the firm's profits may have declined through collusion, but if so, then the other's profits must have increased by more. In such a situation, collusion will still be beneficial to the two firms, but one will have to make a *side payment* to the other to keep it in the cartel.

Depending on circumstances, there may be an incentive for one or both of the firms to attempt to cheat. From Fig. 4.11(a), if Firm 1 cheated and produced more than q_1—and was still able to sell at p_M per unit—both its quantity and its profit per unit would increase, so its profit would also increase. However, even if in the short term it manages to achieve a higher profit, in the longer term it will become clear to Firm 2 that Firm 1 is cheating, because the quantity left for Firm 2 at price p_M will be less than its allotted q_2.

In a market in which there are unstable demand conditions, and/or heterogeneous products, and/or low entry barriers, and/or widely differing firms in terms of size or cost conditions, and/or tight legal restriction on non-competitive behaviour, and/or any other factors that make it difficult for firms to monitor each other's activities, collusion is unlikely.

Fifth variation, conjectural variations   The conjectural variations (CV) approach is a generalization of Sweezy's kinked demand curve model, in that it provides for a range of possible beliefs on the part of the oligopolist as to how his rivals will respond to his actions. The CV approach stresses the interdependence of firms in an oligopoly.

Let $\lambda_{1,2}$ be the conjecture about how Firm 2 would respond to a choice of output by Firm 1. In the Cournot model, Firm 1 assumes that Firm 2 does not respond to Firm 1's actions, in other words the $\lambda_{1,2} = 0$ (the conjectural variation is zero). If $\lambda_{1,2} = 1$, this means that Firm 1 expects Firm 2 to respond to, say, a reduction in Firm 1's output, by an equivalent reduction in its output; $\lambda_{1,2} = -1$ means that Firm 1 believes that a reduction in its own output will be responded to by an equivalent increase in its rival's output.

From Firm i's point of view, where Q_{-1} is the total output of all firms excluding the ith firm

$$\lambda_{i,-i} \simeq \frac{dQ_{-i}}{dq_i}$$

CVs are easily introduced into the Cournot duopoly model. In Cournot's original model (Eqs (4.6) and (4.7)) and in the linear version (Eqs (4.19) and (4.20)), each firm assumes that the other does not respond to its actions. If we now allow Firm 1 to expect some response to its actions on the part of Firm 2, then the change in total quantity arising from a change in Firm 1's quantity is no longer the same as the change in Firm 1's quantity alone. Instead of as in Eq. (4.19), Firm 1 will now maximize its profit for a quantity:[45]

$$q_1 = \frac{(a - bq_2 - c)}{(2b + b\lambda_{1,2})} \tag{4.24}$$

Similarly,

$$q_2 = \frac{(a - bq_1 - c)}{(2b + b\lambda_{2,1})} \tag{4.25}$$

If each firm has an identical conjectural variation then, as before $q_1 = q_2$. Solving, we find the equilibrium output for each firm:

$$q_1 = \frac{(a - c)}{(3b + b\lambda_{1,2})} \tag{4.26}$$

Substituting and solving for p, we get:

$$p = \frac{a - (2a - 2c)}{(3 + \lambda_{1,2})} \tag{4.27}$$

Note that if we set $\lambda_{1,2} = 0$, then q_1 in Eq. (4.26) becomes the same as q_1 in Eq. (4.21) and similarly that p in Eq. (4.27) becomes the same as p in Eq. (4.23).

The conjectural variation approach has been valuable in the theoretical specification of the SCP relationship in oligopolistic industries. Cowling and Waterson's (1976) work on CV and industry structure has been at the forefront of these developments.

Structure is brought in through the following relationship:[46]

$$\frac{p - MC_i}{p} = -\frac{S_i}{\varepsilon} \tag{4.28}$$

That is, the larger a firm's market share, the more market power it has, and the more price elastic the market demand, the less market power it has. As will be recalled from the section on concentration ratios above, $(p - MC)/p$ is a measure of monopoly (or market) power known as the Lerner index.

By multiplying all the terms in Eq. (4.28) by S_i and summing for all n firms, we get:

$$\frac{\left(p\sum_{i=1}^{n}S_i - \sum_{i=1}^{n}MC_iS_i\right)}{p} = -\frac{\sum_{i=1}^{n}(S_i)^2}{\varepsilon}$$

or

$$\frac{(p - \overline{MC})}{p} = -\frac{H}{\varepsilon} \tag{4.29}$$

which shows the relationship between the weighted average industry price-cost margin and the Herfindahl index of industry concentration.

Now, introducing non-zero conjectural variation, it can be shown that:[47]

$$\frac{p - MC_i}{p} = -\frac{S_i}{\varepsilon}(1 + \lambda_{i,-i}) \tag{4.30}$$

This can be aggregated as in Eq. (4.29) to give the following result at market equilibrium:

$$\frac{\left(p\sum_{i=1}^{n}S_i - \sum_{i=1}^{n}MC_iS_i\right)}{p} = -\frac{\sum_{i=1}^{n}S_i^2}{\varepsilon} - \frac{\sum_{i=1}^{n}S_i^2\lambda_i}{\varepsilon}$$

or

$$\frac{(p - \overline{MC})}{p} = -\frac{H}{\varepsilon}(1 + \bar{\lambda}) \tag{4.31}$$

where $\bar{\lambda}$ is a market shares-weighted average conjectural variation.

Cowling and Waterson's (1976) form of Eq. (4.31) has been influential in empirical studies. They show that:

$$\frac{(\Pi + F)}{R} = -\frac{H}{\varepsilon}(1 + \lambda) \tag{4.32}$$

where Π, F and R are, respectively, industry aggregate profit, fixed costs and revenue.[48]

Equation (4.32) indicates thus that 'the profit–revenue ratio is related directly to the Herfindahl index of concentration in the industry and inversely to the industry price elasticity of demand' (Cowling and Waterson, 1976, p. 269). In other words, the firm's profit to revenue ratio is determined by the number and size distribution of firms in the market and by the price elasticity of demand for the product.

There has been a large amount of empirical work using CVs to examine the relationships suggested above.[49] Among the few writers focusing on European data, Haskel and Martin (1994) examine 81 manufacturing industries in the UK. Using a model based on the relationship between λ and capacity constraint, they show that the greater the capacity constraint, the higher the profits. The greater the capacity constraint, the more will competition be quantity-based (Cournot-like), and the less the capacity constraint, the more will competition be price-based (Bertrand-like). These results are intensified by concentration; the higher the levels of concentration in an industry, the more positive the relationship between capacity constraint and profits.[50]

The major criticism of the CV approach, as Fraser (1994) puts it, 'derives from the fact that it is a static equilibrium approach, while oligopolistic interactions are inherently dynamic'. It is for this reason that many industrial economists prefer multi-period game theory to model oligopoly. However, as Fraser argues (agreeing with our conclusion in Chapter 2), game theory does not eliminate the problem of a serious multiplicity of equilibria. Another criticism relates to the assumption inherent in the theory of profit-maximizing behaviour on the part of oligopolists, and assumption which is at best hard to test and at worst inappropriate.

There have been responses to these criticisms. Slade (1987), for example, provided a dynamic analysis by incorporating CVs into a repeated game-based examination of the retail petrol market in Vancouver. The findings were that price responses during a period of price war were greater than would have been the case for a one-play game. The author interpreted this as indicative of 'punishment strategies' to enforce collusion. Shaffer (1991) considers alternatives to profit maximization as the objective of oligopolists in a paper on 'Consistent conjectures in a value-maximizing duopoly'.

We can conclude that the CV approach continues to be one that provides a great deal of work for both theoretical and empirical economists who continue to be interested in fundamental relationships between S, C and P. As to whether oligopolists actually act in accordance with CVs, it is interesting to note 'that management journals now advocate the use of conjectures by businessmen as one way of improving the business planning process and their competitive position' (Fraser, 1994).[51]

4.1.5   Regulation and deregulation[52]

Regulation narrowly defined refers to control by the state or state agency of prices and the imposition by the state of restrictions on entry into certain industries (Shughart, 1990, pp. 175–83). Price controls have been used in many countries, justified by the argument that they help reduce the allocative inefficiency of monopoly. Entry restrictions take the form of occupational licensing requirements, certification and franchising. In the case of monopolies, entry regulation has been justified by the fact that it prevents 'wasteful' duplication of capital investment. Regulation-based entry barriers are found in public utilities (firms supplying electricity, water, natural gas and telephone services), financial services, air and road transport, broadcasting, and business services (lawyers, accountants, pharmacists, etc.).

In neoclassical theory, only perfect competition, and only at long-run equilibrium, provides a situation in which the economic welfare of all the main interests in society are optimized. In all other situations (and, if our critique of perfect competition is correct, this means in all situations) at least one of the parties in the economy is at a less than optimal level of welfare. Most of the economics literature on state intervention is concerned with this failure of the market mechanism to achieve Pareto optimality. There are other theories of state intervention, and, in addition to the *market failure* theory, we will briefly discuss the *paternalist* and *transaction cost* theories of state intervention.

Market failure

The possibility of market failure provides the major justification for government intervention in neoclassical economics. Market failure refers to situations where the market fails to achieve the allocative efficiency standard and where it leads to *misallocation* of resources. We will discuss three types of market failure: external effects, market power and asymmetric information.

External effects (or externalities) arise when the benefits and costs of a given economic activity at the level of the individual differ from those at the level of society.[53] For example, in the case of pollution, there may be zero costs to the individual polluter (if, for example, he or she does not live in the area where the factory is), but substantial costs to society. Government can remedy this market failure by imposing a tax on polluting activities.

However, because so many goods have externalities, both negative (as in the case of pollution) and positive (for example where an apiary is located adjacent to an apple orchard) it is difficult to be precise about what the state can do to bring private and social costs into line with one another. On the one hand this argument can be used to oppose all state intervention to offset externalities (Friedman, 1962), on the other, 'once we begin to accept the pervasiveness of externalities, it seems questionable whether we are justified in having market transactions at all' (Chang, 1994, p. 11).[54]

Collusive behaviour on the part of a group of firms, and/or the existence of economies of scale, will result in firms having an element of *market power*, such as in a monopoly of oligopoly situation, where each firm faces a downward sloping demand curve; price will be greater than marginal cost, and output will be less than it would be under perfect competition. Some of the consumers' welfare is transferred to the firm in the form of supernormal profit. Social welfare would be improved if more resources were used to expand output up to the perfect competition equilibrium point. As discussed above in our explanation of monopoly, there are various means at governments' disposal to correct this second market failure, including taxes, price controls and regulation to provide competition (or deregulation that removes legislation preventing competition). Collusive behaviour of a group of firms is opposed in nearly all countries by anti-trust legislation, prices commissions, monopoly and merger commissions, etc.

The traditional neoclassical view is that government regulation against monopoly and excessive concentration in general will raise consumer welfare. There are a number of arguments against this view. First, as Shughart (1990, p. 169) puts it, it is possible 'that certain industries have become concentrated by virtue of the superior economic efficiency of the established firms'. Public policy to prevent this would be against the interests of consumers. Second, there is the *theory of the second best*, according to which a gain from intervention to 'correct' a non-competitive market can only be guaranteed if all other markets are perfectly competitive. This can be used to justify both widespread intervention, and no intervention. In any case, the theory does not state that there will definitely be no gain, only that gain cannot be guaranteed. Third, Friedman (1962) among others has argued that state intervention is itself a frequent cause of monopoly. Complete absence of intervention is, in this view, the best option. Regulation may indeed be responsible for monopolies in some cases, but, as Chang (1994, p. 10) points out, forces other than collusion and state intervention—including business cycles, structural change and luck—have been far more important in transforming competitive markets into non-competitive ones.

Asymmetric information between two parties involved in a given transaction can also lead to market failure. For example, where one group of consumers of a product are unable to obtain the information (or where the cost of obtaining the information is greater than the potential savings) that there are alternative, lower price suppliers of the product, then a variety of prices, and a degree of monopoly power for sellers, will exist. In a more life-threatening example, someone requiring a doctor for the first time, would, in the absence of occupational licensing, not know which doctor to go to. In both these examples, state intervention is justified, in the first by providing or enforcing the provision of information, and in the second by imposing the need for those wishing to practise as doctors to obtain the appropriate qualifications.

Public goods provide another type of market failure, but it can be considered as a special case of asymmetric information. Public goods are goods whose consumption (or use) by people who have not paid for this use cannot be prevented—unpaid consumption is non-excludable. Examples include public roads, public lighting and public parks (with no gates). A public good leads to market failure because there will tend to be an underestimation of the value (utility) of the good to the consumer when it comes to paying for it, followed by an overutilization by consumers once the good has been provided. The usual solution is for the government to tax people and provide the public good with the revenue. This type of market failure is a special case of asymmetric information in the sense that a good is public because it is impossible for the provider of the good to know who is consuming and how much they are consuming. This leads to the suggestion of improved means of providing that information as a way of correcting the market failure (Peacock, 1979), but this may not always be possible.

Paternalist intervention

There are two main cases of this type of intervention. The first is where there are *merit goods*, that is goods for which it is possible that an individual's consumption decisions will not be in his or her best interests. If education is a merit good, then the possibility that people will consume too little of it is 'an argument for state intervention to ensure that provision is at an optimal level' (Ferguson and Ferguson, 1994, p. 195). In the second case there is a belief that it is *not morally acceptable for certain goods or services to be bought and sold*. Examples include human organs for transplants, and police services. There is a normative argument that the 'state, as the social guardian, should remove such activities from the domain of the market and conduct them itself' (Chang, 1994, p. 12).

Ferguson and Ferguson (1994, p. 195–6) point out that these types of arguments for state intervention ignore the possibility of government failure. They go on to exclude further discussion on the grounds that the argument 'largely turns on paternalistic and normative judgements beyond the scope of economic analysis'. Chang (1994, pp. 13–15) outlines the more detailed, contractarian criticism of paternalist intervention, according to which there should be no interference in the decisions of the individual. He then provides (pp. 15–18) a critique of this argument, based on the idea that an economic theory resting on individualism is no more scientific, and no less moralistic, than one resting on collectivism.

Chang would disagree with Ferguson and Ferguson on the question of whether paternalistic and moral judgements are beyond the scope of economic analysis, but he would agree with them that there has been inadequate attention by economists to the possibility of government failure. He discusses two types of government failure, the *information problem* and *rent seeking*. In the first, there is either insufficient information or asymmetric information within the state apparatus about some market failure. The cost of obtaining (or distributing) the information is greater than the gain from the correction of the market failure. Chang (1994, p. 27) believes that the information problem is exaggerated: 'it is unreasonable to criticise the state for having insufficient information while assuming that decision-makers in private organisations (for example firms) known everything they need to know.' Rent seeking, the second type of government failure, is where regulations by the state result in unproductive activities by private agents to capture what might be called artificial rents.[55] For example, where it is in the power of the state to allocate monopoly rights to a certain industry, the efforts (and expenditures) of individuals attempting to obtain the favourable considerations of politicians, is rent seeking. Chang (1994, pp. 29–31) finds a number of theoretical deficiencies in the rent-seeking argument, one of which is that 'the theory is far too reluctant to acknowledge that the creation of a monopoly by the state may be beneficial for productivity growth if the state can withdraw the rent when necessary.[56] His main criticism of the two theories (information problem and rent seeking) is that neither is concerned with how government failure can be remedied other than by non-intervention.

We can include, as a third type of government failure, *regulatory capture*, where although it might have the intention to act in the public interest, a regulatory body is unduly influenced by firms in the regulated industry. Developed by Stigler (1971), the theory is built on the idea that regulation is a good, supplied by politicians, and demanded by industries. The owners and workers in the industries buy regulation primarily with their votes (though presumably also with bribery). Once they 'own'—or can influence—regulation, producers can use it to their advantage against consumers or other producers. Others have criticized this idea on the grounds that consumers also have votes; that regulation is the product of coalitions between regulated producers and some consumers, at the expense of other unorganized, uninfluential consumers.[57] These criticisms still in general accept the inability of regulation to be in the public interest. It is this fundamental belief that is rejected by Chang (1994) and Tomlinson (1993).

Datta-Chaudhuri (1990) has provided an appropriate conclusion to this section of the chapter. In an article entitled 'Market failure and government failure' he describes the factors giving rise to a successful relationship between the state and the economy in South Korea, and contrasts them with those giving rise to an unsuccessful one in India. He then asks: 'Can a government be relied upon to do the "right" thing and avoid doing the "wrong" thing?' And answers: 'It is impossible to give a context-free answer to this question.'

A transaction cost theory of state intervention

From a neoclassical perspective, there is either an efficient or an inefficient allocation of resources. The costs of achieving either of these allocations is generally ignored. If we reinterpret the costs of state intervention as *transaction costs* (see above, Chapter 3, Section 3.2.3) then 'the real question is whether the state can achieve the same allocative efficiency at a lower cost than the market..., and not whether state intervention is costly *per se*' (Chang, 1994, p. 48). This approach emphasizes a fundamental role of the state in the economy, namely the lowering of general transaction costs. There are three main ways in which the state—in preference to any other actor in the economy—can reduce transaction costs: (1) by establishing and enforcing *property rights*; (2) by reducing *macroeconomic instability*; and (3) by intervening in cases of *co-ordination failure*.

Property rights   A clear and stable set of generally accepted property rights reduces transaction costs because without it individuals would have to expend far more time, effort and money to establish their rights in each transaction.

Douglass C. North (a 1993 Nobel prize winner for economics) provides a clear historical example of institutions of the state in Britain reducing transaction costs through the establishment of property rights. The Stuarts—rulers of England in the early seventeenth century—responded to repeated fiscal crises by practices such as selling various monopoly rights, confiscating property, and forcing the wealthy to make loans to them, 'that rendered property rights less secure'. What followed was a struggle between Parliament and Crown, and civil war, with stability not being re-established until much later in the century, when 'Parliamentary supremacy, central (parliamentary) control in financial matters, curtailment of royal prerogative powers, independence of the judiciary (at least from the Crown) and the supremacy of the common law courts were established'. An immediate consequence of the increased security of property rights was the rapid development of the public and private capital market. These were instrumental factors in England's rise to economic and political dominance (North, 1990, p. 139).

For the systemic reduction of transaction costs by the establishment and enforcing of property rights, it is not essential that the state intervene. However, as the most central institution, with the most pervasive power, it is far more likely that this role would be adopted by the state than by a firm.

Macroeconomic instability To the extent that the actions of governments reduce macro-economic instability (and it is debatable whether in fact they do), this contributes to the reduction of transaction costs. For example, where long-term contracts are concluded in order to achieve the security of known prices or interests rates, the costs of agreeing, monitoring and enforcing such contracts would be avoided if prices and interest rates were stable.

Co-ordination failure The co-ordination problem arises where some people prefer one out-come, others prefer another. If the same number of people prefer each of the two outcomes, and there is no other objective way of distinguishing between them—i.e. there is no way of arguing that one outcome is intrinsically better than the other—then there is a co-ordination problem if only one outcome is possible. To illustrate, let us assume a society in which there is no rule as to which side of the road people must drive. To avoid accidents, a rule must be made, but half the drivers wish to drive on the left, the other half on the right. In such situations, 'superseding private attempts at coordination with state intervention may greatly reduce transaction costs in the economy' (Chang, 1994, p. 52).

Chang (1994, p. 51) provides a game-theoretic example of the co-ordination problem (Fig. 4.12). The video recorder industry requires a national product standard because of network externalities. Firm A would prefer VHS while Firm B would prefer Betamax, but whatever the outcome, each would prefer to use the same, rather than different standards. State imposition of a standard may be a transaction-cost-minimizing way of arriving at a solution, because the alternative, private solution, would involve a great deal of negotiation and bargaining.

A more generalized example is provided by the exit game (Fig. 4.13). Here there is an industry which, because of the contraction of the market, has been reduced to two firms.[58]

Firm B

		VHS	Betamax
Firm A			
VHS		(2, 1)	(0, 0)
Betamax		(0, 0)	(1, 2)

Figure 4.12 A co-ordination problem

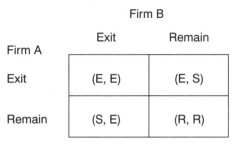

Figure 4.13   The exit game

Further contraction is necessary because only if there is one firm can that firm operate profitably. However, neither firm exits.

There will be a barrier to exit where S > R > E. Even if S is the only positive outcome, a maximum strategy will result in both firms remaining. Firm A, deciding whether to exit or remain will consider its options: if Firm B exits, it will be best for Firm A to remain, because S > E; if Firm B remains, it will be best for Firm A to remain, because R > E. Firm B, by identical reasoning, will also remain. As with the previous example, intervention by the state choosing which firm is to remain, will minimize the transaction costs involved in negotiation and bargaining (and other acts of attrition) between the firms.

In order to reduce transaction costs, the state need not completely replace market transactions. First, it can change institutional configurations, for example encouraging the creation of representative organizations of employers and trade unions, so as to reduce the amount of bargaining. Second, it can attempt to generate, through education and the media, a more homogeneous ideology. The conclusion of 'contracts between agents sharing the same ideology will reduce the bargaining, monitoring and enforcement and other transaction costs required'. Third, the state can provide a focal point around which decisions can be co-ordinated, thus saving transaction costs. French and Japanese planning exercises are examples of such provision of focal points, 'where the state provides a "vision" for the future economy and induces private agents to work toward the same goal' (Chang, 1994, p. 52).

Chang's transaction cost theory of state intervention, drawing on the work of economists like Coase and North, provides a framework for comparing the costs and benefits of intervention. This theory shows that intervention may or may not be justifiable, and provides a means of assessing the extent to which intervention might improve the situation. Such a general framework is necessary, because without it it is difficult to identify where regulation is, and where it is not, appropriate. For example, arguments about the necessity of regulating against entry where there is thought to be a natural monopoly will confront arguments about the need in all cases to encourage competition.[79]

4.2   The EU dimension

4.2.1   Concentration in the EU

The only source of information in the EU that provides measures of market concentration as defined above, is the Annual Reports on Competition Policy published by the European Commission since 1972. Unfortunately, there has been no continuity over time in the

TABLE 4.5   Market leaders in the EC (sample) (*Source: Sixth Report on Competition Policy* (CEC, 1977))

CR1 (%)	Market	Industry	Country	Year	Company
86	Sugar	Food, drink	DK	1975	De Danske Sukkerfabrikker
85	Beverages	Food, drink	B	1976	Coca-Cola
85	Thread	Textiles	F	1973	Dollfus Mieg
85	Electric coffee machine	Electrical machinery	F	1975	Moulinex
25	Car tyres	Transport equipment	F	1974	Michelin

methodologies and definitions of market concentration used in these reports, and comparison of concentration in different periods is therefore difficult.

For example, the Sixth Report (1977) presents a table of all product markets where the leading firm holds more than 25 per cent of the total national market for that product. All the markets in this table were considered by the EC Commission to be characterized by a high level of concentration. A sample of this distribution is given in Table 4.5.

The table shows the importance of certain firms in individual EC markets. As can be seen, the market is very narrowly defined (four or five digits). In the full table, 39 per cent of the leaders are to be found in the food and drink industry, 21 per cent in the chemicals industry, and 6.6 per cent in the paper industry. This suggests that in some industries there are more likely to be large, dominant firms than in others.

The methodology used in subsequent Reports on Competition Policy (nos 12, 13 and 14 for example) relies on the information gathered by the French business magazine, *Le Nouvel Economiste*. The CR4 ratios are calculated on the basis of the ranking, by the magazine, of the 1000 largest companies. The variables used are turnover and numbers employed.

In spite of the discontinuity of methodologies and data, a time-series analysis of concentration can be attempted. Figure 4.14 shows the trend in overall concentration in the EU—based on turnover—from 1972 to 1981, and—based on employment—from 1975 to 1981.

Figure 4.14 is based on shares in turnover and employment. An alternative approach is to calculate the contribution of the largest industrial firms to gross domestic product. This is done by de Jong (1993) for the period 1962 to 1990. Figure 4.15 is based on his data. There is an upward trend in the level of concentration in EU industry during the 1970s. In that period, many large European firms caught up with their British counterparts. From Fig. 4.14 it appears that, in terms of the CR10 ratio for European industry as a whole, the increase in concentration was sharper during the early part of the decade, levelling off to some extent in the latter half. This could be related to the rise in energy prices in 1973 and the subsequent increase in concentration in the oil and coal-mining sectors. In the second half of the 1970s, the growth of concentration either stabilized or reversed (in sectors such as mechanical engineering, and food, drink and tobacco). According to the Commission, in its Sixth Report on Competition Policy:

Since 1972 the process of industrial concentration has been moving clearly towards stability and in some cases even slowing down in those industries which are already highly concentrated. According to modern economic theory, when the level of concentration passes a certain point in a given industry, a trend towards reequilibrium emerges in the form of declining concentration; it has also been found that maturity in an industry generally entails a degree of stability. (CEC, 1977, p. 206)

From Fig. 4.14 it would appear that this slowing down/reversal did not occur until 1976 and from Fig. 4.15, not until 1982. Whether these differences are because of different methodologies

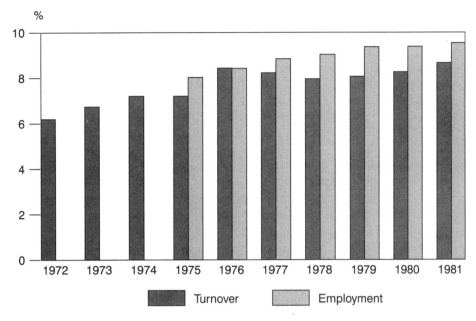

Figure 4.14   Concentration in European industry CR10 (*Source*: 13th Report on Competition Policy)

or different data sources, what follows from all studies is that there is a general upward trend in concentration for European industry as a whole in the 1970s. But, if different industries reach maturity at different times, it is not surprising that concentration in different industrial sectors moved in opposite directions during the period.[60]

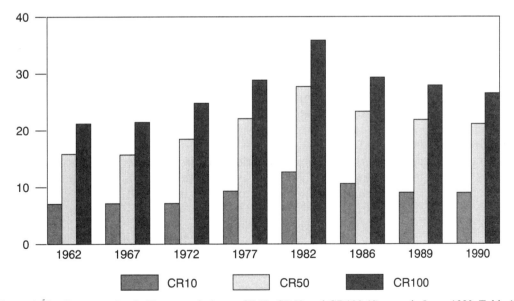

Figure 4.15   Concentration in European industry CR10, CR50 and CR100 (*Source*: de Jong, 1993, Table 1)

TABLE 4.6 Concentration (CR4) in selected sectors, 1973, 1981 and 1989 (*Sources: Twelfth Report on Competition Policy* (CEC, 1983), and for 1989, author's calculations derived from *Le Nouvel Economiste* (Nov. 1990))

	1973	1981	1989
Food, drink and tobacco	33	25	29
Chemicals	25	31	30
Elec. eng., office machinery and data processing	38	43	36
Mechanical and instrument engineering	33	33	36
Production and processing of metals	24	26	44
Motor vehicles and other transport	34	44	44
Wood, furniture and paper	47	45	39
Textiles, clothing, leather and footwear	53	42	38

Table 4.6 shows three sectors in which the CR4 ratio declined during the 1970s, and five sectors in which it either rose or remained stable. During the 1980s the CR4 declined in four sectors and either rose or remained stable in four. The trend seems to have been down in the 1970s and up in the 1980s in food, drink and tobacco,[61] up in the 1970s and down in the 1980s in chemicals and in electrical/electronic engineering, stable or continuously up in mechanical engineering, metals and motor vehicles, and continuously down in wood, furniture and paper and in textiles and clothing.[62]

In the year following the publication of the White Paper on the Completion of the Internal Market (CEC, 1985), concentration in some industries increased through mergers and acquisitions (see Chapter 5, Section 5.3.1). However, Fig. 4.15 convincingly demonstrates that overall concentration, having peaked in the early 1980s, declined thereafter towards levels similar to those of the mid-1970s.

A narrow definition of an industry, either in terms of product or region, can give rise to higher concentration than a more general frame of reference. In the European pharmaceutical industry, for example, concentration ratios in each country are higher than in the EU as a whole; and concentration ratios in each therapeutic market are higher than in the pharmaceutical industry as a whole (de Wolf, 1993; Earl-Slater, 1993).

Concentration can be higher (or lower) in individual member countries than in the EU as a whole. For the manufacturing industry as a whole, the UK, for example, has had a higher level of concentration than other EU economies, at least until recent years. Data (from different sources) put together by Ferguson and Ferguson (1994, p. 54) suggest that the 1982 manufacturing CR100 in the USA was 33, in the UK 41 and in the EC 26. It had reached a peak of 42 in the UK in 1975, and continued to decline to 38 in 1989. It stabilized in the USA much earlier, and in the EC much later.

At a disaggregated level, the concentration ratio varies from industry to industry and from country to country. For example, in 1987, the concentration ratio in the clothing industry, measured using the Gini coefficient, was found to be 0.65 in the UK, against 0.50 in France and 0.61 in Germany (Andréosso, 1991). However, in the software services industry (part of NACE 839), the CR10 ratio in 1992 was only 16.8 per cent in the UK, higher at 23.5 per cent in France, and lower at 13 per cent in Germany. In the EU telecommunication equipment industry (NACE 344), French and German firms are the market leaders; in 1991, the French manufacturer Alcatel had 29 per cent of the European market for transmission equipment against 27 per cent for the top German firm in the industry, Siemens. Finally, the EU market for motor vehicles is probably one of the most concentrated. In 1992, the distribution among domestic firms was as follows: 17.5 per cent to the German Volkswagen, 12.4 per cent to GM-Europe, 12.2 per cent to Peugeot SA, 11.8 per cent to Fiat, 11.2 per cent to Ford-Europe, 10.6 per cent to Renault, the remaining firms being left with less than a quarter of the market (figures from *Panorama of EU Industry*, CEC, 1994).

As argued above, Section 4.1.3), in the context of increasing internationalization, concentration ratios should be adjusted for trade. Marfels (1988) shows that, for example in the automobile industry, adjusting for trade sharply reduces concentration ratios in the USA, Britain and West Germany. The exception, not surprisingly, was Japan. The greater a country's trade surplus, the smaller is the adjusted ratio's denominator and, as a result, the greater the adjusted concentration.

The concentration ratio varies in a number of ways, including overtime at different rates, and even in opposite directions in different industries and countries; it evolves in response to European and global market and specific industrial factors. To explain concentration in the EU, we turn now to these factors.

We will deal here with two EU-specific explanatory variables:

- The change in the dimension of the integrated area
- The change in the intensity of integration in this area.[63]

A number of other factors also influence concentration ratios. There are very broad, global developments like the changes in *enabling technologies* that have facilitated internationalization of production, international division of labour and regional concentrations of rising and declining industries. A narrower focus, on industry-specific technological change, understood to include both production and organizational technology, is also necessary if the interest is in the concentration ratios within that industry. At an even more disaggregated level, differences between firms, and the success or otherwise of the corporate strategies of leading firms can also contribute to changes in concentration in those firms' industries. These factors—not specific to the EU—are discussed elsewhere in this book.[64]

The dimension of the integrated area

Since the degree of concentration is a diminishing function of market size, enlargements should, *ceteris paribus*, reduce market concentration.[65] However, Fig 4.14 and 4.15 suggest that the first enlargement in 1973 was immediately followed by a sharp rise in the level of overall concentration; this trend slowed (at least in terms of turnover) after 1975. Subsequent enlargements, in 1981 and 1986, involved economies too small to influence overall concentration in the integrated area to a great extent, but it is clear from Fig. 4.15 that, whatever the reason, concentration over most of the 1980s declined. The *ceteris paribus* assumption is clearly not valid.

Arguably, spatial dimension and internal economic growth are similar in terms of their expected effect on concentration. This depends, however, on the cause of growth: if it is a consequence of new firms, concentration is diminished; if it is a result of an increase in the turnovers of all firms, then they may be no change in concentration; and if the growth is accounted for by expansion of the larger firms, then concentration will increase.

There is certainly some, albeit sketchy, evidence of an inverse relationship between growth and concentration. During the 1950s the rapidly expanding economies of the Community—Italy, Germany and France—experienced no or only slight increases in concentration. During the mid-1970s, with the post-oil crisis downturn, the CR100 in Germany rose significantly, but in the UK only very slightly. The German increase was, however, accounted for entirely by the six largest firms, possibly increasing their market shares in preparation for the anticipated competition of firms from the recently entered, more highly concentrated, British economy. *Within* industries (globally) over the period 1962 to 1990 'strong growth [was] accompanied by declining concentration, while slow growth, and *a fortiori* decline [were associated with] a rising degree in concentration' (de Jong, 1993, p. 10). But overall, as can be seen from Figs 4.14 and 4.15, there is no indication of concentration increasing during recessions or declining during periods of growth.

We would not expect either spatial spread or internal growth in the Community, by themselves (or even together), to account for the trends in concentration. Mergers and acquisitions, for example, have an obvious impact on concentration, and these types of activities may or may not occur during enlargements or periods of economic growth.

Corporate activity and economic integration

By economic integration in this context, we mean the removal of barriers to the flows of goods, services and factors of production between countries in the region. Some barriers are more amenable to government and corporate action than others. Language and cultural difference are, for example, far more difficult to remove than tariffs.

There was, until relatively recently, very little work on the impact of the Common Market on the structure of European industry. This is in sharp contrast to a wide literature, since the formation of the European Economic Community, on the trade effects[66] of economic integration. One explanation for this difference, given by Pelkmans (1984), is that economists have long been dominated by the static, neoclassical welfare theory of customs unions which ignores intra-union direct investment. Another reason has been the lack of reliable statistics; there seems to be a substantial 'statistical gap' between the EU and the USA.

Economists would expect increasing integration to have an impact on market structure. According to Scherer and Ross (1990, p. 89), during the first two decades of the EC 'the overall impact of integration was almost surely to create market structures more competitive than they otherwise would have been'. While the relationship between how competitive and how concentrated an industry is is not always clear,[67] what Scherer and Ross appear to be arguing[68] is the following: because the concentration ratios for the EC as a whole were much lower than in each of the five main founding member countries, and because the increase in the overall EC ratios over the period 1963 to 1978 was much lower than the increases in the national ratios in any of the five, therefore integration kept concentration down, i.e. it increased competition.

The behavioural aspect of this conclusion is that in the early stages of integration in Europe, characterized by the removal of tariff barriers, the extent to which leading firms dominated in national markets was greater than the extent to which leading firms dominated in the economy of the EC as a whole. Mergers, acquisitions and alliances (MAAs) during this period—in the MAA wave in the early 1970s, for example—were dominated by agreements between firms of the same nation (Hamill, 1992, p. 137; Thomsen and Woolcock, 1993, p. 22). National concentration ratios increased, but because this was happening in most member countries—though to varying extents—overall Community concentration increased less.

A subsequent stage of economic integration[69] deals with the removal of all NTBs (non-tariff barriers), such as legal, technical and financial barriers. Eager to exploit economies of scale in the face of globalized competition, European firms started to implement intensive cross-border strategies. Thus, according to Thomsen and Woolcock (1993, p. 22), 'In 1989–90, for the first time, the largest EC manufacturing firms were more acquisitive abroad than at home.' Hamill (1992, p. 137) more generally concludes that the distinguishing feature of the current [1985–90] boom in MAA activity... is the high proportion of cross-border deals', This suggests expansion of leading firms at the European level, with more of an impact on concentration at that level than the earlier, national mergers. Referring to the most recent merger wave, Shepherd (1990, p. 199) writes that 'the 1980s mergers have probably raised concentration ratios (and equivalent HHI [Herfindahl] values) by 2 or 3 percentage points'.

To summarize the above discussion on economic integration and concentration, in the first decades of the EC integration probably reduced concentration to less than it would have been without integration; more intense integration in the period since 1985 has probably increased concentration to above what it would have otherwise have been. We examine MAAs in more detail in Section 5.3 of Chapter 5 (see also this Chapter, Section 4.3.2).

4.2.2 Barriers to entry in the EU

Barriers to entry (in a particular market) are all types of obstacles at the market edge that make entry for new firms difficult. They consist of all the factors that give incumbent firms advantages over those considering entry into the market. The study of barriers has traditionally been conducted at the level of the single economy.[70] These are the barriers faced by a firm in an economy wishing to gain entry into an industry and, by extension, a product market, in that economy. These barriers, which include economies of scale and product differentiation, can be referred to as *barriers of the first order*.[71] In the case of an open economy, we have to take into account the geographical dimension of the market, and cross-border transactions render the situation more complex.

A firm originating from country A and wishing to expand its activity beyond country A's borders has three broad means at its disposal: foreign direct investment (FDI) (whether through greenfield investments or mergers, acquisitions or joint ventures); other strategic alliances involving, for example, licensing agreements; and trade. In the case of FDI, the firm must overcome the barriers of the first order in the relevant industry in the host country. To some extent these will be similar to the first order barriers in its home country, and to that extent the firm choosing FDI will already have overcome these barriers. Like firms undertaking FDI, firms attempting to enter a foreign market through exporting have usually already gained a foothold (i.e. overcome first order barriers) in their home market. In addition, however, firms choosing exporting as their market entry strategy face barriers through which agents in the target country resist imports. These are *barriers of the second order*.

Barriers of the second order

Barriers of the second order are all restrictions (essentially of an institutional nature) faced by potential entrants into a given geographical market. They prohibit entry of a foreign competitor. They include tariffs,[72] quantitative restrictions and other measures of equivalent effect, and non-tariff barriers (NTBs). The NTBs encompass border checks, administrative procedures such as insurance regimes, differing legal and fiscal regimes, technical standards, public procurement bias, exchange controls and other monetary controls. Cultural and language barriers should also be included in this group.

In some cases, the barriers to entry by international trade into a given geographical market are so numerous and so high that the firm would choose FDI as an alternative strategy. This is particularly true for, but not confined to, non-EU firms attempting to penetrate the EU market. In order to bypass the Common External Tariff constraint, many US multinationals have preferred to establish a presence in the EU market.[73]

The Treaty of Rome, Article 3, Part 1, called for the abolition of tariffs, quantitative restrictions and other measures having equivalent effect, on trade between member states. In the years following its signature, all tariff barriers among the six founding members were removed.[74] In the early years of the EU, it was assumed that NTBs were of limited importance compared with customs duties but, because of the recession in the 1970s, these NTBs multiplied as member states increasingly sought to protect their home markets and industries. Regional integration in the EU could only be strengthened by the abolition of the remaining NTBs. In 1985, the EC Commission produced a detailed legislative programme[75] aimed at the full integration of the economies of the member states of the Community by, among other things, the eradication of all barriers of the second order. The Commission identified among remaining obstacles, impediments not just to the free flow of goods and services, but also to capital and labour. These obstacles have been classified as physical, technical and fiscal barriers.

Physical barriers at customs posts   These are barriers both because they cause delays and because there are formalities like forms and documents that involve administrative costs. The delays include such problems as queues of trucks awaiting inspection at borders, which are costly in terms of drivers' wages and in terms of the opportunity costs of having vehicles unavailable for other uses. Most important in this context is the disadvantage that customs posts impose on suppliers or (consumer and producer) goods from other countries. Many of these problems have been removed by the 1992 programme. For example, in January 1988 member states adopted the single administrative document (SAD) for importing and exporting goods among all members of the EU. However, directives agreed at the EU level still require action on the part of member states to incorporate them into national law and to implement them in practice. Among the five areas that the Commission has identified in which there have been delays at the level of the member states is the suppression of border checks (O'Donnell, 1994). (The others will be mentioned at appropriate points below.)

Technical barriers   These are of two broad kinds: technical regulations and procurement markets.[76] Technical regulations are enacted by national legislators in the interest of health, safety and environment, and often take the form of technical standards. Standards have traditionally been defined by national standards bodies (such as the *Deutsche Industrie Normen*, the *AFNOR* in France and the British Institute of Standards). These national bodies test and certify that a product complies with national standards and/or regulations. National standards are NTBs because when issued at country level, they are not recognized by other member states. The best-known example of stringency embodied in national standards resulting in an NTB was the purity decree of beer in Germany (*Reinheitsgebot*) that almost prohibited imports of foreign beers into the German market.[77] European standardization has enhanced the positions of European bodies such as the CEN (*Centre Européen des Normes*) and the *Cenelec*.[78]

Different national standards have been predominant in the food industry (for example in relation to the marketing of chocolate, beer, pasta and ice cream products), pharmaceuticals, telecommunications equipment, car and building products. Also included in technical barriers are regulations regarding workers' qualifications.

In the view of the Commission, technical barriers

not only add extra costs, but they also distort production patterns, increase unit costs, increase stockholding costs, discourage business cooperation, and fundamentally frustrate the creation of a Common Market for industrial products. Until such barriers are removed, Community manufacturers are forced to focus on national rather than continental markets and are unable to benefit from the economies of scale which a truly unified market offers. (CEC, 1985, p. 17)

The removal of the technical barriers would improve market access; they would remove sheltered dominant positions and lead to a higher degree of competition. Also, a larger market and the restructuring of the EU's productive system would enable firms to undertake and finance costly (and risky) R&D projects. As a result of the full exploitation of economies of scale, prices would be forced down, and would be expected to converge in the medium to long term.

An estimation of possible gains has been attempted by Cecchini (1988).[79] The welfare gains for EC producers and consumers have been estimated at around ECUs 200 billion,[80] representing between 4.3 and 6.4 per cent of the EC's GDP in 1988. Roughly a third of the gains would arise as a result of scale economies and a quarter would stem from increased competition. Given that over 95 per cent of the directives required for completion of the internal market have been passed, many of these gains must already have been achieved.

A key element in the adoption of directives on the removal of technical barriers is the new approach introduced in the programme for the completion of the single market. Up to the mid-1980s, the removal of technical barriers within the EC had been based on attempts to harmonize the technical standards of the member countries. This proved to be an extremely complicated and therefore lengthy process. The new approach was based on *mutual recognition*, where intra-Community trade in products is unrestricted as long as those products meet the technical standards of any member state.

The origin of the mutual recognition principle is the *Cassis de Dijon* case, ruled on by the European Court of Justice in 1978. The ruling was that a product lawfully sold in any one member state must be admitted—and permitted to be sold—in other member states. This principle has increasingly guided international regulation within the EU since 1985.

Some important measures were not agreed by the end of 1992, and some industries (such as the pharmaceutical industry) will not be truly European until well after the year 2000. We have already mentioned the problem of delays in the transposition of EU directives into national laws. The Commission has identified protection of intellectual property as one of the main areas in which these delays have occurred. Another is double taxation of firms, which is discussed under fiscal barriers, to which we now turn.

Fiscal barriers   There have been and continue to be differences in the tax systems (income tax, property tax, corporate tax, VAT and excise duties) of the member states. For example, in 1987, excise duties on wine were zero in Spain, Portugal and Greece. In Ireland, the excise duty was ECUs 2.79 per litre of wine, and ECUs 0.13 in Luxemburg (Emerson *et al.*, 1988). A final agreement on VAT and excise duty harmonization was reached by the 12 Finance Ministers in October 1992. This will involve substantial changes for some member countries.

Another important example of fiscal barriers is the differences between the member states' corporate profit tax rates.[81] In 1991, overall (i.e. central government + intermediate government + local government) corporate profit tax rates ranged from 10 per cent (for manufacturing firms) in Ireland to 57.5 per cent in Germany (Table 4.7).

TABLE 4.7 **Corporate tax rates in the EU (1991)** (*Source*: Supplement to *European Report*, no. 1754, 21 March 1992)

Country	Main rate	Other rate
EU		
Belgium	39	
Denmark	38	
France	34	42[b]
Germany	57.5	45.6[b]
Greece	46[c]	
Ireland	40	10[d]
Italy	47.83	
Luxembourg	39.39	
Netherlands	35	
Portugal	39.6	
Spain	35.34	
UK[a]	33	
Other European		
Austria	39	
Sweden	30	
Switzerland[a]	39.44	13.51[e]

Notes
[a] These countries apply lower rates to corporations with profits below a certain threshold.
[b] On distributed profits.
[c] Varies with activity, status and nature of investment (productive or not).
[d] For manufacturing sector and for certain services (in the International Financial Services Centre in Dublin), 40 per cent otherwise.
[e] Progressive rate schedule, from 13.51 to 39.44 per cent.

The Committee of Independent Experts on Company Taxation, headed by the former Dutch Finance Minister Onno Ruding, was set up in order to advise on the harmonization of company taxation. The Ruding report's recommendations, submitted to the European Commission in March 1992, fall into three categories: elimination of the double taxation of cross-border income flows; harmonization of corporate taxes; and greater transparency between member states on other tax issues. The Committee proposed a three stage approach to harmonization of company taxation: first, that a uniform withholding tax of 30 per cent on all member states' companies be put into effect by January 1994 (whether the profits are distributed in the form of dividends or not); second, that from January 1994, a single type of tax on companies, varying from 30 to 40 per cent, be established; and third, that from the beginning of 1997 (and until full Economic and Monetary Union, or EMU, comes into effect), the scope of the 'parent-subsidiary' directive adopted in July 1990 be extended. The aim here is to eliminate double taxation by giving individual companies the right to claim against such taxation. When double taxation arises, the firm concerned refers its case to the fiscal authorities in the member state where the firm is taxed. If no satisfactory decision is made, the firm refers its case to the authorities in the member state where the associated firm is taxed. As a last resort, the case is referred to an Advisory Commission (comprising a chairman, two representatives of the tax authorities concerned, and an equal number of independent members.

To date, some progress has been made on the transparency front. Since January 1992, a common taxation system on parent companies and their subsidiaries has been agreed (Council

Directive 90/435/EEC).[82] On 1 January 1993, the withholding of tax on interest and royalty payments made between parent companies and their subsidiaries in different member states was abolished (COM (90) 571 final). Important variations still remain however among the fiscal systems and corporate profit tax rates of the member states, and even though many issues have been agreed at the European level, their transposition into national law and implementation by member states has been slower.

The removal of second order barriers can, paradoxically, increase differences between economies, in terms of industrial development. The implementation of the directive relating to the mutual recognition of higher education degrees, for example, would enable firms to recruit their most highly skilled employees from anywhere in the Union. The most profitable and prestigious firms would attract the best European graduates. This may have an adverse effect in some areas that experience a net outflow of such graduates. Most economists expect the net effects to be positive. Adverse effects in disadvantaged areas are expected to be offset by, for example, structural funds aimed at improving the infrastructures of such areas.

Even if the internal market can be fully completed in the near future, other types of barriers will remain: cultural and language barriers will still be a feature of the EU market for the foreseeable future. Cultural and language barriers were important in the ABC/Générale des Eaux and Canal/W.H.Smith TV case (CEC, 1991). Resistance to the removal of other barriers will also continue for many years. Examples include national buying preferences (evidenced in the Aérospatiale/MBB and Alcatel/AEGKabel cases) and different distribution channels and marketing methods in the member states (as in the Otto/Grattan, La Redoute/Empire, Sanofi/ Sterling Drug, and UAP/Transatlantic/Sun Life cases) (CEC, 1991).

Barriers of the first order

The creation of a large European domestic market entails, by definition, the removal of most of the remaining NTBs, the barriers of the second order. It is however interesting to study the significance in the European domestic market of the barriers of the first order, as identified above.

With the elimination of most of the remaining NTBs, the EU is supposedly a quasi-homogeneous geographical market of 350 million people. None the less, intensified competition is expected to change the intensity of other barriers, namely scale economies and product differentiation, the barriers of the first order.

Economies of scale in the EU   Under the assumptions of perfect competition, every firm produces where long-run average cost is at minimum; any increase in output will raise the average cost of the product (diseconomies of scale). In most situations, competition is less than perfect and, as we saw in Section 4.1.4 above, this can result in firms producing under conditions of increasing returns (or economies of scale), that is, above the minimum average cost level (to the left of point *M* on Fig. 4.16). Unexploited economies of scale would then materialize. Since the completion of the European market increases the level of competition, it can be argued that it also drives firms down their average cost curves. Ultimately, even if the result is fewer leading firms in any particular industry in Europe, each will produce greater output at lower average costs. Competition from outside Europe will keep prices close to average cost (i.e. it will keep supernormal profits down).[83]

A number of manufacturing industries have potential for further exploitation of technical economies of scale in the EU.[84] According to Pratten (1987), these industries can be ranked in

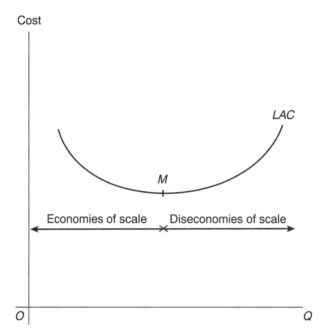

Figure 4.16   Economies and diseconomies of scale

terms of importance of economies of scale. He estimates ranges of potential cost savings from increasing output. Even within industries, these ranges are wide, reflecting the heterogeneous nature of industries in terms of economies of scale.[85]

Broadly, economies of scale are large in motor vehicles, transport equipment, chemicals, mechanical engineering, electrical engineering, instrument engineering, and paper, printing and publishing. These industries accounted for approximately two-thirds of total manufacturing employment in the EU-10 and 55 per cent of industrial production in the EU-12. Production economies of scale are smaller in the more traditional industries: food, drink and tobacco, clothing and leather, timber and wood, and textiles. Economies of marketing and/or of distribution are different from those of production, and are particularly significant in the food industry.

Pratten's (1987) data rest on a strong assumption that the removal of NTBs within the EU has the effect of increasing plant size, enabling plants to realize all significant economies of scale. This hypothesis has been tested by various authors: Schwalbach (1988) for the UK and West Germany, Ranci and Helg (1987) for Italy, and Müller and Owen (1985) for West Germany. Drawing from past experience, their studies confirm the role played by external trade in the expansion of the size of production units.

The larger size of the market, the benefits of which can be reaped by increased exports, and the challenge represented by imports, are the two major explanatory variables. Firms become more efficient and non-viable plants are removed from the respective domestic markets. In France, the average size computed on the basis of sales of the 250 largest domestic companies was $1.3 million at the end of the 1980s; the figures for West Germany and the UK were $2.2 million and $2 million respectively. The 1993 deadline made these differences clear to the French business community. Mergers and acquisitions, as a means of achieving economies of scale, ranked first on the list of French firms' strategies for the early 1990s. The few hundred biggest firms in France acknowledged the fact that 'growth is imperative to achieve dominant positions in [the French] market' (Bain and Company, 1989, p. 98). The necessity to exploit economies of scale increases the average size of production units; this, in turn, tends to raise concentration ratios.

From the completion of the European market arises a potential paradox. Driving costs down makes it even more difficult for new firms to enter the market, because it implies that the volume of output on first entering the industry has to be large. The completion of the Single Market leads to the exploitation of economies of scale which may inhibit competition.[86] Expressed another way, the removal of the barriers of the second order may intensify barriers of the first order.

Product differentiation in the EU   European integration has resulted in an increasing proportion of the total trade of the EU being accounted for by intra-EU trade. How does this relate to product differentiation? If the increasing tendency for member countries to trade with one another is expressed in flows of very different goods out of one member from those that flow out of another, then integration has had no impact on product differentiation. On the other hand, if different members' exports are similar then increasing integration may have increased product differentiation.

The traditional customs union theory (as developed by Jacob Viner in 1950) focused on homogeneous products. The question he asked was whether welfare gains arising from joining a customs union were greater or less than the losses arising from no longer importing from a cheaper source. This question was to be asked for each product affected by joining. Some products would be exported by the new entrant to the customs union, others imported from the customs union. There was no room in the theory for a product to be both exported and imported.[87] In this sense the theory was basically Ricardian; trade would be in accordance with *comparative advantage* within the customs union.

In one respect developments have been predicted by theory; intra-EU trade has continued to increase and now represents almost two-thirds of total EU trade.[88] On the other hand, contrary to the predictions of the customs union theory, the increase in intra-EU trade has been more a result of intra-industry than inter-industry trade.[89]

The expectation was that, say, Germany would become a major European producer of cars and, say, Italy the major European producer of refrigerators. Germany would then be the main source of cars, and most of the imports of cars by member countries would be from Germany, and similarly for refrigerators, most of the imports by members would be from Italy. Instead, all of the large member countries (and some of the smaller ones) have continued to produce and export both cars and refrigerators. They have also continued to import both these products. 'Indeed, the trade figures for all West European countries show that each country has significant exports and imports in most product categories, and this intra-industry trade accounts for a high proportion of total trade' (O'Donnell, 1994).[90] Why?

From a supply perspective, the theory was based on a set of assumptions that were unrealistic. Among these was perfect competition and production at constant returns to scale. Many national markets were closer to monopolistic competition and oligopoly, with economies of scale (EOS) in production (and distribution) and these evolved into similarly structured markets at the European level. With production in different countries, information that firms had about the process, product and distribution strategies of competitors was far less than perfect. This inevitably led to differences between the products (in the same industry) made in different member countries. Firms have acted to maintain these differences, physically differentiating their products from others in the industry, advertising to generate brand loyalty, and investing in R&D in attempts to stay ahead technologically. Finally, one industrial system in Europe may be better orientated towards the achievement of one characteristic of a product (e.g. high quality), while another may be better orientated towards the achievement of another characteristic (e.g. low price).

Among consumers, with increasing incomes there has been an increase in technical knowledge and ability to isolate the many features of the same product; there is, for example, an increased awareness of quality. While some people focus on dependability and price, others focus on 'different, new' for the snob value of being different. Over time, consumer demand interacts with the advertising of the sellers to create brand loyalty.[91]

Intra-industry trade is a consequence of these supply and demand factors, that is, the availability of a variety of EOS products in the same industry in different countries,[92] together with the increasing ability among consumers in different countries to differentiate among products in the same industry.

In his discussion of intra-industry trade, Root (1990, p. 115) emphasizes 'factors that are *specific to the firm* (product differentiation and internal economies of scale)'. Writing of the United States, he points out that the 'firm-specific nature of intra-industry trade is highlighted when we recognize that about one-third of that trade occurs between multinational enterprises and their foreign subsidiaries. Any theory of intra-industry trade, therefore, needs to be linked with a theory of foreign investment that explains the behavior of multinational enterprise.'[93]

The index usually used to measure the intensity of a country's intra-industry trade is the Grubel–Lloyd index. For a single industry, the index is

$$\text{IIT}_{GL} = 1 - \frac{|X - M|}{X + M}$$

where X and M are, respectively, the country's exports and imports of the products of that industry.[94]

The index takes values between zero and one, zero when there are exports but no imports or imports but no exports, and one when exports equal imports. The closer it is to one the higher the level of intra-industry trade. It is in general higher in manufacturing industries than in the primary sector because the production of a particular manufactured good can often in practice be located in any of a large number of different places, whereas primary products must be exported from locations which have a natural comparative advantage for producing them. Arguably, manufactured goods are also subject to a greater degree of product differentiation than primary products. During the first decades of the EC, integration and enlargement were accompanied by a general intensification of intra-industry trade and, by implication, product differentiation.[95]

The degree of product differentiation is likely to be higher in less concentrated, or more competitive industries. In oligopolistic industries (such as microprocessor production), the full exploitation of economies of scale involves product standardization and long production runs; as a result, product differentiation will be much less important than in less concentrated industries, such as office machinery. This raises a problem for EU competition policy; aiming to reduce costs can result in barriers to entry from economies of scale in concentrated industries, but encouraging competition in less concentrated industries can result in product differentiation which can also be a barrier to entry.

The classic example of product differentiation as a barrier to entry is the breakfast cereals market in the USA. The burgeoning number of new brands produced by incumbent firms between 1950 and 1970 was such that entry was deterred. Potential entrants could not find a niche in which to operate profitably, despite the persistently high profits earned by incumbent firms (Schmalensee, 1978a). Shaw (1982) has noticed the same effects in the UK fertilizer industry. In general, as a means of differentiating products, advertising which generates brand loyalty will make it difficult for new brands to compete.[96] In the Commission's examination of the Sanofi/Sterling Drug case (CEC, 1991) national branding was perceived as an entry barrier.

How high are barriers to entry in Europe, and do they differ as between member countries? Barriers of the second order, differentiating between the economies of Europe, have been lowered by the programme for the completion of the Single Market, but the impact has been different in different sectors. In the pharmaceutical industry, for example, both technical and fiscal differences continue to prevent a completely European (as opposed to national) perspective on the part of firms. In some service sub-sectors, such as telecommunications, changes in interpretation of regulations[97] has facilitated the entry of competitors into markets previously reserved for public monopolies.

Geroski and Schwalbach (1989) measured the height of barriers in the UK and Germany for the two periods 1974–79 and 1983–85. They used a model that compared the expected post-entry profits (of the entrant) with the long-run profits that are protected by entry barriers. For the UK, the sample consisted of 3-digit manufacturing industries; for Germany, more disaggregated 4-digit data were available. The results were that in both the UK and FRG entry barriers were 'fairly high', though which specific entry barriers were significant was different in the two countries. In the UK, for example, while the capital requirement did not raise barriers to either domestic or foreign firms attracted by large markets with high demand growth, 'Advertising outlays, on the other hand, are strongly positively correlated with the overall height of barriers.... By far the most powerful entry barrier in the FRG are scale economies. In addition, R&D investments clearly raise entry barriers which is also true for capital intensity, contrary to the UK results' (Geroski and Schwalbach, 1989, p. 73).

4.2.3 Public enterprise and procurement markets

Public sector purchasing embraces all purchases of goods and services by governments and by public enterprise (nationalized industries). Government purchasing may be undertaken centrally, locally or by special agencies. For some products such as defence equipment, the government is the only buyer (monopsony). It has to select a product, a contractor, and must negotiate a contract.

With the exception of important public utilities like telecommunications, water, energy and transport, which the Community had agreed could be excluded, open tendering has theoretically been the rule for public procurement since the 1970s. In practice, however, public procurement has always tended to favour domestic over foreign suppliers. In 1986, for example, public procurement represented 15 per cent of Community GDP, but intra-Community trade in the same area amounted to no more than 0.14 per cent of Community GDP (CEC, 1993a). The White Paper on Completing the Internal Market proposed the enforcement of the rules on open competition for public contracts, and the removal of the exemptions.

Public purchasing is concentrated in some industries: construction and public works account for 29 per cent of total public purchasing in the EU-12. Purchases by governments are also to be found in the defence sector, energy sector, transport equipment and other manufacturing industries (such as electrical goods and chemicals), and services (business services, distribution and telecommunications). It has been estimated that the volume of public procurement that could be opened up to EU-wide competition was between 7 and 10 per cent of Community GDP (CEC, 1993a, p. 2).

Three types of positive effects are expected from an increased degree of competition in the EU procurement markets:

1 The static trade effect whereby public agencies can purchase from the cheapest source, or the lowest cost producer in the EU.
2 The competition effect in which increased competitive pressures felt by the domestic firms force them to reduce prices in order to survive in a non-sheltered European market.
3 The restructuring effect that enables firms to rationalize their production structure in the long term, thereby achieving economies of scale.

Total savings arising from the three effects have been estimated at around ECU 18 billion (at 1984 prices), of which more than a quarter would be represented by savings in the defence sector alone (CEC, 1988). In addition, the dynamic effects of enhanced competition on innovation are other benefits that are difficult to quantify.

4.2.4 Regulation and deregulation in the EU

From Section 4.1.5 above, it is clear that the most commonly argued basis for regulation is market failure. This was, for example, the basis for much of the EU's competition policy as enshrined in particular in Articles 85 and 86 of the Treaty of Rome. These articles aimed to give the Community the power to prevent collusion between firms and to prevent any firm from abusing a dominant position in a market. However, in particular since the mid-1980s and the move towards the Single Market, a great deal of support has been given by the EU to the development of large firms, in the belief that only such firms can compete on world markets with American and Japanese firms. We will discuss these issues in more detail in Chapter 7; they are introduced here to show that there has been, and remains, an explicit acceptance at the European level of the need for regulation. Indeed,

the political will exists to ensure a central role of the EC in economic regulation in a widening range of policy issues, including training, regional policies and local authority networking, consumer protection and employment rights, a process which has been accelerated through the creation of the Single Market however flawed or incomplete that may appear to be at the end of 1992. (Farrands and Totterdill, 1993)[98]

The belief in the need for regulation has, however, varied over time, and is also subject to debate over the nature and extent of regulation at any one time. In addition, some European countries have been consistently more interventionist than others, and more so in some sectors than others. According to Nugent (1994), 'business has traditionally been subject to greater regulation in the more advanced and industrialised countries of Northern Europe than in the poorer and less industrialised countries of Southern Europe. This is still just about so, but—following economic advancement in the South, and a certain amount of deregulation in the North—not so much as previously'.

Even among more industrialized European economies, there have been significant differences in the nature and extent of state regulation, though these also are diminishing. In the UK, regulation has evolved from policies, such as in regional policy, aimed at influencing allocation of resources, to state ownership of major industries like the car and shipbuilding industries.

There have also been corporatist bodies, like the National Economic Development Office (NEDO), but its 'activities have generally been limited to a series of *ad hoc* initiatives' (Farrands and Totterdill, 1993). Potentially more significant was the establishment of the National Enterprise Board, which was supposed to achieve high level economic co-ordination, but it was given inadequate powers and was abolished by the Thatcher government. There has been no consistent theme in regulation in the UK, not even since the advent of deregulation in the early 1980s. Together with the privatizations and general withdrawal from public provision has gone the development of such institutions as the Urban Development Corporations which 'have been highly interventionist in attempting to restructure local land and property markets' (Farrands and Totterdill, 1993).

In *France*, regulation has over the same period been far more direct (or *dirigiste*), through a series of national economic plans, state ownership of a large number of major firms,[99] state influence on the allocation and cost of credit, and significant amounts of state aid to both declining and expanding industries. Since 1986, as in many other countries, there has been a great deal of deregulation. For example, privatizations in the vast majority of state owned firms have been carried out, or announced.

Regulation in *Germany* has been far less intensive than in France. In the post-war period the German economy was among the least influenced by the state until the 1970s when, as in France, tax incentives and subsidies were given to both declining (e.g. steel) and expanding (e.g. electronics) sectors. There has also traditionally been a great deal of encouragement of vocational training and, in recent years, both directly and indirectly, the state has been involved in technological innovation (see also Chapter 5, Section 5.2).

The convergence among the members of the EU in terms of the nature and extent of regulation is due both to global economic forces and developments in the EU itself. At the global level, deregulation is an attraction to mobile capital and if it occurs in some countries, this will force other countries to consider it. This is true at the EU level as well, and in addition, the EU's moves towards the Single European Market involve the removal of national differences in policies towards business.

Deregulation in Europe

The road freight industry provides an example of the international nature of deregulation. It began in the 1960s, among the earliest countries in the OECD to be involved being Switzerland, Sweden and the UK. Subsequently, Belgium (in 1987), Denmark (in 1988), Ireland (in 1988), Norway (in 1987) and Portugal (in 1986), all abolished or reduced quantity or capacity controls or rate-fixing requirements in this sector. In Denmark, the Road Freight Transport Act of 1973, which regulated the issuing of licences, determined freight routes and established a system of approval of freight rates, was invalidated in 1988. In France, less deregulation took place: in 1986, the national quota system for licensing long distance freight transport was reformed to allow more entry (OECD, 1990). Passenger road transport services have been deregulated in the UK; 85 per cent of bus routes were found to be commercially viable after deregulation, and only 15 per cent required a subsidy through a system of public tendering (Balcombe, Hopkins and Penet, 1988).

Despite this deregulation, however, road transport continues to be strongly regulated by national governments particularly in relation to national road transport companies' national activities. According to one analysis (Sleuwaegen, 1993), 'Quantitative, as well as qualitative measures severely impede market entry and free competition'. Harmonization at the European level is occurring, and will eventually lead to developments similar to those in the industry in the USA and Australia. 'The imposition', for example, 'of new harmonized rules with respect to [environmental regulations] is a big step forward in the right direction'. Cole and Cole (1993, p. 181) are more pessimistic, arguing that if 'the desultory progress on the transport infrastructure in the last 20 years is a guide, some drastic changes in priorities and funding are needed'.

Harmonized regulation in the EU

There has been deregulation in the financial services sector too, and this is a sector which provides an excellent illustration of the combination of deregulation and the development—not always successful—of regulation at the EU level.[100] Banking and finance is a sector which has been highly regulated in most countries until relatively recently. Some countries, including Germany, The Netherlands and the UK, had removed controls on capital movements in the 1970s and 1980s. Because of this, and because of deregulation in other key international financial markets for funds, deregulation of this sector in Europe became inevitable in the late 1980s.[101] The 1988 Capital Movement Directive was fundamental, stating among other things that 'Member states shall abolish restrictions on movements of capital taking place between persons resident in member states' (Vipond, 1994). A year later the Second Banking Directive was adopted.[102]

This directive is based on the principles of *single banking licence* and *country of origin regulation*. The single banking licence allows any credit institution to offer services in any member state (host country) so long as it is registered, and permitted to provide those services, in the country of origin (home country). This leaves a great deal of freedom as to the type of regulatory framework the bank can choose. For example, a German bank can set up an Italian subsidiary and operate under Italian rules in Italy; it can, alternatively, operate under German rules in Italy. Under this system, any financial institution is given the opportunity to shop around and choose among the less constraining regulatory frameworks. This is why the 'country of origin regulation will act as a powerful incentive to the Member States of the EC to adopt unified, harmonized regulations' (Gowland, 1991, p. 51). These developments have led to the *Third Banking Directive* which imposes uniform capital adequacy ratios on banks.[103]

It can be argued that the diminution during the 1980s of national powers to regulate financial markets was responsible for the financial and currency crises in the early 1990s. According to Farrands and Totterdill (1993), national regulation proved 'feebly inadequate' in the succession of crises in the City of London in 1990–91. Only regulation at the EU level is appropriate, first because it 'has the information networks and has developed the skilled staff, as well as the legal competences in economic and monetary policy regulation, to take an overall supervisory role' and second, because it is 'at least potentially democratically accountable, whereas the main alternative, the Basle-based committee of European central bankers, is not'.

In some respects, Community regulation has shifted towards the use of fiscal instruments, including charges and levies to prevent pollution at source, penalties for polluters and other fiscal incentives to change firms' behaviour. There have, for example, been proposals for a carbon emission tax in the case of road transport[104] and landing fees for aircraft proportional to noise levels.[105]

The legal status of companies—towards a European company?

In modern European economies, the firm may assume any one of several legal forms. Although it is not possible here to cover all of the bewildering variety of types of companies in the EU, most firms fit the following broad and general pattern:[106]

1 *Sole proprietorship or sole trader*, in which the owner provides all the capital, has sole rights to all profits and is responsible for all losses.
2 *Partnership*, whereby two or more people carry on business in common. A 'general partnership' implies that the partners are personally liable for the debts of the partnership; in a 'limited partnership' the partners are limited in their liability for debts incurred by the firm to the extent of the capital invested. The French *Société en commandite simple* and the German *Kommanditgesellschaft* are examples of limited partnerships.
3 *Limited liability company*, which is distinct from its members. It combines three characteristics (Zaphirious, 1970):

   (a) limited number of members (except in the GmbH)
   (b) the transfer of its shares is subject to some restrictions
   (c) the public does not participate in its shares.

   In the UK, its nearest equivalent is the private limited company; in France, it corresponds to the *Société à Responsabilité Limitée* (SARL), in Germany, to the *Gesellschaft mit beschränkte Haftung* (GmbH), in Belgium, to the *Société de Personnes à Reponsabilité Limitée* (SPRL), and in Denmark to the *Anpartsselskab* (ApS).
4 *Sole member company* is an EU corporate structure created by the Twelfth Company Law Directive. It is an amalgam of a sole proprietorship and a limited liability company, enabling one person to incorporate a business into a limited liability company. Prior to the Twelfth Directive, single member companies existed in Germany and France, among others, but not the UK. The aim is to allow individuals the protection of limited liability 'without the complications of using nominee shareholders' (Andersen, 1993, p. 86). The person setting up a single member company may not set up another single member company, and it therefore cannot be used to set up a chain of companies.
5 *Joint stock company* (either private or public) with or without limited liability. These are companies with a large capital, and a more elaborate management and administration. The public is normally invited to participate in the stock company, whose shares are easily transferable.[107] In France, the stock company includes the *Société en commandite par actions* (SCA) and the *Société Anonyme* (SA), in Germany the *Kommanditgesellschaft auf Atkien* (KGaA), and the *Aktiengesellschaft* (AG), and in Italy, the *Società per Azioni* (SpA). For comparative purposes, the German AG is the equivalent of the French SA and of the British public and private company.

Some legal forms for firms are possible in some countries but not in others. For example, limited partnerships do not exist in the United Kingdom, in Ireland and in The Netherlands, and their existence is only theoretical in Greece. (Individual partners can limit their liability, but at least one partner must assume unlimited liability). The equivalent in Germany of a limited partnership is the *Kommanditgesellschaft auf Aktien* (KGaA), in France the *Société en Commandite par Actions* (SCA), and in Portugal the *Sociedade em Comandita*. In the UK, Ireland, The Netherlands, Denmark and Belgium, the capital of private limited companies is divided into shares. In the other seven countries, the capital is made up of 'quotas' or parts.

Legal aspects of the management structure of firms also differ widely across the EU countries. For example, the French SARL is managed by one or more managers (*gérants*) appointed either by the company's general meeting or through the *status* of the company; it does not have a board of directors unlike equivalent companies in other EU countries. Whereas the Dutch *Anpartsselskab* provides for one management board of directors and for employee representation, the German GmbH is characterized by a two-tier board structure: a management board comprising one or more inside managers; and a second board, the *Aufsichtsrat*, combing supervisory and advisory functions. Members of the latter are outsiders and delegates elected by the company's workers.

The general complexities of, and differences between, the legal aspects of firms in different EU member countries have prompted attempts to regulate at the EU level through the creation of the single legal framework.[108] One aim of such a framework is to remove distortions which give some locations within the EU artificial advantages over others. For example, a firm may avoid locating in a country because of the greater protection allowed to minority shareholders or creditors in that country. A second aim is to facilitate the EU-wide operation of firms by removing the difficulties—and costs—arising from different legal rules in different member states.

Among important steps in the process of harmonizing company law in Europe, is the Second Company Directive, passed in 1976 (in effect since 1983), and stipulating the capital and procedures for the formation of public limited companies. Another, more recent step, was the adoption in 1985 by the Council of Ministers of the EU regulation laying down the concept of a European Economic Interest Grouping (EEIG).[109] Effective since July 1989,[110] the EEIG is aimed at facilitating the economic activities of its members, and is intended to encourage links between small and medium enterprises (SMEs) on matters of common interest such as scientific research, purchasing, production, sales, and mutual administration of specialized services and data processing. Before the EEIG, the two main forms of intra-EC cross-border co-operation between firms were joint venture companies and contractual agreements of co-operation. The EEIG combines the best of these, having the legal form of the company, and the flexibility of the contractual agreement.

The most controversial aspect of the harmonization programme has been the Commission's Fifth Company Directive, the so-called 'structure directive', the first draft of which goes back to 1972.[111] This directive endeavours to harmonize the board structure and administration of public limited companies (PLCs) in the EU. The initial proposal was subsequently amended in depth in 1989, by a directive which would give firms of more than 1000 employees the ability to choose between two types of board structures: a unitary board comprising management members and non-executive members (the Anglo-Saxon type of structure); and a dualistic system composed of a management board and a supervisory board with employee participation (close to the German and Dutch structures). To allow for employee participation, companies who decide for the dualistic structure will be able to choose among three different types of structure. Although the unitary system would be allowed for a certain number of years (after the implementation of the directive), it is envisaged that the dualistic system would predominate in the long term (Werlauff, 1992). The controversial nature of the directive is evident in its continued amendment and deferral: 'by 1993 the Directive itself had gone into seemingly indefinite abeyance' (Manser, 1994, p. 100).

Another harmonization proposal leading to lengthy discussions and inconclusive results has been the proposal for the creation of a European Company Statute. The first Commission proposal on a European Company Statute (*Societas Europaea*, SE) was issued in 1975.[112] Going beyond the approximation of the legal statutes of European companies, the proposal specifies the statutes, structure and workings of a genuinely European company. Its legal form would be that of a company limited by shares, with a minimum paid-up capital such that it ensures adequate resources at its disposal. Its two-tier structure would comprise a Board of Management administering the company's affairs, and a Supervisory Board. The

Supervisory Board would supervise the Board of Management and would appoint its members.[113] In the case where a European company consists of two or more establishments in several member states, each with at least 50 employees, it would then be necessary to form a European Works Council, a body representing the interests of employees of the statutory European Company. The statutory European Company would have its own independent legal structure, separate from the national legal frameworks. It could be formed by such means as the merger of establishments in two or more member states and the formation of a joint venture by two or more companies or establishments. The ultimate aim was to replace different national company legislation, but given the resistance of other states' legislation by members, there was no reason why the SE, to the extent that it was different from any member states' company legislation, would be accepted. In effect, the resistance to accepting different legislation would result in the SE, far from reducing the plethora of different company statutes in Europe, actually adding to it.

Fifteen years after the first draft, the Societas Europaea had still not proceeded much further than the draft stage. The Council stopped the examination of the Commission's proposal on the creation of a European Company Statute in 1982, and returned to it in 1988 (Hitiris, 1994). The Commission's early proposal was redrafted in 1989, revised in 1991, and is supposedly expected to be implemented within the next few years (Werlauff, 1992). Each revision has involved removal of Articles, leaving the text with 137 Articles in 1987, 82 in 1989 and 65 in 1993. Among the sharpest opposition to the SE has been the objection to employee participation. A separate draft directive to which SE is linked, and which forms part of the process of establishing the SE, states among other things, that 'Member states shall take the necessary measures to enable employees of the SE to participate in the supervision and strategic development of the SE'. This met with outright opposition by Germany and the UK, and varying degrees of opposition to the ways in which worker participation would be imposed by most other member states (Manser, 1994, p. 70).

Some initiatives have led to a degree of harmonization, but fundamental revisions have failed. It can be argued that the reason for this failure is that there are, in broad terms, two distinct types of company in the EU, those (with unitary boards) whose source of finance is public capital or shares in equity, and those (with two-tier boards) whose source of finance is bank credit and private capital. The legal and organizational differences, among many others, follow from this distinction. The distinction itself has 'emerged from national history, regulatory tradition and financial evolution' (Manser, 1994, p. 158). Both types are evolving further, and there is some evidence of convergence, such as interest among some UK companies in German-type protection against takeovers, and interest among German companies in stock markets, but differences are likely to remain. The imminent emergence of a European Company to replace national companies is highly unlikely.

Combinations of such factors as the extent and nature of regulation, barriers to entry, nature and performance of firms and market forces in general, have an impact on industrial structure. While some of these have been discussed above, individual firms' strategies and performance are covered in later chapters. We will therefore briefly introduce the topic of industrial structure in the EU here, and return to it in more detail in Chapter 6.

4.2.5 Industrial structure in the EU

Industrial structure refers to 'the relative importance of individual industries or groups of related industries within an economy and to the pattern of transactions between these

TABLE 4.8   Ranking of EU manufacturing industries by output and employment
(*Source*: Panorama of EC Industry, 1994)

NACE code	Description	Employment[ab]	Output[c]
41–2	Food, drink and tobacco	2,376 (2)	337,807
25–6	Chemicals, man-made fibres	1,714 (6)	296,794
35–6	Motor vehicles and other means of transport	1,832 (5)	235,463
34	Electrical engineering	2,695 (1)	181,935
32	Mechanical engineering	2,340 (3)	166,388
31	Metal articles	2,032 (4)	124,559
47	Paper, printing, publishing	1,348 (7)	110,949
43	Textiles	1,271 (8)	89,473[d]
48	Rubber and plastics	993 (11)	71,169
28	Non-metallic minerals	1,008 (10)	69,869
45	Clothing and footwear	1,228 (9)	53,601
46	Timber, wooden furniture	863 (12)	52,450
33	Office machinery and data processing equipment	251 (14)	36,158
37	Instrument engineering	325 (13)	17,737
44	Leather goods	116 (15)	8,971

Notes
[a] Thousands of people employed.
[b] The number in brackets is the rank order in terms of employment.
[c] Output in millions of ECUs.
[d] 1991 figure.

industries' (Devine *et al.*, 1985, p. 27). In this section we will discuss only the relative importance of individual industries in the EU (see Table 4.8). Industry in general (mining, manufacturing, building and construction)[114] in the EU employed over 40 million people (34 per cent of total employment) in 1992, compared with 72 million people in the services sector[115] (62 per cent of the total). Germany is the most industrially oriented country in the EU, its industrial sector (excluding the new länder) accounting for 39 per cent of the workforce. Denmark is at the other extreme, with only 26 per cent of employment in industry. Germany alone accounts for 32 per cent—and Germany, France and the UK together for 72 per cent—of the total industrial workforce in the EU.

In terms of output, the most important manufacturing industries in the EU are food, drink and tobacco, and chemicals and man-made fibres. These are far ahead of all others. Because of different technologies of production[116] (and therefore different productivity levels), the ranking in terms of numbers employed in each industry is different. Electrical engineering and food, drink and tobacco are the largest employers. Note that rankings may change from year to year, first because industries may be at different positions in their business cycles at different times, and second because some industries may be in long-run decline while others are growing. However, in general the larger industries will be in the top half of the table, and smaller ones in the bottom half.

Table 4.9 shows the distribution of the six main manufacturing industries among the five largest EU countries. The only countries that hold their places consistently across all six industries are Germany and Spain.

The relative importance of industries varies among countries. This phenomenon is particularly noticeable for small and open economies (metal processing in Luxemburg, food, electrical engineering and data processing machinery in Ireland, food and mechanical engineering in Denmark, footwear and textile industries in Portugal). As discussed above in Section 4.1, one

TABLE 4.9   The top six manufacturing industries in the largest five EU countries, 1994 (*Source: Panorama of EU industry*, Short-term Supplements, 1995 and 1994)

NACE	Description	Countries	Employment	Turnover (1)
34	Electrical engineering	Germany	912,000	111,129
		France	376,000	52,221
		Italy	308,000	38,189
		UK	392,000	37,691
		Spain	91,000	10,413
35 + 36	Motor vehicles and transport (2)	Germany	867,000	127,962
		France	458,400	82,074
		Italy	262,500	27,503
		UK	424,900	49,468
		Spain	185,400	21,158
41 + 42	Food, drink and tobacco (2)	Germany	504,900	115,130
		France	345,800	96,972
		Italy	215,800	63,415
		UK	490,500	83,022
		Spain	350,200	43,954
31	Metal articles	Germany	664,000	71,302
		France	359,000	30,991
		Italy	233,000	24,307
		UK	302,000	20,995
		Spain	219,000	12,220
32	Mechanical engineering	Germany	881,000	100,112
		France	221,000	28,943
		Italy	260,000	36,050
		UK	334,000	33,526
		Spain	86,000	7,663
25 + 26	Chemicals (2)	Germany	570,500	89,699
		France	282,300	66,938
		Italy	187,000	37,088
		UK	273,400	48,242
		Spain	98,600	19,178

(1) Current prices in million ECUs.
(2) Figures for 1993.

way of answering questions about the relative importance of different industries in different economies is to use location quotients. There are other ways, and we return to this subject in Chapter 6.

The industrial structure of an economy includes the service sector, both in its own right and because of its significant contribution—for example through business services—to the operation of industries. Table 4.10 shows total EU employment in services, by NACE category.

Wholesale/retail distribution, hotels/catering, and repairs account for nearly 30 per cent of service employment. At a more disaggregated (3-digit) level, the ranking, by turnover, of the largest EU service sub-sectors (other than public administration) was as shown in Table 4.11 in 1992.

As with industries, so with service sub-sectors, ranking in terms of turnover may be different from ranking in terms of employment. Life assurance was the largest of all (including agriculture, industry and services) 3-digit sub-sectors, in terms of turnover, although it was

TABLE 4.10 **Service sector employment in the EU (1992)** (*Source*: Eurostat, 1994)

NACE code	Description	Employment ('000s)
61–7	Distribution, hotels, catering and repairs	18,485
71–9	Transport, transport services and communications	7,489
81–5	Banking, finance and rental	9,848
91	Public admin., defence and social services	10,890
92–9	Other services	25,295

TABLE 4.11 **Rank order of services in the EU (1992)**
(*Source*: *Panorama of EC Industry*, 1994)

NACE code	Description
820	Assurance
790	Telecommunication services
838	Advertising
839	Software and computing
923	Industrial cleaning
837	Engineering consultancy

only the sixth biggest employer after industrial cleaning services (923), motor vehicles (351), clothing (453), telecommunications equipment (344), and tools and finished metal goods (316).

In the context of the structure of industries, both theoretically and as applied specifically to the EU, we have referred often to the geographical, spatial and/or locational factors. In Section 4.3, we develop these factors further, clarifying their role in the industrial economics of the regional, national, and European economies.

4.3 Locational categories

4.3.1 Localization

None of the theories of the firm view the geographical dimension as a crucial element; the region in which firms might operate is secondary. In fact, economics as a discipline has paid surprisingly little attention to the location issue. Krugman (1993) has discussed, and attempted to correct, this omission in the context of international economics. It is even more surprising that the industrial economics specialism too has left to others the locational concerns of firms; few industrial economics and industrial organization textbooks have chapters or even sections of chapters on location.[117]

That location is crucial to the organization of production is clear from as far back as Marshall (1898).[118] Marshall identified six main factors in the localization of industries, the first three of which he called causes of, and the second three advantages of localization: physical conditions, demand conditions, political/cultural influences, hereditary skill, the growth of subsidiary trades and the emergency of a local market for the special skills required by the industry.[119]

Physical conditions

An industry requiring raw materials that are expensive to transport is likely to be located near to the source of those raw materials. Similarly other physical conditions, including the climate, the soil and the topography of an area will influence what industries locate in that area. Marshall gave a number of examples, including Sheffield cutlery, which, he wrote, is 'due chiefly to the excellent grit of which its grindstones are made'.

Demand conditions

Under some circumstances, products will tend to be produced close to their market. A high income market for example, Marshall argued, will generate 'a demand for goods of specially high quality, and this attracts skilled workmen from a distance, and educates those on the spot'.[120]

Political/cultural influences

Marshall referred to 'the character of the people, and their social and political institutions', and to individuals' 'ideals of life' as determining how they exploit natural advantages. These factors generate 'industry and enterprise' which, in turn, have 'localized the industrial leadership of the world now in this country and now in that'. Modern developments of these notions include those on culture and institutions by institutionalists like North (1990), and on industry and enterprise by industrial economists/management theorists like Porter (1990).[121]

Once an industry has located, from whatever combination of natural, political, social, cultural and accidental factors, in a particular place, there are cumulative advantages to its continued location in that place.[122]

Hereditary skill

What Marshall was referring to in this context, was the situation in which a large number of people lived and worked—using similar, specialized skills—in close proximity. The skills in production of the particular product become so well known in the area that 'children learn many of them unconsciously'. Inventions 'and improvements in machinery, in processes and the general organization of the business' become quickly known and copied. This is what Krugman refers to as technological spillovers, 'the more or less pure externality that results from knowledge spillovers between nearby firms'.

The growth of subsidiary trades

The localization of an industry attracts firms that supply intermediate goods, including manufacturing equipment, to that industry. As Marshall put it, 'subsidiary industries devoting themselves each to one small branch of the process of production' can employ specialized machinery, and keep it constantly busy if they are supplying a large number of local firms in the main industry. Localization thus also facilitates specialization.

Krugman argues that the concentration of suppliers of intermediate goods in the same location as their customers, 'depends crucially on at least some degree of economies of scale.... It is only the presence of increasing returns that makes a large center of production able to have more efficient and more diverse suppliers than a small one.' We would add to this the possibility of economies of scope but would emphasize the need to distinguish, as Marshall famously did, between internal and external economies. When Krugman writes of a large centre of production, he appears to be referring to a single firm, in which case it is appropriate to invoke economies of scale as prerequisite. However, if we include the possibility of a large number of small producers clustering spatially, and then consider the extent to which this attracts suppliers of intermediate goods, economies of scale as normally understood to mean internal, no longer apply. Instead we must rely on externalities: 'economies...dependent on the general development of the industry' as Marshall defined them. He defined internal economies as those 'dependent on the resources of the individual houses of business..., on their organization and the efficiency of their management'. This distinction and its relevance in terms of size of firm in localized industries is particularly clear in the case of industrial districts, discussed below in Section 4.3.3.

In a second addendum to Marshall's discussion about intermediate inputs, Krugman criticizes the generally accepted view that 'localized industrial complexes will emerge only if it is more costly to transport intermediate inputs than final goods'.[123] He provides both theoretical and historical evidence for the argument that lower transport costs in general—i.e. for both intermediate and final goods—make the localization of industry more likely. Only if the costs of transporting intermediates are particularly low relative to final goods will localization not occur.

Local market for special skills required by the industry

A localized industry, Marshall wrote, 'gains a greater advantage from the fact that it offers a constant market for skill'. The interests of workers with these skills and their employers are mutually reinforced by localization. Employers will tend to locate where the skill is available, and those with the skill will tend to live where employers of the skill are concentrated: 'Social forces here cooperate with economic'. Furthermore, where the skill is very specialized, then other industries, employing other skills, will be attracted by the availability of people in the locality who do not have the specialized skill required by the first industry.

Krugman describes this as labour market pooling, and provides a more formal explanation of the gains from pooling both to workers and firms. He assumes two firms, each producing a different product, but each with an average requirement of labour with the same specific skill of, say, 100 workers, but a peak requirement of 125 and a trough requirement of 75. He shows that all—workers and firms—will gain from both firms locating in a town with 200 workers with the required skill. This results from an additional assumption that the peaks and troughs of the two firms at least occasionally do not coincide. It follows from this assumption that workers laid off by one firm will at times find employment in the other, so they derive an advantage from pooling. Assume the alternative to the two firms and 200 workers in one town is that each firm locates in a different town, each town having 100 workers with the required skill. Then at the peak of its cycle, neither firm will be able to obtain the required number of workers, so the firms also derive a benefit from pooling.

As with intermediate inputs, Krugman argues that in relation to labour pooling, localization requires increasing returns to scale (IRS). Without IRS, he argues, there would be no reason why each firm would locate all its production in one location. A firm could, in the above example, have a plant employing 50 workers (on average) in each of the towns. We would add the proviso that, if the *external* economies are important, then *both* firms would have to locate a 50-person plant in each of the towns. IRS may well be significant, but in the context of localization (or spatial concentration), it must be considered in conjunction with external economies.

Krugman raises two further possible objections to Marshall's labour pooling: flexible wages and exploitation of monopsony power by firms. If wages were flexible in the example, rather than unemployment or excess demand, there would be falls and rises in wages in, respectively, trough and peak times. Does this rule out the gains from pooling? No, Krugman argues, because even though the pooling will mean each firm having to pay a higher wage during the trough than it would if it was isolated and did not have to compete with the other firm for labour, it will also pay a lower wage at the peak. The gain at the peak, from pooling, is greater than the loss at the trough. In general, the 'gains from labour pooling do not rest in any essential way on a failure of labor markets to clear'.

In relation to monopsony, the question is why firms would locate adjacent to other firms that compete for the same labour. Surely, it could be argued, a firm would prefer the monopsony power (and extra profit from paying wages below the value of workers' marginal product) it would derive from being the sole employer of these workers in the town? Where there is labour mobility[124] workers with the required skills will avoid such a town. Firms will locate in the same town as other firms requiring the same skills, in part to avoid such a flight of human capital.

Where a town is dominated by a single firm, as in the case of Dagenham and Ford in England, according to Krugman this is because either there is an important natural resource in that location accessible to only one firm, or IRS is such that the scale of production is so large that the market may be dominated by a single firm that 'agglomerates its plants in order to achieve pooling'. Again, however, Krugman's conclusion requires amendment. Gains from pooling may not rest on the failure of labour markets to clear, but the argument against monopsony and 'company towns' is at least partially offset by unemployment. If there is high unemployment, and firms and workers expect this to persist, then the argument against company towns—multiple firms avoid flight of human capital—does not apply. There will be no such flight if there are no jobs elsewhere.[125]

What follows from Marshall's six localization factors, is that under certain circumstances firms within an industry or in related industries will agglomerate, that is they will locate in the same place, close to one another. The *agglomeration economies* will be greater than the benefits that firms derive from a more diffuse locational distribution. 'When a locality or region constitutes the site for an expansion of the common pools of labour, capital and infrastructure, or when pecuniary externalities can be traced to the new investments made by a firm in some particular place, then the lower unit costs of production facing firms in that place are called *agglomeration economies*' (Harrison, 1992).[126]

Can localization be observed in European industries? In Sections 4.3.3 and 4.3.5 we describe three different types of industrial agglomeration, all of which exist to varying extents within and between different European countries. In addition, it is generally accepted that, at a broader level, there is in Europe a core, or centre, that is relatively developed, industrial and wealthy and a periphery that is less advanced.[127] Increased integration in Europe may or may not reduce/increase the gap between core and periphery. The more important are agglomeration economies and/or increasing returns to scale, and the easier the access to the periphery from the core, the more likely is the gap between core and periphery to increase. In such circumstances large firms in the centre will increasingly dominate the markets of the periphery.

4.3.2   MNEs and European integration

The increasing significance of large, often multinational enterprises (MNEs) in the twentieth century calls for the examination of what appears to be the opposite of localization, namely *globalization*. We have described localization as the tendency for firms to agglomerate. If globalization is simplistically defined as the process whereby the countries, regions and localities of the world are homogenized by changing economic, social, political and technological forces, then these two processes would be opposites. However, as Dicken (1992, p. 2) has pointed out: 'Change does not occur everywhere in the same way and at the same rate; the processes of globalization are not geographically uniform. The particular character of individual countries, of regions and even of localities interacts with the larger-scale general processes of change to produce quite specific outcomes.' Localization and globalization can and do co-exist. Though not attracting mainstream interest in economics, these forces have not been ignored.

The importance of location is clear in the writings of a number of theorists of the firm, who have paid attention to growth in geographically distant markets, particularly foreign markets. This followed the emergence of MNEs in the early part of this century, and their proliferation after the Second World War. The concentration of origins of such firms in the USA, Japan and Europe, has conferred on the regional variable (in its broadest sense) great importance.

In the 1960s there were many attempts to explain the rise in MNEs; the direction of the initial surge of foreign direct investment gave rise to what became known as the American challenge (Servan-Schreiber, 1967). As a result, explanations concentrated on US firms. The pioneering work on endogenous aspects of the IO of MNEs has been attributed to Hymer (1976), and among the most influential theories of internationalization was Vernon's product life cycle model (Vernon, 1966).[128] Dunning (1988), building on the work of others, incorporated the earlier theories of internationalization to develop an 'eclectic' framework for explaining why production is sometimes organized internationally.

Dunning's eclectic framework explains the internationalization of a firm on the basis of ownership (or firm) specific advantages (O), location (or country) specific advantages (L) and internalization (I).[129] O explains why the firm in question, and not some other firm, produces the good. This includes all the reasons why the firm is better at serving the market—domestic and international—for that good than its competitors. There are two types of ownership specific advantages. First, there are those which arise from 'the privileged possession of income generating assets' including patents, the capacity to innovate, superior production technique, exclusive access to raw material and markets, and the systems for buying, producing and marketing. The second arise from a firm's superior ability 'to take advantage of the economies of common governance of separate but related activities which might otherwise have been coordinated through external markets'. These include economies of scale and scope, and diminution of the political and financial risks associated with concentration in a single country.

L explains why the firm wishes to produce the good in the host country. L advantages arise from natural differences between countries including differences in endowments of natural resources, differences in input, production and transport costs, and cultural differences between markets requiring adaptation of the product for specific markets. L advantages also arise from artificial differences, particularly those related to government policies on, for example, trade barriers, technical specifications and other second order barriers.

I explains why the production of a firm's product abroad is done by setting up a subsidiary rather than, for example, licensing some other firm in the host country to produce the good. Here, even more explicitly than in relation to O, Dunning draws on transaction cost analysis. MNEs emerge, he argues, where the 'net production and transaction costs are lower' when the international production and transactions are 'undertaken within internal hierarchies' rather than through the external market.[130] Of the variables which are likely to cause firms to internalize markets, the likelihood and costs of a contractual default and the inability of a contractor to capture the external economies of any transaction are perhaps the two most important (Dunning, 1993, p. 136). The three together (O, L and I) provide a framework for explaining the proliferation and location of subsidiaries of multinational enterprises.

Dunning has for many years had an interest in European integration and in the use of the eclectic framework for examining the position of MNEs in Europe. The increasing significance of MNEs in Europe, particularly since the early 1960s, raised the possibility of an interrelationship with European economic integration (what Dunning called 'regional integration'). Somewhat confusingly, in light of such integration concepts at the corporate level as vertical and horizontal integration, Dunning referred to 'corporate integration' as 'the causes and effects of cross-border activities by and within multinational enterprises' (Dunning, 1988). Dunning's regional integration is the integration of the economies of different countries, arising from formal agreements to remove trade and other barriers—those defined above as barriers of the second order. Although this type of integration involves increasing the extent to which the group of economies together constitute a region, in general it is referred to in the literature as *international (or European) economic integration*. The cross-border activities of MNEs, either internally or with other firms, may both result from or have an impact on the process of removing barriers between economies. This type of integration is not corporate in the sense that it occurs only within a firm, and is more appropriately called *international industrial integration*.[131]

Dunning pointed out that there had 'been few attempts systematically to analyze the interaction between the two kinds of integration', and proceeded to provide a first pass at just such an analysis (Dunning, 1988, Ch. 11).[132] In doing so he distinguished between EC and non-EC firms and concluded that, in general, industrial integration by EC firms *does* aid European integration, where such firms are 'prompted to overcome structural market distortions and transactional markets failure'. However, industrial integration by non-EC firms may or may not enhance European integration. There is a danger, for example, 'of Europe moving down a path towards a decreasing technological capability and a worsening international competitive position' as a result of the shift of high-value parts of the production process from Europe to the USA (Dunning, 1988, p. 300) or Japan (Jacobson and Andréosso, 1988). A recent study by Hamill (1992) shows that of the total value of acquisitions in the EC in 1989 and 1990, US firms accounted for the highest proportion (19 per cent); he concludes with the warning that 'the main beneficiaries of the Single European Market may not be European companies, consumers or workers, but rather non-EC firms which have consolidated their position in the EC through MAAs' (mergers, acquisitions and strategic alliances).

In his recent work Dunning (1993) has contributed further to the systematic analysis of the relationship between the two types of integration. Focusing in different chapters on Japanese, European and US MNEs, and multinational investment in general in the EU, he identifies different effects over time as the EU has developed.[133] He shows that in the early years of integration in Europe, the competitiveness of US MNEs improved to a greater extent than did that of European MNEs, and was exploited by the US firms through foreign direct investment (FDI) in Europe. Over time, the competitive stimulus of the US presence in Europe, together with European integration, 'led to an improvement of ownership advantages of European companies which, by the late 1970s, were increasingly penetrating the US market through direct investment'. The preparations for and implementation of Europe 1992 have had two main consequences for non-EU direct investment. First, there has been an intensification of the fear of 'Fortress Europe'—the fear that the EU will become increasingly protectionist, favouring production within the Union; and second, there has been a recognition of the increasing opportunities arising from the completion of the internal market. From the perspective of non-EU MNEs these underlie 'the astonishingly rapid growth of Europe's L advantages as a production base, for manufacturing and service industry' (Dunning, 1993, p. 159). Together these have resulted in a growth of FDI from both the USA and Japan. FDI into the EU from both the USA and Japan has grown more rapidly than exports from either country.

A concern that the growth of non-EU FDI into Europe might in some way weaken the European economy is offset by the fact that European FDI into the USA has grown even more rapidly than that from the USA into the EU. By 1990, the 'ratio of the US capital stake in the EC to that of the EC stake in the US had fallen to 0.75' (Dunning, 1993, p. 186). This does not, however, remove the need for concern and analysis of the strategic implications of FDI. We would agree with Dunning that it is difficult to generalize. The policy implications will differ, depending on such factors as 'the type of inward direct investment, the extent of the existing foreign investment stake, the sectors in which it is made, the conditions under which it is made, and the home and host countries involved' (Dunning, 1993, p. 382).

The prognosis for the interrelationship between European economic and industrial integration depends on developments at two levels: first, the policies and capabilities of European firms relative to those of other countries; and second, the nature of the collaborative programmes, and competition, merger, tax, technology, trade and investment policies introduced by the EU, at the EU level (Dunning, 1988, p. 303; see also Yannopoulos, 1992; Dunning, 1992; and Dunning, 1993.[134]

Studying the organization and structure of industry within the geographically bounded limits of an increasingly integrated economic area (the EU) compels us to give the regional dimension (understood both in terms of a group of countries, and in terms of regions within countries) a prominent place. In Sections 4.3.3, 4.3.4 and 4.3.5 below we develop this notion further.

4.3.3 Industrial districts[135]

In some cases a relatively large number of independent firms within a region—more locally defined as within a specific country—may act analogously to a large firm (Best, 1990). Work on this phenomenon has focused on the notion of *industrial districts*. These are defined as production systems characterized by a myriad of firms specialized in various stages of the production of a homogeneous product, often using flexible production technology and connected by extensive local inter-firm linkages (Pyke and Sengenberger, 1990; Harrison, 1992). As small, owner-managed firms, often with other members of the family also working in the firm, the communication lines within these firms are short. In addition, flexible production requires most people working in the firm to be able to do most of the jobs. Organizationally, this implies an absence of long top-down chains of authority; firms in industrial districts have relatively flat organizational structures. Between firms, while there is competition at some levels, at others the activities of these independent firms are strongly co-ordinated; they contribute to the production of the same good within the same geographical area (e.g. toys in Canneto sull'Oglio in Lombardy). These geographically defined districts are said to form a 'social and economic whole' and have been at least in part responsible for the rejuvenation of the dormant economy of the 'Third Italy' (Best, 1990, Ch. 7).

The social and political aspects of the industrial district are important. The owners of the small firms are usually artisans (craftsmen-owners), and members of the same artisanal association. The association is one means of distributing information. This sharing of information may also be encouraged by local (municipal or regional) authorities. For all this to exist, there must be a high level of trust; a shared socio-cultural identity 'facilitates trust relations between firms and between employers and skilled workers' (Schmitz and Musyck, 1994). Cooke and Morgan (1990, p. 40), in their analysis of Baden-Wurttemberg, describe *networking* as: 'inter-firm linkages, technology transfer mechanisms, management–labour relations and public–private concertation'. Industrial districts are clearly highly networked systems.

Industrial districts are evidence of the potential for small firms to break into export markets, independent of large firms. More generally, according to those who have examined these regions closely (e.g. Best, 1990, pp. 204–26), they demonstrate the possibility of a high standard of living without corporate giants. The Emilia-Romagna region has been particularly focused upon, because of its furniture, ceramic tile, textiles and clothing, metalworking and machine making, and other industrial districts.

There is some debate over the significance of the industrial districts, both theoretically and empirically. Questions relating to how successful industrial districts are, whether the same processes have given rise to different industrial districts, and whether conceptually or empirically there is anything new in industrial districts, have all been examined with differing conclusions. Amin and Robins (1990) argue critically[136] that an account that 'acknowledges the complex and contradictory nature of the restructuring process—and particularly of its spatial dimensions—must . . . raise considerable problems about the industrial district paradigm'.

While accepting as valid the description of the new *industrial agglomerations* in the Third Italy as new 'Marshallian industrial districts',[137] Amin and Robins (1990) reject the generalization of this to different types of successful regions in different parts of the world. Product pioneering industrial agglomerations, for example, such as Silicon Valley in California, are different from Marshallian industrial districts, they argue, and are more appropriate compared with other areas that have pioneered major products, such as Detroit as the centre of the car industry in the 1930s. Such inter-temporal comparison invalidates the positing of local agglomerations of this type as evidence of a change of an 'epochal' nature in the 1980s and 1990s.

Amin and Robins (1990) are also critical of the view that industrial districts are the way forward, that they are an inevitable consequence of a deepening break-up of large-scale, mass production (Fordism). This argument, based on a variant of transaction cost analysis, identifies a 'progressive externalisation' arising from flexible manufacturing which will lead to industrial districts (Scott, 1988, p. 175). 'Reality', Amin and Robins believe, 'is more equivocal, more ambiguous, more obscure'.

Many writers working on industrial districts do not hold the views that Amin and Robins ascribe to the 'industrial district paradigm'. Benton (1992), for example, emphasizes the 'open-endedness of the widespread process of industrial restructuring' and the 'strikingly different outcomes of industrial restructuring'. Amin and Robins, she argues, focus in their criticism on extreme versions of the industrial district perspective.

Although not engaging in the industrial district debate, Camagni's (1991) analysis supports the views of Amin and Robins. Writing of Toscana and Emilia-Romagna—two of the Third Italy regions—Camagni argues that a new organizational model has emerged in some light industries like clothing and textiles. This is the large, vertically integrated firm, using advanced information and communication technologies to provide remote production control, linking sales with production management, and establishing 'tight relationships with fashion creation and international marketing' (Camagni, 1991, p. 156).

On the other hand, a recent study of the knitwear/clothing district of Carpi found that while there was a crisis in the industry in Europe in general, in Carpi it improved, expanded, increased employment and diversified its product line, despite higher labour costs than elsewhere in Italy. A major advantage of industrial districts in comparison with large firms 'is the presence of numerous centres of strategic decisions.... In a large firm there is only a single strategic centre; in Carpi, these number several hundred. Thanks to this high number of active entrepreneurs, the district can find the best strategies by proceeding through trial and error.' In addition, there is constant experimentation and information circulates rapidly—because 'in such a district everybody knows everybody'—producing 'an environment favouring imitation of the right strategies and innovative change' (Bigarelli and Crestanello, 1994).

Large firms with international links continue to be important, and in some cases are of increasing importance. This is not to argue that industrial districts and other forms of local agglomeration are not important, but that they must be seen as part of the global; 'the product of local, nation-wide and transnational influences' (Amin and Thrift, 1992).

Dunning's work has contributed to an analysis crossing between the theoretical concerns of industrial organization, international trade and international economic integration. Similarly, Pyke and Sengenberger, Best, Benton and others working on industrial districts have contributed to the interdisciplinary integration between industrial economics and regional economics. The next two sections outline industrial/regional concepts which have been considered to be particularly relevant for the development industrial policy.

4.3.4   Filières

French economists, like Montfort (1983), have used the term *filière* to refer to a system in which a good or service 'is supplied to its final consumer through a succession of operations performed by independent units having different activities' (Montfort, 1983).[138] These units of production may belong to different industries linked together by buyer–supplier relationships. A filiére thus consists of a chain of economic activities, ranging from the extraction of natural resources to the distribution of the end product.

While Montfort (1983) and de Bandt (1987) do not, other authors incorporate a technological interrelationship as a part of the definition of the *filière*, e.g. Truel (1983). Thus, referring to Truel (1983), Storper and Walker (1989, p. 133) state that the 'French term "filière" captures the idea of a connecting filament among technologically related activities'. Antonelli, Petit and Tahar (1992, p. 13) seem to accept the broader definition; the concept is, they argue, an attempt to select from and substantiate what is usually meant by the English term 'industry'. In their study of the economics of industrial modernization, however, Antonelli *et al.* (p. 149) use as their unit of focus the *filière* 'taken as a set of interrelated production activities all affected by any sizeable technological change occurring in any of them'.

A *filière* is composed of three poles: upstream, centre and downstream. The upstream pole is a set of supplier industries—they supply to rather than buying from the core industries of the *filière* (though they may buy from or sell to other upstream industries). The downstream pole consists of the industries that buy from, rather than selling to the core industries of the *filière* (though they may buy from or sell to other downstream industries).[139] This leaves the central, or core pole, in which are situated the industries that are involved in the transformation of inputs such as raw materials or primary products into finished goods.

As an example, the agri-food *filière* comprises the following poles:

- The upstream pole, including farming and fisheries activities, agricultural machinery, and animal feed producers
- The downstream pole, including specialized food haulage, catering services, and distribution
- The core, consisting of the food processing industry itself.

The economy does not necessarily divide cleanly into a number of different *filières*. Using input–output tables we can identify how sub-sectors are interrelated; a close relationship among a number of sub-sectors suggests they belong together in a *filière*, but other sub-sectors may display similar linkages with all others across the range of industries, as was found for France. Such sub-sectors, not obviously part of any one *filière*, 'play a special role of inter-mediation' upstream of production (as in the case of electronics, which feeds into a number of different industries) or downstream of production (as in the case of distribution) (Antonelli, Petit and Tahar, 1992, p. 14)[140]

The concept of *filières* was developed in the late 1970s by French economists in the context of the declining competitiveness of French industry. They saw a need to recapture the domestic market,[141] and defined an 'optimal *filière*', among other things as one that is composed of strong and competitive French (as opposed to foreign) firms. The concept was suggestive of nationalistic and interventionist ideas because of its application. The different segment of *filières* were examined, for example, in terms of import penetration. A high import penetration, particularly in the upstream or core poles, would have repercussions for the whole *filière*, and might imply a diminished national industrial independence. The implications for industrial policy were clear: to select important *filières* within which to build up a strong industrial complex of competitive firms able not only to recapture the domestic market, but also to gain increasing shares of the world market.

Despite an interventionist industrial policy, French industry in major *filières* like that of the car and its components, lost shares in international markets during the 1980s.[142] Was this because the wrong policies were adopted, because they were applied incorrectly, or because they were based on misconceptions? A more detailed examination of nation and EU industrial policies will be undertaken in Chapter 7. Suffice to say at this point that it is at least possible that a successful *filière* requires an economic space greater than that provided by the French economy (Andréosso, 1986).

4.3.5 Clusters

Clusters, according to Porter (1990)—who is well known, among other things, for having developed and applied the notion—are related to *filières*.[143] *Filières* as a concept 'was a valuable precursor' to clusters (Porter, 1990, p. 789). Vague though in some ways is the *filière*, the cluster is an even less well-defined concept, referring broadly to 'industries connected through vertical and horizontal relationships' (Porter, 1990, p. 73). A nation's successful industries, Porter argues, 'are usually linked through vertical (buyer/supplier) or horizontal (common customers, technology, channels, etc.) relationships' (1990, p. 149). These links connect the different elements of the cluster. Moreover, because of agglomeration economies, the 'process of clustering, and the interchange among industries in the cluster, ... works best when the industries involved are geographically concentrated' (Porter, 1990, p. 157). This interchange involves 'the exchange and flow of information about the needs, techniques, and technology among buyers, suppliers and related industries', and is a key process underlining the formation of clusters (Porter, 1990, p. 152).

The geographical nature of clusters and the importance of information flows in their formation suggest a relationship with industrial districts, too, though Porter seems to be only vaguely aware of this.[144] One of Porter's examples, the Italian ceramic tile industry (1990, p. 210–25), is, in fact, an industrial district, though he does not say this. It is clear, nevertheless, that industrial districts are clusters or at least parts of clusters.

The cluster is also broader than the *filière*, including as it does horizontal as well as vertical relationships. In this respect the cluster is similar to another French concept, *meso-système*, which is defined by de Bandt (1987, pp. 51–2) in terms of all the vertical and horizontal relationships, direct and indirect—'the agents which are supplying various kinds of inputs: services to enterprises, finance, R&D, training, etc., or which are moulding the market and/or consumer behaviours: distribution, advertising etc.'—competitive and co-operative, in an industry involved in a specific product category. The difference is that the cluster is again a broader concept, including firms in different product categories though this may depend on how the term 'product category' is defined.

Industrial districts are considered to be primarily an Italian phenomenon; *filières* have been examined more in the French than in other economies; clusters are, the work of Porter (1990) suggests, an important characteristic of all successful economies.[145] Porter and his team have examined a number of economies in an effort to identify and explain the existence of clusters, and to underline the implications for policy, both at the level of the firm and that of the government. In this book, strategies of firms are discussed in Chapter 3, policies of governments in Chapter 7, and examples of clusters themselves in Chapters 4 and 6. In what follows we will briefly discuss the identification of and explanation for clusters.

Porter's primary tool for illustrating 'patterns of national advantage' is the *cluster chart*.[146] This chart includes the successful (competitive) industries of a country, identified as such either by having 'a world export share greater than the nation's average share of world exports or an international position based on foreign investment that was estimated to be as significant'. Because demand conditions and vertical relationships among industries (*filières*?) have important roles in his theory, the competitive cluster chart groups industries by end-use application. At the top of the chart are 'upstream sectors', similar to the upstream pole of the *filière*. In the middle are 'broad end-use sectors involving *industrial or supporting functions*'. This, as is the bottom row of Porter's chart, is different from any of the *filière* poles. At the bottom are the 'end-use sectors most associated with *final consumption goods*'.

Using this method, Porter (1990) identifies the clusters of ten different economies, including large ones like the USA, Japan and Germany, and smaller ones like Denmark, Sweden and Switzerland. In Sweden, for example, he identifies (1990, pp. 333–42) five major clusters of internationally competitive industries which are, in order of importance: transportation and logistics (including cars, trucks, engines, distribution services, etc.); forest-related industries (including timber, pulp and paper, paper-making machinery, and furniture); ferrous metals and fabricated metal products (including mining equipment, and metalworking tools); health-related products (including electromedical equipment and pharmaceuticals); and telecommunications (including telecommunications equipment and mobile telephone networks).

The explanation for why Sweden has been successful in these clusters is based, in Porter's model, on an elaboration of developments in Sweden of four factors (which he calls the 'diamond').[147] These factors are: *factor conditions* (including all factors of production, as well as such means as training and education for improving those factors of production); *demand conditions* (for example, the bigger the home demand for an industry's product, the better);

related and supporting industries (the presence in a country of internationally competitive supplier industries, for example, will enhance the competitiveness of the buyer industries); and *firm strategy, structure and rivalry* (including domestic rivalry, and rules and institutions governing that rivalry—the more intense the domestic rivalry, the greater the potential for the firms to be internationally competitive).

The key elements of Porter's explanation for competitiveness and its national and regional specificity are the 'diamond' and clustering. While it is possible for governments to generate clusters, they are 'far more likely to succeed in reinforcing an existing or nascent industry cluster' (1990, p. 655). This, for countries without clusters or at an early stage in industrialization, limits the model's relevance to that of *ex ante* explanation. It has, nevertheless, generated a great deal of interest among policy makers, particularly in advanced countries such as the USA and Canada.

Thus there has been both interest in, and criticism of, Porter's approach. Brittan (1990) and Jacobs and de Jong (1991) have found fault with the criteria for including industries in the chart. Brittan's (1990) view is that 'Porter's measures are too influenced by the sheer size of industries, and countries' changing share in world trade'. Jacobs and de Jong (1991) would agree, pointing out that in Porter's approach an industry may be more competitive in Country A than in Country B, yet appear in B's cluster chart and not A's, 'because of the average performance of the other industries in both countries'.

Jacobs and de Jong (1991) also have two, more fundamental, criticisms of Porter's approach. They argue, firstly, that there is an overemphasis on end-use. In their application of the model to The Netherlands, for example, they find that a cluster may be in an intermediate stage (upstream pole of the *filière*) and not at the end-use stage, which makes it difficult to identify accurately the cluster in Porter's chart. Second, the approach is one-sided in that international diversity is stressed. While Jacobs and de Jong accept that both international divergence and convergence are evident, Porter's approach, in their view, does not capture the dialectic between the two tendencies.[148]

Scassellati (1991) goes even further, criticizing Porter's focus on national entities. Porter fails to incorporate adequately the implications of the new type of corporation—corporations that in 'their inherent drive toward ever expanding accumulation,... simply cannot afford to tie themselves to any territory. 'His applause for the revival of the Swiss watch industry, for example, neglects the fact that several of the most famous Swiss brands are now owned by a US company, North American Watch' (Scassellati, 1991).

In his review of Porter's book, Dunning (1992) agrees with the criticism that Porter's focus does not adequately incorporate MNEs. In an apt example, he points out that Nestlé, though a Swiss company, has 95 per cent of sales accounted for by its foreign subsidiaries. The diamonds of competitive advantage of the host countries in which those subsidiaries operate may therefore have more to do with Nestlé's contribution to Switzerland's GNP than Switzerland's own diamond of competitive advantage. Dunning constructively suggests the addition of a transnational business variable as a separate factor in the diamond of competitive advantages.

Another criticism relates to the limited application of Porter's model to very small, open economies (O'Donnellan, 1994). In such economies there may be too small a domestic market to generate national clusters, and larger economic spaces (e.g. the EU) may have to be analysed to identify the extent to which industries in, say Ireland, are elements in a cluster.

Despite these criticisms, Porter is praised for introducing 'the idea to an audience of economists that globalization somewhat paradoxically leads to more emphasis on local conditions, and moreover, provides a global firm [with] opportunities to take advantage of these' (Jacobs and de Jong, 1991).

TABLE 4.12   Types of industrial system

	Industrial districts	*Filières*	*Clusters*
Horizontal relationships	X		X
Vertical relationships	X	X	X
Implications for internal organization of firm	X		
Marshallian localization	X		
Market or hierarchy?	M/H	M	M

The theories and realities surrounding industrial districts, networks, *filières*, *meso-systèmes* and clusters all underline the need for a sharp awareness of the regional or spatial aspects of industries. Industrial economics must incorporate the fact that different industries are concentrated to different extents, and in different organizational forms, in different locations, but also that these distributions change over time.

We summarize key aspects of the three types of industrial system in Table 4.12. Unlike either of the other types, industrial districts imply various things about the nature of the internal organization of the firms, such as flexible specialization and relatively flat organization structures. Geographical proximity (Marshallian localization) is also far more important for industrial districts than for either of the other two. Like clusters, there are in industrial districts both horizontal relationships—e.g. shared technologies—and vertical relationships—e.g. buying or supplying—between firms. In *filières* there are only vertical relationships between firms. Finally, in view of the greater closeness in the relationships among industrial district firms than is the case elsewhere, we can conclude that industrial districts constitute an industrial system somewhere between market and hierarchy. In both *filières* and clusters relationships are primarily market relationships, though it should be noted that anywhere where firms co-operate closely with other firms—for example where a firm over many years obtains a particular component or input from the same supplier—the relationship can become one somewhere between market and hierarchy.

In this chapter we have discussed the theoretical, empirical—especially European—and geographic aspects of structure. In the next chapter we turn to the behaviour or conduct of firms which, it should already be clear, is interdependent with the structure of industries.

Notes

[1] For a discussion on the problems arising from the difficulty in drawing the boundaries of the market clearly, see Shepherd (1990, pp. 55–60).

[2] For a critical appraisal of the variable definitions of the relevant market, see Fishwick (1986); see also Focsaneanu (1975) and the Commission's Annual Reports on Competition Policy.

[3] This and the cases in the next paragraph are referred to in CEC, 1991, Annex III.

[4] There is, arguably, a fourth, the level of information. This is discussed in Chapter 3, Section 3.1.2.

[5] Product differentiation will be developed further in this chapter in the context of the discussion on monopolistic competition, Section 4.1.4, and again in Section 4.2.2, on the EU dimension.

[6] From: Eurostat, the Statistical Office of the EU, in Luxemburg.

[7] The Gini coefficient and the Lorenz curve are familiar devices for studying the distribution of income and wealth in a nation, and less frequently used to measure concentration in industry.

[8] Above normal profits are also eliminated (and the Lerner index is zero) under contestable market conditions. See Chapter 2, Section 2.2.2.

[9] In Section 4.2.2 below we describe another (though possibly complementary) way of categorizing barriers, in terms of *first order* and *second order* barriers, the former referring to impediments to entry facing firms within the same economy, the latter to impediments facing firms from outside the economy.

[10] There is a substantial literature on the extent to which particular American firms have influenced regulation. For a review and critique of this, the 'regulatory capture' literature, see Tomlinson (1993).

[11] Despite these criticisms, aspects of the exogenous/endogenous classification are widely accepted and, at least from a short-term perspective, appropriately so. See, for example, Sapir (1993), who usefully categorizes barriers to entry into services in Europe as 'natural' (or exogenous), 'strategic' (or endogenous), and regulatory.

[12] This normal amount of profit is defined as just enough to keep existing firms in the industry but not enough to attract additional firms into the industry.

[13] Note that while the price axis for firm and market are identical, the scale of the firm's quantity axis represents a much smaller quantity than that for the market.

[14] Arguably, under conditions of free entry and exit, there is nothing for the leader firm to take over, but once differentiation becomes possible, the condition of completely free entry and exit must also be relaxed. (This, as we show below, is also a criticism of the monopolistic competition market structure.)

[15] Against this and in favour of the perfect competition model, it can be argued that if there are constant returns to scale in perfect competition, then there are no incentives for firms to grow. However, constant returns to scale apply only at the long-run equilibrium and what we are arguing is that it is in moving towards this equilibrium that the model breaks down.

[16] It should be emphasized that the interests of the suppliers in general are optimized by perfect competition; any individual supplier would prefer to be a monopoly.

[17] An example of the welfare economic concept, Pareto optimality, where no change is possible without reducing the welfare of at least some player in the situation.

[18] Chamberlin used the concept product group to refer to products that are close *technical* and *economic* *substitutes*, technical in that they fulfil the same basis function, and economic in that they have similar price ranges; two houses might be technical substitutes in that they both supply shelter, but if the price of one is a million ECU, and the price of the other one-tenth of that, then they are unlikely to be economic substitutes. It should be noted that Chamberlin later abandoned the concept of the product group, though it did at least contribute to the development of ideas on the relationship between firms, industries and markets.

[19] Product differentiation as a basis for establishing a downward sloping demand curve was first introduced by Sraffa (1926).

[20] Note that if the demand curve is downward sloping, the marginal revenue curve is also downward sloping, and below, the demand curve. It can be proved that $MR = p(1 + 1/e)$, where e = price elasticity of demand. Where $MR = 0$, $e = -1$; where $MR = p$, $e \to -\infty$.

[21] Note that if the average selling costs curve is U-shaped, and the average production costs curve is U-shaped, then the sum of the two is also U-shaped.

[22] Note that Cournot had already developed an algebraic model of monopoly in 1838.

[23] This definition implies the absence of externalities. See Section 4.1.5 for a discussion on externalities.

[24] At least in neoclassical economics. There is, as we shall see in Chapter 5, a Schumpeterian view according to which technological change and innovation is best generated by monopolies, in which case there are also social benefits to monopolies.

[25] For diagrammatic and algebraic proofs, see Koutsoyiannis (1979, pp. 186–9).

[26] For diagrammatic and algebraic proofs, see Koutsoyiannis (1979, Ch. 7). The separation of markets is usually considered in geographic terms. For an example based on differentiable characteristics of consumers, see Hirschey and Pappas (1993, pp. 629–37). In this example Hirschey and Pappas show how a university football club could maximize its profits by charging students one price and the general public another (higher) price.

[27] The relationship between S_L and MC_L is analogous to the relationship between demand and marginal revenue.

[28] Since Cournot's work provided a basis (explicitly in places) for arguing that monopoly was better than competition, it would have been seen as contrary to the very strongly held accepted wisdom of time.

[29] It was 40 years after publication in French before Cournot's *Recherches* appeared in Italian, and it was nearly two decades more before the first English version was published.

[30] This is the authors' translation of: 'Le propriétaire (1) ne peut pas influer directement sur la fixation de D_2: tout ce qu'il peut faire, c'est, lorsque D_2 est fixé par le propriétaire (2), de choisir pout D_1 la valeur qui lui convient le mieux, ce à quoi il parviendra en modifiant convenablement le prix' (Cournot, 1980, p. 60).

[31] This is logical, as Cournot writes, 'since the two springs/wells are assumed to be identical and identically located' (translation of: 'ce qui devrait être puisque les deux sources sont supposées semblables et semblablement placées') (Cournot, 1980, p. 61). Cournot's firms each had possession of a natural water source.

[32] The co-operative total revenue is $Q \cdot f(Q)$. Profit is maximized under the condition: $\mathrm{d}TR/\mathrm{d}Q = 0$, i.e.:

$$Q \cdot f'(Q) + f(Q) = 0$$

$$Q \cdot \mathrm{d}p/\mathrm{d}Q + p = 0$$

$$Q + p \cdot \mathrm{d}Q/\mathrm{d}p = 0$$

[33] This is the *prisoner's dilemma* situation familiar from Chapter 2.

[34] Being independent of one another, Pareto argued, meant that their relationship to price would be $p = f(Q_1, Q_2)$ rather than Cournot's $p = f(Q_1 + Q_2)$.

[35] Note, however, that Bertrand was guilty of a similar simplifying assumption, namely that each dupolist acts in the belief that the other's price is fixed.

[36] 'Leur intérêt serait de s'associer ou tout au moins de fixer le prix commun, de manière à prélever sur l'ensemble des acheteurs la plus grande recette possible; mais cette solution est écartée' (Bertrand, 1883, p. 503).

[37] The intuitive notion of a kinked demand curve as an operational tool in economics originated in the early 1930s with the work of Chamberlin, although Chamberlin himself did not use the words 'kinked' or 'kinky' in his analysis. It is only later, in 1939, that Sweezy introduced the kinked demand curve as a workable concept.

[38] Equation (4.14) is obtained as follows:

For Firm 2 (as for Firm 1),

$$p = a - b(q_1 + q_2)$$

Firm 2's profit

$$\pi_2 = \{a - b(q_1 + q_2)\}q_2 - c_2 q_2$$

where c_2 is Firm 2's average cost (and marginal cost if average cost is constant). Firm 2's profit will be maximized where:

$$\frac{\mathrm{d}\pi_2}{\mathrm{d}q_2} = 0 \Rightarrow a - bq_1 - 2bq_2 - c_2 = 0 \Rightarrow 2bq_2 = a - bq_1 - c_2$$

Eq. (4.14) follows.

[39] It can be shown that this result can be generalized for a Stackelberg leader with n followers each with identical cost functions:

$$q_L = \frac{(a - c_L) + n(c_f - c_L)}{2b}$$

where q_L is the quantity and C_L the average (and marginal) cost of the dominant, or leader firm, and q_f the quantity (see fn. 40) and c_f the average (and marginal) cost of each of the follower firms.

[40] Again, as for fn.39, this can be generalized for n followers:

$$q_f = \frac{(a - c_f) - (n + 1)(c_f - c_L)}{2b(n + 1)}$$

[41] For Firm 1, $\pi_1 = (a/4 + 3c/4)q_1 - cq_1$ from which,

$$\pi_1 = \frac{(aq_1 - cq_1)}{4}$$

For Firm 2, $q_2 = \frac{1}{2}q_1$, so:

$$\pi_2 = (a/4 + 3c/4)\tfrac{1}{2}q_1 - c \cdot \tfrac{1}{2}q_1$$

From which,

$$\pi_2 = \frac{(aq_1 - cq_1)}{8}$$

[42] Note that in the 1838 original, which we have more or less reproduced in our discussion of Cournot and Fig. 4.8 above, reaction curves were not linear.

[43] According to Cable, Carruth and Dixit (1994) 'the constraining influence of competition from the fringe is much weakened where products are heterogeneous'. This suggests the need for close attention by anti-trust agencies to cross elasticities of demand. 'However, this recommendation may need to be balanced by dynamic considerations, insofar as it may be argued that new and different products are the lifeblood of dynamic market economies.'

[44] In modern, game theoretic terms, the equivalent of what Chamberlain argued is that a prisoner's dilemma game, where there are repeated plays, will result in a Pareto-efficient solution.

[45] Equation (4.24) is derived as follows:

$$\pi_1 = pq_1 - cq_1$$

$$= \{a - b(q_1 + q_2)\}q_1 - cq_1$$

$$= aq_1 - bq_1^2 - bq_1q_2 - cq_1$$

For profit maximization,

$$\frac{d\pi_1}{dq_1} = a - 2bq_1 - bq_2 - bq_1 dq_2/dq_1 - c = 0$$

i.e.

$$q_1(2b + b\,dq_2/dq_1) = a - bq_2 - c$$

Substituting $\lambda_{1,2}$ for dq_2/dq_1 and simplifying gives Eq. (4.24).

[46] This is derived as follows:

$$p = a - bQ, \qquad \text{where } Q - q_i + Q_{-i}$$

$$\pi_i = pq_i - c_iq_i$$

For π_i max., $d\pi_i/dq_i = p + q_i(dp/dQ)(dQ/dq_i) - c_i = 0$. Now if the only change in Q arising from a change in q_i is q_i itself (i.e. $\lambda_{i,-i} = 0$), then, $dQ/dq_i = 1$, and:

$$p + q_i\, dp/dQ - c_i = 0 \Rightarrow p + p(q_i/Q)(dp/dQ)(Q/p) - c_i = 0$$

$$\Rightarrow p + pS_i/\varepsilon - c_i = 0$$

where S_i is Firm i's market share, and ε is the market price elasticity of demand. With the usual assumption of constant average cost, Eq. (4.28) follows.

[47] As in fn. 46, without the assumption that $dQ/dq_i = 1$.

[48] Note that some economists include the minus sign, and some do not. The market price elasticity of demand is inevitably negative, so the end result with be positive.

[49] Most of this work examines American or Japanese industries. See Fraser (1994) for a brief examination of some of this literature.

[50] Note that the association between higher profits and Cournot competition is consistent with the findings of Cable, Carruth and Dixit (1994) on welfare loss, discussed above, according to which Cournot duopoly is associated with greater welfare loss, and Bertrand with less.

[51] Note, however, that in the special issue of *Strategic Management Journal* on Fundamental Research Issues in Strategy and Economics (**12**, winter 1991), there is not one mention of 'conjectural variation'.

[52] This section relies heavily on Chang (1994, Chs 1 and 2). See also Tomlinson (1993).

[53] See also Chapter 7 for a discussion—and some different examples—of externalities.

[54] Tomlinson (1993) more generally argues that 'to start with "market failure" is precisely to start from an assumption about what markets "should" do and then explain why they do not'. Tomlinson concludes that 'markets never could fulfil this function, so to start from there is a theoretical false step'.

[55] As Tomlinson (1993, fn.7) puts it, the rent seeking approach 'argues that regulation imposes a cost on society because resources are wastefully expended on the fight to obtain the economic rents generated by regulation, hence expanding the harms done by regulation'.

[56] This is a big 'if', particularly in the context of regulatory capture.

[57] See Tomlinson, 1993: see also, Section 4.1.3.

[58] On exit games, see for example, Geroski and Jacquemin (1985).

[59] We will discuss Chang's application of his theory to industrial policy in Chapter 7.

[60] For a brief discussion on product life cycles, industry cycles and concentration, see de Jong, 1993, pp. 16–19.

[61] For more on concentration in the food industry, see Linda (1991).

[62] According to de Jong (1993, Table 5), the curves of the global CR3 ratios (top three firms as a proportion of the output of the top 9, 15, 19 or 20) for the period 1962 to 1990 are, in most major industries, very roughly U-shaped, i.e. concentration has gone down for some years and then up again towards the end of the period.

[63] Integration refers here to spatial (or regional) as opposed to industrial integration. It entails the bringing together of different parts into a whole. The minimalist definition of integration (or the first degree of integration) at the EU level refers to the elimination of tariffs, quantitative restrictions and other measures of equivalent effect, and of non-tariff barriers (NTBs) impeding trade among the 15 European members. A maximalist approach (or a superior degree) would entail the setting up of a European Central Bank (issuing a single European currency), of a European Parliament (as a substitute to 15 national parliaments), etc.

[64] The internationalization of production and issues of location are discussed in Section 3 of this chapter, corporate strategies are covered in Section 1 of Chapter 5, and technological change and innovation in Section 2 of Chapter 5.

[65] The six signatories of the Treaty of Rome in 1957 have subsequently been joined by Denmark, Ireland and the UK in 1973, Greece in 1980, Portugal and Spain in 1986, and Austria, Finland and Sweden in 1995.

[66] They are termed 'static effects' in economic integration theory.

[67] See Table 4.4 above, and the associated discussion on rank mobility. See also the discussion by Auerbach (1988, p. 263), in which he raises and subsequently discusses in detail, the co-existence in the twentieth century of increasing competitive pressure and the emergence of giant enterprises.

[68] Their argument is based in part on Sleuwaegen and Yamawaki (1988).

[69] The '1992 programme'.

[70] A exception to this general rule is the approach followed by Jacquemin (1979).

[71] Barriers of the first order would also include regulation (where this does not distinguish between firms from different countries; if it does so distinguish, it becomes a barrier of the second order), and such strategies of firms as alliances with other firms. Regulation is discussed in Section 4.2.4, and firms' strategies in Chapter 5.

[72] In the case of agriculture, deficiency payments and import levies played a substantial role in restricting trade in the inter-war period.

[73] On this issue, and in particular on the different responses of US, European and Japanese MNCs with subsidiaries in Ireland to the completion of the Single European Market, see Jacobson and Andréosso (1990).

[74] Paradoxically, quantitative restrictions such as production quotas were reintroduced in the 1970s in the EU steel industry and in the 1980s in the agricultural sector.

[75] The 'White Paper on the Completion of the Internal Market' (see CEC, 1985).

[76] Procurement markets will be dealt with below, in Section 4.2.3. Note also that technical regulations are part of regulation in general, a topic which we discuss in Section 4.2.4.

[77] Guinness was one of the few foreign beer products admitted on German soil. In 1986, the European Court of Justice found that the *Reinheitsgebot* violated Article 30 of the Rome Treaty, and the decree had thus to be removed from German legislation. However, the change in German legislation did not lead to the expected entry of foreign beers into the German market. It seems that a successful marketing campaign highlighting the fact that the German beers sold in Germany were, unlike many other foreign beers, brewed according to the defunct law, strengthened the attachment of the German consumers to their domestic product.

[78] EFTA countries are also members of these two bodies.

[79] See, in particular, Cecchini's Table 9.2, p. 84.

[80] At 1988 prices.

[81] Note that high corporate profit tax rates can constitute both first and second order barriers.

[82] Temporary derogations have been granted to Germany, Greece and Portugal.

[83] If the second order barriers are significant enough, however, competition is limited and the dominant firms within Europe, though having lower average costs, may be able, in the absence of regulation, to charge higher prices. This will mean continued supernormal profits.

[84] Most of the discussion on EOS in the context of the European market has focused on technical or production EOS in the manufacturing sector. However, EOS may also be important in relation to R&D, marketing, finance and distribution. For a concise appraisal of price reduction effects in the services sector, see Emerson et al. (1988, pp. 98–122).

[85] For a less aggregated approach, see Pratten (1987).

[86] To the authors' knowledge, Michel Catinat is the only economist who has clearly written about this 'logical incoherence' contained in the White Paper (see Catinat, 1989, p. 104).

[87] Among the vast literature on this subject, see Hitiris (1994).

[88] Total EU exports and imports were respectively ECUs 1136 billion and ECUs 1207 billion in 1992; intra-EU exports and imports were respectively ECUs 696 billion and ECUs 716 billion.

[89] Intra-industry trade means trade between two countries within the same industry (e.g. cars exported by country A to country B, and by country B to country A); inter-industry trade refers to trade between two member countries and between different industries, more or less narrowly defined (e.g. cars exported by country A to country B, and trucks exported by country B to country A).

[90] While much trade in Europe was intra-industry up to the 1980s, there is some evidence of a recent reversal in the growth of intra-industry trade in a number of OECD countries (Globerman and Dean,

1990). For a detailed study of a reversal of this kind in the case of Ireland, see Brülhart and McAleese (1993).

[91] If two goods produced by different firms are in other respects identical, brand loyalty can be defined as that which prevents the cross-elasticity of demand between the two goods from being infinite.

[92] In the incorporation of industrial organization into international trade theory the EOS element is emphasized. 'It is economies of scale that keep each country from producing the full range of products [within an industry] for itself; thus economies of scale can be an independent source of international trade' (Krugman and Obstfeld, 1991, p. 138).

[93] Explanations of the behaviour of MNCs are the subject of Section 3.1.

[94] A single index of intra-industry trade in a number of (or all) industries can also be calculated:

$$\text{IIT}_{GL} = \frac{\sum_{i=1}^{n}(X_i + M_i) - |X_i - M_i|}{\sum_{i=1}^{n}(X_i + M_i)}$$

where X_i and M_i represent the value of the country's exports and imports of the products of industry i.

[95] Grubel and Lloyd (1975) found that the IIT index for all industries in ten industrialized countries in 1967 was 0.48. The index for the EC was 0.67. Thus nearly half the trade among the ten was in goods belonging to the same industry, while among the then six of the EC the figure was two-thirds.

[96] Advertising as strategy of firms is discussed in Chapter 5.

[97] See also, below, on deregulation in Europe.

[98] One reason for the increasing EU interest in regulation is the reduction of intervention at the national level as an attraction to mobile capital: 'the EU has become increasingly involved in regulatory activities...to try to prevent standards being driven down to unacceptably low levels' (Nugent, 1994).

[99] At the peak of state control in the mid-1980s, 'the state owned thirteen of the twenty largest firms in France and had a controlling share in many others' (Nugent, 1994).

[100] Regulation at the EU level in the banking sector began the 1970s with the First Council Directive of 1977 which co-ordinated the laws and regulatory frameworks of credit institutions.

[101] Note that Italy is an exception. In relation to banking 'Italy had the most restrictive regulation in the early 1980s and has undertaken only limited structural deregulation in the course of the last decade...and the Italian market is, if anything rather less integrated with Europe than in the early 1980s' (Gual and Neven, 1992).

[102] It was adopted in December 1989 and had to be implemented by all member states by 1 January 1993. Council Directive 89/646/EEC; see OJCE, 30/12/89.

[103] A bank has three sources of funds: deposits, equity capital, and non-deposit loan capital (such as bonds). The capital adequacy ratio ensures that equity does not fall below a certain percentage of total assets.

[104] This tax is still not implemented in the EU. Because of their lower carbon emission levels, Portugal, Greece, Spain and Ireland will be authorized to defer the application of the tax.

[105] International noise standards were first introduced by the International Civil Aviation Organization (ICAO) in 1971. They have been modified periodically since. In 1980, a Council Directive introduced a noise emission limit at source based on ICAO standards. A noise landing fee was introduced in Paris-Orly in 1973 but had to be removed as it was against French law. (Airbus Industrie: Environmental Protection. France. March 1993.)

[106] For more details on the following, see for example Zaphirious (1970), O'Malley (1982), and Campbell (1983).

[107] In the UK however, a stock company can be either private or public.

[108] Some kind of homogeneous protection ('safeguards') can be traced as far back as the Treaty of Rome, signed in 1957 (see Article 54-3-g). This gave rise to the First Company Law Directive, agreed upon in 1968 and in effect since 1973.

[109] See Council Regulation No. 2137/85 of 31 July 1985 in OJ L 199, pp. 1–9. The EEIG is based on a French legal concept called *Groupement des intérêts économiques*, the most renowned applications of which have been by the Airbus consortium and Ariane Espace where it provided a corporate structure for international cooperation (Andersen, 1993, p. 79).

[110] The delay between 1985 and 1989 was provided for within the regulation itself, to give member states time so that domestic law could be adjusted to allow for EEIGs.

[111] See *EC Bulletin*, Supplement 10/72.

[112] See COM (75) 150 final, Proposal for a Council Regulation on the Statute for European Companies.

[113] The Supervisory Board would have one-third of its members representatives of the shareholders, one-third representatives of employees, and one-third persons representing the general interest (Article 74a).

[114] NACE codes 11 to 50.

[115] NACE codes 61 to 99.

[116] Different traditions and organisation and production, trade unionization, and skill development.

[117] Porter (1990) is among the exceptions; Porter, however, although with a training in formal economics, moved into the management discipline in the 1980s. Note, too, that while economists have, in general, ignored locational issues, economic geographers have not. See, among many examples, Estall and Buchanan (1973), and Dicken and Lloyd (1990).

[118] See Chapter X, 'Industrial organization continued. The concentration of specialized industries in particular localities.'

[119] Krugman (1993, Ch. 2), basing his discussion on Marshall, identifies three sources of industry localization, labour market pooling, intermediate inputs and technological spillover, equivalent, respectively, to Marshall's local market for special skills, subsidiary trades and hereditary skill. Our description of the factors determining localization will be based partly on Marshall (1898, pp. 347–52) and partly on Krugman (1993, pp. 36–63). Quotes from and references to Marshall and Krugman in this section will be from these sources.

[120] Porter's (1990, p. 71) discussion of the importance of demand conditions in a country to the success of that country's industries is similar to, though a modern elaboration of, Marshall's.

[121] Aspects of two parts of Porter's 'diamond'—factor conditions and firm's strategy, structure and rivalry—can be seen as related to this element of Marshall's theory of localization. See Section 4.3.5.

[122] Krugman, too, considers this factor to be of importance. In a discussion about core and periphery in Europe, he writes that 'northwestern Europe is relatively rich for reasons that have to do more with culture than with geography'.

[123] Note that Marshall's point, under Physical conditions above, that an industry requiring raw materials that are expensive to transport will tend to locate near the source of those raw materials, is not necessarily contradicted by this.

[124] Even where there is not labour mobility, the decision of workers as to whether to obtain the skills required by the industry (invest in industry-specific human capital) has the same effect.

[125] It may not be coincidental that the process of establishing the Ford plant in Dagenham took place at the height of the Depression (or trough in the cycle), culminating in the opening of the plant in 1931.

[126] More precisely, the *reduction* in unit costs of production arising from production in that place are the agglomeration economies.

[127] Among attempts to measure and explain core–periphery patterns in Europe, see Jacobson and Mack (1994). Krugman (1993), too, accepts that the 'center–periphery pattern is there: that is, the poorer regions of Europe are in general also relatively distant from markets'.

[128] Hymer (1976) is a reprint of his influential 1960 dissertation.

[129] Our description of Dunning's framework is based on Dunning (1993).

[130] Note the difference between the *O* advantages arising from the *superior ability to take advantage of* the economies of common governance and the *I* advantages which are those *economies of common governance* themselves. Note, too, that transaction cost analysis is not the only one of the theories of the firm that Dunning draws on; his consideration of organizational capabilities as part of *O* advantages suggests a familiarity with the evolutionary theory, too.

[131] For a related discussion on the double process of spatial and industrial integration, see Andréosso and Jacobson (1991).

[132] There has been, as Dunning acknowledged, some work in this area. For some reason, he omitted Dunning and Robson (1987). See also, Jacobson and Andréosso (1990), and Andréosso and Jacobson (1991).

[133] This paragraph draws on Dunning (1993), especially Chs 6 and 7.

[134] We discuss firms' strategies in Chapter 5, and EU policies in Chapter 7.

[135] The scholars most important in the development and application of the concept of industrial districts in recent times are Piore and Sabel (1984).

[136] Note that there are replies to Amin and Robins's attack on industrial district theory by the main proponents thereof, Sabel, Piore and Storper, in the same publication—see 'Three responses to Ash Amin and Kevin Robins' in Pyke, Beccatini and Sengenberger (1990).

[137] Based on Alfred Marshall's work on the 'concentration of specialized industries in particular localities' (Marshall, 1898, pp. 346–56). Not all agree that industrial districts are Marshallian. Harrison (1992) argues that modern industrial district theory implies more than Marshallian (neoclassical) industrial districts, in particular 'interdependence of firms, flexible firm boundaries, co-operative competition and the importance of trust in reproducing sustained collaboration'. Robertson and Langlois (1994) also differentiate between Marshallian and Third Italian industrial districts: 'As applied to the Third Italy, the term indicates a higher degree of cooperative coordination than would be present in a Marshallian industrial district.'

[138] This is our loose translation from Montfort's French.

[139] Some industries may be in both upstream and downstream poles. Transport is particularly pervasive and in the agri-food *filière*, for example, the food-haulage industry may be involved both in upstream delivery of raw materials and in the delivery of end products to distributors.

[140] Antonelli *et al.* use communication, banking and finance as examples of intermediating downstream sub-sectors, but arguably as prerequisites of production they are more important upstream.

[141] See, for example, the article by de Bandt (1983), under the title '*A propos de la reconquête du marché intérieur*'.

[142] On France's industrial policy, see de Bandt (1987). See also Chapter 7.

[143] Note that clustering is not new. It is, according to Storper and Walker (1989, p. 141), rediscovered once a generation.

[144] There is only one mention of industrial districts in the 855-page book, and that is in a footnote (p. 790, fn. 20).

[145] It is worth noting that industrial districts and *filières* are also clusters, or, at least, parts of clusters.

[146] This paragraph draws on Porter (1990, pp. 287–8) and any quotes are from that source.

[147] This paragraph is based on Porter (1990, p. 71). These four factors are the headings under which the successful clusters of any economy can be explained.

[148] This point is very similar to that made, and described by Amin and Robins (1990) and Amin and Thrift (1992), concerning the interrelationship between the local and the global.

Questions

4.1   What is cross elasticity of demand and how can it help to define a market?

4.2   Use Kay's concept of the strategic market to explain why the extent of both market and industry can be defined only on a case by case basis.

4.3   Use the data in Table 4.3 to calculate the CR1, CR3, CR5 and CR7 ratios. What can you say about the results?

4.4   Why is there a need for so many variations on Cournot's basic oligopoly model?

4.5   Why would you expect there to be a difference between concentration at the EU level and concentration at the national level?

4.6   What are the implications for distribution of investment in the EU of different national corporate profit tax rates?

4.7   What are the main features of European industrial structure?

4.8   Marshall developed his approach to localization in the nineteenth century. Is it still relevant?

4.9   What are the relationships between agglomeration economies, networks, industrial districts and clusters?

4.10 Will further integration in Europe encourage or discourage FDI?

5 Behaviour of firms

Among the objectives of the establishment of the Community and, more recently, the Single European Market, is to improve the performance of EU firms, such that they sustain, reinforce, gain or regain a competitive advantage on the international market. As was shown in Chapter 2, a satisfactory level of performance entails, in pure microeconomic terms, determining the most efficient production process, avoiding waste of resources, and responding appropriately and rapidly to new qualitative and quantitative needs of consumers. At the macroeconomic level, good performance of firms can be appraised through their contribution to the long-run growth of GDP per capita, and through their participation in the maintenance of high levels of employment. It should be emphasized that the objective of profit maximization under competitive equilibrium is not often achievable, and the various second bests, towards which competition policy strives, are not always compatible with such goals as the maintenance of high levels of unemployment.

To attain these levels of performance, a variety of conducts, behaviours or strategies can be selected by the firm. Conduct, narrowly defined, refers to *pricing* and/or the setting of *quantity* by the seller *to maximize profits* in a specific market. More broadly, conduct may include *product differentiation and advertising strategies, inter-firm mergers, acquisitions and alliances (MAAs), research and development (R&D), legal tactics*, and pricing strategies such as *predatory pricing* and *price discrimination*. These different conducts are not mutually exclusive. The promotion of newly created products through high advertising expenditures, for example, can go hand in hand with a strategy of price discrimination, and its success can at the same time be partly attributable to R&D.

The conduct of a firm in a perfectly competitive framework is restricted to a minimum. The only actions the firm can undertake are, in the short run, to respond to market price by producing a quantity that maximizes profit and, in the long run, if it is making losses, to leave the industry.[1] In such a market structure, advertising, action to discourage entry of new firms, and reacting to the activities of rivals, are all precluded by definition. In neoclassical theory, firms' conduct depends on the market structure in which they are defined as operating. This is the basis of the Structuralist view, according to which market structure determines conduct. As was shown in Chapter 2, revisions of this view have indicated that a number of different directions of causation are possible in practice.

The specific strategies adopted by EU firms are also, at least in part, influenced by EU-specific institutions and developments. The level of international economic integration and expectations of changes in this level can, for example, constitute an incentive for firms to merge with other firms in order to operate more effectively in the larger market. In particular, among the factors in the late 1980s wave of MAAs in Europe—and between European and US, and European and Japanese firms—were the proposals for the completion of the Single European Market by 1992.

With these observations in mind, the present chapter will examine the various strategies followed by the firms situated in an increasingly integrated region, i.e. the EU. Section 5.1 will explain pricing strategies,[2] advertising and product differentiation strategies, corporate integration and diversification. Section 5.2 will discuss R&D. We turn to the specific strategies of EU firms implemented as an answer to the increase in the level of regional integration in the late 1980s in Section 5.3.

5.1 General strategies

5.1.1 Pricing: a review of neoclassical price theory

Price is the amount that must be paid in exchange for a commodity. The exact amount paid depends on the structure of the market. We turn first to a brief reminder of the two limit cases in neoclassical theory, perfect competition and monopoly.

A *perfectly competitive market* is one characterized by the absence of rivalry between firms, of market barriers, and of product differentiation. Buyers and sellers are so numerous that each individual firm is a 'price taker' (hence the flat, or infinitely elastic, demand curve), and no monopsonic power can affect the working of the market. The individual firm adjusts its sales volume to the profit-maximizing level, i.e. where marginal cost (MC), marginal revenue (MR) and market price (p) are all equal, and because of freedom of entry and exit, this will also be at the minimum average cost (AC), ensuring that no firm earns above the level of profit just sufficient to keep it in the industry (Fig. 4.3).

Monopoly is a market structure characterized by a unique seller, no close substitutes for the product, and high entry barriers. The firm (which is also the industry) demand curve is now downward sloping. By maximizing its profit, the monopolist will choose the price–output combination[3] such that MC is equal to MR (Fig. 4.5). At that point, p will exceed both MC and AC. In the long run, the monopoly firm will earn supernormal profits, represented by the area $p_1 AC_1 BE$.

With both perfect competition and monopoly, once we assume that the firms are profit maximizers, and that they have the required information on supply and demand, there is little remaining choice over price. Firms will produce the quantity at which $MC = MR$, and the price will follow from the market. Alternatively we could argue that firms set the price at which $MC = MR$ and the quantity follows from the market. The point remains: it is $MC = MR$ that dictates price, either directly or via the demand curve. These simple neoclassical models preclude strategic pricing.

5.1.2 Pricing as strategy

The existence of an oligopoly, or of a high level of concentration with the emergence of a *dominant firm*, gives rise to different pricing practices, such as *price leadership*, *price discrimination*, *limit pricing, collusion,* and *predatory pricing*.[4] In the following sections we will discuss first the theoretical aspects of pricing, then the legal aspects.

Price leadership

Price leadership refers to the process by which all price changes in a market emanate from a firm recognized as the leader by other firms, who follow the leader's initiatives. The notion of

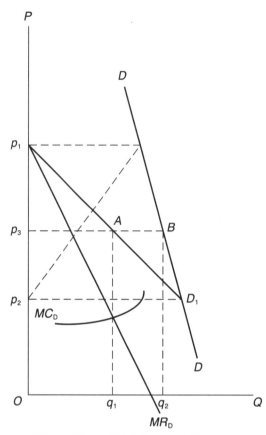

Figure 5.1   Suicidal dominant firm

price leadership normally refers to two different situations: price leadership through a dominant firm; and barometric price leadership.

Dominant firm price leadership   This occurs in an industry characterized by the co-existence of a single large firm and a number of fringe firms, each of which supplies only a minor share of total output. One model—also known as the *suicidal dominant firm* model—assumes first that, below a certain price, the fringe firms produce less than the total quantity demanded, and second, that the dominant firm accepts as the demand for its products what is left of the market after the fringe firms have supplied the quantity they are willing to supply at each price. The dominant firm sets price in response to quantity, the fringe firms set their quantity in response to price. This is shown in Fig. 5.1. The market demand is DD. At price p_1, the fringe firms would altogether produce the entire demand, so there is nothing left for the dominant firm. At price p_2, the fringe firms could not make a profit, so they would not produce at all; the entire demand would be supplied by the dominant firm. At p_1 the demand facing the dominant firm is zero, and at p_2 and below, the demand facing the dominant firm is the entire market. Assuming—as we have done—linear functions, the dominant firm's demand curve is $p_1 D_1 D$. At any price, the quantity indicated by $p_1 D_1$ will be the quantity supplied by the dominant firm, and the quantity indicated by the horizontal distance between $p_1 D_1$ and DD will be the quantity supplied by the fringe firms. The dominant firm will maximize its profits where MR_D, the marginal revenue curve derived from p_1D_1D, intersects MC_D, the dominant firm's marginal cost curve; this occurs at quantity q_1. For a quantity of q_1, the dominant firm can charge a price of p_3. At a price of p_3, the fringe firms will supply the quantity AB, or q_1q_2, and the dominant firm will supply its profit-maximizing quantity of p_3A, or q_1.

Why is this called the suicidal dominant firm model? First, if the price fixed by the dominant firm is such that the fringe firms can earn supernormal profits, this will attract additional firms into the industry. Second, once the dominant firm has fixed the price at p_3, this changes the conditions under which the fringe firms operate. Any uncertainty that existed about price for the small firms in the industry has been removed. They are now willing to supply more at p_3 than they were if p_3 was just one of a series of possible prices. As the quantity supplied by fringe firms increases—to greater than q_1q_2—this reduces the remaining quantity to less than q_1. Acting as a 'quantity taker' and 'price fixer' reduces the dominant firm's market share.[5] It can reduce it—in effect shifting p_1D_1 down and to the left—to such an extent that the dominant firm can no longer produce at a profit.

A dominant firm is unlikely to behave like this in practice. There are other ways in which dominant firms succeed—often illegally—in setting price, and ensuring that their competitors conform to that price or pricing system. This usually involves threats—explicit or implicit—to harm competitors in some way if they do not conform. Thus price leadership in practice often includes other types of anti-competitive behaviour. We will discuss it below in our examination of the legal aspects of various types of pricing.

Barometric price leadership   In this case a particular firm is accepted by the other firms in the industry as the best judge of when to change prices. The firms themselves are assuming asymmetric information, in that they believe that the leader has knowledge or ability that they do not have. Which firm acts as leader can change over time, as different criteria for judging when to alter price come into play. Thus during a period of stability in methods of production a firm with particular expertise in marketing may be seen as price leader, while during a period of rapid technological change, a firm more highly regarded as a production innovator will be watched more closely by the other firms for signals.

If the ultimate price—once the firms have responded to the leader—is close to what it would have been under competitive conditions, then there is generally considered to be nothing anti-competitive about this type of behaviour in an industry.[6] While the leader is likely to be one of the larger firms in the industry, it will not have the power to dominate; there will occasionally be resistance to price initiatives by the leader, possibly leading to a change in leadership; and there will generally be leadership in the raising of prices 'only when rising costs or demand warrant price hikes' (Scherer and Ross, 1990, p. 250). As we shall see, it can be difficult to distinguish between legal and illegal pricing behaviour.

Price discrimination

This occurs where identical products are sold in different markets at different prices. Following the work of Pigou (1932), it is customary to distinguish three types of price discrimination: first, second and third degree price discrimination. First degree price discrimination occurs when each unit of output is sold at a different price. The firm captures all the consumer surplus in the market by selling each unit of output at its maximum demand price. It is difficult to imagine a situation in which this type of price discrimination could be implemented, and it is generally considered to be of theoretical interest only.

Second degree price discrimination is simpler in practice since it requires less information about demand. The firm divides output into successive batches and sells each batch for the highest price consumers are willing to pay. Block pricing and quantity discounts represent two forms of second degree discrimination.[7]

In third degree discrimination the firm segregates customers into distinctive groups characterized by different elasticities of demand, which are explained by exogenous criteria such as location (urban versus rural, residential versus industrial), age, sex or occupation. The diagrammatic representation of third degree discrimination is based on the neoclassical profit-maximizing rule of $MR = MC$. With a different marginal revenue curve in each of the different markets, an appropriate point must be found at which the price-discriminating firm's marginal cost is equal to all of them ($MC = MR_1 = MR_2 = \ldots = MR_n$, for a market segregated into n parts).[8] This is shown in Fig. 5.2, in which we assume a market divided into two parts.

The profit-maximizing quantity is Σq, which is the quantity at which $MC = \Sigma MR$, ΣMR being the horizontal summation of the two marginal revenue curves (MR_1 and MR_2). From E, the point of intersection of MC and ΣMR, a horizontal line is drawn to the left, intersecting with MR_2 at e_2 and with MR_1 at e_1. The quantity at e_1, q_1, is sold for p_1, and the quantity at e_2, q_2, is sold for p_2. The condition for profit maximization, $MC = MR_1 = MR_2$ is satisfied.

Pigou's categorization is not accepted by all economists, and there have been a number of different definitions of price discrimination. Among early definitions was that of Joan Robinson (1933), according to whom price discrimination is 'The act of selling the same article, produced under a single control, at different prices to different buyers...'. This definition is restrictive in the sense that price discrimination can also exist where identical products are sold to the same buyer at varying prices over time, and, as Stigler (1966) points out, where non-identical, but similar, goods are sold at prices which are in different ratios to their marginal costs.

Let us take, for example, the case of a medical service. Robinson's definition applies in the sense that two buyers, one in desperate need of the service and the other considering it worth while but not essential, would be willing to pay different prices for the service. For each patient there is a different demand curve (and marginal revenue curve). The price-discriminating doctor would set her marginal cost equal to marginal revenue, for *each* patient, thus charging each a different price.

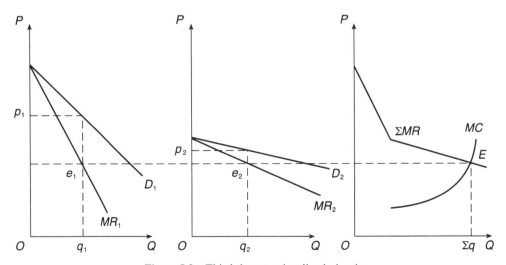

Figure 5.2   Third degree price discrimination

If the second patient becomes ill and also now sees the service—say a check of his blood pressure—as essential, he would also now be willing to pay a higher price. The price-discriminating doctor will charge him more now that he needs the service more (his demand for it is less elastic) than it was before he became ill.

An alternative to the ordinary taking of blood pressure might be a full check of a patient's cardiovascular condition. If, for whatever reason, the demands for these two services are different enough, then the price-discriminating doctor will charge prices such that:

$$\frac{p_1}{MC_1} \neq \frac{p_2}{MC_2}$$

where p_1 and MC_1 are the price and marginal cost respectively of the blood pressure service, and p_2 and MC_2 are the price and marginal cost respectively of the full cardiovascular check-up. As Stigler (1966, p. 209) points out, this definition has the merit of separating the price-discriminator's behaviour into two parts: first, the restriction of output such that price is greater than marginal cost; and second, the misallocation of goods or services among buyers, 'which is zero if prices are *proportional* to marginal costs'.

It is worth noting that where prices for the same good differ, this does not necessarily imply price discrimination, and where the price is identical this does not necessarily imply an absence of price discrimination. An example of identical goods with different but non-discriminatory prices is a bulk buyer obtaining a large quantity of a good at a lower unit cost than a small-scale consumer. The pricing would not be discriminatory if there are lower administrative, transport and other handling costs in the case of the bulk buyer. An example of identical but discriminatory prices is where a college charges the same tuition fees for a large class taught by a junior lecturer, and a small class taught by an experienced (and expensive) professor.[9]

Before a firm can successfully practice price discrimination, three conditions must be satisfied. First, the discriminator must exercise some monopoly power. Without a significant degree of monopoly power in at least one of the markets into which the discriminator is selling its product, attempts to extract supernormal profits in any of the markets will result in competitors undercutting its prices. Second, it must be able to segregate the customers into different sub-groups with different price elasticities of demand. With identical demands in two markets, profit-maximizing behaviour on the part of the firm will result in identical prices in the two markets. Third, the cost of segregating the markets must be less than the gains derived from price discrimination. If the firm can only effectively segregate the markets at very high cost it may not be worth it. Note that the effective segregation of markets implies the elimination of the possibility of arbitrage—the resale of the product by low price customers to high price customers.[10]

The limit price

This is the price set by a dominant firm at a level above costs, but not so high that it encourages new entrants (see Fig. 5.3). It is set, in other words, at a low enough level to block entry. The dominant firm is concerned with determining how far above costs price can be held without inducing entry.

Rather than setting the price at the profit-maximizing level, p_1, where MC_D, the dominant firm's marginal cost, is equal to MR, the dominant firm will set price at some point below p_1. A small, fringe firm would be a price taker, able to enter the market without influencing price. If part of its AC curve is below p_1, then it could profitably enter the market. Note that if fringe

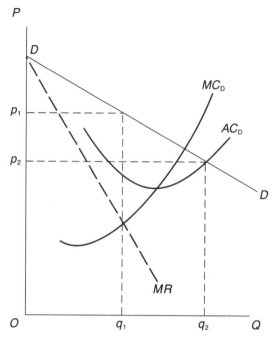

Figure 5.3   Limit pricing

firms do enter, then *DD* is no longer the demand curve facing the dominant firm. Some of the market will have been taken by the fringe firms and the demand now facing the dominant firm will be to the left and below *DD*. If the dominant firm's strategy is simply to set price as above, and then produce whatever quantity is left over after the fringe firms have entered, then it might find itself unable to continue to operate profitably in this market.[11]

To prevent the entry of fringe competitors, the dominant firm must identify the minimum average cost of the typical fringe firm. This will be the limit price. As long as the limit price is between p_1 and p_2 then, by setting a price just below the limit price, the dominant firm will block the entry of the fringe competitors. It will pay fringe firms to produce any quantity for which their average costs are below price; there will be no such quantity if price is below their minimum average cost. If the limit price is below p_2, then the dominant firm cannot use the limit pricing strategy. Any price below p_2 will result—prior to a shift in demand arising from the entry of the fringe firms—in a loss to the dominant firm, because for any quantity greater than q_2 price is less than AC_D.[12]

If fringe firms do enter, and the dominant firm now faces a demand curve below and to the left of *DD*, then this new demand curve will cut AC_D to the left of q_2, and possibly below p_2. However, in terms of pricing strategy to *prevent* entry, the option of setting a price below p_2 is not available to the dominant firm. Either, as shown above, the dominant firm will make losses or, if it restricts quantity to less than q_2, there will be a surplus of demand over supply and market price will be forced up. The limit pricing strategy will thus involve estimating the typical potential entrant's minimum *AC* and, on condition that it is between p_1 and p_2, setting a price just below that minimum *AC*.

In practice, the dominant firm may not be able to find out the minimum *AC* of the potential competitive fringe firms without trial and error. At p_1 fringe firms may begin to enter; the dominant firm will reduce price. Fringe firms may still continue to enter. Once the dominant firm is no longer alone in the market, the strategy it adopts to drive competitors out is called *predation*.[13]

What is the appropriate strategy if a dominant firm wishes to deter the entry of large firms? According to the Sylos-Labini (1962) argument, dominant firms are more likely to use a quantity-based strategy to deter entry where that entry is of relatively large firms. If the potential entrants are small, then no single firm will have a significant impact on quantity and a quantity-based strategy will therefore not be effective. The higher the minimum efficient scale relative to the total market, the more easily will the incumbent firm prevent the entry of newcomers. By continuing to produce the total market quantity (q_1 at p_1 in Fig. 5.3) the dominant firm will directly discourage entry, and if, as might reasonably be assumed, there are cost rigidities, the dominant firm will in any case wish to produce the full quantity because any less will result in under-utilization of capacity.

Collusive pricing

Collusive pricing is illegal in most countries. It consists of agreement among a group of firms to charge the same or similar prices for the same or similar products. Agreements for which documentary evidence can be found—which can occur only if the agreement is explicit—are easier to prosecute than cases in which the collusion must be inferred.

We have already presented, in Chapter 4 (Fig. 4.11), a diagrammatic model of collusive pricing as an example of oligopolistic behaviour. This was an explicit agreement to set price as though the firms were a monopoly. Arguably, price leadership also involves collusion, either explicit or tacit, in that other firms in the industry allow the leader to set price, and then follow (or collude), rather than set different prices. It has long been known that price leadership can be 'in lieu of overt collusion'[14] and it is often adopted in order to avoid (or reduce the likelihood of) prosecution.

The main reason for colluding is to increase profits by avoiding competition but, at least in the short term, there may be even more profit for the individual firm if it cheats, either by charging a higher price and selling the same quantity, or charging the same price and selling a higher quantity than that agreed by the cartel. A collusive duopoly in which the likely outcome is that both firms cheat on the agreement to collude would have a payoff matrix as shown in Fig. 5.4. This shows collusive duopoly as a (symmetric) prisoner's dilemma with the Nash equilibrium where both firms cheat, if:

$$N_c < C_c < N_n < C_n$$

Firm B

	Cheat	Not cheat
Firm A		
Cheat	$(C_c,\ C_c)$	$(C_n,\ N_c)$
Not cheat	$(N_c,\ C_n)$	$(N_n,\ N_n)$

Figure 5.4 Payoff matrix of a collusive duopoly

where N_c is the payoff if the firm does not cheat and its competitor cheats, C_c is the payoff if the firm cheats and its competitor also cheats, etc. The Pareto optimal position for the two firms is where they both do not cheat (N_n, N_n), but because N_c is the worst possible outcome for either firm, they will both avoid the strategy that contains that possibility and cheat (C_c, C_c).

A wide range of factors can increase or reduce the possibility of stable collusion. How stringently law against collusion is implemented is a major factor. Even before collusion is considered, however, the parties to the agreement must believe that it is capable of succeeding. Each firm must believe that the others can and will stick to the agreement, and that they will be able to be seen to be sticking to the agreement. Any factors that make it difficult for firms to adhere to the conditions of the agreement, or difficult to know whether others—or which of the others—have broken the agreement, will reduce the likelihood of collusion. A product subject to highly volatile demand, for example, will be unlikely to be produced by a collusive oligopoly; prices and quantities agreed in conditions of high demand are unlikely to be maintained in a slump.

Predation

This normally involves the use or the threat of use by the dominant firm—or the firm attempting to become dominant—of one of the following variables: price, quantity supplied, quality. In particular, predatory pricing is a strategy that calls for reductions of price to below the short-term profit-maximizing position, so that other firms are driven out of the market or weakened to the point of being taken over by the dominant firm. It is sometimes referred to as a 'pricing-below-cost' strategy. Based on Areeda and Turner's (1975) influential contribution to the debate on predation, Fig. 5.5 defines predatory pricing as any price below average variable cost (AVC).[15] At any price between p_1 and p_2 the firm is covering its short-run variable costs. It can remain in business in the short run since although there will be a loss on each unit, the excess of price over average variable cost will partly offset average fixed cost.[16] At any price below p_2, the firm may be engaged in predatory pricing.

Two separate—though related—debates in relation to predation deserve our attention. The first is theoretical, based around the Chicago School argument that, in the *absence of barriers to entry*, and under *conditions of perfect information*, predation can not occur.[17] The second is practical, empirical and legal, and rests on the need for competition law to distinguish between illegal predation and legitimate business practice aimed at gaining competitive advantage. This second debate will be discussed in Section 5.1.3, under the law in relation to dominant position and predatory pricing in Europe.

In essence, the Chicago School argument is anti-interventionist; predation is unlikely, and therefore policy to prevent it is unnecessary. Let us assume that a firm incurs losses in the short run, with the expectation of driving out or taking over its competitors so that in the long run it can increase price and derive supernormal profits. To make this worth while, the long-run profits will have to more than make up for the short-term losses. However, in the absence of barriers to entry, there is nothing to stop new firms from continuing to enter, even after the first competitors have been eliminated. So the dominant—or would-be dominant—firm will have to incur losses in the long run, as well.

Perfect information has a similar effect to the absence of entry barriers, because if the dominant firm's decision makers know that it will be able to improve its long-run position by predation, then so will the other firms and/or consumers. For example, consumers, aware of the

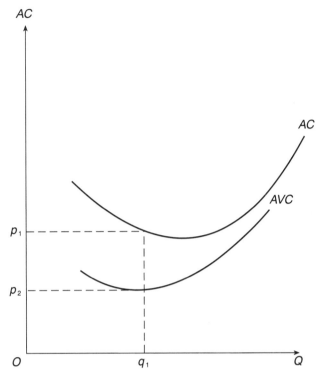

Figure 5.5 Predatory pricing

potential in the predatory activity of the dominant firm to monopolize the market, may support the competition and prevent monopolization.

The counter-arguments to the Chicago School's objection to predation in theory aim primarily at the improbability of the School's assumptions. The first is similar to that against contestable market theory (see Chapter 2), namely that entry is rarely completely free. If barriers exist, then the dominant firm *will* be able to raise prices after eliminating the competition. The extent to which supernormal profits can be extracted will be directly related to the height of the barriers. As long as the barriers are imperfect, however, it may be that predation is unprofitable. It will depend on the level and duration of short-term losses, the discount rate, and the subsequent level and duration of supernormal profits, as well as the height of the barriers to entry. The basic point is that if there are entry barriers, predation as a rational strategy cannot be ruled out.

If information is imperfect, then this, too, means that predation as a rational strategy cannot be ruled out. Information is, moreover, likely to be asymmetric as between the firms in an industry and potential providers of capital. This is exacerbated when the firms in question are under threat to a dominant firm's predatory strategy. Their self-interest will make it difficult for the capital market to trust the information they provide, but there will be transaction costs in obtaining the information independently. As Martin (1994, p. 464) puts it, 'The result is that while a target might be able to acquire additional funds, it can do so only at a cost of capital greater than that available to the predator firm. This cost differential will make predation a feasible strategy.'

Entrant

	Stay out	Enter
Incumbent		
Resist	-- --	(−5, −5)
Co-operate	-- --	(20, 20)
Stay in	(50, 0)	-- --

Figure 5.6   Chain store paradox

We have shown that, under certain circumstances, predation is rational. Even if it is not, an aggressive firm by behaving irrationally can drive out the opposition.[18] Aggressive price reductions might convince competitors that the aggressor will 'stop at nothing' to eliminate opposition. Rather than suffering the consequences of a struggle in which, although the aggressor will lose, so will the competitor, the competitor may simply leave the market. The aggressor becomes a monopoly supplier without the loss and its apparent irrationality turns out to have been rational.

This kind of argument about strategy suggests the usefulness of a game theoretic approach to the problem. Selten (1978) introduced what has become known as the 'chain store paradox' to examine in game theoretic terms a situation in which a firm in a number of markets faces possible entrants in each of them.[19] He assumed that the firm faced the entrants, one after the other, for example first in Market 1, next in Market 2, and so on up to Market N. So, there is a firm with N branches, facing other firm(s) considering entry into each of its N markets, in turn.

What we have is a game with up to N moves. The first move might have a payoff matrix as shown in Fig. 5.6. Prior to the entry of competition, the firm was making a profit of 50,000 ECUs in Market 1. Following entry it has a choice between price cutting to resist the entrant (in which case both will make losses of 5000 ECUs), and co-operating (in which case both will make profits of 20,000 ECUs). Faced with these payoffs, and ignoring for a moment the other $N - 1$ markets, the entrant will enter, and the incumbent will co-operate (and both will make profits of 20,000 ECUs); this is the Nash equilibrium.

Adopting what is called a *repeated game* approach,[20] Selten (1978) showed that this result would hold for each of the N moves. Assuming the firms are in the last (or Nth) market, if the payoff matrix is similar to that in Fig. 5.6, than the competitor will enter and the incumbent will co-operate. The alternative, aggressive pricing strategy will result only in a loss to the incumbent, with no possibility of later gain. If, instead of the Nth market, we assume that the firms are in the $(N - 1)$th market, the incumbent might consider the aggressive strategy as a means of frightening the entrant away from the Nth market. The incumbent and the entrant would both lose 5000 ECUs in the $(N - 1)$th market and, if the entrant does in fact take the warning and refrain from entering the Nth market, then the incumbent will have a payoff of 50,000 ECUs in the Nth market. The incumbent's total payoff for the Nth and the $(N - 1)$th markets will be 45,000 ECUs. This is shown in Table 5.1.

If the entrant does not take the warning (indeed, if the entrant realizes that he *should not* take the warning) then the incumbent will again be faced by the entrant in the Nth market. With no possibility of recouping losses (the Nth being the last market), the incumbent will co-operate.

TABLE 5.1   Incumbent's payoffs from the last two markets

Market	Strategy	Payoff	Total
Nth	Monopoly	50	
$(N-1)$th	Resist	−5	45
Nth	Resist	−5	
$(N-1)$th	Resist	−5	−10
Nth	Co-operate	20	
$(N-1)$th	Resist	−5	15
Nth	Co-operate	20	
$(N-1)$th	Co-operate	20	40

And if he co-operates in the Nth market, then he will surely co-operate in the $(N-1)$th market. Choosing the aggressive strategy in the $(N-1)$th market and the co-operative strategy in the Nth market will give him a total payoff of only 15, instead of 40 by co-operating in both. Similarly, beginning in the $(N-2)$th—or any other, back to the first—market, we can show that if it is likely that the entrant would not 'take the warning', then the rational incumbent will choose the co-operative strategy.

The rational (and Nash equilibrium) solution, argued in this way, is for the incumbent to co-operate in all N markets. Selten called this a paradox because, he argued, in reality the incumbent firm would be much more likely to adopt an aggressive strategy from the beginning, in Market 1.

One resolution of the paradox is that, as we argued above, a dominant firm might act apparently irrationally, adopting a 'stop at nothing' approach to eliminating competition. This, in effect, uses a different paradox to explain that of Selten's chain store, namely one described by Schelling (1960, p. 22) as follows: 'that the power to constrain one's adversary depends on the power to constrain oneself irrevocably'. The more convinced the entrant is that the incumbent means to resist in all N markets if necessary, the more likely the entrant is to withdraw rather than face losses (unless the entrant, too, adopts a similarly aggressive and irrational approach in which case they both do, in fact, turn out to have been behaving irrationally). If the incumbent manages to convince the entrant that no matter what the entrant does, he or she (the incumbent) will not back off, then the entrant will withdraw, and they will both have behaved rationally. This resolution of the paradox also results from imperfect information where the entrant is uncertain about the incumbent's payoffs (Kreps and Wilson, 1982; see also Milgrom and Roberts, 1982). If the entrant believes that the incumbent's payoffs are such that the incumbent is more likely to resist repeatedly following resistance in an early game/market, then the entrant will withdraw. If the entrant believes that the incumbent is bluffing, or playing at being aggressive just to frighten him or her, but that the incumbent will behave rationally in the end, then the entrant will continue to compete. In general, where there are two firms competing in a single product market in a number of different locations, the fewer the locations that are left following earlier struggles between the firms, the less likely they are to adopt aggressive strategies.

5.1.3   Pricing and competition law in Europe

The law in Europe broadly aims to prevent firms from using strategies to reduce competition, except where these strategies improve the production or distribution of goods, or lead to technical progress. European competition law is closer to the German approach than to that of the UK (Pearson, 1994, p. 327), though in some respects, as we will show, American law is the precedent followed by Europe. All collusive agreements or practices are covered by Article 85, and situations in which a firm or firms achieve a dominant position are covered by Article 86 of the Treaty of Rome. (Both these Articles are discussed further in Chapter 7.)

Collusion

In general, collusion is prohibited by competition law in Europe. There have been a large number of cases of collusive oligopoly, successfully pursued by the Commission under Article 85. Here we discuss two such cases.

1 'The plastics cartel was possibly one of the most spectacular illicit cartels to have been blown open by the Commission ...' (Welford and Prescott, 1994, p. 92).[21] This case involved a group of 23 large companies accounting for a very high proportion of the total European supply of PVC. There had been a substantial expansion of the industry immediately prior to the oil crisis in 1973; then, costs had increased and there was a downturn in demand. The firms responded by secretly agreeing quotas for each firm, and by fixing prices across Europe which were sufficiently harmonized to discourage buyers from switching suppliers. Despite this, many firms in the industry continued to make losses, and the best of them (such as BASF of Germany) experienced stagnation in profits. Some firms contravened the quota and price agreements, but frequent meetings kept this to a minimum.

   The Commission in turn responded by monitoring the industry closely, and imposing a series of fines, totalling 120 million ECUs for the period 1984 to 1987. Finally, following raids in January 1987 by the Commission on the firms involved in the cartel, there has apparently been an end to collusion, over-capacity has been corrected by lay-offs, plant closures and general rationalization. There has also been an upturn in demand and an improvement in the industry's profitability. Arguably the collusion achieved for the industry stability during a period of slack demand, at the cost of the fines levied by the Commission.

2 In 1989 the Commission concluded an investigation of the Italian flat glass industry, finding that the firms in the industry had practised parallel pricing. The firms had offered the defence that while their prices were identical, they had arrived at their decisions independently. It had earlier been established by the European Court of Justice (ECJ), in a number of cases, that circumstantial evidence of concerted practice—such as where firms adopt the same prices—is insufficient. A key principle is that 'each economic operator must determine independently the policy which he intends to adopt on the Common Market'.[22] Where this holds, there is no collusion. In the Italian flat glass industry case, firms admitted that because of their fear of loss of market share, when price rises were being considered 'each producer [took] the precaution of checking whether the others [were] prepared to increase prices as well'.[23]

Restrictive practices other than price collusion

In the words of Article 85 'all agreements ... and concerted practices which may affect trade between Member States and which have as their object or effect the prevention, restriction or distortion of competition within the Common Market are prohibited'. This includes more than just collusion. Perhaps among the most contentious are sole agency—or 'exclusive distribution'—agreements, where a manufacturer gives to an agent the exclusive right to distribute the product in a particular country. In the Consten and Grundig (1966) case, Grundig provided Consten with the sole right to distribute Grundig products in France and, in addition, the two firms attempted to prevent parallel importing.[24] Pearson's (1994) discussion of this and related cases suggests that it is this last element, the attempt to provide 'absolute territorial protection', that contravenes European competition law. In a 1987 case, *Pronuptia de Paris* v. *Schillgalis*, where such territorial protection was not a part of the distribution agreement, the Court found that it was not restrictive.[25]

The basic economic point of Article 85 is that competition must be possible. As for collusion, so for other restrictive practices, where the actions of firms prevent fair competition by other firms, then such actions are prohibited.

Exemptions and exceptions

Exemptions and exceptions to the prohibition of restrictive practices are allowed in some cases. Pearson (1994, p. 333) outlines the two ways in which an agreement can obtain exemption from Article 85.[26] First, the firms involved can submit their agreement for individual exemption; second, an agreement can be automatically exempt if it conforms to the criteria issued by the Commission for block exemptions.

Individual exemptions can be permitted where four conditions are satisfied:

1 The *benefit* from agreement or concerted practice is greater than the losses arising from the restriction of competition. Examples include agreements that achieve standardization and simplification, improvements in distribution, and rapid diffusion of new technology.
2 The *consumer receives a fair share* of the benefit arising from the restrictive practice.
3 The agreement must contain only *indispensable restrictions*, i.e. only those absolutely necessary to achieve the benefit.
4 Competition must not be *eliminated* by the agreement. It may restrict competition, if it also provides broad benefits, including consumers in the share of those benefits, and if only indispensable restrictions are included in the agreement. But even if the other criteria are satisfied, an agreement that also eliminates—or almost eliminates—competition, will not be exempt from prohibition under Article 85.

Block exemption has been granted for six types of agreements:

1 *Specialization agreements*   This is where, for example, two firms that produce a product that has two components, agree that one will produce all the requirements of the first component for both firms, and the other firm will similarly produce the other component. The restriction must not, however, exceed 20 per cent of the market, and the total turnover of all participating firms must not exceed 500 million ECUs.
2 *Exclusive distribution agreements*   These are subject to a block exemption only where: competition is not wholly eliminated;[27] the agreement is bilateral; and the two parties are not competing manufacturers.
3 *Exclusive purchasing agreements*   Two firms agree that one (say, A) will buy a good—either for resale or as an input into its production process—only from the other firm (say B). B may sell the good to other firms in the same area. The benefits are that A has continuity of supply and B is better able to plan production. Such agreements must be bilateral to be subject to block exemption.

4 *Research and development (R&D) agreements*   A wide range of R&D agreements is subject to block exemption but they must satisfy a number of conditions, including precise ones such as that all parties to the agreement must have access to the results, and more contentious ones such as that the results 'must be decisive for the manufacture of the product or application of the process (Pearson, 1994, p. 336). The regulations under which R&D agreements are subject to block exemption are valid until 1997.

5 There are special regulations for the block exemption of motor vehicle distribution and servicing agreements.

6 *Licence agreements*   The holder of a patent may license another undertaking to make or use the patented invention, exclusively in the licensee's territory. The licensee may be prohibited by the agreement from exploiting the licensed product or process in other territories, though the licensee can, in general, respond to unsolicited orders from other territories.

The prohibition of restrictive practices and the accompanying exemptions constitute two sides to competition policy. On one hand there is a set of principles, according to which both consumers' and producers' interests are met by competition in which there are as many firms as possible, each independently making decisions about price and quantity. On the other hand, efficiency, competitiveness, and even in some cases the interests of consumers, are best achieved by restricting competition. The problems arising from this contrast are discussed in Chapter 7.

The law in relation to dominant position and predatory pricing

The legislatures and judiciaries of various countries have attempted to make laws and pass judgments as to where the activities of firms become illegal monopolization, exceeding legitimate competition. Among the earliest laws and policies of this type were those in the United States, and in particular the Sherman Antitrust Act of 1890.[28] Much has been written about what the legislators intended and what the results of the Act were.[29] Much has also been written—by economists and others—about how the courts should interpret the law, and these normative injunctions now apply not only to American law, but also, for example, to the laws promulgated in the process of economic integration in Europe.[30]

An important early application of the Sherman Act[31] led to what has become known as the *rule of reason doctrine*. According to the Supreme Court, a company or group of companies contravened the law if it (a) acquired a monopoly position and (b) did so with the intention of excluding rivals from the market. The question was how to tell whether there was such intent in the monopolization activities. This is where the rule of reason came in: 'if the acts unduly restrained competition, going beyond normal business practice, intent could be inferred' (Scherer and Ross, 1990, p. 450).

It is not always clear when a firm's activities go 'beyond normal business practice', however, and, as a result, prominent cases have been decided on split decisions by the judges, in some cases in favour and in some against the dominant firms.[32] According to Scherer and Ross (1990, p. 478), neither the Areeda–Turner marginal cost rule nor its average variable cost surrogate has 'demonstrably superior welfare effects' yet these are the rules 'adopted most often by U.S. courts'. Other rules have been proposed. We will briefly discuss four such alternatives.

First, Williamson's (1977) quantity rule forbids dominant firms from increasing output for 12 to 18 months following the entry of competitors. This prevents the dominant firm from driving price down by flooding the market. Second, Baumol's (1979) price rule permits the dominant firm to reduce price following the entry of competitors, but if the competitors then leave the market, the rule forbids post-exit real price increases on the part of the dominant firm. This would prevent below-cost pricing in the short run by ensuring that the level to which price is reduced is maintained in the long run. Third, Joskow and Klevorick (1979) propose a two-stage rule. In the initial stage an analysis of market structure and the dominant firm's market power is undertaken to determine whether predatory pricing would be a reasonable strategy.[33] Only if it can be shown that it would be, should the court proceed to the next stage, where the rule is a combination of the Areeda–Turner average cost rule and Baumol's no post-exit price increase rule. Fourth, Dodgson, Katsoulacos and Pryke (1990) apply a framework very similar to that of Joskow and Klevorick—which they call a 'Modified Rule of Reason'—in which the first step is to determine whether in the given industry, and in particular in the firm under consideration, there are specific factors that render predation a feasible and rational strategy. If there are such factors, an economic model of oligopolistic rivalry is constructed and used to verify that predation did in fact occur. Ideally this model is based on information about the nature of demand and costs prevailing in the market and is used to estimate the incumbent firm's (or firms') and new entrant's (or entrants') profits in a situation of competitive equilibrium (the so-called *anti-monde* hypothesis). The estimated normal equilibrium profits of an additional firm $\hat{a}_e$ are compared with the actual profit level of the new entrant a_a. If $\hat{a}_e$ is greater than a_a, there is a strong suggestion of predation, assuming that all other possible variables explaining the difference between the two levels of profits (e.g. price discrimination, mismanagement) have been discarded. The first stage for Joskow and Klevorick on the one hand, and Dodgson *et al.* on the other, is very similar, but while the former focus on the pricing activity of the dominant firm, the latter focus on the entrant's profit level. Joskow and Klevorick also incorporate, as does Baumol, a temporal dimension, suggesting the need for a time series of prices before predation can be identified.

Of the many alternatives, no single rule has been shown to be economically best in all cases. Martin (1994, p. 484) concludes that each rule has costs and benefits, and that which 'rule one prefers depends on the importance one attaches to different costs and benefits *and* on one's political preferences concerning the role of antitrust policy'.

In the EU, predatory pricing is condemned under Article 86 of the Treaty of Rome because it is anti-competitive (see Chapter 7). As in the Sherman Act, it is not the existence of a dominant position that contravenes competition law, but abuse of that position. In the *AKZO Chemie* v. *Commission* case (1985), AKZO appealed against the imposition by the Commission of a fine of 10 million ECUs for predatory price cutting. AKZO Chemie BV, a Dutch-based multinational, is the biggest producer in the EU of a chemical, benzoyl peroxide, which is used both as a flour additive and in the production of plastics. ECS, a firm based in the UK, sold into the flour additives market and was attempting to break into the plastics market. The Commission found that, to deter ECS, AKZO implemented a campaign of price cuts—to 'uneconomic levels'—targeted at the smaller firm's main customers in the flour additives market in Britain and Ireland; this AKZO did in spite of injunctions obtained by ECS in the English Courts against such action. AKZO's appeal before the European Court of Justice against the Commission's decision was unsuccessful. The ECJ upheld the decision of the Commission, and clarified its position in stating that a pricing strategy of a dominant firm is predatory pricing:

- if pricing is below average variable cost, or
- if the price is above average variable cost, below average total cost, and is part of a plan of the dominant company to eliminate a competitor.[34]

This ruling is close to those in the United States under the Sherman Act, in particular in its focus on the intent of the dominant firm's strategy. It also follows more recent cases in the US in the extent to which it relies on the Areeda–Turner rule.

Intent was again an important factor in the *Napier Brown* v. *British Sugar* case, in which the Commission focused on the intention of the dominant firm's strategy.[35] In this case, the Commission found against British Sugar with the argument that 'should British Sugar have maintained this margin in the long term, Napier Brown, or any company equally efficient in repackaging as BS without a self-produced source of industrial sugar, would have been obliged to leave the United Kingdom retail sugar market' (OJCE 1988 L284/41, pp. 54–5). The point was that, as in the *Alcoa* case (1945) in the United States,[36] it was found against the dominant firm because of the firm's control over the industry's main ingredient (industrial sugar).[37]

Predation is just one type of abuse of a dominant position. Before such abuse can be considered, the existence of dominance must be shown. What is meant by dominance is market power so great that the firm possessing that power can, if it so wishes, eliminate or control competitors in its industry. This gives rise to problems of definition of market, already discussed in Chapter 4 (Section 4.1.2).[38] Once the market has been defined, the Commission must decide whether the firm under consideration has a dominant position. A first indication is market share, dominance being indicated by a share in excess of 40 per cent. A large firm with as little as 20 per cent of the market can, however, have a dominant position if its competitors are highly fragmented. In some cases dominance can be inferred from behaviour as in the *Eurofix-Bauco* v. *Hilti* (1988) case, in which the Commission found that Hilti's behaviour—insisting that purchasers of Hilti nail cartridges use only Hilti nails—was evidence of its 'ability to act independently of, and without due regard to, either competitors or customers'; in other words, it was evidence of Hilti holding a dominant position.

Having defined the market and ascertained that the firm has a dominant position, the next question is whether the actions of the firm constitute abuse of that position. We have shown how predation has been identified in European competition law, but it is just one of many types of abuse of dominant position. In the next section we consider two more, price leadership and price discrimination.

Price leadership and price discrimination

There is a great deal of evidence of price leadership and price discrimination in Europe, both from empirical research published in the industrial economics literature and from cases pursued by the Commission. Among the sectors in which economists have identified price discrimination are retail banking, conveyancing, and the car industry. Heffernan (1993), analysing competition in British retail banking, suggests that if savers could switch easily between products and, perhaps, banks, they would be better off. There are, however, high information and transaction costs, which contribute to consumer inertia. The result is different groups of consumers with different elasticities of demand for loans (and different elasticities of supply of deposits) enabling the banks to practise price discrimination. In conveyancing, Stephen *et al.* (1993) show that deregulation in England and Wales was responded to differently by different firms, increasing the extent of price discrimination.

The car industry has been the subject of particular attention. Kirman and Schueller (1990) show how the segregation of markets through price leadership in the European car industry tends to perpetuate itself. Specifying a theoretical model in which they assume, among other things, that all (but one) of the markets are characterized by a Stackelberg equilibrium, the authors reach the following conclusions:

1 In markets where the dominant producer has high costs, the prices of all competing products will be higher.
2 In markets where the tax rate is high, pre-tax prices will be lower.
3 In the market where there is no dominant individual producer prices will be lowest.

In a comparison of these theoretical results with the empirical evidence, Kirman and Schueller conclude that there *is* price leadership, usually with the domestic manufacturer the leader in its home market, and that there *is* price discrimination, there being significant differences in the pre-tax prices of cars in the different European markets.

In his description of pricing behaviour in the European car industry, Rhys (1993) suggests four factors that make price discrimination likely. First, there are different levels of sales tax on cars, from as low as 15 per cent in Germany to as high as 197 per cent in Denmark; second, there are price controls in some countries (Belgium); third, because of a combination of product differentiation and consumer preferences manufacturers sell cars with slightly different specifications into the different EU markets; and fourth, the manufacturers and distributors have different discount schemes in different markets. These factors make it difficult for consumers to know whether, and to what extent, the prices paid to the manufacturers vary between markets. It is this ignorance on the part of the consumers (or information asymmetry between sellers and buyers), together with the selective distribution system that the car firms are permitted to adopt, that enables these firms to separate markets. According to Rhys (1993), the selection of distributors in different countries enables 'the car-makers [to] determine who can sell their cars, thereby restricting entry to the new car retail sector. This prevents independent retailers buying cars in a cheap market and selling them in a dear one, undercutting the price in the official network.'[39]

There is an increasing awareness of price discrimination in the car industry, and it has received the attention of the Commission. The Commission is particularly sensitive to geographical price discrimination because this type of price discrimination involves the partitioning by firms of the EU market along geographical boundaries, which contravenes the fundamental principles of European integration and the Single European Market.

In relation to the car industry, the Commission has examined, among other things, the actions of the manufacturers and 'official' distributors (i.e. those appointed by the manufacturers) to prevent parallel imports. As between the Continent on the one hand, and Britain and Ireland on the other, discrimination was maintained by such devices as delivery of right-hand drive vehicles only in bulk, refusing warranty services unless the car was bought from the distributor or one of its 'official' dealers, and withdrawing credit and discount facilities from dealers who imported directly. 'Such practices are now illegal, as a result of pressure from the Commission and the verdict of the Court' (de Jong, 1993, p. 408). Price discrimination will, however, probably continue to be practised to some extent in this industry as long as the selective distribution system remains.[40]

The Chiquita case (1976) is another example of geographic price discrimination. United Brands, a banana producer, was selling its produce under the brand name Chiquita to distributors/ripeners at different prices in various member states. The lowest prices were charged in Ireland, while the highest prices were charged on bananas destined for the West German market. The differences in price could not be explained by transport costs, since it actually costs more to transport goods to the Irish market than to any other member state. The Commission argued that:

differences in transport costs, taxes and duties or marketing conditions might justify different levels in price or resale at the retail level. These differences can, however, never justify objectively UBC's different prices to its distributors/ripeners for equivalent transactions at Bremerhaven and Rotterdam, and still less so given that the quantities of bananas sold to each such distributor/ripener are approximately the same. (OJCE 1976 L95/1 p. 15.)[41]

The judgment could be criticized in that it was inducing United Brands to charge a uniform price higher than that charged in its low-price markets, in order to avoid losses in Germany, leading to detrimental effects for the Irish consumer. The welfare effects of price discrimination are in fact ambiguous, and therefore so are the welfare effects of the removal of price discrimination. This has been shown by Armstrong and Vickers (1993), both for situations in which the dominant firm is a pure monopoly and where the incumbent firm faces competition as a result of regulation to remove the discrimination. If a result of the introduction of uniform pricing is that the previously lower-priced markets are no longer supplied, then it can be shown (see Layson, 1994) that price discrimination is preferable from a welfare point of view. In general, however, unless regulation to prevent price discrimination results in a substantial reduction in output, it will be preferable to price discrimination (Schmalensee, 1981).

Many cases of price discrimination involve other types of anti-competitive behaviour as well. A recent example of this was brought to light following the Commission's examination of the ice cream market in Ireland. Unilever's Irish ice cream subsidiary, HB, provides retailers with freezers, but insists that these hold only HB products. The prices paid for HB products by retailers that accepted this arrangement were the same as the prices paid by retailers that did not agree to the condition (and therefore did not have HB freezers). Other ice cream companies—including the Mars subsidiary, Master Foods (Ireland)—issued a formal complaint to the Commission. The Commission upheld the objection on two grounds. First, 'exclusivity'—the preclusion of non-HB ice creams from HB freezers—and second, 'inclusive pricing'—in effect price discrimination in favour of those retailers who accept the freezers. If both sets of retailers nominally pay the same price for the ice creams, but one set also gets free freezers, then those who have to pay for their own freezers are, in effect, paying more for ice creams.

In upholding the objection, the Commission left the door open to HB to respond to the criticisms. It was reported in March 1995 that HB had agreed to alter its distribution system as follows:

1 By giving rebates to retailers who do not use HB freezers who sell a reasonable amount of HB products.
2 Introducing similar non-discriminatory pricing schemes in all other EU countries during 1995.
3 Selling freezers to the retailers who accepted them, at the wholesale price.
4 In future, giving retailers the option of taking freezers under hire purchase terms, which would include the condition that exclusivity be limited to the five-year purchase period.

These changes were sufficient, in the view of the Commission, to justify exemption from 'EU rules barring anti-competitive practices', but a final decision awaited responses from the other parties involved. According to Mr Karel Van Miert, Competition Commissioner, the new pricing arrangements will result 'not only in the redressing of the current discrimination against retailers offering Unilever products from their own cabinets but will also reduce the incentive for retailers to take or retain Unilever-supplied cabinets' (McGrath, 1995).

Pricing is, in practice, clearly a complex aspect of an overall strategic approach to marketing products. The resultant price per unit of the product may well, as would be expected from neoclassical theory, involve less profit the more intensive the competition, but the evidence suggests that pricing—among other strategies—can actually be used to ameliorate competition. We turn next to advertising and product differentiation.

5.1.4   Product differentiation and advertising

The way a firm's products are priced is often part of a broader strategy aimed at distinguishing that firm's products from those of its competitors. The non-price parts of the strategy are our concern in this section. A list of all such non-price factors would be extensive, including, for example, physical characteristics like colour, size, quality and packaging, and aspects of the services provided with the product such as delivery time and after sales service. One type of non-price strategy is to differentiate any of these for products that are in other respects identical. In addition, firms may make an effort to differentiate their product in some more fundamental way. For example, a breakfast cereal firm could develop a new product, say oat flakes, as an alternative to corn flakes. All R&D expenditure on product innovation is, in this sense, an attempt to differentiate products. Even R&D on process innovation can contribute to differentiation by, for example, improving the quality or reliability of the product.[42]

In the perfect competition model, the product is homogeneous; each firm sells a product identical to that sold by the other firms. This identity goes all the way through, from production to sale. There is no incentive for any individual firm to expend special effort in increasing sales, because inherent in the model is the assumption that each firm can sell as much as it wants without such extra effort. Only in imperfectly competitive models can firms rationally implement strategies to increase sales. In both monopolistic competition and oligopoly, for example, a firm often develops strategies to avoid competition, making its product (or products) special to more and more consumers, so that its sales increase. These strategies can involve both changes in the product, and advertising to change the public's perception of the product. Other firms then have the choice of making their products as similar as possible, so that they gain the advantage of the efforts of the first firm to increase sales, or of implementing their own strategies to make their product (or products) special to consumers. The former—similar or identical product—strategy is more likely to lead to price competition. Among the interesting questions in this part of industrial organization theory, is under what circumstances product differentiation (and advertising) strategies will be adopted.

Product differentiation

Product differentiation, according to Bain, 'refers to the extent to which buyers differentiate, distinguish, or have specific preferences among the competing outputs of the various sellers' (1968, p. 223). This is consistent with Chamberlin's (1933) view that much of product differentiation is *perceived* rather than *real*. Following a discussion of (a) the differences between real and perceived differentiation, this section will next examine (b) horizontal and vertical differentiation, (c) measures of differentiation and (d) product differentiation in the EU.

Real and perceived differentiation   Real differences include those in quality, as expressed in reliability and/or performance. An example of this is where one make of car (or computer) is less likely to break down, and/or is faster than another, even if it is identical in other respects. In services associated with the product, real differences include those in delivery time, in after sales service and in proximity/accessibility of the supplier or distributor to the end customer.

Perceived product differentiation is less easy to specify,[43] since it refers to the subjective appreciation of a product: two products A and B may perform in an identical way, and yet consumers may perceive a difference between them because of the presence of other factors, such as colour, packaging and design. For example, certain characteristics of a product may establish a link in the mind of the consumer between the product itself and some other, well-known, prestigious brand. Marketing theorists have shown that even apparently 'meaningless' differentiation can be used as a brand strategy, producing under certain conditions a separate brand identity which consumers will see as being relevantly and valuably different from competing brands (Carpenter, Glazer and Nakamoto, 1994). Distribution can also be used to generate perceived differences, such as where a manufacturer of a mediocre product attempts to impress the consumer by distributing the product through prestigious retail outlets. This last example emphasizes the analytical problem in distinguishing between real and perceived differences. A 'prestigious retail outlet' may, in fact, be a real difference, because it provides better advice and other services related to the sale of the product.[44]

Horizontal and vertical differentiation   For analytical purposes, product differentiation is usually divided into these two types. Horizontal differentiation, based on perceived differences, is where a product is assumed to have a number of key characteristics in relation to which consumers' tastes and preferences vary.[45] The colour, style and design characteristics of men's shoes are an example. Shoes by different manufacturers, at similar prices, with different mixes of these characteristics are said to be horizontally differentiated. Within this product range, an increase in the number of products offered will increase the likelihood that any individual consumer will find the pair of shoes that exactly fits his preferences.

Vertical differentiation is based on real differences; it refers to quality differences between brands, in relation to which all consumers agree. Vertically differentiated shoes would be ranked, in order of quality, in the same way by all buyers of shoes. This might refer, for example, to comfort and durability. If the only differentiation was vertical, then lower quality products would only sell if they were priced less than higher quality products. Some men would be willing to pay more for higher quality shoes, others would not, but all would agree with the ranking, both of brands of shoes and their associated prices.

The origins of the *theoretical work on horizontal differentiation* lie in Hotelling's (1929) duopoly model in which the firms produced identical goods, and consumers were assumed to be uniformly distributed along a street.[46] Hotelling argued that both firms would choose the mid-point as the location of their sales outlet. This is called the 'principle of minimum product differentiation'.[47] D'Asprement, Gabszewicz and Thisse (1979), using a slightly different model and correcting a mathematical error in Hotelling's model, came to the opposite conclusion, namely that each firm would choose a location as far away from the other as possible: 'maximum product differentiation'. Most recently, Böckem (1994), with a slight adjustment in turn to the d'Asprement *et al.* model, has arrived at an intermediate conclusion: that the two firms may adopt neither minimum nor maximum product differentiation. All three models assume simultaneous choice of locations and Bertrand competition. Böckem's (1994) addition is to generalize the earlier models by allowing consumers the option of not buying the goods of either of the two firms. The result is a trade-off for firms between avoiding price competition and 'bringing the product closer to consumers' locations'. In terms of product differentiation, the more that firms wish to avoid price competition the more they will differentiate their products. The degree of product differentiation, *ceteris paribus*, will depend on assumptions about how price is determined.

Recent *theoretical work on vertical differentiation* has focused on the relationship between differentiation and industrial concentration. Shaked and Sutton (1987) have shown that the nature of product differentiation, and the way in which quality is improved, are important factors in market structure. Where there is only horizontal differentiation, an increase in market size is likely to attract new entrants, as long as there are no significant barriers to entry. On the other hand, if the main costs of improving products are fixed costs,[48] and if consumer preferences are such that at least some buyers will be willing to pay more than the increase in variable costs for an improvement in the product, then an increase in the size of the market will not—as might otherwise be expected—mean more firms and lower levels of concentration. Firms will compete by incurring higher fixed costs, and improving their products; overall there will be higher fixed costs in the industry, and improved products, but no increase in the number of firms, and no decline in the level of concentration. The high fixed costs of improvement are not necessarily the cause of high levels of concentration. It is the nature of competition in the industry, and in particular the strategic choices of the firms—to compete via vertical differentiation—that are the main factors in determining both high fixed costs and high levels of concentration.

Measures of differentiation   In practice, products are often both horizontally and vertically differentiated. Firms will adopt mixed strategies of quality and other differences, charging higher prices for both. *Measures of product differentiation* do not, therefore, distinguish between horizontal and vertical differentiation. One such measure, already defined at the beginning of Chapter 4, is CED, *cross elasticity of demand*. This measures the responsiveness of the quantity demanded of a product to changes in the price of another product. The greater (smaller) the difference between the products the lower (higher) the value of CED.

Another measure, introduced in Chapter 4 as a measure of concentration, is the *entropy index*. The entropy-based measure of the degree of product differentiation was proposed by Bernhardt and Mackenzie (1968). It is based on the randomness of consumers' choice of retail outlet. At maximum entropy ($E = 1$), customers always buy certain products from the same store. There is very high differentiation. At minimum entropy ($E = 0$), customers distribute their purchases of those products evenly among all stores. There is homogeneity.

Thirdly, because of the close link between advertising and product specification/differentiation, the advertising-to-sales ratio can also provide an indication of the degree of differentiation.[49] It is reasonable to expect that the more that is spent by a firm on advertising, the more its product will be differentiated—at least in terms of consumers' perceptions—from the products of the firm's competitors.

Product differentiation and the EU   What are the implications of product differentiation for European integration, and vice versa? Product differentiation has long been accepted by industrial economists as having a role in the strategies of firms to improve the competitiveness of their products. For many economists writing on *international trade*, this eventually translated into the fact that product differentiation itself—even in the absence of comparative advantage—could cause trade.[50] However, the theory of comparative advantage, in particular in its modern guise as the Heckscher–Ohlin–Samuelson theory, remained dominant until the 1980s. According to this theory, countries' factor endowments are main determinants of what goods countries will export or import. The work of Krugman (1980, 1987a) has been important in developing international trade theory beyond these foundations. In his examination of the implications of this work for industrial economics (1989) he shows that economies of scale and product differentiation—and imperfect competition in general—must be added to comparative advantage as factors in determining what goods countries will trade.

At a simple level, empirical evidence for these new theories lay in the growth among EU member countries of trade in similar products. Comparative advantage theory led economists to expect that international trade within a barrier-free Europe would be increasingly inter-industry, but there was a great deal of evidence of intra-industry trade. Among other factors, product differentiation led to exports and imports of similar goods. From the perspective of firms, there were declines in shares of local markets, and increases in shares of foreign markets; from the perspective of consumers, there was an increase in the variety of goods available.[51]

From the perspective of Europe as a whole, it is arguable that a strong historical tradition of product differentiation—particularly in high quality products—has constituted a comparative advantage *vis-à-vis* other major trading blocs. This tradition led to European leadership in, for example, luxury goods industries where product differentiation is high. Closely associated with this, brand awareness became highly developed in Europe. High quality products and high income markets reinforce one another. French luxury goods industries, for example (including fashion clothing and footwear, leather wear, and food and drink), export nearly three-quarters of their output, mainly to high income countries (Japan, USA, and other European countries). Even in markets like Japan, in which indigenous products have very high market shares, European branded goods in general are considered to be 'sophisticated', 'chic' and to express a 'good sense of design'. This applies not only to such hand-crafted luxury goods as clothing, but also to complicated industrial products like Mercedes-Benz cars.[52]

The completion of the Single Market in Europe raises a number of difficulties for firms adopting product differentiation strategies:

1 Increasing homogenization of markets suggests the need for increasing scales of production to compete in these markets; but in the different member countries—and even in some regions within member countries—there are continuing cultural and linguistic differences that call for strategies to differentiate products to match the preferences of local consumers. Should firms develop Euro-brands, and/or should they modify generic brands to suit local differences in tastes? The optimum strategy depends on what Kay (1990a) calls the strategic market.[53] Comparing, say, a hairdresser with a precision tool manufacturer, it is clear that the market for the former will be a local one, while that for the latter will be a much wider one. The size of the industry depends on economies of scale and scope; the size of the market on such factors as whether it is a consumer or producer good, and the degree of homogeneity of tastes of consumers. A firm already producing more than enough for its share of a local market, and with significant economies of scale, will attempt to identify products that can be mass marketed under Euro-brands; if, instead, it has significant economies of scope, it may attempt to identify a range of differentiated products for local markets.

2 Even where all other factors suggest the distribution of a product throughout Europe, the plurality of languages can cause problems. If companies have to print the majority of EU languages on the package, the wording related to the specifications of the product can become confusing, the amount of text can be excessive and the design of the package distorted. It has been suggested that to overcome the language barrier, firms operating on the European market should use strong visual design elements that do not rely on languages, in order to present a single visual identity across Europe (Lynch, 1990).

3 A successful product differentiation strategy in Europe can be hampered by the remaining non-tariff barriers (NTBs). For example, exchange rate movements and different VAT rates create price distortions in the EU, which can distort the 'value for money' element that would otherwise contribute to the differentiation of certain products.

4 Pan-European product differentiation strategies involve greater physical distances in Europe, and hence higher costs. Since American firms have historically been accustomed to the long distances between different markets, they have had time to consolidate this comparative advantage over their EU counterparts.

For this reason, the determination of the optimal distribution channel has been of particular concern to EU firms eager to benefit from the completion of the Single Market. A firm based for example in Hamburg has to determine the appropriate type of sales back-up that can be provided in the event of its entry into the Spanish market. (Should it use an independent local agent? Can it rely on a large, well-established distributor, still under-represented in Spain? Should it set up its own sales network?) In general, under what circumstances will a firm wish to distribute its product through its own retail outlet (downstream vertical integration)?[54]

There may be a relationship between product differentiation and the way in which firms choose to distribute their products. According to Welford and Prescott (1994, p. 178), in an industry in which, because of limited scope for product differentiation, there is mainly price competition, firms will produce (or license other firms to produce) their product in final markets rather than using wide distribution networks. This is because, under such circumstances, 'there is little scope to support transportation costs across wide distances'. It follows that the less differentiated a product is, the more likely it is to be produced in final markets, rather than be exported to, and distributed by agents in, those markets. This, however, contrasts with the view of Anderson and Coughlan (1987) that if non-differentiated products 'are sold through middlemen, ... the manufacturer's ability to respond to price changes (wage price wars) is inhibited, thereby protecting the manufacturer's product'; the greater the extent to which competition is through product differentiation, the more likely it is that the product will be sold by the manufacturer itself,[55] rather than be exported to and sold by agents in, foreign markets.

The historical evidence provides more support for Anderson and Coughlan than for Welford and Prescott. As Chandler (1990, p. 263) has shown, during the second half of the nineteenth century, when transport systems improved rapidly, firms like the chocolate manufacturer, Cadbury Brothers, adopted improved, high volume production processes to take advantage of the expanding markets. They began to brand their products and advertise nationally—their main competitors in Britain were Fry and Rowntree—and 'took over the marketing functions that, until then, had been handled by intermediaries'. Thus the increasing importance of differentiation was associated with greater control by the manufacturer over distribution.

In addition, there is anecdotal evidence from some highly product differentiated markets like those for fashion items. Here retail specialization through the segmentation of markets into specific niches has been adopted by a number of European firms in recent years (Body Shop from the UK, Bally from Switzerland).

This conclusion is far from final, however. It may be that in different industries, with greater economies of scale relative to economies of scope, firms will be less likely to take control of downstream distribution. This would depend on the nature of the economies of scope; as Porter (1991) has argued, 'it would be useful to learn whether economies of scope result from the production technology, or whether economies of scope in distribution and marketing are more important empirically'.

Advertising

It is important at the outset of the discussion on advertising to note that there is no necessary relationship between the promotion of a product and its social desirability or usefulness. Products are advertised because the owners of firms manufacturing those products wish to sell (more of) them. The normative question of the desirability of advertising is more complicated than the question of the desirability of the products themselves. Most people might agree that cigarettes are harmful, and that means should be found to reduce their consumption,[56] but there could still be an argument that among those continuing to smoke, competitive advertising by different cigarette manufacturers performs a useful function. It might inform smokers of changes in price and innovative new products that reduce health risk. If advertising achieves these ends without inducing non-smokers to start smoking, then few would argue against such advertising. On the other hand, milk is generally accepted as healthy. This does not necessarily mean that people's welfare is enhanced by the advertising of milk. It is at least conceivable that advertising results in people buying (and consuming) more milk than is optimal given their incomes and nutritional needs.

A simple neoclassical approach to advertising   Adopting neoclassical conventions, from the firm's point of view advertising might be considered as just another part of the costs of getting the product from raw material, via manufacturing, distribution and sale, to the consumer. Whether to advertise, and how much to advertise, can then be answered by the question: is the marginal cost of advertising covered by the marginal revenue from the additional sales generated by the advertising? From the consumer's point of view, advertising does not change significantly the neoclassical condition for optimization: that the marginal utility derived from the consumption of the good be equal to the price paid for the last unit. If advertising increases that marginal utility, then the producer will be able to charge a higher price, and the consumer will be willing to pay that higher price because of the additional satisfaction he or she gets as a result of the advertising.[57] From this perspective a producer may increase profits, and consumers may or may not increase consumer surplus, depending on the impact of the advertising on the demand curve.

This is most simply represented in the case of monopoly. Figure 5.7 shows that if the firm advertises, the marginal cost curve will shift from MC_1 to MC_2; advertising also shifts the demand curve to the right, from D_1 to D_2. Both the firm's revenue and its costs will increase, but its revenue by more than its costs. If not, then the firm will not advertise. Consumer surplus—the area of the triangle below the demand curve, above price—is also increased. To reduce consumer surplus, advertising would also have to significantly reduce the elasticity of demand.

The usual way of presenting the neoclassical perspective on advertising is with the Dorfman–Steiner (1954) condition. According to this condition, *the optimal level of advertising* for a profit-maximizing firm, is where the advertising to sales ratio is equal to the price cost margin multiplied by the advertising elasticity of demand.

$$\frac{p^A A}{PQ} = \frac{P - c}{P} E_{QA} \qquad (5.1)$$

where: E_{QA} is the advertising elasticity of demand, p^A is the per unit price of advertising, P is the per unit price of the advertised product, and c is its average cost.

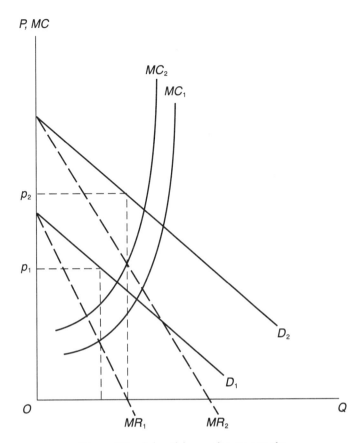

Figure 5.7   Advertising under monopoly

The more sensitive the quantity demanded is to advertising, and/or the more firms can make on the sale of the marginal unit, the higher the level of advertising.

The relationship also suggests that any of the factors that affect the market structure—such as product differentiation and barriers to entry—will affect advertising if, and to the extent that, they have an impact on the advertising elasticity of demand. As will be shown below, advertising intensity is not only a result but also a cause of market structure. The effects of advertising on market structure and welfare must also be appraised.

Recent work on advertising, often using game theoretic techniques, builds on two separate perspectives: one, originating from Stigler (1961), focuses on advertising as information; the second, at the root of which is the work of Bain (1958), sees advertising primarily as persuasion.

Advertising as information   Stigler (1961) showed that if consumers lack information about the prices charged by different sellers of a product, then the sellers will, in general, be able to charge higher prices than if the consumers had perfect information. Moreover, the more a consumer intends to spend on the product, the more he or she will be willing to spend on the search for the lowest price. The more consumers in general spend on their search, the less will the prices vary. From this analysis, Stigler concluded that advertising of prices by competitors provides the information necessary for consumers to decide on which outlet to choose. Advertising thereby reduces search costs. By improving consumers' information, advertising will also reduce the range of prices. If we see search costs as part of the costs of the transaction, then advertising reduces transaction costs.

Nelson (1974) also considered advertising as a means of providing information, but rather than price information, he emphasized advertising as a signal that the product exists and that the advertiser's confidence in the product is such that he is willing to spend money on it. If it is impossible to know in advance how good the product is (i.e. if it is an *experience good*) then consumers must buy it and try it. The more satisfied the consumers are, and the more they repeat their purchase, the higher the stream of profits the firm will make. The more confident the firm is that there will be repeat purchases, the more it will be willing to spend on advertising. From this Nelson concluded that high expenditure on advertising is in fact a signal of high quality of the product.

Building on Nelson's work, Bagwell and Ramey (1994) argue—for retail advertisers—that even where advertising is ostensibly uninformative, if it directs consumers towards the firms that offer the best deals it will achieve *co-ordination economies*. This is where increased expenditure on advertising reduces selling costs, results in an expansion of the product line and an expansion in sales per customer. The firms offering the best deals will gain, there will be higher levels of concentration, and consumers will also gain because of greater variety and lower prices.

It might reasonably be argued, in relation to both Nelson's and Bagwell and Ramey's models, that once it becomes established that high expenditure on advertising is a signal of high quality, some firms will raise advertising to high levels despite the low quality of their products. They will expect thereby to attract a large number of buyers expecting high quality products (or the best retail deals). Indeed Hertzendorf (1993), also using a signalling model, concludes that when the 'advertising channel is noisy' the low-quality firm is able 'to take advantage of consumer ignorance by partially mimicking the strategy of the high-quality firm'.

The economic condition for firms selling low quality products to be able to adopt this approach profitably is that the extra returns from sales to first-time buyers be greater than the extra costs of advertising, which is close to the original neoclassical condition introduced above.

Advertising as persuasion   This approach sees advertising as a means of establishing brand loyalty, as a result of which there will be barriers to entry. Assume for example that a contact lens manufacturer develops a new type of lens. It may be difficult to patent because it is so easily copied. The firm may therefore decide to advertise heavily, attempting to establish in the minds of consumers that its brand of the new contact lens, as the first one, is the best, most reliable, etc. If this advertising campaign is successful, it will make entry by new firms into the market difficult. By persuading the consumers (i.e. altering what would otherwise be their preferences), the firm increases its market power. Again advertising leads to higher levels of concentration, but in this view it does not lead to gain for the consumer. In the tradition of Bain, the early work on advertising as a means of creating barriers to entry was reviewed by Comanor and Wilson (1979), who were themselves seminal contributors to the empirical literature in this field (Comanor and Wilson, 1967).

Among the main scholars laying down markers on the key questions in this area was Kaldor (1950). He was one of the first to see in advertising a means of increasing entry barriers through the building up of *consumer loyalty* or *inertia*[58] for a particular product. In his own words:

Advertising makes the public 'brand conscious'; it is not so much a question of making the consumer buy things he would not have bought otherwise; but of crystallizing his routine habits, or making him conscious that keeping to a certain routine in consumption means not only buying the same commodities in a vague sort of way, but sticking to the same brand.

Because of unconscious 'routine buying' or a deliberate fervour to stick to a product on the part of consumers, potential new firms are barred by the practice of 'packing the product space'; a proliferation of differentiated (branded) items makes no niches available for new firms who want to gain a foothold in that market.[59]

Using a variety of techniques, a number of economists have, since Kaldor, and Comanor and Wilson, provided arguments critical of advertising. Dixit and Norman (1978) used conventional welfare-theoretic methods to study advertising that leads to changes in consumer tastes. Their conclusion was that it pays firms to advertise to a level which is socially excessive, and that this is true for monopoly, oligopoly and monopolistic competition.

Shapiro (1980) criticized this result on the grounds that the analysis assumed that pre-advertising consumption is distributed efficiently according to post-advertising tastes. If this is not the case—and Shapiro argued that it was generally not—then there were additional gains to advertising not accounted for by Dixit and Norman's approach.

Using an approach not susceptible to Shapiro's criticisms, Kotowitz and Mathewson (1979)—assuming that the consumer has imperfect information—also conclude that advertising, at least in the short run, can be profitable for the seller, but misleading to the consumer. Taking the limitations of consumers even further, Nagler (1993) develops a model of advertising and consumer reactions in which consumers exhibit a form of bounded rationality. On the basis of a set of reasonable assumptions he shows that there will be firms that have an incentive to advertise deceptively, causing a net welfare loss to society in the absence of corrective policy. This is further substantiated by Ordonez de Haro (1993), who uses a horizontal differentiation model to consider the strategic effects of persuasive advertising, and concludes that 'even under "benevolent" interpretation of persuasive advertising, a threatened monopolist, in order to deter the entry of potential competitors, will undertake too much advertising relative to a social planner'.[60]

It would appear that advertising—whether as provision of information or means of persuasion—can, under certain conditions, reduce consumer welfare. It should also be emphasized that it is possible under different conditions that advertising, even if intended to persuade, does not reduce consumer welfare. It may, for example, fail to raise barriers to entry. Among the key factors in determining the results of advertising are how informed the consumers are—and assuming there are asymmetries, how rapidly they learn—and how easy it is to imitate the advertiser's product. Mizuno and Odagiri (1990) show that the more rapidly consumers learn, the less likely they are to be misled by advertising; and the greater the ease with which the product can be imitated, the less able will the seller be to mislead the consumer.

Advertising, then, informs and persuades; it may also change the structure of the industry if, for example, it enables one firm to obtain a dominant share of the market. How is advertising measured? How important is it in the EU? How might firms choose an advertising strategy? What are the effects of advertising? It is to such questions that we now turn.

Measures of advertising intensity   There are broadly two different ways of measuring the advertising intensity of firms. The most common is the *advertising to sales ratio*. This ratio, A/S, varies with the type of industry. Luxury goods industries tend to spend more than others, for example. (The perfume industry spends as much as 15 per cent of turnover on advertising.) Some toiletries and food products are also heavily advertised.

TABLE 5.2   Total advertising spending in million ECUs in selected economic areas (*Source*: Waterson, 1992)

	1981	*1990*
EC-11 (1)	17,105.2	44,026.3
of which:		
Germany	4,987.9	10,009.0
UK	4,548.4	9,162.8
France	2,516.6	7,342.9
Spain	1,052.8	6,490.2
EFTA (2)	2,789.1	6,148.7
USA	33,634.0	59,740.1
Japan	7,610.7	20,521.0
TOTAL	61,139.0	130,436.1

(1) Luxemburg excluded.
(2) Only Austria, Finland, Norway, Sweden and Switzerland are recorded here.

As Cowling (1976) has noted, in spite of its popularity this indicator is less appropriate the more diverse in size is the cross-section of industries or firms covered. The EU car industry has a low A/S (less than 1 per cent), compared with 15 per cent for the perfume industry, but the number of car advertisements is indubitably greater than the number of perfume advertisements. Being much bigger than the perfume industry, the car industry devotes a far larger budget (in absolute terms) to advertising than the perfume industry does. Thus A/S ratios should be used carefully and should be weighted in order to eliminate the size effect.

A *second* way of measuring advertising intensity is by comparing advertising spend in different countries, and over time.

In 1990, total advertising spending in the three major economic blocs (EC + EFTA, USA and Japan) was over 130 billion ECUs (Table 5.2). The share of the USA in total advertising expenditures was still the highest in 1990, at 46 per cent. However, the share of the EC-11, an economic area with a comparable size and economic development, had increased sharply over the previous ten years. Advertising spending in the EC represented in 1990 one-third of the total, against less than 28 per cent in 1981. The growth rates in advertising spending were particularly high in the Mediterranean countries of the EC, namely: Portugal (+592%), Spain (+387%), Italy (+342%) and Greece (+315%). The lower growth rate of Ireland (+193%), which was less than that of France, suggests that the relationship between advertising expenditure and level of economic development is not straightforward. We elaborate on this point with Table 5.3.

While Greece, Portugal and Ireland, with lower GDPs per capita than the rest of the EU, had relatively low advertising per capita, there is not in all cases a clear, direct relationship between GDP per capita and advertising per capita. Spain, with a GDP per capita very close to that of Ireland, for example, had an advertising expenditure per capita higher than that of Japan and France, and the ratio for Italy is lower than that of Ireland. A possible explanation for this paradox is the control (restrictions) exercised by various governments on advertising. For example, the total ban on alcohol advertising on French television could partly explain the relatively low ratio for this country. On the other hand, there has been a relatively liberal attitude to advertising in post-Franco Spain.

Controls have been operated with different degrees of strictness according to the medium used. The control of advertisements on TV is more stringent in the Scandinavian countries

TABLE 5.3   **Total advertising spending in local currency as a percentage of GDP, and in ECUs per capita (1990)** (*Source*: Waterson, 1992)

		Advertising spending as % of GDP	Advertising spending per capita
EC-11			
	Belgium	0.61	85.2
	Denmark	1.57	295.1
	France	0.76	130.1
	Germany	0.83	158.7
	Greece	0.91	49.2
	Ireland	0.99	97.6
	Italy	0.61	92.4
	The Netherlands	0.94	140.9
	Portugal	0.81	37.2
	Spain	1.88	166.9
	UK	1.16	159.6
EFTA-5			
	Austria	0.91	152.0
	Finland	1.01	212.6
	Norway	0.69	146.3
	Sweden	0.85	173.0
	Switzerland	1.03	269.4
USA		1.39	237.6
Japan		0.88	166.1

(Sweden, Norway, Denmark, Finland), in The Netherlands and in Switzerland than in Italy, USA, Japan or the UK (Table 5.4). Table 5.4 highlights a clear split: with the exception of Germany, in the wealthiest European countries the press tends to be more used as an advertising medium, whereas in the relatively poorer European economies advertisements through the audio-visual mediums (TV and radio) have a greater share. Also, the importance of the public transport system in large urban areas (Tokyo, Brussels, Paris) explains the relatively high shares of advertising through this medium for the corresponding countries.

It should be pointed out that the medium used depends on the type of product: fast moving consumer goods would tend to be advertised on TV and radio, whereas consumer durables (computers, cars) and to an even greater extent capital goods (industrial machinery, equipment) would mostly be advertised in specialized magazines, at fairs, but only marginally on TV and radio.

Finally, the last challenge facing EU firms pursuing a strategy of pan-European differentiation emanates from another aspect of the Completion of the Internal Market: the EU legislation affecting advertising.

EU legislation affecting advertising   The Cross-frontier Broadcasting Directive (proposed under Article 100(A)), adopted on 3 October 1989, restricts advertising in the following areas:

- It bans tobacco advertising: the content of advertisements in the press/magazines would be restricted, and a list of health warnings would be used.
- It bans prescription pharmaceutical advertising, and calls for the inclusion of detailed label information in advertising.
- It introduces guidelines on alcohol advertising.

TABLE 5.4   Distribution of advertising expenditures by medium and country (in %, 1990)*
(*Source*: Authors' calculations based on Waterson, 1992)

	Newspapers	*Magazines*	*TV*	*Radio*	*Cinema*	*Outdoor/transport*
EC-11						
Belgium	37	25	23.5	0.8	1.4	12.3
Denmark	73	19.1	5.3	0.9	0.5	1.2
France	28.6	27.5	24.8	6.6	0.8	11.7
Germany	46	27.9	15.8	5.0	1.2	3.9
Greece	26	28.2	35.3	5.7	na	4.8
Ireland	63.7	5.5	19.6	6.2	na	5.0
Italy	27.8	24	43.1	1.4	na	3.6
The Netherlands	50.3	27.8	8.9	2.2	0.3	10.4
Portugal	25.1	21.7	37.1	6.7	na	9.4
Spain	47.9	16	23.0	8.5	0.6	3.9
UK	44.1	19.3	30.5	2.2	0.5	3.4
EFTA-5						
Austria	51.6	18.0	17.7	8.0	0.4	4.3
Finland	69.9	10.4	13.2	3.9	0	2.6
Norway	77.2	15.7	2.5	1.0	1.2	2.2
Sweden	79.0	15.0	1.4	na	0.7	3.8
Switzerland	61.1	16.8	6.7	1.7	0.9	12.7
SA	41.4	13.4	33.3	10.7	na	1.2
Japan	34.0	9.2	36.7	5.6	na	14.5

* The totals by line may not amount to 100 due to roundings.

- It introduces guidelines on advertising to children.
- It introduces rules for sponsorship.

This Directive also introduces a minimum quota for programmes of European origin content. Finally, the Misleading Advertising Directive aims at controlling misleading advertising (*International Journal of Advertising*, 1991, **10**, 79–87).

These restrictions clearly impinge on the plans of the pharmaceutical, drink/tobacco and toy firms.

5.1.5   Corporate integration

The transformation of a combination of inputs into a marketable output involves several stages: a product moves along the transformation line from the conception and design stage, through the production stage to the distribution stage.

The production process itself comprises many different steps, that range in the case of a car, for example, from the cutting of metals, stamping of body parts (and the production of machine tools required for these tasks) to the various operations performed at the finishing stage (painting and polishing) (Fig. 5.8). These different functions can either be performed by a single firm, or by several separate specialized firms, each one at a different stage of the transformation process. If the former, then the firm can be viewed as a *vertically integrated*

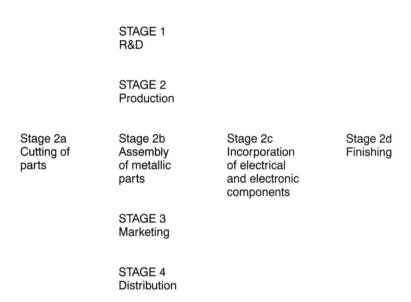

Figure 5.8   Stages in the product transformation process in the car industry

organization. Of particular interest is the dynamic process of integration; this is the actions that the firm undertakes, including changes in the organizational characteristics of production, in order to incorporate different parts of product transformation into the firm. It is appropriate to differentiate between *corporate integration* in which different stages are incorporated into a single firm, and *industrial integration* in which the different stages are undertaken by separate firms in a particular industry in a particular region or country.[61]

There are three types of corporate integration:

1 Horizontal integration is the combination, by acquisition or merger, of two or more distinct firms that lie at the same stage of the same transformation process.
2 Vertical integration is the combination, by acquisition or merger, of two or more firms that are at separate stages of the same process.
3 Conglomerate integration is the combination, by acquisition or merger, of two or more firms that are involved in different product areas.

Much of the discussion on corporate integration is similar, irrespective of whether the focus is horizontal, vertical or conglomerate integration. In all three, there is the possibility of two broad effects: an increase in market power and an increase in efficiency arising from economies of scale and/or scope. Much of the theoretical work on horizontal integration is closely related to the oligopoly models discussed above in Chapter 4, and horizontal integration in practice is included in Section 5.3 of this chapter. Moreover, aspects of both horizontal and conglomerate integration are covered in the discussion on diversification, below. We therefore concentrate here on vertical integration.

Vertical integration can be upstream (backward) or downstream (forward). Fiat (motor car) merging with Comau (machine tools) provides an example of upstream vertical integration. Downstream vertical integration is where, for example, a car company acquires a distribution company. Two-way vertical integration is also possible. An example of this would be the merger of a petroleum refiner with a company owning oil reserves (upstream) and with retail petrol stations (downstream).

It may be required, under certain circumstances, to measure the degree of vertical integration. One way of doing so is to use a vertical integration ratio:

$$VI \text{ ratio} = \frac{\text{value added of a firm}}{\text{final sales revenue}}$$

Computing the value added to a product by a single firm, as a proportion of the final cost to the consumer of that product, gives an indication of the significance of that firm (as a vertically integrated entity) in the production of that product. A similar ratio can be computed—as industrial, rather than corporate integration—for a group of firms, or a region, to identify their significance in the total industry.

Among the problems with such ratios is that value added is not necessarily synonymous with vertical integration; one firm that has resulted from a series of upstream and downstream mergers or acquisitions—and which is therefore the result of a great deal of vertical integration—could still be adding less value than another firm that works only on one part of the product transformation process. Design, for example, may add more value than assembly, distribution and retail sales together. Another problem is that it is not always easy to distinguish between corporate and industrial integration.

This problem is discussed by Robertson and Langlois (1994) who contrast the 'nexus-of-contracts' view of the firm with the 'property-rights' view of the firm. The former is close to what we called, in our description of different theories of the firm in Chapter 3, the principal–agent theory, and the latter, to the transaction cost theory. The point is that if the firm is seen in terms of contracts, then what goes on inside the firm differs from how the firm relates to other firms only in degree, not fundamentally. Both are governed by contracts, those governing the firm's interactions with other firms usually having a greater degree of specificity than those governing the firm itself. On the other hand, the transaction cost view of the firm sees it in terms of ownership of assets; assets are either owned by the firm or they are not. In the transaction cost view, the firm does differ fundamentally from other firms. Vertical corporate integration is clear from a property rights perspective: 'two stages of production are held to be vertically integrated when the assets involved are under common ownership'. But the 'boundaries of the firm [are] rather fuzzy under the "nexus" view' (Robertson and Langlois, 1994).

Recalling the continuum between market and hierarchy introduced in Chapter 3, vertical corporate integration is apparently within a hierarchy. The process of upstream or downstream vertical integration is the process of removing transactions from the market and internalizing them into the firm. However, a firm could own one of its suppliers, but deal with it in the same way as it deals with other suppliers, in terms of market criteria. Moreover, there are many situations in which firms control other firms without owning them. Jacobson and O'Sullivan (1994), for example, describe the relationship between subsidiaries of software multinationals and small software manual printing firms in the host country, as one in which the former to a great extent control the latter through demand for high quality and exclusive dealing. Robertson and Langlois (1994) conclude that there are two types, or dimensions, of integration, ownership and co-ordination integration. Let us call them OI and CI. A holding company, which merely owns a number of different, and perhaps unrelated businesses for investment reasons, has a high degree of OI, but virtually no CI. A large, vertically integrated firm that is involved in all the stages of the transformation of a product will have a high degree of both OI and CI. An industrial district of the type we discussed in Chapter 4 is a group of firms that has a high degree of CI, but no OI.

Whether directly through ownership, or indirectly through control, there are three broad types of reasons why a firm will attempt to achieve greater vertical integration: to increase efficiency; to bypass government regulations; and to reduce uncertainty.

Efficiency

We can understand efficiency in this context as relating to minimum efficient scale (MES), that is, the smallest size of firm for which average cost is minimized. In an enlightened discussion of this concept and its role in the evolution of large, modern, industrial enterprises in the late nineteenth and early twentieth centuries, Chandler (1990, pp. 21–38) points out, among other things, the following:

1 Independent intermediary firms can have *scale* advantages through buying finished goods from, or selling inputs to a number of different manufacturers of the same product.
2 Such intermediary firms can also have *scope* advantages through buying from or selling to manufacturers of different products.
3 Where specialized knowledge about a particular product or about any part of that product's transformation process is required, or where some specialized system of buying inputs or selling the finished product is necessary, then this can offset intermediaries' scope advantages and lead to vertical integration by the manufacturer.
4 To be successful, vertically integrating firms of this kind require highly skilled management.[62]
5 There is a complex relationship between the MES of the plant and the MES of the firm.[63]

A somewhat different, though not necessarily contradictory, view of vertical integration as a means of increasing efficiency, is to see efficiency in terms of the minimizing of transaction costs.[64] If the transaction costs in using the price mechanism exceed the costs arising from the non-market co-ordination of exchanges within a firm, then ownership integration is likely. From our earlier discussion, note that this non-market co-ordination may in some cases be between firms, in which case it is CI and not OI.

Introducing *asset specificity* into the discussion shows a degree of overlap between Chandler's and the transaction cost perspectives on vertical integration. What Chandler shows is that vertical integration is more likely when some specialized knowledge or system, specific to the product manufactured by that firm, is required. A transaction cost approach can lead to the same conclusion: where there is asset specificity, such as where equipment or skills are required only for the production of a particular product, then where technology is such that only one firm uses that equipment or those skills, they are more likely to be internalized than become the property of a separate firm. In other words, if a transaction requires an investment in a specific asset, internalization of the asset by the firm is more likely than ownership of the asset by a second, separate firm and purchase of the product of the asset on the market by the first firm.

Jacobson and O'Sullivan's (1994) study of the software manual printing industry again illustrates. The highly specific nature of the machinery required for the high quality printing of manuals led to the close relationship (CI rather than OI in this case)[65] between the host country printing firms and the subsidiaries of the software multinationals. If the printing firms could have used their manual-printing equipment for other purposes, the tight, often exclusive sub-contracting relationships between them and the software firms would not have developed.

That the nature of the technology is crucial is shown by reference to the neoclassical literature on *fixed* and *variable proportion technologies*[66] and their implications for vertical integration.[67]

We assume, for simplicity, that the product transformation process has only two stages. In the case where production is subject to fixed proportion technology, it can be shown that an incentive to integrate vertically exists if there is a monopoly at each of the stages prior to integration. Integration would lead to the upstream output being transferred to the downstream division at its marginal cost of production,[68] the price of the final product would be reduced, and the final output would expand. As a result, the total profit of the vertically integrated monopoly would exceed the sum of the profits of the two monopolies prior to integration. Under these assumptions there is clearly an incentive to integrate vertically, though it is arguable that there will be efficiency/welfare costs associated with increasing monopolization.

Scherer and Ross (1990, p. 526) argue that where there is variable proportion technology, 'the efficiency gain from improved input proportion choices [as a result of vertical integration] at least partly offsets the efficiency loss from elevated end product prices...'. Here there is more than one input, and the production of one of them is monopolized. Vertical integration between the upstream and downstream monopolies leads to control by the vertically integrated firm of *both* inputs. It can now—following vertical integration—determine the proportions in which to combine the two inputs undistorted by one of the input suppliers being a monopoly.

There are two factors at work: how variable the proportions are, and how competitive production at each of the stages is. If there are variable proportions, we have shown that vertical integration can improve efficiency. It depends, however, on what the market structures at the various stages of production were before vertical integration. For example, if the down-stream market was competitive prior to integration, vertical integration can lead to efficiency losses—from the point of view of the industry and consumers—that more than offset the gains from improved choice of input proportions (Waterson, 1982). The cost reduction trans-lates into increased profit for the firm (Vernon and Graham, 1971), but not necessarily to reduced prices for the consumer.

We can conclude that the impact of vertical integration on efficiency (and welfare) depends, among other things, on the variability of proportions (or the elasticity of input substitution) and on how competitive the various markets up and down the product transformation process are, before and after integration.

Bypassing government regulations

The avoidance of government regulations is another incentive for vertical integration. This is best explained in terms of actions by firms to overcome or exploit differences in tax and price control regulations in different countries or regions, or in relation to different parts of the product transformation process. Where such differences exist, they can be overcome or exploited by vertically integrated firms in ways that would not be open to separate firms inter-acting on the basis of market criteria.

By vertically integrating across the boundaries between regions or countries (and/or between upstream and downstream) in which the different regulations exist, firms can remove the buying and selling of the product of the upstream part of the production process from open market transactions. That product is now transferred downstream *within* the firm for further processing. The firm can determine for itself—internally, administratively—at what price this transfer should take place. This internal transfer price can be used to switch profits from a high tax location or part of the production process to a low tax location or part of the production process.

According to Shepherd (1990, p. 366) this type of profit switching transfer pricing (PSTP) has been a common practice in the USA, where oil extraction has been taxed at lower rates than refining. In the EU, where corporate profit tax rates are significantly higher in some member countries than in others (see Table 4.7), firms can reduce their global tax payments by switching profits between high tax areas like, say, Germany, and low tax areas like Ireland. There is, in fact, a great deal of evidence that Ireland is used as a location into which to switch profits using PSTP (Stewart, 1989). The formation of multinational corporations through the establishment of subsidiaries in Ireland (i.e. corporate vertical integration into Ireland) is at least in part in order to exploit the differences in corporate profit tax rates.[69]

Where the government regulation is through price controls, similar arguments can be used to explain the advantages of vertical integration. Where, for example, an input is subject to price controls, vertical integration will enable the firm to use transfer pricing to insulate itself from these controls. More generally, to the extent that EU-wide competition leads to downward pressures on prices, this will further encourage 'firms to internalise their production or down-stream functions and embark upon a period of manipulative transfer pricing to make up the short-falls in their profitability' (Welford and Prescott, 1994, p. 145).

Note that vertical integration to avoid government regulations, as discussed in this section, must be OI, and not just CI. It is the internalization into the single firm's information systems of what had been separate operations that makes possible the avoidance of the regulations.

Uncertainty

Uncertainty can also be a factor in vertical integration. Transactions between firms at different stages of the product transformation process are all subject to uncertainty. For example, the supply of some raw materials (uranium, bauxite, oil, coffee) is highly variable in nature. Political as well as climatic considerations explain this volatility. The demand for the final good is also often uncertain. As Chandler (1990, p. 24) points out, maintaining the throughput at the level of MES over time requires careful co-ordination not only of production, 'but also of the flow of inputs from suppliers and the flow of outputs to intermediaries and final users'. If, because of the independence of those suppliers, intermediaries or final users, the supply of inputs or demand for outputs is uncertain, then vertical integration is likely to reduce the uncertainty and improve co-ordination. Chandler goes on to show (1990, p. 25) that it was in order to improve this type of co-ordination that the Standard Oil Trust (the precursor of Exxon) was formed in the late nineteenth century.

Uncertainty can lead to vertical integration, but it can also explain why that vertical integration is CI and not OI. In the context, for example, of rapid technological change, a man-ufacturer can reduce uncertainty by buying inputs from a subcontractor rather than itself investing in the possibly short-lived technology required to produce those inputs. Once again the software manual-printing industry illustrates the point. The major software firms, like Microsoft and Lotus, avoided setting up their own printing divisions and instead bought in printing services from local firms, often established entirely for that purpose. The uncertainties in relation to the life-expectancy of the technology—and of the product—were borne by the printers. In the event of the displacement of printed manuals by manuals and on-line help functions in various types of machine-readable formats, the manual printers' investments in specialized printing equipment become sunk costs. Under these circumstances, the software firms themselves, on the other hand, can simply shift their demand to the new type of input (Jacobson and O'Sullivan, 1994).

The literature on corporate integration has traditionally focused on factors giving rise to increases in the size of firms. Large-scale production developed in the context of technologies which increased the MES. These technologies were usually based on assembly lines, and came to be known as Fordist production methods. In practice, as we saw in our discussion of industrial districts in Chapter 4, in some circumstances small firms can be more successful than large ones. Some writers, including Piore and Sabel (1984), have gone so far as to argue that new technologies in recent decades have provided the basis for disintegration, for a new industrial era in which small firms, using sophisticated production, distribution, marketing and co-ordination technologies, will *in general* be more successful than large firms.

These new, post-Fordist systems of organization have come to be known as *flexible specialization*. They are based on small firms because, it is argued, small firms can respond more rapidly both to changes in consumer tastes and to process innovations. Moreover, the argument continues, new production technologies—and the application of computers to all stages in the product transformation process—are accessible to small firms, or at least to groups of small firms.[70]

While there is some validity in the argument that new technologies can facilitate the development of smaller firms,[71] there is little evidence in such indicators as concentration ratios of radical shifts in the relative importance of small firms overall. It seems more appropriate, therefore, to conclude (along with Best, 1990, and Robertson and Langlois, 1994) that different technological, cultural, institutional and market conditions can result in large firms predominating in some circumstances and small firms in others. 'There is no single degree of integration, or form of firm or industry organization, that suits all purposes' (Robertson and Langlois, 1994).

5.1.6   Diversification

Diversification refers to the movement of a firm into new, related or unrelated product areas (product extension); and/or, less frequently, to the movement of a firm into a different geographic market (geographic extension). When the firm diversifies into an unrelated field of production, this is called pure or conglomerate diversification. In most cases, however, firms tend to diversify into adjacent product lines.

Diversification as an increase in the number of product lines may be through internal expansion into the production of different products, or through mergers or acquisitions. Diversification through mergers or acquisitions is also a form of corporate integration, more horizontal where the firms are in related areas, more conglomerate where they are in unrelated product areas. There have been a number of examples of this latter type of diversification (horizontal and conglomerate integration) in the merger and acquisition (M & A) boom of the late 1980s and early 1990s: Guinness (stout beer producer) acquired the Bell Scotch whisky company; Louis Vuitton (up-market manufacturer of morocco leather articles) merged with the champagne producer Moët et Chandon which had earlier acquired the Hennessy brandy company; LVMH (Louis Vuitton Moët Hennessy) then acquired the up-market French couturier, Givenchy; Guinness acquired LVMH; Pernod-Ricard acquired Irish Distillers; a number of pharmaceutical majors acquired biotechnology companies, Roche, for example, acquiring

Genentech; the Ferruzzi Group of Italy in 1987 acquired the chemical firm Montedison, took control of some 20 per cent of the EC sugar market through its participation in the French firm Beghin-Say, and established a strong foothold on the world market of soyabeans, after the purchase in 1987 of the American firm Central Soya (Linda, 1988); the Swedish vacuum cleaner company, Electrolux, acquired or merged with a number of companies including Zanussi (Italian, 1984), Servis (UK, 1985), the domestic appliance division of Thorn-EMI (UK, 1987), and two Italian companies, Alfatec and AlpenInox in 1988. Electrolux's aggressive diversification through acquisition moved it from being among the leaders in the vacuum cleaner market to world leadership in the entire domestic appliance sector, with around 18 per cent of the world market (Bianchi and Forlai, 1993). All these are diversifications into more or less closely related adjacent—or complementary—markets; in other words they are examples of horizontal integration. An example of pure diversification (conglomerate integration) is acquisition by the Swedish car manufacturer Volvo of firms in the food and drinks sector in Sweden.[72]

Examples of diversification through internal expansion are given by Chandler (1990). Focusing on the emergence of modern, giant, industrial enterprises in the first half of this century, he writes that 'Product diversification came from opportunities to use existing production, marketing and research facilities and personnel by developing products for new and more profitable markets' (1990, p. 39). This is closely related to economies of scope, for where a number of different products could be produced using at least some of the same production, marketing, etc., facilities, then this sharing of resources would reduce the average costs below what they would be if each product line were to have its own production, marketing, etc.

In the 25 years after the Second World War, most diversification in Europe was through internal expansion. Moreover, while in the 1970s in the USA a great deal of conglomerate diversification through acquisition took place, in Europe there was much less expansion through acquisition. There was, as in the USA, some overdiversification by European firms, but because they—and this applies particularly to German firms—'continued to rely on long-established relationships with banks and other financial institutions, they were able to pull back when such expansion did not prove profitable, and they appear to have done so in a more orderly fashion than their American counterparts' (Chandler, 1990, p. 626).

There is an interesting question arising from the discussion of diversification thus far: why in some cases—and during some periods—is diversification through mergers or acquisitions, and in others through internal expansion? In answer to this question, de Jong (1993) suggests that the choice is related to the industry life cycle.[73] When an industry is new, firms will be optimistic, and expand capacity. Growth will occur, but for no product is there indefinite market growth. Eventually, demand will cease to expand. Arguably (though de Jong does not say so), at some point between the new and the mature phase of the industry, when there is still optimism about its future, if diversification takes place into related product lines, it will be through internal expansion. However, in the mature phase,

large, financially strong firms with uncertain or unpromising prospects diversify into other industries by means of takeover. As the invention of basically new products cannot be achieved at will and the means of production of a new product cycle are not instantly available for such mature firms, despite extensive research facilities, external diversification is often considered to be a way out of the mature phase. (de Jong, 1993, p. 19)

According to Chandler (1990, p. 626), one reason for the predominance of mergers and acquisitions in the USA and of internal expansion in Europe during the 1960s and 1970s is the 'smaller size of the European capital markets, in terms of volume and turnover of transactions, and the continuing strength of the banks (particularly in Germany) and of the financial holding companies'. Unlike in the USA, as a result, in Europe there was little development of an active market for corporate control.

We have shown that, since the mid-1980s, a large number of firms have diversified through acquisition in Europe. Either the industries in which these firms operate are in mature phases (if de Jong is correct) or the size of the capital markets of Europe have grown since the 1970s (if Chandler is correct). Both the explanations are to some extent correct. First, in relation to the argument that diversification through mergers and acquisitions is more likely in the mature phase, while there has been a general increase in the number of mergers and acquisitions in most sectors in the second half of the 1980s and early 1990s, the increase has been most notice-able in mature, slow growth sectors (Jacquemin and Wright, 1993). In particular, chemicals, a mature industry experiencing low growth since the 1970s, had a significantly higher number of mergers and acquisitions in the second half of the 1980s than any other industry (an annual average of 88, over 17 per cent of the total; de Jong, 1993, Table 2). Second, with respect to the growth in the European financial market, a combination of the integration of the financial markets of Europe since the mid-1980s, and increasingly free flows of capital internationally, both within and beyond Europe, have provided large firms, even national ones, with new options (Vipond, 1994).

Using the number of mergers and acquisitions is only a partial measure of diversification, excluding as it does all diversification through internal expansion. There are two other measures commonly used by industrial economists (see, e.g., Scherer and Ross, 1990, pp. 91–2). The first is based on a system of classification of activity of firms. The European system, already discussed in Chapter 4, is called NACE. At the three-digit level there are 130 different activities or product/service categories. The first measure simply asks in how many of these 130 different categories each firm operates. The result of such a count clearly depends on the classification system. The more disaggregated the system, the higher will be the number. The International Standard Industries Classification (ISIC),[74] for example, has 512 different categories.

The weakness of this measure is that it does not take into account the relative importance of the different activities of the firm. A firm realizing 90 per cent of its turnover in the sale of one product i, and 1 per cent in the sale of each of 10 other products, will appear as diversified as another firm engaged equally in 11 product lines.

Because of this weakness, a second, weighted, measure of diversification is sometimes used. This diversification index, di, derived from the Herfindahl index of seller concentration, is found as follows:

$$di = \frac{1}{\displaystyle\sum_{j=1}^{n} Z_{ij}^2}$$

where Z_{ij} is the fraction of firm i's sales in the jth activity or product. If the firm operates in only one activity, then $di = 1$. If the firm had 10 activities, each accounting for one-tenth of total turnover, then:

$$di = \frac{1}{\displaystyle\sum_{j=1}^{10} \left(\frac{1}{10_j}\right)^2} = 10$$

Similarly, whatever the number of activities in which the firm has equal shares, the di will equal that number. A very high fraction of the firm's activities in one activity, and low fractions in others will bring the diversification index near to one.

The few empirical studies on diversification in Europe reveal that, as we have already suggested, diversification has proceeded by spurts, and along different paths in different European countries, at different times and in different industries.

In the UK, Kumps (1975) found that between 1958 and 1963, the degree of diversification increased. During this period, the number of lines of business in which firms were involved increased by 33 per cent. In the case of German firms, the increasing degree of concentration in the second part of the 1960s went in parallel with an increasing degree of diversification (Schwartz, 1973).

During the same period of time, diversification in France was not a common strategy, with the exception of the luxury goods industry (Dior and Cartier diversifying into spectacles, Porsche into watches and spectacles), and the food industry. The aggressive strategy of BSN (world-wide leader of mineral water drinks) was unusual for the period in Europe. As a French firm, it was also unusual in diversifying through acquisitions abroad. Most acquisitions by French firms during that period were of other French firms, and it was not until the late 1980s that international mergers and acquisitions by French firms—for example Sodima–Yoplait and Pernod–Ricard—became common.

As a strategy of firms, diversification opens up the possibility of a number of other strategies already discussed in this chapter. Where diversifications are successful—and they are not always—then *cross-subsidization* is often a factor (Edwards, 1955). Diversified firms can transfer resources across divisions situated in the various markets in which they operate. This gives them an incentive to carry out discriminatory strategies such as predatory pricing, price discrimination, and non-price strategies such as R&D and advertising.

The division engaged in predatory pricing can afford to do so because it can rely on funds coming from the other divisions of the firm. Once the other firms have been evicted from the market, the division can set monopoly prices—unless there are low entry costs, in which case the threat of entry will keep prices low; predatory pricing is unlikely in contestable markets.

The cross-subsidization argument, and the suggestion that it underlies a positive relationship between diversification and profitability, have been the subject of criticism.[75] First, as already suggested, while diversification can facilitate cross-subsidization, and cross-subsidization makes predatory pricing easier, predatory pricing is only profitable where there are significant entry barriers (see also Weston, 1973). Second, Cowling *et al.* (1980, p. 331) argue that diversification is intrinsically related to firm size, and that 'the effects of diversification can be analysed initially within the framework of traditional analysis in which relative size is a major determinant of a firm's monopoly power[;] ... this is implicit in the cross-subsidisation analysis but not fully recognised'. In other words, for small firms with little monopoly power, advantages to be gained from diversification and cross-subsidization are limited.

We have so far identified two main *reasons for diversifying*: to gain the benefits of economies of scope, and to facilitate other strategies like cross-subsidization and predatory pricing. A third reason is to reduce risk.

The profitability of a diversified firm may be raised (or the variability of profits may be diminished), because of a reduction in risk; with a presence in a number of markets, the likelihood of the firm as a whole failing, is diminished. The reduction of risk is greater the more disconnected are the markets in which the diversified firm operates. The three reasons for, or advantages of, diversification thus apply to three broadly different situations. The more complementary the diversification, the more the gains from economies of scope; the greater the barriers to entry, the more the potential gains to diversification from such strategies as cross-subsidization and predatory pricing; the more conglomerate the diversification, the more the gains from reduction of risk.

5.2   R&D and innovation[76]

Interest in technology and technological change and innovation as a strategy of firms is probably as old as firms themselves. But an intensification of interest in this issue in Europe in recent times stems from concern that a *technology gap* may be opening up between EU firms on the one hand, and Japanese and US firms on the other. What is meant by technology gap is a disparity in the levels and rates of change of technology (a more detailed discussion will be found in Chapter 6).

In this section we will examine the level of technology and innovation within Europe, and compare Europe with other regions. To prepare the ground we begin with some basic definitions followed by an account of the development of ideas about technological change.

5.2.1   Basic definitions

Technology has been defined in a number of different ways. Dosi and Orsenigo (1988) define it in terms of information about input combinations, in Germany it is generally regarded as a body of knowledge and skill applicable in the production of goods (Warner, 1994), and Woods (1987) defines it as 'the systematic organisation of the production process'. We accept a wide definition, including all the above, that is, one that incorporates both the technical, production engineering information and the organizational aspects.

Another concept that has different definitions is *high technology*. While it would be preferable to define this—as does the US Congress (1982)—in terms of new and/or innovative products or processes, this is, in practice, very difficult to measure. No data are kept on new and/or innovative products or processes; it is not clear whether such data could be kept in any comprehensive way. As a result, it is more usual to define a high technology industry as one with a high level of R&D (OECD, 1986).

This leads to the identification of high technology industrial sectors as those which have three characteristics:

1 A higher-than-average investment in R&D, with a R&D-to-production ratio of over 4 per cent.
2 A greater propensity to obsolescence due to a higher-than-average introduction of new products and processes.
3 A greater share of government outlays on R&D (Woods, 1987, p. 17).

Industries that correspond to these characteristics are: aerospace, office machinery and computers, electronics, pharmaceuticals, precision and measuring instruments, and electrical machinery. The problem with this definition is that it excludes advanced technology activities in traditional industries like clothing, textiles and furniture.

A *key technology* is 'the specific knowledge that enables a firm to keep up with or ahead of its competitors' (Pavitt and Sharp, 1992). Similar to this is a *core technology* which is a technology the 'mastery of which is essential to the development of an industrial sector. Some may be specific to a given industry, while others may have more general application' (Woods, 1987, p. 17). The idea of a widespread application across many sectors leads to the notion of a *generic technology* or a *pervasive technology* (Pavitt and Sharp, 1992). Generic technologies are most evident in the mechanical engineering, chemicals, and office equipment sectors. A *strategic technology* is one that enables a nation (or an economically integrated area) to keep its economic independence *vis-à-vis* the rest of the world. The concept was developed for use in conjunction with the notion of *filière* developed by French economists (see Chapter 4, Section 4.3.4).

5.2.2   Some contributions to the development of ideas about technology

That our interest in technological change and its causes is not new, is clear from the following—amazingly modern-sounding—sentence written in 1826: 'The rapidity with which during the last twenty years invention has followed upon invention may be taken as one of the signs of the increased quantity of knowledge and ingenuity which, by means of improved education, has been introduced into the community' (Ellis, 1826).

However, economists have differed and ideas have changed about what technological change and innovation are and how they should be studied. Ellis was interested in the relationship between the quality of labour and capital on one hand, and productivity and profitability on the other, and he focused on the consequences of the introduction of new machinery. This typically classical perspective related closely to the material conditions that prevailed at the time. Many classical economists asked whether industrialization could generate as much work as it was displacing through mechanization.

Following the marginalist revolution in economics in the late nineteenth and early twentieth centuries, the focus shifted to the theory and measurement of the relationship, at a point in time, between the inputs of factors of production and the resulting level of output. This relationship—the neoclassical production function—was based on the assumption of fixed technical knowledge. A change in technology would shift the production function. Technological change and innovation were exogenous to this static conception of how industrial economies evolve.

Working within the neoclassical tradition, Robert Solow (1957) attempted to measure the contribution of technological change to productivity. What he showed was that over a period of decades, the increase in output was far more than could be accounted for by the increases in the inputs. In particular, labour productivity could not be explained by increases in the capital/labour ratio alone. There had to be some 'residual' factor accounting for a large part—as much as 90 per cent—of the productivity change. 'This residual comprised all those awkward hard-to-measure elements other than labour and capital, such as technical and institutional change' (Freeman, 1994). Solow's analysis was extended and refined by Denison (1985) who attempted to break up the residual into its various components.

Earlier, and working within a different, empirical/historical tradition, Kuznets (1930) had already identified a relationship between technology and economic growth. His view was that the output of a good tends to follow an S-shaped pattern over time, with eventual stagnation or decline—at the top of the S-curve—explained by the exhaustion of the inventive potential of that industry. These ideas were related to those of Schumpeter who, as we saw in Chapter 2, was interested in innovation and in the relationship between innovative industries and the economy in general.

What Kuznets and Schumpeter had in common was the view that this type of cyclical pattern underlies the growth of new industries and that technological change is a cause rather than a result of a whole range of other economic phenomena. This distinguished them from the mainstream, neoclassical approach to technology.[77]

At the intersection between the neoclassical and Schumpeterian traditions, economists like Rosenberg (1963) and Mansfield (1968) undertook both theoretical and empirical work in the 1960s and 1970s, paving the way for what Freeman (1994) calls 'a wave of neo-Schumpeterian research [that] gathered force in the 1970s and 1980s'.

In recent years, at the forefront of this research have been economists like Freeman (1988a) himself, Nelson (1993) and Lundvall (1992). Among the earlier criticisms of the neoclassical production function approach was that it did not adequately account for the interdependence and complementarity of all the factors involved in technological change and innovation. The work of Freeman, Nelson and Lundvall avoids this problem by explicitly considering innovation and the general level of technology in a country to be systemically related to a whole series of institutional and cultural factors. Rather than focusing exclusively on narrow, quantifiable variables like expenditure on R&D, patents, etc., these writers have developed the idea of 'national systems of innovation'. The national system of innovation (NSI) is the set of institutions, within an economy, 'whose interactions determine the innovative performance of national firms', where innovation is understood to refer to 'the processes by which firms master and get into practice product designs and manufacturing processes that are new to them, whether or not they are new to the universe, or even to the nation' (Nelson, 1992). This is the perspective we will adopt in this section, using but identifying the weaknesses of quantitative measures and comparisons, and elaborating on them with descriptions of the nature and development of some of the major innovation systems in Europe.

A fundamental aspect of this approach is that the success or otherwise of firms' innovative activities is tied up in the system in which they operate. Firms' innovative strategies must therefore be based on awareness and understanding of systems of innovation.

5.2.3   Invention, innovation and diffusion

The procedure of developing new processes and products has traditionally been divided into three stages: invention, innovation, diffusion. In this view, *invention* is understood as the creation of a new idea, or of a new way of combining technical operations. *Innovation* is seen as the transformation of the idea into practical use; it is the application of the invention in new, improved or just different products or processes. *Diffusion* is 'the process by which the use of an innovation spreads and grows' (Mansfield *et al.*, 1977).

The diffusion of an innovation can be inter-industry or spatial diffusion. Within a single nation, a new product or process, generated in a given industry, can spread across the industrial structure of that nation. Improvements in machine tools or in computers, for example, while the results of innovation in those—or supplier—industries, will lead not only to process improvements but also to product upgrading within the user industries. Innovation and diffusion of this type can occur almost simultaneously as, for example, where increased precision in production of a product arising from a particular innovation necessitates the introduction of the same or similar innovation in the firms supplying sub-components.

Spatially, and, specifically internationally, diffusion is enhanced by transfers through foreign direct investment (FDI), joint ventures (JVs), licensing, and other strategic alliances. Diffusion can be both inter-industry and, simultaneously, international, as for example when it is a by-product of 'normal' market operations, such as the purchasing of capital equipment or of intermediate inputs into a production process. In addition to imitation, scientific exchanges, specialist publications, and the inter-firm mobility of employees at various levels, all also enhance the diffusion process.

The perfect knowledge assumption of the neoclassical theory implies that imitation will be instantaneous. In practice, the diffusion of innovations across economies can be rapid or slow. According to the cross-industry study carried out by Mansfield (1961), the time required for the adoption of an innovation by imitators can vary from one year (packaging beer in tin cans), to twenty years (continuous annealing of tin-plated steel). The lag depends on the height of entry barriers and on the nature of the innovation. Among other early work on diffusion was that by Griliches (1957) on the agricultural sector. Studies of diffusion in manufacturing became more common in the 1960s and 1970s.

The early diffusion model used by economists was developed by Mansfield in 1961.[78] In this model, $x(t)$ is the fraction of firms that have adopted the innovation at time t. The rate of diffusion of the innovation is $dx(t)/dt$. This rate will be proportional to both the fraction of early adopters $x(t)$ and to the fraction of potential adopters remaining, $[1 - x(t)]$, so that

$$dx(t)/dt = bx(t) \cdot [1 - x(t)]$$

where b is constant.

Now, as $x(t)$ rises, $[1 - x(t)]$ falls. As time passes, there are more and more adopters, and therefore greater likelihood that a non-adopter will come into contact with an adopter and itself become an adopter. On the other hand, there will be fewer and fewer non-adopters, so that beyond a certain point the likelihood of further adoptions diminishes. This relationship is represented in the S-shaped logistic curve shown in Fig. 5.9.

The curve shows how the proportion of firms that introduce the new process or product innovation changes over time. The stages in the life cycle of an innovation can be described as the introduction, growth, maturity and—though this is not shown in the figure—decline stages (see Robertson, 1971). In certain circumstances innovations do actually diffuse in an S-shaped manner,[79] not necessarily through the 'epidemic' process described in the paragraph above. According to Stoneman (1983), for example, firms below a certain size will not be able to intro-duce the innovation until it becomes less expensive. So large firms adopt the innovation first, followed at a later stage (the growth stage) by smaller firms. Here cost, rather than contact, is the key factor.

Other factors in the diffusion of innovations include the nature of the innovation, the internal structures of firms, relations between firms, and legal protection for the innovator. According to Lane (1991), for example, 'in a long-term stable contractual arrangement, such as vertical integration, firms are more likely to adopt firm-specific new technologies'. Similarly, Jacobson and O'Sullivan (1994) show that demand for high quality on the part of industrial buyers can lead to the adoption of new technology by suppliers where there is a close—and/or uneven[80]—contractual relationship between buyer and supplier.

Legal protection of innovators is usually in the form of patents. *Patents* are a device aimed at protecting the innovator against quick diffusion; they also constitute an indicator of innovative performance. One risk faced by the innovating firm is fast imitation before the costs of innova-tion have been retrieved, sometimes referred to as the 'free rider problem'. The more effectively patents can prevent free riding, the slower will be the rate of diffusion.

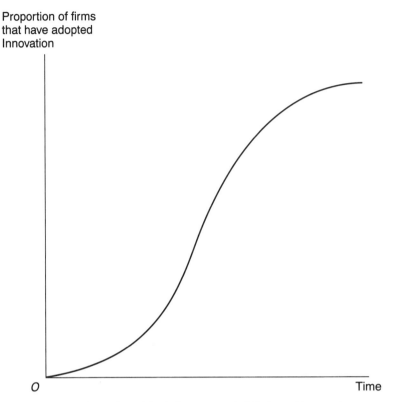

Figure 5.9   The S-shaped logistic curve and diffusion of innovations

Lissoni and Metcalfe (1994) show that there are different ways of studying diffusion, and that each approach emphasizes different key factors. Evolutionary theorists, for example, emphasize selection rather than imitation; the path-dependency approach focuses on increasing returns and technological 'lock-in'; and among spatial approaches are those of the industrial district analysts, who emphasize innovation and diffusion as agglomeration effects.

The different approaches to diffusion are beginning to converge, or at least to agree that diffusion is based on more than just adoption behaviour; 'A much richer pattern is emerging which distinguishes technology in terms of knowledge and skills as well as discrete artefacts' (Lissoni and Metcalfe, 1994). Human, social and even cultural factors are increasingly being accepted as important in technology, innovation and diffusion.

5.2.4   Measuring innovation in Europe

Research and development (R&D) spending is usually considered to be a precondition for successful patent performance. Table 5.5 shows R&D expenditure as a percentage of GNP in the major European countries, Japan and the USA.

During the 1980s, Japan, West Germany and the USA had significantly higher R&D expenditures as a percentage of GNP than France and the UK. Moreover, West Germany and Japan, in terms of this indicator, came from behind France and the UK in the 1960s to

TABLE 5.5   R&D expenditure as a percentage of GNP (*Source*: Nelson (1993), various tables)

Year	France	W. Germany	UK	Japan	USA
1964	1.8	1.6	2.3	1.5	2.9
1975	1.8	2.2	2.1	2.0	2.2
1986	2.3	2.7	2.4	2.8	2.7
1989	2.3	2.9	2.2	2.7	2.8

equal or exceed the USA by the end of the 1980s. Since its reunification, Germany has declined somewhat, due to the relatively lower level of R&D expenditure in East Germany. The use of R&D as a percentage of GNP to measure innovativeness has limitations. In what follows, in the context of comparing Europe with Japan and the USA, and the major European countries with one another, some other ways in which R&D and innovativeness can be measured will be considered.

Expenditure by governments accounts for more of R&D in some countries than in others. Table 5.6 shows a general decline between 1985 and 1991, but in France, government still accounts for half of total R&D expenditure. In the US the Federal government's share also still accounts for nearly half of all R&D. In both Germany and the UK, the figure is closer to one-third. The Japanese government's contribution to R&D expenditure is lower than that in other industrialized countries. In other respects, however, the role of the government in Japan is greater than in most other industrialized countries.

The pattern is somewhat different in relation to defence R&D, and, to quote Nelson (1993, p. 508), defence R&D 'accounts for the majority of the differences among the countries in government funding on industrial R&D, and the presence of large military programs thus explains why government industrial R&D spending in the United States, and the United Kingdom, and France is so much greater than in Japan and Germany'. For most of the countries in Nelson's study, 'military R&D accounts for the largest portion of government funding of industrial R&D' (Nelson, 1993, p. 513); Japan and Germany are exceptions. This is reflected in Table 5.7, showing percentage of government R&D expenditure accounted for by defence. The USA is by far the highest, followed by the UK and France. Germany and Japan, as a continuing legacy from their post-Second World War demilitarization, are the lowest. The figure for the EU as a whole, at around 25 per cent, is between Germany and France.

Tables 5.5, 5.6 and 5.7 together raise two key questions. First, does the high proportion of R&D accounted for by government, particularly in France and the USA (Table 5.6), reflect strengths or weaknesses in the national innovation systems of those countries?[81] Second, do the high proportions of government R&D expenditure accounted for by defence in France and the UK, and particularly in the USA (Table 5.7), enhance or reduce the innovativeness of these economies? In short, to what extent do Tables 5.6 and 5.7 change the picture presented in Table 5.5? These questions will be returned to later in this section.

TABLE 5.6   Government funding as a % of GERD* 1985–91 (*Source*: OECD, 1993)

Year	France	Germany	UK	Japan	USA
1985	52.9	36.7	42.7	21.0	48.3
1991	48.8	36.5	34.2	18.2	46.8

* Gross domestic expenditure on R&D, based on constant 1985 $.

TABLE 5.7   Defence as a % of government expenditure on R&D, 1991 (*Source*: OECD, 1993a)

France	Germany	UK	Japan	USA*
37.4	11.0	44.3	5.7	59.7

* Federal government only, excluding capital expenditure.

In the 1950s and 1960s, the USA and Britain had the highest R&D expenditure to GNP ratios and yet, at the same time, showed the lowest rates of productivity growth. As Lundvall points out, the measure 'reflects only an input effort and does not say anything about what comes out of the effort' (Lundvall, 1992, p. 6). Using R&D expenditure as a proxy of innovation intensity also implies the existence of the following linear pattern:

R&D ► new idea ► new product ► market definition ► product launch

This is associated with a smooth flow of operations from the research laboratory, to the design and then the market analysis departments. However, this linear pattern does not hold true in all cases. In many instances innovations are born in the production department (factory floor) itself; many others are suggested by end users (customers), or by suppliers. Some innovative firms do not have research departments and, thus, apparently no R&D expenditure at all. To quote Lundvall again, 'R&D expenditure is not the only kind of relevant input to the process of innovation—learning in connection with routine activities may be more important than R&D' (Lundvall, 1992, p. 6). Even in industries in which there is a research function, such as the pharmaceutical industry, there have been changes in traditionally understood patterns of development from invention to product launch. The market is an increasingly important first element in the very identification of the need for research. Moreover, there are many ways of differentiating pharmaceutical products, including different types of delivery systems (e.g. liquids, tablets, patches), different strengths, packaging, distribution outlets, and, more fundamentally, research to slightly alter molecular structure—which, in many cases, is influenced by national regulations. This means that the linear pattern outlined above is an over-simplification. The reality is often far more complex, with most of the stages able to influence developments in most other stages.

The fact that different elements of the technology change process, though located within a single company, may be located in different countries, also reduces the accuracy of R&D data. The UK, for example, is an R&D base for many firms whose headquarters are elsewhere. As a result, the expected relationship between R&D expenditure and innovation may not be realized within the UK because the results of the research in the UK may be used to develop products and processes which are introduced in the countries where these firms' headquarters are located.

It is clear, then, that as an alternative to R&D expenditures, other indications of innovativeness, and of the level of technology in an economy in general, must sometimes be used. One such alternative—which can be considered an output of R&D effort—is trade in high technology products. Over the 1980s and early 1990s, EC imports in high technology products, and particularly information technology, grew faster than exports. The exception was high technology trade with the USA which, as shown in Fig. 5.10, improved marginally but the export/import ratio remained well below one. The greater this ratio is above one, the greater is Europe's surplus in high technology trade, and the further below one, the greater Europe's deficit. The most significant deterioration in Europe's high technology balance of trade was

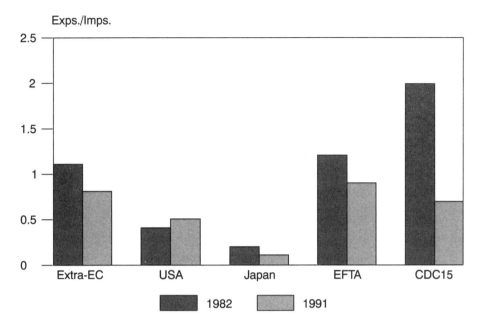

Figure 5.10   EC trade in high technology products—export:import ratio (*Source: European Economy*, 1993, no. 52)

with CDC15, 15 competitive developing countries. Note that with Sweden, Finland and Austria leaving EFTA to join the EU in 1995, the EU's high technology balance of trade with EFTA will have improved. However, in relation to Japan, the USA and competing developing countries, the EU continues to have deficits in high technology trade.

Research, done in universities, national research laboratories, and to a significant extent in a limited number of large firms, is at least the foundation for innovation. It 'provides the knowledge and skills on which national systems of business R&D can build' (Patel and Pavitt, 1991, p. 42). The number of people employed in research is another way of indicating the level of technology and potential for technological development of an economy.[82] This is shown in Fig. 5.11, in terms of research personnel per 1000 in the labour force. Two different indicators are used in the figure: all personnel in R&D, and scientists, engineers and other graduates in R&D (S, E and G). Figure 5.11 confirms that most European countries lag behind the USA and Japan. Germany is again the highest in Europe but, in terms of scientists, engineers and other graduates per 1000 labour force, it is well below both the USA and Japan.

R&D expenditure data and alternative indicators of levels of technological development like high technology trade balance and employment in R&D all show the EU to be behind the USA and Japan. They also show wide disparities within Europe. Thus both research inputs and outputs point to the same disparities.

Patel and Pavitt (1991) have suggested ways of measuring research productivity, relating inputs to outputs. Table 5.8, for example, relates research inputs as measured by government funding to outputs as measured by scientific publications. According to Patel and Pavitt, the table is 'based on the most thorough attempts made so far to compare per capita inputs and outputs of basic research' in these countries (Patel and Pavitt, 1991, p. 42). The figures for Japan and the USA are an index with Western Europe (France, UK, Germany and The Netherlands) set equal to 100. The publications' indices are based on the CHI/NSF Science

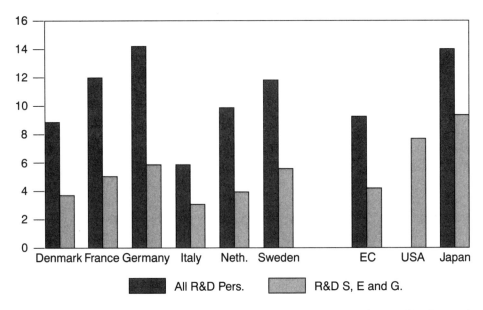

Figure 5.11   R&D personnel per 1000 labour force 1991: S, scientists; E, engineers; G, other graduates

Literature Indicators Database. The table suggests that the USA is the most productive of the three and that Japan became relatively more productive, over the 1980s. One reason for the apparent improvement in Japan may be the English language bias of the literature base, publications by Japanese scientists in English language journals having become more common over time.

How do the major European countries compare to each other? Patel and Pavitt combine a number of different indicators in order to identify aspects of the inputs into and results of R&D. Some of their data substantiates the findings of Tables 5.5 to 5.7. Germany spends most, and has the highest proportion of R&D accounted for by non-governmental sources; France has the lowest proportion accounted for by non-governmental sources. What Patel and Pavitt add, is that there are very sharp differences in the basic indicators of industrial technology among the three main European countries. Germany's industry-funded R&D is nearly twice that of the UK and more than twice that of France. In relation to the granting of patents in the USA, there is an even larger gap between Germany and the other two. The largest gap of

TABLE 5.8   Per capita inputs and outputs of basic research: West Europe, Japan and USA
(*Source*: Patel and Pavitt, 1991, Table 3.2)

Measure	West Europe	Japan	USA
Government funding (inputs)			
1987	100	52	104
1980	100	55	97
Publications (outputs)			
1986	100	51	118
1981	100	46	125

all is that between Germany and the UK in craft and technician level qualifications; and, with respect to this last measure, the UK is significantly below France as well.[83] The only measure in relation to which the UK appears to be ahead of France and Germany, is the output of scientific publications, and here, as mentioned before, there is an English language bias—though it may not account for all the difference.

The reason why US patents granted to France, Germany and the UK respectively, is used, rather than patents granted within each of these countries, is because data on the latter are distorted by different national systems of registration of patents. In Japan, for example, 'patents are granted separately even when inventions behind them were closely related technologically' (Odagiri and Goto, 1993, p. 104). For the same reason, in Fig. 5.12, only external patent applications per capita are used as a measure of research output. These are applications by residents of each country for registration of patents abroad. What Fig. 5.12 shows is that, from more recent data, Germany has higher external patent applications than its European partners but also that it has higher external patent applications than either Japan or the USA. (The figure also shows that Japan has had a more substantial growth in gross domestic expenditure on R&D per capita than either the European countries or the USA.)

In the EU, the problem of different patent rules is gradually disappearing since a European patent system is being implemented. The principle of this patent system was agreed in Luxemburg in 1975 and was completed in 1989; it represents a serious attempt at transnational harmonization of patent systems. Normal patent life throughout the EU is now 20 years, though in some cases this can be extended. A directive relating to pharmaceutical products, for example, proposes Summary Protection Certificates, which could be issued in certain cases to provide an *effective patent life* of 15 years. This is the period covered by patent protection following the introduction of the medicine to the market.

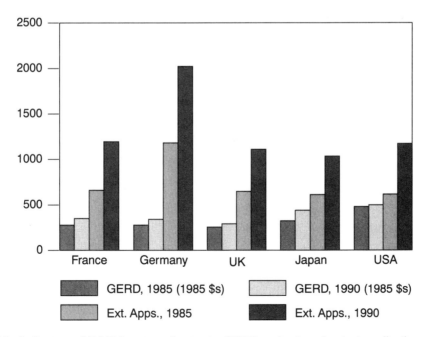

Figure 5.12 Indicators of R&D inputs and outputs. GERD and external patent applications per capita (*Source*: OECD, 1993a)

The most important advantage of a European patent system in which the patents of each member are recognized by all others—not yet fully implemented—is that firms' costs and the administrative effort they expend in obtaining patent protection in each country would be removed.

Even when there is a uniform European parent system, the use of patents as an indication of the output of R&D, or of innovativeness, will continue to suffer from the problem that many patents issued are not actually used in products or processes within firms. A tendency to apply for patents may be a characteristic of a particular (national or sectoral) group of firms, without that group of firms necessarily being more innovative—in the sense of actually implementing change—than less patent oriented groups of firms.[84]

Another way to indicate the inputs and outputs of R&D is to compare the change in Gross Domestic Expenditure on Research and Development (GERD) per capita over a period with the change in the Technology Balance of Payments (TBP) over the same period. The TBP 'registers the commercial transactions related to international technology and know-how transfers. It consists of money paid or received for the use of patents, licences, know-how, marks, models, designs, technical services and for industrial R&D carried out abroad, etc.' (OECD, 1993a, p. 333)

There are differences in coverage from country to country, and there may also be problems arising from profit switching transfer pricing, where firms adjust prices so as to shift profits to low tax areas. This measure is therefore also not perfect, and should be used in conjunction with others to give broad indications. Figure 5.13 shows, first, how GERD per capita has changed between 1985 and 1990. (Greater than one is an increase, and less than one is a decrease.) It has increased in all the countries, but particularly in Japan. Second, it provides through the TBP, an indication of change in the output of R&D. (Here the ratio of receipts to payments for 1990 is divided by the ratio of receipts to payments for 1985.[85] An index greater than one suggests an improvement in the TBP, and less than one, a deterioration in the TBP.) Only Germany and Japan have improved.

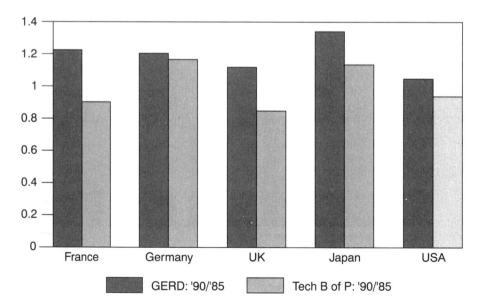

Figure 5.13 Indicators of R&D inputs and outputs. GERD per capita and technology balance of payments (*Source*: OECD, 1993a)

It is clear, even from the partially comparable data that is available, that in terms of innovation intensity—whether measured in terms of research inputs, outputs or productivity—there are significant differences among the three industrialized world regions, and among the countries of Europe itself. In terms of most indicators Germany is among the most advanced technologically, though Europe as a whole is behind both the USA and Japan.

Most indicators would also show significant differences between industries. A technological specialization index, for example, shows that among 15 selected industries, European invention activity is highest in agricultural machinery, with woodworking machinery second; it is lowest in office machinery with consumer electronics the second lowest (Panorama, 1993d, p. 87). Japanese and American invention activity would show a very different rank order of industries, consumer electronics in Japan in particular being much higher.

We have shown that among the three major countries within the EU there are significant differences. Nevertheless, in the wider European context, Germany, the UK, and France are among the most innovative; data similar to those presented in the tables above would show that, in most respects, Portugal, Greece and Ireland are least innovative. On the basis of many of the measures introduced above, Italy and Denmark are also well below Germany, the UK and France, but as will be shown below, Italy and Denmark are, in other respects, more innovative than their major neighbours.

5.2.5 National systems of innovation (NSIs)

Lundvall (1992, p. 12), emphasizing the importance of learning in NSIs, differentiates between narrow and broad definitions of NSI. The narrow definition is the one underlying most of Section 5.2.4, including, as it does, only those organizations and institutions directly involved in 'searching and exploring—such as R&D departments, technological institutes and universities'. The broad definition, which is close to that of Nelson, 'includes all parts and aspects of the economic structure and the institutional set-up affecting learning as well as searching and exploring'.

Given that historical, social, cultural and other factors—many aspects of which are nation-specific—influence the development of institutions, it follows that any country's NSI will be unique. In an attempt to operationalize this notion, Niosi *et al.* (1992) suggest that NSIs can be differentiated on the basis of a number of criteria. Somewhat adjusted, these are as follows:

- *Size of the country*   A large country (like the USA) is characterized by a more diversified system than small ones (like Austria or Finland) which have tended to focus on particular sectors.
- *Role of the country in the world*   In the UK, France and the USA, past colonialism/imperialism explains the development of R&D in military-based technology.
- *Existence and nature of natural resources*   The nuclear programme in France was developed because of the lack of fossil fuels; the success of the petrochemical industry in the USA is linked to the abundance of petrol in that country.
- *Socio-cultural factors*   Culture or 'habits of thought' are specific to societies, interacting with institutions to process information. Know-how or learned routines are as important as knowledge and can be communicated to the population as a whole. This places the training and education systems at the centre of the innovation process.
- *Political factors*   These have a substantial impact on the institutional framework of a nation (role of the state, banking system, education system) and, through policy, on its economic features as well.

These ideas will inform the examination of some of the NSIs in Europe, to which attention is now turned. France and the UK are examined first, followed by a brief discussion of some of the other NSIs. Next, the international level is the focus of attention. The aim is to identify the significant aspects of the technological environments within which firms in each of these countries operate, and to consider the relative importance of the national and European scopes of those environments.

The national system of innovation in France

As we saw above, France has a lower R&D/GNP ratio than Germany, and a higher government R&D/Total R&D ratio than either Germany or the UK; its defence R&D is as significant as that of the UK, well above that of Germany. From these findings, a number of more detailed questions suggest themselves. Why is the state so important in R&D in France? Does this have positive or negative implications for the output of R&D? Does France's military R&D produce commercial results exploitable by French companies? Other questions are suggested by the criteria for assessing NSIs. How is France's R&D distributed? How successful is the French education system? Is there a culture of innovation within firms, and to what extent is it diffused among firms?

The significance of the state in the French economy in general, and in science and technology in particular, has roots in the Colbertism of the seventeenth century. Features were added by the *Ancien Régime* in the eighteenth century and Napoleonic governments in the nineteenth century. Apart from the education system, the actual organizations and mechanisms involved in the production and distribution of R&D have evolved since the Second World War but the broader institutional and socio-cultural aspects of innovation developed over centuries.[86]

At the centre of the NSI (narrowly defined) is the National Centre for Scientific Research (CNRS) which, while established in 1939, in its present form dates from 1945. It has had a pervasive effect on the organization of basic and long-term research in science, and on the availability of scientific and technical personnel. In particular the CNRS directly administers laboratories and research facilities in areas not covered by universities and, in addition, it funds university research and makes its own personnel and equipment available to universities for specific projects. More broadly, the CNRS provides services to the scientific community, including documentation, training and 'assistance on patentable inventions' (Chesnais, 1993, p. 203).

That an institution such as the CNRS was necessary was a consequence of the weaknesses in R&D in the third level education system. This system contains two separate types of institution, the professional schools (*Grandes Ecoles*), established by Napoleon, and the universities. The *Grandes Ecoles* gave priority to technical education, and French engineers were among the best in the world in the nineteenth century. French scientists, too, were very advanced, and the *Ecole Normale Supérieure* became a leading scientific institution. In terms of science graduates, however, it was too small, providing '*much too narrow a base on which to build a sound scientific edifice*' (Chesnais, 1993, p. 198; emphasis in original). The university system remained secondary to the *Grandes Ecoles*, and had a tradition of small, personal laboratories that went with the professorial chair and reflected the interests of individual professors. This situation was not corrected until the formation of the CNRS.

Despite the weakness of science in the higher education system, there is little evidence of attempts within industry to undertake scientific research. This contrasts sharply with the situation in the USA, where, at much the same time (late nineteenth and early twentieth centuries), a large number of corporate research laboratories were established.[87] Where France did excel during the first half of the twentieth century, was in areas in which the engineering skills, built up over the previous 100 years, could impinge on product and process development. French inventors and entrepreneurs were most active in 'sectors where technological development took the form of pragmatic, step-by-step innovations as in automobiles and aeronautics' (Chesnais, 1993, p. 199).

Immediately after the Second World War, France, despite its defeat, thus had a continuing tradition in engineering-based industries, based on expertise built up over the nineteenth century,[88] and, with roots as far back as the seventeenth century, the remnants of and potential for a chemical industry. One large firm still in existence today, Saint-Gobain, was established during the Napoleonic wars as a direct result of efforts by the government at the time to 'root science-based innovation in industry' (Chesnais, 1993, p. 195). The combination of the centrality of the state and selective areas of scientific and technological excellence in large firms continued into the decades after the Second World War. In the period immediately after the war, the emphasis was on the creation of state institutions. To the extent that firms derived advantages through diffusion of innovation from these state activities, it was primarily in state-owned enterprises, nationalized during this period.

In addition to the CNRS, the French government established a number of research institutions, both civil and military. Among these were the Energy Commission (CEA), which included R&D into and production of nuclear energy, a National Centre for the Study of Telecommunications (CNET), and a National Office of Aeronautical Studies and Research (ONERA). These, and a number of others in such areas as tropical agriculture, health sciences, and military research, were mostly under the relevant government ministries. In the international scientific context, the most significant step was the establishment of the Saclay R&D laboratories by the CEA. In a country where no large firm, even at this late stage, had yet set up a major industrial R&D laboratory based on the US and German model, 'Saclay was France's first real step into twentieth-century fundamental and applied science' (Chesnais, 1993, p. 202).

Driven in part by a desire for technological independence from the United States, the state began to select particular firms and particular industries. 'National champions'—some publicly and some privately owned—were selected for support by the state, both directly and through state-owned financial institutions. From the 1960s onwards, this evolved into a planned restructuring of French industry in general, and a sharpening of French technological competitiveness in particular. In the late 1960s and early 1970s, four *grands programmes* were developed, covering the nuclear, aerospace, space technology and electronics industries—each of which, it should be noted, has significant military aspects.

Industrial policy in the period since the early 1980s has witnessed significant changes, but the principal features of the technological environment in France have not varied greatly.

With respect to the overall structure and working of the French innovation system, the 1970s and 1980s have essentially brought about only *shifts in emphasis* in the area of overall R&D resource allocation and the location of entrepreneurial capacity, along with a clearer spelling out of features that were already contained within the system ... (Chesnais, 1993, p. 204)

There are a number of weak elements to this system, which arise from the fundamental nature of the control and organization of French industry. First, there is the extremely important role of the state.[89] From the end of the Second World War to the end of the 1960s, both through the establishment of institutions and the implementation of policies, the state contributed an essential co-ordination role to the success of the French economy. However, this role also enhanced features of the system which would later emerge as weaknesses (de Bandt, 1987).

Nelson's (1992) conclusion from studies of systems of innovation in 15 countries is that few have 'active coherent industrial policies', and government policies supporting industrial innovation are 'generally fragmented'. This concurs with de Bandt's assessment of the role of the state in the relative lack of success of French industrial innovation since the early 1970s: 'While the transfers from the state to enterprises remain very important, no attempt is now being made to define and implement a consistent industrial policy' (de Bandt, 1987, p. 49). The nationalizations by the Socialist government in 1981–82 were aimed at integrating 'some of the big firms into a consistent plan-rational approach for the redeployment and further development of the French industrial system' but they were followed by an industrial policy of 'hesitations and obfuscation' (de Bandt, 1987, p. 48). Since the early 1980s, France—along with virtually all other governments in Europe—has reduced the degree of direct intervention and progressively privatized its nationalized industries.

Given its importance in military-related technologies, the state's role has become associated with a need for secrecy.[90] This is a second weakness, because technological information that might have contributed to commercial innovations remained within organizations developing and implementing those technologies for military purposes. Moreover, the significance of the military in directing the sub-systems of innovation in France, is increasing. The *Délégation Générale à l'Armement* (DGA) plays a key role, in most cases along with other government agencies, in innovation sub-systems of nuclear power, telecommunications, defence electronics, aerospace, and aeronautics. The increasing influence of the military, 'even in telecommunications and nonmilitary space [is] a result of the current post-Gulf war reorientation of military-strategic priorities to space observation and telecommunications systems' (Chesnais, 1993, p. 214).

As with government involvement in general, military control of R&D is not *ipso facto* negative. There might be different contributions to commercial competitiveness of military R&D, depending on whether this R&D aims at 'opening up a broad new generic technology', or whether it goes into 'highly specialized systems development'. The former is associated with greater 'spinoff', the latter with less. French and British military R&D have 'from the beginning focused largely on the latter', and 'most of the companies [from those countries] receiving R&D contracts have shown little capability to crack into non-military markets' (Nelson, 1992).

An exception to this generalization about limited spinoff of military R&D in France, is the case of aerospace. Aerospace and drugs and medicines (on which, see below) are the only two industry groups in the high technology sector that have positive trade balances. Strong institutions, established relatively early, form the background to the success of the aerospace industry in France. The first such institution was ONERA in the immediate post-war period (see above), followed by the establishment of a Committee for Space Research in 1959, and a National Centre for Space Studies (CNES) in 1961. A key difference in aerospace was that the CNES, unlike other state institutions, involved 'public and private firms in the program from the outset by contracting out a large part of the R&D to the business sector' (Chesnais, 1993, p. 203). The main firms were Matra, Aérospatiale and Thomson-CSF. A second difference is in the scale of this industry which is such that, from the beginning, international partners were sought. This led to the central role that France has played in Arianespace, the European competitor to the US satellite launchers.[91]

A third broad weakness of the French NSI, is its organization into vertical sub-systems. Both industrial and technological policies have been implemented through programmes aimed at particular industries, and on the basis of the 'national champion' ethos, at particular large firms. While the overall economic 'plan' approach in the early post-war period also relied on large firms, this was appropriate and successful in the context of the French economy in that period. However, both the 'programme' and large-firm aspects of state intervention in the later period, resulted in an overly vertically organized set of sub-systems in the 1970s and 1980s, when increasing flexibility, rapid change and globalization required a different type of state intervention. The vertical organization of industries reduced the rate of diffusion of innovation between industries.

Closely related to this is the over-specialization engendered by French industrial policy: 'firms such as Schneider or Thomson or CGE deliberately abandoned the machine tool industry, the equipment industry, and consumer electronics and invested the money provided by the state in the nuclear power industry, military electronics and telecoms' (Cohen, 1995). As a result, private industrial R&D has been weak in France, and there has been a collapse in particular of the machine tool industry.

The state is not exclusively responsible for problems in the French system of innovation. Among other aspects of French industry that impede the diffusion of innovations are: the absence of an integrated industrial infrastructure at decentralized geographical levels; the poor relations between big and small firms, particularly in the case of subcontracting; the unfavourable power relations between industry and distribution; and the weak research–business relations (de Bandt, 1987, p. 54). To these may be added characteristics of French firms and industry that reduce innovation in general: the 'more hierarchical and bureaucratic attributes of French enterprises (compared with German firms) prove particularly ill-suited to the needs of advanced technological change' (OECD, 1988, p. 79); and the influence of stock markets which (as in the UK, but unlike Germany and Japan), impose short time horizons and deter changes or investments that might reduce current profitability, but enhance future competitiveness.

The focus has thus far been on R&D undertaken or controlled by government and the military. The pharmaceutical industry is the main high technology industry which is, at least in part, outside the state's system of innovation.[92] While in some ways this industry builds on France's traditional strengths in the chemical sciences, in other ways it differs from the typical French pattern. Like other research-based industries in France, it is dominated by large firms, the main ones being Rhône-Poulenc (which merged with the American firm Rorer in 1989) and Sanofi. They have strong in-house R&D capacity, and in this are unusual (though not unique) in France. R&D expenditure as a percentage of sales (around 19 per cent) for both these firms is well above the average for the top 25 pharmaceutical companies in Europe (16.8 per cent) (Sharp, 1991, Table 13.5). This R&D is largely self-funded by the industry and this also differentiates pharmaceuticals from most of the other innovation sub-systems, including electronics, armaments and aerospace. It does obtain transfers of technology from its joint ventures with the public sector's *Institut Pasteur—Pasteur-Mérieux-Sérums et Vaccins* in the case of Rhône-Poulenc, and *Diagnostics-Pasteur* in the case of Sanofi—but in the allocation of state R&D funding: 'one finds an *overwhelming bias in favor of the nuclear, aeronautics, space, telecommunications, and electronics sectors* to the detriment of the chemical, biological, and life science based sectors ... as well as to that of the machine tool and robotics industries and other small firm dominated industries ...'[93] (Chesnais, 1993, fn.18; pp. 207–8).

In terms of competitiveness, the pharmaceutical industry in France has a positive trade balance, but there appear to be long-term problems—which the merger with Rorer may reduce at least for Rhône-Poulenc. First, while French companies tend to have very high numbers of compounds under development, the proportion of these that are successful in world markets when launched is smaller than that of Germany or the UK. According to Sharp (1991, p. 218), French companies 'have introduced many new drugs but mainly for local market needs; they were not sufficiently innovative to reach world markets'. As compared to the UK's 12 and Germany's 10, French companies did not have one drug in the world's top 50 best-selling drugs in 1990 (Sharp, 1991, Table 13.3A). The second problem facing the French pharmaceutical industry is that France has not experienced the same 'swarming' of new, innovative firms in biotechnology as the USA. France shares this weakness with the other major European countries, but biotechnology research in new firms has been even less prevalent in France than elsewhere in Europe. Established European firms in general also responded late to this new area, Rhône-Poulenc not until 1989 when it acquired Connaught Biosciences of Canada (Sharp, 1991, pp. 222–3).

It would appear that the French NSI is dominated by state institutions and particularly the military. The pharmaceutical industry is to some extent outside this. Even more independent, though largely unresearched, is the innovative activity of small firms. A key to this is the development and transmission of skills. The French system of vocational education is, as would be expected, public, and although work experience contracts have been used since the late 1970s to combine workplace and school-based learning, this has tended to reproduce the large-firm, narrowly defined skills, Taylorist mentality that impedes innovation.

The national system of innovation in the UK

The UK national system of innovation is in some respects even weaker than that of France. French industry-funded R&D was below that of the UK at the beginning of the 1980s, and it declined relative to that of the UK into the 1990s (OECD, 1993a). But, while overall R&D expenditure as a percentage of GNP (Table 5.5) grew substantially in France from the 1960s to the 1990s, in the UK it was at best constant. Also, in terms of external patent applications, while the UK was ahead of France in 1985 (though both were, and remain, behind Germany), by the 1990s, the UK had been overtaken by France (Fig. 5.12). More significantly, in terms of number of people obtaining mechanical and engineering qualifications at the craft and technician level, the UK, well below either France or Germany in the 1970s, also grew much slower than either over the period up to the late 1980s (Patel and Pavitt, 1991, Table 3.8) and, between 1985 and 1990, the UK's Technology Balance of Payments deteriorated to a greater extent even than that of France (Fig. 5.13).

How does an examination of the British NSI contribute to our understanding of the strengths and weaknesses of R&D inputs and outputs in the UK? Does it facilitate a better understanding of technological aspects of the business environment in the UK? Does the less interventionist role of the state mean a greater rate of diffusion? Is there more commercialization of the results of military R&D in the UK? As with France, the discussion begins with the historical background, followed by a description of relevant aspects of the educational system and key R&D institutions, and concludes with some indication of the innovativeness of the UK economy.

The UK has not had the 'étatist' tradition of France. While the reasons for this are complex, they are related to Britain's position as the first industrialized nation, and its early and long-standing commitment to free trade. The economic role of the state in Britain between the mid-eighteenth and last quarter of the nineteenth centuries was confined to the regulation of a small number of markets, including financial and property markets, and to the advancement and protection, by military means where necessary, of foreign trade. While intervention increased over the next 100 years, it was never as coherent or determined as in France or Japan. Whether despite or because of this,[94] for much of the 200 years up to the end of the nineteenth century, the national system of innovation in Britain 'had no match, generating revolutionary changes in the techniques of energy and material transformation (the coal, iron, and steam nexus), in the organization of production (the factory system), and in transportation (railways and the steam ship)' (Walker, 1993, pp. 187–8).

Britain has not declined since then, but it has lost its leadership position.[95] There are different theories as to why this change occurred, though few attribute a significant role to the British state. Among the main explanations are the inappropriateness of culture and institutions to the conditions of the twentieth century, despite their success in the previous two centuries; a change in attitude from industrial enterprise to a rentier mentality; and the inevitable catch-up of competitor nations as industrialization spreads.[96] While there is an element of truth in each of these explanations, the first fits best with the NSI framework's focus on culture and 'habits of thought'. Chandler (1984) provides a material basis to the argument by suggesting that 'Britain was the only nation to industrialize before the coming of modern transportation and communication. So its industrialists had become attuned to a slower, smaller-scale process of industrial production and distribution.'

Some writers have emphasized the weakness of education and training in Britain as reasons for its loss of leadership.[97] One weakness is that, although having a long and excellent tradition, particularly in science, the Oxford and Cambridge universities are part of an élitist system, access to which is obtained as much through wealth as ability. The private education system, small in comparison to the total, nevertheless still provides a disproportionately large part of the country's economic and political élite. The system is, moreover, more service than production oriented. 'The French phenomenon of bright young Polytechniciens developing careers that span both government service and industrial management has no parallel in Britain.'[98] A second weakness is that, while at the highest level (doctorate), the UK education of scientists and engineers is comparable in terms both of quality and quantity with other European countries, at the middle level (bachelor, technician and craft), it is relatively weak. Engineering in particular is weak at the technician and craft levels. This reflects the low standing of the engineering profession in British society.

Why engineering underwent such a decline, having been a part of Britain's earlier success story, may be attributable to the onset of the rentier mentality.[99] Thus it is not just the weaknesses in the education and training systems themselves that account for the low level of engineering skills. It is also the lack of recognition of the need for a more highly skilled labour force on the part of employers. This is illustrated in the contrast between an estimated investment in training by industry of only 0.15 per cent of revenue in Britain and 2 per cent in Germany. Intervention by the state could have imposed selective qualification prerequisites, but the state has traditionally had a *laissez faire* attitude to the economy. This does not mean that there are no significant state institutions in the NSI, nor that government policy has never impinged on innovation. Policy and institutions in the UK are almost inseparable, with the latter more or less determined by the former.[100]

As in France, policy has been inconsistent. In the 1960s, the state was more interventionist than at any other time. Industrial policy (industrial restructuring, corporation tax, capital grants), particularly under the Labour government between 1964 and 1970, aimed to reorganize industry through consolidation in particular sectors—notably steel, cars, machine tools and computers—to form national champions. At the same time, science and technology (S&T) policy (S&T education, public sector laboratories, patent laws) acting through the education system, direct support of R&D, and other measures, attempted to regain technological leadership for Britain. Generally, however, there was a lack of co-ordination, with industrial policy under the Department of Trade and Industry and S&T policy under the Department of Education and Science. In the late 1960s, an attempt was made to simplify matters by the creation of a Ministry of Technology. In the 1970s direct intervention continued. The National Enterprise Board (NEB), set up in 1974—also by a Labour government—had, among others, the role of acting as a catalyst for investments in advanced technology areas. This it attempted, for example through Inmos, a state semiconductor development company, and Celltech in the biotechnology area.

Under the Conservative governments since 1979, direct intervention has been largely ruled out, and a policy of creating the right environment, or climate, for encouraging innovation has been adopted. The NEB was initially instructed to act commercially, but its most public function became the bailing out of failing companies such as Rolls-Royce. Partly in consequence of this, in 1981 it merged with another state corporation to became the British Technology Group (BTG), providing venture capital through equity mainly in small firms. By the mid-1980s, BTG had an investment portfolio of about £230 million in 430 companies. Other schemes introduced in the 1980s with the aim of advancing venture capital to facilitate the introduction or development of new technologies included the Loan Guarantee Scheme and the Business Expansion Scheme. One problem with all these schemes is that many of the firms which have obtained capital through them are not actually innovative in terms of products, processes or structures.

Among the important institutions in the British system of innovation under the Conservatives have been, at various times, the Advisory Council for Applied Research and Development (ACARD), the Advisory Committee on Science and Technology—both advising the Cabinet Office—and, as before, the Department of Trade and Industry. Significant programmes, like the Alvey Programme for information technology, were launched (in 1981, becoming 'one of Britain's largest efforts to strengthen national technological capabilities' (Walker, 1993, p. 184)); and defence R&D expenditure remained high—a higher proportion of government R&D than in France and much higher than in Germany. But despite these elements of continuity in innovation policy, during the second half of the 1980s and into the 1990s, there has been a substantial reduction in the state's role in the innovation system. Moreover, as Table 5.6 shows, the decline in the government's contribution to R&D in the UK has been much greater than that in any other major country. A number of initiatives, including many begun by the Conservative government itself during the early 1980s, have been terminated. Most significant among them was the Alvey project. The state continues to have a role, the Office for Science and Technology (OST) distributing the nation's £1.2 billion science budget, mainly for basic research, to a number of research councils.

In recent years there has been a growing awareness of problems in the British system of innovation. The Conservative government issued a White Paper on science and technology in 1993, calling for a strengthening of links between academia and industry, and proposing the Technology Foresight Programme.[101] This programme resulted in the spring 1995 publication of reports on the likely technological developments in each of 15 sectors of industry. The objective of the programme is to stimulate investment by British firms in R&D so that they will be ahead of their rivals in the markets for the new products and processes. The programme was orchestrated by the OST. This, according to some commentators, confuses matters because the OST deals mainly with basic science and Foresight is about applications and innovations for industry. The suggestion is that it should have been organized by the Department of Trade and Industry. There is also concern that the government will not fully support the implementation of Foresight. A key element in implementation is the Chamber of Commerce one-stop-shops called Business Links, 'where local firms are supposed to be able to find advice about anything from new technology to staff training'. But of the planned 200 Business Links, only 75 are operating, and many of these are under-funded. The success of Foresight will depend on 'whether its message becomes embedded in the industrial culture'. There is little evidence from the past performance of the British NSI that this is about to happen.

How important has defence R&D been to the British NSI and how much spinoff has there been? The answer to this question is very similar to that for France. Most defence R&D goes on development rather than basic or applied research, and there is a sharp distinction between civil and military activities. Defence R&D may occupy an even greater proportion of Britain's technological resources than in France, and almost certainly defence procurement absorbs a higher proportion of high technology *engineering* resources. There 'is broad agreement that defense spending has sapped, rather than strengthened, Britain's industrial economy' (Walker, 1993, p. 177). Among significant differences between the UK and France in relation to defence technology, is that while the UK was willing in certain key areas to remain dependent on the USA—such as nuclear missiles—France went for independence across the board, and solved the scale problem by relying to a greater extent than the UK on exports. This is changing as 'recently a French-style policy of export maximization has been adopted that discourages product complexity' (Walker, 1993, p. 177).

Among similarities between the two countries is that the only high technology industries with positive trade balances are aerospace and pharmaceuticals and that, therefore, aerospace is an exception to the generalization that there is little spinoff of military R&D.[102] Britain's heavy post-war commitment to defence procurement has contributed directly to the strength of this industry. The main firms benefiting from this procurement have been British Aerospace, Rolls-Royce, and Lucas Aerospace. As in France, the pharmaceutical industry is the only high technology industry that has performed well in international terms. Companies like ICI, Glaxo and Beecham have been aggressive investors in R&D and have established close links with university researchers in related fields. In comparison to France, British companies have far fewer new drugs under development, but the drugs they do develop have greater success in world markets. One reason for this is the British companies' strict policies of dropping products which, from the early screening process, seem unlikely to be successful.

A key difference in the pharmaceutical industries, and of the two national economies in general, is in the significance of multinational enterprises (MNEs). Subsidiaries of MNEs are far more important to the UK economy than they are either to France or Germany. There has been a long tradition, beginning in the late nineteenth and early twentieth centuries and increasing sharply after the Second World War, of American direct investment. With companies like Ford and General Motors—and, more recently the Japanese car companies—owning manufacturing subsidiaries in the UK, it is not surprising that foreign companies account for 45 per cent of gross value-added in motor vehicles. But even in chemicals and pharmaceuticals, dominated by the giant UK companies like ICI and Glaxo, foreign companies account for 32 per cent of value-added (Walker, 1993, Table 5.5).

There are differences of opinion as to the implications of a significant presence of MNEs, particularly in high technology areas. Vernon's (1966) product cycle model suggested that the more sophisticated parts of a MNE's production process, including R&D, would be located in the country of the firm's headquarters. Porter elaborates on this, arguing that production of sophisticated components, and core R&D, are activities, 'first and foremost, for either the multinational's home base, or nations with attributes (such as demand conditions) that make locating in them important to innovation. In addition, foreign subsidiaries do not necessarily breed managers with an orientation toward exports and international competition' (Porter, 1990, p. 679).

Vernon himself, among others,[103] now disagrees with this view: 'explanations of the behaviour of TNCs which draw on the national origins of the enterprises as a major explanatory variable are rapidly losing their value, to be replaced by an increased emphasis on the characteristics of the product markets in which the enterprises participate' (Vernon, 1992).

Dunning, whose work on MNEs has been seminal, takes a position somewhere between those of Porter and Vernon. He argues that an increasing proportion of economic activity is potentially footloose in its location, though the extent to which enterprises 'are able and willing to switch locations varies according to industry, firm and country-specific differences' (Dunning, 1992).

In a detailed case study of foreign owned firms in the UK machine tool industry, Young and Dunlop (1992) point out that 'most UK production of machining centres ... is under licence from Japanese makers'. Young and Hood (1992), referring to the same study, conclude that UK competitiveness in this industry will depend on the extent of Japanese FDI, and sourcing strategies—which, in turn, may depend on EU local content rules. What emerges is a picture of an industry in which the presence of foreign, and particularly Japanese, firms may have reduced—or been a result of a decline in—the competitiveness of the indigenous machine tool industry in the UK. As the industry has advanced technologically, so has it become, in the UK, more dependent on foreign owned firms.[104] Thus, whether as a causal or resultant factor, the high proportion of foreign owned firms in this high technology industry in the UK is an expression of the relative weakness of the innovativeness of the indigenous industry. At least in this industry, location of ownership is important.

Walker generalizes this finding by emphasizing the importance of distinguishing between those competitive manufacturing industries in the UK in which the strengths are indigenous—chemicals and pharmaceuticals, aerospace, and food, drink and tobacco—and those in which they derive from foreign multinationals—motor vehicles and electronics (1993, pp. 167–8). He goes further than Young and Hood by stating that Britain's entire industrial development in the 1990s (not just in the machine tool industry) will depend on the behaviour of foreign multinationals and in particular, on the decisions of Japanese companies.

How these conclusions relate to the particularly British state and policy context is suggested by Grant (1995). Grant characterizes Britain as a neo-liberal 'spectator state' whose policy towards globalization has been 'welcome'. Among the results of this, he argues, has been the breaking down of indigenous networks, adversely affecting, in particular, equipment suppliers.

As with foreign direct investment, so with foreign investment specifically in R&D in the UK, there is no consensus as to its effect on UK indigenous technological capabilities. Either way, it is a significant characteristic of the British system of innovation, that the proportion of UK patents registered in the US accounted for by foreign owned firms in the UK, is far above the European average, and that the proportion of large British firms' patents registered in the US accounted for by those firms' foreign subsidiaries, is also above that average (Patel and Pavitt, 1991, Table 3.6). These characteristics firmly underline the relatively international nature of the British NSI. Yet, at least in the high technology sectors, Britain has very few 'giant' manufacturing companies. At the other end of the scale, while there is a profusion of dynamic small firms in the service sector, in manufacturing 'Britain is relatively poorly endowed with small firms' (Walker, 1993, p. 167).[105]

There are weaknesses in Britain's indigenous NSI. One must conclude that the possibility of regenerating British technological leadership is slight, notwithstanding the improvements that may be achieved by the Foresight Programme. Among the key weaknesses are those in the areas of technical education and training and, more broadly, general attitudes to technical skills. As to what the impact of European integration will be, therefore, positive results will be derived more from effective institutional developments than from the further extension of market mechanisms.

Other European systems of innovation

Both France and the UK have strengths and weaknesses in their NSIs. In this section these will become clearer through comparisons with aspects of the NSIs of other European countries, in particular Germany and Italy.

Germany and the importance of the financial system   The control and financing of firms and, in particular, of investment in R&D and innovation varies from country to country. Moreover, different systems of control and financing—or governance—may be associated with different rates and types of innovation. According to Ozaki:

Management of the capitalistic firm is constrained by the propensity of the institutional investors or major individual capitalists to intervene in management decisions (they may, for example, opt for higher dividends and object to a proposed increase in R and D expenditures). The same management also faces another interventionist force, the union, which, concerned with job security of its members, may oppose management's attempt to introduce a new automation technology. (Ozaki, 1991, p. 58)

Ozaki's argument is that Japan has had innovative success because of a hybrid form of enterprise, the 'humanistic firm', in which these problems are obviated by the fact that management and unions all act in the long-term interests of the firm. While this may be part of the explanation, others (e.g. Christensen, 1992) emphasize the close relationships of Japanese firms to banks.

Germany's innovative success, it can be argued, has also been based, among other factors, on aspects of industrial relations and banking. In Germany, too, there has been a 'system of industrial relations that has limited trade union conflict within industries' and a 'banking system that enables the banks to support the restructuring of industries' (Keck, 1993).[106]

Christensen's (1992) analysis suggests that the role of finance is particularly important in Germany.[107] The German tradition of strong banking influence in the process of industrialization goes back to the middle of the nineteenth century. As to whether there is still an important, direct influence by banks on large firms in recent years, there is some doubt. Firms like Siemens, for example, are largely internally financed. However, the banks (and, to some extent, government grants) remain important in the financing of small and medium enterprises. Moreover the German financial system continues to have an indirect influence on large firms. In contrast to the financial systems in the UK and the USA, for example, the institutional features of the German system make takeovers difficult. This lower frequency of takeovers means less disruption in the establishment of reputations and the building of relations—inter- and intra-firm—that arises from frequent changes in ownership.

A distinction can be drawn between credit-based and capital-market-based financial systems. In the first, firms' financing is based mainly on bank credit, and in the second, firms raise funds mainly through the stock market. It is inappropriate to identify the German (or Japanese) system as exclusively credit-based, and the UK (or US) system as exclusively equity-based. However, to the extent that the UK is more capital-market-based than Germany, the problem of 'diverse shareholders who take little interest in the development of the firm, except for the short term prices of their shares' (Christensen, 1992, p. 161), will be more a British one than a German one. And to that extent, investment in R&D with returns expected over a long time horizon will be more likely in Germany than in the UK.

The picture is more complicated than this suggests, because each of the two systems, credit-based and capital-market-based, has advantages—the former in financing of R&D within existing firms, and the latter in the one-off selection of projects, such as new firms based on single innovations. Furthermore, financial systems may emerge from, as well as influence, industrial development. The expertise that financial institutions have in relation to the business of their clients, and the relationships between credit institutions and the firms they finance, will also influence the efficacy of credit-based systems. What is clear, at least, is that there is an interrelationship between the development of a country's financial system, and its industrial and technological change. Despite a great deal of internationalization of financial markets and institutions, national financial systems—with all the historical, cultural, legal, linguistic and economic factors that go into differentiating them—continue to be of primary importance.[108]

German success relative to other European countries is thus based, in part, on its financial system. The technical education system is also usually mentioned as a basis of that success. Ironically, the German perspective on the German NSI emphasizes its weaknesses relative to Japan rather than its strengths *vis-à-vis* its European partners: 'Japan has caught up with Germany or overtaken it on nearly all counts that make up for a strong national technological capability: business financed R&D as percentage of gross domestic product, patents held in the United States, scientists and engineers in nonacademic jobs per 10,000 labor force ...' (Keck, 1993, p. 146).

With respect to some indicators of technological capability, Germany has outperformed even Japan, as can be seen from Table 5.5, Figs 5.12 and 5.13 above. The Japanese system is also not without faults, and Odagiri and Goto (1993), for example, fear that the sharp diminution in the share of universities in basic research in Japan may not augur well for the future of the Japanese NSI. Germany's continuing success over a much longer period than Japan, notwithstanding the increasing challenges it faces in the context of its reunification, increasing European integration, and the intensification of technological competition from South-East Asia, leave room for confidence about the future of its NSI.

Italy and industrial districts   Thus far, attention here has been on national, and to some extent sectoral factors in systems of innovation. There are also, however, in most EU countries, important sub-national, regional systems of innovation. In Italy, for example, in addition to a NSI which is comparable (though inferior) to those of the UK, France and Germany, there is also a second, much more successful, system of innovation, a small firms network.

These two systems are quite different in terms of capabilities, organization, and performance. The small firms network is composed of a large population of small and medium size firms (in some cases located in industrial districts), which interact intensively at the local level.... Firms in the network are engaged in rapid adoption of technology generated externally and in the adaptation and continuous improvement of this technology. (Malerba, 1993, p. 230)

Within the small firms network, Malerba identifies three types of firms: first, those in industrial districts: second, the equipment manufacturers (some of which are also in industrial districts); and third, non-industrial district firms in traditional sectors.

Industrial districts have already been defined and discussed in some detail in Section 4.3.3 of Chapter 4. They are an empirical phenomenon, identified in what has become known as the

Third Italy, and particularly the Emilia-Romagna region. Each industrial district contains a number of firms of different sizes, but all small or medium, all producing all or part of the same product, and all in close proximity to one another. They are closely related to Marshallian industrial districts. Emilia-Romagna has been a particular focus of attention, because of its ceramic tile, textiles and clothing, metalworking and machine making industrial districts, among others. As can be seen from the traditional nature of some of these products, the innovativeness of the industrial districts is concentrated in their processes. There are other industrial agglomerations (or regional innovation systems), like Silicon Valley in California, in which product innovations are more prevalent.

Metalworking and machine making firms are examples of the large number of innovative, internationally competitive, small and medium sized *equipment manufacturers* which are common in a number of different regions in the Third Italy. Among these firms, those in the machine tool industry have been particularly successful. This is illustrated by the growth in the Italian share of machine tool production—which, in contrast to UK machine tool production, is accounted for almost exclusively by indigenous firms. In 1986 the Italian share of world machine tool production was 5.6 per cent; by 1990 it had grown to 8.5 per cent (*American Machinist*, various issues). The success of these firms derives partly from the high levels of skill among technicians and engineers—which transfers rapidly horizontally where the firms are part of an industrial district—and partly from the needs of sophisticated users in close vertical relationships with the suppliers. Major Italian firms like Fiat and Olivetti, and the flexibly specialized, small-firm districts (such as the textile machinery district in Biella), interact closely with machinery designers and manufacturers. This provides 'an innovative stimulus and a continuous feedback on the use of the machinery' (Malerba, 1993, p. 239).

Benetton has been cited as an example of an innovative firm in the *traditional sector*. But many of these firms are not particularly innovative. Those like Benetton that are, represent a new organizational model for the Third Italian regions in which they have emerged in recent years—including Emilia-Romagna and Toscana—particularly in sectors such as clothing and textiles. This is the large, vertically integrated firm, which has been more typical of other regions. Using advanced information and communication technologies to provide remote production control, linking sales with production management, this type of firm has also established 'tight relationships with fashion creation and international marketing' (Camagni, 1991, p. 156). Such firms use the most sophisticated telecommunications and/or production technologies to emulate some of the flexibility of the industrial districts.

Industrial districts are a very important part of the recent innovative success of small firms in Italy. Other examples of localized agglomerations of innovative firms in Europe that have been discussed, either as extant or potential, include those in Spain (Benton, 1992), Germany (Schmitz, 1992) and Denmark (Hansen, 1991; Kristensen, 1992).

Among others, two questions emerge from the discussion thus far. First, are small firms, such as those in industrial districts, more innovative simply because of their size? Second, has the local focus of many of the innovative systems within Europe impeded the emergence of an integrated European system of innovation?

Firm size, market structure and innovation

A traditional, neoclassical view would be that competition is the major spur to innovation, and that monopoly retards it. In much recent work on technological change, culture, tradition and other elements inherent in NSIs may be key factors, rather than market structure (though market structure may itself be a factor in NSIs). But firm size and market structure continue to be of interest. If very large firms are more likely to generate innovation, then innovation will be more common in oligopolistic and monopolistic structures. If small size of firm is associated with innovativeness, then competitive, or industrial district-type structures are the more likely milieu for innovations.

The debate on firm size, market structure and innovation has already been referred to, in Chapter 2 in relation to Schumpeter, and in Chapter 3 in relation to Lazonick and Best. The early Schumpeter believed that innovations were more likely to emanate from small, new firms. Later, coming to the view that high levels of investments were required for successful innovation, he concluded that large firms, possibly in collusion with others, or as monopolies, were more likely to generate innovations. Schumpeter had 'observed that the locus of innovative activities [had] shifted from the talented individual entrepreneur to the organized R&D laboratory' (Pavitt, 1994).

Whether or not Schumpeter's change of mind was a reflection of a real change in the sources of innovation, there continues to be a debate about the significance of size of firm. This debate in some ways is reflected in the work of Lazonick and Best. Lazonick's (1991) view favours large firms, while Best's (1990) favours small firms. Lazonick summarizes his theory of the innovative organization as one 'in which the organizational capability of the business enterprise influences the extent to which the enterprise can transform the high fixed costs of its innovative investment strategy into high-quality products at low unit costs' (1991, p. 198). A high fixed cost innovative investment strategy is a fundamental part of this theory. High fixed costs suggest the need for firms to be large scale.[109]

Best's view of innovative (or entrepreneurial, or learning) firms is shown in the criteria he uses to distinguish them from hierarchical firms. As we showed in Chapter 3, he identifies these firms as ones that seek strategic advantage through continuous product, process and organizational innovation, maintaining organizational flexibility at all levels, including the micro production level (1990, pp. 11–14). This emphasis on organizational flexibility and relatively flat organization structures, underlines the advantages of small firms.[110]

Another difference between Lazonick (and others, like Chandler, who focus on large firms) and Best (and others who emphasize flexible specialization), is that Lazonick attaches more importance to management decisions and strategies than Best, while Best attaches more importance to innovation as a social process than Lazonick. Only a relatively open (and preferably small?) firm can conform to Best's 'learning firm' in which 'ideas for improvement can come from everyone, including consumers, workers, suppliers, staff and managers. As a social process, innovation involves the interaction of people engaged in functionally distinct activities' (1990, p. 13).

A third difference in this context relates to market structure. While Lazonick and Chandler's views favour a small number of large firms, Best's favour the industrial district concept of large numbers of small firms, competing and co-operating in a market structure undefined in neo-classical theory.

Rothwell and Dodgson (1994) summarize and compromise by suggesting that in some cases large firms, and in other cases small firms are more innovative: 'The innovatory advantages of large firms are in the main associated with their relatively greater financial and technological resources, i.e. they are *material* advantages; small firm advantages are those of entrepreneurial dynamism, internal flexibility and responsiveness to changing circumstances, i.e. they are *behavioural* advantages.'[111]

Empirical work on firm size, market structure and innovation faces all the same complications—and more—already discussed above in relation to measurement of R&D, innovation and technological change.

1 *Differences between countries*   Gellman Research Associates (1976) found that the percentage of innovations accounted for by firms with annual sales of less than $50 million was as high as 57 per cent in France, as low as 20 per cent in Japan, with the United States, Germany and the UK in between.
2 *Differences between industries*   Industries like chemicals, pharmaceuticals and electronics, in which expensive R&D laboratories are required, favour large firms;[112] industries in which mass production, continuous process, high capital costs and/or high advertising costs are present, also favour large firms, and innovations in those industries are therefore likely to emanate from large firms;[113] in industries like scientific instruments, specialist machinery and software, where there are relatively low entry costs and/or where niche markets exist (because, for example, of specific customer requirements for producer goods), small firms' share of innovation is high.
3 *Differences over time, even within industries*   In general, small firms predominate in the early stages of a new technology, and larger firms when the technology is more mature. The new biotechnology industry, for example, came about through the inventive/innovative activities of new technology-based firms (NTBFs)—small and medium enterprises established specifically to create, exploit or develop new technologies. The production, distribution and advertising to larger markets—the general commercialization—of such products of the new industry as new drugs, are being handled by large, established firms in the pharmaceutical industry.[114] In some cases, the original invention/innovation occurs in large firms, and the diffusion is through NTBFs. According to Dodgson and Rothwell (1994), this is what happened in relation to semiconductor devices and computer aided design (CAD) systems.

Whether innovations originate in small or large firms, both types of firms have roles in the development and diffusion of innovations. Indeed, successful innovation will often depend on the relationships between small and large firms. Close contacts between an industry and its upstream suppliers, for example, can speed innovations. An illustration is the clothing and textiles industries, in which new products have resulted from such developments in the chemical industry as rayon, nylon and polyester. There are similar examples in the printing and publishing, and wood and furniture industries.

Innovation in an industry can be dependent both on its upstream suppliers and downstream customers. In the software manual-printing industry for example, improvements in printing technology developed upstream were introduced into the relatively small software manual-printing firms because of the insistence of the large software producers downstream (Jacobson and O'Sullivan, 1994).

Despite the complexity of the relationship between firm size and innovation, attempts are made to generalize. Dodgson and Rothwell (1994) conclude from available data that the relationship between firm size and innovation share is U-shaped, that is that small and large firms have higher shares of total innovations than medium-sized firms. The value of such generalization is, however, limited because of the national, industrial and dynamic differences already explained. It follows that, for managers trying to identify appropriate innovation strategies for their firms, 'There are', as Pavitt (1994) concludes, 'no easy and generalizable recipes for success'.

A European system of innovation?

Impediments to flows of information about innovations have been shown in this chapter to exist both within and between countries. The dual systems of innovation in Italy, and subnational regional systems of innovation elsewhere in Europe, reduce the flow of information about innovations within these countries. Military R&D and other institutional factors also impede diffusion to varying extents in each EU country. Between EU members such impediments exist to an even greater extent, despite the completion of the Single European Market (SEM). The role of the military in the innovation system can, as has been shown, limit spillover into commercial applications, but it has also limited international diffusion: 'Despite belonging to the same military alliance, countries lent a high degree of protection to their defence industries, thereby placing limits on the international division of labour, multinational investment and the diffusion of technology. Within countries, a high degree of tolerance was shown to monopolistic supply structures' (Walker, 1991, p. 367).

Nationally focused assistance for defence industries has continued despite the efforts within NATO of the Independent European Programme Group (IEPG), and largely failed exercises like the European Fighter Aircraft project. The military aspects of the NSI have thus enhanced national, and diminished international, aspects of systems of innovation in Europe. However, given the end of the cold war and the collapse of the Soviet bloc, this particular obstacle to diffusion is declining. Also, according to Harbor (1990, p. 145), the European Commission 'cannot afford to cede national autonomy in defence industrial matters, for to do so would be to create a massive loophole through which governments and companies could circumvent EC legislation on the single market on the grounds of national security'.

While it is not clear that such autonomy is in the Commission's power to cede (and such loopholes are therefore likely to continue to exist), there are at the same time a number of other factors that are contributing to the generation of elements of a European system of innovation. Such factors include the development of institutions and programmes in the EU, and the improvements in information and communication technologies. In the context of defence matters, an important development is the increasing co-ordination of defence policy via the Western European Union and—since the Treaty on European Union entered into force—via the EU itself.

European integration and technology—the impact of EU policy   The relationship between technology and integration can be examined in two separate ways: first, in terms of attempts within the EU to 'Europeanize' (or de-nationalize) efforts to influence firms to create, produce, and introduce new technologies; second, and in the opposite direction, in terms of how new technologies have brought firms to focus on Europe (or even the world) as a terrain, both for production and distribution. The two directions of causality—from EU institutions to firms to technology, and from technology to firms to EU institutions—reinforce one another but, for the sake of presentation, this section will examine the former, and the next section the latter.

During the 1970s and early 1980s, it began to be perceived that a technology gap existed, with Europe lagging behind the US (and Japan), particularly in the area of microelectronics.[115] There were a number of unsuccessful attempts, including Unidata, to generate research cooperation within Europe. There was also success, like the European Space Agency and the Arian rocket but, as suggested above, though these did include technological collaboration among firms and governments of different European countries, they were more or less dominated by France. Concorde, an Anglo-French technological success of the 1960s, was a commercial failure. More recently, Airbus has also been a technological success, and may become a commercial success. But if it does, it will do so on the basis of a great deal of support by a number of European governments, as well as by the EU. In the midst of this very mixed record, through EC Commissioner Davignon's initiative, discussions were held at the beginning of the 1980s with the managing directors of the 12 leading electronics firms in Europe. Davignon's aim was to reduce the fragmentation arising from the support for national champions provided by individual member states.

Out of these discussions emerged a collaborative R&D programme, the European Strategic Programme for Research in Information Technology (ESPRIT). Starting as a small pilot programme, ESPRIT grew into a significant institutional context for co-operation between the major European firms, involving Community expenditure of 750 million ECUs in 1984–88, and 1.6 billion ECUs in 1988–92. More important than either the expenditure or the projects generated, was ESPRIT's symbolic value: first, ESPRIT was the first EC programme providing funds on the ('demand-led') basis of competitive bidding by groups of firms and researchers; second, subsequent programmes, such as RACE (Research in Advanced Communications for Europe) and BRITE (Basic Research in Industrial Technologies of Europe), were modelled on ESPRIT; third, it provided a context for co-operation and encouraged converging technological expectations; and fourth, it helped generate support among large firms—accepting that for success they had to be competitive beyond their national markets—for the completion of the SEM.[116]

The 1986 Single European Act formalized and intensified much of this collaborative R&D effort. In the words of Riccardo Petrella, Head of the EC's FAST programme (Forecasting and Assessment in Science and Technology), 'For the first time since the creation of the EC, member countries have decided to adopt a common European policy for research and technological development' (Petrella, 1991, p. 10). In particular, under the Framework Programme, beginning in 1984 all EC R&D and Science and Technology (S&T) programmes were brought together, with a 1987–91 budget of 5.6 billion ECUs. The Third Framework Programme had a similar budget for the years 1990–94, its main features responding to a 1989 review of the first programme by, among other things, giving more attention to the creation or support of 'European centres of excellence'. The Fourth Framework Programme (1994–98) was allocated a budget by the December 1993 Brussels European Council of 'not less than 12 billion Ecu'. The guidelines of the Fourth Programme include, in addition to a number of specific technology-related focuses, greater co-ordination of the research being undertaken in the context of the national programmes of member countries.

Another programme under which funding is obtained for R&D collaboration among West European firms and institutions is the European Research Coordinating Agency (EUREKA). EUREKA, which includes countries outside the EU, does not fund research, but merely acts as a match-maker. The funding comes from the national governments and participating firms and institutions. There is some overlap between the EU programmes and EUREKA, but the former concentrate on pre-competitive R&D and the latter on the competitive end of R&D.

In general, Sharp's conclusions about the impact of integration on the technology and competitiveness of European industry are positive and optimistic.[117] Others are less optimistic. Petrella (1991, p. 13), for example, sees dangers in the fact that 'the process of globalization of competition and technological strategies seems as yet to be happening faster than European economic integration'. There are a number of grounds for moderating optimism about the impact of EU programmes and institutions. First, as Petrella (1991, p. 15) has pointed out, most inter-firm collaborative agreements have been between European firms on the one hand, and US or Japanese on the other.[118] Secondly, there are vastly greater levels of public expenditure on R&D within individual countries than there are in the Framework Programme and

EUREKA combined. Thirdly, there is little in the present EU technology policy that will offset the imbalance between the technological capacity of the European core and that of the periphery.[119] Fourthly, EU member countries and regions continue to compete through various incentives for the mobile investment projects of US and Japanese firms. Finally, there is the unsolved problem of actual and potential national support for nationally based MNCs that continue to be seen as national champions.

Technology and European integration—the technological drive to internationalization   The development of certain technologies has greatly facilitated the emergence of firms whose terrain of activity transcends national boundaries. The most important 'enabling technologies' are transportation and communications. In relation to transportation, jet aircraft have significantly reduced the time taken to move people and goods from one part of the world to another. In communications, the application of information technology, and the convergence between computer and communication technologies into information and communication technologies (ICT), have facilitated the transmission, virtually instantaneously, of spoken and written words and data, and of images. While these technologies by themselves have not made inevitable the emergence of MNCs, the growth in scale and number of these firms would certainly not have been possible without such technologies. Related to the ways in which enabling technologies have given rise to MNCs, particularly during the second half of this century, are the developments in production processes which have required large volumes of output—and hence large firms and large markets—for competitiveness, and the continued accumulation of technologies by firms in their attempts to remain competitive (Cantwell, 1989).

Among the practical results of these forces acting on the advanced technology firms in the member countries of the EU, has been the support that many of these firms have offered for the removal of trading and other barriers. To some extent this support, as shown above, is attributable to the efforts of the Commission, and to the ESPRIT programme, which 'created an important constituency in big business, pressing for the completion of the internal market and the abolition of all remaining internal barriers to trade, such as divergent standards and regulations' (Sharp, 1990, p. 59). At least some of this constituency, irrespective of ESPRIT, would have been pressing for these ends because of technological and competitive imperatives. Indeed, some authors go so far as to suggest that firms' needs resulted in such programmes as ESPRIT: 'Market pressure and rising R&D cost were among the main factors [in the 1980s] underlining the willingness of both managers and politicians to engage in (international) inter-firm collaboration. Shared-cost R&D programmes like ESPRIT and EUREKA are a very clear expression of this phenomenon' (Roscam, Schakenraad and Schakenraad, 1991, p. 27).

International, inter-firm collaboration in Europe does not unequivocally enhance European integration, however. Thus alliances of various kinds were much more common, at least until the mid-1980s, between European firms on the one hand and non-European (and particularly US) firms on the other. On the basis of a study of the ICT industry in the second half of the 1980s, there were, according to Petrella (1991, Table 2 and p. 17), some signs of change towards intra-European agreements, but it was not yet clear whether this was an emerging trend.

Hamill (1992, p. 137), apparently confirming this trend, writes of recent years having 'witnessed a wave of mergers, acquisitions and strategic alliances (MAAs) in Europe'. This includes a growth in intra-EU cross-border MAAs, but some of the most significant MAAs he identifies are, as in the early 1980s, between non-European firms (US and Japanese) and EU firms. He concludes that the rationalization arising from intra-EU MAAs may have an adverse effect on employment and on concentration, and that there may be a loss of EU sovereignty arising from non-EU acquisitions of EU firms. The 'main beneficiaries of the Single European Market may not be European companies, consumers or workers, but rather non-EC firms which have consolidated their market positions in the EC through MAAs' (Hamill, 1992, p. 158). This rather negative view is consonant with that of Kay (1990b), who finds, among other things, that high technology firms are particularly likely to collaborate with firms 'outside their natural market sphere'. On the basis of this and other similar findings, Kay concludes that, in the aftermath of the Single European Market, it could, ironically, 'be easier and cheaper to stimulate joint ventures between EC and non-EC firms than between EC firms' (1990b, p. 269). This may make an EU science and technology policy of encouraging intra-EU collaboration more difficult and expensive, notwithstanding the aims and objectives of the Fourth Framework Programme.[120]

This doubt about the extent to which increasing European integration and technological development can interrelate with European firms to create a European system of innovation is strengthened by the organization and behaviour of most of the large, research-based companies. While many MNCs with headquarters in EU member countries have supported increasing integration, there has not emerged a significant number of integrated European firms. The national base of advanced technology firms remains important. As Petrella (1991, p. 91) shows, for example, 'the country of origin remains the preponderant site of location of R&D units in Europe, USA and Japan'.

What the apparently contradictory evidence suggests, is that individual European firms may support and gain from EU S&T policies in particular and European integration in general. However, pressures arising from technological change, while they may contribute to MAAs, are—by themselves—unlikely to generate industrial integration in Europe. As a context within which R&D and innovation take place, the European system of innovation, for most research and for most firms, is far less significant than national—and in some cases subnational regional—systems of innovation.

5.3   Strategic responses to regional integration

In the context of Europe, the 1980s were marked by the revival and intensification of the integration process. Among the immediate aims of the EC Commission's White Paper on the 'Completion of the Internal Market' in 1985 was the removal of remaining non-tariff barriers. This would create a Single European Market and, as a result, would encourage European firms to see themselves increasingly as European, rather than as German, French or Dutch. This was based on a belief that the fragmented nature of European markets put European firms at a disadvantage *vis-à-vis* American and Japanese firms; the more significant were increasing returns to scale in the major industries, the more would European firms in these industries gain from an expansion of their markets.[121]

The integration process does not seem to have been impeded by expansion, from a Community of 9 at the beginning of the decade, to 10 with Greece joining in 1981 and 12 with Spain and Portugal joining in 1986. More recently, the EU has grown to 15 member countries, with Austria, Finland and Sweden joining in 1995. European integration and expansion, together with various global forces, have been a spur to a wave of mergers, acquisitions and strategic alliances among European firms, and between European and non-European firms since the mid-1980s.[122]

5.3.1   Mergers, acquisitions and joint ventures

Mergers, acquisitions and alliances (MAAs) have already been discussed in a number of places in this book. Chapter 4, which was mainly about structure, mentioned mergers and acquisitions (M&As) first in Section 4.2.1, in the context of a brief discussion about corporate activity and European integration, and second, in Section 4.3.2, in the context of a discussion about globalization. In the present chapter, mainly about strategy, MAAs have again been discussed, first, as vertical integration in Section 5.1.5, second, as horizontal and conglomerate integration in Section 5.1.6, and third, as an expression of increasing European integration driven by technological change in Section 5.2.5. Here we will examine the major trends in mergers, acquisitions and joint ventures (MAJVs) before and since the upsurge in this type of corporate activity in the mid-1980s. In Section 5.3.2 we will briefly examine other types of alliances.

An early example of empirical work on the strategy of European multinational enterprises (MNEs) after the first stage of integration was that of Franko (1976). Based on data covering the period 1958–71, his study concentrated on the conduct of over 80 European MNEs having their headquarters in the six founding members of the EC. He found that although there had been a substantial increase in European multinational operations in the EC, intra-EC operations were relatively limited and confined only to a few sectors such as cars and electrical appliances. Given that most foreign direct investments are made through acquisitions, these findings are likely also to reflect mergers and acquisitions (see Thomsen and Woolcock, 1993, p. 22).

That the EC was not seen as an integrated entity within which to develop corporate strategy is confirmed by work specifically on M&As. There was a merger and acquisition wave in the 1960s in some ways analogous to that since the mid-1980s. They both followed significant steps in European economic integration. But the post-1958 wave was based decidedly on intra-national mergers, while the post-1985 wave has been much more evenly distributed among national, intra-EC, and extra-EC M&As.[123] The national concentration of mergers, even in the UK, the most international of European economies, is shown by Hannah's (1983) data:[124] in the decade of the 1960s, 5635 firms disappeared in the UK as a result of mergers, more than the 5468 firms that disappeared as a result of mergers during the previous six decades.

Tracking MAAs in any international context is a complex task. Once the definitional problem has been solved, one has to deal with the lack of comparative statistical data.[125] Despite these problems, reasonable data are compiled by the Commission. These show a substantial increase in MAJVs during the second half of the 1980s. A growing number of cross-border deals were within the boundaries of the EC, though even in 1990, intra-EC deals were the equivalent in value of only half the deals in America. The more cross-border nature of MAJVs since the mid-1980s is reflected in the fact that, in 1983/84, 65 per cent of mergers (by number) in the EC were between firms within the same EC member country, while in 1989/90 the percentage of mergers accounted for by intra-national deals had gone down to less than 39 per cent. However, 1989/90 was the only year in which this figure dipped below 40 per cent; it rose again to 41 per cent in 1990/91, and 51 per cent in 1991/92 (see Table 5.9).

The aggregate EC trend in *industrial* MAJVs during the 1980s and early 1990s is shown in Fig. 5.14. The figure is based on numbers of mergers, minority acquisitions and joint ventures.[126] Data for the figure, given in detail in Table 5.9, refer to the industrial sector only, and are based on operations involving the 1000 leading firms in the Community, ranked according to turnover, and the 500 largest industrial firms worldwide. It is clear from the figure that the trend during the second half of the 1980s was upwards, peaking in 1989/90, and that

TABLE 5.9 National, community and international MAJVs: (a) mergers; (b) acquisitions of minority holdings; (c) joint ventures in industry in the EC (*Source*: EC Reports on Competition Policy (various years))

Domain	1986/87	1987/88	1988/89	1989/90	1990/91	1991/92
National[i]						
(a)	211	214	233	241	186	175
(b)	84	115	102	73	60	60
(c)	29	45	56	41	33	29
Sub-total	324	374	391	355	279	264
Community[ii]						
(a)	75	112	197	257	170	119
(b)	21	37	37	62	55	34
(c)	16	31	36	55	49	33
Sub-total	112	180	270	374	274	186
International[iii]						
(a)	17	57	62	124	99	49
(b)	12	29	20	45	31	27
(c)	45	35	37	60	45	41
Sub-total	74	121	119	229	175	117
Total						
(a)	303	383	492	622	455	343
(b)	117	181	159	180	146	121
(c)	90	111	129	156	127	103
Grand total	510	675	780	958	728	567

Notes
(i) Deals among firms from the same member state.
(ii) Deals among firms from different member states.
(iii) Deals including firms in member states and third countries, with effects on the Community market.

mergers in general far outweighed either acquisitions of minority holdings or joint ventures. (The number of mergers in 1982/83—117—is included for comparative purposes.)

Cox and Watson (1995) point out that the preference for mergers over joint ventures is uneven across sectors. They calculate the ratio of number of mergers to number of joint ventures, for the period 1986 to 1990, and show that in high technology sectors (chemicals, electrical and electronic engineering, computers and data processing, and mechanical engineering) the ratio is much lower—3.8—than in the rest of industry—6.4. What this means is that while all firms prefer mergers and acquisitions to joint ventures, firms in high technology sectors are more likely to opt for joint ventures than firms in other sectors.

Firms in industries with rapidly changing technologies will wish to 'hedge their bets' by co-operating in various ways with their competitors. They will, however, wish to select the projects in relation to which to co-operate. They may co-operate with one competitor in one project and another competitor in another. This way they will maintain independence but learn from their associations with other firms. This explains the choice of JVs over mergers.[127] As de Bandt (1987) has argued, success is achieved by high levels of both competition and co-operation.

The merger/JV ratio also varies in terms of degree of internationalism. Figure 5.15 is based on the data from Fig. 5.14, for 1991/92, broken down into the three categories or *domains*,

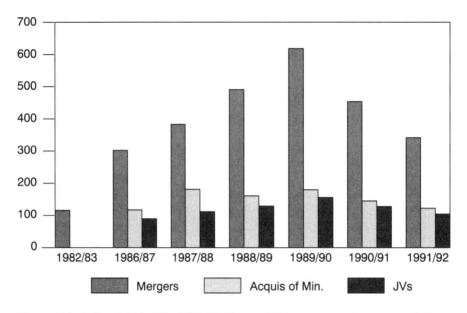

Figure 5.14   Industrial MAJVs, 1982–92 (*Source*: EC Reports on Competition Policy)

national, EC and international. National refers to MAJVs between firms within the same EC member country; EC refers to cross-border MAJVs between firms within the EC; international refers to cross-border MAJVs in which one of the firms is an EC firm and the other a non-EC firm. Figure 5.15 shows that the difference between number of mergers and number of JVs is

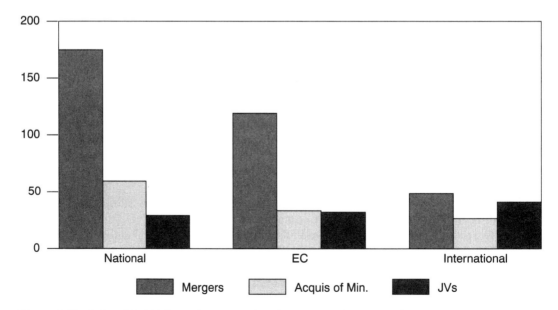

Figure 5.15   Industrial MAJVs, 1991/92: national, EC and international (*Source*: EC Reports on Competition Policy)

greatest for national, and least for international deals; the more international the MAA, the more likely are firms to opt for JVs rather than mergers. Cox and Watson (1995) show similar results for aggregated 1986–90 data. In their terms, the more distant the firms from each other, the greater the aversion to mergers. Firms may begin with JVs to gain familiarity with a foreign market and/or foreign competitor. The greatest familiarity (and therefore greatest likelihood that the deal is a merger/takeover) is in relation to co-national firms, the next in relation to other EC firms, and least in relation to non-EC firms.

Thomsen and Woolcock (1993), use the same Commission breakdown between national, EC and international, to examine trends in mergers in manufacturing and in services. Rather than number of mergers, they obtained data on value of mergers. This confirms that mergers increased during the 1980s peaking in 1989/90 (1988/89 for services). It also shows that, as for mergers by number, cross-border intra-EC mergers in manufacturing increased in value at a greater rate than intra-national mergers up to 1989/90 but that that year—1989/90—was the only year in which EC exceeded national mergers. Thereafter, the value of intra-EC cross-border mergers again declined to below that of intra-national mergers.

To summarize thus far, MAJVs increased during the 1980s, peaking in 1989/90; mergers were more important than JVs; high technology firms were more likely to use JVs than other firms; national deals are least likely to be JVs, EC deals more likely, and international deals most likely; intra-EC, cross-border mergers peaked in 1989/90, exceeding intra-national mergers only in that year.

In the context of the completion of the SEM, one objective was to facilitate the emergence of European firms. 'There is increasing recognition within the European Commission ... of the need for MAAs to allow EC firms to compete more effectively with non-EC firms' (Hamill, 1992, p. 155). The increase in cross-border, intra-EC mergers and acquisitions could therefore be seen as success. However: (i) intra-EC mergers have declined since 1989/90; (ii) other aspects of MAA trends may suggest a decline in European competitiveness; and (iii) it may be inappropriate to see intra-EC MAJVs as a general means of improving the competitiveness of EC firms.

Decline in intra-EC mergers since 1989/90

While the programme for the completion of the SEM by 1992 was a significant factor in the increase in MAJVs in the mid-1980s, it was not the only factor: 'despite the role of the SEM, there remains an important, outward-looking, global dimension to most recent MAAs' (O'Donnell, 1994). Global restructuring during a period of economic growth in the second half of the 1980s also encouraged the MAA boom. This suggests that one reason for the decline in MAAs was the worldwide recession in the early 1990s. It is also possible that most MAAs in response to the SEM had already occurred by 1990. But why, following the 1989/90 peak, did mergers decline faster than acquisitions of minority holdings and JVs?

A new set of powers for the European Commission—The Merger Control Regulation—was agreed in December 1989, coming into effect in September 1990 (see Chapter 7 for further details). It is quite possible that many firms planning cross-border mergers or acquisitions implemented these plans in 1989/90 in order to avoid being subject to the new regulations. Only mergers and majority acquisitions in which the combined global turnover of the firms is over ECUs 5 billion are subject to the Merger Control Regulation. The number of such mergers in 1990/91 was over 30 per cent less than in the previous year. The number of mergers below

ECUs 5 billion was around 40 per cent less than the previous year. In value terms, however, the decline in ECUs 5 billion plus mergers was greater.

Another consideration in the decline in cross-border intra-EC mergers as a proportion of the total after 1989/90 is the sectoral breakdown. For the first time in 1991/92, for example, the food and drink sector overtook the chemical sector as the leader in takeover activity. Deals in the food and drink sector are more commonly domestic than are deals in the chemicals sector.

Other aspects of MAJV trends

Our earlier discussion of mergers (in Section 5.2.5) suggested that mergers/majority acquisitions by/of non-EC firms of/by EC firms, even though in number and value less than intra-EC mergers, may be more significant, particularly in certain sectors. By analogy with the dominance by Japanese firms of the UK machine tool industry, the danger is that non-EC firms will undertake the higher value-added, more technologically sophisticated parts of the production process outside the EC, and use their association with EC firms to gain access to the EC market.

The first point to note—referring again to Figure 5.15—is that, while EC MAJVs increased over the second half of the 1980s, so too did international MAJVs. Cox and Watson (1995) show that in major high technology industries like computers and electronics, among EC firms looking for cross-border MAJVs there is a marked preference for association with non-EC firms. This is explained by the fact that the leading firms in these industries are non-EC firms. In chemicals, where European—and especially German and British—firms are the world leaders, the data suggest a preference for intra-EC deals. Cox and Watson also show that, for the period 1989–90, the industries in the EC which stood 'to gain the most from a round of merger activity—electronics, computers, chemicals, automotive, and aerospace are clearly those industries which experienced the highest level of cross-border deals'. In other words, while in some industries non-EC firms may be gaining from the MAJVs, in the key sectors— at least up to 1990—there was some Europeanization of industry.

However, this Europeanization was far from evenly spread among members. In 1991/92, nearly 87 per cent of mergers (including majority acquisitions) involved firms in the four largest EC countries, i.e. Britain, Germany, France and Italy. Although the figure for 1986/87 is similar (nearly 85 per cent), an important change took place over the period. The share of deals accounted for by Britain fell sharply from nearly 30 per cent in 1986/87 to just over 12 per cent in 1991/92. This drop was matched by an unprecedented increase in the number of acquisitions taking place in Germany. The share of majority acquisitions in Germany increased from 23 per cent of the total in 1986/87 to 45 per cent in 1991/92.

German firms themselves have been the major acquirers of other firms in Germany (93 such deals in 1991/92), followed by French firms (19), and Dutch firms (9). This upsurge of acquisitions by German firms is at least in part accounted for by the acquisition of newly privatized firms in the new German länder, a process that began with the reunification of Germany.

At the beginning of the 1990s, deals accounted for by French firms began to outnumber the British ones. Again, this is partly explained by acquisitions in the new German länder. In 1991/92 more than half the acquisitions by French firms were of firms outside France: in Germany, and in particular the new German länder (25%), Spain (13%), Italy (6%) and the UK (6%). French firms were beginning to make up for a long period of excessively nationally orientated strategies. The decline in the predominance of the UK in international acquisitions is confirmed by Thomsen and Woolcock (1993), who note in relation to foreign direct investment outflows, that the 'leading role of the United Kingdom [has] been usurped by Germany and France'.

Indigenous firms in other countries, like Spain (because of a protectionist tradition) and Ireland (because of a dependence on foreign direct investment), have traditionally been inward looking. Here, too, changes have occurred: for example, Ferry in Spain, and the Kerry Group in Ireland, have adopted strategies of aggressive cross-border acquisitions. Firms in the five largest European countries continue to account for the largest shares of MAJVs, but this is to be expected given that the majority of firms are located in these countries.

The unevenness in the geographic location of acquisitive firms is even more noticeable when different industries are compared. In the period 1989–90, for example, the highest proportions of acquisitions and mergers in which EC firms were targets were accounted for by British (19.4%) and French (17.6%) firms in electronics and computers, by American (17.8%) and British (16.6%) firms in pharmaceuticals, by German (17.2%) and British (15.3%) firms in chemicals, and by German (17.6%), Japanese (13.7%) and American (13.3%) firms in the automotive and aerospace industries (Cox and Watson, 1995, Table 11.6). British firms remain by far the most important in acquisitions in the food and drink sector: 'three British companies, Grand Metropolitan, Hillsdown Holdings and Northern Foods accounted for 14 of the 52 takeovers and mergers registered in the Community in 1991/92' (CEL, 1993d, p. 501).

France, Germany, Italy, the UK and Spain accounted for the vast majority of the target firms, though again unevenly across industries. For example, German firms were the leading targets in electronics/computers with 22.5 per cent of the total, and British firms by far the leading targets in automotive/aerospace, with 25.2 per cent of the total (Cox and Watson, 1995, Table 11.6).

Intra-EC MAJVs as a means of improving the competitiveness of EC firms?

We have already mentioned that EC mergers exceeded national mergers only in 1989/90. Figure 5.16 shows that this is also true for total deals, that is, that the total of mergers, acquisitions and JVs that were cross-border, but intra-European, exceeded the intra-national total only in 1989/90. The figure also shows that national deals declined far less rapidly than either EC or international deals following the peak. As a percentage of total deals, national deals had declined to 50 per cent in 1988/89 and 37 per cent in 1989/90, but was up again to 47 per cent in 1991/92. This could be interpreted as a degree of scepticism following the 'Euro-optimism' of the late 1980s. It could also suggest that minimum efficient scales can in many cases be achieved by national companies.

Why do firms undertake MAAs? From an economic point of view, MAAs improve efficiency and/or increase market power. To the extent that they improve efficiency without increasing market power, welfare economics holds that they improve welfare; to the extent that they increase market power without improving efficiency, welfare economics holds that they reduce welfare. From the point of view of the firm, the reasons for MAAs are more complex.[128]

1 To improve efficiency through economies of scale and scope.
2 To facilitate technological development through exchange of information.

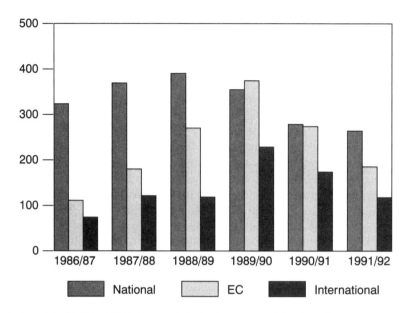

Figure 5.16 Industrial MAJVs, 1986–92: total deals, by year and by domain (*Source*: EC Reports on Competition Policy)

3 To reduce risks ('hedge bets') by co-operating with one or more competitors.
4 To increase control over the market through agreement (collusion) with competitors.
5 To expand the range of markets accessible to the firm's products.[129]
6 To improve access to (or terms for borrowing) capital.
7 To avoid various types of government control, for example over trade.

The main motives for MAJVs in 1989/90, according to the 1991 Report on Competition Policy, were to 'strengthen market position' and 'expansion'. These are most similar to items 4 and 5, and 1, respectively. In many cases, as we showed in our discussion of Kay's (1990a) notion of *strategic market* in Chapter 4, the geographic dimension of the industry is not the same as that of the market, and the appropriate market may be the same, smaller than, or greater than the EU. The reported motives suggest that, at least in that year, the peak year of intra-EC MAJVs, firms identified their appropriate scales of activity, and strategic markets, as greater than their national markets. The subsequent decline in intra-EC MAJVs suggests that expansion into the pan-European market became a less important motivation, i.e. that for most firms the appropriate scales of activity were their national markets. The industrial districts of the Third Italy, for example, in most cases remain very localized networks of small firms. Yet many of them compete successfully in European and world markets.

At the other end of the scale, in some industries the most successful firms are neither national nor European but global. The dominant MAJVs in these industries have been between European on the one hand and American or Japanese firms on the other. In the pharmaceutical industry—in which we have already shown that American firms are the leading initiators of takeovers of European firms—many of the top firms are results of Euro-American mergers and/or acquisitions, and all the top firms have alliances of various kinds across the Atlantic, and often with Japanese firms as well. For example, SmithKline Beecham and Glaxo Wellcome are Anglo-American, Rhône-Poulenc Rorer is Franco-American.

The assessment of trends in industrial MAJVs in Europe suggests a mixed reception: there has been a degree of Europeanization, but national MAJVs still predominate; international MAJVs have in no years been more substantial in number than either of the other two domains (national or EC), but in some sectors mergers and acquisitions involving non-EC firms have been predominant; and the emphasis on intra-EC, cross-border MAJVs is in some cases inappropriate.

The data compiled by the EC Commission in its overview of MAJVs in the *services sector*, refer to three sub-sectors: distribution, banking and insurance. The data for each year from 1986/87 to 1991/92 are presented in Table 5.10. (Data for the year 1984/85 are included for the sake of comparison.)

Table 5.10 shows that, as for industrial MAJVs, mergers are by far the most important type, and 1989/90 was the peak year both for mergers and MAJVs in general. Unlike industrial MAJVs, in the service sector there was another upturn in 1991/92. This was due primarily to an increase in mergers and minority acquisitions in banking accounted for, in the main, by banking institutions in Italy and in France. Banking in the early part of the period and insurance in the latter part stand out as sub-sectors in which acquisitions of minority holdings are more common than in industry, in some years preferred even to mergers.

TABLE 5.10 Distribution, banking and insurance MAJVs: (a) mergers; (b) acquisitions of minority holdings; (c) JVs in the EC service sector (*Source*: EC Reports on Competition Policy (various years))

Sub-sector	1984/85	1986/87	1987/88	1988/89	1989/90	1990/91	1991/92
Distribution							
(a)	34	49	57	58	52	38	36
(b)	9	11	22	22	21	14	8
(c)	4	5	7	14	13	9	7
Sub-total	47	65	86	94	86	61	51
Banking							
(g)	18	35	78	83	113	75	97
(b)	21	33	81	62	96	57	66
(c)	13	24	30	24	30	16	19
Sub-total	52	92	189	169	239	148	182
Insurance							
(a)	15	28	40	33	46	28	31
(b)	8	11	19	29	44	30	24
(c)	1	2	16	16	11	14	16
Sub-total	24	41	75	78	101	72	71
Totals							
(a)	67	112	175	174	211	141	164
(b)	38	55	122	113	161	101	98
(c)	18	31	53	54	54	39	42
Grand total	123	198	350	341	426	281	304

Note
As for Table 5.9, the data are based on deals involving at least one of the 1000 largest firms in the Community.

From other data[130] it is clear that, again as for industrial MAJVs, among national deals mergers are far more common than among EC or international deals. MAJVs in the distribution sub-sector are particularly national.

5.3.2 Other strategic alliances

In addition to MAJVs, firms can also adopt alliance strategies that involve less commitment, control or interdependence, for example, licensing and cross-licensing, subcontracting and other collaboration.

Licensing and cross-licensing

In a standard *licensing* agreement, a company having proprietary rights (the licensor) gives another company (the licensee) the right of use in return for a fee. Usually in industry[131] there is a product or process over which the licensor has a patent or trademark. This firm gives the information on how to produce the product or use the process to the licensee firm in return for a fee. Along with technical know-how, the licensor often provides support services. The fee can be a lump sum or a payment per unit sold (royalty). A firm would license rather than produce because transaction costs in licensing the particular product are lower—using both direct and indirect costs—than internalizing the operation.[132] There are a number of reasons why this might be the case:

1 While the licensor may have the knowledge, the licensee may have the experience in that type of production. A software firm, for example, may produce a new type of programme, but have no experience—or capacity—to manufacture and distribute multiple copies of the programme.
2 The licensor may have the knowledge and experience, but not have a production presence in the location of the licensee. Because of lack of familiarity or other factors leading to high start-up costs, licensing rather than direct production takes place.
3 The licensor may be fully utilizing its production capacity, but not wish to expand because, for example, it believes that the need for extra capacity will be temporary. This type of licensing is also known as *second-sourcing*.

Licensing is in general more common where the product (or service) is clearly defined, and where the product or process is not technologically strategic, i.e. where the firm holding the proprietary right sees no further development of the product or process that may be usurped by the licensee.

In the context of the completion of the SEM, licensing only becomes a more attractive strategy to licensors because it is a means of getting access to a larger market. However, the licensing strategy 'is particularly effective for smaller markets (niches) and in countries with which a firm is not sufficiently familiar to enter alone' (Jacobson, 1991). It is therefore particularly appropriate for small or medium sized enterprises (SMEs) who have products with narrow markets. For example, SMEs in the Japanese pharmaceutical industry, of which there are a large number, are most likely to use licensing to gain access to the European market. Larger Japanese pharmaceutical companies have had their products manufactured and distributed by Western companies in Europe for many years. They have, through this, gained familiarity with the European market. With the advent of the SEM, they have seen a need for greater control and are using other strategies to maintain or increase their presence in the EU, like greenfield investments and MAJVs.

Cross-licensing is used, for example, as part of a technology exchange agreement. With cross-licensing, each company has something the other requires; they agree to exchange the information, usually as the start of an alliance the next step in which would be a joint venture (Hagedoorn and Schakenraad, 1990). In ordinary licensing, the licensor is usually more technologically advanced, or in some other respect ahead of the licensee; the former, after all, has something the latter wishes to acquire. Cross-licensing is usually an agreement between firms on a more equal footing. Cross-licensing is one of many types of agreement that firms in high technology industries have used to ensure that they keep in touch with what their competitors are doing. Along with MAJVs, there has been an increase in cross-licensing, both among European, and between European and non-European firms, since the mid-1980s.

Subcontracting

Like licensing, *subcontracting* is a form of co-operation whereby in-house production is rejected, reduced or expanded less, in favour of production by independent firms. Also, as with licensing, the transaction cost analysis—compare all costs of 'make' with all costs of 'buy' to arrive at the 'make or buy' decision—is crucial. Often the job is tendered for, i.e. the firm makes it known to a number of other firms that it will require a certain quantity of some product, usually a component of some larger product; the other firms respond by informing the first firm as to cost, quality and timing conditions under which they can produce the product. The first firm then chooses to whom to give the contract. If the contract is fulfilled satisfactorily, it can lead to exclusive supply agreements (see Jacobson and O'Sullivan, 1994).

According to Semlinger (1991), out-sourcing (i.e. 'the market procurement of formerly in-house produced goods and services') and subcontracting have been on the increase in recent times. This is explained mostly by more intense competition on world markets, and the rise of Japanese firms as competitors in these markets. An important aspect of Japanese business organization is that firms often have extensive networks of affiliated subcontractors. American and European firms have responded by developing similar networks.

The nature and importance of subcontracting in the EC has been analysed by Charbit, Ravix and Romani (1991). They found that, over the period 1980 to 1986, intra-EC subcontracting increased sharply. (This is where both the principal—the firm for which the work was being done—and the subcontractor were EC firms.) The major principals were British, German and French firms.[133] The nature of the subcontracting networks differed:

1 Those between Benelux, French and German firms involved a wide range of different industries, and were of a 'circular' type; there were principals and subcontractors in each of these member states.
2 Subcontracting networks involving firms from Spain, Portugal and Greece were limited to a much smaller range of industries, and were 'centrifugal'; the firms in these countries were mainly subcontractors, with the principal firms predominantly in Germany, France and Benelux. Spain is particularly important as the home of subcontractor firms in parts of the car, metal and mechanical engineering industries.
3 Because of strong links between the UK and Ireland on one hand and North America on the other, firms in these economies did not appear to have strong subcontracting links with

the rest of Europe. It is likely that a more recent analysis would find a strengthening of all intra-EC subcontracting networks since the mid-1980s.

Other types of collaboration

Collaboration between firms can include vague discussions between managers at the simplest, most casual level, and formal exchange of information in preparation for a merger at the most intense level. The advantage of collaboration is that the firms maintain independence; the disadvantage is that success for all the collaborators depends on high levels of trust and integrity. It is relatively easy, for example in collaboration over R&D, for one party to obtain from the collaboration disproportionately more than it puts into it.

Collaboration is seen as particularly important in high technology industries, and in R&D in general. Jacquemin (1987a) has pointed out, among other advantages of technological collaboration, the 'dynamic economies', whereby the collaboration accelerates invention and innovation through learning effects of working together. This can lead to increased market power.

Another advantage of collaboration is the support that it provides in the establishment and imposition of technical standards. Well-known standards like VHS for video recorders and the DOS and Windows operating systems for computers, although resulting from the efforts of leading firms, also required collaboration from other firms. A recent example of this type of collaboration has been evident in the attempt to establish Microsoft's Windows 95 as the new standard operating system. Although Microsoft is the owner, initiator and main driving force behind Windows 95, there is evidence of the assistance of other software majors that produce for PCs. A newspaper headline 'Caring about Sharing—Even with Rivals'[134] summarizes the attitude of Novell, for example, which is a key competitor in the software market. Novell, like Lotus and Symantec, want to see the new standard established so that they can sell new products based on that standard. One way in which Microsoft and Novell have collaborated is in providing each other with early copies of software, so that they can be cross-tested. Any conflicts in the operation of the software can then be ironed out, in the interests of both sets of customers,[135] before the products are released.

Intra-EC collaboration, particularly in R&D, has been emphasized as an important, positive result of increasing economic integration in Europe (Hayward, 1995). The idea was to encourage the emergence of 'Euro-champions' in high technology sectors. In sensitive sectors such as armaments, aerospace, machine tools, biotechnology and electronics, technological collaboration would enhance EC sovereignty. Once European firms had become the equals of their Japanese and American competitors they could then enter into various kinds of alliances with them. The fear was that if they did so too early, they would become merely subcontractees. In addition, collaboration would help in the achievement of the large and more integrated European domestic market by removing diverging technical standards.

ESPRIT and other such programmes discussed in Section 5.2 of this chapter (and in Chapter 7) aimed to encourage intra-EC collaboration in R&D, but such efforts have been limited. While there was an increase in all types of strategic alliance, including collaboration, among EC firms in the late 1980s, there were also increases in collaboration between EU and non-EU firms.[136] Of MAJVs, trends in joint ventures are probably most indicative of trends in collaboration. Table 5.9 shows that during the period 1986/87 to 1991/92, JVs were higher in most years in international than in either of the other two domains. Our earlier discussion on the differences between mergers and JVs also suggests that collaboration, like JVs, would be a preferred choice among firms in the international domain in comparison to firms in closer proximity.

5.3.3 Conclusion

As with other aspects of the behaviour of firms, so with strategic alliances, European integration has been just one of a number of factors influencing firms. EU policy may influence firms to collaborate, for example, but firms will participate in EU programmes only to the extent that it is in their interests. They will continue to hold options open, including among these options participation in all sorts of alliances with both European and non-European firms. It may in some sub-sectors be in the general European interest for greater industrial integration—including corporate integration—to take place. It may, however, not be in the interests of individual firms to follow this route. We discuss this issue in more detail in Chapter 7. First we turn to the performance of firms in Chapter 6.

Notes

[1] This is from a Cournot-type perspective; a Bertrand-type perspective would be that firms can adjust price until their optimal quantity is sold.

[2] Note that prices and pricing are discussed in various other parts of the book as well. See, for example, the 'Impediments to profit maximization' in Chapter 3 and 'Maximum price to regulate monopolies' (Fig. 4.6) in Chapter 4.

[3] The monopoly firm can set either the price or the quantity, but not both, for whichever it sets, the other will depend on the market demand.

[4] For a discussion of the behaviour of firms under the conditions of oligopoly, see Chapter 4, Section 4.1.3.

[5] Note that in planning to produce q_1 at price p_3, the dominant firm is assuming that there will be no response on the part of the fringe firms to its action of setting price, i.e. it has a conjectural variation of zero.

[6] Lanzillotti (1957) considers competitive price leadership to be most likely.

[7] Block pricing entails a decreasing average price with increasing use. Public utilities often use this pricing practice. Note that there is an underlying assumption in this definition of price discrimination that the costs are the same irrespective of whether the sale is in batches or in units. We will argue below that if different prices for batch than for single units are a result of different costs, then this is not discriminatory.

[8] See the discussion on monopoly in Chapter 4, Section 4.1.4.

[9] This example was originally suggested by Stigler (1966, pp. 209–10), but there continues to be a great deal of interest in US colleges as a monopolistic price discriminating cartel. See, for example, Brimelow (1994). Note that as with many other examples of anticompetitive practices, this one includes more than one: collusion and price discrimination.

[10] Services are consumed during the process of delivery and are, therefore, not susceptible to arbitrage. Price discrimination is thus easier to implement in relation to services than goods.

[11] That is why this strategy of the dominant firm—to set price on the assumption that no other firms will enter (i.e. zero conjectural variation), and if they do, to respond by keeping price where it is and producing the remaining share of the market—is known as a suicidal dominant firm pricing model.

[12] Thus the limit pricing strategy can only be used if the dominant firm can make a profit at prices at which potential entrants would make a loss

[13] Predatory pricing is discussed later in this chapter.

[14] Markham (1951) as quoted in Scherer and Ross (1990, p. 249).

[15] Actually Areeda and Turner argued that predatory pricing was being practised when price was below marginal cost. However, MC is more difficult to estimate, so they settled for AVC as the value below which predatory pricing could be said to exist.

[16] In the short run there are fixed costs; in the long run all costs are variable. The average fixed cost (AFC) is the vertical distance between the AVC and the ATC.

[17] See Martin (1994, Ch. 16) for a detailed discussion of this debate.

[18] See Schelling (1960), who gives examples of such strategies as that of a driver at an intersection. The driver makes it clear to oncoming traffic that he cannot see that traffic by turning his head the other way. As long as he either knows, or is willing to take the chance that, oncoming drivers (a) can see his head is averted, and (b) can stop in time, then he can enter the intersection. Not looking at the oncoming traffic may seem to be irrational, but it can achieve the driver's aim of quickly entering the intersection.

[19] Note that if the incumbent remains a monopoly in this example then it is, in fact, a case of deterrence, rather than predation.

[20] There are two types of multi-period (or multi-move) versions of single-period (or single-move) games: repeated game, in which the players must choose a strategy for a single-period game, for each game in succession, up to the total number of games (in our example, N games); and *super game*, which is an infinitely repeated single-period game.

[21] The rest of the discussion on this case is from the same source.

[22] This quote, and the related discussion, is from Pearson (1994, pp. 328–36).

[23] Quoted by Martin (1994, p. 178) from OJ L 33/47 4 February 1989. The Italian flat glass industry's price fixing is also mentioned in Reekie and Crook (1995, p. 518).

[24] This is where, though not being supplied by Grundig in France, another distributor imports Grundig products from another country into France for sale in France.

[25] As will be mentioned below, exclusive distribution agreements are subject to a block exemption.

[26] This discussion draws heavily on this source.

[27] As discussed above, absolute territorial protection—or the prevention of parallel importing—is an example of total elimination of competition, which if it is part of an exclusive distribution agreement would render it ineligible for exemption.

[28] Note, however, that in Britain and the United States, unlike in continental Europe, 'Under common law, combinations in restraint of trade were illegal' (Chandler, 1990, p. 72). This made it impossible for aggrieved members of cartels to use the courts to get retribution, but, until the Sherman Act, no government had the power to prosecute alleged offenders (restrainers of trade). There was, moreover, no comparable law anywhere until the 1940s (Chandler, 1990, p. 73).

[29] See, for example, Telser (1987), especially Ch. 2. Chandler is convinced that the Act 'and the values it reflected' were extremely important in explaining the differences between the long-term evolution of firms in the United States on one hand, and Germany and Britain on the other (Chandler, 1990, p. 73).

[30] See, for example, the debates in the *Harvard Law Review* and *Yale Law Journal* in the late 1970s, often between economists and lawyers; and, on Europe, Dodgson, Katsoulacos and Pryke (1990).

[31] In which the United States Supreme Court in 1911 held that the Standard Oil Company of New Jersey had contravened the law by monopolizing the petroleum refining industry.

[32] Standard Oil (1911), against; American Tobacco Company (1911), against; Eastman Kodak (1915), against; US Steel (1915 and 1920), in favour; American Can Company (1916), in favour; Alcoa (1945), against; IBM (case began in 1975, prosecution case dropped in 1982); AT&T (1981), against; *Zenith* v. *Matsushita* (1986), in favour of Matsushita. For a summary of these cases, see Scherer and Ross (1990, Ch. 12).

[33] For example, if it is a contestable market (zero sunk costs), then predatory pricing is unlikely. A dominant firm under such circumstances may set a below-cost price to drive one competitor out, but will be unable to follow this with an increase in price to recoup the losses. Relatively free entry will prevent such price increases. However, on the critique of contestable market theory, see Chapter 2.

[34] The fine on AKZO was however reduced because the law on predatory pricing was not clear at that time.

[35] A fine of 3 million ECUs was imposed on the vertically integrated firm British Sugar for reducing its margin between the raw material and the final product to an amount that could not cover its own transformation costs.

[36] The crucial issue leading the Court to decide against Alcoa was the firm's control over the main input (aluminium ingots) into the aluminium production process.

[37] Note that in this case the UK was identified as the market, because of the high cost of transporting the product. BS would not have been able to control the British market for industrial sugar if the transport costs—second order barriers to entry—were not high.

[38] See also, Pearson (1994, pp. 336–8). The following discussion of dominant position is drawn from Pearson (1994, pp. 338–41).

[39] See also Besanko and Perry (1994) who analyse exclusive dealership in a model with product differentiation by manufacturers and geographic differentiation by retailers. There is shown to be an incentive for manufacturers to insist on exclusive dealing because this type of relationship with retailers generates higher profits for manufacturers. Exclusive dealing also increases prices to consumers, but this may to some extent be offset by the reduction in fixed costs of retailing.

[40] Rhys (1993) discusses the conflict between competition policy and industrial policy in relation to the car industry, the former aiming to prevent anti-competitive behaviour within the EU on the part of the firms in the industry, and the latter encouraging the development of a European car industry competitive with those of Japan and the US. This may account for the continuation of the selective distribution system which the Commission might otherwise have prohibited.

[41] United Brands was also accused of trying to prevent arbitrage among the distributors/ripeners by not allowing them to transport unripened bananas.

[42] Though note that if process innovation merely reduces the costs of production, then it does not contribute to the differentiation of the product.

[43] Note that the terms themselves can be confusing. By 'perceived' in this paragraph, we are implying 'perceived but not real'. Real differences are, after all, also perceived differences, otherwise they could not be associated with different prices.

[44] For more on the role of the retailer in product differentiation, see Porter (1974). See also the section on differentiation in the EU.

[45] An individual consumer's tastes and preferences may vary over time, but this is not the issue here. Here the variation is between consumers.

[46] This paragraph draws on Böckem (1994).

[47] The distance between the firms is a proxy for the degree of product differentiation.

[48] To illustrate, they contrast the high fixed costs in R&D required to speed up a computer, with the increase in variable costs involved in improving the quality of furniture by improving the quality of the raw materials.

[49] We will return to discuss this measure in more detail.

[50] This awareness of the role of factors such as product differentiation and increasing returns to scale was not incorporated into international trade theory until the 1980s. For discussions on product differentiation and international trade, see Krugman (1983), and McGovern (1994). McGovern points out that Lovasy (1941) had already, decades before the 'new international trade theorists', used product differentiation to explain aspects of international trade. Laussudrie-Duchêne (1971) had as well.

[51] For a discussion on these and related issues on the economics of European integration, see Krugman (1987b).

[52] This begs the question of why in so many other high quality products Europe lost its leadership to Japan, for example in electronics and cameras. It nevertheless provides some indication of why European firms in some industries continue to be internationally competitive. According to a survey by Insead (1990), European manufacturers may even overemphasize the quality element at the expense of flexibility and design. The Insead analysis points to the fact that design for manufacture, or value analysis and product redesign was near the bottom of manufacturers' priorities at the beginning of the 1990s. The average European manufacturer did not see that a better integration between design and manufacturing was essential to superior technology management.

[53] See above, Chapter 4, Section 4.1.2, for a detailed discussion of Kay's approach. See also Chapter 4, Section 4.3.2 for a discussion on globalization and localization.

[54] This is where a firm sets up, takes over, or otherwise takes control of a part of the production/distribution process closer to the final consumer than itself.

[55] Whether directly or by wholly owned distribution channels.

[56] Economists would wish to compare the gain in welfare from reduction of cigarette consumption—improvements in health, reduction in expenditure on public health, etc.—with the reduction in welfare arising from unemployment in the tobacco industry.

[57] Alternatively, the consumer will consume more of the good until the marginal utility for the last ECU spent on the good is the same as the marginal utility for the last ECU spent on all other goods.

[58] 'Loyalty' is defined as a rational (non-impulsive) preference, whereas 'inertia' involves routine buying.

[59] Also, a proliferation of brands creates confusion among consumers.

[60] This is a quote from the English summary of the article, which is in Spanish.

[61] In this latter sense we might say that a particular group of firms in a country or region is more industrially integrated if together they contribute all the stages of the product transformation process. There may not be vertical corporate integration, because there are many different firms, but there may be vertical industrial integration, because that region or country provides all the inputs, processing and marketing of the final product. *A filière* is an example of vertical industrial integration, and not necessarily vertical corporate integration.

[62] 'The combined capabilities of top and middle management can be considered the skills of the organization itself. These skills were the most valuable of all those that made up the *organizational capabilities* of the new modern industrial enterprise' (Chandler, 1990, p. 36).

[63] 'The potential economies of scale and scope, as measured by rated capacity, are the physical characteristics of the production facilities. The actual economies of scale or scope, as determined by throughput, are organizational' (Chandler, 1990, p. 24).

[64] Chandler's view of vertical integration is the *evolutionary* perspective. For explanations of both evolutionary and transaction cost theories of the firm, see Chapter 3.

[65] As to whether the vertical integration induced by asset specificity is OI or CI, this may depend upon uncertainty.

[66] A fixed proportion production function describes how one—and one only—combination of inputs is needed to produce a given level of output, for example, two wheels and a frame to produce one bicycle. A variable proportion production function describes how different combinations of inputs can produce a specific output. In this case, inputs can be substituted for one another, as for example where labour and machines can be mixed in different ways to produce that same good.

[67] See Blair and Kaserman (1985), and Shughart (1990).

[68] If they were two separate firms, transfer would be something above marginal cost.

[69] Attempts by the EU to monitor and control PSTP are discussed in Chapter 7; see also Welford and Prescott, 1994, p. 28; Manser, 1994, pp. 146–7.

[70] See the discussion on industrial districts in Chapter 4 for references to the literature in which these arguments are common. See also, in particular, Sabel (1989).

[71] The question of size of firm and innovation is discussed in some detail in Section 5.2.5 of this chapter under the heading firm size, market structure and innovation.

[72] More aggregate data on the merger and acquisition boom are presented in Section 5.3 of this chapter.

[73] 'The growth cycle concept focuses attention on the various stages through which products, processes and sometimes whole industries pass from birth to death' (de Jong, 1993).

[74] See OJEC, No. L.293/4, 24.10.90.

[75] For contradictory empirical work in this area, see Cowling *et al.*, 1980, p. 327.

[76] Parts of this section draw closely on Jacobson (1994).

[77] According to Freeman (1994), among economic theorists, 'only Marx in the 19th century and Schumpeter in the 20th could be said to place innovation at the very centre of their growth theory'.

[78] For a critique of this model, see Freeman (1988b); for a brief but comprehensive review of approaches to diffusion, see Lissoni and Metcalfe (1994).

[79] Investigations in agricultural technology, medicine, computers, nuclear power, energy, man-made fibres and plastics support the existence of this type of pattern.

[80] Uneven in the sense of power derived from market structure. A monopsony can clearly impose the introduction of new technology on its suppliers; perfect competition in an industrial buyers' market will leave each of the buyers unable to influence the suppliers.

[81] Precisely what is meant by 'national system of innovation' will be discussed in the next section of the chapter.

[82] It is also a non-financial input indicator.

[83] Barnett (1986, pp. 204–5) points out a similar disparity just *before* the Second World War, when there were 39,000 students between the ages of 13 and 21 in full-time vocational education in England and Wales, and 164,000 in Germany.

[84] On other limitations of patents, see Lamberton (1994).

[85]

$$TBP = \frac{Receipts_{1990}/Payments_{1990}}{Receipts_{1985}/Payments_{1985}}$$

[86] This paragraph and much of the rest of this section are drawn from Chesnais (1993).

[87] In Germany too, to a greater extent than the UK, there was growth in industrial research during the first half of the century (Mowery, 1990).

[88] This engineering tradition was at the level of trained engineers; in general in France, as argued by de Bandt, even after the Second World War, 'The level of industrialisation was quite low and the industrial traditions—cultural, behavioural, institutional—were rather poor' (1987, p. 46).

[89] For more on the role of the state in Europe in general and in France in particular, see Nugent (1994).

[90] De Bandt (1987, p. 50) writes of the absence of transparency in the decision-making process because it is 'internalised within the state apparatus'.

[91] French shares in the Arianespace industrial consortium, held by CNES and the four main contractors, are still 48 per cent, having been reduced from 60 per cent. It should be noted that the French leadership in Europe in relation to space research was not least a result of the Gaullist search for a leadership role for France in Europe in general.

[92] It is part of the chemicals, pharmaceutical and agrochemicals complex, which, Chesnais (1993, p. 220) suggests, is a partly separate innovation sub-system. It should be noted that while the state has had significant shares in the major French pharmaceutical companies, particularly since 1982, these firms have behaved by and large commercially.

[93] It may well be that in the absence of state funding, and even in the absence of self-funded R&D, these firms are nevertheless innovative. There is, indeed, some evidence that the innovative activity of small firms is 'much greater … than that reflected in the formal R&D data'. (Chesnais, 1993, p. 222)

[94] It could be neither despite nor because of the role of the state from the mid-eighteenth century; the success of the British economy in the eighteenth and nineteenth centuries could be a result of—among other things—the role of the state during the mercantilist period up to the second half of the eighteenth century.

[95] Losing its leadership means, as McCloskey (1990) points out, a relative decline, though some writers fail to emphasize the fact that it is relative. See for example, Porter: 'Britain declined because of growing disadvantages in each part of the "diamond"' (1990). The diamond is Porter's explanatory framework, consisting of firm strategy, structure and rivalry, related and supporting industries, factor conditions, and demand conditions.

[96] See Walker (1993, pp. 158–9) for a brief elaboration of these three theories. Porter (1990, p. 506), in some ways combines each of them when he states that the most significant causes were 'weaknesses in human resources, low motivations, the lack of rivalry, and eroding demand conditions'. The main factor according to Chandler (1984) was the continuation of control by the owning families of the main corporations, long after control by salaried managers had become the norm in Germany and the USA.

[97] See, for example, Barnett (1986, Ch. 11). The discussion on the British education and training systems that follows, draws mainly on Walker (1993). See also Porter (1990, pp. 497–8).

[98] This quote from Walker (1993) shows that he sees this characteristic of the French system as a strength. Chesnais (1993, p. 214) sees the same characteristic as a weakness of the French system.

[99] Walker (1993), referencing Hobsbawm (1987), writes: 'resources became overextended as the Empire grew, middle class culture turned against industrial enterprise, and a rentier mentality took hold'. See also Lazonick (1990a, p. 90): 'The heads of the most successful firms, typically of middle-class origin, sought to have their sons educated at the élite public schools, and Oxford and Cambridge—institutions that remained firmly under the control of an aristocracy of landowners and financiers who had little use for industry or technology.'

[100] The discussion that follows draws on Rothwell (1987), Porter (1990, pp. 504–6) and Walker (1993).

[101] This paragraph draws on Coghlan (1995). All the quotes are from this source.

[102] There is an interesting contrast within this similarity, though. Chesnais (1993) identifies French success in aerospace as having derived, in part, from the need for international collaboration. The result, he writes, is that, in this area 'the French subsystem of innovation has *provided the overall structure and represented the backbone of Europe's involvement in space*'. On the other hand, Walker (1993), using similar evidence of need for international collaboration, concludes that it has led to a diminution in the 'autonomy of the British innovation system'. We will discuss this point further.

[103] See, for example, Robert Reich's argument that 'the important question—from the standpoint of national wealth—is not which nation's citizens own what, but which nation's citizens learn how to do what' (1992, p. 137).

[104] We argued in 1988 that the conclusion of agreements between British and Japanese firms in the UK machine tool industry in order to give the British firms access to the newer technologies, amounted, in some respects, 'to the "peripheralisation" of Europe. The high-skill, advanced-technology parts of the production process will end up being located outside Europe—in the US and Japan' (Jacobson and Andréosso, 1988). See also Andréosso and Jacobson (1991). For a detailed discussion of the relationships between multinational corporations and national systems of innovation, see Chesnais (1992).

[105] The argument that manufacturing is the source of innovation in industry and services is presented in Coriat and Petit (1991, pp. 30–2).

[106] Keck considers the industrial relations and banking systems to be 'other factors', outside the 'national system for technical innovation'. According to Nelson's definition of NSI quoted above, they would fall within the national system of innovation. Industrial relations in particular deserves more attention than we have space for here. See Lazonick (1990b).

[107] There are, as is clear from the early part of this section, other important characteristics of Germany's NSI. Particularly significant is technical education. This is discussed by Keck (1993) in some detail.

[108] In addition to Christensen (1992), on the relationship between financial systems and innovation, see also Zysman (1990) and Dosi (1990).

[109] Notwithstanding Lazonick's insistence that 'scale economies are *economies only because of the dynamic interaction of organization and technology* that transforms high fixed costs into low unit costs' (1991, p. 229).

[110] It does not preclude large firms. Microsoft, for example, is a huge organization, but purportedly remains relatively flat (non-hierarchical) in its organization structure, with electronic mail facilitating open communications among all departments and all levels.

[111] Note, however, that this is a generalization. Pavitt (1994), for example, agrees that 'continuous organizational redesign to exploit emerging technological opportunities' can be a problem for large firms, but adopting an evolutionary approach he argues that successful large innovating firms can and do 'assimilate major technological discontinuities'. The rest of this discussion, unless otherwise specified, is from Dodgson and Rothwell (1994) and Pavitt (1994), the two main entries of relevance to firm size and innovation in the *Handbook of Industrial Innovation*.

[112] Note that, according to Scherer and Ross (1990), US data suggest that in relatively smaller firms, R&D expenditure is more efficient.

[113] For example, car industry (mass production), glass, steel and pharmaceuticals (continuous process), shipbuilding and aerospace (high capital costs), food, cosmetics and washing powders (high advertising costs).

[114] In most cases this has occurred through major pharmaceutical companies taking over small, innovative biotechnology firms.

[115] This discussion draws heavily upon Sharp (1990, pp. 57–60). See also Sharp (1991), pp. 60–7.

[116] In addition to the manufacturers, research institutions and small and medium firms have also gained from ESPRIT: 'The SMEs in particular are very positive about ESPRIT and the Commission now claim that 70 per cent of the ESPRIT budget goes to SMEs, a considerable turn-around from its early days' (Sharp, 1991, p. 67).

[117] This optimism is tempered only by doubts about the outcome of the dialectic between 'the pressures towards liberalisation and deregulation on the one hand and towards collaboration and concentration on the other' (Sharp, 1991, p. 75).

[118] More recent data may show a change in the late 1980s and early 1990s.

[119] 'The gap ... between technology-rich and technology-poor countries in Europe is not likely to diminish as a result of *à la carte* programmes [like] EUREKA or technology specific programmes [like] ESPRIT' (Roscam Abbing and Schakenraad, 1991, p. 27).

[120] We examine MAAs in more detail in Section 5.3 of this chapter.

[121] The notion that there are large economies of scale waiting to be exploited has been questioned. See for example, Cox and Watson (1995), in particular their discussion on pp. 306ff. under the heading 'European industrial concentration in the 1960s: the cult of scale'.

[122] European and non-European firms have also responded to the SEM by foreign direct investment. This is discussed in Section 4.3 of Chapter 4, and Section 5.2.5 of this chapter. There is a vast literature on the subject; for example, Thomsen and Woolcock (1993), Young and Hamill (1992) and Cantwell (1992). Note also that cross-border mergers and acquisitions are also forms of FDI.

[123] For the earlier period, see Cox and Watson (1995), Geroski and Jacquemin (1985) and, on the UK, Hannah (1983).

[124] As reported by Cox and Watson (1995).

[125] According to *Panorama of EC industry* (1991) (CEC), two countries only, the UK and the USA, produce sufficient data to make long-term comparisons possible. Unless otherwise specified, data for this section are drawn from the EC Reports on Competition Policy.

[126] Note that mergers include majority acquisitions (or takeovers), and a joint venture between two or more firms involves the amalgamation of their business interests in a specific area, product or project, through the creation of a separate company. We will call mergers, acquisitions and JVs *types* of MAJVs; the *domain* of MAJVs refers to location, i.e. national, EC or international—see below for full explanation of domain.

[127] Note that often firms will undertake JVs with other firms in which they hold minority shares. This may lead to acquisition or merger. The pharmaceutical giant, Glaxo Wellcome, for example, with a 17 per cent stake in the Canadian biotechnology company Biochem Pharma, also had, in the summer of 1995, two joint ventures with that company. In August 1995 newspaper reports suggested that Glaxo Wellcome was considering a complete takeover of Biochem Pharma (e.g. *The Sunday Times*, 13 August 1995).

[128] See also the discussion on reasons for diversification.

[129] This is an application of economies of scope: where the distribution system of one firm facilitates access to markets of the products of its new partner, then the alliance is distributing two products (or ranges of products) cheaper per unit than if they were distributed separately.

[130] See EC Report on Competition Policy, 1993, Annex iv, Table 1.

[131] In the service sector it is more common for the licensor to control a brand name. It *franchises* another firm or individual to use that brand name.

[132] See also the discussion of the transaction cost theory of the firm in Chapter 3.

[133] Italian firms are also important subcontractors, but the data for Italy are limited.

[134] See *The Sunday Times*, 27 August 1995.

[135] Note that in the case of Novell customers using their products running on PCs with Microsoft operating systems, the firms share the customers.

[136] Note, however, that intra-EC collaboration was very low during the first half of the 1980s. Mytelka and Delapierre (1987) estimate that less than one-third of all agreements in the information technology

industry were intra-EC agreements. The non-EC agreements were mostly with American firms. Over this period 52 per cent of the agreements signed by the Dutch firm Philips, for example, were with American firms. Japan was also important; nearly one-fifth of agreements signed by the British firm STC were with Japanese firms.

Questions

5.1 What is the difference between dominant firm pricing and barometric pricing?

5.2 Compare game theoretic with the diagrammatic models of duopolistic collusion? Which explains the situation better?

5.3 Explain why, in a repeated game, the incumbent will co-operate, while in a single play he or she will not. Do you agree with these results?

5.4 What are the differences between incremental and radical technological changes? What are the implications for measurement of these two kinds of technological change?

5.5 Is the concept NSI helpful in explaining differences in technological performance?

5.6 What are the main strengths and weaknesses of the UK, French and German NSIs?

5.7 What can we learn from trends in mergers, acquisitions and joint ventures?

5.8 Why might mergers not be successful?

5.9 How would you—if you were a company's decision maker—decide between a merger and a strategic alliance?

6 Performance of firms

Performance is the firm's and the nation's ultimate concern. It refers to the degree of success in achieving stated objectives. Good performance is the result of successful, efficient conduct. The essential consideration is how efficient firms are in producing the 'right' good in the 'right' quantity at the 'right' cost.

Studying the results obtained by firms can be done at three different levels:

- At the firm (or microeconomic) level
- At the industry (or mesoeconomic level)
- At the level of a country or group of countries (macroeconomic level).

Section 6.1 of this chapter will review the possible criteria that can be used to define performance in general, and will discuss the link between performance and market power. As will be seen, each measure of performance has advantages and disadvantages. In the light of this discussion, Section 6.2 will examine the results achieved by EU firms and industries compared with their major competitors. Finally, in Section 6.3 we will study the relationships between market structure and performance in the EU.

6.1 Measuring performance and the debate on market dominance versus competitive success

6.1.1 Indicators of performance

There are several performance indicators, at the firm, industry and national levels:

- Measures of profitability
- Productivity measures
- Market shares and competitiveness
- Efficiency
- Technological advance.

For cross-country comparisons, there are several:

- International trade-based indicators.

Estimates of performance can be undertaken as time series or cross-sectionally. A firm's profit rate, for example, can be presented on an inter-temporal basis (giving a firm's profit rate at various points in time) or on a cross-sectional basis (comparing it, at a point in time, to the profit rates of other firms).

Since Bain's seminal work from the 1940s on, most analyses of the structure–performance relationship have used cross-sections of firms or industries. However, cross-sectional data often lead to like not being compared with like. They should therefore be limited to firms or industries selling almost identical (or comparable) products in distinctive geographic markets. Combining times series data with cross-sectional data enables us to determine whether the performance of a given corporation has improved or disimproved when compared with the results of rival firms.

We will consider each of the above indicators in turn.

Profit rates and profitability

Since profit maximization has normally been assumed to be the single most important objective of the firm, profit rates and profitability have been treated as the primary barometers of the success of a firm. Changes in profit rates have been used, for example, as indicative of the success or otherwise of mergers.

Profit is defined by the economist as the excess of revenue over cost, including the cost represented by the income foregone from using the capital in the firm rather than in the best alternative use. A simple computation of *profit rate* is given by r_1, which provides an assessment of the effectiveness of the utilization of the resources used:

$$r_1 = \frac{\text{Profits (before interest payments)}}{\text{Total real capital employed}}$$

Computing this rate involves choosing between the evaluation of the firm's assets (in particular capital equipment) either in terms of their cost of acquisition or in terms of their replacement cost[1] to the firm. As demonstrated by Machlup (1952), high profit rates may be the result of undervalued assets, rather than the result of pure economic efficiency. To bypass this difficulty, economists have turned to a second profit rate r_2, which is the accounting rate of return on stockholders' equity.[2]

$$r_2 = \frac{\text{Accounting profit}[3]}{\text{Stockholders' equity}}$$

$$= \text{Rate of return on equity}$$

But this rate depends on *debt/equity ratio* variations as well as on *accounting regulations and conventions*. The debt/equity ratio is problematic because one firm might raise capital by borrowing, and a second by selling shares; the first will have a high debt/equity ratio and the second, a low one. Their performance in making and selling products may be identical, but the first firm may have a higher r_2 than the second—depending on the cost of the debt. How accounts are prepared can also cause problems when comparing the performance of firms. Different regulations in relation to tax in different countries, for example, can result in two firms with identical 'real' performance, reporting different accounting profits. Some tax rules, such as those on transfer pricing, allow large profits to be reported as small ones.

The most popular measure of profitability (and by extension, of market power)[4] in industrial economics was devised by Bain (1941, pp. 276–7): the rate of profit is 'that rate which, when used in discounting the future rents of the enterprise, equates their capital value to the cost of those assets which would be held by the firm if it produced its present output in competitive equilibrium'. This index facilitates the calculation of profits earned in excess of 'ordinary' or 'normal' returns on invested capital (i.e. the returns derived in a perfectly competitive framework).

The data available on firms' balance sheets enable the accountant to write the following identity:[5]

$$\pi_a = p \cdot Q - [c \cdot Q + D]$$

where $p \cdot Q$ is total revenue; $c \cdot Q$ is the total accounting cost including wages, salaries, raw materials, rent on land, electricity and water, etc.; and D is depreciation on fixed capital.

The economist also includes the opportunity cost in the profit function. Economic profit becomes:

$$\pi_e = \pi_a - r \cdot I$$

where r is the rate of return that could have been earned, had capital been used in the best alternative, and I is the value of the investment in the firm.

From the above, *Bain's excess profit rate* is derived:

$$\pi_b = \pi_e / I$$

In computing this rate, it is again necessary to decide whether the firm's investment is to be evaluated at its original purchase cost or in terms of an estimate of its replacement cost.

To avoid many of the problems of profit measures, another ratio, known as *Tobin's q*, was devised in the 1960s.[6] It is defined as the ratio of market value of assets to their replacement cost:

$$q = \frac{\text{Firm's market value}}{\text{Cost of replacing total assets}}$$

where the firm's market value is determined by the value of its shares on the stock markets, and where its total assets comprise buildings, equipment, inventories and outstanding debts.

If a firm's stock is composed of 1 million shares with a market price of ECU 50 per share in time period t_1, the firm's market value in t_1 will be ECUs 50 million. Assuming that it would cost ECUs 20 million to replace all the firm's assets, the q ratio will be equal to 2.5. This particular example illustrates the case of a firm that has managed to develop in such a manner as to be now valued more than twice as much in the marketplace than in terms of the value of its investments. Its market value is far in excess of the replacement cost of its assets. A high q ratio indicates some degree of 'extra profitability'; to have a market value higher than the value of its investments, the firm must be selling its product at prices above long-run costs, i.e. it must be earning supernormal profits.[7]

In a perfectly competitive market, the ratio will be equal to 1 for all firms operating in this market; this is the case where the market value of the firm is just equal to the value of the capital resources owned by the firm. When q is greater than 1, and entry is free, new firms will have an incentive to enter the industry, by purchasing the same capital stock as the incumbent firms, and by anticipating an increase in the market value of their investment. Also, the incumbent firms will have an incentive to expand, because of the higher return on investments. If entry barriers are low, new entry (as well as expansion) will bring the q ratio down, and the adjustment process will stop when the ratio reaches unity. If the ratio persistently assumes a value above 1, this may indicate the exercise of monopoly power characterized by the ability to bar entry. On the other hand, 'q may exceed 1 for a price-taking firm that earns economic rents because it possesses unique, efficiency-producing assets' (Martin, 1993, p. 515). This is the familiar Demsetz efficiency argument: a firm may be making supernormal profits because it is more efficient than its competitors, rather than because it has some means of holding on to market power. While Tobin's q is indicative of a firm's profitability, it does not reveal the reason for that profitability.

Economy-wide variations of the q ratio have been empirically estimated by Tobin and Brainard (1977), von Fürstenberg (1977) and Lindenberg and Ross (1981) for the US economy. Lindenberg and Ross (1981) based their analysis on a sample of 257 firms over a period of 17 years. They found the q ratio to be above 1 for most firms in the sample. It was particularly large for firms with either significant monopoly rents or with rents resulting from the use of special factors that can act as entry barriers (such as control of distribution, and patents). In a second category, with lower q ratios—but still above 1—the authors found firms using product differentiation (cereals, cosmetics), and/or enjoying strong patent protection (photographic equipment, drugs). Low values of q were associated with declining industries, e.g. steel and primary metal manufacturing, as well as for regulated industries, such as electric utilities.

Lindenberg and Ross's results indicate a declining value of q over the period of their study. The average value of the ratio was 1.5; the average firm's value was approximately 50 per cent above the replacement cost of its assets. Other studies have found a cyclical pattern of change in q, but with substantial and consistent differences among them.[8]

Tobin's q ratio does not always reflect the level of competition in an industry. As we have argued, all that q shows is the relationship between the value of the firm and the replacement costs of its assets. Among the reasons why this might differ from unity are the following:

1 That a rent[9] is earned on certain factors of production. These factors will lower the cost function of the firm relative to that of the marginal firm. The existence of such rents will tend to bias q upwards. In addition, these rents may not be captured in the replacement cost figure (Lindenberg and Ross, 1981).
2 That the industry is a mature one, facing a permanent decline in demand. This will drive q to a value below 1.
3 That there is technical change which makes the capital stock of the firm not worth replacing. The q ratio will be less than unity.

In addition, it may be difficult to calculate the ratio because of one or more of the following considerations:

- Replacement costs are difficult to estimate.
- Information on the market value of the firm is available only for publicly traded firms.
- The value of the firm (the numerator of the q ratio) is prospective, or forward-looking. Since it indicates the investors' evaluation of the probable future profitability of the firm, the ratio is sensitive to errors in market valuation. Estimates may be subject to the method used for calculating depreciation expenses, or for valuing inventories (Shughart, 1990). They can also be distorted by manipulations, mistakes, and 'all the strange things that happen in Wall Street' (Shepherd, 1990, p. 115).

Another method of assessing the extent to which profits are above normal is the *Lerner index*. This index measures the excess of the firm's price over its marginal cost.[10] Because marginal cost data are not generally available, we usually use average variable costs. The Lerner index becomes:

$$L = (P - AVC)/P$$

Multiplying numerator and denominator by the number of units sold gives the following ratio, the data for which are readily accessible:

$$\text{Price-cost margin} = \frac{TS - (CM + PR)}{TS}$$

where TS refer to total sales (of either the plant or the firm), CM denotes material costs, and PR is payroll costs.

The most complete measure of profitability would be given by a comprehensive price–cost margin (PCM) index capturing, in addition to all material and payroll costs, advertising, R&D, and capital costs.

While there are pitfalls in relation to each of the measures of profitability, some of these can be overcome by using more than one measure. Results are, however, decidedly mixed. McFarland (1988), for example, finds quite high levels of correlation between q and the accounting rate of return, and finds q to be a better estimate than the accounting rate of return, but also finds errors in both to be high. According to Rob (1992), on the other hand, sales and current profits account for a much larger proportion of the variation in investment decisions than q. Some studies using these measures have arrived at conclusions that contradict the underlying theory. Chen, Hite and Cheng (1989), for example, using Tobin's q to investigate the relationship between barriers, concentration and profitability, obtain results at odds with the theory that greater concentration is associated with price collusion and monopoly profits. And, adding further complexity to the picture, Stevens (1990) concludes that 'positive returns to market shares... depend on a high level of market concentration, suggesting that collusion and efficiency explanations are not clearly separated'; his results from the use of Tobin's q suggest that market power and efficiency together explain performance.

We saw in earlier chapters that there are difficulties in assuming that the maximization of profits is the primary motivation of firms. It follows from our discussions on the measures of profitability that even if a high profit rate is indicative of success from the point of view of the individual firm, it may not be so from the *social* standpoint (Devine *et al.*, 1985). The less the extent to which the Demsetz efficiency argument explains profitability, and the greater the extent to which higher profits may have been achieved through the exercise of market dominance—through the eviction of other firms, and other anti-market strategies discussed in Chapter 5—arguably the more anti-social are supernormal profits. However, even this is not the whole story. Supernormal profits, which may be anti-social in the short run, may contribute to the long-run success of the firm, which in turn may have social benefits through, for example, contributions to employment, to the national system of innovation via technological development, and to other firms through buyer–supplier linkages.

Measures of performance based on profitability also have the failing—common in neo-classical economics in general—that they focus on the firm as a single, homogeneous entity. Other theories of the firm, as we saw in Chapter 3, focus on the structure of the firm. Productivity measures of performance at least recognize that different elements of the firm may have different contributions to make to performance.

Productivity measures

Productivity is normally defined as the ratio of one unit of output to one or more units of the inputs necessary for the production of the product. Partial as well as total factor productivity indices can be computed (Devine *et al.*, 1985).

The total factor productivity index is defined as:

$$P_T = \frac{Q}{\alpha L + \beta K}$$

with $\alpha + \beta = 1$, where α and β are weighted coefficients, and L and K are the labour and capital inputs used in the production process.

Productivity measurements lead to a host of difficulties, in particular in relation to the selection and measurement of factor inputs, and to the measurement of output. For example, the total number of employees in a firm/plant/industry may be used as a measure of labour inputs; but if two firms have the same number of employees, and the same output, and in one firm the workers work a 35 hour week, while in the other they work a 45 hour week, labour productivity is not the same in the two firms. In this case total hours worked, rather than number of employees, would be a more appropriate measure of labour input.

There are similar problems in relation to measures of capital productivity—and of capital in general. Is the capital input the replacement cost of the capital stock, or its original cost? What happens to the value of machinery if more advanced machinery becomes available? How should the fact that people have become adept at using the old machinery be taken into consideration?

In relation to either capital or labour, a major problem associated with the use of productivity indicators is that they do not reflect the qualitative differences among factor inputs used. They generally assume that both labour and capital are homogeneous factors of production. An ideal labour productivity index would reflect the many different skill categories in the labour force.[11]

However they are measured, labour and capital productivity as indicators of performance suggest that the greater the output per unit of input (person or hour of labour, 1000 ECUs of value of capital), the more successful the firm.

The measurement of output is also subject to problems.[12] For example, the use of price deflators to correct for a change in the general price level only partly solves the problems associated with increasing prices. Price increases may be associated with quality upgrading and exchange rate movements (in the case of a cross-country study), as well as with domestic inflation.

Market shares and competitiveness

Firm i's *market share* is the percentage share of total sales revenue held by firm i in a given market j. For any given product, this percentage share can be written as:

$$m_s = \frac{S_{ij}}{S_j}$$

where S_{ij} is the sales revenue of firm i on market j and S_j is the total sales revenue earned by all the firms in market j.

A firm's market shares can vary from 0 to 100 per cent. In everyday business practice, the relative success of a firm is often measured by its market share (as much as in terms of profits and stock prices).

Competitiveness is not a well-defined concept. Some see it as a broad idea, incorporating industry- or economy-wide productivity, living standards and economic growth; others focus more narrowly on success in international trade (Bailey, 1993). For the present purposes let us define competitiveness as the ability to sustain and increase market shares on both the national and the international markets. This can be applied to individual firms (microeconomic level), to industries (mesoeconomic level) and to the economy—or group of economies—as a whole (macroeconomic level). For a group of economies like the EU, for example, we may talk of competitiveness being determined by the ability of EU firms to sustain and increase market shares in EU and international markets.

A distinction can be drawn between *price* competitiveness and *structural* competitiveness. Price competitiveness refers to all factors enabling a firm to price its products at prices below those of its competitors. Structural competitiveness refers to all the non-price elements of competitiveness, i.e. all the factors that contribute to product (or process) differentiation, including quality, durability, brand and design. Normally, price competitiveness and structural competitiveness are important in different product areas:

prices are most important in standardised and commodity-type goods which vary little in quality, and in the lower quality range of more differentiated consumer products such as clothing. [There are other] industrial products—including most capital goods, consumer durables and other branded consumer goods—in which factors such as quality, reliability, after-sales service, innovation and marketing exert a strong influence on competitive ability. (O'Malley, 1989, p. 225)

In some industries, recent trends show that a new form of competitiveness has emerged in which firms must achieve both price and structural competitiveness to succeed (Andréosso, 1991).[13]

At the macroeconomic level, and assuming an open economy, the study of the price competitiveness of a nation leads us to the notion of *real exchange rates*. This is defined as the ratio of prices prevailing in two countries, expressed in a common currency. The real exchange rate is:

$$RER = (P_i \cdot e)/P_j$$

where P_i is the general price level in country i, P_j is the general price level in country j and e is the nominal exchange rate.

For country i, an increase in RER means a loss in price competitiveness *vis-à-vis* country j, and a decrease in RER means that country i becomes more price competitive.[14]

The link between price competitiveness and volume market shares in the 1980s, in both the EU-12 (Fig. 6.1) and the USA (Fig. 6.2), has been analysed in the European Commission journal, *European Economy* (No. 52, 1993).

Change in market shares is defined as the difference between the average annual export volume growth (for the EU-12, extra-EU exports) and the weighted world import volume; where this is positive, it indicates an increase in the market share of the country (or group of countries). Change in price competitiveness for the EU is defined as the difference between the (weighted) average annual growth of the competitor's export prices and the export price of the EU; where this is positive, it indicates an increase in the EU's price competitiveness.

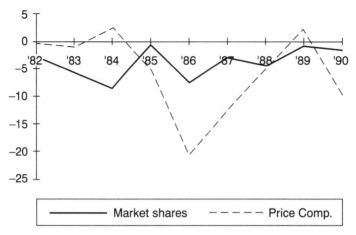

Figure 6.1 Gains and losses in export volume market shares and price competitiveness in the EU-12, 1982–90 (*Source*: CEC, 1993c)

There is a better correlation between the two variables in the USA over the period than in the EU-12. In both cases changes in price competitiveness—in particular through changes in exchange rates—seem to have influenced market shares, but more closely in the USA. The depreciation of the US dollar during the second half of the 1980s contributed to the recovery of American export market shares since 1986. In the EU price competitiveness deteriorated continuously during the 1980s. This had an adverse impact of the export market shares.

However, although there is a correlation between price and market shares, this has too often been exaggerated at the expense of other factors that also contribute to competitiveness. The EU share of world manufacturing exports decreased continuously from nearly a quarter in 1979, to approximately 18 per cent in 1992; in the same period, the exchange rate of the ECU against the currencies of Europe's major trading partners oscillated widely. The ECU index (1987 = 100) fluctuated from approximately 100 in 1979, to around 80 in 1984 and to 110 in 1992 (UNICE, 1994).

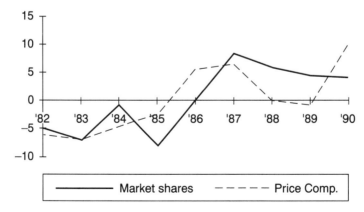

Figure 6.2 Gains and losses in export volume market shares and price competitiveness in the USA, 1982–90 (*Source*: CEC, 1993c)

Exchange rates do have an impact on short-term price competitiveness, but long-term competitiveness is based on a number of other factors. Among the determinants of long-term, or structural, competitiveness are:

1 Management practices and the organization of relationships within and between firms (e.g. clusters, industrial districts, etc.—see Chapter 4).
2 The ability of firms to meet changing demand patterns, and in particular their aptitude to innovate and to move to higher quality goods (produced among other things by a strong NSI—see Chapter 5).
3 An appropriate macroeconomic infrastructure (i.e. public expenditure, tax system, optimal regulation and the correct industrial policy—see Chapter 7).
4 In some cases the cost structures of firms and their investment levels, though note that these are related to 1 above.

Competitiveness is a complex notion; this brief discussion shows that much of this book is of relevance in explaining why some firms/industries/regions are, and other are not, competitive. As with other approaches to the performance of firms, price competitiveness should be used in conjunction with other measures to provide a comprehensive picture.

Efficiency

Measuring efficiency is another way to assess performance. In common parlance, an efficient firm is one that produces its goods or services quickly, smoothly and with a minimum of waste. In economics there are a number of efficiency concepts, each defined differently. We will here explore in turn productive, technical, allocative, dynamic and X-efficiency.

Productive efficiency has two main components: *technical* and *factor price* efficiency (see for example, Devine *et al.*, 1985, p. 321). Technical efficiency entails deriving a maximum level of output from any given set of inputs, for a given state of technology. Factor price efficiency measures the ability to use the best combination of inputs, given their relative prices. The concept of productive efficiency implies producing a specific level of output at minimum cost, for any given technology. This concept is derived from the neoclassical theory of the firm, and can be shown graphically using the production function (represented by the *isoquant*) and the *isocost line*. The isoquant—or equal quantity curve—is the curve showing the different ways in which two factors of production can be combined to produce, optimally, the same quantity of output. The isocost line is the line along which the relative prices of the two factors of production are constant.

In Fig. 6.3, the curve QQ is the isoquant; it indicates the minimum combinations of factor inputs X and Y that allow the firm to produce a given level of output Q, for a given state of the technology. The isocost line AB measures the relative price of the two inputs. Let us assume that the firm produces quantity Q at point F. It will use quantities OX_1 and OY_1 of X and Y respectively. The technical efficiency of the firm is given by the ratio OC/OF. Factor price efficiency is measured by the ratio OI/OC. The productive efficiency of the firm is:

$$\text{Productive efficiency} = \frac{OC}{OF} \cdot \frac{OI}{OC} = \frac{OI}{OF}$$

The closer the ratio to unity, the higher the productive efficiency of the firm. At equilibrium, i.e. at point E, the ratio is equal to unity, which implies that the productive efficiency of the firm is maximum.

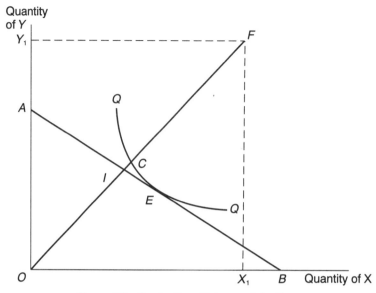

Figure 6.3 Productive efficiency of the firm

The theory underlying the notion of productive efficiency has been criticized by Tomlinson (1993). In this theory, he writes, production 'is conceptualized in terms of a combination of factors, where those factors are disembodied from any organization or calculative framework'. They will be optimized as a result of market forces. 'But markets cannot be seen as compelling either organizational and calculative homogeneity or optimum efficiency. The problem with the neo-classical theory of production is that it excises crucial features of the enterprise which matter for efficiency.'

Productive efficiency, while in theory determined by factors outside the firm (market forces), refers to decisions made in relation to intra-firm operations. *Allocative efficiency* goes beyond the boundaries of the firm. The concept of allocative efficiency has been developed in the framework of General Equilibrium Analysis (GEA), the roots of which are found in the work of Léon Walras. According to GEA, a competitive market system leads to an optimal allocation of resources and income distribution. In each market, each level of output is reached by equating marginal cost to price, for each consumer the marginal benefit is equal to the price, and the relative marginal benefits are the same to all consumers. This is allocative efficiency, which maximizes consumer welfare.[15] It is tempting to conclude from this that removing imperfections will improve allocative efficiency, but Lipsey and Lancaster's (1956) famous *theory of the second best* implies that, given one market imperfection, it will not necessarily improve total welfare to remove other imperfections. 'This is an awkward conclusion because it yields so little guidance on appropriate action in the real world. However, it does at least suggest that competition will not solve all individual allocative inefficiency problems' (Waterson, 1993).

The concept of X-*efficiency*, introduced by Leibenstein in 1966, is best explained in relation to the average cost curve. This curve shows the lowest average cost at which each different level of output can be produced. The neoclassical firm is always on its average cost curve; it is X-efficient. For all sorts of reasons, however, a firm may in practice not be on its average cost curve. Inefficient contracts between principals (owners) and agents (managers) may result in managers being able to operate at less than the lowest costs for each level of output; for example they may be able to give themselves perks over and above what is normally available to equivalent managers. If competition is not very intense, both owners and managers may be able to relax, and instead of keeping employees, plant and equipment optimally utilized, allow some slack; the absence of competition will allow the price to be kept high enough to cover any extra costs. Hicks's (1935) famous line, 'The best of all monopoly profits is a quiet life' reflects this. In these cases there is X-*inefficiency*. In a recent review of the literature, Button and Weyman-Jones (1994) show that there is substantial theoretical and empirical evidence for the existence of X-inefficiency.

Firms that operate in industries under government protection—such as regulated monopolies—are likely to have higher levels of X-inefficiency than those in competitive industries; they will, for example, be less cost conscious. This has led to the notion that deregulation will reduce X-inefficiency. The concern over efficiency has, arguably, been a major driving force behind the regulatory reforms, and privatization measures in Europe in recent decades.[16]

X-efficiency and allocative efficiency are different, but they are related. An improvement in allocative efficiency (for example through the removal of a monopoly) drives prices down, and in turn leads to an improvement in X-efficiency. Leibenstein (1966) showed however that the welfare gain resulting from improvements in allocative efficiency is substantially smaller than that resulting from improvements in X-efficiency.[17]

The degree of X-inefficiency is measured by the extent to which actual average costs exceed the optimal average costs indicated by the average cost curve (see Fig. 6.4). The higher above the AC curve the firm's average costs are, for any given level of output q_1, the more X-inefficient the firm is.

Note that anywhere on the cost curve is efficient. The minimum point on the average cost curve is the *minimum efficient scale*. This is the point towards which, according to neoclassical theory, perfectly competitive firms will be driven by market forces. They will even move from

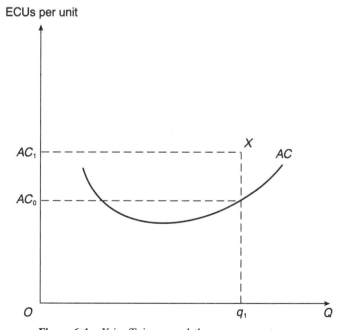

Figure 6.4 X-inefficiency and the average cost curve

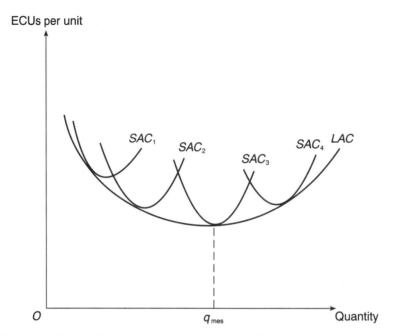

Figure 6.5   The envelope curve and the minimum efficient scale in the long run

short-run average cost curve to short average cost curve (or from one sized plant to another sized plant) in order to achieve lower unit costs; such firms will ultimately settle at the minimum point, q_{mes}, of the long-run (envelope) average cost curve—see Fig. 6.5.[18]

Not only do firms often not operate along their average cost curves, they often do not operate at the level of output appropriate to minimum efficient scale. This would imply no remaining economies of scale to exploit, and the decision makers in the firm knowing that this is the case. Even if it were possible for firms temporarily to be at minimum efficient scale, constant change in prices, inputs, products, processes and technologies cause fluctuations which shift them from this ephemeral point.

Another distinction in the use of the term efficiency relates to that between dynamic and static efficiency. *Static efficiency* refers to efficiency in the production and allocation of resources, given an existing technology, and therefore depends on both productive and allocative efficiency. With *dynamic efficiency* technology changes, a firm or economy is more dynamically efficient, the better it utilizes resources in improving organization systems, and introducing new and better products and processes. Static and dynamic efficiency are not always directly related. The routines that improve static efficiency can result in inertia that prevents dynamic efficiency.[19] As a result, the instruments of competition and industrial policy needed to promote static efficiency may be different from those required to promote dynamic efficiency (see Chapter 7).

One way of measuring efficiency is the *capacity utilization rate*. This shows the extent to which productive capacity is being realized in practice. Excess capacity is a sign of sluggish economic activity. It is, on the other hand, also an entry deterrent since potential entrants who are aware of its existence know that if they enter the industry, the incumbent firms can immediately expand output. This is likely to impose downward pressure on prices, which the incumbent firms are more likely to survive than the new entrants.

Technological advance

As a measure of performance, what technological advance refers to is closely related to dynamic efficiency; it is the result of that efficiency. Hall (1994) provides a detailed account of various ways in which neoclassical and new growth theories can be used to measure technological advances. He praises evolutionary theories for having contributed to change in other theories, but seems to conclude that technical—diagrammatic, algebraic and statistical—economic models hold out hope for better understanding of technological advance. Much of the work on national systems of innovation (see Chapter 5) contradicts this and some of the work on technological advance in the context of close buyer–supplier relationships also calls for a more case-based approach. For example, if factors such as trust and the level of commitment between firms—factors which cannot be measured—are key determinants of the rate at which firms introduce new products, processes and organizational systems, then a case study approach is indicated (Lorenz, 1994). Despite these comments, attempts have been made, with some success, to compare firms, industries or countries in terms of quantitative estimates of their *technological intensity* (see, for example, Davis, 1991).

Technological intensity refers to the extent to which output—or exports—are accounted for by high technology firms or industries. At the macroeconomic level, for example, technological intensity can be measured by the relative proportion of high technology[20] industries in the industrial structure of a country or countries. R&D expenditures, patents, percentage shares of research personnel per industry (or per country) and percentage shares of countries in international publications in technologically advanced fields, are all common measures of technological advance. Their merits and limits have been discussed in Chapter 5.

Trade-based indicators

The *trade balance* (exports – imports, or $X - M$) is a first, and imprecise, barometer of a nation's performance on international markets. For industrial economic purposes it is more interesting to focus on the specific products or industries in relation to which an economy is relatively successful in international competition.

According to the Ricardian model of trade specialization (as revised by Heckscher and Ohlin), a country specializes in the production of, and exports, the goods for which it has a comparative advantage; the country's comparative advantage lies, according to the theory, in being able to produce those goods relatively cheaply because it is relatively well endowed with the factor of production used most intensively in the production of those goods. More recent trade theory takes into account product differentiation and intra-industry trade.

Empirical attempts to identify in relation to which industries a country has comparative advantage have used Balassa's (1965; 1977) *revealed comparative advantage* formula:

$$RCA_i = \frac{X_i/X_{iw}}{\sum X_i / \sum X_{iw}}$$

where X_i = country's exports of industry i, X_{iw} = world exports of industry i, $\sum X_i$ = country's total exports of all industries, $\sum X_{iw}$ = world total exports of all industries.

Where $RCA_i > 1$, the country has a comparative advantage in relation to industry i.

Examples of such studies include Thornhill (1988), in which the author concludes that in relation to manufactured goods, during the 1970s Ireland's comparative advantage shifted strongly towards high-skill, capital intensive industries, and away from low-skill, labour intensive industries. Using revealed comparative advantage specifically to examine questions of technology transfer, Klodt (1990) shows that West Germany maintained a comparative advantage to a greater extent in those industries in which the technology was less mobile. Hibou (1993), however, calls into question the empirical use of revealed comparative advantage, and in particular the drawing of policy implications from such studies.

On the basis of traditional theory, it would be expected that there would be *inter-industry specialization* in trade between countries. What this means is that one country would specialize in and export one product, while its trading partner would specialize in and export another, different product. In practice, a great deal of international trade is based on *intra-industry specialization*, in which countries export and import similar goods to and from one another.[21]

Whatever the industrial specialization of a country actually is, the normative question can be asked as to whether that structure is 'appropriate'/'optimal' and if not, to what extent, and for what reasons, it is 'defective'. One criterion for the normative assessment of a country's industrial structure is its international competitiveness in strategic industries, where strategic industries refers to industries lying at the root of technological change. Another criterion relates to the growth of demand in international markets for its competitive industries. Declining demand for the products of a country's best industries suggests a weak industrial structure.

Another criterion for assessing a country's industrial structure is the *revealed technological comparative advantage (RTCA)*. This index measures the comparative advantage of a nation in innovative activity, as opposed to its advantage in high technology industries. For a given country *i*, the index is computed as follows:

$$RTCA = \frac{\text{Country } i\text{'s share in world trade of high tech product}}{\text{Country } i\text{'s share in world trade of manufactured products}}$$

If, for the EU, the index is above the critical value of 1, this implies that the EU has a comparative advantage, or is relatively specialized, in high technology goods. A country for which the index is less than 1 is specialized in traditional goods, i.e. encompassing a low technological content. The measurement of this index suffers from limitations in the availability of statistics; high technology products are generally defined, as we have seen, as products of industries with high R&D content. Ideally, the *RTCA* should give an indication of a country's ability to sell the goods and services that are growing in importance in world markets, or that use production technologies that are growing in importance in world markets. This would indicate that country's dynamic potential to compete in markets of the future.[22]

With all the limitations of each of the measures of performance, it is appropriate to use more than one such measure in any one study. In relation to the individual firm, the conclusion that it has—in whatever sense—performed well, raises the question as to why.

6.1.2 The debate over market dominance and competitive success

A firm performing well in terms of profit-based measures of performance may be performing well, we have shown, either because of its efficiency, and/or because of its own (or some regulatory authority's) ability to suppress the competition of other firms. In general, a high market share held by a firm is taken as indicative of its ability to dominate the market. A firm with a low market share (10 per cent or less) has little or no market power. This situation is graphically depicted by a relatively flat demand curve facing the firm. As market share increases, control over quantities or prices increases and the demand curve facing the firm becomes less and less elastic. The higher the firm's market share, the closer it comes to being a monopoly. As a monopoly, with 100 per cent of the market, the firm's demand curve coincides with the market demand curve.

We can consider a firm to be *dominant* when it has over 40 per cent of the sales of the market, no close rival, and the ability to control pricing (for example by engaging in price discrimination).[23] Dominant firms are *near-monopolies*, in that although their control of the market is less than complete, they set the profit-maximizing decisions unilaterally, which raises the level of prices. Such firms derive supernormal profits from their ability to dominate the market.

When a firm does have dominance, for how long does this dominance persist? A Chicago school/efficient market approach would suggest the answer: dominance will not persist, there will usually be a rapid rate of erosion of monopoly positions.

Studying a sample of 47 firms in the UK, Shaw and Simpson (1985) found that the rate of decline of market dominance averaged 0.3 to 0.8 percentage points per year. Shepherd's (1975) estimate was around 1 percentage point per year; Geroski's (1987) study, based on 107 firms, obtained results closer to Shaw and Simpson's lower estimate, namely that the decline in market shares was only around 0.3 percentage points per year. Geroski's conclusion is that if market shares and dominant positions decline, they do so only at a 'glacial pace'.[24] Looked at from this point of view of the dominant firms themselves, Chandler's (1990) work confirms that certain firms, in certain industries, have been able to maintain their leading positions over many decades.

The empirical results thus contradict the efficient market view of competition. For whatever reasons, firms in dominant positions are able to maintain that dominance over long periods of time. Organizational, intra-firm factors, explained for example by the evolutionary theories of the firm, are more consistent with the maintenance of dominant positions by leading firms. Jacquemin (1987b, p.129), following an examination of the theoretical underpinnings of the process of dominance, concludes that there is a need 'to be more open to an evolutionary perspective in which the competitive process is more important than equilibrium and in which cumulative interactions among economic agents' vast strategy space and industrial structure have no chance of leading to an optimum'.

6.2   Performance of EU firms and industries

We will assess the performance of EU firms and industries at two different levels:

- At the intra-EU level
- At the international level, allowing for a comparison between EU industry as a whole and its major competitors in the world.

In Section 6.2.1 we will highlight the relative importance of manufacturing industries for the individual EU member countries, as well as their relative performance in terms of turnover. In Section 6.2.2, the position of EU industry as a whole is compared with that of Japan (and other Asian economies) and the USA. In the last part of this chapter, we use trade-related performance indicators to examine industrial specialization of the EU.

6.2.1 Performance of firms and industries at the intra-EU level

The importance of various industries for the EU as a whole has been discussed already (see Chapter 4). The analysis here will highlight the differences among EU countries.

The relative importance of manufacturing industries varies among member countries, with Germany being the most industrially oriented country of the EU. The four largest countries combined (Germany, France, the UK and Italy) account for more than three-quarters of total EU manufacturing turnover. The largest companies (in terms of turnover) tend also to be concentrated in these countries, although the importance of The Netherlands, Switzerland and Sweden as bases for large companies should not be underestimated. Table 6.1 depicts the manufacturing significance of a selected group of European countries.

The largest companies are found in the iron and steel industry (NACE 221), and petroleum products (NACE 13) where technical indivisibilities predominate.[25] Other than these, in the manufacturing sector, the highest average sizes are recorded for motor vehicles (144 employees per enterprise), metal processing (69 employees), office machinery (54), and other transport equipment (50). At the other end of the spectrum lie the leather industry (with an average size of 9 employees), the clothing industry (11), and the food industry (12).[26] The predominance of large firms in the motor vehicle industry is clear from Table 6.2.

The smaller countries appearing in Table 6.2 (Switzerland and The Netherlands) have large food companies. Crossing the two variables—geographical location and industry size—leads to the study of industrial specialization.

Industrial specialization can be defined at both the production and trade levels. The industrial specialization of a country at the production level is the extent to which its industrial structure is dominated by a few large industries; it is the extent to which output (or employment, or value added) is concentrated in the top few industries. Defined on the basis of trade results, the indicator reflects the performances of a given national industry on the world market. Normally, the trade specialization performances of a country mirror its specialization intensity at the production level.

Industrial specialization (at the production level) is particularly noticeable for small and open economies; for example, Luxemburg tends to be specialized in metal processing, the Republic of

TABLE 6.1   The 200 largest companies in Europe by country (1990)
(*Source: Panorama of EC Industry*, 1993)

	Number	Turnover (million ECUs)	%
W. Germany	42	470,077	24.9
France	45	397,503	21.1
UK	47	392,538	20.8
Italy	13	214,520	11.4
The Netherlands	10	118,024	6.3
Switzerland	10	92,646	4.9
Sweden	12	67,456	3.6
Spain	8	48,458	2.6
Belgium	6	33,401	1.8
Norway	2	16,761	0.9
Austria	2	16,046	0.9
Finland	2	14,139	0.8
Luxemburg	1	4,912	0.3
Total	200	1,886,482	100.0

TABLE 6.2 Top firms in selected industries in the EU-12, ranked by turnover (1992)
(*Source*: *Le Nouvel Economiste*, Novembre 1993, Spécial 5000)

Company	Country	NACE	Industry	Turnover (million FF)
1 Royal Dutch Shell	NL	13	Petroleum	512,842
2 IRI	I	—	Diversified	358,259
3 Daimler Benz	D	35	Motor car	333,915
4 British Petroleum	UK	13	Petroleum	309,890
5 Volkswagen	D	35	Motor car	289,516
6 Siemens	D	34	Electrical	266,454
7 Fiat	I	35	Motor car	254,510
8 Unilever	NL	41/2	Food	230,552
9 VEBA	D	—	Diversified	221,769
10 ENI	I	—	Diversified	214,348
11 Nestlé	CH	41/2	Food	205,465
12 Elf Aquitaine	F	13	Petroleum	200,563
13 Renault	F	35	Motor car	179,449
14 EDF	F	16	Electricity	177,463
15 Philips	NL	34	Electrical	176,225

Note The Istituto per la Ricostruzione Industriale (IRI) is a highly diversified group. The Ente Nazionale Idrocarburi (ENI) and VEBA are also diversified, albeit to a lesser extent, since they are still relatively concentrated in oil products and chemicals.

Ireland in electronic and electrical engineering, Denmark in food and mechanical engineering, and Portugal in the footwear and textile manufacturing industries. Table 6.3 gives a rough summary of the patterns of industrial specialization in the manufacturing sector for a selected number of EU countries during the second half of the 1980s.[27]

Two interesting points emerge from Table 6.3. First, France is not relatively specialized when compared with the other large EU countries. Even with a more detailed breakdown of industries (3 digit) France is less specialized in general than the European countries of comparable size (Lafay and Herzog, 1989). Second, many countries seem to be specialized in the same industry

TABLE 6.3 Industrial specialization in the EU manufacturing sector—selected countries, 1987 (*Source*: Adapted from *Panorama of EC Industry*, 1990)

Country	Major, NACE two-digit, areas of specialization
Denmark	Food, drink and tobacco (0.2)
France	Office and data processing machines precision and optical instruments (0.1)
Germany	Transport equipment (1.3); Electrical goods (1.2)
Spain	Food, drink and tobacco (1.3); Textiles–clothing and footwear (0.5)
Italy	Textiles–clothing and footwear (1.9)
Luxemburg	Ferrous and non-ferrous metals (11.2)
Portugal	Textiles–clothing (6.0); Food (2.0)
UK	Food, drink and tobacco (1.3); Paper and printing products (0.3)

Note The specialization indicator (in brackets) is here defined as the difference between the share of the value-added (VA) in the GDP of a given industry in a given country and the total EU-12 share of the sector. The higher the indicator, the higher the level of specialization.

TABLE 6.4   Export specialization in the EU services sector—average for 1987–89, selected results (*Source*: Adapted from CEC (1993e, Table 5.2, p. 50))

Country	*Major area(s) of specialization*
A. *High specialization*	
UK	Insurance (288)
	Banking (232)
	Communications (195)
Denmark	Sea transport (250)
	Road transport (215)
The Netherlands	Road transport (286)
	Business services (177)
Greece	Sea transport (207)
	Tourism (153)
Portugal	Tourism (234)
Spain	Tourism (231)
B. *Low specialization*	
Ireland	Road transport (172)
	Air transport (162)
	Tourism (155)
	Insurance (104)
Italy	Sea transport (173)
	Construction (158)
	Tourism (124)
France	Banking (118)
	Road transport (116)
C. *Intermediate specialization*	
Germany	Construction (238)
	Communications (182)
	Air transport (151)
	Trade (120)
BLEU	Sea transport (220)
	Business services (190)
	Trade (154)
	Banking (144)

Note   The export specialization index (in brackets) compares a sector's share in total services exports with the corresponding figure for the Community as a whole. The higher the index for a given industry i, the more specialized the country in industry i. BLEU: Belgium–Luxemburg Economic Union.

(Denmark, the UK and Spain in the food industry; Italy, Portugal and Spain in the textile–clothing and footwear industry). This reflects the importance of intra-industry specialization.

Trade specialization patterns in the EU services sector are summarized in Table 6.4.

Table 6.4 groups the EU-12 into three broad categories:

1 Type A encompasses countries that are highly specialized in a few service activities. These countries have at least one service area in relation to which the specialization index exceeds 200.

2 Type B groups countries that are only loosely specialized; they tend to be slightly specialized in many different services sub-sectors. As a result, the specialization indices tend to be low (the maximum being around the 170).

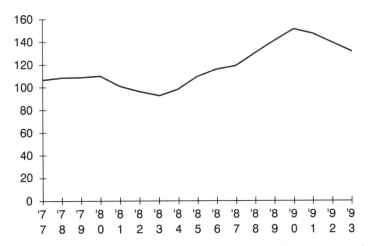

Figure 6.6 Index of investment in EU-12 manufacturing industry (in constant prices, 1981 = 100) (*Source*: European Community Investment Survey)

3 Type C gathers countries that are in an intermediate situation. These countries have distributed their strengths over a limited number of different service sub-sectors, but have succeeded in achieving relatively high specialization indices, for at least one service activity above 200.

The table confirms British leadership in the EU insurance and banking industries. Denmark, The Netherlands and Greece have a strong position in the transport industries, whereas Portugal, Spain and, to a lesser extent, Greece are heavily and primarily involved in tourism. At the other extreme lie Ireland (loosely specialized in transport and tourism), Italy and France. Ireland's specialization can be called *pole specialization*[28]—specialization in a small number of related products or services—in that air transport and tourism are mutually reinforcing. Here again, France appears very poorly specialized. The French manufacturing and services sectors lack strong positions in a few selected industries, a feature which is not common to the other large EU economies. Germany has particularly strong positions in relation to construction, and communications; BLEU's strengths are in sea transport and business services, and, to a lesser extent, in trade and banking.[29]

We now turn to *change over time* in the performance of European industry, focusing in particular on investment trends, production growth and change in productivity.

Between 1983 and 1989, investment in the EU-12 manufacturing sector increased by more than 50 per cent whereas between 1991 and 1993, it dropped by more than 15 per cent (Fig. 6.6). The decline of manufacturing investment has been particularly acute in France and in the UK. When data on the new German Länder are integrated into the study, the decline becomes much less pronounced in Germany.

One would expect the growth in investment during the 1980s to be paralleled by an equally impressive growth of output in the EU manufacturing industry. However, manufacturing production increased by an annual average of 1.8 per cent over the last decade, and by an even lower 0.5 per cent in the important mechanical engineering industry (see Appendix 6.2, Table A6.3). Note that all manufacturing industries except footwear and clothing have experienced output growth over the same period.

During the early 1990s, investment and turnover in the capital goods sector, and in particular in the mechanical engineering industry, have been particularly depressed (Table 6.5). This is of

TABLE 6.5   Trends in investment and turnover in selected EU manufacturing industries (annual percentage change, 1989–93) (*Source*: CEC, *Panorama of EC Industry. Short-term Supplements (1993 and 1994)*)

NACE code		Investment 89	Turnover				
			89	90	91	92	93
24	Non-metal mineral products	21.3	9.8	4.3	2.4	−0.2	−4.1
25/6	Chemicals and man-made fibres	16.2	9.1	1.2	−1.2	1.4	−2.9
31	Metal articles	21.4	14.5	6.9	2.0	−0.1	−7.3
32	Mechanical engineering	18.6	13.4	8.8	−1.7	−2.6	−4.9
34	Electrical engineering	10.7	9.4	6.1	2.7	−0.7	−2.6
35/6	Transport	16.5	11.6	6.7	4.0	1.4	−11.8
37	Instrument engineering	17.6	9.6	4.3	5.4	2.7	na
41/2	Food	10.0	8.9	5.4	5.6	3.0	na
47	Paper	11.3	11.3	6.1	5.2	−1.0	−2.4
48	Rubber	15.5	12.2	6.8	6.2	2.4	−4.3
45	Clothing	9.4	10.3	6.4	4.2	5.3	9.6

great concern to the entire EU manufacturing industry since performance in this particular industry is likely to affect performance in other industries that use the products of the mechanical engineering industry and, through multiplier effects, other industries as well. The greater the output of industries like mechanical engineering and office and data processing equipment and, by implication, the greater the introduction of the products of these industries into downstream industries, the greater the impact on productivity in those downstream industries.

Figure 6.7 shows the recent trends in labour productivity of selected EU-12 manufacturing industries. Labour productivity is defined as the ratio of gross value-added at factor cost to

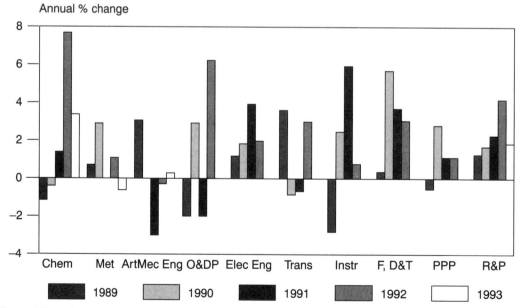

Figure 6.7   Labour productivity in selected EU-12 manufacturing industries (*Source*: *Panorama*, 1993, 1994)

the number of employees. In chemicals and man-made fibres (Chem) productivity increased sharply following declines in 1989 and 1990. Metal articles, mechanical engineering and office and data processing equipment all performed unevenly, O&DP in particular falling and rising in alternate years, with a sharp rise in 1992. Electrical engineering increased each year over the period, as did food, drink and tobacco (F,D&T) and rubber and plastics (R&P). In the remaining industries, instrument engineering (Instr) and paper, printing and publishing (PPP), like chemicals and man-made fibres, productivity increased following declines in the early years of the period.

Unless accompanied by more than proportionate increases in output, labour productivity improvements are associated with declining manufacturing employment. Job contractions can also be due to restructuring, or the reorganization of firms, a widespread phenomenon in the EU in the late 1980s.

6.2.2   Comparative performance: EU, USA and South-East Asia

In order to study the relative importance of the EU in the world, the most appropriate criteria are those relating to its comparative performance on the world market. The world export share and the trends in world industrial production of the EU will be examined first, followed by factor productivity and specialization; next, our performance indicators will be broadened to include the trade specialization of the EU as a whole.

World importance of EU industrial and service sectors

The EU Commission forecasts that during the 1990s the Asian nations will be responsible for more than one-third of world economic growth,[30] as opposed to one-quarter for the EU as a whole, one-sixth for North America and slightly more than 4 per cent for the EFTA countries. There will be three main poles of industrial and international economic activity: the EU and its associates (mainly EFTA and Eastern Europe), NAFTA (North American Free Trade Area, comprising the USA, Canada and Mexico) and Japan and East Asia.[31] Wherever possible, our analysis will be based on a comparison of the industrial structures and performances among the three major industrial poles of the triad.

Proportion of employment   Industry accounts for a smaller proportion of employment in the USA than in the EU or Japan (Table 6.6). The importance of manufacturing to employment in the economies of the countries with a manufacturing tradition has been shrinking since the first oil shock (1973). This phenomenon of *de-industrialization* has been more important in the USA than in either Europe or Japan.

TABLE 6.6   Share (%) of industrial and service sectors in employment (1992) (*Source*: Basic statistics of the Community, 1994)

	EU-12	*USA*	*Japan*
Manufacturing	32.8	24.6	34.6
Services	61.4	72.5	59.0

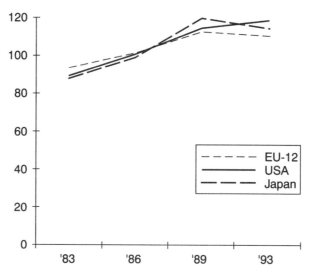

Figure 6.8   Change in manufacturing production, EU, USA and Japan (1985 = 100) (*Sources*: Eurostat, Basic Statistics of the Community, Luxemburg; OECD, Main Economic Indicators (various issues))

Size of firms   Within manufacturing, size of firms is an important characteristic on the basis of which to compare the EU with its competitors. European firms are generally smaller than their American or Japanese equivalents. For example, in the late 1980s, 9.5 per cent of EU firms in the food industry were medium or large size enterprises (i.e. 100 employees or more), compared with 19 per cent in the USA, and 11 per cent in Japan. Small enterprises (i.e. employing 10 to 19 people) accounted for 57 per cent of employment in the clothing and footwear industry in the EU, compared with 9 per cent in the USA. Wide disparities can also be noted in the textile industry.

Growth of industrial production   Growth of industrial production since 1985 has been slower in the EU than in the USA or Japan. This is shown for manufacturing (industry less building and construction) in Fig. 6.8. This figure confirms the sluggish growth rate of industrial production in the EU over the past decade, compared with that of either Japan or the USA. EU industrial production actually declined during the very beginning of the last decade; in 1984, EU industrial production was back to the 1980 level. In Japan, industrial production was almost flat between 1980 and 1982. The year 1983 marks the recovery of industrial production for both Japan and the USA (roughly 9 per cent increase each). EU recovery was less sharp (less than 2 per cent growth in 1983). In the second half of the 1980s there was, in all three areas, substantial expansion in industrial production sustained by a parallel increase in investment. This increase has been very marked in Japan, where the share of investment in GDP rose to 32 per cent in 1990, compared with approximately 27 per cent in the mid-1980s. In the EU, it increased slightly, and went above the 20 per cent mark in 1990 (CEC, 1993a).

International variations in productivity and efficiency

Table 6.7 compares *total, labour and factor productivity* changes in the USA, Japan and Europe. Over the last 20 years, Europe has consistently ranked midway between a very

TABLE 6.7   Annual average percentage changes in factor productivity (*Source*: OECD, *Economic Outlook*, No. 54, December 1993)

	Total factor productivity[a]		Labour productivity[b]		Capital productivity	
	1974–79	*1980–91*	*1974–79*	*1980–91*	*1974–79*	*1980–89*
USA	0.2	0.5	0.5	1.0	−0.5	−0.4
Japan	2.1	1.9	3.6	2.9	−2.2	−1.4
Europe[c]	1.6	1.3	2.0	1.7	−1.1	−0.6

[a] TFP growth is the weighted average of the growth in labour and capital productivity.
[b] Output per person at work.
[c] This corresponds to the EU-15 plus EFTA countries.

productive Japanese economy and a less productive American economy in terms of changes in productivity.

In trying to measure the level of *technical inefficiency*[32] in the UK manufacturing industry, Green and Mayes (1991) concluded that similar levels of inefficiency can be observed across countries (in particular in the UK, the USA, Japan and Australia). The authors found, for example, that the average level of inefficiency at the plant level in the UK is similar to that in Japan.[33]

6.2.3   Trade-based indicators of performance

If we focus on a single year, the EU seems to have performed relatively well, and to be relatively important in the world, in terms of trade related indicators. In 1990, total extra-EU exports exceeded ECUs 400 billion[34] (Table 6.8). The EU merchandise trade in that year represented 20.7 per cent of world trade, compared with 16.8 per cent for the USA and 9.7 per cent for Japan (*European Economy*, 1993). Since more than 90 per cent of EU merchandise exports are composed of manufacturing goods, these figures suggest that EU manufacturing industry is still relatively significant worldwide.

The EU is the world leader not only for merchandise trade, but also for commercial services. In 1990 the EU accounted for 27.1 per cent of world trade in services, compared with 16.1 per cent for the USA and 10.2 per cent for Japan.

Given these high levels of contribution of the EU to world trade, it is not surprising that the EU is economically more open than either the USA or Japan. In 1990, the trade to GDP ratio in the EU was above 25 per cent, against roughly 20 per cent for both the USA and Japan.[35]

TABLE 6.8   Exports, imports and trade balance of the EU (billion ECUs)
(*Source*: *European Economy* (1993) The European Community as a World Trade Partner, No. 52, adapted from Table 82, p. 205)

	Extra-EU exports	*Extra-EU imports*	*Balance*
1970	54.2	61.8	−7.6
1975	118.5	132.9	−14.4
1980	216.7	282.5	−65.8
1985	378.7	406.6	−27.9
1990	419.8	462.7	−42.9

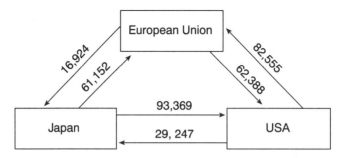

Figure 6.9 Manufacturing exports of the triad in million ECUs, 1990 (*Source: European Economy*, CEC, 1993c)

If we analyse EU trade over a longer period of time (1970–90), we can see that the EU manufacturing industry has been losing ground on several fronts. First, the trade balance of the EU deteriorated gradually during the 1970s (Table 6.8). During the 1980s, the deterioration seems to have been halted, but not reversed. Following some improvement in the first half of the 1980s, it worsened again between 1985 and 1990. The trade deficit in 1990 is still important, amounting to ECUs 43 billion.

Most of the EU deficit is explained by the bilateral trade situation of the EU *vis-à-vis* Japan (Fig. 6.9). In relative terms, the EU's share of world exports came down to less than one-third in 1989, against more than 34 per cent in 1980. In the same period the Japanese share of world exports nearly doubled, and the share of Asia pacific countries[36] increased from 15 per cent in 1980 to 24.5 per cent in 1990 (World Bank Statistics). Because some countries in the world have been growing much faster than the EU, and because the improvement of their trade balance is even more spectacular than that of the EU, the trade position of the EU during the 1980s is best characterized by loss minimization on world markets rather than by any substantial improvement.

6.2.4 Revealed comparative advantages of EU industry

There is a great deal of diversity, involving strengths and weaknesses of particular industrial sectors, and of particular countries underlying the performance of the EU as a whole. The study of production and trade performance by type of industry enables us to look at the EU's sectoral specialization.

Patterns of trade specialization

Table 6.9 summarizes the major patterns of trade specialization for a number of EU countries, for the USA and for Japan in the second half of the 1980s. The food and armament industries are not taken into account in this table.

Table 6.9 shows how trade in the bigger EU countries and in their major competitors is normally polarized around a few industries only. Probably the most striking feature of this table is the different intensity of trade specialization of Italy and Japan on the one hand, and France, the UK, West Germany, and the USA on the other. Italy and Japan are heavily engaged (and widely successful) in a small number of selected industries. These two countries have been able to become dominant in a few specific industries: Italy is heavily engaged in the manufacture and

TABLE 6.9 Major areas of trade specialization of selected EU countries versus the USA and Japan
(*Source*: Adapted from Turpin, 1989)

Country	Products (three-digit classification)
Italy	Knitting (370); cement (320); leather products (312); furniture (245); domestic type electric appliances (200); clothing (197); ceramics (142)
France	Rubber products (93); cement (83); aerospace equipment (81); motor vehicle components (73)
W. Germany	Machinery for use in specific industries (107); motor vehicles (93); paints (82); motor vehicle components (74)
UK	Aerospace (139); consumer electronics (76); pharmaceutical products (67)
Japan	ODPM(*) (604); optical instruments and photographic equipment (278); motor vehicles (214); telecommunications equipment (210)
USA	Aerospace (289); consumer electronics (163); precision mechanical instruments (130); fertilizers (124); motor vehicle components (89); organic chemical products (72)

(*) ODPM: Office and Data Processing Machinery.

Note The index shown in this table is a *global specialization index*. It is the difference between the export specialization index (calculated as the share of a product in the exports of a given country, over the share of this product in the total exports of a reference group, the OECD) and the import specialization index (calculated in the same way). The advantage of using this global index is that it takes into account intra-industry trade. A high global index indicates a high trade specialization level.

exports of consumer goods where design and product differentiation are high (clothing, leather, furniture and domestic appliances); Japan has strong positions in high technology sectors (computers and optical and photographic equipment). This type of specialization can be called *product specialization* (or *spécialisation de créneau*). The trade specialization intensity of both the USA and West Germany is lower, but these two countries have succeeded in building *pole specialization* (or sectoral specialization, i.e. specialization in a small number of related products). The USA is specialized in different segments of the transport equipment and chemical industries, whereas West Germany has a number of dominant positions in the mechanical sector. France, and to a lesser extent the UK, appear to be the 'generalists' of the group. The fragile trade specialization in France is explained by a number of factors, among the most important of which is the industrial policy of France in the 1960s and 1970s which was excessively geared towards the objective of industrial independence.

Whereas Italy has strong positions in the production and export of unrelated products scattered along its industrial structure, this is less true for Japan, which has succeeded in creating a bridge between its various areas of specialization. Although the Japanese products do not belong to the same broad sector, they are technologically interrelated (improvements in the ODPM industry can be diffused to the optical instruments industry, to the telecommunications equipment industry and to the motor car industry). This is why Japanese trade is characterized by both product specialization and pole specialization (Turpin, 1989).

There is clearly a great deal of diversity in relation to specialization. The *specialization intensity*[37] as between the EU, the USA and Japan is no exception. Lafay and Herzog (1989) have calculated that the USA is 2.5 times less specialized than Japan, which in turn is three times less specialized than the Newly Industrializing Countries (NICs). Europe's specialization intensity is close to that of Japan, in spite of very wide intra-EU differences.

The Japanese strength is still found in the electronics, motor cars and electrical equipment industries. The NICs tend to be heavily involved in the textile–clothing, steel and paper-printing *filières* (after having reduced their dependence on the raw materials sector). Textile and clothing represent today more than 30 per cent of total export earnings in China. Clothing only overtook crude oil in 1991 as China's biggest export item.[38] The EU as a whole is relatively specialized in the mechanical industry (more than 15 per cent of its total merchandise exports in 1989/90), and in the chemical industry (12 per cent of its exports).

Is the EU's industrial specialization optimal?

From a normative point of view, optimal specialization of a given country or group of countries is one that orientates the industrial structure, to some extent, towards strong demand industries: industries with high, sustained levels of growth of demand. We can roughly categorize industries according to intensity of demand into three groups:

1 *Strong demand industries* are in many cases technology driven industries (computers and electronics, chemicals, electrical equipment).
2 *Low demand industries* are the declining industries (textile–clothing, steel, metal products); they are the industries where world competition is mature, or where decline has set in.
3 *Medium demand industries* encompass industries in which emerging new producers in the last decade have started to displace traditional EU leaders; this is the case for industrial machinery, transport equipment, motor vehicles, telecommunications equipment. In this category we also find the food industry.

Into which of these three categories do the EU's main industries fall, and are any of its strong demand industries competitive? A study done at the NACE three-digit level for the second part of the 1980s enables us to draw up and categorize a list of more than 100 different products (CEC, 1990).[39] As to which of these industries is competitive, we can use a combination of two ratios:

- The exports to imports ratio (i.e. the *cover rate*)
- The exports to production ratio.

On the basis of these ratios, a set of selected EU industries can be grouped into four columns (see Table 6.10):

- Column 1 includes industries which are highly competitive. These industries tend to export a high share of their production (more than 10 per cent) and the exports to imports ratio is also high (i.e. above 3). At the end of the 1980s, there were five such industries: textile machinery, rubber and material manufacturing machinery, iron tubes, ceramic products, and railway equipment.
- Column 2 refers to industries performing more than moderately well, but not as competitively as column 1 industries. They export more than 10 per cent of their production and their cover rate is above 1. This describes 17 industries including a relatively high R&D group: machine tools, precision instruments, farming machinery, pharmaceutical products, chemical products, shipbuilding, cars and spare parts, and domestic appliances, a more traditional, less R&D intensive group of industries such as timber and wooden furniture, glass and rubber products. These latter are, however, industries where product differentiation and quality would play a substantial role. The machine tool industry displays one of the highest cover rates of this class (around 1.6 in 1988). However, this cover rate has been decreasing at a steady pace over time. Because of the emergence of new competing nations,

TABLE 6.10   EU manufacturing specialization (a sample) (*Source*: Adapted from CEC, 1990)

	Column 1 $X/P > 10\%$ $X/M > 3$	*Column 2* $X/P > 10\%$ $X/M > 1$	*Column 3* $0\% < X/P < 10\%$ $X/M > 1$	*Column 4* $0\% < X/P < 10\%$ $X/M < 1$
High demand		Chemicals Precision instruments Telecomm equipment		EEEng(*) Consumer electronics OEDP(**) Musical instruments
Medium demand	Textile machinery Ceramic products Railway equipment	Machine tool Cars & spare parts Furniture	Construction material Wood, paper, printing Food, drink, tobacco	Aerospace
Low demand	Iron tubes	Shipbuilding		Textile, clothing, and footwear

Key: (*) EEEng: Electrical and Electronic Engineering.
    (**) OEDP: Office Equipment and Data Processing Machinery
    X = exports
    P = production
    M = imports

a not-negligible proportion of industries of this class is in a critical position; this is the case for shipbuilding, cars, machine tools, but this is also increasingly true for telecommunications equipment.

- Column 3 groups industries that export only a moderate part of their production (i.e. $0\% < X/P < 10\%$), and for which the cover rate is greater than 1. These industries are moderately competitive on the world market. Fifteen industries fall into this category. These are semi-finished goods industries (semi-finished wooden products, non-metallic minerals, construction materials), or they are part of the food–drink–tobacco, paper–printing and timber–wood industries. It should be noted that most of these moderately competitive industries owe their relative success to the fact that their products are non-tradable on a large scale, either because of their weight (construction materials, boiler construction, foundries, non-metallic minerals), or because of their perishability (dairy products, sugar and other foodstuffs); they have a degree of natural protection. Because of this, although apparently performing less well than column 2 industries, those in column 3 are in some cases less threatened by outside competition.

- Column 4 industries are those which export less than 10 per cent of output and import more than they export. These industries are either unable to consolidate their international position, or they have been displaced already by new international competitors. The former includes electrical and electronic engineering, electronic components and, even more critically, consumer electronics and office equipment and data processing. The latter includes aerospace, textiles, man-made fibres, clothing, footwear, toys and musical instruments. We should note that a large proportion of industries in column 4 are information technology (IT) related industries, and that their output and development is important for further productivity increases throughout the economy. As a result, demand growth facing these industries is high.

An example will illustrate the inability of EU industry to respond adequately to the changes at both the technological and demand levels. In the market for musical instruments, apparent

EU consumption (production + imports − exports) almost doubled in the 1980s. However, production in the EU grew over the period by only 5 per cent, as compared to over 11 per cent in Japan. In the USA, production actually declined over the last decade. With increasing EU demand for musical instruments, and a strong EU production base, nevertheless imports, particularly from Japan, were a major contributor to the growth in apparent consumption.

The empty top left-hand corner of Table 6.10 shows the dearth of high demand, technology related industries among those in which Europe was globally competitive at the end of the 1980s. This suggests the conclusion that, at that time, EU industrial production structure and specialization were in some sense not optimal. Data for the early 1990s show that the EU performance is still relatively weak in technology oriented, high demand industries. This is the subject of the next section.

6.2.5   The EU's position in high technology industries

Computing the RTCA *index*

We can explore the EU's technological performance on foreign markets with the help of the index of revealed technological comparative advantage.[40] For the EU as a whole, the index is computed as follows:

$$RTCA = \frac{\text{EU share in world trade of high technology products}}{\text{EU share in world trade of manufactured products}}$$

For the EU, this index was slightly above the critical value of 1 in 1963; it declined to 0.88 in 1980 (Heertje, 1983). This implies that the EU lost ground in relative terms on the world market for high technology products. But so did the USA, for which the index declined from a value of 2 to 1.2 over the same period. These results are partly explained by the increasingly high technology industries of Japan (office and data processing machinery, electronic equipment, telecommunications equipment). For Japan, the index went from 0.56 in 1963 to 1.41 in 1980. These trends continued into the 1980s and early 1990s, as can be seen from Tables 6.11 to 6.13, and Fig. 6.10. See also Fig. 5.9 in Chapter 5.

At first sight, the technological effort of EU industry throughout the 1980s appears remarkable. Between 1980 and 1990, EU exports of high technology products more than doubled (Table 6.11); however, EU imports over the same period more than trebled. The result was an increase in trade deficit for high technology products of from ECUs 5 billion to ECUs 23 billion.

Although its share has declined, in 1990 the USA was still the major supplier of high technology products into the EU (35 per cent of all EU high technology imports). Japan and the

TABLE 6.11   EU trade in high technology products (ECUs, billions)
(*Source*: Adapted from *European Economy*, 1993, p. 213)

	Extra-EU exports	Extra-EU imports	Balance
1980	35,413	30,345	+5,068
1990	72,509	95,794	−23,285

TABLE 6.12   Cover rates (X/M) for four selected R&D intensive industries (*Source*: OECD (1995)
Main Science and Technology Indicators)

	1984				1992			
	EU	NC(*)	USA	Japan	EU	NC	USA	Japan
Aerospace	1.31	0.24	2.98	0.10	1.30	0.65	3.47	0.21
Electrical and electronic engineering	1.09	0.73	0.52	10.55	0.85	0.80	0.58	5.56
O&DP Machinery	0.47	0.39	1.38	5.61	0.37	0.38	0.67	4.42
Pharmaceuticals	2.26	1.10	1.70	0.27	1.67	1.62	1.12	0.39

(*): Nordic countries (i.e. Finland, Iceland, Norway, Sweden).

NICs have accounted for an increasing proportion of EU high technology imports, the share of the NICs having almost doubled between 1978 and 1990 (CEC, 1993b).

Table 6.12 highlights the main feature of Japanese industrial policy (see also Chapter 7); selectivity has resulted in strong positions (pole specialization) in electronics and in office machinery, two industries where the cover rates are still impressively high, 5.56 and 4.42 respectively in 1992. On the other hand, Japanese industrial policy has so far devoted only marginal consideration to the pharmaceuticals and aerospace industries. Nevertheless, the Japanese cover rates for these two industries have grown substantially during the period. Table 6.12 also shows that the EU pharmaceuticals industry, an area of European excellence in the past, is losing ground in relative terms.

**TABLE 6.13   Rank and share of exporting country in OECD imports of
R&D-intensive products, selected countries** (*Source*: OECD (1992)
Science and Technology Policy. Review and Outlook)

	1969 1987			
	Rank	%	Rank	%
South-East Asia (*)	—	11.70	—	28.97
USA	1	29.26	2	17.34
ex-EFTA-5	—	8.44	—	6.69
EU-8	—	43.26	—	35.35
of which:				
Germany	2	15.95	3	12.59
UK	4	8.70	4	6.52
France	5	5.77	5	6.41
Italy	8	4.35	7	3.55
The Netherlands	6	5.15	8	3.14
BLEU	10	2.15	13	2.04
Denmark	12	1.19	18	1.10
Switzerland	7	4.91	9	3.10
Sweden	11	2.15	16	1.75
Austria	14	0.89	17	1.10
Finland	19	0.15	19	0.44
Norway	17	0.34	21	0.30

(*) I.e. Japan, Taiwan, South Korea, Singapore and Hong Kong.
EU-8 excludes Ireland, Spain, Portugal and Greece.

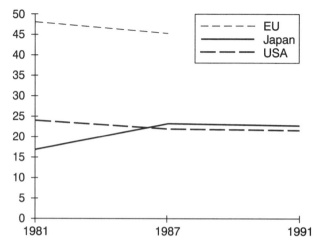

Figure 6.10 Share of the OECD market for high technology products (OECD = 100) (*Source*: OECD Main Science and Technology Indicators (various issues))

Table 6.13 shows that the EU and ex-EFTA countries account for only 42 per cent of R&D intensive exports into the OECD area in 1987, a decline from 52 per cent in 1969. Over this period, only Italy improved its rank (from 8th to 7th) among leading sources of high technology imports into the OECD area.

Figure 6.10 shows graphically the continuous decline in the EU's share of high technology markets in the OECD. This graph also shows that the Japanese rise reached a plateau in the late 1980s. A graph in this figure for the NICs would show their share rising.

To summarize, all indicators related to the performance of the EU high technology sector reflect a similar pattern. The major conclusions are as follows:

- Cover rates for high technology products have declined in the EU.
- The EU's increasing dependence in high technology on imports is largely explained by its weakness in the office and data processing machinery sector;
- The rate of introduction of the newest processes of production has been slower in the EU than in either Japan or the USA over the last 20 years.
- Although the EU as a whole is still the biggest world exporter of high technology products, its leadership is being eroded by the rise of the South-East Asian countries (Japan in the 1960s and 1970s, the rest since then).

The technology gap

All these, together with the fact that the EU's world share of inventions and innovations has decreased faster than that of the USA gave rise to concern about the *technology gap*. We introduced this topic briefly in Chapter 5. The idea is that the EU as a whole systematically lags behind Japan, and to a lesser extent the USA, in a number of 'key' or 'strategic' industries; and that the EU is less innovative[41] than its major competitors.

The theme of the technology gap is not new. The threat represented by the technology gap and/or the national challenge to overtake and surpass the world technology leaders had been made clear already in the middle of the nineteenth century by Friedrich List (1841). Obsessed by the technological superiority of Britain over Germany during the first half of that century, he was the first economist to identify the main features of what could be called a 'catching up strategy'; this strategy relied essentially on a technology policy.

A more modern version of this theme can be traced back to the work of Lovasy (1941).[42] Lovasy's paper on product differentiation and international trade, highlighted the fact that a firm which introduces a *new, differentiated, product* enjoys an export monopoly situation until imitators come into the market. Product innovation highlights the importance of non-price elements. Once imitation and adoption set in, price elements become of primary importance again. Much of trade performance can thus be explained by product superiority or product uniqueness: a new high quality product emerges, making substitutes obsolete. Process innovation is equally important here. Process innovation leads to a cost squeeze. This, in turn, enhances price as a variable explaining performance in international trade.

Following this line of thought, Posner (1961) developed a technology gap theory of foreign trade. At the microeconomic level, the technology gap between one firm and another could be sustained for a period of time *depending on the imitation lag*. The longer the imitation lag, the higher the export gains. Hufbauer (1965) found empirical evidence in a clear-cut relationship between trade performance and innovative leadership, for 60 synthetic materials.

In the 1970s, the idea of the technology gap was revived and applied to the EU as a whole. It gradually gave rise to support for the promotion of technology. Its acknowledgement by EU governments gave birth to ESPRIT, BRITE and all other similar technology programmes in the EU (see Chapters 5 and 7). By the 1980s, a plethora of studies had highlighted the existence of, or concern about, the technology gap, particularly between the EU and Japan.[43]

A number of these and other studies focused on the relationship between innovative performance and trade performance. For example, Soete (1981) regressed variations in export performance on variations in innovativeness for each of 40 industrial sectors in 22 OECD countries; he demonstrated the crucial role of the technology variable in explaining differences in export performance in most of the industries studied, but in particular in the high technology industries.[44] Freeman (1987) agreed that innovation was of fundamental importance, arguing that it explained, for example, the predominant position of the West German and US chemicals industries in the early decades of the new synthetic material era.[45] Marbach (1990) further substantiated this general view; basing his analysis on a group of French SMEs, he showed that the most successful exporters are also the major innovators.

While much attention has been devoted to the relative inability of the EU to innovate, and to its related weak trade performances, little evidence has been gathered on whether there is a *managerial and marketing gap*. Positing something of a counter-argument to the technology gap view, Lewis (1957) suggested that:

it is not necessary to be a pioneer in order to have a large export trade. It is sufficient to be a quick imitator. Britain would have done well enough if she merely imitated German and American innovations. Japan, Belgium and Switzerland owe more of their success as exporters of manufactures to imitation than they do to innovation.

However, because production in advanced industries is technically demanding, imitation is not as easy as it was. Imitation and innovation require equivalent levels of technical skill. It may well be, then, that imitation—and managerial and marketing ability—is particularly strong in some national systems of innovation, while innovation is strong in others, and invention in yet others. (The ideal is to have strengths in all three!) A number of notorious past cases such as penicillin, TV, VCRs, compact disks, videotex and high-definition television, in which

Europe was the inventor, often even the innovator, but rarely the market leader, may lead us to conclude that the EU has a comparative advantage in inventing, whereas Japan has a comparative advantage in fast imitation, and marketing.

The EU as a whole, in terms of growth of high technology industries, appears to have been overtaken by other parts of the world (USA from the early part of the century, Japan since the 1960s, South-East Asia today). However, as we saw in Chapter 5, the EU is a set of heterogeneous countries, with varying technological and industrial performances.

A country by country analysis reveals strong positions held by firms in some EU countries: German and Italian firms still have a leading edge in some types of machine tools; UK firms are aggressive competitors in the food and biotechnology sectors; French firms have strengthened their position in the telecommunication equipment and transport sectors; Swedish motor-vehicle firms do not seem to have been outstripped by their Japanese competitors. A long-term perspective enables us to see how some European firms have regained a strong competitive position in the world in the last 30 or so years. The cross-border movement of goods, services and factors of production is partly responsible for this catching-up by European firms. The arguments of this paragraph suggest the need for combining industry specific, country or region specific, and long-term perspectives, and to this we now turn.

International trade promotes the diffusion of innovations on a global scale. The spatial diffusion of technology led to a worldwide reorganization of production patterns. In the recent past, the spatial spill-over effects have been beneficial to some countries[46]—in particular, in recent decades, Japan and South-East Asia—and to some local regions—in particular *technopoles* like Silicon Valley in the USA, Montpellier in France, Cambridge in England, Taedok in South Korea, and Kansai Science City in Japan.[47] Technological developments, together with increasing international movement of goods, services and factors of production have been responsible for a *historical shift* in the competitive positions of firms, regions and countries.

Shifts in the location of the world's leading growth poles are not new.[48] Economic and industrial dominance has historically been associated with techological dominance and as the location of the latter changed, so has that of the former. In the nineteenth century, most technological innovations were pioneered by firms in Europe (mainly in the UK and, later, in Germany); but by the turn of the century, the USA had caught up (Buckley and Roberts, 1982). During the post-Second World War period, the USA consolidated its supremacy. This dominance took the form of a new pattern of production: the gradual emergence of a new international division of labour under the institutional control primarily of multinational enterprises (MNEs). While the century or so up to the middle of the twentieth century was characterized by the internationalization of exchange, the period since then has been characterized by the internationalization of production. International trade between independent firms (inter-firm trade) has been supplanted by international trade between subsidiaries of the same MNE (intra-firm trade).

The technological superiority, and more rapid internationalization of American firms left European firms with a new challenge: they had to narrow the technological and managerial gaps with their large American counterparts. According to Cantwell (1989), from the mid-1950s there was in fact a relative resurgence of some industries in Europe. The growth rate of manufactured exports of the six founding members of the EC between 1955 and 1975 was twice as high as that of the USA. Firms in the aircraft, coal and petroleum products, tobacco products and pharmaceuticals industries in Europe experienced the fastest growth rates relative to their equivalents in the USA (see Table A6.4 in Appendix 6.3). However, two factors militate against an optimistic assessment of Europe's performance in this period. First, the performance of firms in the office machinery industry in the EC-6 was very poor; and, as a 'generic' or 'pervasive' industry, office machinery was particularly important. Second, American MNEs' subsidiaries that had been set up in Europe during the period were partly responsible for the improvement in the trade performance of Europe. Cantwell (1989) estimated that over half of the increase in Europe's share of total European and US manufacturing exports, over the period 1957–75, was due to an increase in the exports of US-owned affiliates in Europe. The contribution of US affiliates is marked in all industries, with the exception of transportation equipment (see Table A6.5 in Appendix 6.3). Only in this industry did the share of US affiliates fall; this is the one industry in which an indigenous revival did occur. Cantwell goes on to analyse the variation in the competive response to the 'American Challenge'[49] among European firms and nations:

- In West Germany, indigenous firms performed well in food products, motor vehicles, mechanical engineering and chemicals.
- In France, improvements were discernible in electrical equipment, and non-metallic mineral products.
- In Italy, the performances of indigenous firms improved in motor vehicles and electrical equipment.
- In the UK, good results were achieved in food products, chemicals, and electrical equipment.

The revival of indigenous firms in response to the American challenge was strongest among the firms of the big four EC countries. There was, however, also some success in The Netherlands, where firms achieved quite satisfactory results in electrical equipment (radio and TV receivers), and coal and petroleum products (Royal Dutch Shell), and in Belgium–Luxemburg, where firms in the non-metallic mineral products and professional instruments sectors were also quite active.

Cantwell (1989, p. 86) summarizes the pattern as follows: 'While in the case of the larger industrialised countries the presence of US affiliates tended to act as a spur to the technological capacity of indigenous firms, in the smaller countries indigenous competition has been inhibited.'

Theoretical explanations

In the 1950s, a number of theories of international trade and investment, enriched by the introduction of technical change as a crucial and new explanatory variable, followed a more dynamic approach than the traditional theories. Among these were theories that also provided frameworks for analysing the existence and behaviour of MNEs. We have already described Dunning's eclectic model in Chapter 4.

The eclectic model   The eclectic model provides a good framework for explaining the existence of American MNEs in Europe and reasons for their presence there.[50] It does this by focusing on country or region specific advantages in Europe, the ownership advantages that gave American MNEs the competitive edge in the first place, and the advantages of internalization that explain why they set up subsidiaries rather than licensing European firms to produce for them.

Product life cycle model (PLCM)   Another influential theory was the product life cycle model (PLCM) developed by Vernon (1966); it was the best known of the so-called 'new technology' theories of international trade emerging in the 1960s.[51] According to the PLCM, a new product will originate in a high income country (the USA), where there is a demand for it (with a high income elasticity) and superior skills to produce the good. In the early stages, the manufacture of the new product will take place in the country of origin because any adjustments that need to be made at this—the prototype product, and not yet standardized process—stage will need to be made quickly, in response to the home market. Production will be at relatively high unit costs but costs are less significant in the early stages of marketing because the demand for innovations is price inelastic. In the next stage of the cycle, production of the product becomes standardized. The market widens as demand for the new product develops in other relatively high income countries. This is at first met by exports (from the USA). A wider market will give rise to economies of scale, and hence to a falling price. This will widen the market still further, making possible the sale of the product in lower income countries. A combination of increasingly international distribution of the product, and the relatively lower unit costs of production outside the USA, will result, in the next stage of the cycle, in relocation of the standardized (vertically integrated) production to a country where factor—and mainly labour—costs are lowest.

The PLCM was useful in explaining the pattern of post-Second World War US foreign direct investment (FDI) in Europe and South-East Asia. It also helped explain international trade, in the 1950s and 1960s, in that more sophisticated, innovative products and products of innovative processes tended to be exported from advanced countries, but some manufactured goods were produced by and exported from less developed countries. There were also other applications, Buckley and Roberts (1982), for example, finding the model useful in explaining the case of European FDI in US manufacturing industry before 1914 (Buckley and Roberts, 1982).[52]

The PLCM has, however, been criticized, not least by Vernon himself:

- It focuses on a discontinuity created by the emergence of an entirely new product. However, technological innovation can also be viewed as a continuous, gradual and cumulative process.
- The PLCM leaves unanswered the question of why the international relocation of production is done through FDI rather than, say, through licensing.
- The PLCM does not take into consideration oligopolistic market structures in determining the location strategies of MNEs.
- While the PLCM may have had some explanatory power for the 1950s to the 1970s, increasingly rapid changes in technology, and the multiplicity of new locations (in particular Japan and the NICs) from which competitive firms have originated since then, have made the model less and less applicable.[53]

Vernon posited an alternative explanation, based on the oligopolistic behaviour of MNEs, though he believed that strong traces of his original PLC sequence would remain.[54] In the alternative he suggested that there were three phases in the development of MNEs: *innovation-based oligopolies*, when production will tend to be in the home market, whether that be US, Japanese or European; *mature oligopolies*, when pricing, investment and locational decisions are made in response to expectations about the behaviour of competitors—for example, a follow-the-leader strategy might result in a firm setting up in a location simply because a competitor set up there; and *senescent oligopolies*, when differences in costs determine the location of production. This, Vernon's second PLCM, does 'describe today's oligopolistic global MNEs. It is surprising that the second version of the model still receives less attention than the first' (Eden, 1991).

Structural changes in the 1980s   Another reaction to the inadequacies of the first PLCM was that of Susan Strange (1991), who argued that, over the 1980s, there were radical and irreversible changes in global structures, in particular the *production structure* and the *financial structure*. In relation to the first, she theorized that the increasingly rapid changes in technology meant that local, national markets were insufficient to recoup in profits the R&D costs of creating or installing new products or processes. If this is so, then internationalization is essential. The financial structure changed through 'the integration of capital markets into one, worldwide market for savings and credit'. Albeit partial and incomplete, this integration gave MNEs 'far greater possibilities than smaller local concerns of raising money wherever they operate' (Eden, 1991). These two structural changes reinforce one another, and make likely increasing significance of MNEs' global economic activity.

The theory of technological accumulation   The last of the reactions to the first PLCM that we will deal with is the theory of technological accumulation. The notion of technological accumulation is based on the idea that the development of technology within a firm is a continuous and cumulative process. In Cantwell's (1989, p. 16) words:

the industrial composition of innovative activity in a given location or amongst a given national group of firms reflects past technological accumulation. This suggests that international patterns of technological advantage, having been established, will remain relatively stable over time. The sectors in which each group of firms is technologically strongest change only gradually.

In order to assess the 'stability over time of technological advantage', Cantwell (1989, p. 19) uses the following methodology:

1 First, he constructs an index of *revealed technological advantage* as follows:[55]

$$RTA_{ij} = \frac{P_{ij} / \sum_{j} P_{ij}}{\sum_{i} P_{ij} / \sum_{i} \sum_{j} P_{ij}}$$

where P_{ij} is the number of US patents in industry i granted to residents of country j.

The USA is taken as a country of reference, because it grants a higher number of patents to non-residents than any other country.

If i is the chemicals industry, and j is Germany then the RTA is calculated as the share of US patents taken out by German firms in this industry, divided by the total share of US patents due to non-US residents. Cantwell (1989) calculated an index of 1.68 and 1.18 for the time periods 1890–1912 and 1963–83 respectively. This means that in spite of a decrease of the index over time, Germany still holds a relative innovative advantage in this particular industry.

2 Second, Cantwell measures the stability of the sectoral distribution of the RTA index over time. The more stable this is, the better will be the correlation of RTA indices calculated for a national group of firms at two different points in time.[56] The correlation between the sectoral distribution of the RTA index at time t and at the earlier time $t - 1$ is estimated through a linear equation of the form:

$$RTA_{it} = \alpha + \beta RTA_{it-1} + \epsilon_{it}$$

where i refers to a specific industry, and t to a particular time.

Cantwell found a positive and significant correlation between the two *RTA* distributions (i.e. $b > 0$) for 15 out of 16 countries; Pavitt (1987), in a similar study, found a positive and significant correlation for nine out of ten countries.[57]

Cantwell's conclusion is that past success in an area strongly determines future innovation and growth in that or adjacent areas.[58] In his view, the gradual change in the nature of technology 'disturbed only slightly the pattern of technological advantage held by the firms of the major industrialised countries in the 20 years between the early 1960s and the early 1980s' (Cantwell, 1989, p. 45).

There are criticisms of Cantwell's work. First, he himself acknowledges that the statistical link becomes 'tenuous over longer periods'.[59] Second, and more fundamentally, he calculates innovative output solely on the basis of patents. The limits of patents as an indicator of innovative output were discussed in Chapter 5. Ironically, his results may not be indicative of the type of gradual accumulation of technology and skill that, for example, underlies the success of industrial districts.[60]

With these reservations, we agree that there is evidence for a degree of stability in the global distribution of production of innovations, at least over the short to medium term. For example, the ability of European firms in some industries to catch up with their American counterparts depended on the accumulation of technological experience over years and decades. To take another example, this time looking into the future rather than the past, it may be that, based on cumulated technological experience in the chemical and pharmaceutical industries, Europe will have a relatively greater potential to exploit discoveries in the new biotechnology field than will other regions of the world.

6.2.6   Summary and consolidation: competitiveness of EU industry

We have at various points highlighted the strategic role played by some industries in the economy of a given nation. Most important are those that form the technological core of a country's industrial structure; they are crucial to the improvement of the country's competitive edge *vis-à-vis* the rest of the world. We have also emphasized the importance of the structural— as opposed to price—elements of competitiveness.

This conclusion has been well stated by the Commission's Directorate General for Economic and Financial Affairs: 'Although price remains an important element of competitiveness, non-price factors, like the ability to innovate in the presence of rapid technological progress, play a major role in determining the overall level of competitiveness' (CEC, 1993b, p. 17). It follows from this that at least one appropriate way of defining the competitiveness of an economy is on the basis of the performance of its high technology industries. Together these arguments lead to the conclusion that one expression of improvement in the competitiveness of the EU is improvement in its trade position in high technology industries.

In terms of high technology industries, Japan was the most export oriented of OECD countries between 1970 and 1986, and the least open to foreign competition (OECD, 1992). Relying on the above definition of competitiveness, Japan was thus the most competitive of the major OECD economies. OECD (1992) also showed that the high technology competitive position of the USA deteriorated, that Germany remained 'technology competitive', and that both the United Kingdom and Italy declined in competitiveness over the period.

At a more global level, the emergence of the dynamic Asian economies (DAEs) leaves logically a smaller proportion of world exports to the traditional exporters of manufactured goods: the EU, but also the USA and Japan. What is of major concern is the inability of the

EU as a whole to respond adequately to changing demand patterns in international markets, and in particular to focus satisfactorily on high technology industries. It seems indeed that the EU has been encouraging intra-EU trade, since exports of high technology products within he EU grew more quickly than EU exports to the rest of the world.

6.3   Relationship between market structure and performance

The question under investigation in this section is: how and to what extent do specific elements of market structure shape performance in a given market?

6.3.1   Structure and performance

Early studies in industrial organization focused on the simple profit–concentration relationship, which is summarized by the form:

$$P = f(S)$$

where price–cost patterns were taken as a measure of performance (P), and where concentration was taken as an indication of market structure (S). In empirical work this equation involved the use of simple regression analysis (s regressed on p). It was much easier to test than the more complete version, S–C–P, because data on conduct (strategies) were non-existent and in any case would have been difficult to integrate into the equation. It was expected that there would be a positive association between S and P. Firms operating in highly concentrated industries were expected to earn higher profits than firms in industries with a lower concentration ratio. The performance of firms measured by profit rates, it was thought, was determined by the market structure in which firms operated.

Early empirical work included Epstein (1931) and Summers (1932), who found evidence of an inverse relationship between firm size and profit rates—suggesting that high concentration was not necessarily related to high profit rates—and Crum (1933), whose results were that there was a positive relationship between firm size and profit rate, supporting the high concentration–high profit hypothesis.

Bain's painstaking empirical work, particularly in the 1950s, focused not just on concentration, but also on entry barriers; again not surprisingly, he found a strong, positive relationship between high concentration and high entry barriers on the one hand, and high profit rates on the other. Later work in the Bainian tradition (for example Qualls, 1972; and Weiss, 1974) in general supported this conclusion.

In the 1970s, the conclusions about the relationship between structure and performance underwent serious reconsideration, primarily on the basis that even if there was general agreement on the existence of a strong positive relationship between the two variables,[61] there was no consensus on the underlying cause of this relation.

Disagreement over cause of structure–performance relationship

We have already at various points in earlier chapters discussed this issue. It suffices here merely to reiterate that: (a) in Bain's view—and in the Harvard tradition—concentration was associated with high entry barriers. This gave the firms in the industry a degree of market power which they exerted to achieve higher prices and higher profits; (b) in Demsetz's[62] (1973) view—and in the Chicago tradition—concentration was itself the consequence of the greater efficiency of the successful firms. It was lower costs that enabled such firms to make higher profits. A generalized form of the Chicago view was that concentration is the result of superior competitive performance, arising not just from greater efficiency in production, but also, for example, from better management practices and better choice of strategies.

This disagreement shifted attention towards conduct, behaviour and strategy, all of which had been ignored by the simple structuralist perspective. This in turn generated a demand for more sophisticated techniques in the study of the structure–performance relationship. This demand was met by an increasing supply of statistical data and of the means to analyse the data—more availability of and better access to computers.

Improvement of techniques and disagreement over results

During the 1970s, multiple regression techniques were introduced into the empirical research on the determinants of profit. The simple, two-variable models were replaced by models of the form:

$$\text{Profit rate on equity} = a + b \cdot \text{market share of firm } i + c \cdot \text{concentration on market } j$$
$$+ d \cdot \text{barriers to entry to market } j + e \cdot \text{growth rate of } j + \dots$$

The constant term, a, denotes the minimum competitive profit rate that a firm with no market power can attain.

There have been various ways of measuring the variables, and more and more variables have been added to improve the explanatory power of the model. Among significant empirical efforts in the 1970s were those by Shepherd (1975), who found that entry barriers had a significant 'yet secondary effect on profitability', and Scherer (1979), who added a new independent variable to the model: the proportion of each industry's sales going to final demand.

In the 1980s, further sophistication was added by Bradburd and Over (1982), who found ways of incorporating into the explanation of profits such factors as capital intensity, buyer concentration and vertical integration. Smirlock, Gilligan and Marshall (1984) used Tobin's q in an attempt to distinguish between efficiency and market power: a significant positive correlation between market share and q, they assumed, reflected efficiency, and a significant positive correlation between concentration and q, market power. By the end of the 1980s, three-equation simulations S–C–P models had become common (Martin, 1993, Ch. 17). In the 1990s, among others, linear and non-linear, static and dynamic, stochastic and chaotic models were being used, or proposed for use, in researching these basic questions in industrial economics (Byers and Peel, 1994).

The increasing sophistication of empirical technique has done little to settle the basic issues. Thus, for example, Dickson (1991), in his model of the relationship between unit cost and market concentration, finds evidence to support the efficiency hypothesis; Martin (1993, p. 498), though aware of Dickson's study, concludes that the efficiency hypothesis 'has a weak theoretical foundation and little empirical support'.[63]

6.3.2 Is growth a better performance indicator? Testing Gibrat's law

Are small firms more likely to grow than big firms, or is it more likely that industries become increasingly concentrated as large firms grow, keeping ahead of, and ultimately removing small firms? Some analysts have found no relationship between size and mean growth rate of the firm (Simon and Bonini, 1958; Hymer and Pashigian, 1962).[64] These studies have in fact reiterated the validity of Gibrat's law—also referred to as the law of 'Proportionate Effect'[65]—which states that the probability of a firm growing x per cent is independent of the size of that firm.

According to Hymer and Pashigian's study, the continuous decline of the $LRAC$ curve is related to the fact that the variability of small firms' growth rates is larger than that of larger firms' growth rates. The authors explain this higher variability of growth rates among small firms by the fact that, being at a sub-optimal scale of production, they have to bear high unit costs of production; consequently, many of these firms would experience negative growth rates until they are driven out of the market. Different results were obtained by Singh and Whittington (1968); in testing the law for UK firms, they showed that larger firms grew at a faster rate than smaller firms.

Other studies have investigated the link between the firm's growth rate and the growth rate of their national economies.[66] Rowthorn (1971), for example, found that the largest firms' growth rates were correlated with the national growth rates; he stressed also the fact that this link weakened with foreign trade and investment.

Caves's work (1991) assesses the closeness of association between a large firm's growth rate and the growth rate of its national market, as well as the link between the firm's and the industry's growth rates. Using data from a set of 280 manufacturing firms compiled by *Fortune* magazine for the years 1973–88, he finds that the growth rates of both industries and national economies have a strong influence on the growth results of firms. However, contrary to the results of Rowthorn, he concludes that the growth of industry output has more explanatory power than the growth of real gross domestic product.

6.3.3 Reasons for controversies

Even with improvements in data and techniques, disagreements remain. We discuss here some of the reasons for these disagreements.

Mis-specifications and omission of variables

The imperfect nature of the data used and the mis-specifications of the variables are still the most important reasons for the inconsistency of results. For example, misuse of concentration ratios, as discussed in Chapter 3, can cause errors and inconsistencies.

Variables are mis-specified in the sense that they are defined in different ways. Most industry studies, for example, use three-digit industry groups, which are much broader than markets. Even in a four-digit classification, some industries must be excluded because the data do not correspond to any economic reality (Jacquemin, 1979). Only a minority of studies have used firm-level data despite the fact that, as Martin (1994, p. 212) points out: 'The advantage of using firm-level data is that one can examine the effect of changes in market share, rather than market concentration, on market performance. [O]ligopoly models ... suggest that market share will be one of the critical structural determinants of the degree of market power.'

Numerous variables have traditionally been omitted; for example, only a minority of studies have integrated trade performance data. This variable has a crucial importance for the EU as a whole and for individual European countries in particular. Intra-EU and international competition reduces the dominance of firms in national markets. Buyer concentration, vertical integration, diversification and elements of public policy have largely been ignored, and if they were, or could be included, they could have an effect on results. These factors have an impact, and their impact may vary from industry to industry; not including them in the models can result in similar studies having different results.

The intrinsic nature of different industries: consumer v. producer goods; durable v. non-durable goods

Bain's seminal work suggested that the effect of concentration on profitability in producer-good industries is less than in consumer-good industries. This may be related in some way to lower barriers to entry in producer-good industries. Product differentiation, as a major source of entry barriers, is less important for industrial purchasers than it is for individuals.[67]

Stressing differences between industries, Brooks (1973) confirmed the fact that the strength of the relationship between concentration and performance depends upon the nature of the industry studied. Working on a sample of 417 four-digit Standard Industrial Classification manufacturing industries in 1963, Collins and Preston (1969) reached the following conclusion: the most significant impact of concentration on price–cost margins occurred in the large firms of the consumer-good industries. For small firms of the same industries, market concentration did not translate into greater margins.[68] The fact that market concentration raises price–cost margins only where small firms are at a competitive disadvantage, suggests that product differentiation is itself an important source of competitive (dis)advantage.

In their study, Domowitz, Hubbard and Petersen (1986) reiterate the differences related to the intrinsic nature of industries: they found no significant profitability–seller concentration relationship for producer goods industries over the period 1974–81. Their distinction between producer and consumer goods industries is based upon the use of industry shipments: they assume that if more than 50 per cent of an industry's output was bought for direct use and not for further production, then this industry was a consumer goods industry.

Cowling (1976) warns that the differentiation between consumer and producer goods may be less relevant in the context of distributors' increasing power. Price–cost margins are indeed normally measured at the wholesale rather than at the retail level. The necessity to go beyond the consumer/producer distinction is reiterated by Cowling and Waterson (1976). In their study referring to UK industry, these authors split their sample into durable and non-durable goods industries. In addition, they highlight the major weakness of earlier studies (in particular, Collins and Preston's) which lies in the fact that they do not measure the price elasticity of demand on an industry-by-industry basis. Cowling and Waterson's (1976) results run counter to those of many other studies. They find a significant relationship between price–cost margins and concentration in the durable goods industries, whereas in the case of non-durable goods industries, their equations showed no explanation of changes in the price–cost margin. They conclude that 'The results are consistent with the view that durables show greater price flexibility via quality change than do non-durables . . .' (Cowling and Waterson, 1976, p. 273).

It may well be that in some respects, each industry—or even sub-sector, perhaps even firm!—is unique, requiring separate examination of its SCP relationships. In relation to the question of the potential for deriving efficiency gains from increasing concentration in Europe, for example,

Jacquemin (1990) shows that there is such a potential for some European industries (telecommunications) but not for others (metal products).

The critical concentration level as a proof of discontinuity in the profit–concentration relationship

Bain's 1951 pioneering study clearly stated that the concentration–performance relationship held primarily for large firms. His first conclusion was that firms operating in concentrated industries were substantially more profitable than firms operating in less concentrated industries. The critical level of market concentration above which industries were concentrated—and above which concentration did explain profitability—was a CR8 of 70 per cent. Below this, concentration did not explain profitability.

Numerous empirical studies have investigated the existence of the critical level of market concentration (see in particular, Schwartzman, 1959; Mann, 1966). The studies of Meehan and Duchesneau (1973) and Dalton and Penn (1976) found evidence of discontinuity, but no significant profitability increases beyond the threshold level. Other studies disagree even with the existence of a discontinuous relationship (Collins and Preston, 1968).

The validity of studies highlighting the existence of a *single* critical concentration level has been questioned by Phillips (1976) and by Bradburd and Over (1982). Bradburd and Over's work brings evidence of two critical CR4 levels, K_I and K_D, and of a 'critical region of concentration' defined as $K_D < K < K_I$. K_D is referred to as the 'disintegrative' concentration ratio, and K_I as the 'integrative' concentration ratio. Their model defines two 'sticky' equilibria (a non-co-operative and a co-operative equilibrium) contained within this 'critical region'. They estimate the values of K_D and K_I at 0.46 and 0.68 respectively. Their results can be summarized as follows:

- An industry starting from a low level of concentration (below 0.46) will generate profits 'sticking' to a lower price–cost margin; its concentration level must increase to the value 0.68 before profits shift upwards to the higher value.
- Conversely, an industry moving from a high concentration level (above 0.68) will generate profits 'sticking' to the higher price–cost margin value; profits will not fall to their lower value until CR4 falls below 0.46.

In his 1981 article, Geroski widens Bain's 'critical concentration ratio' hypothesis. Introducing seven independent variables likely to have an impact on profitability (five-firm concentration ratio, advertising–sales ratio, capital intensity, import–sales ratio, export–sales ratio, average industry sales growth rate and an index of industry diversification), and breaking the concentration variable into seven size classes, Geroski finds the relationship between price–cost margin and industry concentration in the UK to be as follows:

- Up to levels of concentration of about 0.35 there is weak evidence of a U-shaped relation with a local maximum at 0.35; there is also weak evidence of a second convex segment between 0.35 and about 0.75 (which is also a local maximum).

At higher levels of concentration (greater than 0.75) one can observe a decline in profits followed immediately by a much sharper rise.

Geroski's major conclusions are as follows:

- The profit–concentration relationship is positive overall.

- The Bainian 'critical concentration ratio' hypothesis is only a special case of his model.
- His model rests on a non-linear functional form of the profit–concentration relationship.

Note, however, that even in 1994 Geroski could write: 'At the moment, we know relatively little about intra-industry market dynamics, or about the nature of the selection process that operates within industries.'

The critical concentration ratio (or ratios) hypothesis can explain some of the controversy over the relationship between concentration and performance; if they exist in practice, then not allowing for them in models can give rise to spurious results.

The relevance of business cycles in the study of the structure–performance relationship

Studies finding different relationships between concentration and performance may be doing so because the time periods on which their studies are based are at different points on the business cycle. Weiss (1974) noted that the strength of the profit–concentration relationship highlighted in earlier industry cross-section studies seemed to vary over time. The inclusion of business cycles in the study of the relationship has thus become a requirement. This is illustrated in the study by Domowitz, Hubbard and Petersen (1986): using a sample of 284 industries, they found that over the period 1958–81, the relationship between industry average price–cost margins and seller concentration weakened considerably. According to the same authors, cross-sectional studies drawn from relatively prosperous years (such as 1963) show a stronger link between profitability and concentration than would cross-sectional studies based on recession years (such as the mid-1970s).

Perhaps in the 1970s, weak demand combined with rising costs squeezed concentrated industry profit margins. This is consistent with the view that larger firms, having higher capital to sales ratios than smaller firms, are more vulnerable to the burden represented by fixed costs during an economic recession. During a recession, weak demand is likely to generate more intense competition; strategies based on price become more important to capture more market shares (Green and Porter, 1984).

Even incorporating the business cycle does not, however, dispel controversy. One view, as we have seen, is that during a recession, competition intensifies. This view is contested by other authors (e.g. Rotemberg and Saloner, 1986) who argue that oligopolies tend to behave in a more competitive manner during boom periods.

Co-existence of several 'strategic groups of firms' in a specific industry

Again this is a factor that may explain different results because it was not incorporated into the models. An industry in one country may exhibit very different SCP characteristics from those of the same industry in another country because, for example, a higher proportion of the firms are foreign owned in one country than the other. In some situations, firms can and should be separated and classified to form different homogeneous groups of actors. Firms belonging to a distinct group, defined on the basis of certain criteria (such as nationality) will have similar patterns of behaviour.

In attempting to allow for such differences between firms that have already entered an industry, Caves and Porter (1977), for example, put the emphasis on barriers to mobility rather than on entry barriers. In the same stream of studies, Donsimoni and Kambouri (1989) isolated domestic firms from foreign firms, and assumed that their belonging to different home countries explained different behaviours. Geroski (1991a) similarly distinguished between domestic and foreign firms, though his results were that because the heights of entry barriers facing the two types of entrants were broadly similar across industries, foreign owned firms did not appear to behave differently from domestically owned firms in Britain.

6.3.4   Summary and conclusion

In relation to both the theory and empirical results on SCP relationships in Europe there is a marked absence of unanimity. Among the important questions in relation to which there is still some dispute are: How and why do firms (and industries) grow? How important is size of firm? How stable are concentration levels in different industries (and regions) over time, and why? How important is clever strategy as opposed to efficient production?

One important conclusion that can be derived from the continuing controversy in so many areas, is that we require more disaggregated studies. Our own research on particular industries (Andréosso, Storey and Fitzpatrick, 1991; Jacobson, 1991; Jacobson and O'Sullivan, 1994) has convinced us that this type of temporally and spatially aware, industry-specific work has much to commend it. Fisher (1991) has written that 'In the absence of strong guidance from theory, we need to know what happens in fact. This surely requires the detailed study of particular industries.' While we believe an entirely inductive, empirical approach is inappropriate, and epistemologically impossible, a shift in this direction is appropriate at this time in the development of industrial economics.

In addition to these methodological conclusions, there are also policy conclusions. For Europe, the implications of the empirical studies on SCP are, among others, the following:

- Because of intra-industry (and also inter-firm) differences, the struggle for growth should not be seen as something that policy should *generally* support. *EU firms should rather concentrate on other complementary strategies* in order to sustain or increase their profitability.
- Since there is no consensus on the relationship between concentration and performance, how much importance should EU competition and industrial policy attach to the prevention of concentration?

It is to this and similar policy questions that we turn in Chapter 7.

Notes

[1] 'Replacement cost is the ECU outlay needed to purchase the current productive capacity of the firm at minimum cost' (Lindenberg and Ross, 1981, p. 12).

[2] Equity is the 'net worth' of the firm; it is equal to: total assets – all short-term and long-term liabilities.

[3] The 'accounting profit' captures all information available on a balance sheet and relating to revenue, cost and depreciation.

[4] Though note that profitability could arise from efficiency—see the discussion on the Demsetz efficiency problem.

[5] The following draws on Shughart (1990, p. 86).

[6] See Lindenberg and Ross (1981).

[7] Unless the value of the shares is based on expectation of future profit.

[8] Tobin and Brainard's (1977) estimations are consistently higher, whereas von Fürstenberg's (1977) are consistently lower. Note that Tobin's q has also been used in studies of investment in Europe; see Funke, Wadewitz and Willenbockel (1989) on Germany and the UK, and Chan-Lee and Torres (1987) on France.

[9] Arising, for example, from learning effects, or from access to better quality inputs.

[10] We introduced this index as a measure of concentration in Chapter 4.

[11] One way to capture these differences is to incorporate data on wage differentials. For a cross-country comparison including skill differences, see Freeman, R. (1994).

[12] We are referring, in general, to products. In relation to services—especially publicly provided services like health, education, defence—the measurement of output is particularly problematic.

[13] Note that most studies of competitiveness are quantitative studies, in which price (or cost) competitiveness alone is used, mainly because it is difficult to measure intangibles like quality and design.

[14] An increase in the real exchange rate can be due to: *ceteris paribus*, an increase in the general price level in country i, or an appreciation of the nominal exchange rate (i.e. j's currency becomes more expensive in terms of that of i).

[15] Consumer surplus is defined as the excess of value received by consumers over what they must pay for a good. The magnitude of the consumer surplus depends in part on the elasticity of demand.

[16] For an examination of this argument in the case of the UK, and in particular the electricity supply industry in the UK, see Button and Weyman-Jones (1993). An industry like electricity supply is particularly amenable to estimation of actual and optimal average costs because of the standardized nature of the output.

[17] There is also a difference between X-efficiency and technical efficiency. For a theoretical discussion and empirical evidence, see Kalirajan and Varagunasingh (1992).

[18] For a critique of this view of the behaviour of the firms in relation to average cost curves, see Lazonick (1991, Ch. 3).

[19] See our discussion on the evolutionary theory of the firm in Chapter 3.

[20] As in Chapter 5, and in line with practices in both the OECD and the EU, we define a high technology industry on the basis of its R&D intensity. The six high technology industries identified by the OECD (1992) are: aerospace, electrical machinery, electronics and components, office machinery and computers, pharmaceuticals, scientific instruments.

[21] For recent work on improvements in measuring intra-industry specialization, see Brulhart and McAleese, 1993.

[22] See Chapter 5, Section 5.2, for more on technological comparisons between countries; in particular, for example, see Figs 5.10 and 5.13.

[23] For a discussion on market dominance in the EU, see Chapter 4, especially Table 4.4, and Chapter 7. We can consider there to be effective competition when the four-firm concentration ratio is below 40 per cent, entry barriers and profit rates are low, and market shares fluctuate.

[24] See also Pascoe and Weiss (1983) and Geroski and Jacquemin (1988). Note that rate of decline in market dominance strongly depends on antitrust legislation.

[25] In these particular industries, technical indivisibilities are the result of large plant or machine size, implying high levels of output to obtain reasonable levels of capacity utilization.

[26] All these figures are for the year 1988, and are extracted from Eurostat (1992). See also *Panorama of EC Industry*, 1994, p. 75.

[27] See also Table A6.2 in Appendix 6.2, which provides a list of the top 25 European firms ranked by employment.

[28] See Turpin (1989).

[29] A split between Belgium and Luxemburg would show a definite involvement of Belgium in sea transport and of Luxemburg in banking.

[30] The World Bank forecasts that between 1993 and 2001, Thailand, Taiwan and South Korea will all have annual average growth rates of around 6 per cent. China will grow at more than 7 per cent per annum. According to the same source, the Asian Pacific countries (Japan excluded) accounted for a quarter of world exports in 1990 compared to 15 per cent in 1980.

[31] For our purpose, East Asia or the Asian Pacific countries will encompass the six "Dynamic Asian Economies", to borrow an expression used by the OECD. These are: South Korea, Taiwan, Hong Kong, Singapore, Thailand and Malaysia.

[32] Defined as the failure to achieve a maximum level of output from a given combination of inputs.

[33] The authors also try to explain the variables that affect the level of inefficiency. According to their study, the degree of competition, the intensity of international trade, product differentiation, the rate of structural change, the size of markets and the organization of firms within the industry explain half the differences in inefficiency levels across industries.

[34] Since the pace of economic integration has increased substantially in the last 10 to 15 years, making the EU with its common external tariff (CET) one single trading bloc, it is more accurate for the purpose of international comparisons to refer to extra-EU trade rather than intra-EU trade. Intra-EU exports are exports originating from one EU country and the destination of which is another EU partner country. Extra-EU exports are all EU exports directed towards the rest of the world.

[35] It should be noted however that the degree of openness varies according to the changes in the relative prices, and according to exchange rate movements.

[36] i.e. China, Hong Kong, Malaysia, Indonesia, Korea, Taiwan and Thailand.

[37] For a given country, the specialization intensity is calculated on the basis of the relative position of the various industries in world trade (see Lafay and Herzog, 1989, p. 34).

[38] *People's Daily* (overseas edition, 11 January, 1994).

[39] Even this classification may be too aggregated. For example, the agricultural machinery industry (NACE code 321) is composed of many different types of sub-products or segments. All results should thus be interpreted with great caution, since an apparently weak industry for the EU as a whole can conceal many very competitive positions in specific segments of this particular industry as well as in specific countries.

[40] See also the high technology balance of trade (Fig. 5.10) and the high technology balance of payments (Fig. 5.13).

[41] In the sense of conversion of inventions into marketable products.

[42] Recently rediscovered (see McGovern, 1994).

[43] See for example Richonnier (1984), Woolcock (1984), Woods (1987), and Sharp and Shearman (1987).

[44] Exceptions were found for food, petroleum and stone, clay and glass, where natural resource endowments play a significant role, and also for mature industries such as textiles and clothing.

[45] See also Walker's (1979) study for the OECD area, and Mayes, Buxton and Murfin (1990) for the UK.

[46] Assisted by appropriate industrial policies.

[47] For a detailed discussion of the *Technopoles of the World*, see Castells and Hall (1994); see also Scott (1988).

[48] On this theme, see for example the work of Fernand Braudel in France and of Immanuel Wallerstein in the US.

[49] To borrow an expression from Servan Schreiber (1967).

[50] See, for example, Jacobson and Andréosso (1990), for an application of the eclectic framework to the analysis of US MNEs in Ireland.

[51] The PLCM has been credited to Vernon, but see also Hirsch (1967) and Hufbauer (1965); for an application of the PLCM to early American investment in Europe (that of Ford in Ireland in 1917), see Jacobson (1977).

[52] Among the original aims of the PLCM was to explain the famous Leontief paradox.

[53] Walker (1979) in relation to the reaction of Japanese firms to US FDI in the car industry, and Baba (1987) on the response of Japanese firms to US penetration of the Japanese TV market, both provide evidence for this point.

[54] For a summary of Vernon's work in this area, from 1966 to the end of the 1970s, see Dicken (1992, pp. 139–42); for a more detailed discussion of Vernon's work, up to 1990, see Eden (1991).

[55] This index was first used by Soete (1981).

[56] The statistical methodology used in the Galtonian regression model (see Cantwell, 1989, p. 25).

[57] Pavitt regressed the *RTA* index in 1975–80 on the equivalent *RTA* index in 1963–68, whereas in Cantwell's study, the two *RTA* distributions relate to the periods 1977–83 and 1963–69.

[58] He has developed this idea further in an article entitled 'The international agglomeration of R&D' (1991).

[59] What exactly is meant by 'longer periods' is very unclear in Cantwell's study.

[60] We have, despite our reservations, included details of his statistical analysis as it represents a significant proportion of the work in this area.

[61] Though even this was, and is, still disputed.

[62] See also Brozen (1970).

[63] Martin (1993, Chs 17 to 19) is a detailed and advanced survey of the recent literature in this area.

[64] Hymer and Pashigian's findings imply that the long-run average cost (*LRAC*) curve of the firm declines continuously. Their explanation is that small firms typically grow very rapidly because they want to avail themselves of the scale economies implied by the negatively sloped part of their *LRAC* curve.

[65] See Gibrat (1931).

[66] In the case of equi-proportionality, national economic expansion is distributed evenly among firms, and by extension, the firm's growth rate coincides with the growth rate of the national economy.

[67] The relationship between the industrial buyer and supplier is more important than the characteristics of the intermediate product. This relationship seems to be increasingly important, as evidenced, for example, in the growth of sub-contracting—see Section 5.3.2

[68] See criticism of this study in Shepherd (1990, p. 116) and Martin (1988, pp. 167–72).

Questions

6.1 Why is the profit rate, by itself, an inadequate measure of performance?

6.2 What is competitiveness?

6.3 What are the advantages and disadvantages of using RTCA ratios?

6.4 The UK has more firms in the European top 200 than Germany, but the UK firms are, on average, smaller. Which country, on the basis of this information alone, is more competitive?

6.5 In which industries are the largest European firms to be found, and why?

6.6 Is the EU's industrial specialization optimal?

6.7 Why is there disagreement on the relationship between structure and performance?

Appendix 6.1

List of high-tech industries as defined by EUROSTAT (*Source*: Eurostat (1989) *Statistical Analysis of extra-EC Trade in High-tech Products*)

1 Aerospace industry, aircraft piston engines
2 Automatic data processing machines and units, and office machinery
3 Electronic equipment
4 Telecommunications equipment, TV, gramophones
5 Drugs
6 Scientific instruments
7 Electrical machinery
8 Non-electrical machinery
9 Chemicals.

Note This list is based on SITC (Standard International Trade Classification). This classification is essentially based upon the R&D intensity of each industry defined as the ratio of R&D expenditure to turnover or output. The approach of the Statistical Office of the European Communities is interesting in that it splits the high-tech products into consumer products, capital products, and intermediate products.

List of high-tech industries as defined by the OECD (1987–89) (Source*: OECD (1994) *Science and Technology Policy; Review and Outlook*)

1 Aerospace
2 Computers
3 Electronics
4 Pharmaceuticals.

Medium high tech industries

5 Instruments
6 Motor vehicles
7 Chemicals
8 Electrical machinery.

Note This list is based upon R&D expenditures in various industries.

Appendix 6.2

TABLE A6.1   Ranking of EU manufacturing industries by production (1992, three-digit level)[1]
(Source: Panorama of EC Industry, 1994, p. 19)

NACE Manuf. industry		Production (2)	Employment (3)	AAGR (4)
351	Motor vehicles	216,122	1,163,899	3.4
251	Basic industrial chemicals	112,098	607,098	2.7
344	Telecom equipment	85,225	880,785	5.4
483	Plastics processing	84,280	771,598	7.1
412	Meat	79,382	436,685	4.2
328	Other machinery	79,341	770,324	1.7
316	Tools	71,730	781,332	4.2
257	Pharmaceuticals	68,601	408,008	7.3
413	Dairy products	67,815	241,968	1.6
353	Motor vehicle parts	49,521	516,491	4.8
453	Clothing	45,973	734,348	1.8
472	Paper & board processing	44,879	401,386	3.5
364	Aerospace equipment	43,543	389,854	1.6
325	Iron & steel machinery	41,792	388,144	1.8
345	Consumer electronics	39,684	356,893	3.2
467	Wooden furniture	39,171	466,379	3.3
429	Tobacco	38,992	77,257	0.4
258	Soaps, detergents, perfumes, toiletries	38,079	196,135	4.0
423	Other food	36,621	190,045	6.2
471	Pulp, paper & board	30,453	184,714	4.0
314	Constructional steelwork	30,203	337,053	4.4
324	Food & chemical machinery	30,131	227,397	3.1
422	Compound feed	29,202	87,132	3.7
243	Concrete, cement, plaster	27,955	242,091	4.2
419	Bread & flour	27,437	456,197	4.3
427	Brewing & malting	26,099	132,190	0.0
313	Secondary transformation of metals	24,525	346,323	5.7
421	Cocoa & sugar confectionery	24,497	174,091	4.5
346	Domestic electrical appliances	23,722	222,645	3.8
247	Glass	22,224	236,693	3.3
322	Machine tools	20,969	280,933	−1.6
436	Knitting	20,235	284,231	0.3
315	Boilers & metal containers	19,498	216,866	1.0
311	Foundries	19,111	250,260	0.6
451	Footwear	18,689	234,453	2.6
414	Fruits & veg processing	18,471	128,166	4.9
428	Soft drinks, mineral waters	18,064	98,368	5.0
361	Shipbuilding	17,991	204,909	2.0
411	Oils & fats	17,833	49,378	4.3
432	Cotton	16,450	221,157	−2.5

TABLE A6.1 (Continued)

NACE Manuf. industry		Production (2)	Employment (3)	AAGR (4)
248	Ceramic goods	16,265	240,086	1.6
242	Cement, lime, plaster	15,103	77,044	1.9
312	Forging	14,583	164,988	3.9
424	Alcohol & spirits	13,756	46,439	−0.2
463	Carpentry	12,643	159,482	3.8
352	Bodies for motor vehicles	12,611	140,386	4.8
321	Agricultural machinery	12,026	122,297	−4.0
437	Textiles	11,768	110,849	7.0
326	Transmission equipment	11,640	155,232	−0.3
416	Grain milling	11,567	36,213	1.8
431	Wool	11,300	123,672	−1.6
433	Silk	10,111	83,030	0.9
425	Wine	9,910	46,483	0.1
440	Leather & leather goods	9,777	105,005	−0.2
371	Measuring & precision instruments	9,483	121,881	0.8
347	Electric lighting	9,075	101,110	4.6
415	Fish	8,836	82,893	3.7
323	Texile machinery	8,483	93,713	−0.2
462	Semi-finished wood products	8,128	66,572	4.6
372	Medical & surgical equipment	7,796	104,354	6.2
438	Carpets, linoleum	7,697	66,255	3.3
491	Jewellery	7,326	58,485	8.2
441	Tanning, dressing of leather	6,094	45,880	−1.1
373	Optical & photographic equipment	6,090	78,349	2.6
241	Clay products	6,016	75,026	1.6
461	Sawing & processing of wood	5,846	72,347	4.3
494	Toys & sports goods	5,668	67,373	1.2
417	Pasta	5,551	19,282	3.9
362	Railway rolling stock	5,349	62,315	1.2
363	Cycles & motorcycles	4,664	44,875	1.5
464	Wooden containers	3,198	43,339	4.4
466	Cork & straw articles	2,146	31,927	1.9
246	Grindstones	1,577	19,446	0.2
374	Clocks & watches	1,356	18,241	−2.9
492	Musical instruments	797	12,787	−1.4
244	Asbestos articles	637	12,113	−11.9
456	Fur & fur goods	521	6,985	−5.3

(1) Estimated
(2) In current prices, million ECUs
(3) Number of employees
(4) Annual average growth rate. Calculated using production in constant prices (1985 = 100)

TABLE A6.2   The 25 biggest employers in the EU + EFTA (1990)
(*Source*: *Panorama of EC Industry*, 1993, p. 38)

1	IRI	I	419,500
2	Daimler-Benz	D	376,785
3	Siemens	D	373,000
4	FIAT	I	303,238
5	Unilever	UK/NL	301,000
6	Deutsche Postdienst	D	300,019
7	La Poste (PTT)	F	298,000
8	Philips	NL	272,800
9	Volkswagen	D	267,997
10	Deutsche Bundesbahn	D	235,975
11	SNCF	F	230,221
12	British Telecom	UK	226,900
13	BAT Industries	UK	217,373
14	ABB (Asea Brown Boveri)	CH/S	215,154
15	Deutsche Telekom	D	212,217
16	British Post Office	UK	207,438
17	Alcatel-Alsthom	F	205,500
18	Nestlé	CH	199,021
19	Robert Bosch	D	179,636
20	Compagnie Générale des Eaux	F	173,105
21	Hoechst	D	172,890
22	Bayer	D	171,000
23	Peugeot	F	159,100
24	Renault	F	157,378
25	France Télécom	F	156,615

TABLE A6.3   Manufacturing production: annual average percentage change 1980–89 in EU-12 (*Source*: CEC, 1990, p. 45)

Manufacturing industry	1.8
Mineral oil refining	1.1
Processing of metals	0.8
Non-metallic minerals	0.4
Chemical industry	3.2
Metal products	0.5
Mechanical engineering	0.5
Electrical engineering	3.6
Motor vehicles	3.5
Other means of transport	0.0
Food-drink-tobacco	2.0
Textile industry	0.2
Footwear & clothing	−2.0
Pulp and paper	2.3
Printing publishing	3.3
Rubber and tyres	4.1
Plastic products	5.8

Appendix 6.3

TABLE A6.4   A comparison of export growth rates: USA and EEC-6, 1955–75 (selected products) (*Source*: Calculated from data in UN, *Commodity Trade Statistics*)

Product	Export growth EEC-6/US export growth*
Aircraft	8.45
Coal and petroleum products	8.06
Tobacco products	5.29
Pharmaceuticals	4.24
Motor vehicles	3.24
Rubber products	3.17
Food and drink	2.45
Mechanical engineering	2.35
Electrical equipment	1.96
Chemicals	1.93
Professional instruments	0.60
Office machinery	0.18
Total manufacturing	2.00

* The figure for Aircraft, for example, shows that the rate of growth of EC-6 exports over the period was 8.45 times that of US exports in this industry.

TABLE A6.5   The contribution of US affiliates in Europe to total European and US exports of selected manufactured products, 1957–75 (%)
(*Source*: Calculated from data in UN, *Commodity Trade Statistics*)

	1957	1975
Food products	0.6	2.0
Chemicals and allied	3.1	14.2
Primary and fabricated metals	1.8	3.5
Mechanical engineering	2.7	11.4
Electrical equipment	3.4	6.5
Transportation equipment	16.3	12.1
Rubber products	7.4	16.6
Paper and allied products	0.5	6.3
All products	3.8	8.8

7 Aspects of industrial policy

7.1 Introduction

State intervention in economic activity can be traced as far back as the time of the Egyptian pharaohs. The nature of intervention has of course changed over time. Industrial policy, in particular, is a much more recent phenomenon. By industrial policy we mean something close to Johnson's definition (1984, p. 8): 'Industrial policy means the initiation and co-ordination of governmental activities to leverage upward the productivity and competitive-ness of the whole economy and of particular industries in it.' Industrial policy can refer to all activities of public authorities that affect, directly or indirectly, the performance (e.g. productivity, profitability, international competitiveness) of the manufacturing and service sectors.[1]

The expressions 'industrial strategy', launched in the early 1970s in Canada (Grant, 1989), and '*Strukturpolitik*', officially used in the German language, are euphemisms aimed at subduing objection to the interventionist element. That there is a range of views on how interventionist industrial policy might be is clear from Harrop's (1989, p. 86) definition: 'Industrial policy creates the condition in which industry can flourish and its main concern has been to create a competitive and efficient industrial structure.' Johnson's definition allows for much more active intervention than Harrop's; Johnson's suggests, for example, policies aimed at particular industries, while Harrop's implies only a general policy environment. These are just two views; there is a whole range of views. One reason for the diversity of views is that the notion of industrial policy is a confusion of three types of policies:[2]

- 'policies designed to shape the environment in which the company operates'.

This is part of industrial policy because, as we already mentioned in relation to Johnson's definition, macroeconomic and macrosocial policies affect industrial activity.

- 'sectoral policies (structuring, promotion of high tech industries, aid to lame ducks)'; and
- 'the strategy of the shareholding state'.

We will expand on this point, providing a taxonomy of industrial policy types, but first, let us raise the question as to why governments might intervene at all.

7.1.1 Why do governments intervene?

In Chapter 4 we showed that explanations for state intervention could be discussed under three main headings: *market failure*, *paternalist intervention*, and *transaction cost*. We will again use these headings, though the discussion will differ somewhat from that of Chapter 4. Here we are concerned more directly with a general perspective on state intervention as a backdrop to industrial policy in particular.[3]

Market failure

Imperfect markets are markets other than those in which the conditions of perfect competition apply. They are characterized by varying degrees of oligopolistic and monopolistic conditions. Examples of market failure include:

- The existence of externalities
- Prohibitively large sums of capital needed to start up production or to engage in research and development (sunk costs)
- The existence of increasing returns to scale
- Information imperfections.

Externalities   In its narrowest sense, the concept of external economies (and diseconomies) refers to the effect the production of a good or service has on the production or consumption of another good or service. Externalities can be external economies (also called *benefit externalities*) or external diseconomies (also called *cost externalities*).[4] For example, a firm investing in R&D may derive direct benefits from this investment; if the R&D results in a better way of producing its product, it will have reduced its costs. Now other firms, close to the first one—geographically and/or sectorally—learn about the improvements.[5] Without having spent any money on the R&D, the other firms derive some of the benefits; these are benefit externalities. This example provides one of the explanations for the success of *industrial districts*, discussed in Chapter 4; the community is so integrated that there are external economies to all improvements any of the firms introduce.

The most common example of cost externalities is pollution, where the polluter does not pay to remove these negative consequences of production. Ideas can also, in a sense, pollute. Let us take, for instance, a clothing industrial district, in which one firm introduces a new design for a shirt, convinced that it is going to be the latest fashion. Many other firms hear about (and copy) the new design. If it succeeds, there will have been benefit externalities; if it fails, however, and no consumers buy the product, then there will have been cost externalities.

What have externalities to do with state intervention? If a private economic activity can have implications—positive or negative—for a wider community, and if it is difficult or impossible for markets to cost these implications, then the state intervention may be appropriate. The state can, for example, ensure that the actions inducing cost externalities are reduced, by charging for them.

It is important to emphasize that just because there are externalities does not mean there is a case for state intervention. The case of the new shirt design in an industrial district emphasizes the complexity of the issue: it may not be clear until after the event whether the externalities are positive or negative. Intervention by an authority to ensure that the other firms pay the first firm for the new design—and so reduce the extent of the copying—may reduce losses if the new design fails. But such intervention may reduce the gains if the new design succeeds. Arguably, reducing the general gains does not matter, as long as the creator of the new design is rewarded. However, if—as in industrial districts—individual success is dependent on general success then by reducing general gains the intervention will also reduce individual gains. Even at the risk of failure of the entire district, this type of intervention would not be appropriate.[6]

Large sunk costs   Sunk costs explain why a firm may be reluctant to enter an industry. The point is that if there is some sense in which this industry is socially necessary, but is not (or not sufficiently) profitable to justify the entry into the industry of a profit-maximizing firm, then the state must intervene. The state can, in a sense, create a contestable market by providing the sunk capital; the airline industry could, after all, become a contestable market if the state provided the airports, runways, air traffic control and so on. More realistically, in train transport, privately owned firms could offer the service, if the government invests in electrification, stations and tracks.

Increasing returns to scale   If the technology for producing a particular good or service is such that even at levels of output that would capture substantial shares of the market, the firm is still experiencing increasing returns to scale—i.e. it has not yet reached the minimum point on the average cost curve—then this is a *natural monopoly* (see Chapter 4). The nature of the technology—indivisibilities—prevents more than one firm from entering and competing in the industry without substantially increasing costs. Following this line of thinking, Forte (1967) argued that in the case of an indivisible or very large-scale project, public sector production is the best choice. Alternatively, the state could intervene by regulating a private, natural monopoly firm.

Information imperfection   Where a market could exist, but it is not known—and not reasonably knowable—to potential investors that this is the case, then there is an argument for intervention by the state to provide the information. In the absence of a stock market, for example, information about the nature and price of potential investments would be very difficult to obtain. This is an argument for the public provision—though not necessarily operation by the state—of a stock market.

Paternalist intervention

A second broad set of reasons for government intervention in industry stems from socio-political and ethical considerations. Since the competitive process results in a misallocation of resources, with high levels of unemployment, a shortage of particular skills, and regional disparities, it was increasingly accepted in the 1970s that it was up to governments to ensure that the distribution of welfare emerging from the economic process was in accord with the concepts of equity.[7] A major problem was (and is) how to define equity.

Political concern, sometimes about unemployment, sometimes about the strategic need to prevent a firm from becoming foreign-owned, was a key motivation in the rescuing of ailing companies by the state. Such state rescues were carried out by both Labour and Conservative governments in Britain, particularly in the 1970s. Several companies were taken wholly or partly into public ownership: Rolls-Royce (aero-engines), British-Leyland (motor-cars), Ferranti (electronics), Alfred Herbert (machine tools), and ICL (computers) (George, 1991).

Another political reason for takeovers by the state was prevalent in France after the Second World War; the state in France transferred some firms into public ownership because these firms had collaborated with the then enemy during the war. The 'nationalizations-sanctions' affected Renault, and the builder of aircraft engines Gnome et Rhône, which became SNECMA.

The same kind of political argument applies—though *ex post*—where the private production of a good or service may give private individuals access to political influence or power beyond their constitutional rights. This has particular relevance in the case of the defence sector and its related armaments industry.

The existence of what Musgrave (1959) called 'merit and demerit wants' also explains some direct state involvement in industry. *Merit and demerit goods* are particular goods for which the state makes the (normative) judgment that they are 'beneficial' (merit goods) or 'detrimental' (demerit goods) to the individual. This will lead to public spending on merit goods, such as education and basic research, and taxes on demerit goods, such as alcohol and tobacco.

Transaction costs

Chang (1994) introduced a transaction cost theory of state intervention.[8] It was already clear, long before Chang, that transaction costs—or the costs associated with any market transaction—which are generated by imperfect information call for state ownership. For example, rather than allowing firms to struggle over the establishing of rules of conduct in a particular market, by intervening to establish the rules of the trading game the state may actually improve the functioning of the market. This type of transaction cost argument belongs in the same category as information asymmetry, imperfect market explanations for intervention. Chang's theory goes farther, arguing that markets are just one allocative mechanism, the state is another. Markets are imperfect, leading to a degree of allocative inefficiency; state intervention, with costs measured in terms of transaction costs, can reduce this allocative inefficiency. This provides a framework for questioning where and whether state intervention is justified—if the net improvement through transaction cost reduction resulting from state intervention is greater than if left to the market, then such intervention should be made.

7.1.2   Results of industrial policy

A quick glance at the record of post-war economic development suggests that best-performing countries in terms of growth and international trade shares were the countries which implemented some kind of an industrial policy: Japan and other East Asian countries, Germany, France and Italy. The USA maintained its leadership only in areas where it did have an industrial policy, or at least a significant amount of state intervention and support (aerospace, armament, nuclear energy, and related electronic fields). In contrast, British Conservative governments were sceptical about the merits of an industrial policy and the British economy was among the worst performers in the EC and the OECD.

This very cursory view suggests that industrial policy may improve an economy's performance. In practice, however, nearly all economies have some degree of intervention that impacts on industry. The dilemma is not between implementing an industrial policy or not having an industrial policy at all, but rather it involves choosing among the various degrees of industrial policy, at appropriate times.

7.1.3   Types of industrial policy

Table 7.1 shows the main features of the five types of industrial policy to be described in this section. These types of policies are not necessarily mutually exclusive; the broad range of

TABLE 7.1   Various degrees of government intervention in industry

1 Passive and negative	Control, restriction, penalization of dominant positions, regulation of monopolies (competition policy)
2 Passive but positive	Creation of a favourable economic environment (degree 1 + fiscal, financial, legal measures; deregulation). Also monetary policy
3 Active but negative	Sectoral policies, and trade policies (defensive) (with rising barriers) to curb threats from new emerging economies
4 Active and positive	Co-ordination of national economic policies. The state as a supplier of capital. Picking the winner policy
5 Active, positive and directly involved	The state as an entrepreneur and innovator

policies adopted in any one country at any one time could—and usually does—include more than one type of industrial policy.

A minimalist approach

The least interventionist industrial policy seeks to improve industrial performance through the creation of a favourable macroeconomic environment. This encompasses an appropriate fiscal policy, the attainment of adequate technological and educational standards, and a good infrastructure. We can call this, the first degree of industrial policy, a minimalist approach to industrial policy. Under this approach, monopolies are condemned because they result in a misallocation of resources; they restrict output to below the competitive level, and set prices above the competitive level. Nothing ensures that, in the long run, the monopolist will move towards its minimum efficient scale. A minimalist approach to industrial policy thus usually includes competition policy, for example to monitor mergers and acquisitions and prevent the formation of monopolies.

Although it appears that this policy is active in, for example, implementing competition policy, we consider it more appropriate to identify the policy as passive. It does not initiate any industrial activity, merely waits for firms to act. If the actions of the firms bring them into the net of competition policy, they will be examined, if not they are left alone. It is negative in that it prevents some actions, penalizes others; competition policy does not involve any positive encouragement.

Note that even a minimalist approach, even if it includes nothing other than competition policy to prevent the emergence of monopolies, has international implications, all the more so in the absence of trade and other barriers between countries. At the European level, the adoption of a competition policy by one country, for example, will have serious negative implications for that country. A simple prisoner's dilemma game illustrates how the co-ordination of monopoly policies by various governments, or indeed a common monopoly regulation, leads to the best payoff for all concerned.[9]

Beginning with the top, right-hand cell in Fig. 7.1, if the home country regulates monopolies and the trading partner country does not, then monopolies in the partner country will be able to make more profits and, ultimately, out-compete the home country monopolies. There will be a high positive payoff to the partner, and a negative payoff to the home country. The home country will not choose the monopoly regulation strategy for fear that the partner country will

		Partner country	
		Monopoly regulation	No monopoly regulation
Home country	Monopoly regulation	(10, 10)	(–10, 20)
	No monopoly regulation	(20, –10)	(0, 0)

Figure 7.1   Effects of monopoly regulation: an international prisoner's dilemma

choose the no regulation strategy. The same considerations will face the partner country. In the absence of discussion and binding agreement to opt for monopoly regulation, the countries will settle in the bottom, right-hand cell. This is the non-Pareto optimal equilibrium point. With such discussion and agreement, they will settle in the top, left-hand cell, which is Pareto optimal.

The favourable economic environment approach

In this approach there may be, in addition to competition policy, fiscal and other policies that encourage certain actions. Usually these policies are very broad, rather than focused. For example, a fiscal policy relieving all new firms of tax liability in the first two years of operation is positive in that it encourages or generates certain actions—the starting up of new firms; it is general in that it applies to all firms, rather than being focused, say, on SMEs in the textile industry. It is passive in that once the environment—fiscal policy—has been set, it is up to the firms to respond. This type of policy is closest to that implemented by governments apparently ideologically opposed to industrial policy, but faced with problems like industrial decline and unemployment that are seen to require intervention.

The active, negative sectoral policy approach

The rise of the Japanese and East Asian economies in the 1950s and 1960s, and the structural adjustments of the early 1970s, gave birth to a new form of industrial policy in Western Europe. The newly industrialized countries (NICs) were gradually encroaching on the established markets of the traditional world manufacturers (the USA, and Northern Europe). Some industries in Europe began to be referred to as 'traditional' or as 'declining' industries. These developments were in line with Rostow's (1960a, 1960b) stages approach to economic development, expanded later by Balassa (1977) in what became known as 'the stages approach to comparative advantages'.[10] Industrial restructuring in Europe, or the phasing out of non-viable sectors, was hampered by social considerations, and the EC industrial policy took the form of a defensive policy. Vertical or sectoral policies were implemented and were combined with restrictive trade policies. For example, in order to protect North America and Europe against cheap imports from Japan and other LDCs, a long-term arrangement regarding international trade in cotton textiles was concluded in 1962. This arrangement introduced the philosophy embodied in what later became the Multi-Fibre Agreements (MFAs).

This type of industrial policy, usually including such trade policies as MFAs and voluntary restraint agreements (VRAs), is activist in the sense that it allows for a more determined involvement of the state in specific activities, but negative because it is aimed at restricting the degree of competition worldwide. It does not directly encourage domestic producers, but changes their competitive environment by reducing the impact of foreign competition.

The active co-ordinator approach

An active and positive industrial policy has a number of aspects. Broadly speaking, the state remains outside the industrial framework itself. It does not directly own or control production, but it does influence it, sometimes directly. As co-ordinator, the state ensures consistency between policies (e.g. industrial and educational) and actively focuses such policies on achieving industrial outcomes (e.g. by encouraging research in universities to be applied to the needs of industry). This encouragement may be by providing funds through an appropriate channelling of credit, or by directly covering—usually only partially—the cost of a project. The state also acts as counsellor and information provider to firms in this type of policy. In order to act in all these ways, the state is required to actively select the sectors—or sub-sectors—to support. The notion of the state 'picking winners' usually refers to state support for individual firms. This is not quite what occurs here, but it is close to it. To provide special support for a particular sub-sector, for example, the state must have—or have access to—expert knowledge on the activities and potentials of this sub-sector. It must know about the industry worldwide, as well as about the strengths or potential strengths of the domestic firms in the industry.

Direct involvement in production

The most intense degree of industrial policy involves the building up of public enterprises.[11] Following Parris, Pestieau and Saynor (1987, p. 23), public enterprises can be grouped into three distinct categories:

1 Enterprises 'directly managed by a government department or semi-public authority'. This is the case of, for example, the railway and postal systems in Italy, and of telecommunications in The Netherlands, where such undertakings are called 'state enterprises'.
2 Enterprises 'with a special legal status, subject to a public authority but possessing also a measure of managerial autonomy'. This is the case for most public enterprises in Ireland where they are also called 'state-sponsored bodies'; those involved in production of goods and services—other than public services—are called 'commercial state-sponsored bodies'. In the UK these are known as QUANGOs—quasi-autonomous non-governmental organizations.
3 Companies 'with the same legal status as those in the private sector and enjoying a substantial degree of managerial autonomy, whose shares are owned (wholly or partly) by the state'. These include British Leyland (private today), Air France, the French SNCF; they are referred to as 'mixed-societies' or 'state-owned companies'.

Totally or partially owned and controlled by the state, the public enterprise may pursue other goals besides the economic goal of producing a good or service efficiently and selling it at prices compatible with cost and demand conditions. The typical public firm also serves a social purpose. It is as concerned about the availability of the good or service as about profitability. A state-owned bus company, for example, will provide a service throughout the day. If it was profit maximizing, it would have no—or fewer—buses running outside peak hours. The public pays for the use of the good or service on a payment-for-use basis and/or by means of subsidies which are raised through national, regional or local taxation.

7.1.4 Public versus private firms

An endless debate about the type and extent of public enterprise a nation should have—and about the role of the state in an economy in general—has been the feature not only of modern economics, with the privatization era in the 1980s, but of politics and political economy since the time of Plato and Aristotle.[12]

Even those in the classical and neoclassical traditions have accepted economic and non-economic arguments in favour of public enterprise as a second best. In his *Wealth of Nations*, Adam Smith (1776) himself advocated government intervention in four types of economic activity: defence, justice, certain public works and education. It was up to the government, he argued, to create and maintain defence, justice and educational institutions as well as to engage in some public works that are not economically profitable but may be socially desirable and advantageous.

Up to 1939, public enterprises in Europe were rare and were usually in the first category of public enterprises—directly managed by public or semi-public authorities. They included postal services, armaments and arsenals, and financial institutions, often created during the nineteenth century. In addition, public firms were created in France in 1919, the role of which was to exploit the German assets taken over as war payments (e.g. potash in Alsace). After the Second World War, the public sector was extended to cover many more areas: utilities (supply of water, gas, electricity, rail and air transport);[13] defence; finance and insurance; social services (transport, health, education); telecommunications; and nuclear energy.[14]

In the late 1940s and 1950s, public enterprises in France and Italy were formed in order to serve the major concern which was the rebuilding of the devastated economies. The public sector played a major role in the reconstruction and modernization of French industry during that time. French and Italian state capitalism served as a model for British Labour Party policy makers (Hager, 1982).

One way this was expressed in Britain was in successive waves of nationalizations and privatizations.[15] In some cases, usually relating to whether there were Labour or Conservative governments, firms were transferred back and forth between private and public ownership in just a few years; British Steel, for example, was nationalized in 1949, de-nationalized in the mid-1950s, nationalized again in 1967, and re-privatized in the 1980s (George, 1991).

During the 1960s, trade performance and technological independence (*vis-à-vis* the USA, and the increasingly challenging Japan) came to the fore as new objectives of industrial policy.[16] The formation of *national champions* was favoured as one means of achieving these objectives. National champions have been described by Hager (1982, p. 241) as 'large firms favored by national procurement policies, capital sources, etc., and able to negotiate with American companies on the terms under which US technology was utilized'.

In the 1970s, the economic crisis reinforced the role of the public sector. The aim of narrowing the technology gap led to support for the creation of large *European champions*—Airbus is one example—that would open up to the world market and respond to the challenge of the American and Japanese competitors. At the purely national level in Europe, various nationalization programmes increased the number of state-owned multinationals. In the second half of the 1970s, British Leyland was nationalized, the shipyards and steelworks in Sweden were nationalized (despite the advent to power of a Conservative government), and

TABLE 7.2   Public enterprises in Europe, 1985 (*Source*: Adapted from Anastassopoulos, Blanc and Dussauge, 1987)

Enterprise	Sector of activity	Country of origin
IRI (1)	Iron & steel aeronautics, shipyards, electronics, communications	Italy
ENI (2)	Oil products, chemicals	Italy
Elf Aquitaine	Oil products, chemicals	France (*)
Voest Alpine	Metals–machine tools	Austria
Renault	Motor-car	France (*)
CGE (3)	Electrical, electronic engineering	France (*)
Saint Gobain	Glass, cast iron, building materials	France (*)
DSM (4)	Chemicals, fertilizers, plastics	The Netherlands (*)
Thomson	Electrical, electronic engineering	France (*)
Rhône-Poulenc	Chemicals	France (**)

(1): Istituto per la Ricostruzione Industriale (see below)
(2): Ente Nazionale Idrocarburi
(3): Compagnie Générale d'Electricité
(4): Dutch State Mines
(*): Companies that have since 1985 been partly de-nationalized.
(**): Privatization plans exist for these companies

there was a wave of nationalizations in Portugal (this time ideologically based, following as it did the Portuguese revolution of 1974).

European public enterprises in general grew—and grew in number—over the period between the 1960s and the 1980s. In 1965, only 19 of the 200 largest companies in the world outside the USA were publicly owned; in 1975 and 1985, there were respectively 29 and 38 such companies (Anastassopoulos, Blanc and Dussauge, 1987). The number of state-owned firms among the world's top enterprises outside the USA thus doubled over the two decades; the number of all state-owned multinationals increased six-fold in the same period. Economic internationalization and political nationalization combined to put state-owned multinational enterprises at the forefront of European industrial development.

The 10 largest public enterprises in Europe in 1985, ranked by size of turnover, are represented in Table 7.2. These are publicly owned firms that 'have industrial subsidiaries in at least two countries other than the country of origin and [that] conduct 10 per cent of their activity abroad' (Anastassopoulos, Blanc and Dussauge, 1987, p. 25).

It is clear that the biggest public multinationals were to be found in the traditionally interventionist countries, namely France and Italy. Austria has also traditionally been a country with a strong public sector. The countries the least represented are Germany, the UK and The Netherlands, countries where the *laissez-faire* attitude has been more pervasive. It should be noted that if the 1970s and the 1980s saw ideologically inspired waves of nationalizations and privatizations in countries such as the UK, France and Portugal, the attitude of politicians in Germany and The Netherlands was probably more balanced. In these latter countries, 'It is as though [the public firms] had been accepted as belonging to the industrial landscape' (Anastassopoulos, Blanc and Dussauge, 1987, p. 59). As pointed out by the same authors, the managements of these firms (e.g. DSM in The Netherlands) require that they be as efficient as if they were private companies.

However, political ideology opposing state intervention probably reached its apogee in the 1980s, resulting in a radical break with the past in some European countries. The case against state enterprises led to massive privatization programmes, starting in Thatcherite Britain and spreading over Europe.[17] Among the questions addressed in relation to privatization, are: How important is the social service provided by the postal system? Should the likes of tennis courts and universities (used only by a minority of the public), be subsidized by all taxpayers? Is it socially desirable to continue to subsidize the steel industry?

7.1.5 The wave of privatization

A non-exhaustive list of companies that have been sold off wholly or in part in the past five years or so is given in Appendix 7.1. As one would expect, the number of public companies de-nationalized or privatized is quite high in the *United Kingdom*. British privatized companies include: British Airways, British Aerospace, British Telecom (the biggest sale), BP, Cable & Wireless, Ferranti, International Computers Ltd, Jaguar Cars (part of British Leyland), Rolls-Royce, Amersham International, and British Gas Corporation. The shipbuilding yards Sealink and Inmos have been partly de-nationalized. Following the privatization of the public utilities (water, gas and telecommunications), the UK government set up new regulatory bodies to control prices, and to limit diversification. In the telecommunications sector, together with the privatization of BT, the government also facilitated the establishment of another company, Mercury. Now in many segments of the British telecommunications sector, a duopoly exists. This calls for a new regulatory framework controlling the private duopolies. Only a few large concerns are still in public ownership today:[18] British Rail, National Coal Board, Post Office, and London Regional Transport.

In *France*, a list of '*privatizable*' companies was determined by the law of 31 July 1986. A list of French companies privatized between 1986 and 1988 can be found in Appendix 7.1. In 1993 alone, 22 companies were sold. In January 1994, the share of manufacturing employment in state firms had dropped to 7 per cent (*Le Monde*, 13 January 1994) from 16 per cent in 1984, i.e. shortly after the wave of nationalizations. More companies were being privatized in 1994, of which Compagnie des Machines Bull, Banque Nationale de Paris, Crédit Agricole, and Renault were most important. Ironically, while in the latter part of 1993, the Minister for Trade and Industry was confirming these future privatizations, he was also corroborating the fact that the French state was going to increase its capital participation in SNECMA and Aérospatiale.

The reunification of the two *Germanies* prompted intense efforts to privatize the 13,400 previously state-owned firms of the eastern länder. The *Treuhandanstalt* (privatization agency) played a major role in this process. During the first six months of 1991, the Treuhand Agency managed to sell some 2600 companies. The assets sold by the agency between 1991 and 1994 have been valued at DM 45 billion, i.e. DM 275 million short of the expected figure, leaving an equivalent deficit to the German taxpayer. Of the 4 million people originally employed in these firms, the privatized firms planned to keep roughly 1.5 million jobs (*Le Monde*, 25 January 1994). The agency temporarily held minority shares in the de-nationalized firms; for example, it held 40 per cent of the shares in EKO, a steel company, 60 per cent of which had been sold to the Italian firm, Riva.

The mission of the Treuhand Agency came to an end at the end of 1994, when it was taken over by the German authorities. Although costly in the short term, the agency achieved a great deal, in a short time-period. When it was dissolved, it had sold 17,000 firms or parts of firms, mostly to German firms; only 700 passed into foreign ownership.

In France, where right-wing and left-wing governments have alternated in the 1980s and 1990s, in Thatcherite UK, and in East Germany, the privatization wave was intense. Elsewhere, European governments have privatized more cautiously, selling only part of their assets and retaining a substantial share of public interest. In Spain, and to a certain extent Italy, de-nationalization has been seen as a means to reduce the public deficit in order to comply with the convergence criteria for participation, first, in the European Monetary System, and, more recently, in moves towards economic and monetary union.

In *Italy*, the massive losses of the IRI, amounting to FF35 billion (*Le Monde*, 1 February 1994), has prompted the sale of 14 of its smaller companies to private interests (such as Alitalia, Aeritalia, SIRTI telecommunications). The privatization programme is planned to lead to the sale of 57 per cent of the capital of IRI. A quarter of the stake of the largest bank in Italy, Il Banco Nazionale del Lavoro, has been sold. Other privatizations in the banking sector include Il Credito Italiano and l'Istituto Immobiliare. In the early part of 1994, the government announced the sale of the main Italian industrial bank, the Banca Commerciale Italiana (known as Comit).

Austria is another country with a relatively large public sector. In 1987, of the nine largest enterprises, five were totally state owned, one was under majority state ownership, two others were state controlled through large nationalized banks, and only one was privately owned. Following the crisis of Voest-Alpine (steel and engineering group) in the 1980s, the Austrian government announced that it would introduce private funding in the companies owned by the state.

Unlike other countries in Europe, *Dutch* governments never implemented large programmes of nationalization. This explains why the public sector in this country has always been relatively small, and why privatization has only been very slight. In the past few years, the Dutch state reduced its stake in KLM to 55 per cent, and two-thirds of the chemical firm DSM was sold to the public.

The *Spanish* government's majority stake in the car manufacturer SEAT was sold to Volkswagen in 1986. SKF Española (tyre manufacturer) was de-nationalized, and 39 per cent of ENCE was sold on the stock exchange. Negotiations for the sale of a minority stake in ENASA (motor-car) and MTM (railway equipment) started in the late 1980s. The Spanish government did not follow a systematic strategy of de-nationalization of public enterprises, but rather followed a 'process of clarification of their objectives that necessitated the de-nationalization of some of them' (García Delgado *et al.*, 1989, p. 496).

In *Belgium*, the sale of 50 per cent of the stock of the country's second largest state bank, Société Nationale de Crédit à l'Industrie (SNCI) began in December 1993.

In *Denmark*, one enterprise, Statsangstalten for Livsforsikring (State Life Insurance Company) was sold to a private firm. In 1993, the Danish government sold 25 per cent of the shares in Kobenhavns Lufthavnsvaesen (KLV), 25 per cent of Postgiro, and 49 per cent of the shares in TeleDanmark.

The impact of the privatization and de-nationalization programmes in the last decade is shown in Tables 7.3 and 7.4.

It is clear that the most spectacular decline in the impact of state-owned enterprises took place in the UK. There were also declines in France, Spain and Ireland and, to a very small extent, in Denmark. Note that even where firms remain in state ownership, EU rules prevent the state from intervening in the operation or financing of these firms in any way that might improve their competitive position.

7.2   History of industrial policy in Europe

There was a near consensus on industrial policy in Europe and, in general, on the role of the state in economic affairs during the period of the Renaissance. A divergence of views developed

TABLE 7.3   **Numbers employed, value added, and gross fixed capital formation (GFCF) in European public enterprises (1991)** (*Source*: Centre Européen des Entreprises à Participation Publique, Bruxelles. (Les Entreprises à Participation Publique dans l'Union Européenne. Annales du CEEP 1994. Résumé des Études Nationales)

	Share of non-agricultural employment (%)	*Value added as a % of total manufacturing and service industry (at current prices)*	*Share in non-agricultural GFCF (%)*
Belgium	9.8 (*)	7.5	8.4
Denmark	8.2	8.7	17.6
France	13.4	15.1	24.2 (*)
Greece	14.7	17	30
Ireland	8.7	11.5	16.9
Italy	13.5	20	23.5
Luxemburg	3.2	5.2 (**)	4.6
The Netherlands	5.1	8.0	9.2
Portugal	10.6	21.5	30.0
Spain	6.0	7.5 to 8.5	12.5 to 13
UK	4.6	4.0	5.0

(*): Total CFCF.
(**): Percentage share in non-agricultural turnover.
NB: For Denmark and Italy, estimates by CEEP.

during the Industrial Revolution, and marked differences have persisted since. In the twentieth century, even with the spread of widely influential schools of thought, there is no unanimity on what constitutes appropriate intervention. First, Keynes's thinking influenced the national policies of virtually all West European and North American countries after the war, providing support for anti-cyclical budgetary policies. More recently, since the early 1980s, the neo-liberal, anti-interventionist, 'new classical economists' have convinced the governments of Europe—and elsewhere—of the merits of deregulation. The significance of Robert Lucas's

TABLE 7.4   **Average index measuring the impact of public enterprises on the economy (agricultural sector excluded), 1982, 1988, and 1991 (1)** (*Source*: Compiled from information released by CEEP, Brussels)

	1982 (%)	*1988 (%)*	*1991 (%)*
Denmark	12	11.9	11.5
France	22.8	na	17.6
Greece	na	na	21.0
Ireland	na	14.4	12.4
Italy	20.3	20 (3)	19.0
Portugal	na	>21.0	20.7
Spain	na	ca 10.0	8.5 to 9.0
UK	15 (2)	na	4.5

(1): This share is the non-weighted average of the three indicators shown in Table 7.3 for each given year.
(2): Figure for 1979.
(3): Figure for 1985.

contribution to this school of thought, through his theory of 'rational expectations', was recognized in the award of the 1995 Nobel Prize for Economics to Robert Lucas.

Modern economic thought about intervention has emerged from a number of earlier schools of thought. Mercantilism, prevalent up to the eighteenth century, held that a country's wealth was represented by the wealth of the state—controlled by the sovereign. This was an interventionist, protectionist doctrine, owing much, among others, to Machiavelli.[19] The state had power and used it to determine which individuals or groups obtained trading and other commercial rights. This led to the enrichment of a mercantile *bourgeoisie* and possibly to an increase in general welfare. In the seventeenth and early eighteenth centuries, many merchants, bankers and industrialists were in favour of a strong state because they felt that the commercial prosperity of a nation was strictly linked to the political power of the monarch and to the success of its military conquests abroad.

The physiocrats in France in the eighteenth century and the classical political economists in Britain in the eighteenth and nineteenth centuries vigorously opposed state intervention. Their views are expressed in the famous saying, *laissez-faire, laissez-passer*, strongly advocating free trade, the freedom of the individual and the freedom of enterprise. This was a philosophy and ideology consistent with what was required for the Industrial Revolution. By the late eighteenth and early nineteenth centuries, the emerging commercial and industrial *bourgeoisie* saw itself as inhibited by various economic and social regulations of the state. Different paces of industrialization in Europe, as well as different degrees of penetration of the ideas of the classical economists, resulted in the twentieth century in Keynesian policies being applied to differing extents in different countries. Together, these all explain the differences in national industrial policies. Such differences have persisted, and underlie the difficulties in designing an industrial policy for the EU.

7.2.1 Major historical trends in national industrial policies

Germany

Post-Second World War Germany became one of the major proponents of a free market economy in Europe. In official language, *Strukturpolitik* is today the word used to refer to industrial policy in Germany. But in the 100 years or so before the war, Germany had had an intensely interventionist, centralist state. State intervention, and constraints on competition, started in Bismarckian Germany and culminated in the 1930s. The Zollverein, established in 1834 under Prussian leadership, began the process, also providing the opportunity to build a strong industrial economy.

The central philosophy embodied in the Erfurt Programme, adopted in 1891, was to develop public enterprises as a means to bring about production on a large scale and also as a means to improve general social welfare (Russell, 1965). The Erfurt Programme remained in force until 1921; it was then replaced by the Goerlitz Programme which endorsed the principle of public ownership. In the late-nineteenth century cartels, *Syndikate, Konzerne* and monopolies were formed in heavy industries.[20] The *Syndikat* is a superior form of cartel, in which the total production of a firm, of an industrial sector and of a stage of production is transferred and sold to a common point of sale (Maschke, 1914). In the late nineteenth century, *Syndikate* were formed in the coke and coal industries (called *Kokssyndikat* and *Kohlensyndikat*) (Hallgarten and Radkau, 1974). By the end of the century, German coal production was the second largest in the world. Friedrich List's ideas, and in particular his criticism of the 'dwarf economy', had a definite influence on the constitution of large groups in German industry at that time.[21] The 'Kartellgesetz' of July 1933 increased state intervention in the economy, which further intensified under Hitler.

Breaking radically with this interventionist, authoritarian system, post-war Germany dedicated itself to the building of as free as possible a domestic economy within the Common Market. The necessity to reconstruct a devastated economy explains the continued and concentrated aid to some industrial sectors (coal, shipbuilding and steel). The year 1957 is crucial for German industry as it marks, through the Rome Treaty, the launching of unprecedented opportunities for German industrial goods, and the determined dismantling of large groups and conglomerates. The 1957 'Kartellgesetz'—prohibiting anti-competitive behaviour—was subsequently amended and passed by the Bundestag in 1964 (Hallgarten and Radkau, 1974). An anti-merger bill was passed in the early 1970s.

The first wave of privatizations began in 1958, and was revived in 1982 with the coming into power of a right wing coalition. For example, the oil company VEBA was privatized in 1983. From the 1960s onwards, the German *Strukturpolitik* gave the government only a supporting role. Even after the late 1960s, with the advent of the SDP (*Sozial Demokratische Partei*) as the dominant partner in a coalition with the Free Democrats, the public sector did not increase. Over all these years, the preferred form of support was tax relief; the major aims were to increase productivity, and to promote innovation and technological development. This was made possible by the existence of three circumstances:

1 The federal structure of the country which gives the various Länder a large margin of manoeuvre. The federal structure of the country allows a *Strukturpolitik* to be carried out at the state level coupled with actions at the level of the Länder. The German Constitution gives the Länder the responsibility for education and vocational training.

2 The apparent absence, *in the past*, of acute regional problems. Before the reunification of the two Germanies, industrial activity was more or less evenly distributed. In 1978, one-third of the German population lived in assisted areas, which covered more than 60 per cent of the German territory (regional aid represented 40 per cent of total federal and Länder aid). However, since reunification, the regional problem has become severe. Today, the politicians of the new Länder want more decentralization *vis-à-vis* Bonn, regional initiatives taken by more independent regional bodies, and a more active and positive industrial policy aimed at rescuing the remaining public companies.[22]

3 The cooperation between different partners involved in the design and implementation of the policy, i.e. government, industry, research institutes, universities, trade unions and large banks. In particular, the role of the banking system is crucial to industrial development in Germany. Since the middle of the nineteenth century, large banks have exercised a 'weeding-out' function. In Hager's words (1982, p. 240):

The ability of the big German banks to have detailed knowledge of all major firms in the key sectors of the economy (through their representatives on the boards of directors) and their willingness to go for long-term capital gains rather than short-term high dividends are examples of the many fortunate historically derived arrangements that lessen the need for active industrial policies in that country.

The efficiency of the banking system meant financial support could be extended to many more industrial sectors, including nuclear power, aircraft, computer and ocean-related industries, than was the case in most other countries. Although today many large companies (e.g. Siemens) are internally financed, banks remain important in financing SMEs (as does the government, within EU constraints).

One area where the state's contribution was important was in education and training. Even here, however, success was due, at least in part, to close relationships between education and training on the one hand and industry on the other. One result was the predominance of German firms in technology-orientated industries.[23] As pointed out by Freeman (1982, p. 100) 'by the late nineteenth century, Germany had developed a "national system of innovation" which proved superior to the British in terms of the education and training system, as well as the organisation of in-house R&D in the new chemical and electrical industries'.

The absence of intervention in Germany should not be overemphasized. An important *social market economy* co-exists with the market economy. In the social market economy competition is limited—through state regulation and direct intervention—in the interests of political or social goals. 'These types of politically regulated enterprises can be found in the services sector (transport, postal services, telecommunications, energy supply, banking, and insurance)...' (Esser, 1995). However, even in the regulated industries there is now, in the 1990s, a mix of private and public enterprise.

Another, more centralized, example of state intervention in Germany is in research and technology. Through the Federal Ministry for Research and Technology (*Bundes Ministerium für Forschung und Technologie*—BMFT), the research and technology policies have been the major ingredients of the German *Strukturpolitik* since the 1950s. The leading technological position of Germany is credited to its technological and educational policies. In 1988, German industry spent around DM 35 billion on R&D programmes, of which two-thirds were government funds (Schuster, 1990).[24] The BMFT co-ordinates all federal expenditures on R&D, and can be seen, to some extent, as actively and positively interventionist, because the allocation of funds is based—not entirely, but preferentially—on the government's calculated guesses about winners of the future.

The German *Strukturpolitik* has been primarily of the first and second types of industrial policy, but also with minor elements of the third, fourth and fifth types. It has, in general, been a more *laissez-faire* than interventionist approach; where there have been government subsidies, they have been limited in scope and have attempted to leave most decisions to market forces, with the exception of the social market areas.

The United Kingdom

There has long been a commitment to free trade in the UK, and a widespread scepticism as to the ability of the state to intervene beneficially in economic matters has always been widespread.[25] This is normally seen as the legacy of Adam Smith (1776), and he was no doubt influential. However, it is not coincidental that the UK was the most powerful trading country in the world and the one most strongly in favour of free trade. The intense intervention of the mercantilist era provided the foundation on which private entrepreneurs and individuals could build the first industrialized nation. The Victorian values spread through the nineteenth century dominated the govenment–industry relationship (Grant, 1989). The result, as Walker (1993) writes, was that the role of the state in Britain 'was confined to some regulatory functions (financial markets, property law, etc.) and to the advancement and military protection of foreign trade'. More recently, the British commitment to as little government intervention as possible is exemplified by the 1965 anti-merger legislation, and by the Industry Act passed in 1972.

In the 1960s, the National Economic Development Council, the Industrial Reorganization Corporation and other bodies were set up to help companies to catch up with their European and international counterparts (Hager, 1982). This suggests an active, positive policy, but in the view of many commentators, government intervention in Britain (be it under the leadership of the Labour Party or of the Conservative Party) has often occurred as a policy of last resort. In Grant's words (1989, p. 87), 'the main motive for intervention has been the collapse of an enterprise [...], or at least the fact that it is in such a poor state that it would be unable to continue without government aid'.

There are exceptions to this such as the steel industry which was built up as part of a national industrial strategy under Labour immediately after the war. From then on, Grant may be correct even for the steel industry. The 1951 Conservative government de-nationalized the industry. When the 1964 Labour government re-nationalized it, at least part of the reason, unlike the earlier nationalization, was the need to support the industry because it had been technologically backward and generally uncompetitive. Under the Thatcher government, restructuring and radical rationalization were required to bring British Steel Corporation towards profitability. This prepared it for re-privatization in 1988 (Grant, 1995). In relation to steel, and to the other industries in which nationalizations had taken place, the extraction of the state in the 1980s was thorough. Of the major countries of Europe, 'Britain is the one in which the transition from the old conception of a "national champion" to that of the international firm has gone furthest' (Grant, 1995).

Where policy was active and positive, as for example in the nuclear and aircraft industries, large amounts of resources were inappropriately committed by the state. In Hager's (1982, p. 238) view, this aspect of industrial policy was an outstanding failure, since 'it drained the rest of the economy of scarce engineering talent'.

In summary, British industrial policy, like Germany's, has been more about attempting to get the environment right for industrial success, than intervening actively or positively. Where intervention has been active and positive, unlike in Germany it has generally failed in Britain.

France

It has been customary to view industrial policy in France as an extension of the seventeenth-century mercantilist 'Colbertist policy'. It should be remembered however that Colbert, minister of Louis XIV, applied the same protectionist policy as his predecessors (Sully for example). The originality of Colbert's approach lay in the fact that manufactures were, in his time, the key sector to be developed. In order to protect and promote the domestic manufacturers, high and prohibitive tariffs were imposed on imported manufactured goods. This trade policy was supplemented by a meticulous industrial policy aimed in particular at raising the quality of products.[26] The consolidation of the state led to unprecedented wars and to distress and famine in the countryside. An anti-Colbertist movement arose, which nourished the emerging physiocratic doctrine. Turgot, the minister of Louis XVI, demonstrated an indisputable efficiency in restoring free trade, and in de-regulating manufactures.

Among Napoleon's legacies to France was an educational system—the *Grandes Écoles*—which was to constitute an indirect means of intervention by the state; in these colleges was to be created a new elite, the civil servants who were to administer industrial (and other) policies. They remain today a most important training ground for senior administrators of the state apparatus in France.[27]

After the Second World War, France isolated itself from the international community. It experienced enormous difficulties in breaking with the protectionist era inherited from Méline,[28] but this isolationist policy did enable France to consolidate trade links with its colonies, and to strengthen the role of the state (Eck, 1990). State intervention became embodied in the French planning system. It may seem ironic that the *Commissariat au Plan*, created in 1946, had as its first director the businessman Jean Monnet, one of the founding fathers of the European Union.[29] However, this illustrates the fact that planning in France involved a social compromise (Cohen, 1995).

The French planning system is best characterized by its three closely associated epithets: it is flexible, indicative, and concerted, as it involves the co-operation of different economic partners. The plan involves non-binding quantitative targets for global, sectoral and regional production, investment, and employment. These targets normally cover a period of five years.[30]

An objective of the first French plan was to modernize some industrial sectors and industrial infrastructure (railway, electricity, coal and steel). Among major objectives in subsequent plans, was to create industries capable of withstanding international competition through the supply of capital to industries that needed to replace old capital stock, through incentives to merge, and through the provision of technological know-how. In the 1950s, France imitated Britain by laying the ground for the active development of the nuclear and aerospace industries. This latter was militarily motivated.

During the 1960s, the 'German miracle' and the 'American challenge' led the French government to focus on the building up of technologically advanced national champions able to reap the full benefits arising from the associated economies of scale. Among the candidates for national champion status were CGE (electrical), PUK (aluminium and chemicals), Saint-Gobain (glass), Rhône-Poulenc (chemicals), SNIAS, Dassault and Bréguet (Messerlin, 1987).

Although one of the objectives of French planning was to build up strong national groups, and although the French state has been a major actor in the shaping of industrial policy and industrial structures in post-war France, the state gradually changed its philosophy. It was more *dirigiste* than other European governments throughout the period since the war, but it was less so later than earlier. According to Eck (1990), from France's participation in the EEC in 1958 onwards, the French state became more respectful of the principles and mechanisms of the market.

The French government's answers to the oil crisis were many, and sometimes contradictory policies. Under the presidency of Giscard d'Estaing (1974–81), a policy of specialization in selected sectors was favoured (the so-called *politique de créneaux*). Public funds were poured into the mechanical equipment industry. For military and strategic reasons, the French industrial policy of the 1970s was also geared towards the objective of import substitution. The Electronic Components Plan was drawn up for that purpose. Large sums of public funds were also allocated to rescue the ailing textile companies (*Plan Textile*). Most of these policies, though in practice aspects of industrial policy, were 'largely outside the remit of the ministry supposedly in charge of industry' (Cohen, 1995). Radically opposed to Giscard d'Estaing's conception of industrial policy, the socialist governments in the early 1980s favoured a policy of *filières*.

Other contradictions arising in the conduct of industrial policy in the 1980s centred on the role of the state as entrepreneur. For the first socialist governments of the early 1980s, public firms were seen as an essential instrument in boosting economic growth. Through its 1981–82 policy of nationalizations, the government gained control, wholly or partially, of 12 large industrial groups, 2 financial groups and 36 banks.[31] Although this new wave of nationalizations had economic objectives, it was overshadowed by political ideology. In 1986, the short-lived conservative government de-nationalized all the above, with the exception of Sacilor and Usinor. Its privatization programme was very comprehensive since it was extended to cover companies and banks that had been under state control since the 1940s (Agence Havas,

Banque Nationale de Paris, Crédit Lyonnais). A new form of pragmatism emerged in the latter part of the decade as the new socialist governments also partly privatized some state companies.

The role of the French state in economic development in general, and in industrial development in particular, has often been overemphasized. The French planning system is not coercive, but indicative, and based on consensus. But though not focused, the power of the state in France is pervasive. On the basis of the index of impact of public enterprises calculated in Table 7.4, France is not far below Italy, and well above the UK. On the basis of ECUs per employee of subsidy to manufacturing industry, France (1380) is again below Italy (over 2175), and above Germany (984) and the UK (582) (see Table 7.5).

Industrial policy in France is mixed. It has varied over time, to some extent dependent on which government was in power. There have also been a number of different instruments of policy at any one time. So, like the UK, there are elements of all five types of industrial policy in France. Like the UK, too, industrial policy is not concentrated in the fourth and fifth types, but rather the first, second and third. However, French industrial policy has been more interventionist than Britain's; greater weight has been put on the fourth and fifth types than in the UK.

Italy

Italy is another country with a relatively long tradition of state intervention in the economy. The depression of the early 1930s, with a generalized downward movement of shares on the stock exchanges explains the creation in 1932 of the *Istituto per la Ricostruzione Industriale* (IRI) which soon controlled part of the banking system in Italy (Corbino, 1962). The first mission of the IRI was to integrate the large, newly constituted public firms who had a participation in its capital, and eventually to control them totally. The IRI gained control, albeit indirectly, of the shipbuilding industry (Fincantieri), of the maritime transport industry (Finmare) and of the steel industry (Ilva) (Corbino, 1962).

The IRI, in a sense a legacy of Fascism in Italy, in more recent times, developed interests in the car and civil aviation industries (by controlling Alfa Romeo and Alitalia) and in the food industry (SME). It also helped to establish a modern heavy and light engineering industry, as well as technologically advanced sectors such as computing, electronics and telecommunications (STET). It developed extensive interests in the banking sector, becoming the majority shareholder of the Credito Italiano, Il Banco di Roma, and of La Banca Commerciale.

In the 1950s, as the Italian economy was starting to register unprecedented growth rates, massive state intervention was developed in order to solve two of the major domestic problems at the time: the transformation of the economy from an agricultural based economy to an industrialized economy, and the increasing *mezzogiorno*[32] issue. The law of October 1950, known as the *legge stralcio*, facilitated the expropriation, improvement and redistribution of land to farmers. Public concern about the less developed regions of Italy, and in particular about the *mezzogiorno*, led to the creation of the *Cassa per il Mezzogiorno* and to the involvement of the state holding company, IRI, in the industrialization of the south (Ranci, 1987). The objective of the *Cassa* was to develop infrastructure and industry in the south of the country. The IRI represented a driving force in southern industrialization until the early 1970s. It supported the development of heavy industries (chemicals, steel, aluminium, oil and gas) mainly in the south. A study by Del Monte (1977) estimated that between 1953 and 1971, regional investment incentives generated between 79,000 and 124,000 manufacturing jobs in the *mezzogiorno*.

Until the early 1970s, industrial policy in Italy was intimately conducted in relation to regional policy. After 1973, a radical change was implemented: industrial policy became essentially defensive. As an aftermath of the economic recession, the state sought to avoid too many bankruptcies, by simply taking over large private firms.

Government intervention in Italian industry is best represented as a network of multi-focal relationships. The IRI has certainly been a mainstay in industrial development in Italy. For example, SGC, a subsidiary of IRI, became in 1983 the 20th largest producer in the area of semiconductors (Anastassopoulos, Blanc and Dussauge, 1987).

In the second phase of its existence (since the 1980s), the IRI became subject to intense political influence. Corruption[33] helped to create massive losses and debts, which represented 5 per cent of Italian GDP in January 1994. The large size of the public deficit, the inefficiency of public administrations, and a faster pace of European integration, radically changed the nature of industrial policy in the 1980s. Italian industrial policy has become more market oriented (Ranci, 1987).

Since the mid-1980s, the combination of the completion of the Single Market and the general intensification of global competition has forced restructuring on Italian industries. It was just in these years, however, that 'the internal crisis of the Italian political system exploded and made the development of national strategies for international economic growth extremely difficult to carry out' (Bianchi, 1995). There is something of a vacuum, with all awaiting the outcome of the political struggles.

Though not necessarily coherent, Italian intervention has been intense, greater than in any other major European country. The data in Table 7.4 show that the impact of public enterprise in Italy has been greater than in other major European countries; and the data presented above on ECUs per employee of subsidy to manufacturing industry show the same picture. This puts Italy more into industrial policy types four and five than its European partners, at least until recent years.

Spain

State intervention in the Spanish economy has been a creation of twentieth-century economics. Before the civil war, the state had only a marginal impact on Spanish economic life. Its activities were limited to justice, defence, police, and to infrastructural works which were not profitable enough to be carried out by private initiatives. According to García Delgado *et al.* (1989), the optimal state during that time was seen as one that exercised the lowest possible level of interference with private initiatives, and that could protect the domestic market against foreign competition.[34]

State intervention intensified as a result of the Great Depression of the early 1930s and of the diffusion of Keynes's ideas. The action of the state took three forms:

1 Protection against foreign competition through trade barriers, such as import quotas, which became even more popular later under Franco's rule.
2 Stimulation of national production, through fiscal and financial aid to domestic enterprises.
3 Regulation of production and commercialization through corporatism.

State regulation and state intervention increased sharply under the Franco dictatorship; it reached its peak during the 1940s and 1950s. The creation of an intrepreneurial public sector—an expression of which was the *Instituto Nacional de Industria* (INI)—is the very peculiar characteristic of Francoism (García Delgado *et al.*, 1989). The INI was set up in 1941. In the 1950s there was a gradual liberalization of the Spanish economy, culminating in the 1959 *Plan de Estabilización y Liberalización* (García Delgado *et al.*, 1989). This plan initiated the de-regulation of both production on the domestic market and international economic transactions. Quantitative restrictions on imports and custom duties were reduced, imports of financial capital and of technology were facilitated.

This liberalization trend was short lived, since the subsequent decade brought with it a new wave of protectionism and regulation, to such an extent that in the mid-1970s, the Spanish economy was still characterized by many institutional rigidities and by many administrative controls. In particular, its public sector was totally inefficient.

A new era opened for Spain with the advent of a democracy, and with the prospect of joining the EC. There was a definite opportunity to de-regulate and liberalize the economy.[35] Spain joined the EC, together with Portugal, in 1986.

Public enterprises in Spain are an integral part of the industrial policy. Born in the period 1941–61, they are organized around holding companies as is the case in Italy, Germany and Austria. There are three existing holding companies: INI, *Instituto Nacional de Hidrocarburos* (INH) and the *Dirección General del Patrimonio del Estado* (DGPE) (García Delgado *et al.*, 1989). These holding companies control roughly two-thirds of the value added of state-owned enterprises. State-owned enterprises have been assigned clear and determined objectives, which are: to be export-driven, to maintain a high level of employment, to combat the regional inequalities, to improve the balance of technological trade, to re-industrialize the country, and to provide an example of the 'work ethos' (García Delgado *et al.*, 1989).

Ireland

There have been four main periods—and types—of industrial policy in Ireland since independence:

1 From the beginning of fiscal autonomy in 1923 to 1932 the policy was one of agriculture-led growth, with little or no industrial intervention and a very low tariff regime. With the changes in the world economy following the depression in 1929, Irish policy, like most others in Europe, changed.

2 The second policy period was from 1932 to 1958, during which import-substituting industrialization (ISI) was implemented. Industrialization, based on indigenous firms, was to be achieved through protectionism. A set of Control of Manufactures Acts (1932 and 1934) aimed—with only limited success—to keep ownership of the protected industries in Irish hands. This was also a period during which a number of public enterprises were established.

When all the employment that could be created through ISI had been created, the combination of outflows of people from the land, and high natural population growth still left Ireland in the 1950s with very high unemployment rates, and high net emigration. A net emigration rate of around 1 per cent of the population left Ireland every year between 1951 and 1961. At the same time, developments in Europe—like the formation of the EEC—expressed a general movement towards more liberal trade policies. This combination of factors resulted in a sharp change in Irish industrial policy.

3 The third policy period, 1958 to 1990, was one of export-led industrialization. Through a semi-autonomous government agency, the Industrial Development Authority, foreign direct

investment was encouraged. There were high, though varying, rates of inflow of foreign capital, and America replaced the UK as the main origin of foreign economic interest in Ireland. The task of encouraging FDI was assisted by Ireland—along with the UK and Denmark—joining the EC in 1973. Today subsidiaries of American companies account for more than half of all employment in foreign-owned firms in Ireland; foreign-owned firms account for over 40 per cent of all manufacturing employment and for over 70 per cent of all manufactured exports.

4 Since the early 1990s, a fourth policy period has been introduced. The roots of the change were in the questioning of the concentration in industrial policy on encouraging FDI. Already in the early 1980s a report commissioned by the National Economic and Social Council—and carried out by the American consultancy group, Telesis—had recommended a shift in favour of the development of internationally trading indigenous firms. A number of steps were taken in this direction, and over the 1980s the proportion of capital grants going to foreign firms declined from over 90 per cent to around 50 per cent, with the other 50 per cent going to indigenous firms. The change gathered pace in the early 1990s, culminating in reorganization of the industrial development agencies in 1994/5. A separate agency was established to encourage the development of indigenous firms, and both this new agency—Forbairt—and the IDA, came under the control of an industrial policy and planning agency, Forfas.

Recent years have also seen Irish governments following European privatization trends. Sales of shares of previously state-owned enterprises have occurred in insurance and in sugar production, for example.

Denmark

Danish industrial policy integrates some elements found in the German *Strukturpolitik*. Traditionally liberal, it aimed at creating a favourable economic and industrial environment for firms, through fiscal and monetary instruments. During the Second World War, the state had a massive involvement in technological matters; it designed a 'Science Policy' which later became a 'Research Policy' (Braendgaard, 1986). Post-war Danish industrial policy concentrated on technology promotion schemes.

In the 1980s, Danish industrial policy changed from a more *laissez-faire*, to a more interventionist approach. The new policy had three main elements:

• A general model using the market mechanism
• A selective strategy (a large part of public spending for industrial policy benefits only a small part of manufacturing industry)
• A social need-orientated strategy.

As summarized by Braendgaard (1986, p. 181), 'the public sector has, directly or indirectly, helped create many of the strong competitive positions of Danish industry in international markets'.

The major state-owned enterprises are found in the postal, telecommunications, transportation and energy sectors. Their combined annual turnover is quite small in European terms, since it amounts only to 5 to 6 per cent of GDP (OECD, 1993b). In the beginning of the 1990s, the government started to transform the legal status of public enterprises. Tele Sonderjylland

(Telecom Southern Jutland), Københavns Lufthavnsvaesen (Copenhagen Airport), Statens Teletjeneste (Telecom covering wireless communication) and Postgiro have all become limited liability companies.

The Danish Competition Act of 1990 has replaced the Monopolies Act of 1955 and the Prices and Profits Acts of 1974. Its aim is to promote competition and to strengthen the efficiency of production and distribution. Collusive tendering and resale price maintenance (i.e. binding resale) agreements are prohibited. It leaves companies free to engage in all kinds of business agreements provided they are registered with the competition authorities (OECD, 1993b). Cartels are thus widespread in Denmark.[36]

The Netherlands

Although The Netherlands is one of the most *laissez-faire* orientated European countries in terms of industrial policy and economic policy in general, it also provides an example of planning. Integrated projection planning is used. This is a set of conditioned, mutually compatible sectoral forecasts ascertained econometrically (Franzmeyer, 1979). The projections are only decisional aids. This country tries to overcome its regional problems by encouraging investment in the less-developed regions with the help of the Investment Grant Scheme (IPR).

East European countries[37]

In the early 1990s, the economies of Poland, Hungary, the Czech Republic, Slovakia, Bulgaria, Romania, and the ex-USSR (all former CMEA countries) initiated programmes of structural reform that are supposed to culminate in the emergence of a market-led economy, and minimal intervention by the state in economic and industrial affairs.

Although the pace of economic reform is very unequal in the former centrally planned economies, there are some common features: the major instruments put forward to enable the industrial and economic transition were privatization, attraction of FDI, reform of the legal system, measures to support SMEs, the signing of Europe Agreements[38] with the EU, and fiscal and monetary reforms with the creation of a competitive capital market.

The prospects for these countries have not been helped, however, by the bleak macroeconomic results achieved in the early 1990s, with soaring levels of inflation, large declines in national output and rising unemployment in countries once characterized by a theoretical full employment. The reasons for such results are predominantly the many distortions inherited from the inefficient centrally planned economic system prevailing in the past. At the core of the economic systems of these countries was central planning—embracing the most extreme *dirigiste* industrial policy—the importance of which varied from country to country. Its characteristics were the quasi-absence of private enterprise, administratively set prices, production which generated negative value-added (the so-called 'Value Subtractor'), labour hoarding, and centrally managed international trade.

Not surprisingly, since between one-half and three-quarters of all Hungarian, Bulgarian, Czechoslovakian, and Polish trade was conducted within the sphere of the former CMEA, a distorted industrial structure emerged in these countries. Intra-CMEA trade was concentrated essentially on the more industrially advanced products and resulted in the predominance—or 'over-representation'—of industries such as mechanical engineering and heavy chemicals. Trade with Western Europe was limited and was concerned only with primary products (minerals), and with labour intensive, low value-added products (e.g. clothing and footwear).

Little room was accorded to production and trade in industries such as computers, instrument engineering and food processing.

According to Economist Intelligence Unit (EIU) forecasts, inflation may have been brought down to acceptable levels in both the Czech Republic and in Slovakia where it is expected to be less than 10 per cent in 1995. However, the inflation rate is forecast to be still as high as 70 per cent in Bulgaria and 45 per cent in Romania during the same year. According to estimates emanating from the same source, all countries—with the exception of Bulgaria—have experienced positive growth rates in real GDP in 1994, ranging from 4.7 per cent for Poland, to 1.0 per cent for Romania. Some economic recovery seems to be on the way, although the unemployment rates are still comparable to those of the poorer states of the European Union; unemployment affects more than 15 per cent of the Polish, Slovak and Bulgarian labour forces.

It has been widely acknowledged that the leaders in the reform process were the Visegrad four, namely Hungary, Poland, Slovakia and the Czech Republic. While the majority of countries opted for 'Shock Therapy' reforms, characterized by large privatization programmes, others were more gradual in their approach. The transition from a centrally planned to a market economy started almost 25 years ago in Hungary. Although Hungary has today been outpaced by some other countries in its progress towards economic reforms, it is seen as the most successful country in having set up a relatively sophisticated banking and financial system, an attractive element for would-be foreign investors. Also, recent trade patterns between Hungary and the EU-12 show that motor vehicles, office machinery and optical instruments were among the fastest growing exports between 1990 and 1993.

Hungary, and to a lesser extent the former Czechoslovakia, seem to show a clear commitment to becoming the East European leaders in the high technology industries. The emergence of high technology industries in Hungary is partly explained by the superiority of its System of Innovation when compared with other Central and East European countries. 'Hungary took an early interest in the development of technology, and a National Committee for Technological Development (OMFB) was set up as far back as 1964' (OECD, 1994, p. 295).

There have been only a limited number of domestic investors in the privatization of the Hungarian state companies' assets (Blaho and Halpern, 1995); the Czech Republic and Romania have tried to make their privatization programmes more popular by, for example, distributing some company shares among the population.

Much of production and trade reorientation occurring in the Central and East European Countries (CEECs), and facilitated by the privatization programmes, can be explained by: (a) the importance of FDI; (b) the Europe Agreements; and, the expectation ultimately of (c) a combination of both (i.e. intensive trade flows between the two Europes facilitated by West European Direct Investment).

The Europe Agreements, signed on a bilateral basis between December 1991 and March 1993, are seen as a first step towards the integration of the Central and East European countries into a wider EU. These agreements allow for a gradual tariff reduction and elimination of all quantitative restrictions for the CEEC signatories' exports. However, trade liberalization with the EU will be slower for certain 'sensitive products' (textile, clothing, iron and steel), and delayed for agricultural products.

Geographical reorientation of CEEC trade in favour of the EU has anticipated the coming into effect of the Europe Agreements. The EU is today the major trading partner of the CEECs. For example, the share of the EU-12 in total Czech and Slovak exports (imports) increased from 9 per cent (10 per cent) to 49.4 per cent (42.1 per cent) between 1989 and 1992 (Andréosso and Noonan, 1995). Trade flows between the EU and the six CEECs mentioned above, and assessed with the help of cover rates and Grubel and Lloyd (GL) indices, show a clear division of manufacturing competence between the six CEECs.

Broadly, Bulgaria could potentially become the CEEC leader in the chemicals sector, Poland in the area of transport, Hungary in the food and in the electrical engineering sectors, and the Czech Republic in the mechanical engineering, as well as in the instrument engineering sectors. Low GL indices in some high technology industries show that the potential for the CEECs in terms of product differentiation is immense, whereas high GL indices in other industries suggest that the CEECs must aim at reducing the technology and quality gaps which exist in relation to the EU.

Reducing the technology and quality gaps through the intensification of trade relations with the EU implies designing a coherent industrial structure at the pan-European level. Indeed, transition in the CEECs from centrally planned systems to market economies corresponds, from an industrial policy standpoint, to the passage from too much state intervention to too little organization of industrial affairs. This implies that a European Industrial Policy (EIP) needs at least to take cognizance of the Central and East European countries and their problems.

Summary

In general, there appears to be a trend in the development of industrial policies in different countries: government intervention reaches a peak in the early 1950s—this period of intervention being explained by the need for post-war reconstruction—and in the mid-1970s—following the oil crisis. During the 1960s, the major objective of industrial policy in Europe was to catch up with the more technologically developed USA, and the increasingly threatening Japan. During the 1980s and early 1990s there has been a general withdrawal of the state, represented by de-regulation and privatization.

Have industrial policies in Europe converged during the period since the Second World War? According to Hager (1982), if there is a trend, it is not to be found in the amount of intervention as such, but rather in the fact that the increasing importance of the international environment provides incentives for developing industrial policy.

In *Germany*, the view is that the role of the government is to provide an adequate 'framework' or 'climate' conducive to innovation and investment by firms. The government is to provide a research base, but not direct research towards a particular industry; positive financial assistance (i.e. state subsidies), and a 'picking the winner' strategy is to be the exception rather than the rule. Protection of infant industries will not be allowed.

The *British* view is close to the German one in that it advocates total freedom to be given to firms. The British government has become heavily involved in supporting research directed at developing technology. However, the British attitude is the least European oriented of all since it stresses that in sectors where Europe has fallen behind its competitors, the only way to catch up is to welcome direct investment from the United States or Japan. Also, some officials in the UK have traditionally been sceptical with regard to the development of further European R&D and technological initiatives.

In some ways, the *French* attitude is radically opposed to that of Germany and the UK. With its tradition in government interventionism, and in planning, France strongly recommends the transfer of the national tools of industrial policy to the European level. It calls for further European industrial integration, and for external protection (Fortress Europe).

The clear differences in industrial policy prospects even among the three major European countries suggests difficulties in the building of a positive European industrial policy.

7.2.2 Competition policy in the European Union

During the first 15 years of its existence, the EC did not have an industrial policy in the sense of drafting the course of and stimulating industrial development.[39] This was not necessary because the favourable macroeconomic conditions of the 1960s (low inflation and unemployment rates, stable currencies, catching-up of European firms with their US counterparts) created a healthy competitive environment that would have kept prices down and have assured the efficient use of factors of production. To the extent that there was a EIP, it was confined to Competition Policy (first type of industrial policy in Table 7.1), and to Commercial Policy.

Horizontal measures, i.e. measures with a wide and universal application throughout the Common Market, such as the harmonization of company laws, were almost non-existent. Vertical measures, i.e. measures implying a selective Community intervention in depth in particular sectors or industries, were kept to a minimum. For security and strategic reasons, the atomic energy sector, the coal and steel industries and the agricultural sector were given special treatment.[40] It was not until the 1970s that it began to be seen that an adequate response at the European level to structural changes required more than provided for by the Competition Policy.

Ten articles in the Rome Treaty (85 to 94) were devoted to the designing of the EU Competition Policy.[41] The philosophy of the Community Competition Policy is based on the *laissez-faire* approach: the free interplay of supply and demand in all EU markets[42] is expected to provide the major ingredient for economic efficiency. Any firm willing to engage in some arrangement with another firm in the EU must notify the Commission, through the relevant national body. The Commission stipulates the incompatibility of such arrangements with the essence of the Common Market. *Article 89* specifies that 'the Commission shall investigate cases of suspected infringement of these principles' [of competition], and 'shall propose appropriate measures to bring [them] to an end'. It provides for action to be taken in cases where strategies followed by EU firms violate the principles of Competition in the Common Market, and for exemptions in some specific circumstances. The Community Competition Law has precedence over national legislation, although it does not annul it.[43]

Articles 85 and 86 (see Appendix 7.2) prohibit every agreement (or strategy) that appreciably distorts open competition or that creates unfair competition in the member states. In particular, Article 85 of the Rome Treaty deals with collusive behaviour. All practices that affect trade (price fixing, market sharing, control of production markets and investment, joint selling and joint purchasing agreements...) are 'incompatible with the common market' in the sense that 'they affect trade between Member States' and limit the degree of competition. Article 85 clearly aims at controlling cartels; for example, it was found that in 1986 the EU market for polypropylene, a key product used in the manufacture of a wide range of plastics, was controlled by four EU-based firms, Royal Dutch Shell, Imperial Chemicals International, Montedipe and Hoechst. The Commission sought to prove that these four firms were operating a cartel with a view to fixing prices. However, price agreements have been more difficult to prove; some price movements may only be coincidental. In the case of a tight oligopoly, the price takers will often react instantaneously to the signals of the price leader.

Minor exceptions were envisaged under paragraph 3 of the same Article: some restrictive agreements, of minor importance, and/or encouraging co-operation between small and medium sized enterprises, such as R&D agreements, were permissible. To qualify for exemption from the prohibitions of Article 85/1 a co-operative research agreement must satisfy certain conditions (for example, the co-operation should have a specific objective). Finally, a 1968 Notice on Co-operation Between Enterprises states that co-operative agreements relating exclusively to basic research and development do not fall under Article 85.

Article 86 deals with the *abuse of a dominant position*. This refers to concentration or monopoly power that enables any firm, as a buyer or seller, to influence the outcome of the market. The essence of this Article has to be found in the early days of the ECSC when France feared any renewed concentration of the German coal and steel industries. No precise definition of the level of concentration is given. There is, for example, no mention of the market share that a firm must have before it can be called a dominant firm. Such a general definition would be impossible, because a market share required for a firm to be dominant in one industry will be different from that required in another; it varies from product to product, industry to industry, market to market. In any case, it is not the existence of dominance that is prohibited, but the *abuse* of the dominant position. This view enables the Commission to intervene after a firm has acquired dominance and has sought to abuse it; it does not enable the Commission to prevent the emergence of that dominance in the first place.

Dominant firm abuse is illustrated, for example, by the case of Hoffman La Roche, a Swiss firm dominating the market for vitamins, that abused that position by charging different prices in different markets (price discrimination), and by the case of Commercial Solvents which controlled materials and refused to supply them freely to other firms. However, this view has been challenged in the Continental Can case in 1973 and in the Philip Morris–Rothmans case in 1987. In the Continental Can case,[44] the Commission argued that a dominant firm necessarily abused its position by seeking a merger with another firm (and that a merger between a dominant firm and another was in itself an abuse of dominance). In this particular case, the judgment of the European Court of Justice (ECJ) made it clear that proof of dominance required a definition of the market, and that the determination of the relevant market was essential (see discussion in Chapter 4).

The verdicts issued under these two cases opened the possibility for the use of Article 86 (and also 85) for *ex ante* EU control in some specific cases.

Article 90-2 allows certain firms providing services of 'general economic interest' to exempt themselves from the general competition rules and to conduct purely national policies.

The EU position with regard to the competition rules has become somewhat ambiguous and unclear. Firms appreciably distorting or impeding the smooth functioning of a competitive environment are penalized, and yet it is recognized at the same time that large firms are necessary in some sectors to compete technologically and efficiently with US and Japanese firms. Large firms are more able to benefit from economies of scale and scope, and are more able to spend on R&D. The 1985 White Paper on the Completion of the Internal Market endorsed the view that the EU needs companies of a sufficient size to compete with the large international corporations. This makes unequivocal opposition to all restriction of competition more and more difficult.

Free and undistorted competition in the Community requires strict monitoring and surveillance of state aids. *Article 92* (in Appendix 7.2) forbids any government aid to EU enterprises. In that regard, a very cautious approach was at first adopted by the Commission. The philosophy of the Commission was to try to limit subsidization and to try to incorporate it into the context of restructuring. Exemptions were allowed for particular economically weak industries and regions of the Community. National governments have to notify the Commission about any intention to allocate or alter existing aid schemes to particular industries, and the Commission decides on the compatibility of these aids with the provisions of the Treaty of Rome. If incompatibility arises, the member state is asked to amend or to abolish the aid. For example, in 1986 the EU Commission asked 'the West German government for an explanation of its alleged subsidy to Daimler Benz to build a new plant in Baden Würtemberg, an area not eligible for special regional assistance. The local authorities replied that it was merely a general aid to improve the region's industrial infrastructure' (Harrop, 1989, p. 112). Bianchi (1995, Table 4.9) shows that of 15 disputes between Italy and the EC over subsidies to industry, in four cases (clothing and textiles, leather and footwear, man-made fibres and paper production) the national subsidies were forbidden. In four other cases various restrictions were imposed.

During the 1970s, on the onset of the recession, it was perceived that much state aid (in the steel industry in particular), was in fact 'sustaining lame ducks'. In subsequent years, the Commission looked for a tougher stance: state aids should be carefully monitored and controlled; they should decrease in size and importance. In its first comprehensive report on state aids published in 1989, the Commission described the structure of state aids to firms in the EU.[45] According to the report, total public aid amounted to an average of 3.0 per cent of EU-10 GDP during the years 1981–86. Two other surveys have been undertaken by the Commission since. In the second survey, total national public aid was found to amount to 2.2 per cent of EU GDP. The third survey displays some information on aid during the period 1986–90. Roughly 40 per cent of aid went to the manufacturing sector.[46] It encompasses, *inter alia*, aid to the shipbuilding, steel, synthetic fibres, motor vehicle industries, energy sector, and services (mail and special delivery services, banking and insurance, audio-visual industry, tourism, craft activities). When measured in terms of ECUs per person employed, aid in general, and to the manufacturing industry in particular, decreased between 1986 and 1990. As revealed by Table 7.5, the differences among member states are important.

The countries with the highest shares in value added are Italy, Ireland and Greece, because of the predominance of regional aids, and Belgium, because of the importance of steel in this country. A difficulty that arose in the past with regard to the computation of state aids was that in the case of nationalized firms, it was difficult to distinguish between pure investments

TABLE 7.5   State subsidies to the EU manufacturing sector (annual averages 1988–90) (*) (*Source*: CEC (1992), *Third Survey on State Aids in the EC in the Manufacturing and Certain Other Sectors*)

	In % of value-added	In ECUs per person employed
Belgium	4.1	1655
Denmark	2.1	634
Germany	2.5	984
Greece	14.6	1502
Spain	3.6	936
France	3.5	1380
Ireland	4.9	1734
Italy	6.0	2175
Luxemburg	2.6	1270
The Netherlands	3.1	1327
Portugal	5.3	758
UK	2.0	582
EU	3.5	1203

(*): Refer to subsidies that are subject to Community rules.

(legitimate) and state aids (illegitimate). In spite of the recent privatization movement, this problem has not disappeared.

Aids to the manufacturing sector also differ by type. For the EU as a whole they are distributed as follows: 47 per cent are grants, 32 per cent tax reductions, 7 per cent equity participations, 7 per cent soft loans, 2 per cent tax deferrals and 6 per cent guarantees. Equity participation includes financial allocation for privatization purposes.

7.2.3   Merger and takeover policy

The Commission at first had to direct power to control mergers *ex ante*. This is understandable in the light of the long history of cartelization in the steel industry. The first proposals for EC anti-merger legislation were initiated in 1973. During that year, the Commission introduced a draft regulation on the control of concentrations between undertakings.[47] This draft was vehemently criticized by both industry and the member states. However, the Commission remained determined to have an agreement reached at some stage. Proper European merger legislation was becoming a prerequisite for the efficient functioning of a single market free of internal frontiers. Increased cross-border merger and acquisition activity of European firms in the second half of the 1980s made European legislation an urgent matter. In the absence of European legislation, the cross-border deals would be subject to the jurisdiction of more than one country, which would make control increasingly complex.

The Commission had to wait until 1989 to see the Council of Ministers finally move in favour of merger legislation. At that stage, only Britain, Ireland, France and Germany had legislation on this type of activity. Many of the other EU countries seldom took action in this regard. Greece and Portugal still did not exercise any merger control; the Belgian and Danish Competition laws were much more permissive, since merger controls were exercised only over banking (Belgium) and under some specific circumstances (Denmark). Spain had very recently drafted a law on mergers. The Commission's Merger Regulation (Regulation No. 4064/89) was adopted in December 1989, and came into force in September 1990.[48]

Under Article 1 of the Regulation, all mergers having a 'community dimension' are covered. A 'community dimension' is defined as where:

(i) 'the aggregate world-wide turnover of all the undertakings concerned is more than ECU 5 billion, and
(ii) the aggregate Community-wide turnover of each of at least two of the undertakings concerned is more than ECU 250 million,
unless each of the undertakings concerned achieves more than two-thirds of its aggregate Community-wide turnover within one and the same Member State'. (OJ L 395/3)[49]

The Regulation also applies to concentrations resulting from undertakings which do not have their principal field of activity in the Community, but are likely to have an effect within the Community. It is estimated that between 50 and 60 mergers will have to be notified each year to the Commission.

The definition of the Community dimension helps member states decide which legislation—national or Community—should be used. Member states shall not apply their national legislation on competition to concentrations which have a Community dimension, as defined in Article 1. Mergers which fall outside the scope of application of the Regulation can be dealt with by member states. The EU Commission will not, as a matter of policy, apply Articles 85 and 86 to them. The EU Merger Regulation reflects a preference for more competition and acknowledges the fact that large size is no guarantee of international competitiveness. A strong German influence can be detected in the drafting of this Regulation. The EU merger legislation still leaves a lot of room for decisions by national authorities; as in other respects, the EU regulatory legal framework here co-exists with strong national regulation.

EU policy on acquisitions is covered by the 13th Council Directive on Company Law, concerning takeovers and public bids (see OJ C 64, 14/03/89, and its amendments in COM (90) final). This new piece of legislation aims at creating a more liberal takeover market in the EU; it tries to establish certain minimum standards for the conduct of takeover bids, with the objective of ensuring equality of treatment for shareholders. Defensive measures (in Germany and in The Netherlands), and all barriers to takeovers, such as closely held ownership in Italy, will be on the decrease (Moerland, 1991).

7.2.4   A move towards a positive industrial policy

The EU industrial policy (EIP) has graduated from having mainly a supervisory function in the 1960s, to adopting a defensive stance in the 1970s, and to becoming more positive in the 1980s. For example, although the need for Community initiatives in the area of R&D as a vital facet of the process of economic integration was appreciated by the original founders of the EU,[50] the Treaty of Rome did not give the Commission and the Council of Ministers explicit powers to promote research, and indeed, industry. In this section, we will study how the European industrial policy, as a simple competition policy in its early days (type 1), evolved from being a vague regulatory framework aimed at shaping the right market environment, to becoming a more positive industrial and technological policy.

The Colonna Report (1970): a first attempt at designing a EIP

By the mid-1960s, 'the EC Commission had begun working out a coherent industrial policy concept for the Community' (Franzmeyer, 1979, p. 116). In 1967, the Commission established the General Directorate for Industrial Affairs, which, among other objectives, sought to encourage cross-border industrial co-operation. During the same year, the first Council of Science Ministers met; it commissioned studies in six broad areas of technological development (of which data processing and telecommunications were two), and its initiatives led to the establishment of COST (European Co-operation in the field of Science and Technical Research).

The first working documents on industrial policy appeared. In particular the second programme for medium-term economic policy (OJ L 129, 30-5-69) laid down the cornerstone for the memorandum on 'The industrial policy of the Community' known as the 1970 Colonna Report (CEC, 1970). This constitutes the first attempt by the commission to define and to implement a Community industrial policy. This very ambitious Report emphasizes six broad needs:

1 To create a single market based on the elimination of intra-Community barriers to trade.
2 To harmonize company laws, banking laws and taxation if the free movement of capital is to become a reality.
3 To promote trans-EC mergers in order to enable European firms to adapt to the needs of the Common Market and to international competition.
4 To have the Community play a role in the promotion of new technology.

5 To integrate social and regional policies.

6 To develop the Community's commercial policy with third countries.

After the 1972 Paris Summit, a Communiqué explicitly called for a common policy in the sphere of science and technology. This gave birth to a Commission memorandum (the Spinelli Memorandum) which set out the parameters of a Community Policy. The 1973 Spinelli *Memorandum on the Technological and Industrial Policy Programme* (CEC, 1973) put the emphasis on some elements of the Colonna Report, but the essence of the document was the promotion of a free-market-orientated common industrial policy based on:

- The elimination of technical obstacles to trade and the harmonization of national regulations
- The opening up of national markets for purchasing by public sectors
- The harmonization of company laws and the liberalization of capital markets
- The encouragement of trans-EC enterprises
- The encouragement of co-operation and mergers between Community firms through the diffusion of information.

In December 1973, a programme was adopted by the Council of Ministers along these lines, which partially reconciled the French *dirigism* with the German views influenced by the virtues of the *laissez-faire* approach. In spite of its adoption by the Council, its implications were kept to a minimum, since no real consensus on the necessity for or on the form of a common industrial policy existed at the time (Hitiris, 1994). The oil crisis and its concomitant economic recession made it fall short of its declared objectives. Both national governments and the Community were forced to divert attention, energy and investment from the 'sunrise' technologies, to the 'sunset' industries which were being seriously hit by the recession. However, one concrete proposal that emerged was the creation of the European Economic Interest Group (EEIG), which was finalized (i.e. adopted by the Council of EU Ministers) in 1985, and which came into effect in July 1989. The EEIG is the first harmonized legal framework facilitating co-operation of EU firms. It enables EU companies, and more particularly SMEs, to merge part of their economic activities in a structure with full legal standing, while retaining their independence.

There had long been a need for such a framework. When the theme of the technological gap emerged, European governments initiated the promotion, via mergers and subsidies, of a series of national champions, as well as of cross-national groupings in key technological sectors. One of these early collaborative ventures was the Eurodata consortium which comprised Philips, AEG-Telefunken, ICL, CII, Olivetti and Saab. Its aim was to gain a contract in order to provide for the computer needs of the newly established European Space Research Organization.[51] Among the early collaborative attempts in the field of technology and industry, many, like the Eurodata Consortium, did not meet with much success, but the aerospace sector became a notable exception (see discussion on technological collaboration, below p. 304).

The 1970s: a 'defensive' EIP

The American challenge, as well as the gradual shift of comparative advantages, gave birth to a defensive industrial policy, centred mostly on vertical actions. However, timid and unfruitful attempts were made to instigate and consolidate mergers in the EU. The Dunlop–Pirelli merger of 1971 dissolved in 1981 (Harrop, 1989). In 1973, Bull, Siemens and Philips tried to form the first computer group in Europe, Unidata. Its aim was to challenge the American IBM, but the group sank very quickly.

Limited traditionally to the coal and steel sector, more sectoral policies were introduced with the advent of the economic recession. Vertical actions were implemented to remedy the problems of the 'crisis industries' such as:

- The shipbuilding industry from 1969
- The textile and clothing industry, with the Multi-Fibre Agreements (MFAs) signed in 1974
- The motor car and machine tools industries, where quotas and VERs (Voluntary Export Restraints) limit the annual imports of Asian products into each individual EU country.

According to Balassa's 'stages approach to comparative advantage' and to economic development (Balassa, 1977), these industries are all declining industries. Since they are bound to contract in a given period of time, is it worth promoting them? Some economists have criticized the many bail out actions in these industries, and have equated them to measures sustaining 'lame ducks'. British Steel, British Coal, Sacilor, Usinor, ENI Quimica in Italy and RUMASA in Spain are all well-known examples of firms where a poor strategy and a poor management have led to nationalizations as the only solution for their survival.

In the *shipbuilding* industry, Japan overtook Western Europe as a major world producer in the 1960s. The shift in comparative advantage, which moved in favour of Asian countries (first Japan, and more recently South Korea and China) and, more recently, of East-European countries (Poland), produced the first alarming signs for the European shipyards. The 1973 economic recession accentuated them. The growing difficulties of the industry in the 1970s are best summarized by Edwards (1982, p. 85):

Demand in the shipbuilding industry has traditionally been cyclical. Rarely, however, has the collapse of the market been as severe as in the mid-1970s [...]. The expansion in merchant shipbuilding during the 1960s and early 1970s was rapid [...]. With the 1973–74 oil crisis [...] demand for new shipping collapsed. While orders derived from the earlier optimistic forecasts of continued expansion cushioned the immediate impact, by 1978 the world order book was at its lowest in 13 years.

In 1992, the EU world market share, computed on the basis of order book, was close to its 1976 level, at slightly over 22 per cent. Over the same period of time, Japan's market share stabilized at roughly 28.6 per cent, whereas Korea's and China's shares were multiplied by 2.5 and 5 respectively. Employment in the construction of new vessels in the EU plummeted from roughly 209,000 in 1975 to 77,000 in 1992 (CEC, 1993b).

Over-capacity, losses and redundancies nurtured a host of generous government subsidies in both the European countries and the rest of the world. The influx of state capital into the industry went totally against the initial objective of the Commission which was to liberalize the market by 1975, through the phasing out of state aids. These state aids or 'crisis aid' were to be temporary, since they were to enable the restructuring of the industry in the long term.[52] In the late 1980s, talks with Japan and Korea were initiated for the purpose of stabilizing the international market.

In the *steel* industry, one of the most important industries for the Community in the past, a similar scenario existed. Soon after the creation of the ECSC in 1952, demand expanded considerably until the oil recession.

TABLE 7.6   Loss per ton (£) in the European steel industry (1977–78)
(*Source*: British Steel Corporation Annual Press Conference, 4 July 1978,
as reported in Woolcock, 1982)

Sacilor	42
Usinor	29
BSC (Italsider)	25
Cockerill	24
Kockner	21
Ensidesa	16
Estel	13
Arbed	11
Salzgitter	11

In the 1970s, falling demand, technological change, increased competition from composite materials and other substitutes, and increased global competition all led to over-capacity (up to 30 per cent for certain products), losses (Table 7.6), contraction in the workforce (by 50 per cent between 1974 and 1986), and a slump in prices.

The Commission attempted to regulate the market by introducing indicative targets for the major sub-products by country in 1975. Three years later, the Davignon Plan was introduced establishing minimum prices for some sub-products, increased guidance prices, import quotas, as well as anti-dumping duties on steel imports.[53] Bilateral agreements were concluded with EFTA, East European and developing countries. These various measures kept imports at their traditional level and increased prices successfully (Woolcock, 1982).

During the early 1990s, the signing of the Europe Agreements with East European countries has initiated new turbulences in the market. Since 1990, prices in the EU-12 have decreased by 30 per cent. Imports from Central and Eastern Europe rose by 40 per cent in 1992. However, recent negotiations with East European producers (Czech Republic, Slovakia, Poland, Russia, Ukraine and Kazakhstan) focusing on the 'smooth reorganization' of their exports into the EU enabled the Commission to implement safeguard measures and stabilized imports from these countries.[54]

The Braun Report of November 1992[55] estimated over-capacity of crude steel at 30 million tons, and of rolled products at between 19 and 26 million tons (*Le Monde*, 11 February 1993). For all steel products combined, the capacity utilization rate was down to two-thirds. The Report calls for a drastic reduction of numbers employed (−50,000 in three years), for a reduction of over-capacity through plant closures, and for the reorientation of the market, as various means to rescue the European industry. Market orientation involved recommendations made by the Commission on the level of production required and was to be aimed at redressing prices. The Braun Report, and its subsequent Council meeting of February 1993, led to the recent reorganization of the market. For example, between February 1993 and April 1994, the production of hot-rolled products went down by 11 million tonnes. This resulted from the partial closures and privatizations of Freital, EKO-Stahl, ILVA, Sidenor, CSI and Siderurgia Nacional.[56] The recent changes in the numbers employed are shown in Table 7.7.

If in the 1970s and in the early part of the 1980s, the political support of declining industries was explained mostly by protectionist motives (Hillman, 1982), the late 1980s and 1990s have introduced a more pragmatic approach, making structural adjustment a requirement. This is reflected in the new type of industrial policy pursued in the past 10 years.

TABLE 7.7   Changes in the numbers employed in the steel industry (*Source*: Eurostat (as reproduced in *European Report*, no. 1972, 3 September 1944))

Member state	Number of employees and reference months		Change (%)
Belgium	25,300 (Dec. 92)	24,000 (Dec. 93)	−5.1
Denmark	1,300 (Dec. 92)	1,100 (Dec. 93)	−15.4
Germany (1)	126,400 (Jan. 93)	105,000 (Jan. 94)	−16.9
Greece	3,000 (Jan. 93)	2,800 (Jan. 94)	−6.7
Spain	35,200 (Jan. 93)	27,300 (Jan. 94)	−22.4
France	42,800 (Dec. 92)	40,500 (Dec. 93)	−5.4
Ireland	600 (Mar. 93)	500 (Mar. 94)	−16.7
Italy	50,700 (Sep. 92)	49,900 (Sep. 93)	−1.6
Luxemburg	7,600 (Dec. 92)	7,100 (Dec. 93)	−6.6
The Netherlands	15,500 (Jan. 93)	13,500 (Jan. 94)	−12.9
Portugal	3,300 (Dec. 92)	3,100 (Dec. 93)	−6.1
United Kingdom	40,700 (Jan. 93)	39,100 (Jan. 94)	−3.9

(1): Including the new Länder.

Technological collaboration in the 1980s and early 1990s

While in the 1970s EIP was fundamentally negative, as it was endeavouring to apply short-term remedies to the 'problem industries',[57] the 1980s have introduced a more constructive approach to industrial policy. A wide range of new technological programmes has been set up. Some degree of technological collaboration and co-ordination has been achieved in the EU, through the launching of, *inter alia*, ESPRIT, RACE, BRITE–EURAM, COMETT.[58]

The technological gap discussed above, and the sluggish improvement in competitiveness of European industry generally—and of the information technology (IT) sector in particular—led to a complete rethinking of the appropriate strategies for EU industry. In particular, it was thought that the lack of European collaboration widened substantially the technological and competitive gaps (Mytelka and Delapierre, 1987). By the early 1980s, 12 major European IT companies had begun to collaborate under the instigation and with the assistance of the then Commissioner for Industrial Affairs, Etienne Davignon.[59] The group produced the first set of technological programmes which ran from 1984 to 1987 (OJ L 208, 25-07-83). ESPRIT was the information technology component in this programme.

ESPRIT was in fact the first technological programme ever implemented in the EU. Launched in 1984 with a financial base of ECUs 750 million, the programme is based upon the idea of *pre-competitive* and collaborative research.[60] Its purpose is ultimately to enable European firms to collaborate and through that to catch up in the field of IT and information processing. Pre-competitive research refers to research conducted at a sufficient distance from the market so as not to infringe antitrust laws or competition policy; such research is targeted at a specific problem whose results may not lead directly to commercial products. This notion is distinct from the one of basic research, and of scientific research whose application leads to commercially useful results. Building on the German experience, the implementation of ESPRIT involves the co-operation of firms, research centres, governments and trade unions.

ESPRIT was a 'source of inspiration' for other programmes such as RACE in the field of telecommunications, BRITE on the introduction of new technologies in traditional industries, BAP (Biotechnology Action Programme, 1985–89), and later, FLAIR (Food Linked Agro-Industrial Research for Innovation, Development and Growth in Europe, 1989–93), ECLAIR

(European Collaboration Linkage of Agriculture and Industry through Research), and MEDIA 2 in the audiovisual field.[61]

The idea of inserting an explicit commitment to research and technology into European legislation originated from a Memorandum that the Commission presented at the Milan Summit in 1985.[62] Subsequently endorsed by the Council of Ministers, it became one of the basic documents which provided for the foundations of the Single European Act (SEA). The ratification by all member states of the SEA in 1987 rendered the proliferation of technological programmes easier. The SEA explicitly legitimated the scientific and technological dimension of the EU; this first revision of the Rome Treaty introduced an item on 'Research and technological development'.[63] Article 130f of the revision of the Treaty made clear the objective of 'strengthening the scientific and technological bases of Community industry and encouraging it to become more competitive at international level'. A means of achieving this aim is through the common technology programmes, grouped from 1987 onwards under the umbrella of the so-called 'Framework Programme' (Article 130I).

Almost 10 years later, attempts at evaluating the relative success of the EU technological programmes can be made. In particular, the ESPRIT Review Board, composed of an independent panel, is given the task of evaluating the impact of the programme. In its first mid-term review (1986), the Board concluded that ESPRIT was on its way to meeting its objectives, and that it led to a significant increase in R&D activity in the EU (through spill-over linkages between EU companies outside the programme).

Many criticisms have, notwithstanding, been addressed to this programme. As pointed out by Amin, Charles and Howells (1992), among others, large firms in the core IT-based regions have received more money than firms situated in Spain, Greece, Portugal and Italy. In their review of EU technological policy, Grahl and Teague (1990) argue similarly that Davignon's policy has privileged the largest and most powerful companies.

Not surprisingly, ESPRIT-II and III were subsequently designed to amend and improve ESPRIT-I. ESPRIT-II (1988–92) focused on the necessity to lessen regional disparities.[64] ECUs 1600 million were allocated to this second phase of the programme, which involved the participation of nearly 1500 organizations, two-thirds of which were SMEs. Finally, ESPRIT-III (1990–94) placed more emphasis on the application of research and on the improvement of the 'manufacturing capability of the European integrated circuit industry' (OJ C 30, p. 17, 1991).

We should note that intra-European R&D co-operation in sectors characterized by new technologies, and actively promoted by the programmes launched and implemented by the Commission, has not been restricted to the EU. These programmes have had a EEA (European Economic Area) dimension since firms like Volvo, Asea, Brown Boveri and Nestlé have all been involved (prior to the most recent expansion of the EU).

European technological collaboration also took the form of the building up of government-supported multinationals created by countries who came together to form an economic association and who developed a project of common interest.[65] Well-known examples are Concorde and Airbus in the field of aeronautics, Arianespace which was developed to design and market a space-launcher, and Eurodif, a European consortium that has produced a uranium enrichment process.

Originally set up by France, Germany, the UK, the Benelux countries, and subsequently Spain, Airbus Industrie is a European consortium designed to face the challenge of the American monopoly Boeing, and aimed at increasing the productivity of European producers. A subsequent deal with Pan Am gave the group a strong foothold in the market for intermediate-range commercial airliners (Jacquemin, 1987b). Its success can be judged by the fact that it has achieved substantial market shares.

In its last document submitted to the Council and to the European Parliament on the theme of industrial policy, the EU Commission defined the broad orientations of an EIP compatible with a global competitive environment.[66] In this document, the Commission endeavours to develop and give precision to the concept of a common industrial policy in three distinct steps.

First, it stresses that an industrial policy should be built around the essential task which is that of 'maintaining a favourable business environment'. The merits of the common competition policy (Articles 85, 86 and 92) are reiterated, but in addition the need to 'promote economic and social cohesion', i.e. the necessity to introduce and to deal with the problem of regional disparities, is acknowledged. Also, the objective of achieving a high level of economic growth in parallel with a high level of protection for the environment is clearly voiced.

Second, it sees the process of completion of the internal market as a 'catalyst for adjustment'. Third, it refers to a 'positive approach' to industrial adjustment; this implies the implementation of policies that will help accelerate the process (such as technology policies, a dynamic policy towards SMEs, etc.).

Aimed at securing a stimulating economic environment, the 'new' approach of the Commission is again in essence inspired by the virtues of the free market economy. In placing the emphasis on the creation of a sound economic environment, the Commission reiterates a view inherited from the traditional and highly criticized S-C-P paradigm. The approach is 'new' in that the Commission's document asserts for the first time the necessity of conducting a more positive EIP, in the sense of attempting to bring about a convergence of views between member states that had until then often followed rather different industrial policy approaches. Another new feature of the document is the fact that it incorporates both a regional and an environmental dimension.[67] It should be remembered that these two dimensions had emerged at an early stage of the process of European construction. The Community Environmental Policy began in 1973. It was agreed that the 'polluter pays' principle should be used as much as possible. The concern of 'Economic and Social Cohesion' precedes the Commission's 1990 document and finds its roots in the regional policy of the EU set up in 1975. Apart from these three elements, the Commission's document on industrial policy lacks originality. According to Bance (1992), the Commission's proposals do not break with the previous strategy of the Commission in the area of industry.

Technological collaboration remains the mainstay of what we have called a positive EIP. However, technological co-operation between EU firms cannot be simply equated to the willingness to build a sound EU technological base. It has been argued that co-operation in science and technology in the EU has been driven more by negative elements than by positive ones. Williams (1989) writes that in many instances, fear of the USA, Japan, and latterly of the NICs, exorbitant costs attached to the development of some projects, and risk aversion have explained the European orientation of firms.

Other criticisms have centred on the restricted financial resources devoted to the Community technology policy. Representing only 4 per cent of total civilian private and public spending in Europe, EU financing of research programmes is indeed very modest. Bance (1992) argues that this results in an industrial policy with 'deprived financial means'. EU financing of technological programmes has increased since the birth of the Common Market but it is still minuscule. The EU budgetary expenditure on industry, energy and research increased from 1.6 per cent of all EU budgetary expenditure in 1973, to a mere 3.5 per cent in 1992.

In summary, EIP in the 1980s has become more positive, through the development of common technological programmes and projects, but has been hampered by restricted financial means, by the wrong motivation (fear instead of confidence in a more integrated Europe), and by other European developments which lie outside the industrial field and which in the view of the Commission can be used as substitutes for a more positive EIP. Before we give details of these other developments, it is worth recalling the experience of other non-European countries; this may reveal the weaknesses and limits of the European approach.

7.2.5 Industrial policies in other countries: the experience of the USA, Japan and East Asian newly industrialized countries (NICs)

US industrial policy

The English trade policies of the seventeenth and eighteenth centuries were perceived to favour England at the expense of its overseas colonies (Miller, 1943). The newly independent federal state lived its first decade 'under the Articles of Confederation, which denied the central government both the power to tax and the ability to regulate trade' (Diebold, 1982, p. 159). These historical developments partly explain why US industrial policy is weak and non-interventionist by tradition.[68] According to Grant (1989, pp. 115–16), 'The dominant values of US society are at odds with any interventionist industrial policy. [. . .] The episode of the New Deal [. . .] cannot be said to have created a legitimate interventionist tradition in the USA.'[69]

Notwithstanding, Alexander Hamilton's *Report on Manufactures* of 1791 is a first proposal for an American industrial policy. It advocated the use of tariffs, and the selection of industries that best suited the country at the time. Although Hamilton's Report had no lasting impact on the conception of industrial policy in the USA (Hudson, 1985), it did provide a basis for industrial development in the newly independent federal state. A decade after its publication, the Report came back to the forefront of discussions on American industrial policy. The 1816 tariff protected new (or infant) industries; trade protection gave American industry the ability to produce a wide range of products, and to focus on the domestic market (Diebold, 1982).

In the latter part of the nineteenth century, antitrust laws formed the fundamental pillar of US industrial policy. A new type of industrial policy emerged with the Interstate Commerce Act of 1887, and antitrust policy was created with the 1890 Sherman Act. It was designed to reduce monopoly and dominant positions in the economy. In 1914, both the Clayton Act and the Federal Trade Commission Act emerged from the dissatisfaction generated by judicial interpretations and enforcement of the Clayton Act (Shughart, 1990). The Clayton Act (amended partially in 1936 by the Robinson Patman Act) prohibits all discriminatory practices that reduce competition substantially. In short, antitrust policies are aimed at punishing price fixers and at preventing anti-competitive practices.[70] These laws still play an important part in contemporaneous American economic policy. Post-war American industrial policy has many features: a secular devotion to antitrust laws, an increased commitment to tariff reduction, and a more interventionist policy, the driving force of which has been the defence industry and its space-related programmes.

Since the Second World War, defence spending has been massive. In the 1960s, government financial assistance was extended with the introduction of the space programmes. At the peak of this phenomenon, more than 50 per cent of all US engineers and scientists were directly involved in government supported R&D programmes. This effort has generated many civilian spinoffs in the fields of advanced materials, high technology computer languages and semiconductors. Other aspects of post-war American interventionist industrial policy include: quotas on foreign oil aimed at import substitution, and subsidies for the shipping and shipbuilding industries.[71] The watch industry was protected on the grounds that only the watch makers had the appropriate skills for the manufacture of bomb sights (Diebold, 1982).

The energy crisis, the monetary disorder, and the emergence of NICs in the 1970s introduced the themes of 'American industrial decline', and 'loss of US technological leadership'.[72] In the 1970s, the terms 'industrial policy' and 'industrial strategy' re-emerged in the official language (Diebold, 1982). In the 1980s, these expressions were overshadowed by the notion of 'competitiveness'. The new Reagan administration focused on macroeconomic issues, such as tax cuts and the reduction of government expenditure. Although these measures were aimed at expanding industrial production and productivity, 'they were not thought of as "industrial policy", a term abjured by many in the new administration' (Diebold, 1982, p. 181). In spite of its negative attitude towards the concept of industrial policy, the new federal administration continued intervening in the defence-related industries.[73] In some ways it is as if the American government had proceeded all along with an industrial policy, without it having been either deliberate or acknowledged.

MITI (Ministry of International Trade and Industry) and the Japanese model of industrial policy

Hosomi and Okumura (1982) view industrial policy in Japan as 'constructive', and as a well approved and purposeful tool for the advancement of the national economy. In Japan, industrial policy (*Sangyo Seisaku*) is anchored on a societal consensus and on a network of extended economic and business relationships. The Japanese production model is based on a co-operative form of capitalism.

The two pillars of the Japanese business model are: social consensus—which entails that all the employees of a corporation, not only the top managers, are involved in the determination of the long-term objectives of the firm—and a network structure of business relations. The Japanese business network (*keiretsu*) is best represented as a series of concentric circles (Imai, 1989). The core is a bank or an insurance company, surrounded by large firms, controlling other firms of equal dimension or smaller. Each firm is then connected to a myriad of suppliers. In turn, the suppliers develop strong relations with the trading houses (*sogo shosha*).[74] The Japanese banking institutions are strongly involved in industrial policy offering cheap long-term capital through modest interest rates. There are many business networks of this kind or industrial conglomerates, one competing with another.

The Japanese model of industrial policy is based on government–business synergies. The Japanese state is neither dominant/coercive nor submissive to private firms. In Kitschelt's words (1991, p. 478), 'the Japanese state contributed more intelligence than funding to economic development, backed up by sanctions if industries failed to comply with market-conforming government programs, primarily those of the revered Ministry of International Trade and Industry (MITI)'. Market-conforming government programmes entail the specification of long-term objectives of industrial policy by MITI. Firms belonging to competing networks try to meet these objectives.

Japanese industrial policy is best represented by its three major components: general measures, sectoral measures, and organizational measures (Hosomi and Okumura, 1982). The general measures—such as quality standardization—are designed to promote industry as a whole. Sectoral measures aim to improve the productivity and the employment opportunities of specific sectors (modernization and rationalization of the steel and textile industries; import restrictions on computers, etc.). Institutional measures ensure the non-disruption and the smooth functioning of competition (antitrust laws). These measures also encompass taxation and financial actions to promote SMEs.

One of the major roles of the Japanese state is to *create comparative advantages* for Japanese industry. This role is best summarized by a statement of the Japanese minister, Ojimi, more than 20 years ago (OECD, 1972, p. 149):

The MITI decided to establish in Japan industries which require intensive employment of capital and technology, industries that in consideration of comparative cost of production should be the most inappropriate for Japan, industries such as steel, oil-refining, petro-chemicals, automobiles, aircraft, industrial machinery of all sorts, and electronics, including electronic computers. From a short-run, static viewpoint, encouragement of such industries would seem to conflict with economic rationalism. But, from a long-range viewpoint, these are precisely the industries where income elasticity of demand is high, technological progress is rapid, and labor productivity rises fast.

The launching by MITI of the Very Large Scale Integration Initiative (VLSI) in the 1970s which brought together the major electronics manufacturers proved very successful. It supported the entry of Japanese firms into volume commodity chip manufacture with the 64K-RAM chip. The fifth generation computer program was launched in October 1981. It was backed by some US $200–300 million of government financial investment. Industrial planning in Japan always incorporated a long-term view.[75]

The Asian NICs

In all East Asian newly industrializing economies (Hong Kong, Korea, Singapore, Malaysia, Philippines, Thailand), with the exception of the *laissez-faire* Hong Kong, active industrial policies with selective industrial targeting have been set in place; they were aimed at promoting specific industrial activities at different times (Chowdhury and Islam, 1993).

There are important differences, but also common features in the industrial policies of these countries.

Selection by the government of industrial growth sectors, target industrial areas or priority industries   In the mid-1960s, the 'strategic' industries of Korea were identified as textiles and consumer electronics. This policy of selecting priority industrial activities was repeated again in the early part of the 1970s. Capital-intensive activities, such as steel, non-ferrous metals, chemicals, machinery, shipbuilding and electronic industrial equipment, became the priority. The Taiwanese government played an important role in promoting capital and technology-intensive industries in the 1970s. In Singapore, the Economic Development Board (EDB) 'lays down its priorities for industrial activities in anticipation of changes in Singapore's comparative advantage' (Chowdhury and Islam, 1993, p. 96).

Flexibility in the industrial policy philosophy   This flexibility has materialized at three different levels:

1 A change from import substitution towards export led growth. In 1964, Korea underwent this change which involved selecting new target industries such as textiles and consumer electronics. The Taiwanese economy experienced the same transformation in the mid-1960s. In addition, to facilitate exports, the exchange rate systems have been reformed.
2 A change from labour-intensive to capital-intensive and to R&D (or high skills)-intensive industries. This was expressed in the shift from textiles, to steel, shipbuilding, petrochemicals, and finally to electronics, biotechnologies, new material sciences. In Taiwan, the government

promoted the expansion of capital-intensive industries in the 1970s, whereas the 1980s have witnessed an expansion of high technology and skill-intensive activities (IT, electronics, machinery and biotechnology). The 1973 industrial restructuring programme launched by the Korean government put the emphasis on the development of new priority sectors: steel and non-ferrous metals, chemicals and petrochemicals, machinery, shipbuilding and electronic industrial equipment. In Singapore, the 1979 industrial restructuring programme was aimed at discouraging labour-intensive activities. High wages, a payroll tax and a Skill Development Fund levy on the employers of unskilled labour were all measures intended to shift industrial activities towards skill- and technology-intensive activities.

3 A change from sectoral objectives to horizontal measures, such as R&D support, promotion of SMEs, introduction of new technologies (automated manufacturing systems). But, as noted by the OECD (1991c, p. 66) 'the R&D and technology support measures often have a marked sectoral bias, with the focus on electronics, IT and biotechnologies'.

Instruments

1 *Financial instruments*   The regulation of the financial sector, taking the form of investment funds channelled in favour of the target industries, has been documented by Wade (1988, 1990). Through tight control over the financial sector at the end of the 1960s, the Korean government was able to administer preferential credit to the industries it had identified as being strategic. In Singapore, the Economic Development Board allocates selective grants and loan schemes to the target industries.

2 *Training*   In Korea, through active R&D and human resource development (HRD) programmes in the 1970s, the government played a crucial role in expanding engineering education. In Taiwan, R&D activities were promoted by the establishment of publicly funded industrial and technological parks. During the early 1990s, the erosion of the competitiveness of the East Asian economies on international markets and the gradual liberalization of their domestic markets called for a renewed interest in R&D programmes.

   R&D centred programmes and programmes aimed at upgrading the skills of workers have had such an impact that shortages of unskilled or semi-skilled workers are a concern for the future. In Taiwan, the shortage of unskilled and semi-skilled staff is expected to be 120,000 by 1996. The limits of automation and drastic immigration controls also offer a partial explanation for these shortages.

3 *The state as an investor*   Government enterprises are non-existent in Hong Kong, and are of minor importance in Korea. In Taiwan, government enterprises are present in heavy industry (steel and petrochemicals) and in advanced sectors (components, silicon smelting) (OECD, 1991c). In Singapore, the state has heavily invested in construction, iron and steel, and ship repair industries.

   It has often been alleged that in Hong Kong, economic growth has been achieved with minimal state intervention. The role of the state has been mainly confined to creating an appropriate economic environment, with low (ideally zero) price distortions. But even in this *laissez-faire* colony, the government did have an input in the shaping of the industrial structure through, for example, a sectoral policy to promote the electronics industry (OECD, 1991c, p. 65).

   In the last decade, industrial policies of the Asian countries have changed with the introduction of privatization programmes. These programmes were implemented in the 1980s in Singapore; they began in March 1989 in Taiwan. What is interesting to note is that the privatization of state enterprises in the East Asian countries has responded less to a general ideological and fashionable trend, which was very pronounced during these years, than to a logical requirement. State involvement in the early stages of industrial development is seen as a prerequisite for growth. Once the industry has become viable, private entrepreneurs are encouraged to take over. This is why in Singapore, for example, the recent and current privatization programmes affecting some industrial sectors, such as the firms associated with the defence industry, and the rubber association, are totally compatible with the creation or development of public enterprises in other new sectors—the leading edge industries.

7.3   The debate over industrial policy

Among EU scholars and politicians, there has been and still is an endless debate between those who want as little industrial policy as possible and those who wish to give it a more positive, constructive and indeed interventionist role. The first group is predominant in Germany, in The Netherlands and in the UK; the second group would be found in France and in other Mediterranean countries. The first group is in favour of developing a range of substitutes for an EIP, such as a trade and competition policy, and/or an Economic and Monetary Union (EMU). The second group calls for increased financial means—for fiscal federalism, for example—and for a greater political consensus and commitment. The view of the Commission is an attempted compromise, but it is in fact closer to the liberal German philosophy than to the French 'Colbertist' approach.

Since we have discussed the EU Competition Policy earlier, we will here briefly explore whether budgetary and monetary integration can be seen as a substitute for a more positive EIP. In subsequent paragraphs of this section, we will venture into the many facets of a more positive EIP: European *filières* and districts, the optimal mix between private and public firms, the financial constraints, and the implications for third countries.

7.3.1   Is EMU (Economic and Monetary Union) a substitute for a more positive EIP?

The primary aim of budgetary and monetary integration is to create a favourable economic environment. This is theoretically achievable if:

- Budget deficits are contained within 'reasonable' limits
- Price stability is achieved throughout the Union, and inflation rates are minimal
- Interest rates are kept low
- Realignments of European currencies (or devaluations) are the exception rather than the rule.

All these positive conditions would boost business confidence, would increase growth and per capita income, and would obviate the need for a more positive EIP. On the other hand, the adjustable peg as implemented within the framework of the European Monetary System (EMS), and the irrevocable fixing of exchange rates as provided for under Economic and Monetary Union (EMU) arrangements, lessen and eliminate respectively the possibility of compensating losses in industrial competitiveness by a decline in the exchange rate. Since the competitive devaluation[76] will not be seen as a viable option in the future of the European Union, economic adjustments will increasingly have to take place at the structural or industrial levels. Accordingly, monetary integration clearly calls for a more positive EIP.

As can be seen, EMU brings radically antagonistic results. Are EMU and a more positive EIP incompatible, or can they be mutually reinforcing policies? Under EMU there will be both macroeconomic stability and the impossibility of using the national exchange rate as an instrument for adjustment to macroeconomic shocks. In the absence of stability, some means other than exchange rate adjustment will be necessary to respond to macroeconomic shocks. A quick move towards EMU (now planned for 1999) will indubitably necessitate industrial adjustments and thus a more positive EIP, if all European countries are to participate in the Monetary Union.

7.3.2   An active, positive European industrial policy

The EU has developed in the past a strong competition policy, but what is lacking today is the same legal basis for the development of a strong industrial policy. Is it possible that support will be generated for the development of such a policy? 'If, in future, a more interventionist-minded Commissioner were to be appointed to DGIV [Competition Policy], this could tip the balance in favour of a more industrial-policy-based EC' (Woolcock and Wallace, 1995). A more constructive and positive EIP should not be confused with systematic government intervention and with protectionism. In addition to a stronger technological policy, such a policy could entail:

- The completion of a 'favourable European business environment'
- The building up of European *filières*, clusters and industrial districts
- The building-up of 'Euro-champions'
- The allocation of greater levels of finance, in order, *inter alia*, to develop a European system of innovation
- A concerted policy *vis-à-vis* third countries.

A favourable business environment

In spite of all progress made in trying to build a more integrated EU—i.e. a European Financial Area, and monetary–budgetary–fiscal integration—problems still remain which prevent the attainment of even a minimalist EIP. These problems relate to the many different regulations with respect to the functioning of stock exchanges, to conflicting labour laws, to institutional factors, and also to continued absence of full fiscal harmonization. For example, the various stock exchanges in the EU maintain national characteristics: the French stock exchange (*Bourse de Paris*) imposes legal restrictions on hostile bids in France, the Milan stock exchange devotes a lot of importance to family shareholding and to non-voting shares. In particular, they impose major restrictions on the control and ownership of private firms and impede or retard cross-border acquisitions. Some of the differences between EU countries can be explained by their different relationships between capital markets and corporate control.

European filières, *clusters and industrial districts; the role of European MNEs*

A more constructive EIP must integrate spatial parameters. The concept of *filière* has been defined above (Chapter 4). We have stressed the limited validity of the concept at the national level and its relevance at the European level. Andréosso and Jacobson (1991) explore the way a peripheral country such as Ireland could become more integrated in the EU at both the spatial and corporate/industrial levels. Our argument rests on the examples of two 'strategic' industries: the computer/office equipment industry and the machine tools/robotics industry. The point we make is that spatial and corporate integration could eventually lead to the constitution of a European *filière*. It is thus essential that all types of alliances between European firms be fostered in order to build a series of European *filières*.

As we saw above, subcontracting is one of the lowest degrees of firms' interdependence; it could thus represent a first step in the constitution of European *filières*. Where the relationship between firms spreads beyond that of buyer–supplier, the potential exists for the formation of clusters which, as we saw in Chapter 4, incorporates horizontal as well as vertical relationships. The consequence of this type of cross-border activity is ultimately the formation of European MNEs, as European, rather than as German, British or French firms with a presence elsewhere in Europe.

Where small, local firms exist on the basis of traditional crafts, the potential exists under a positive EIP to incorporate a regional element and find ways of encouraging the development of competitive industrial districts among such firms. Research is unfortunately not yet sufficiently advanced to enable us to identify where the potential for successful industrial districts exists.

Picking winners and Euro-champions

The instruments of a policy favouring Euro-champions could include public aid, fiscal exemptions, and public (EU) procurements. Dierickx, Matutes and Neven (1991) show that the design of an appropriate policy based on the selection of potential winners is a very complex task. In their simple duopoly model with a single homogeneous commodity, the appropriate intervention in a declining industry depends upon the interplay of cost differences, the amount of production of the low variable cost firm, the discount rate, and the rate and pattern of demand decline. Their work highlights the fact that 'simple rules for picking survivors based on current unit cost, profitability, or productive efficiency simply do not provide sound guidance for policy' (Dierickx, Matutes and Neven, 1991). The technical complexity of the task is only one of the many difficulties that such a policy encounters. Other obstacles are of a political and institutional nature. Such obstacles should not, however, prevent the continuing efforts to develop such a policy.

It is increasingly felt in the EU that without a strong supranational co-ordination (i.e. some kind of European Political Union (EPU)) it is impossible to design a more positive industrial policy. EPU is a prerequisite for a stronger European Technological Collaboration. For instance, Tsoukalis (1991) is very sceptical as to the development of Euro-champions in present circumstances. Since the EU is characterized by a weak state, it can only have a weak industrial policy, so that it does not have at its disposal many instruments to promote such an active policy. Bance (1992) underlines this with a description of the minimalist role of the EU Competition Policy as a '*chasse aux gros*' (Bance, 1992, p. 7). The EU Competition Policy does not contribute greatly to the possibility of agreement on other issues in industrial policy.

The financial constraint

Related to the fact that the EU has a weak state, the weak EU budget and its minuscule share devoted to industry, energy and research, hamper the development of a more positive EIP. It is felt that quicker adjustments in the agricultural sector should naturally redistribute European resources towards other programmes (of an industrial and regional nature). However, costly R&D in the aircraft industry, nuclear energy, armament, and biotechnology sectors need more than a redistribution of funds.

Many economists and politicians are hostile to increased financial resources being provided, either via the EU budget or via national budgets, because of the financial burden on the tax-payer implied by such a policy. Indeed, 'picking winners' and/or promoting Euro-champions may lead to a high level of public spending incompatible with the EMU convergence criteria, and may also lead to a familiar harmful consequence known as the 'crowding-out' effect.[77] To avoid this recessionist effect, private funding can be increasingly sought. This is particularly plausible in the case of public works that have a high rate of return. The most famous example in the EU is certainly the FF90 billion Eurotunnel project, in which more than 200 banks in the world have participated (*Le Monde*, 25 May 1993). Large sums of money are available on the international capital markets for other projects of this nature.

Policy vis-à-vis *third countries*

Economic relations with third countries range from pure trade relations to direct investment. The trade relations of the EU countries are organized within the framework of the Common Commercial Policy (CCP) of the EU, and are influenced by the broader international framework under the aegis of the World Trade Organisation (WTO). Article 110 of the Rome Treaty stipulates that 'by establishing a customs union [...] Member States aim to contribute to the harmonious development of world trade, the progressive abolition of restrictions on international trade and the lowering of customs barriers'. The CCP ensures that the Customs Union, and possibly EMU in the future, is compatible with free trade at a global level. One of the major instruments of the CCP is the Common External Tariff (CET), established for each category of manufacturing product as an arithmetic average of the tariffs applied by the different member states (Article 19/1). In the past, the successive GATT rounds have progressively diminished the incidence of the CET. The Dillon Round (1960–62) and the Kennedy Round which started in 1963 cut the tariffs on manufacturing goods by about half. The Tokyo Round of the mid-1970s led to a further cut of 30 per cent.[78] Since the setting up of the EEC in 1958, the average level of CET on manufacturing products has decreased from 40 per cent to less than 5 per cent. In the same period, the dispersion has narrowed considerably; only a few (sensitive) products are today subject to the so-called 'peak tariffs', i.e. those close to or above 15 per cent. These tariffs are today the exception rather than the rule. Still subject to these tariffs are some motor vehicle products, articles in the footwear, clothing and textile industries, and in the electrical and electronic industries (TV receivers, electronic circuits). It can thus easily be ascertained that since its inception, the CCP has worked towards freer trade on a global scale in the manufacturing sector. There is some foundation for the criticism aimed at the EU for its protectionist stance (Fortress Europe) only if a minority of products—the sensitive manu-factured goods, and agricultural products—are referred to. Progress was made during the Uruguay Round (1986–93) to decrease the level of tariffs in these industries as well.

However, it should be borne in mind that tariff cuts do not equate simplistically with trade liberalization. Many other non-tariff barriers (NTBs) have been increasingly used by all nations in general and by the EU in particular to protect the vulnerable industries. In Lindert's (1991, p. 152) words: 'By the time the Kennedy Round of tariffs cuts was consummated in 1967, non-tariff barriers had emerged as the main roadblocks in the way of trade. Since the early 1970s, non-tariff barriers have been getting even more formidable.' NTBs can be expressed as tariff equivalents (see Whalley, 1985; Deardorff and Stern, 1983; Balassa and Balassa, 1984).[79] The oldest and most popular form of NTBs used by the EU are (import) quotas, but today the EU operates also 'voluntary export restraints' (VERs) and 'orderly marketing arrangements' (OMAs), which are negotiated on a bilateral basis, and which exist outside the GATT/WTO framework.

Export promotion, through the use of export credits, and the implementation of a minimum EU content can also be viewed as non-tariff obstacles to trade. The minimum content clause specifies that for a product to be considered as European, 80 per cent at least of its final value must originate from the EU; such a product can thus escape the realm of the CET. This rule is aimed at restricting the practice of 'screwdriver' plants or low-skilled assembly operations set up by Japanese and American multinationals in the EU. Import quotas still exist on Japanese cars.[80]

It has been widely acknowledged that the existence of the CET has provided an additional reason for the location of American and Japanese plants in the EU (Jacobson and Andréosso, 1990). Foreign Direct Investment (FDI) is one of the many strategies offered to MNEs facing high trade barriers. The study of FDI trends in the EU is a complex task explained by the ambiguity of the concept. Nicolaides (1993) notes that official statistics relate only to investment registered in the balance of payments. Concentrating solely on externally financed greenfield investment, they omit all financing performed through the international capital markets. Léonard (1990) proposes two definitions of FDI: a 'narrow' or more traditional definition, and an 'enlarged' definition. The 'narrow' definition of FDI refers to the MNE's participation in the capital of a firm, the benefits reinvested in the host country, as well as the loans granted by the headquarters of the MNE. The 'expanded' definition encompasses all types of contracts such as joint venture agreements (where foreign participation does not exceed 50 per cent), licence agreements, franchising and other agreements, as well as international subcontracting practices (Léonard, 1990). Since all data relating to FDI are based on the traditional or restricted definition, official statistics underestimate the true extent of FDI. Since even a biased measurement of the phenomenon is preferable to no measurement at all, we can rely on the traditional definition and state that during the second half of the 1980s, Japanese and American direct investment in the EU has doubled from the 1980–84 period to the 1985–89 period (UNCTC, 1991).

An appropriate tool of EIP would be to design a *concerted and appropriate FDI policy*. FDI brings both positive and negative effects to the economy of the recipient country. On the positive side, benefits include job creation, positive net foreign exchange earnings, technological flows, possibilities of sourcing materials and inputs locally (linkages), development of an adequate educational base, and taxes on rents or profits earned by foreign enterprises (MacDougall, 1960; Dicken, 1992). Some of these positive effects should however be carefully assessed. In many instances, MNEs have not met the objectives of the national governments. Many jobs created have been low-skilled jobs ('screwdriver plant syndrome'), and linkages have been poor.[81] On the purely negative side, FDI may result in negative balance of payment earnings,[82] and may destroy jobs. It will certainly weaken the domestic industrial structure and lead eventually to a loss of national industrial identity. This loss will in turn reduce the breadth of the national industrial policy. To take Ireland as an example again, the Irish government can use fiscal incentives to attract MNEs and can improve the domestic educational base; it *cannot* however build up strong indigenous firms on a basis comparable to that of France and Denmark. De Bernis (1990) refers to the 'destructuring effect of foreign investment'. The structure of the Japanese MNEs, investing in the EU, is represented by concentric circles of firms–banks who possess their own networks of sub-suppliers. This implies that a Japanese MNE setting up a motor-car plant, say, in the UK, will not only directly compete against the domestic manufacturers of cars, but to the extent that it succeeds against those domestic manufacturers, it may gradually (and indirectly) evict other domestic manufacturers of sub-supply products, since it may source its inputs increasingly from Japanese firms.[83]

A concerted and appropriate FDI policy must not be equated with a protectionist policy. Too often, the EU has taken protectionist stances, as a result of its inability to devise a sound, positive EIP. A positive and active EIP gives priority to policy instruments that are exercised upstream,[84] e.g.: increased technological collaboration; lending facilities on capital markets in the EU (through a greater synergy between banks and firms à la the German or Japanese models); and fiscal allowances. These instruments are aimed at making the strategic industries more competitive. In particular, the technological policy of the EU should be reviewed. We have seen that ESPRIT-III has initiated a move, but a much greater emphasis should be placed on the applied and scientific research as opposed to 'pre-competitive' research.

In the same way, too often the development of common (industrial) policies has been perceived by non-EU countries as the building of 'fortress Europe' (Curzon Price, 1991). Co-operation with third countries should be encouraged provided this co-operation maximizes the benefits of the Union. In the light of the recent association agreements signed recently with the East European economies, the concept of a European *filière* could be extended not only to the EFTA countries but also to Eastern and Central Europe.

The crux of a positive and constructive EIP rests on technology and finance. Extended financial means in the EU would facilitate more coherent technological programmes, and the design of a strong European technological system. Referring to the case of the UK only, Geroski (1991b) is of the opinion that an appropriate industrial policy aimed at stimulating the diffusion of existing technology would 'prove more effective' than a policy designed to foster the generation of new knowledge. However, in the case of the EU, stimulation of the creation as well as the diffusion of new knowledge, is required.

Success (and failure) depends 'not only on a match between the properties of technology in individual sectors and the national institutional capabilities but also on the ability to translate these properties and capabilities into efficient sectoral governance structures' (Kitschelt, 1991, p. 490).

Notes

[1] Note that among policies that can impact on the performance of firms and industries are fiscal, monetary and other aspects of macroeconomic policy in general. While we must, in examining industrial policy, be aware of these impacts, macroeconomic policy is not the primary concern. We are more concerned with policy designed to influence industry directly.

[2] The quotes are from Cohen (1995), who was referring specifically to French industrial policy, but it seems to us that his point is valid for all industrial policy.

[3] We urge the student to refer back to Chapter 4 for a more detailed account of state intervention.

[4] In Chapter 4 we used the terms positive and negative external effects.

[5] This might, for example, be through an employee from the first firm leaving and joining another firm.

[6] Another type of intervention may be appropriate, such as improved information and skills for all firms so as to reduce the likelihood of a bad design.

[7] Though see the theory of the second best.

[8] Discussed in some detail in Chapter 4, Section 4.1.5

[9] This example is borrowed from Nielsen, Heinrich and Hansen (1991), Ch. 5.

[10] According to this approach, a country's comparative advantage evolves in stages: first, a typical developing country will have comparative advantages in labour-intensive industries (e.g. clothing and textiles); with rising living standards and wages, these labour-intensive activities will be phased out, and the country will develop capital and subsequently technology and skill-intensive activities.

[11] There is no common legal definition of a public enterprise in the EU. However, a 1980 Directive (OJCE, 29-07-80) stipulates that a public undertaking is one 'over which the public authorities may exercise directly or indirectly a dominant influence by virtue of their ownership of it, their financial participation therein, or the rules that govern it'. Public authorities are the state: government, central, regional or local authorities.

[12] For Plato, the state and the individual are both subservient to the attainment of the objective good. The tasks of the ideal state, as defined by Plato, are: to maintain the equality between individuals (excluding slaves!), divided into different social classes, to supervise the production and distribution of commodities—for example, to fix the conditions if agricultural production takes place—and to authorize exports and imports. Despite his strong advocacy of private property, Aristotle asserted even more strongly than Plato the existence of the state as a spiritual reality.

[13] In France, Air France and the SNCF (Société Nationale des Chemins de Fer Français) are mixed societies that were created in the 1930s.

[14] The 'Commissariat à l'Energie Atomique' was founded in 1945.

[15] Nationalization is the taking into state ownership of private firms; in privatization ownership is transferred back into private hands; de-nationalization refers to that type of de-regulation that removes the barriers preventing private firms from entering a nationalized industry; it allows for some private ownership, whereas privatization implies no state ownership.

[16] The publication in 1967 of Servan-Schreiber's book *Le défi américain* partly explains the formulation of this new objective; it culminates in the resurgence of the theme of the 'technological gap'. For more on the significance of Servan-Schreiber's book, see Hayward (1995).

[17] Note that the recent wave of privatization started in Pinochet's Chile in the mid-1970s. Privatizations are still on the agenda of many countries for the coming years. Solomon Brothers estimated at $120 billion the world sale of public assets in the years 1993–95, compared with $250 billion between 1984 and 1991.

[18] Essentially, because the privatization plans of some of them have been delayed.

[19] Niccolò Machiavelli (1520) saw in the co-existence of a rich state and of poor citizens the condition for an increasingly vast and powerful empire (cf. Discorsi sopra la prima deca di Tito Livio, Libbro II, Capitolo 19).

[20] For a history of the emergence of cartels and syndicates in Germany, see for example Chandler (1990).

[21] See List (1842).

[22] It is not necessarily contradictory to want more decentralization—more power for the Länder—and a more active, positive industrial policy which includes financial flows from the centre.

[23] For an influential early view on the importance of technology, see List (1841); see also Section 7.2.3.

[24] Government contribution to R&D is somewhere between that of France and the UK—see Table 5.6.

[25] An exception being the period of the 1930s, when free trade was abandoned to leave way for the Import Duties Act (see Gribbin, 1991).

[26] Colbert's economic policy was subsequently jeopardized by the religious policy of Louis XIV. The revocation of the 'Edit de Nantes' in 1685 led to a massive emigration of the industrially oriented Huguenot elite, to the benefit of the neighbouring countries (England, Holland, Prussia and Switzerland).

[27] For more on the *Grandes Écoles*, see Chapter 4, in the discussion on the French NSI.

[28] Having signed the Havana Charter in 1948, France kept on imposing substantial customs barriers. Although France was a member of the the European Payment Union from 1950, it did not implement the 1955 monetary agreement. The French franc remained non-convertible, unlike the DM and sterling.

[29] Jean Monnet was in fact an influential businessman and politician who played a leading role in keeping sound relations with the USA at the time.

[30] During the 1950s, indicative planning was adopted, with many variations, by Italy, the United Kingdom, Ireland and Belgium. These planning systems did not however reach the same sophisticated degree as in the French system (Franzmeyer, 1979).

[31] Among which were: Usinor and Sacilor (steel); CGE, Thomson, PUK; Paribas, Indosuez; CII-Honeywell-Bull.

[32] The *mezzogiorno* is the poorer, more agricultural, southern part of Italy.

[33] With the *lottizzazzione* (i.e. attribution) of posts on the basis of political affiliation.

[34] Authors' translation of: '*El mejor Estado era el que menos interfería la iniciativa privada; ni siquiera para proteger el mercato interior de la competencia extranjera*' (García Delgado et al., 1989, p. 435).

[35] Article 149 of the 1978 Constitution specifies the restricted role of the state.

[36] It should be noted that Danish companies are generally small or medium-sized by European standards. SMEs with fewer than 200 employees absorb 78 per cent of total manufacturing employment, compared with 55 per cent in Belgium, 47 per cent in Germany, and 45 per cent in the UK.

[37] This section draws on Andréosso and Noonan (1995). Note that CMEA was the Council for Mutual Economic Assistance.

[38] Above and beyond the Europe Agreements, the financial assistance of the EU takes the form of the PHARE programme (Pologne Hongrie: Assistance à la Reconstruction Economique) and the TACIS programme (Technical Assistance to the Commonwealth of Independent States). (See: *Revue du Marché Commun*, 1993; OECD, 1991c.)

[39] The Rome Treaty does not provide for a European Industrial Policy (EIP), if we conceive a EIP as a complete set of horizontal and vertical measures. Horizontal measures are measures with a wide and universal application throughout the Common Market, such as the harmonization of company laws. Vertical measures require a selective Community intervention in depth in particular industries.

[40] The pooling of the European coal and steel industries gave birth to the ECSC (European Coal and Steel Community) in 1952. The ECSC was *supranational*—it was empowered to intervene directly in the industries of member countries. Integration in the EC agricultural markets took the form of the Common Agricultural Policy (CAP).

[41] We will discuss only the main articles here.

[42] These articles do not apply to the coal and steel, and nuclear energy industries, which are subject to the rules laid down in the ECSC (European Coal and Steel Community) and Euratom Treaties.

[43] Article 177 of the Rome Treaty stipulates that the implementation and enforcement of EU law is left to the national courts, whereas the European Court of Justice plays a residual and guiding role.

[44] Continental Can, a large American manufacturer, took over a German firm that had a dominant position in the market for preserved meat and fish (and for metal caps for preservative jars). This was followed by another takeover on the Dutch market, and resulted in a dominant position held by Continental Can on both markets.

[45] See: CEC (1989) *First Survey on State Aids in the European Community*, Luxemburg.

[46] The rest is distributed as follows: coal industry 16 per cent, transport sector 30 per cent and agriculture 13 per cent.

[47] See the Council Regulation COM/73/1210 final.

[48] See: *Official Journal* L 395, 30.12.1989.

[49] A review of the policy is due to take place in 1995. One possible change is that the ECU 5 billion threshold will be reduced to 2 billion.

[50] As illustrated by the fact that R&D formed an important part of Jean Monnet's Action Committee for a United States of Europe.

[51] Formed in 1969, the Consortium subsequently fell apart partly because of the pressure from the German government as Siemens had been left out.

[52] Several Directives have provided the legal framework for the attribution of state aids to the shipbuilding industry in the 1980s and early 1990s. In particular, the seventh Directive on aid to shipbuilding creates special arrangements for the former GDR in order to allow it to restructure.

[53] Anti-dumping duties on imports are permitted under GATT (General Agreement on Tariffs and Trade), provided that it can be shown that imports are entering at a price below cost.

[54] The safeguard clause, enabling any party to curb temporarily its imports of steel and coal products originating from the associated area, has been integrated *ab initio* in the Europe Agreements signed subsequently with Bulgaria and Romania (Andréosso, 1993).

[55] For more details, see 'Towards greater competitiveness in the steel industry: the need for further restructuring' (SEC (92) 2160).

[56] CEC (1994) *Intermediate Report on the Restructuring of the Steel Industry* (COM (94), 125 final, Brussels).

[57] A notable exception is the establishment in 1978 of the JET (Joint European Torus), an experimental fusion tokomak at Culham, England.

[58] ESPRIT: European Strategic Programme for Research in Information Technology; RACE: Research and Development in Advanced Communications Technology for Europe; BRITE–EURAM; Basic Research for Industrial Technology in Europe and European Research on Advanced Materials; COMETT: Community Programme in Education and Training in Technology.

[59] The 'Big Twelve' comprised the heads of Bull, Thomson, and CGE from France; AEG, Nixdorf, and Siemens from Germany; ICL, Plessey, and GEC from Britain; Olivetti and STET from Italy; and Philips from The Netherlands.

[60] Note that under Articles 85 and 86 of the Treaties, collaboration for the purpose of competitive research (i.e. at the later development stage), is expressly prohibited, whereas collaboration at the pre-competitive stage may be granted a block exemption.

[61] For a more comprehensive approach, see Sharp and Pavitt (1993).

[62] See CEC (1985b) *Towards a Technology Policy* (COM (85) 530 final).

[63] The second revision of the Rome Treaty gave birth to the Maastricht Treaty signed in February 1992.

[64] Although the substance of ESPRIT-I remained unchanged, ESPRIT-II aimed at upgrading the IT programme. New areas were covered (microelectronics and peripheral technologies), EFTA participation was fully acknowledged.

[65] The creation of consortia is not limited to the EU. Other integrated areas have experienced the same. The ASEAN countries (Singapore, Indonesia, the Philippines, Malaysia, Thailand and Brunei) have set up a network of industrial enterprises in priority sectors (copper, chemicals). (Anastassopoulos, Blanc, Dussauge, 1987).

[66] CEC (1990): *Industrial Policy in an Open Competitive Environment. Guidelines for a Community Approach*. COM (90) 556 final, Brussels, 16 November.

[67] It should be noted that from the awareness of 'economic and social cohesion' emerged the STRIDE programme. With a fund of ECUs 400 million over the years 1990–93 (extended to the year 1994 since), it is aimed at increasing the research, technological and innovatory capacity of less developed regions in the Union. (See OJ C 196, 4/08/1990.)

[68] For a contrary view, see Solo (1982).

[69] On the New Deal experience, see also Hawley (1966), and Diebold (1982).

[70] For more on the origins and specifications of US antitrust policies, see Shepherd (1990, Ch. 19), and Shughart (1990, pp. 199–202).

[71] There are only a few cases of bailing out by the federal government; one is the Lockheed Company (see Diebold, 1982, p. 172).

[72] It is not possible to refer to the plethora of studies related to these themes. However, the reader can refer for example to Prestowitz (1988), and Nelson (1993).

[73] The Pentagon's long lasting commitment to technology is reflected through various programmes, among which are the Strategic Defense Initiative (see Colijn, 1987) and the Navy's programme called the Rapid Acquisition of Manufacturing Parts (RAMPs).

[74] The *sogo shosha* have at their disposal a very dense and developed network of information. They can respond very quickly to changes in the foreign demand and they help Japanese MNEs in their location decisions (see, for example, Kojima, 1978; Peyrard, 1990).

[75] For more on Japanese industrial policy, see Okuno (1988). On historical developments of Japanese industrial policy, see Hosomi and Okumura (1982).

[76] The cascade 'competitive devaluations' of sterling, the Irish punt, lira, escudo, peseta, Swedish krone, during the fourth quarter 1992 and the first quarter 1993, with the exit from the Exchange Rate

Mechanism of sterling and the lira had to be seen as an attempt to regain structural/industrial competitiveness by means of currency devaluation. See the limits of such a policy in the case of Ireland in Andréosso (1993).

[77] When the government sells bonds to the public to finance its industrial programme, this can result in higher interest rates which may in turn reduce private sector investment. Note that in the case of the reunification of the two Germanys, the 'crowding out' effect has not occurred at all in spite of an unprecedented budgetary deficit.

[78] The last GATT agreement, known as the Uruguay Round and concluded in December 1993, leads to a commitment to cut tariffs by more than one-third. With the exception of 'sensitive' products (see below) the general level of tariff protection of the EU at present is very low.

[79] The results of these studies are summarized in Molle (1990, p. 445).

[80] The market for motor-cars in the EU will be liberalized in 1999.

[81] See for example O'Malley (1989) in the case of Ireland.

[82] The net foreign exchange earnings of FDI encompass capital inflow and export earnings on the one hand, balanced against foreign royalty payments and profit outflows (due to profit repatriation) on the other hand. It is clear that if profit outflows are nil, and if all production is for export, these effects are positive and are at their maximum. Conversely, if profit outflows are high, and all the production is absorbed by the domestic market, the balance of payments effects will be negative.

[83] See a concrete example in Andréosso and Jacobson (1991).

[84] Policy instruments that are exercised downstream attempt at minimizing the losses of the 'problem industries'. Such instruments refer to any kind of protective measure, and such a policy is what we have termed an 'activist but negative' policy (Table 7.1).

Questions

7.1 Can economics adequately explain why states intervene in the economy?

7.3 Are there particular reasons why states have intervened in the economies of the EU?

7.3 Compare and contrast the industrial policies of any two European countries.

7.4 What is the difference between competition policy and industrial policy?

7.5 Are there important differences between the industrial policies of European countries on one hand and those of the NICs on the other? If yes, what are they, and why do they exist?

7.6 What special problems must be faced in the setting of industrial policies in East European countries?

7.7 Discuss the argument that if and when full EMU is achieved, an industrial policy will not be necessary.

7.8 Could there be an active, positive European industrial policy? What would be its main features?

7.9 Should the rules, taxes and grants offered to non-EU multinationals be harmonized? If yes, describe the policies that would/should emerge from this harmonization.

Appendix 7.1

TABLE A7.1   Sales of public assets in European countries (1) (*Source*: OECD, 1990 (Department of Economics and Statistics, Working Papers, No. 90: The Public Sector: Issues for the 1990s). Complemented with national sources)

Country	*Utilities*	*Manufacturing and others*
Austria	Graz-Koflacher Kisenbahn[P]	Bayou Steel Co.
	Bergau Gmbh[P]	Fepla Hirsch Gmbh[P]
	ÖMV (oil products)[P]	Futurit Werk AG[P]
Denmark		Kryolitselskabet
	Statsangstalten	Kobenhavns Lufthavn
	Livsforsikring	Postgiro
		TeleDanmark
France	TF1	Elf-Aquitaine
		CGCT
		St Gobain-Pont-à-Mousson
		Compagnie Générale d'Electricité
		Matra
		Crédit Commercial de France
		Société Générale
		Caisse Nationale de Crédit Agricole
		SOGÉNAL
		BBTP
		BIMP
		Paribas
		Indosuez
		Dassault
		Mutuelle Générale Française
		Agence Havas
		BNP
		Rhône-Poulenc
		UAP
		AGF[P]
		Bull[P]
		Framatome[P]
		Renault[P]
Germany	I.V.G.	VEBA (totally private)
		VIAG (totally private)
		Volkswagen (totally private)
		Deutsche Pfandbriefantstalt
		Deutsche Siedlungs und Landesrentenbank
		Deutsche Industrieanlagen
		Salzgitter (totally private)
		Lufthansa
		Schenker & Co.[P]
		Deutsche Verkehrskreditbank[P]

TABLE A7.1   (*continued*)

Country	Utilities	Manufacturing and others
Germany		Treuarbeit
Italy		Alitalia[P]
		Aeritalia
		Sirti
		Selenia
		Alfa Romeo
		Banco Nazionale del Lavoro[P]
		Credito Italiao
		Istituto Immobiliare
		Comit[P]
The Netherlands	KLM	Stoovaart Maatschappij Zeeland
		NMB Postbank
		NV Gerofabriek
		Hongovens
		DSM II
		NIB
		Vredestein
		DSM I
Spain	MIPSA	IGFISA (food)
	FOVISA	Frigsa (food)
		Olcesa (food)
		Gypsa (food)
		SEAT (motor car)
		SECOINSA (electronics)
		SKF Española
		Industrias Semimetalicas (aluminium)
		REMETAL, ALUFLET (aluminium)
		Textil Tarazona (textiles)
		Hilaturas Gossypium (textiles)
		PAMESA (paper)
		ENTURSA (hotels)
		Viajes Marsans (tourism)
UK	Associated British Ports	BP (Petrol)
	British Gas	Cable & Wireless
	British Telecom	Britoil
	Sea Link	Enterprise Oil
	National Bus Company	British Aerospace
	British Airways	Jaguar
	British Airports Authority	Inmos
	British Steel	International Aeradio
	Water (England and Wales)	British Shipbuilders
	Electricity (England and Wales)[P]	
	North of Scotland	British Sugar Corp.
	Hydro-Electric Board[P]	Fairey Engineering
	South of Scotland Electricity	Ferranti
	Board[P]	ICL
	Forestry Commission	Wytch Farm
	Scottish Bus Group	Scott Lithgow
		Vosper Thorneycroft
		Vickers Shipbuilding
		Yarrow Shipbuilders
		Leyland Bus Company
		BA Helicopters

TABLE A7.1 (*continued*)

Country	Utilities	Manufacturing and others
UK		Swan Hunter
		British Rail Hotels
		Unipart[p]
		Shorts[p]
		Rolls Royce
		Royal Ordnance
		North Sea Oil Licence
		Amersham International
		Council House
		Girobank[p]
		Istel
		Rover Group
		National Freight Company
		Plant Building Institute
		National Enterprise Board
		General Practice Finance

(1): Partial sales of public assets correspond to de-nationalizations whereas full sales are privatizations.
[p] Prospective sales.

Appendix 7.2   Treaty of Rome

PART THREE—COMMUNITY POLICY
TITLE I—Community Rules
Chapter I—Rules on Competition
Section I
Rules applying to undertakings

Article 85

1. The following shall be prohibited as incompatible with the common market: all agreements between undertakings, decisions by associations of undertakings and concerted practices which may affect trade between Member States and which have as their object or effect the prevention, restriction or distortion of competition within the common market, and in particular those which:

(a) directly or indirectly fix purchase or selling prices or any other trading conditions;
(b) limit or control production, markets, technical development, or investment;
(c) share markets or sources of supply;
(d) apply similar conditions to equivalent transactions with other trading parties, thereby placing them at a competitive disadvantage;
(e) make the conclusion of contracts subject to acceptance by the other parties of supplementary obligations which, by their nature or according to commercial usage, have no connection with the subject of such contracts.

2. Any agreements or decisions prohibited pursuant to this Article shall be automatically void.
3. The provisions of paragraph 1 may, however, be declared inapplicable in the case of:

- any agreement or category of agreements between undertakings;
- any decision or category of decisions by associations of undertakings;
- any concerted practice or category of concerted practices;

which contributes to improving the production or distribution of goods or to promoting technical and economic progress, while allowing consumers a fair share of the resulting benefit, and which does not:

(a) impose on the undertakings concerned restrictions which are not indispensable to the attainment of these objectives;
(b) afford such undertakings the possibility of eliminating competition in respect of a substantial part of the products in question.

Article 86

Any abuse by one or more undertakings of a dominant position within the common market or in a substantial part of it shall be prohibited as incompatible with the common market in so far as it may affect trade between Member States.

Such abuse may, in particular, consist in:

(a) directly or indirectly imposing unfair purchase or selling prices or other unfair trading conditions;
(b) limiting production, markets or technical development to the prejudice of consumers;
(c) applying dissimilar conditions to equivalent transactions with other trading parties, thereby placing them at a competitive disadvantage;
(d) making the conclusion of contracts subject to acceptance by the other parties of supplementary obligations, which, by their nature or according to commercial usage, have no connection with the subject of such contracts.

Article 92

1. Save as otherwise provided in this Treaty, any aid granted by a Member State or through State resources in any form whatsoever which distorts or threatens to distort competition by favouring certain undertakings or the production of certain goods shall, in so far as it affects trade between Member States, be incompatible with the common market.
2. The following shall be compatible with the common market:

(a) aid having a social character, granted to individual consumers, provided that such aid is granted without discrimination related to the origin of the products concerned;
(b) aid to make good the damage caused by natural disasters or other exceptional occurrences;
(c) aid granted to the economy of certain areas of the Federal Republic of Germany affected by the division of Germany in so far as such aid is required in order to compensate for the economic disadvantages caused by that division.

3. The following may be considered to be compatible with the common market:

(a) aid to promote the economic development of areas where the standard of living is abnormally low or where there is serious under-employment;
(b) aid to promote the execution of an important project of common European interest or to remedy a serious disturbance in the economy of a Member State;
(c) aid to facilitate the development of certain economic activities or of certain economic areas, where such aid does not adversely affect trading conditions to an extent contrary to the common interest. However, the aids granted to shipbuilding as of 1 January 1957 shall, in so far as they serve only to compensate for the absence of customs protection, be progressively reduced under the same conditions as apply to the elimination of customs duties, subject to the provisions of this Treaty concerning common commercial policy towards third countries;
(d) such other categories of aid as may be specified by decision of the Council acting by a qualified majority on a proposal from the Commission.

References

Abegglen, J. C. and G. Stalk Jr. (1985) *Kaisha: The Japanese Corporation*. Basic Books, New York.

Aiginger, K. (1991) 'Concentration et Profitabilité: Leçons de l'Expérience Autrichienne'. *Revue du Marché Commun et de l'Union Européenne*, no. 350, September, pp. 639–45.

Aitken, N. D. (1973) 'The effects of the EC and EFTA on European trade: a temporal cross-section analysis'. *American Economic Review*, vol. 63, pp. 881–92.

Alchian, Armen A. (1950) 'Uncertainty, evolution and economic theory'. *Journal of Political Economy*, vol. 58, June, pp. 211–21.

Alchian, A. (1984) 'Specificity, specialization, and coalitions'. *Zeitschrift für die gesamte Staatswissenschaft (JITE)*, vol. 140(1), pp. 34–49.

Alchian, A. A. and H. Demsetz (1972) 'Production, information costs and economic organization'. *American Economic Review*, vol. 62(5), pp. 777–95.

Alchian, A. A. and S. L. Woodward (1988) 'The firm is dead; long live the firm: a review of Oliver E. Williamson's *The Economic Institutions of Capitalism*'. *Journal of Economic Literature*, vol. 26(1), pp. 65–79.

Amin, A., D. R. Charles and J. Howells (1992) 'Corporate restructuring and cohesion in the new Europe'. *Regional Studies*, vol. 26, no. 4, pp. 319–31.

Amin, A. and M. Dietrich (1991) 'From hierarchy to "Hierarchy": the dynamics of contemporary corporate restructuring in Europe'. In A. Amin and M. Dietrich (eds), *Towards a New Europe?* Edward Elgar, Aldershot.

Amin, A. and K. Robins (1990) 'Industrial districts and regional development: limits and possibilities'. In Pyke et al. (eds), *Industrial Districts and Inter-Firm Co-operation in Italy*. International Institute for Labour Studies, Geneva.

Amin, A. and N. Thrift (1992) 'The local in the global'. Paper presented at the Fourth Annual Conference of the European Association for Evolutionary Political Economy, Paris, November.

Anastassopolous, J. P., G. Blanc and P. Dussauge (1987) *State-owned Multinationals*. Wiley, New York.

Andersen, C. (1993) *Getting European Community Help for Your Company: A Guide for Small and Medium-Sized Businesses*. Kogan Page, London.

Anderson, E. and A. T. Coughlan (1987) 'International market entry and expansion via independent or integrated channels of distribution'. *Journal of Marketing*, vol. 51, January, pp. 71–82.

Andréosso, B. (1986) 'Une Structure Industrielle Européenne Optimale: Concepts et Application á la Machine Outil/Robotique'. Unpublished PhD dissertation, University of Lille, France.

Andréosso, B. (1993) Dévaluation: l'Irlande est-elle un "cas spécial"? *Revue Banque*, no. 539, July, pp. 62–4.

Andréosso, B. (1993) 'Aperçu sur les relations CE-Bulgarie'. *Revue du Marché Commun et de l'Union Européenne*, no. 369, June, pp. 516–519.

Andréosso, B. and D. Jacobson (1991) 'Le double processus d'intégration spatiale et industrielle à la lumière du cas Irlandais'. *Revue du Marché Commun et de l'Union Européenne*, no. 350, September, pp. 648–58.

Andréosso, B. and C. Noonan (1995) 'Industrial specialisation and intra-industry—Central and Eastern Europe and the EU'. Paper read at Development Studies Association Annual Conference, September, University College, Dublin.

Andréosso, B. (1991) *The Clothing Industry and the Single European Market*. Special Report no. 2081, Economist Intelligence Unit, London and Fitzpatrick and Associates, Dublin.

Antonelli, C., P. Petit and G. Tahar (1992) *The Economics of Industrial Modernization*. Academic Press, London.

Aoki, M. (1984) *The Co-operative Game Theory of the Firm*. Clarendon Press, Oxford.

Aoki, M. (1990) 'Toward an economic model of the Japanese firm'. *Journal of Economic Literature*, vol. 28, no. 1, pp. 1–27.

Areeda, P. and D. F. Turner (1975) 'Predatory pricing and related practices under Section 2 of the Sherman Act'. *Harvard Law Review*, vol. 88, February, pp. 697–733.

Armstrong, M. and J. Vickers (1993) 'Price discrimination, competition and regulation', *Journal of Industrial Economics*, vol. 41, no. 4, pp. 335–59.

Arrow, K. J. and G. Debreu (1954) 'Existence of an equilibrium for a competitive economy'. *Econometrica*, vol. 22, pp. 265–90.

Asanuma, B. and T. Kikutani (1992) 'Risk absorption in Japanese subcontracting: a micro-econometric study of the automobile industry', *Journal of the Japanese and International Economies*, vol. 6, no. 1, pp. 1–29.

D'Asprement, C., J. J. Gabszewicz and J. F. Thisse (1979) 'On Hotelling's "Stability in Competition"'. *Econometrica*, vol. 47, pp. 1145–50.

Auerbach, P. (1988) *Competition: The Economics of Industrial Change*. Basil Blackwell, Oxford.

Axelrod, R. (1984) *The Evolution of Cooperation*. Basic Books, New York.

Baba, Y. (1987) 'Internationalisation and technical change in Japanese electronics firms, or why the product cycle does not work'. Paper presented at EIASM meeting on Internationalisation and Competition, Brussels, June.

Babbage, C. (1832) *On the Economy of Machinery and Manufactures*. Knight, London. Reprinted (1993) Routledge/Thoemmes Press, London.

Bagwell, K. and G. Ramey (1994) 'Coordination economies, advertising and search behaviour in retail markets'. *American Economic Review*, vol. 84, no. 3, pp. 498–517.

Bailey, E. E. (1981) 'Contestability and the design of regulatory and antitrust policy'. *American Economic Review*, vol. 71, no. 2, pp. 179–83.

Bailey, E. E. and J. C. Panzer (1981) 'The contestability of airline markets during the transition to deregulation'. *Law and Contemporary Problems*, vol. 44, no. 1, pp. 125–45.

Bailey, M. N. (1993) 'Review of: *International Productivity and Competitiveness*'. *Journal of Economic Literature*, vol. 31, no. 3, pp. 1483–4.

Bain, J. S. (1941) 'The profit rate as a measure of monopoly power'. *Quarterly Journal of Economics*, vol. 55, February, pp. 271–93.

Bain, J. S. (1951) 'Relation of profit rate to industry concentration: American manufacturing 1936–40'. *Quarterly Journal of Economics*, vol. 65, August, pp. 293–323.

Bain, J. S. (1956) *Barriers to New Competition*. Harvard University Press, Cambridge, MA.

Bain, J. S. (1958) *Industrial Organization*. Wiley, New York.

Bain, J. S. (1968) *Industrial Organization*, 2nd edition. Wiley, New York.

Bain and Company (1989) French industry in the global marketplace. Strategies for the future. France 300 Research Programme carried out on behalf of the French Ministry of Industry, Paris, September.

Balassa, B. (1965) 'Trade liberalisation and "revealed" comparative advantage'. *The Manchester School Economic and Social Studies*, vol. 33, pp. 99–124.

Balassa, B. (1967) 'Trade creation and trade diversion in the European Common Market'. *Economic Journal*, vol. 77, pp. 1–21.

Balassa, B. (1975) 'Trade creation and trade diversion in the European Common Market: an appraisal of the evidence'. In Balassa (ed.), *European Economic Integration*. North-Holland, Amsterdam.

Balassa, B. (1977) 'A stages approach to comparative advantage'. World Bank Staff Working Papers, no. 256.

Balassa, B. and C. Balassa (1984) 'Industrial protection in the developed countries'. *World Economy*, vol. 7, no. 2, pp. 179–96.

Balcombe, R. J., J. M. Hopkins and K. Penet (1988) *Bus Deregulation in Great Britain*. Research Report, no. 161.

Bance, P. (1992) 'Europe industrielle: la politique communautaire en question'. *Problèmes Economiques*, no. 2261, February, pp. 1–9.

Barnett, C. (1986) *The Audit of War*, Macmillan, London.

Baumol, W. J. (1967) *Business Behavior, Value and Growth*. Harcourt Brace Jovanovich, New York.

Baumol, W. J. (1979) 'Quasi-permanence of price reductions: a policy for prevention of predatory pricing'. *Yale Law Journal*, vol. 89, no. 1, pp. 1–26.

Baumol, W. J. (1984) 'Towards a theory of public enterprise'. *Atlantic Economic Journal*, vol. 12, no. 1, pp. 13–19.

Baumol, W. J. and R. D. Willig (1986) 'Contestability: developments since the book'. *Oxford Economic Papers*, vol. 38, November, supplement, pp. 9–36.

Baumol, W. J., J. C. Panzar and R. D. Willig (1982) *Contestable Markets and the Theory of Industrial Structure*. Harcourt Brace Jovanovich, New York.

Becattini, G. (1990) 'The Marshallian industrial district as a socio-economic notion'. In Pyke, Becattini and Sengenberger (eds), *Industrial Districts and Inter-Firm Co-operation in Italy*. International Institute for Labour Studies, Geneva.

Beggs, J. (1982) 'Long run trends in patenting'. Working Paper no. 952, National Bureau of Economic Research, Washington DC.

Beije, P. R. *et al.* (eds) (1987) *A Competitive Future for Europe? Towards a New European Industrial Policy*. Croom Helm, New York.

Benton, L. (1992) 'The emergence of industrial districts in Spain: industrial restructuring and diverging regional responses'. In Pyke and Sengenberger (eds) *Industrial Districts and Local Economic Regeneration*. International Institute for Labour Studies, Geneva.

Benzing, C. (1990) 'The determinants of aggregate merger activity: before and after-Celler-Kefauver'. *Review of Industrial Organization*, vol. 6, no. 1.

Berle, A. A. and G. C. Means (1932) *The Modern Corporation and Private Property*. Macmillan, New York.

Bernard, J. and A. Torre (1991) 'L'Enigme du Chainon Manquant, ou l'Absence des Strategies dans les Verifications Empiriques du Paradigme S.C.P.'. *Revue d'Economie Industrielle*, no. 57, 3rd quarter, pp. 93–105.

Bernhardt, I. and K. D. Mackenzie (1968) 'Measuring seller unconcentration, segmentation, and product differentiation'. *Western Economic Journal*, vol. 6, December, pp. 395–403.

Bernstein, J. and M. Nadiri (1989) 'Research and development and intra-industry spillovers: an empirical application of duality theory'. *Review of Economic Studies*, vol. 56, pp. 249–69.

Bertrand, J. (1883) 'Théorie mathématique de la richesse sociale'. *Journal des Savants*, September, pp. 499–508.

Besanko, D. and M. K. Perry (1994) 'Exclusive dealing in a spatial model of retail competition'. *International Journal of Industrial Organization*, vol. 12, no. 3, pp. 297–329.

Best, M. H. (1990) *The New Competition*. Polity Press, Cambridge.

Bianchi, P. (1995) 'Italy: crisis of an introvert state'. In Hayward (ed.), *Industrial Enterprise and European Integration*. Oxford University Press, Oxford.

Bianchi, P. and L. Forlai (1993) 'The domestic applicance industry 1945–1991'. In de Jong, (ed.), *The Structure of European Industry*. Kluwer, Dordrecht.

Bigarelli, D. and P. Crestanello (1994) 'An analysis of the changes in the knitwear/clothing district of Carpi during the 1980s'. *Entrepreneurship and Regional Development*, vol. 6, no. 2, pp. 117–44.

Bingham, T. (1985) *Banking and Monetary Policy*. OECD, Paris.

Blahó, A. and L. Halpern (1995) 'Stabilisation, crisis and structural change in Hungary'. In Landesmann and Székely (eds), *Industrial Restructuring and Trade Reorientation in Eastern Europe*. Cambridge University Press, Cambridge.

Blair, R. D. and D. L. Kaserman (1978) 'Uncertainty and the incentive for vertical integration'. *Southern Economic Journal*, vol. 45, July, pp. 266–72.

Blair, R. D. and D. L. Kaserman (1985) *Antitrust Economics*. Richard D. Irwin, Homewood, Ill.

Böckem, S. (1994) 'A generalized model of horizontal product differentiation'. *Journal of Industrial Economics*, vol. 42, no. 3, September, pp. 287–98.

Bradburd, R. M. and A. M. Over (1982) 'Organizational costs, "sticky" equilibria and critical levels of concentration'. *The Review of Economics and Statistics*, vol. 64, February, pp. 50–8.

Braendgaard, A. (1986) 'Danish industrial policy: liberalism revised or revisited'. In G. Hall (ed.), *European Industrial Policy*. Croom Helm, London.

Brimelow, P. (1994) 'Taxation without representation'. *Forbes*, vol. 153, no. 2, pp. 74–5.

Brittan, S. (1990) 'Conditions of progress: determinants of industrial success'. *Financial Times*, 24 June, 1990.

Brooks, D. G. (1973) 'Buyer concentration: a forgotten element in market structure models'. *Industrial Organization Review*, vol. 1, no. 3, pp. 151–163.

Brozen, Y. (1970) 'The Antitrust Task Force Deconcentration Recommendation'. *Journal of Law and Economics*, vol. 13, October, pp. 279–92.

Brülhart, M. and d. McAleese (1993) 'Intra-industry trade, adjustment and the EC Single Market: the Irish experience'. Unpublished, Trinity College Dublin, December.

Buckley, P. J. and B. R. Roberts (1982) *European Direct Investment in the USA Before World War 1*. Macmillan, London.

Bugbee, B. W. (1967) *Genesis of American Patent and Copyright Law*. Public Affairs Press, Washington DC.

Bullock, C. J. (1901) 'Trust literature: a survey and criticism'. *Quarterly Journal of Economics*, vol. 15, February, pp. 167–217.

Button, K. J. and T. G. Weyman-Jones (1993) 'X-inefficiency and regulatory regime shift in the UK'. *Journal of Evolutionary Economics*, vol. 3, no. 4, pp. 269–84.

Button, K. J. and T. G. Weyman Jones (1994) 'X-efficiency and technical efficiency'. *Public Choice*, vol. 89, nos 1–2, pp. 83–104.

Byers, J. D. and D. A. Peel (1994) 'Linear and non-linear models of economic time series: an introduction with applications to industrial economics'. In Cable (ed.), *Current Issues in Industrial Economics*. Macmillan, London.

Caballero, S. F. and M. Catinat (1992) 'European technology policy and cohesion: a reconciliation in practice'. *Revue d'Economie Industrielle*, no. 59, 1st quarter, pp. 192–203.

Cable, J. (1994) 'Introduction and overview: recent developments in industrial economics'. In J. Cable (ed.), *Current Issues in Industrial Economics*. Macmillan, London.

Cable, J., A. Carruth and A. Dixit (1994) 'Oligopoly and welfare'. In J. Cable (ed.), *Current Issues in Industrial Economics*. Macmillan, London.

Camagni, R. P. (1991) 'Regional deindustrialization and revitalization processes in Italy'. In L. Rodwin and H. Sazanami (eds), *Industrial Change and Regional Economic Transformation: The Experience of Western Europe*. HarperCollins, London.

Campbell, D. (ed.) (1983) *Legal Aspects of Doing Business in Western Europe*. Kluwer, Dordrecht.

Cantwell, J. (1989) *Technological Innovation and Multinational Corporations*. Basil Blackwell, Cambridge and Oxford.

Cantwell, J. A. (1991) 'The international agglomeration of R&D'. In M. Casson (ed.), *Global Research Strategy and International Competitiveness*. Basil Blackwell, Cambridge and Oxford.

Cantwell, J. (ed.) (1992) *Multinational Investment in Modern Europe: Strategic Interaction in the Integrated Community*. Edward Elgar, Aldershot.

Carlton, D. W. (1979) 'Vertical integration in competitive markets under uncertainty'. *Journal of Industrial Economics*, vol. 27, March, pp. 189–209.

Carpenter, G. S., R. Glazer and K. Nakamoto (1994) 'Meaningful brands from meaningless differentiation—the dependence on irrelevant attributes'. *Journal of Marketing Research*, vol. 31, no. 3, pp. 339–50.

Castells, M. and P. Hall (1994) *Technolopoles of the World: The Making of 21st Century Industrial Complexes*. Routledge, London.

Catinat, M. (1989) Les conditions de réussite du grand marché intérieur. Concrétiser les opportunités. *Economie et Statistique*, nos 217–218, January–February, pp. 97–115.

Caves, R. E. (1971) 'International corporations: the industrial economics of foreign investment'. *Economica*, vol. 38, February, pp. 1–27.

Caves, R. E. (1991) 'Growth of large enterprises and their market environments'. In P. de Wolf (ed.), *Competition in Europe: Essays in Honour of H.W. de Jong*. Kluwer Academic, Dordrecht.

Caves, R. E. and M. E. Porter (1977) 'From entry barriers to mobile barriers: conjectural decisions and continued deterrence to new competition'. *Quarterly Journal of Economics*, vol. 91, pp. 241–61.

Caves, R. E. and M. E. Porter (1978) 'Market structure, oligopoly and stability of market shares'. *Journal of Industrial Economics*, vol. 26, no. 4, pp. 289–313.

CEC (Commission of the European Communities) (1965) *Mémorandum sur le problème de la concentration dans le marché commun*. CEC, Brussels.

CEC (1970) *Industrial policy in the Community: Memorandum from the Commission to the Council*. Colonna Report, CEC, Brussels.

CEC (1973) *Memorandum on the Technological and Industrial Policy Programme*. Spinelli Memorandum, CEC, Brussels.

CEC (1977) *VIth Report on Competition Policy*. CEC, Brussels.

CEC (1983) *XIIth Report on Competition Policy*. CEC, Brussels.

CEC (1985a) *Completing the Internal Market*. COM (85) 310 final. CEC, Brussels.

CEC (1985b) *Towards a Technology Policy*. COM (85) 530, final, CEC, Brussels.

CEC (1988) *The Cost of Non-Europe in Public Sector Procurement*, vol. 5, Part A. CEC, Brussels.

CEC (1989) *First Survey on State Aids in the European Community*. Luxemburg.

CEC (1990) *Industrial Policy in an Open Competitive Environment. Guidelines for a Community Approach*. COM (90) 556 final. CEC, Brussels.

CEC (1991) *XXIst Report on Competition Policy*. CEC, Brussels.

CEC (1992) *Third Survey on State Aids in the EC in the Manufacturing and Certain Other Sectors*. Luxemburg.

CEC (1993a) *The Opening-up of Public Procurement*. DG Internal Market and Industrial Affairs, Luxemburg. CEC, Brussels.

CEC (1993b) *Report from the Commission on the State of the Shipbuilding Industry in the Community—Situation in 1992*. COM (93) 562 final, Brussels, 16 November 1993. CEC, Brussels.

CEC (1993c) *The European Community as a World Trade Partner*. European Economy, no. 52. CEC, Brussels.

CEC (1993d) *XXIIIrd Report on Competition Policy*. CEC, Brussels.

CEC (1993e) *European Economy, Social Europe*. CEC, Brussels.

CEC (1994) *Intermediate Report on the Restructuring of the Steel Industry*. COM (94), 125 final, CEC, Brussels.

CEC (various years) *Panorama of EC Industries*. CEC, Brussels.

Cecchini, P. (1988) *1992: The European Challenge: The Benefits of a Single Market*, Gower, Aldershot.

Chamberlin, E. H. (1933) *The Theory of Monopolistic Competition*. Harvard University Press, Cambridge, MA.

Chamberlin, E. H. (1962) *The Theory of Monopolistic Competition, 8th edn*. Harvard University Press, Cambridge, MA.

Chandler, A. D., Jr (1984) 'The emergence of managerial capitalism'. *Business History Review*, vol. 58, no. 4, pp. 473–503.

Chandler, A. D., Jr (1990) *Scale and Scope: The Dynamics of Industrial Capitalism*. Belknap/Harvard University Press, Cambridge, MA.

Chandler, A. D. (1992a) 'What is a firm?' *European Economic Review*, vol. 36, nos 2/3, pp. 483–92. (This is a paper presented at the Sixth Annual Congress of the European Economics Association, Aug./Sept. 1991, and is an earlier version of Chandler, 1992b.)

Chandler, A. D. (1992b) 'Organizational capabilities and the economic history of the industrial enterprise'. *The Journal of Economic Perspectives*, vol. 6, no. 3, pp. 79–100.

Chang, Ha-Joon (1994) *The Political Economy of Industrial Policy*. Macmillan, London.

Chan-Lee, J. and R. Torres (1987) 'q de Tobin et taux d'accumulation en France'. *Annales d'Economie et de Statistique*, no. 5, Jan./March, pp. 37–48.

Charbit, C., J. Ravix, and P. M. Romani, (1991) 'Sous-traitance et intégration industrielle européenne'. *Revue d'Economie Industrielle*, no. 55, 1st quarter, no. spécial, pp. 178–89.

Chen, K. C., G. L. Hite and D. C. Cheng (1989) 'Barriers to entry, concentration, and Tobin's q ratio'. *Quarterly Journal of Business and Economics*, vol. 28, no. 2, pp. 32–49.

Chesnais, F. (1992) 'National systems of innovation, foreign direct investment and the operations of multinational enterprises'. In B.-Å Lundvall (ed.), *National Systems of Innovation*. Pinter, London.

Chesnais, F. (1993) 'The French national system of innovation'. In R. R. Nelson (ed.) *National Innovation Systems*. Oxford University Press, Oxford.

Chowdhury, A. and Y. Islam (1993) *The Newly Industrialising Economies of East Asia*. Routledge, London.

Christensen, J. L. (1992) 'The role of finance in national systems of innovation'. In B.-Å Lundvall (ed.), *National Systmes of Innovation*. Pinter, London.

Church, C. H. and D. Phinnemore (1994) *European Union and European Community*. Harvester Wheatsheaf, Hemel Hempstead.

Clark, J. M. (1940) 'Towards a concept of workable competition'. *American Economic Review*, vol. 30, pp. 241–56.

Clark, N. and C. Juma (1987) *Long Run Economics: An Evolutionary Approach to Economic Growth*. Pinter, London.

Coase, R. H. (1937) 'The nature of the firm'. *Economica*, vol. 4, November, pp. 386–405. Reprinted as Chapter Two in Coase, R. H. (1988) *The Firm, the Market and the Law*. University of Chicago Press, Chicago.

Coase, R. H. (1992) 'The institutional structure of production'. *American Economic Review*, vol. 82, no. 4, September, pp. 713–19.

Coghlan, A. (1995) 'A very British tragedy?' *New Scientist*, no. 1973, 15 April, pp. 12–13.

Cohen, E. (1995) 'France: national champions in search of a mission'. In J. Hayward (ed.), *Industrial Enterprise and European Integration*. Oxford University Press, Oxford.

Cohendet, P., P. Llerena and A. Sorge (1992) 'Technological diversity and coherence in Europe: an analytical overview'. *Revue d'Economie Industrielle*, no. 59, 1st quarter, pp. 9–26.

Cole, J. and F. Cole (1993) *The Geography of the European Community*. Routledge, London and New York.

Colijn, G. J. (1987) 'Non-strategic aspects of SDI'. Working Paper no. 45, Department of Politics, University of Warwick.

Collins, N. R. and L. E. Preston (1968) *Concentration and Price–Cost Margins in Manufacturing Industries*, University of California Press, Berkeley.

Collins, N. R. and L. E. Preston (1969) 'Price–cost margins and industry structure'. *Review of Economics and Statistics*, vol. 51, August, pp. 271–86.

Comanor, W. S. and T. A. Wilson (1967) 'Advertising, market structure and performance'. *Review of Economics and Statistics*, vol. 49, pp. 423–40.

Comanor, W. S. and T. A. Wilson (1979) 'The effect of advertising on competition: a survey'. *Journal of Economic Literature*, vol. 17, pp. 453–76.

Cooke, P. and K. Morgan (1990) 'Learning through networking: regional innovation and the lessons of Baden-Wurttemberg'. Regional Industrial Research, Cardiff, Report no. 5, May.

Corbino, E. (1962) *L'Economia Italiana dal 1860 al 1960*. Zanichelli Editore, Bologna.

Corden, W. (1972) 'Economies of scale and customs union theory'. *Journal of Political Economy*, vol. 80, pp. 465–75.

Coriat, B. and P. Petit (1991) 'Deindustrialization and tertiarization: towards a new economic regime?' In A. Amin and M. Dietrich (eds), *Towards a New Europe?* Edward Elgar, Aldershot.

Cournot, A. (1838) *Recherches sur les Principes Mathématiques de la Théories des Richesses*. Hachette, Librairie de l'Université Royale de France, Paris. Reprinted in 1980 by Librairie Philosophique J. Vrin, Paris.

Cowling, K. (1976) 'On the theoretical specification of industrial structure–performance relationship'. *European Economic Review*, vol. 8, July, pp. 1–14.

Cowling, K. and M. Waterson (1976) 'Price–cost margins and market structure'. *Economica*, vol. 43, August, pp. 267–74.

Cowling, K. *et al.* (1980) *Mergers and Economic Performance*. Cambridge University Press, Cambridge.

Cox, A. and G. Watson (1995) 'The European Community and the restructuring of Europe's national champions'. In J. Hayward (ed.), *Industrial Enterprise and European Integration: From National to International Champions in Western Europe*. Oxford University Press, Oxford.

Crum, W. L. (1933) *Corporate Size and Earning Power*. Harvard University Press, Cambridge, MA.

Cubbin, J. (1981) 'Advertising and the theory of entry barriers'. *Economica*, vol. 48, August, pp. 289–98.

Curzon Price, V. (1991) 'The threat of "Fortress Europe" from the development of social and industrial policies at a European level'. *Außenwirtschaft*, St Gallen. vol. 46, no. 2, July, pp. 119–38.

Dalton, J. A. and D. W. Penn (1976) 'The concentration–profitability relationship: is there a critical concentration ratio?' *Journal of Industrial Economics*, vol. 25, December.

Dankbaar, B., J. Groenewegen and H. Schenk (eds) (1990) *Perspectives in Industrial Organization: Studies in Industrial Organization*, vol. 13. Kluwer Academic, Dordrecht.

Datta-Chaudhuri, M. (1990) 'Market failure and government failure'. *Journal of Economic Perspectives*, vol. 4, no. 3.

Davies, S., P. Geroski and A. Vlassopoulos (1991) 'La concentration au Royaume-Uni'. *Revue du Marché Commun et de l'Union Européenne*, no. 350, September, pp. 646–7.

Davies, S. and B. Lyons (1988) 'Introduction'. In Davies *et al.* (eds), *Economics of Industrial Organisation*. Longman, London.

Davis, L. A. (1991) 'Technology intensity of US, Canadian and Japanese manufacturers output and exports'. In J. Niosi (ed.), *Technology and National Competitiveness: Oligopoly, Technological Innovation and International Competition*. McGill-Queen's University Press, Buffalo.

Deardorff, A. and R. Stern (1983) 'Economic effects of the Tokyo Round'. *Southern Economic Journal*, vol. 49, no. 3, pp. 605–24.

de Bandt, J. (1983) '*A propos de la reconquête du marché intérieur*'. *Les Cahiers français*, no. 212, pp. 62–73.

de Bandt, J. (1987) 'French industrial policies: successes and failures'. In Beije *et al.* (eds), *A Competitive Future for Europe?* Croom Helm, New York.

de Bernis, G. (1990) 'Investissement extérieur direct et systèmes productifs en France et au Japon'. In A. Androuais (ed.), *L'Investissement extérieur direct*. University Press, Grenoble.

Demsetz, H. (1973) 'Industry structure, market rivalry and public policy', *Journal of Law and Economics*, vol. 16.

Demsetz, H. (1974) 'Two systems of belief about monopoly'. In H. Goldschmid, H. M. Mann and J. F. Weston (eds), *Industrial Concentration: The New Learning*. Little Brown, Boston.

Demsetz, H. (1988) 'The theory of the firm revisited'. *Journal of Law, Economics and Organization*, vol. 4, no. 1, pp. 141–61.

de Jong, H. W. (1990) 'The takeover market in Europe: control structures and the performance of large companies compared'. *Review of Industrial Organization*, vol. 6, no. 1.

de Jong, H. W. (ed.) (1993) *The Structure of European Industry*. Kluwer Academic, Dordrecht.

Del Monte, Alfredo (1977) *Politica Regionale e Sviluppo Economico*, F. Angeli, Italy.

Denison, E. F. (1985) *Trends in American Economic Growth, 1929–1982*. Brookings, Washington DC.

Devine, P. J. *et al.* (1985) *An Introduction to Industrial Economics*. Allen and Unwin, London.

de Wolf, P. (ed.) (1991) *Competition in Europe: Essays in Honour of Henk W. de Jong*. Kluwer Academic, Dordrecht.

de Wolf, P. (1993) 'The pharmaceutical industry: towards one single market?' In H. W. de Jong (ed.), *The Structure of European Industry*. Kluwer Academic, Dordrecht.

Dicken, P. (1992) *Global Shift*. Macmillan, London.

Dicken, P. and P. E. Lloyd (1990) *Location in Space: Theoretical Perspectives in Economic Geography*. Harper and Row, New York.

Dickson, V. A. (1991) 'The relationship between concentration and prices and concentration and costs'. *Applied Economics*, vol. 23, no. 1A, pp. 101–6.

Diebold, W. (1982) 'Past and future industrial policy in the United States'. In J. Pinder (ed.), *National Industrial Strategies and the World Economy*. Croom Helm, London.

Dierickx, I., C. Matutes and D. Neven (1991) 'Cost differences and survival in declining industries: a case for "picking winners"?' *European Economic Review*, vol. 35, pp. 1507–28.

Dixit, A. (1979) 'A model of duopoly suggesting a theory of entry barriers'. *Bell Journal of Economics*, vol. 10, Spring, pp. 20–32.

Dixit, A. and V. Norman (1978) 'Advertising and welfare'. *Bell Journal of Economics*, vol. 9, Spring, pp. 1–17.

Dodgson, J. S., Y. Katsoulacos and R. W. S. Pryke (1990) *Predatory Behaviour in Aviation*. Report for the Commission of the European Communities.

Dodgson, M. and R. Rothwell (eds) (1994) *Handbook of Industrial Innovation*. Edward Elgar, Aldershot.

Doeringer, P. and M. Piore (1971) *Internal Labour Markets and Manpower Analysis*. D.C. Heath and Co., Boston, MA.

Domowitz, I., R. G. Hubbard and B. C. Petersen (1986) 'Business cycles and the relationship between concentration and price–cost margins'. *Rand Journal of Economics*, vol. 17, spring, pp. 1–17.

Donaldson, G. and J. W. Lorsch (1983) *Decision Making at the Top*. Basic Books, New York.

Donsimoni, M. P. and M. Kambouri (1989) 'The SCP paradigm revisited'. Working Paper no. 8506, University Catholique de Louvain.

Dorfman, R. and P. O. Steiner (1954) 'Optimal advertising and optimal quality'. *American Economic Review*, vol. 44, December, pp. 826–36.

Dosi, G. *et al.* (eds) (1988) *Technical Change and Economic Theory*. Frances Pinter, London.

Dosi, G. (1990) 'Finance, innovation and industrial change'. *Journal of Economic Behavior and Organization*, vol. 13, no. 3, pp. 299–313.

Dosi, G. and L. Orsenigo (1988) 'Structure Industrielle et Evolution Technologique'. In A. Heertje (ed), *Innovation, Technologie et Finance*. Basil Blackwell, Oxford.

Douma, S. and H. Schreuder (1992) *Economic Approaches to Organizations*. Prentice-Hall, Hemel Hempstead, UK.

Downie, J. (1958) *The Competitive Process*. Duckworth, London.

Duchêne, F. and G. Shepherd (eds) (1987) *Managing Industrial Change in Western Europe*. Pinter, London.

Dunning, J. H. (1988) *Explaining International Production*. HarperCollins, London.

Dunning, J. H. (1992) 'The global economy, domestic governance strategies and transnational corporations: interactions and policy implications'. *Transnational Corporations*, vol. 1, no. 3, pp. 7–45.

Dunning, J. H. (1993) *The Globalization of Business*. Routledge, London and New York.

Dunning, J. H. and P. Robson (1987) 'Multinational corporate integration and regional economic integration'. *Journal of Common Market Studies*, vol. 26, no. 2.

Earl-Slater, A. (1993) 'Pharmaceuticals'. In P. Johnson (ed.), *European Industries*. Edward Elgar, Aldershot.

Eatwell, J., M. Milgate and P. Newman (eds) (1987) *The New Palgrave*. Macmillan, London.

Eck, J. F. (1990) 'Forces et Faiblesses de l'Industrie'. In *Histoire de l'Economie Française depuis 1945*, pp. 82–110. Cursus, Paris.

Eden, L. (1991) 'Bringing the firm back in: multinationals in international political economy'. *Millenium: Journal of International Studies*, vol. 20, no. 2, pp. 197–224.

Edquist, C. and B.-Å. Lundvall (1993) 'Comparing small Nordic systems of innovation'. In Nelson (ed.), *National Systems of Innovation*. Oxford University Press, Oxford.

Edwards, C. D. (1955) 'Conglomerate bigness as a source of power'. In *Business Concentration and Price Policy*. National Bureau of Economic Research conference report, Princeton University Press, Princeton NJ.

Edwards, G. (1982) 'Four sectors: textiles, man-made fibres, shipbuilding, aircraft'. In J. Pinder (ed.), *National Industrial Strategies and the World Economy*. Croom Helm, London.

Ellis, W. (1826) 'Effect of the employment of machinery upon the happiness of the working classes'. *Westminster Review*, vol. 5, January, Article IV. (Ref in B. L. Anderson (ed.) (1974) *Capital Accumulation in the Industrial Revolution*, J. M. Dent & Sons.)

Emerson, M. *et al.* (1988) *The Economics of 1992. The EC Commission's Assessment of the Economic Effects of Completing the Internal Market*. Oxford University Press, Oxford.

Epstein, Ralph C. (1931) 'Profits and size of firms in the automobile industry, 1919–27'. *American Economic Review*, vol. 21, December, pp. 636–47.

Esser, J. (1995) 'Germany: challenges to the old policy style'. In J. Hayward (ed.), *Industrial Enterprise and European Integration*. Oxford University Press, Oxford.

Estall, R. C. and R. O. Buchanan (1973) *Industrial Activity and Economic Geography*. Hutchinson, London.

Eurostat (1989) *Statistical Analysis of Extra-EC Trade in High-Tech Products*. Eurostat, Luxemburg.

Eurostat (1992) *Enterprises in Europe, 2nd Report*, Luxemburg.

Fama, E. F. (1980) 'Agency problems and the theory of the firm', *Journal of Political Economy*, vol. 88, April, pp. 288–307.

Fama, E. and M. C. Jensen (1983) 'The separation of ownership and control'. *Journal of Law and Economics*, vol. 26, no. 2, pp. 301–325.

Farrands, Chris and Peter Totterdill (1993) 'A rationale for an appropriate level of regulation in the European Community'. In R. Sugden (ed.), *Industrial Economic Regulation*. Routledge, London.

Ferguson, P. R. and G. J. Ferguson (1994) *Industrial Economics: Issues and Perspectives*. Macmillan, London.

Fisher, F. M. (1991) 'Organizing industrial organization: reflections on *The Handbook of Industrial Organization*'. *Brookings Papers on Economic Activity: Microeconomics*, pp. 201–225.

Fisher, F. M. and J. J. McGowan (1983) 'On the misuse of accounting rates of return to infer monopoly profits'. *American Economic Review*, vol. 73, no. 1, pp. 82–97.

Fisher, F. M., J. W. McKie and R. B. Mancke (1983) *IBM and the US Data Processing Industry: An Economic History*. Praeger, New York.

Fishwick, F. (1986) *Definition of the Relevant Market in Community Competition Policy*. Commission of the European Communities, Brussels.

Fishwick, F. (1993) 'The definition of the relevant market in the competition policy of the European Economic community'. *Revue d'Economie Industrielle*, no. 63, 1st trimester, pp. 174–192.

Focsaneanu, L. (1975) 'La jurisprudence de la Cour de Justice des C.E. en matière de concurrence: Marché des produits en consideration'. *Revue de Marché Commun*, no. 191, December.

Forges, F. and J.-F. Thisse (1992) 'Game theory and industrial economics: an introduction'. In G. Norman and M. La Manna (eds), *The New Industrial Economics*. Edward Elgar, Aldershot.

Forte, F. (1967) 'Should public goods be public?' *Papers on Non-Market Decision Making*, vol. 8, pp. 39–46.

Fox, E. M. (1983) 'Abuse of a dominant position under the Treaty of Rome—a comparison with US Law'. *Annual Proceedings of the Fordham Corporate Law Institute*, pp. 367–421.

Franko, L. G. (1976) *The European Multinationals: A Renewed Challenge to American and British Big Business*. Harper & Row, New York.

Franzmeyer, F. (1979) *Industrielle Strukturprobleme und sektorale Strukturpolitik in der Europäischen Gemeinschaft*. Duncker & Humbolt, Berlin.

Fraser, C. D. (1994) 'Conjectural Variations'. In J. Cable (ed.), *Current Issues in Industrial Economics*. Macmillan, London.

Freeman, C. (1982) *The Economics of Industrial Innovation*. Pinter, London.

Freeman, C. (1987) *Technology Policy and Economic Performance: Lessons from Japan*. Pinter, London and New York.

Freeman, C. (1988a) 'Japan: a new national system of innovation?' In G. Dosi *et al.* (eds), *Technical Change and Economic Theory*. Pinter, London.

Freeman, C. (1988b) 'Diffusion: La Propagation des Nouvelles Technologies dans les Entreprises, les Différents Secteurs et Etats'. In A. Heertje (ed.), *Innovation, Technologie et Finance*. Basil Blackwell, Oxford.

Freeman, C. (1994) 'Innovation and growth'. In M. Dodgson and R. Rothwell (eds), *Handbook of Industrial Innovation*. Edward Elgar, Aldershot.

Freeman, C., M. Sharp and W. Walker (eds) (1991) *Technology and the Future of Europe: Global Competition and the Environment in the 1990s*. Pinter, London.

Freeman, R. B. (ed.) (1994) *Working Under Different Rules*. Russell Sage Foundation, New York.

Friedman, M. (1962) *Capitalism and Freedom*. University of Chicago Press, Chicago.

Funke, M., S. Wadewitz and D. Willenbockel (1989) 'Tobin's Q and sectoral investment in West Germany and Great Britain: a pooled cross-section and time series study'. *Zeitschrift fur Wirtschafts und Sozialwissenschaften*, vol. 109, no. 3, pp. 399–420.

García Delgado, J. L. *et al.* (1989) *España—Economia*. Espasa-Calpe, Madrid.

Gardner, R. (1995) *Games for Business and Economics*. Wiley, New York.

Geithman, F. E., H. P. Marvel and L. W. Weiss (1981) 'Concentration, price, and critical concentration ratios'. *Review of Economics and Statistics*, vol. 63, August, pp. 346–53.

George, K. (1991) 'Public ownership versus privatisation'. In P. de Wolf (ed.), *Competition in Europe: Essays in Honour of Henk W. de Jong*. Kluwer, Dordrecht.

George, K. D., C. Joll and E. L. Link (1992) *Industrial Organisation: Competition, Growth and Structural Change*. Routledge, London.

Geroski, P. A. (1981) Specification and testing the profits–concentration relationship: some experiments for the UK. *Economica*, vol. 48, August 1981, pp. 279–288.

Geroski, P. A. (1987) 'Do dominant firms decline?' In Hay and Vickers (eds), *The Economics of Market Dominance*, Basil Blackwell, Oxford.

Geroski, P. A. (1991a) 'Domestic and foreign entry in the UK: 1983–1984'. In P. A. Geroski, and J. Schwalbach (eds), *Entry and Market Contestability: An International Comparison*. Blackwell, Oxford.

Geroski, P. A. (1991b) 'Innovation and the sectoral sources of UK productivity growth'. *Economic Journal*, vol. 101, Nov., pp. 1438–51.

Geroski, P. A. (1994) 'Entry and market share mobility'. In J. Cable (ed.), *Current Issues in Industrial Economics*. Macmillan, London.

Geroski, P. A. and A. Jacquemin (1985) 'Industrial change, barriers to mobility, and European industrial policy'. *Economic Policy*, vol. 1, November, pp. 169–218.

Geroski, P. A. and A. Jacquemin (1988) 'The persistence of profits: a European comparison'. *Economic Journal*, vol. 98, June, pp. 375–89.

Geroski, P. A. and J. Schwalbach (eds) (1991) *Entry and Market Contestability: An International Comparison*. Blackwell, Oxford and Cambridge.

Gibrat, R. (1931) *Les Inegalités Economiques*. Receuil Sirey, Paris.

Globerman, S. and J. W. Dean (1990) 'Recent trends in intra-industry trade and their implications for future trade liberalization'. *Weltwirtschaftliches Archiv*, vol. 126, no. 1, pp. 25–49.

Gowland, D. H. (1991) 'Financial policy after 1992'. In D. H. Gowland and S. James (eds), *Economic Policy after 1992*. Brookfield, Aldershot; Dartmouth, USA.

Grahl, J. and P. Teague (1990) *1992: The Big Market*. Lawrence and Wishart, London.

Grant, W. (1989) *Government and Industry: A Comparative Analysis of the US, Canada and the UK*. Edward Elgar, Aldershot.

Grant, W. (1995) 'Britain: the spectator state'. In J. Hayward (ed.), *Industrial Enterprise and European Integration*. Oxford University Press, Oxford.

Green, A. and D. Mayes (1991) 'Technical inefficiency in manufacturing industries'. *The Economic Journal*, vol. 101, May, pp. 523–38.

Green, E. J. and R. H. Porter (1984) 'Non-cooperative collusion under imperfect price information'. *Econometrica*, vol. 52.

Grether, E. T. (1970) 'Industrial organization: past history and future problems'. *American Economic Review*, vol. 60, p. 83.

Gribbin, D. (1991) 'The contribution of economists to the origins of UK competition policy'. In P. de Wolf (ed.), *Competition in Europe: Essays in Honour of Henk W. de Jong*. Kluwer, Dordrecht.

Griliches, Z. (1957) 'Hybrid corn: an exploration in the economics of technical change'. In Z. Griliches, (1988) *Technology, Education and Productivity: Early Papers with Notes to Subsequent Literature*. Blackwell, Oxford and New York.

Grubel, H. G. and P. J. Lloyd (1975) *Intra-Industry Trade: The Theory and Measurement of International Trade in Differentiated Products*. Macmillan, London.

Grünsteidl, W. (1990) 'An industrial policy for Europe'. *European Affairs*, Autumn.

Gual J. and D. Neven (1992) 'Deregulation of the European Banking Industry (1980–1991)'. CEPR Discussion Paper no. 703, August.

Hagedoorn, J. and J. Schakenraad (1990) 'Strategic partnering and technological co-operation'. In B. Dankbaar, J. Groenewegen and H. Schenk (eds), *Perspectives in Industrial Organization*. Kluwer, Dordrecht.

Hager, W. (1982) 'Industrial policy, trade policy, and European social democracy'. In J. Pinder (ed.), *National Industrial Strategies and the World Economy*. Croom Helm, London.

Haines, W. W. (1970) 'The profitability of large-size firms'. *Rivista Internazionale di Scienze Economiche e Commerciali*, vol. 17, no. 4, pp. 321–51.

Hall, M. and L. W. Weiss (1967) 'Firm size and profitability'. *Review of Economics and Statistics*, vol. 49, August, pp. 319–31.

Hall, P. (1994) *Innovation, Economics and Evolution: Theoretical Perspectives on Changing Technology in Economic Systems*. Harvester-Wheatsheaf, London.

Hall, R. L. and C. J. Hitch (1939) 'Price theory and business behaviour'. *Oxford Economic Papers*, vol. 2, May, pp. 12–45.

Hallgarten, G. W. F. and J. Radkau (1974) *Deutsche Industrie und Politik von Bismarck bis heute*. Europäische Verlagsanstalt, Frankfurt.

Hamill, J. (1992) 'Cross-border mergers, acquisitions and alliances in Europe'. In S. Young and J. Hamill (eds), *Europe and the Multinationals*. Edward Elgar, Aldershot.

Hannah, L. (1983) *The Rise of the Corporate Economy*, 2nd edn. Methuen, London.

Hansen, N. (1991) 'Factories in Danish fields: how high-wage, flexible production has succeeded in peripheral Jutland'. *International Regional Science Review*, vol. 14, no. 2, pp. 109–132.

Harbor, B. (1990) 'Defence electronics before and after 1992'. In G. Locksley (ed.), *The Single European Market*. Belhaven, London and New York.

Harrison, B. (1992) 'Industrial districts: old wine in new bottles?' *Regional Studies*, vol. 26, no. 5, pp. 469–83.

Harrop, J. (1989) *The Political Economy of Integration in the European Community*. Edward Elgar, Aldershot.

Hart, P. and R. Clarke (1979) 'Profit-margins, wages and oligopoly: a survey of the evidence for the UK'. Working Paper, University of Reading.

Hart, P. E. and E. Morgan (1977) 'Market structure and economic performance in the UK'. *Journal of Industrial Economics*, vol. 25, no. 3, pp. 177–193.

Haskel, J. and C. Martin (1994) 'Capacity and competition: empirical evidence on UK panel data'. *Journal of Industrial Economics*, vol. 42, no. 1, pp. 23–42.

Hawley, E. W. (1966) *The New Deal and the Problem of Monopoly*. Princeton University Press, Princeton.

Hay, D. A. and D. J. Morris (1991) *Industrial Economics and Organization: Theory and Evidence*. Oxford University Press, Oxford.

Hayek, F. A. (1949) *Individualism and Economic Order*. Routledge and Kegan Paul, London.

Hayward, J. (1995) 'Introduction: Europe's endangered industrial champions'. In J. Hayward (ed.), *Industrial Enterprise and European Integration. From National to International Champions in Europe*. Oxford University Press, Oxford.

Heertje, A. (1973) *Economics & Technical Change*. Weidenfeld and Nicolson, London.

Heertje, A. (ed.) (1983) *Investing in Europe's Future*. Blackwell, Oxford.

Heertje, A. (ed.) (1988) *Innovation, Technologie et Finance*. Published (in French) for the European Investment Bank by Basil Blackwell, Oxford.

Heertje, A. and M. Perlman (eds) (1990) *Evolving Technology and Market Structure: Studies in Schumpeterian Economics*. University of Michigan Press, Ann Arbor.

Heffernan, S. A. (1993) 'Competition in British retail banking'. *Journal of Financial Services Research*, vol. 7, no. 4, pp. 309–32.

Hertzendorf, M. N. (1993) 'I'm not a high-quality firm—but I play like one on TV'. *Rand Journal of Economics*, vol. 24, no. 2, pp. 236–47.

Hibou, B. (1993) 'Indicateurs d'avantages comparatifs et contrainte extérieure'. *Economies et Sociétés*, vol. 27, no. 9, pp. 41–68.

Hicks, J. R. (1935) 'Annual survey of economic theory: the theory of monopoly'. *Econometrica*, vol. 3, no. 1, pp. 1–20.

Hillman, A. (1982) Declining industries and political support for protectionist motives. *American Economic Review*, vol. 72, no. 5, pp. 1180–7.

Hirsch, S. (1967) *Location of Industry and International Competitiveness*. OUP, Oxford.

Hirschey, M. and J. L. Pappas (1993) *Instructor's Manual to Accompany Managerial Economics*. Dryden Press, Fort Worth.

Hitchens, D. M., K. Wagner and J. E. Birnie (1992) Measuring the contribution of product quality to competitiveness: a note on theory and policy. *The Economic and Social Review*, vol. 23, no. 4, July, pp. 455–63.

Hitiris, T. (1994) *European Community Economics*. Harvester Wheatsheaf, Hemel Hempstead.

Hobsbawm, E. J. (1987) *The Age of Empire 1875–1914*. Weidenfeld and Nicolson, London.

Hofstede, G. (1983) 'The cultural relativity of organizational practices and theories'. *Journal of International Business Studies*, vol. 14, no. 2, pp. 75–89.

Holmstrom, B. R. and J. Tirole (1989) 'The theory of the firm'. In R. Schmalensee and A. Willig (eds), *Handbook of Industrial Organization*. North-Holland, Amsterdam.

Hosomi, T. and A. Okumura (1982) 'Japanese industrial policy'. In J. Pinder (ed.), *National Industrial Strategies and the World Economy*. Croom Helm, London.

Hotelling, H. (1929) 'Stability in competition'. *Economic Journal*, vol. 39, pp. 41–57.

Hudson, W. E. (1985) 'The feasibility of a comprehensive US industrial policy', *Political Science Quarterly*, no. 100, pp. 461–78.

Hufbauer, G. C. (1965) *Synthetic Materials and the Theory of International Trade*. Duckworth, London.

Hunt, E. K. and H. J. Sherman (1990) *Economics: An Introduction to Traditional and Radical Views*. Harper & Row, New York.

Hurdle, G. J. *et al.* (1989) 'Concentration, potential entry, and performance in the airline industry'. *Journal of Industrial Economics*, vol. 38, no. 2, pp. 119–39.

Hyman, D. (1992) *Economics*. Irwin, Homewood, Ill.

Hymer, S. (1976) *The International Operations of National Firms: A Study of Direct Foreign Investment*. MIT Press (reprint of 1960 dissertation), Cambridge, MA.

Hymer, S. and P. Pashigian (1962) 'Firm size and rate of growth'. *Journal of Political Economy*, vol. 70, December, pp. 556–69.

Ijiri, Y. and H. A. Simon (1977) *Skew Distributions and the Sizes of Business Firms*. North-Holland, Amsterdam.

Imai, K.-I. (1989) 'Evolution of Japan's corporate and industrial networks. In Bo Carlsson (ed.) *Industrial Dynamics: Technological, Organizational and Structural Changes in Industries and Firms*. Kluwer, Dordrecht.

Insead (1990) *Removing the Barriers in Manufacturing*. Report on the 1990 Manufacturing Futures Survey, Fontainebleau.

IRDAC (1992) *Skill Shortages in Europe*. Industrial Research and Development Advisory Committee of the CEC, Special Report to the EC Commission, Brussels.

Ireland, N. J. (1992) 'Product differentiation and quality'. In Norman and La Manna (eds), *The New Industrial Economics*. Edward Elgar, Aldershot.

Itoh, M. *et al.* (1991) *Economic Analysis of Industrial Policy*. Harcourt Brace Jovanovich/Academic Press, San Diego.

Iwanek, M. (1992) 'Some issues in the transformation of ownership institutions in Poland'. *Journal of Institutional and Theoretical Economics*, vol. 148, no. 1, pp. 52–65.

Jacobs, D. and M. W. de Jong (1991) 'Industrial clusters and the competitiveness of The Netherlands'. TNO Policy Research, 90/NR/064, May.

Jacobson, D. S. (1977) 'The political economy of industrial location: the Ford Motor Company at Cork 1912–1926'. *Irish Economic and Social History*, vol. 4, pp. 36–55.

Jacobson, D. (1991) *Europe's Pharmaceutical Industry: Tackling the Single Market*. Special Report no. 2085, Economist Intelligence Unit, London.

Jacobson, D. (1994) 'The technological and infrastructural environment'. In N. Nugent and R. O'Donnell (eds), *The European Business Environment*. Macmillan, London.

Jacobson, D. and B. Andréosso (1988) 'Investment and industrial integration in Western Europe'. *Administration*, vol. 36, no. 2, pp. 165–85.

Jacobson, D. and B. Andréosso (1990) 'Ireland as a location for multinational investment'. In A. Foley and M. Mulreany (eds), *The Single European Market and the Irish Economy*. Institute of Public Administration, Dublin.

Jacobson, D. and R. Mack (1994) 'Core–periphery analysis: a tale of two nations'. Paper to the Regional Science Association International Conference in Dublin, October.

Jacobson, D. and D. O'Sullivan (1994) 'Analysing an industry in change: the Irish software manual printing industry'. *New Technology, Work and Employment*, vol. 9, no. 2, pp. 103–14.

Jacquemin, A. (1979) *Economie Industrielle Européenne: Structures de Marché et Stratégies d'Entreprises*, 2nd edn. Dunod, Paris.

Jacquemin, A. (1987a) 'Comportements collusifs et accords en recherche–développement'. *Revue d'Economie Politique*, vol. 97, no. 1, pp. 1–23.

Jacquemin, A. (1987b) *The New Industrial Organization: Market Forces and Strategic Behavior*. MIT Press, Cambridge, MA.

Jacquemin, A. (1990) 'Mergers and European policy'. In P. H. Admiraal (ed.), *Merger and Competition Policy in the European Community*, Basil Blackwell, Oxford.

Jacquemin, A. and H. W. de Jong (1976) *Markets, Corporate Behaviour and the State*. Nijhoff, The Hague.

Jacquemin, A. and L. Philips (1974) 'Concentration, size and performance of European firms'. Working Paper no. 7409, Institut des Sciences Economiques, Louvain.

Jacquemin, A. and A. Sapir (1987) 'Intra-EC trade: a sectoral analysis'. CEPS Working Paper, no. 24, January.

Jacquemin, A. and D. Wright (1993) 'Corporate strategies and European challenges—post-1992'. *Journal of Common Market Studies*, vol. 31, no. 1, pp. 525–73.

Jenny, F. and A. P. Weber (1974) 'Taux de profit et variables structurelles dans l'industrie manufacturiere française'. *Revue Economique*, November, Paris.

Johnson, C. (1984) 'The idea of industrial policy'. In C. Johnson (ed.), *The Industrial Policy Debate*. Institute for Contemporary Studies, San Francisco.

Johnson, P. (ed.) (1993) *European Industries: Structure, Conduct and Performance*. Edward Elgar, Aldershot.

Joskow, P. L. and A. K. Klevorick (1979) 'A framework for analyzing predatory pricing policy'. *Yale Law Journal*, vol. 89, no. 2, December, pp. 213–70.

Kaldor, N. (1934) 'The equilibrium of the firm'. *Economic Journal*, vol. 44, March, pp. 60–76.

Kaldor, N. (1950) 'The economic aspects of advertising'. *Review of Economic Studies*, vol. 18, pp. 1–27.

Kalirajan, K. P. and T. V. Varagunasingh (1992) 'In pursuit of identifying technical efficiency and X-efficiency'. *Journal of Economic Development*, vol. 17, no. 2, pp. 81–92.

Kay, J. A. (1990a) 'Identifying the strategic market'. *Business Strategy Review*, spring, pp. 2–24.

Kay, N. (1990b) 'Industrial collaboration and the Single European Market'. In G. Locksley (ed.), *The Single European Market*. Belhaven, London and New York.

Keck, O. (1993) 'The national system for technical innovation in Germany'. In R. R. Nelson (ed.), *National Innovation Systems*. Oxford University Press, Oxford.

Khalilzadeh-Shirazi (1974) 'Market structure and price–cost margins in UK manufacturing industries'. *Review of Economics and Statistics*, vol. 56, no. 1, pp. 67–76.

Khün, T. S. (1962) *The Structure of Scientific Revolutions*. Chicago University Press, Chicago.

Kim, E. H. and V. Singal (1993) 'Mergers and market power: evidence from the airline industry'. *American Economic Review*, vol. 83, no. 3, pp. 549–69.

Kirman, A. and N. Schueller (1990) 'Price leadership and discrimination in the European car market'. *Journal of Industrial Economics*, vol. 39, no. 1, pp. 69–91.

Kitschelt, H. (1991) 'Industrial governance structures, innovation strategies, and the case of Japan: sectoral or cross-national comparative analysis?' *International Organization*, vol. 45, no. 4, pp. 453–93.

Klein, B., R. G. Crawford and A. Alchian (1978) 'Vertical integration, appropriable rents and the competitive contracting process'. *Journal of Law and Economics*, vol. 21, no. 2, pp. 297–326.

Klodt, H. (1990) 'Technologietransfer und internationale wettbewerbsfähigkeit'. *Aussenwirtschaft*, vol. 45, no. 1, pp. 57–79.

Koch, J. V. (1980) *Industrial Organization and Prices*. Prentice-Hall, Englewood Cliffs, NJ.

Kojima, K. (1978) *Direct Foreign Investment, a Japanese Model of Multinational Business Operations*. Croom Helm, London.

Kotowitz, Y. and F. Mathewson (1979) 'Advertising, consumer information, and product quality'. *Bell Journal of Economics*, vol. 10, no. 2, pp. 566–88.

Koutsoyiannis, A. (1979) *Modern Microeconomics*. Macmillan, London.

Kreps, D. M. and R. Wilson (1982) 'Reputation and imperfect information'. *Journal of Economic Theory*, vol. 27, August, pp. 253–79.

Kristensen, P. H. (1992) 'Industrial districts in West Jutland, Denmark'. In F. Pyke and W. Sengenberger (eds), *Industrial Districts and Local Economic Regeneration*. International Institute for Labour Studies, Geneva.

Krugman, P. R. (1980) 'Scale economies, product differentiation and the pattern of trade'. *American Economic Review*, vol. 70, no. 5, pp. 950–9.

Krugman, P. R. (1983) 'New theories of trade among industrial countries'. *American Economic Review*, vol. 73, no. 2, pp. 343–7.

Krugman, P. R. (1987a) 'Is free trade *passé?*' *Journal of Economic Perspectives*, vol. 1, no. 2, pp. 131–44.

Krugman, P. R. (1987b) 'Economic integration in Europe: some conceptual issues'. In Tommaso Padoa-Schioppa (ed.), *Efficiency, Stability, and Equity: A Strategy for the Evolution of the Economic System of the European Community*. Oxford University Press, Oxford, pp. 117–40.

Krugman, P. R. (1989) 'Industrial organization and international trade'. In R. C. Schmalensee and R. D. Willig (eds), *Handbook of Industrial Organization*, vol. 2. North-Holland, Amsterdam, pp. 117–250.

Krugman, P. R. (1993) *Geography and Trade*. Leuven University Press, Leuven/MIT Press, Cambridge, MA.

Krugman, P. R. and M. Obstfeld (1991) *International Economics: Theory and Policy*. Harper-Collins, New York.

Kumps, A. M. (1974) *Le Conglomérat*. La Renaissance du Livre, Bruxelles.

Kumps, A. M. (1975) *Conglomerate Mergers: The Case of Great Britain*, Document de Travail, CRIDE, no. 751.

Kuznets, S. (1930) *Secular Movements in Production and Prices*. Houghton Mifflin, Boston and New York.

Lafay, G. and C. Herzog (1989) 'Vingt ans d'échanges internationaux. L'Europe sur la défensive'. *Economie et Statistique*, nos 217–18, January–February, pp. 29–36.

Lamberton, D. (1994) 'Innovation and intellectual property'. In M. Dodgson and R. Rothwell, (eds), *Handbook of Industrial Innovation*. Edward Elgar, Aldershot.

Lambin, J. J. (1976) *Advertising, Competition and Market Conduct in Oligopoly Over Time*. North-Holland, Amsterdam.

Lane, S. J. (1991) 'The determinants of investment in new technology'. *American Economic Review*, May, pp. 262–5.

Lanzillotti, R. F. (1957) 'Competitive price leadership: a critique of price leadership models'. *Review of Economics and Statistics*, vol. 39, February, pp. 56–64.

Lanzillotti, R. F. (1959) 'Pricing objectives in big companies', *American Economic Review*, vol. 48, December, pp. 921–40.

Lassudrie-Duchêne, B. (1971) 'La demande de différence et l'échange international'. Cahiers de l'ISEA, *Economies et Sociétés*, June.

Layson, S. K. (1994) 'Market opening under third-degree price discrimination'. *Journal of Industrial Economics*, vol. XLII, no. 3, pp. 335–40.

Lazonick, W. (1990a) 'Organizational integration in three industrial revolutions'. In A. Heertje and M. Perlman (eds), *Evolving Technology and Market Structure*. University of Michigan Press, Ann Arbor.

Lazonick, W. (1990b) *Value Creation on the Shop Floor: Organization and Technology in Capitalist Development*. Harvard University Press, Cambridge, MA.

Lazonick, W. (1991) *Business Organization and the Myth of the Market Economy*. Cambridge University Press, Cambridge.

Leibenstein, H. (1966) 'Allocative efficiency vs "X-efficiency"', *American Economic Review*, vol. 56, pp. 392–415.

Léonard, J. (1990) Mutations de l'investissement direct international et processus d'endettement du Tiers-Monde: des ambiguïtés théoriques aux difficultés de la mesure. In A. Androuais (ed.), *L'Investissement extérieur direct*. University Press, Grenoble.

Leonard, R. J. (1995) 'From parlour games to social science: von Neumann, Morgenstern, and the creation of game theory 1928–1944'. *Journal of Economic Literature*, vol. 33, no. 2, pp. 730–61.

Lerner, A. (1934) 'The concept of monopoly and the measurement of monopoly power'. *Review of Economic Studies*, vol. 1, June, pp. 157–75.

Levin, R. C. (1988) 'Appropriability, R&D spending and technological performance'. *American Economic Review*, vol. 78, no. 2, pp. 424–8.

Lewis, W. A. (1957) 'International competition in manufacturers'. *American Economic Review*, Papers and Proceedings, vol. 47, May.

Linda, R. (1988) 'The food and drinks industry: large firm strategies'. In H. W. de Jong (ed.) *The Structure of European Industry*. Kluwer, Dordrecht.

Linda, R. (1991) 'Industrial and market concentration in Europe'. In P. de Wolf (ed.), *Competition in Europe: Essays in Honour of Henk W. de Jong*. Kluwer, Dordrecht.

Lindenberg, E. and S. Ross (1981) 'Tobin's q ratio and industrial organization'. *Journal of Business*, vol. 54, January, pp. 1–32.

Linder, S. (1961) *An Essay on Trade and Transformation*. John Wiley, New York.

Lindert, P. H. (1991) *International Economics*, 9th edn. Irwin, Boston.

Lipsey, R. and K. Lancaster (1956) 'The general theory of the second best'. *Review of Economic Studies*, vol. 56, pp. 11–32.

Lissoni, F. and J. S. Metcalfe (1994) 'Diffusion of innovation ancient and modern: a review of the main themes'. In M. Dodgson and R. Rothwell (eds), *Handbook of Industrial Innovation*. Edward Elgar, Aldershot.

List, F. (1841) *Das nationale System der politischen Ökonomie*. Published in English (1909). Dent, London.

List, F. (1842) 'Die Ackerverfassung, die Zwergwirtschaft, und die Auswanderung'. *Deutsche Vierteljahrschrif*, vol. IV, pp. 106–91.

Loasby, B. J. (1990) 'Problem-solving institutions'. *Scottish Journal of Political Economy*, vol. 37, May, pp. 197–202.

Locksley, G. (ed.) (1990) *The Single European Market and the Information and Communication Technologies*. Belhaven, London and New York.

Lorenz, E. H. (1994) 'Review of: *Prices, Quality and Trust: Inter-firm Relations in Britain and Japan*, by M. Sako. Cambridge University Press, Cambridge'. *Journal of Economic Literature*, vol. 32, no. 4, pp. 1918–20.

Lovasy, G. (1941) 'International trade under imperfect competition'. *Quarterly Journal of Economics*, vol. 55, August, pp. 567–83.

Lundvall, B.-Å (1992) 'Introduction'. In B.-Å Lundvall (ed.) *National Systems of Innovation: Towards a Theory of Innovation and Interactive Learning*. Pinter, London.

Lynch, R. (1990) *European Business Strategies: An Analysis of Europe's Top Companies*. Kogan Page, London.

Lyons, B. R. (1984) 'The pattern of international trade in differentiated products: an incentive for the existence of multi-national firms'. In H. Kierzkowski (ed.), *Monopolistic Competition and International Trade.* Clarendon Press, Oxford.

McCloskey, D. N. (1990) *If You're So Smart*. University of Chicago Press, Chicago.

MacDougall, G. D. A. (1960) 'The benefits and costs of private investment from abroad: a theoretical approach'. *Economic Record*, vol. 36, pp. 13–35.

McFarland, H. (1988) 'Evaluating *q* as an alternative to the rate of return in measuring profitability'. *Review of Economics and Statistics*, vol. 70, no. 4, pp. 614–22.

McGovern, S. (1994) 'A Lakatosian approach to changes in international trade theory'. *History of Political Economy*, vol. 26, no. 3, pp. 351–68.

McGrath, B. (1995) 'HB still freezing out ice cream competition'. *Irish Times*, 11 March.

McGuire, J. W., J. S. Y. Chiu and A. O. Elbing (1962) 'Executive incomes, sales and profits'. *American Economic Review*, no. 52, September, pp. 753–61.

Machlup, F. (1946) 'Marginal analysis and empirical research'. *American Economic Review*, vol. 36, September, pp. 519–54.

Machlup, F. (1952) *The Political Economy of Monopoly*. Johns Hopkins, Baltimore, MD.

Machlup, F. (1967) 'Theories of the firm: marginalist, behavioral, managerial'. *American Economic Review*, vol. 57, March, pp. 1–33.

Malerba, F. (1993) 'The national innovation system: Italy'. In R. R. Nelson (ed.), *National Innovation Systems*. Oxford University Press, Oxford.

Mann, H. M. (1966) 'Seller concentration, barriers to entry, and rates of return in 30 industries, 1950–1960'. *Review of Economics and Statistics*, vol. 43, August, pp. 296–307.

Mannering, F. (1991) 'Brand loyalty and the decline of American automobile firms'. *Brookings Papers on Economic Activity*, Washington, no. 1, pp. 67–114.

Manser, W. A. P. (1994) *Control from Brussels*. Addison-Wesley (and Economist Intelligence Unit), Wokingham, Berkshire.

Mansfield, E. (1961) 'Technical change and the rate of imitation'. *Econometrica*, vol. 29, no. 4, pp. 741–66.

Mansfield, E. (1968) *The Economics of Technical Change*. Norton, New York.

Mansfield, E. (1971) *Research and Innovation in the Modern Corporation*. Norton, New York.

Mansfield, E. (1986) 'Patents and innovation: an empirical study'. *Management Science*, vol. 32, February.

Mansfield, E. (1993) *Managerial Economics: Theory, Applications, and Cases*. Norton, New York.

Mansfield, E., J. Rapoport, A. Romeo, S. Wagner and G. Beardsley (1977) 'Social and private rates of return from industrial innovations'. *Quarterly Journal of Economics*, vol. 10, pp. 221–40.

Marbach, Ch. (1990) 'L'industrie de l'après-1990'. *Politique Industrielle*, no. 21, pp. 71–88.

March, J. G. and H. A. Simon (1958) *Organization*. Wiley, New York.

Marcus, M. (1969) 'Profitability and the size of the firm'. *Review of Economics and Statistics*, vol. 51, pp. 104–7; reprinted in B. Yamey (1973).

Marfels, C. (1988) *Recent Trends in Concentration in Selected Industries of the European Community, Japan and the United States*. Luxemburg, EC.

Markham, J. W. (1951) 'The nature and significance of price leadership' *American Economic Review*, vol. 41, December, pp. 891–905.

Marris, R. (1963) 'A model of the "managerial" enterprise'. *Quarterly Journal of Economics*, no. 77, May, pp. 185–209.

Marris, R. (1966) *The Economic Theory of Managerial Capitalism*. Macmillan, London.

Marshall, A. (1898) *Principles of Economics*, Macmillan, London.

Marshall, A. (1961) *Principles of Economics*, 8th edn. Macmillan, London.

Martin, S. (1988) *Industrial Economics*. Macmillan, London.

Martin, S. (1993) *Advanced Industrial Economics*. Blackwell, Cambridge, MA.

Martin, S. (1994) *Industrial Economics: Economic Analysis and Public Policy*. Macmillan, New York.

Marx, K. (1972) *Capital*. J. M. Dent, London, (First published, in German, in 1867.)

Maschke, E. (1914) Grundzüge der deutschen Kartellgeschichte bis 1914, Dortmund.

Maskin, E. and J. Tirole (1992) 'The principal-agent relationship with an informed principal, II: common values'. *Econometrica*, vol. 60, no. 1, pp. 1–42.

Mason, E. S. (1939) 'Price and production policies of large scale enterprise'. *American Economic Review*, supplement 29, pp. 61–74.

Mason, E. S. (1949) 'The current state of the monopoly problem in the United States'. *Harvard Law Review*, vol. 62, pp. 1265–85.

Mayer, T.F. and Y. Varoufakis (1993/94) 'Game theory: an exchange'. *Science and Society*, vol. 57, no. 4, pp. 446–60.

Mayes, D. G., T. Buxton and A. Murfin (1990) 'R&D, innovation and trade performance'. In B. Dankbaar, J. Groenewegen and H. Schenk (eds), *Perspectives in Industrial Organization*. Kluwer, Dordrecht.

Meehan, J. W. and T. D. Duchesneau (1973) 'The critical level of concentration: an empirical analysis'. *Journal of Industrial Economics*, vol. 22, September, pp. 21–30.

Messerlin, P. (1987) 'France: the ambitious state'. In F. Duchêne and G. Shepherd (eds), *Managing Industrial Change in Western Europe*. Pinter, London.

Milgrom, P. and J. Roberts (1982) 'Limit pricing and entry under incomplete information: an equilibrium analysis'. *Econometrica*, vol. 50, pp. 443–59.

Milgrom, P. and J. Roberts (1992) *Economics, Organization and Management*. Prentice-Hall, Englewood Cliffs, NJ.

Miller, J. G. (1943) *Origins of the American Revolution*. Little, Brown, Boston.

Mirrlees, J. (1976) 'The optimum structure of incentives and authority within an organization'. *Bell Journal of Economics*, vol. 7, pp. 105–31.

Mizuno, M. and H. Odagiri (1990) 'Does advertising mislead consumers to buy low-quality products'. *International Journal of Industrial Organization*, vol. 8, no. 4, pp. 545–58.

Moerland, P. (1991) 'Efficacy and freedom of mergers and acquisitions'. In P. de Wolf (ed.), *Competition in Europe*. Kluwer Academic, Dordrecht.

Molle, W. (1990) *The Economics of European Integration: Theory, Practice, Policy*. Brookfield, Aldershot/Dartmouth, USA.

Montfort, J. (1983) 'A la recherche des filières de production'. *Economie et Statistique*, no. 151, January, pp. 3–12.

Mowery, D. C. (1990) 'The development of industrial research in US manufacturing'. *American Economic Review*, vol. 80, no. 2, pp. 345–54.

Mowery, D. C. and N. Rosenberg (1993) 'The U.S. National Innovation System'. In R. Nelson (ed.), *National Innovation Systems*. Oxford University Press, Oxford.

Müller, J. and N. Owen (1985) 'The effect of trade on plant size'. In J. Schwalbach (ed.), *Industry Structure and Performance*. Sigma, Berlin.

Murphy, K. J. (1985) 'Corporate performance and managerial remuneration'. *Journal of Accounting and Economics*, vol. 7, April, pp. 11–42.

Musgrave, R. A. (1959) *The Theory of Public Finance*. McGraw-Hill, New York.

Mytelka, Z. and K. M. Delapierre (1987) 'The alliance strategies of European firms in the information and technology industry and the role of ESPRIT'. *Journal of Common Market Studies*, vol. 26, no. 2, December, pp. 231–53.

Nagler, M. G. (1993) 'Rather bait than switch: deceptive advertising with bounded consumer rationality'. *Journal of Public Economics*, vol. 51, no. 3, pp. 359–78.

Nash, J. F. (1951) 'Non-cooperative games'. *Annals of Mathematics*, vol. 54, no. 2, pp. 286–95.

Nelson, P. (1974) 'Advertising as information'. *Journal of Political Economy*, vol. 82, July/August, pp. 729–54.

Nelson, R. R. (1984) *High Technology Policies: A Five Nation Comparison*. American Enterprise Institute, Washington DC.

Nelson, R. R. (1992) 'National innovation systems: a retrospective on a study'. *Industrial and Corporate Change*, vol. 1, no. 2, pp. 347–73.

Nelson, R. R. (ed.) (1993) *National Innovation Systems: A Comparative Analysis*. Oxford University Press, Oxford.

Nelson, R. R. (1995) 'Recent evolutionary theorizing about economic change'. *Journal of Economic Literature*, vol. 33, no. 1, pp. 48–90.

Nelson, R. R. and S. G. Winter (1982) *An Evolutionary Theory of Economic Change*. Harvard University Press, Cambridge, MA.

Neumann, M., I. Böbel and A. Haid (1979) 'Profitability, risk and market structure in West German industries'. *Journal of Industrial Economics*, vol. 27, March, pp. 227–42.

Nicolaides, P. (ed.) (1993) *Industrial Policy in the European Community: A Necessary Response to Economic Integration?* Martinus Nijhoff, Dordrecht.

Nielsen, J., H. Heinrich and J. Hansen (1991) *An Economic Analysis of the EC*. McGraw-Hill, Maidenhead, Berkshire.

Niosi, J., B. Bellon, P. Saviotti and M. Crow (1992) 'Les systèmes nationaux d'innovation: à la recherche d'un concept utilisable'. *Revue d'Economie Française*, vol. 7, no. 1, pp. 215–50.

Norman, G. and M. La Manna (eds) (1992) *The New Industrial Economics*. Edward Elgar, Aldershot.

North, D. C. (1990) *Institutions, Institutional Change and Economic Performance*. Cambridge University Press, Cambridge.

Nugent, N. (1994) 'The political environment'. In N. Nugent and R. O'Donnell (eds), *The European Business Environment*. Macmillan, London.

Nugent, N. and R. O'Donnell (eds) (1994) *The European Business Environment*. Macmillan, London.

Odagiri, H. and A. Goto (1993) 'The Japanese system of innovation: past, present and future'. In R. Nelson (ed.) *National Innovation Systems*. Oxford University Press, Oxford.

O'Donnell, R. (1994) 'The economic environment'. In N. Nugent and R. O'Donnell (eds), *The European Business Environment*. Macmillan, London.

O'Donnellan, N. (1994) 'The presence of Porter's clustering in Irish manufacturing'. *Economic and Social Review*, vol. 25, no. 3, pp. 221–32.

OECD (1972) *The Industrial Policy in Japan*. OECD, Paris.

OECD (1985) *The Semi-Conductor Industry, Trade and Related Issues*. OECD, Paris.

OECD (1986) *Science and Technology Indicators II: R&D, Invention and Competitiveness*. OECD, Paris, pp. 58–61.

OECD (1988) *New Technologies in the 1990s: A Socio-economic Strategy*. OECD, Paris.

OECD (1989) *Predatory Pricing*. OECD, Paris.

OECD (1990) *Competition Policy and the Deregulation of Road Transport*. OECD, Paris.

OECD (1991a) *Trade, Investment and Technology in the 1990s*. OECD, Paris.

OECD (1991b) *Science and Technology Indicators Report*. OECD, Paris.

OECD (1991c) *Industrial Policy in OECD Countries. Annual Review*. OECD, Paris.

OECD (1992) *Science and Technology Policy—Review and Outlook*. OECD, Paris.

OECD (1993a) *Basic Science and Technology Statistics*. OECD, Paris.

OECD (1993b) *OECD Economic Surveys*: Denmark. OECD, Paris.

OECD (1994) *Science and Technology Policy—Review and Outlook*. OECD, Paris.

OECD (1995) *Main Science and Technology Indicators*. OECD, Paris.

Okuno, M. (ed.) (1988) *Industrial Policy of Japan*. California Academic Press, San Diego.

O'Malley, E. (1989) *Industry and Economic Development; the Challenge of the Latecomer*. Gill and Macmillan, Dublin.

O'Malley, L. (1982) *Business Law*, Sweet & Maxwell, London.

Ordonez de Haro, J. M. (1993) 'Effectos de la publicidad estrategica en una industria con producto diferenciados'. *Investigaciones Economicas*, vol. 17, no. 3, pp. 527–49.

Ornstein, S. I. (1977) *Industrial Concentration and Advertising Intensity*. American Enterprise Institute, Washington DC.

Ozaki, R. (1991) *Human Capitalism: The Japanese Enterprise System as World Model*. Kodansha International, Tokyo.

Pagoulatos, E. and R. Sorenson (1976) 'Foreign trade, concentration and profitability in open economies'. *European Economic Review*, vol. 8, pp. 255–67.

Panorama of European Industry, 1993 (1993) Commission of the European Communities.

Pareto, V. (1911) 'Economie mathématique'. *Encyclopedie des Sciences Mathematiques*, tome 1, vol. 4, Paris.

Parris, H., P. Pestieau and P. Saynor (1987) *Public Enterprise in Western Europe*. Croom Helm, London.

Pascoe, G. and L. W. Weiss (1983) 'The extent and permanence of market dominance'. Federal Trade Commission, Washington DC (unpublished paper).

Pashigian, B. P. (1968) 'Limit price and the market share of the leading firm'. *Journal of Industrial Economics*, vol. 16, July, pp. 165–77.

Patel, P. and K. Pavitt (1991) 'Europe's technological performance'. In C. Freeman, M. Sharp and W. Walker (eds), *Technology and the Future of Europe*. Pinter, London.

Pavitt, K. (1982) 'R&D, patenting and innovative activities: a statistical exploration'. *Research Policy*, vol. 11, no. 1.

Pavitt, K. (1985) 'Patent statistics as indicators of innovative activities: possibilities and problems'. *Scientometrics*, vol. 7, nos 1–2, January.

Pavitt, K. (1987) 'International patterns of technological accumulation'. In N. Hood and J. E. Vahne (eds), *Strategies in Global Competition*. Croom Helm, London.

Pavitt, K. (1994) 'Key characteristics of large innovating firms'. In M. Dodgson and R. Rothwell (eds), *Handbook of Industrial Innovation*. Edward Elgar, Aldershot.

Pavitt, K. and M. Sharp (1992) 'Key technologies and new industrial policies'. Paper at Conference, Europe and Global Economic Interdependence, Brugge, January.

Peacock, A. (1979) 'The limitations of public goods theory: the lighthouse revisited'. in A. Peacock (ed.), *The Economic Analysis of Government*. Martin Robertson, Oxford.

Pearson, E. S. (1994) *Law for European Business Studies*. Pitman, London.

Pelkmans, J. (1984) *Market Integration in the European Community*. Martinus Nijhoff, The Hague.

Penrose, E. T. (1959) *The Theory of Growth of the Firm*. Blackwell, Oxford.

Petrella, R. (1991) *Four Analyses of Globalisation of Technology and Economy*. FAST, Commission of the EC, Brussels.

Peyrard, J. (1990) 'Les théories des investissements directs à l'étranger dans les pays industrialisés depuis 1950'. In A. Androuais (ed.) *L'Investissement extérieur direct.* University Press, Grenoble.

Philipps, A. (1976) 'A critique of empirical studies of relations between market structure and profitability'. *Journal of Industrial Economics*, vol. 24, June, pp. 241–9.

Phlips, L. (1971) *Effects of Industrial Concentration: A Cross Section Analysis for the Common Market.* North-Holland, Amsterdam.

Phlips, L. (1983) *The Economics of Price Discrimination.* Cambridge University Press, Cambridge.

Pigou, A. C. (1932) *The Economics of Welfare.* Macmillan, London.

Pinder, J. (ed.) (1982) *National Industrial Strategies and the World Economy.* Allanheld, Osmun Publishers, Croom Helm, London.

Piore, M. J. (1990) 'Work, labour and action: Work experience in a system of flexible production'. In F. Pyke *et al.* (eds), *Industrial Districts and Inter-Firm Co-operation in Italy.* International Institute for Labour Studies, Geneva.

Piore, M. and C. F. Sabel (1984) *The Second Industrial Divide: Possibilities for Prosperity.* Basic Books, New York.

Poirier, D. (1976) *The Econometrics of Structural Change.* North-Holland, Amsterdam.

Porter, M. E. (1974) Consumer behavior, retailer power and market performance in consumer goods industries'. *Review of Economics and Statistics*, vol. 56, no. 4, pp. 419–36.

Porter, M. E. (1990) *The Competitive Advantage of Nations.* Macmillan, London.

Porter, M. E. (1991) 'Towards a dynamic theory of strategy'. *Strategic Management Journal*, vol. 12, winter, pp. 95–117.

Porter, R. H. (1991) 'A review essay on *Handbook of Industrial Organization*'. *Journal of Economic Literature*, vol. 29, no. 2, pp. 553–72.

Posner, M. V. (1961) 'International trade and technical change'. *Oxford Economic Papers*, vol. 13, October, pp. 323–41.

Posner, R. A. (1969) 'Natural monopoly and its regulation'. *Stanford Law Review*, vol. 21, February, pp. 548–643.

Prakke, F. (1988) 'Le Financement de l'Innovation Technologique'. In A. Heertje (ed.), *Innovation, Technologie et Finance.* Basil Blackwell, Oxford.

Pratten, C. (1987) *A Survey of Economies of Scale.* Report prepared for the EC Commission, Brussels.

Prestowitz, C. V. (1988) *Trading Places: How we Allowed Japan to Take the Lead.* Basic Books, New York.

Pyke, F. and W. Sengenberger (eds) (1992) *Industrial Districts and Local Economic Regeneration.* International Institute for Labour Studies, Geneva.

Pyke, F., G. Becattini and W. Sengenberger (eds) (1990) *Industrial Districts and Inter-Firm Co-operation in Italy.* International Institute for Labour Studies, Geneva.

Qualls, P. D. (1972) 'Concentration, barriers to entry and long run economic profit margins'. *Journal of Industrial Economics*, vol. 20, April, pp. 146–58.

Radner, R. (1992) 'Hierarchy: the economics of managing'. *Journal of Economic Literature*, vol. 30, no. 3, pp. 1382–1415.

Ranci, P. (1987) 'Italy: the weak state'. In F. Duchêne and G. Shepherd (eds), *Managing Industrial Change in Western Europe.* Pinter, London.

Ranci, P. and R. Helg (1987) *Economies of Scale and the Integration of the European Economy: the Case of Italy.* Report prepared for the EC Commission, Brussels.

Ray, G. F. (1984) *The Diffusion of Mature Technologies.* Cambridge University Press, Cambridge.

Reekie, W. D. and J. N. Crook (1995) *Managerial Economics*. Prentice Hall, Hemel Hempstead.

Reich, R. (1992) *The Work of Nations*. Vintage Books, New York.

Rhys, G. (1993) 'Motor vehicles'. In P. Johnson (ed.), *European Industries: Structure, Conduct and Performance*. Edward Elgar, Aldershot.

Richonnier, M. (1984) 'Europe's decline is not irreversible'. *Journal of Common Market Studies*, vol. 22, no. 3.

Rob, R. (1992) 'Sales, uncertainty and the determinants of investment'. Univ. of Pennsylvania CARESS Working Paper, 92-03.

Robertson, P. L. and R. N. Langlois (1994) 'Institutions, inertia and changing industrial leadership'. *Industrial and Corporate Change*, **3**, no. 2, pp. 359–378.

Robertson, P. L. and R. N. Langlois (1995) 'Innovation, networks, and vertical integration'. *Research Policy*, vol. 24, no. 4, pp. 543–62.

Robertson, T. S. (1971) *Innovative Behavior and Communication*. Holt, Rinehart & Winston, New York and London.

Robinson, E. A. G. (1958) *The Structure of Competitive Industry*. University of Chicago Press, Chicago.

Robinson, J. (1933) *The Economics of Imperfect Competition*. Macmillan, London.

Robinson, J. (1956) *The Accumulation of Capital*. Macmillan, London.

Root, F. R. (1990) *International Trade and Investment*. South-Western, Cincinnati, Ohio.

Roscam, A., M. Schakenraad and J. Schakenraad (1991) *Intended and Unintended Effects of Participation in ESPRIT and EUREKA for Small Countries' Industrial Policies*. MERIT, Maastricht.

Rosenberg, N. (1963) 'Technological change in the machine tool industry'. *Journal of Economic History*, vol. 23.

Ross, S. A. (1973) 'The economic theory of agency: the principal's problem'. *American Economic Review*, vol. 63, no. 2, pp. 134–9.

Rostow, W. W. (1960a) *The Process of Economic Growth*. Clarendon Press, Oxford.

Rostow, W. W. (1960b) *The Stages of Economic Growth*. Cambridge University Press, Cambridge.

Rotemberg, J. J. and G. Saloner (1986) 'A supergame-theoretic model of price wars during booms'. *American Economic Review*, vol. 76, pp. 390–407.

Rothwell, R. (1987) 'Technology policy in Britain'. In P. R. Beije *et al.* (eds), *A Competitive Future for Europe?* Croom Helm, New York.

Rothwell, R. and M. Dodgson (1994) 'Innovation and size of firm'. In M. Dodgson and R. Rothwell (eds) *The Handbook of Industrial Innovation*. Edward Elgar, Hemel Hempstead.

Rowthorn, R. (1971) 'International Big Business 1957–1967: A Study of Comparative Growth'. Occasional Paper, No. 24, University of Cambridge, Cambridge University Press, Cambridge.

Russell, B. (1965) *German Social Democracy*. Allen and Unwin, London.

Sabel, C. F. (1989) 'Flexible specialisation and the re-emergence of regional economies'. In P. Hirst and J. Zeitlin (eds), *Reversing Industrial Decline? Industrial Structure and Policy in Britain and Her Competitors*. Berg, Oxford.

Saloner, G. (1991) 'Modeling, game theory and strategic management'. *Strategic Management Journal*, vol. 12, winter, pp. 119–36.

Samuels, J. M. and Smyth, D. J. (1968) Profits, variability of profits and firm size. *Economica*, vol. 35, pp. 127–39.

Sapir, A. (1993) 'Regionalism and the new theory of international trade: do the bells toll for GATT? A European outlook'. *World Development*, vol. 16, no. 4, pp. 423–38.

Say, J.-B. (1803) *Traité d'économie politique ou simple exposition de la manière dont se forment, se distribuent et se consomment les richesses*, 1st edn. Paris.

Scassellati, A. (1991) 'European integration in the context of international capital'. *Socialism and Democracy*, no. 13, May, pp. 159–65.

Schelling, T. C. (1960) *The Strategy of Conflict*. Harvard University Press, Cambridge, MA.

Scherer, F. M. (1965) 'Firm size, market structure, opportunity, and the output of patented inventions'. *American Economic Review*, pp. 1097–126.

Scherer, F. M. (1970) *Industrial Market Structure and Economic Performance*. Rand McNally, Chicago.

Scherer, F. M. (1979) 'The causes and consequences of rising industrial concentration'. *Journal of Law and Economics*, vol. 22, April, pp. 191–211.

Scherer, F. M. (1992) *International High-Technology Competition*. Harvard University Press, Cambridge, MA.

Scherer, F. M. and D. Ross (1990) *Industrial Market Structure and Economic Performance*. Houghton Mifflin, Boston.

Schmalensee, R. L. (1973) 'A note on the theory of vertical integration'. *Journal of Political Economy*, no. 81, March–April, pp. 442–9.

Schmalensee, R. (1974) 'Brand loyalty and barriers to entry'. *Southern Economic Journal*, April, pp. 579–88.

Schmalensee, R. (1978a) 'Entry-deterrence in the ready-to-eat breakfast cereal industry'. *Bell Journal of Economics*, vol. 9, autumn, pp. 305–27.

Schmalensee, R. (1978b) 'A model of advertising and product quality'. *Journal of Political Economy*, vol. 86, pp. 485–504.

Schmalensee, R. (1981) 'Output and welfare implications of monopolistic third-degree discrimination'. *American Economic Review*, vol. 71, pp. 242–7.

Schmalensee, R. (1987) 'Industrial organization'. In J. Eatwell *et al.* (eds), *The New Palgrave Dictionary of Economics*. Macmillan, London.

Schmalensee, R. and R. D. Willig (eds) (1989) *Handbook of Industrial Organization*, vol. 1. North-Holland, Amsterdam.

Schmitz, H. (1992) 'Industrial districts: model and reality in Baden-Württemberg, Germany'. In F. Pyke and W. Sengenberger (eds), *Industrial Districts and Local Economic Regeneration*. International Institute for Labour Studies, Geneva.

Schmitz, H. and B. Musyck (1994) 'Industrial districts in Europe: policy lessons for developing countries?' *World Development*, vol. 22, no. 6, pp. 889–910.

Schumpeter, J. A. (1912) *Theorie der Wirtschaftlichen Entwicklung*. Duncker & Humboldt, Leipzig.

Schumpeter, J. A. (1934) *The Theory of Economic Development*. Harvard University Press, Cambridge, MA.

Schumpeter, J. A. (1939) *Business Cycles*. McGraw-Hill, New York.

Schumpeter, J. A. (1943) *Capitalism, Socialism and Democracy*. Allen and Unwin, London.

Schuster, G. (1990) 'Technology policy'. In C. C. Schweitzer and D. Karsten (eds), *FRG and EC Membership Evaluated*. Pinter, London.

Schwalbach, J. (1988) 'Economies of scale and intra-community trade'. In *Research on the 'Costs of non-Europe'*. CEC, vol. 2, Ch. 3.

Schwartz, D. (1973) 'Zum Stand der Wirtschaftskonzentration im Gemeinsamen Markt'. *Der Bürger im Staat*, vol. 4.

Schwartzman, D. (1959) 'Effect of monopoly on price'. *Journal of Political Economy*, vol. 67, August, pp. 352–62.

Scitovsky, T. (1943–44) 'A note on profit-maximization and its implications'. *Review of Economic Studies*, no. 11, pp. 57–60.

Scott, A. J. (1988) *New Industrial Spaces: Flexible Production Organization and Regional Development in North America and Western Europe*. Pion, London.

Selten, R. (1978) 'The chain store paradox'. *Theory and Decision*, vol. 9, pp. 127–59.

Semlinger, K. (1991) 'New developments in subcontracting: mixing markets and hierarchy'. In A. Amin and M. Dietrich (eds), *Towards a New Europe?* Edward Elgar, Aldershot.

Servan-Schreiber, J.-J. (1967) *Le défi américain*. Denoël, Paris.

Shaffer, S. (1991) 'Consistent conjectures in a Value-Maximising Duopoly'. *Southern Economic Journal*, vol. 57, no. 4, pp. 993–1009.

Shaked, A. and J. Sutton (1987) 'Product differentiation and industrial structure'. *Journal of Industrial Economics*, vol. 36, no. 2, pp. 131–46.

Shapiro, C. (1980) 'Advertising and welfare: comment'. *Bell Journal of Economics*, vol. 11, no. 2, pp. 749–52.

Sharp, M. (1990) 'Technology and the dynamics of integration'. In W. Walker (ed.), *The Dynamics of European Integration*. Pinter (for RIIA), London.

Sharp, M. L. (1991) 'Pharmaceuticals and biotechnology: perspectives for European industry'. In C. Freeman, M. Sharp and W. Walker (eds), *Technology and the Future of Europe*. Pinter, London.

Sharp, M. and K. Pavitt (1993) 'Technology policy in the 1990s: old trends and new realities'. *Journal of Common market Studies*, vol. 31, no. 2, pp. 129–51.

Sharp, M. and C. Shearman (1987) *European Technological Collaboration*. Routledge & Kegan Paul, London.

Shaw, R. (1982) 'Product proliferation in characteristics space: the UK fertilizer industry'. *Journal of Industrial Economics*, vol. 31, nos 1–2, pp. 69–92.

Shaw, R. and P. Simpson (1985) 'The Monopolies Commission and the persistence of monopolies'. *Journal of Industrial Economics*, vol. 34, pp. 355–72.

Shepherd, W. G. (1972a) The elements of market structure. *Review of Economics and Statistics*, vol. 54, no. 1, February 1972, pp. 25–37.

Shepherd, W. G. (1972b) 'Structure and behaviour in British industry'. *Journal of Industrial Economics*, vol. 21, pp. 35–54.

Shepherd, W. G. (1975) *The Treatment of Market Power*. Columbia University Press, New York.

Shepherd, W. G. (1990) *The Economics of Industrial Organization*. Prentice-Hall, Englewood Cliffs, NJ.

Shetty, Y. K. and V. M. Buehler (eds) (1983) *Quality and Productivity Improvements: US and Foreign Company Experiences*. Manufacturing Productivity Center, Chicago.

Shughart, W. F. (1990) *The Organization of Industry*. Irwin, Boston.

Simon, H. (1959) 'Theories of decision-making in economics and behavioral science'. *American Economic Review*, vol. 49, June, pp. 253–83.

Simon, H. A. and C. P. Bonini (1958) 'The size distribution of business firms'. *American Economic Review*, vol. 48, September, pp. 607–17.

Singh, A. (1972) *Takeovers: Their Relevance to the Stock Market and the Theory of the Firm*. Cambridge University Press, London.

Singh, A. and G. Whittington (1968) *Growth, Profitability and Valuation*. Cambridge University Press, Cambridge.

Singh, A. and G. Whittington (1975) 'The size and growth of firms'. *Review of Economic Studies*, vol. 42, no. 1, pp. 15–26.

Slade, M. (1987) 'Interfirm rivalry in a repeated game: an empirical test of tacit collusion'. *Journal of Industrial Economics*, vol. 35, no. 4, pp. 499–516.

Sleuwaegen, L. (1993) 'Road Haulage'. In CEC (1993e), pp. 215–250.

Sleuwaegen, L. and H. Yamawaki (1988) 'The formation of the European Common Market and changes in market structure and performance'. *International Journal of Industrial Organization*, vol. 32, no. 7, pp. 1451–75.

Smith, A. (1776) *An Inquiry into the Nature and Causes of the Wealth of Nations*. Reprinted 1976. Chicago University Press, Chicago.

Smirlock, M., Th. Gilligan and W. Marshall (1984) 'Tobin's q and the structure–performance relationship'. *American Economic Review*, vol. 74, December, pp. 1051–60.

Soete, L. (1979) 'Firm size and inventive activity: the evidence reconsidered'. *European Economic Review*, pp. 312–90.

Soete, L. L. G. (1981) 'A general test of technological trade theory'. *Weltwirtschaftliches Archiv.*, vol. 117, no. 4, pp. 638–66.

Solo, R. A. (1982) *The Positive State*. Cincinatti, South-Western Publishing.

Solow, R. M. (1957) 'Technical change and the aggregate production function'. *Review of Economics and Statistics*, vol. 39, pp. 312–20.

Spence, A. M. (1977) 'Entry, capacity, investment and oligopolistic pricing'. *Bell Journal of Economics*, vol. 8, pp. 534–44.

Sraffa, P. (1926) 'The laws of returns under competitive conditions'. *Economic Journal*, vol. 26, pp. 535–50.

Steedman, H., G. Mason and K. Wagner (1991) 'Intermediate skills in the workplace: deployment, standards and supply in Britain, France and Germany'. *National Institute Economic Review*, May, pp. 60–73.

Steiner, R. L. (1973) 'Does advertising lower consumer prices?' *Journal of marketing*, vol. 37, October, pp. 19–26.

Stephen, F. H., J. H. Love, D. D. Gillanders and A. A. Paterson (1993) 'Deregulation and price discrimination in the conveyencing market'. *Managerial and Decision Economics*, vol. 14, no. 4, pp. 365–75.

Steuart, S. (1767) *An Inquiry into the Principles of Political Economy: Being an Essay on the Science of Domestic Policy in Free Nations*, 1st edn. London.

Stevens, J. L. (1990) 'Tobin's q and the structure-performance relationship: comment'. *American Economic Review*, vol. 80, no. 3, pp. 618–21.

Stewart, J. C. (1989) 'Transfer pricing: some empirical evidence from Ireland'. *Journal of Economic Issues*, vol. 16, no. 3.

Stigler, G. J. (1947) 'The kinky oligopoly demand curve and rigid prices'. *Journal of Political Economy*, vol. 55, October, pp. 444–6.

Stigler, G. J. (1961) 'The economics of information'. *Journal of Political Economy*, vol. 69, June, pp. 213–25.

Stigler, G. J. (1963) *Capital and Rates of Return in Manufacturing Industries*. Princeton University Press, Princeton, NJ.

Stigler, G. J. (1966) *The Theory of Price*, 3rd edn. Macmillan, London.

Stigler, G. J. (1968) *The Organization of Industry*. Irwin, Homewood, Ill.

Stigler, G. J. (1971) 'The economic theory of regulation'. *Bell Journal of Economics*, vol. 2, no. 1, pp. 3–21.

Stiglitz, J. (1974) 'Incentives and risk sharing in sharecropping'. *Review of Economic Studies*, vol. 64, pp. 219–56.

Stiglitz, J. E. (1991) 'Symposium on organizations and economics'. *Journal of Economic Perspectives*, vol. 5, no. 2, pp. 15–24.

Stiglitz, J. E. and G. F. Mathewson (eds) (1986) *New Developments in the Analysis of Market Structure*. Macmillan, London.

Stoffaes, C. (1980) 'Politique industrielle et filières'. *Revue d'Economie Industrielle*, no. 13, 3rd quarter.

Stolper, W. F. (1994) *Schumpeter*. Princeton University Press, Princeton.

Stoneman, P. (1983) *The Economic Analysis of Technological Change*. Oxford University Press, Oxford.

Storper, M. and R. Walker (1989) *The Capitalist Imperative: Territory, Technology and Industrial Growth*. Blackwell, Oxford.

Strange, S. (1991) 'Big business and the state'. *Millenium: Journal of International Studies*, vol. 20, no. 2, pp. 245–50.

Sugden, R. (ed.) (1993) *Industrial Economic Regulation: A Framework and Exploration*. Routledge, London.

Summers, H. B. (1932) 'A comparison of the rates of large-scale and small-scale industries'. *Quarterly Journal of Economics*, vol. 46, May, pp. 465–79.

Sweezy, P. (1939) 'Demand under conditions of oligopoly'. *Journal of Political Economy*, vol. 47, no. 4, pp. 568–73.

Sylos-Labini, P. (1962) *Oligopoly and Technical Progress*. Harvard University Press, Cambridge, MA.

Teece, D. J. (1982) 'Towards an economic theory of the multiproduct firm'. *Journal of Economic Behavior and Organization*, vol. 3, pp. 39–63.

Teece, D. J. (ed.) (1987) *The Competitive Challenge*. Ballinger, Cambridge, MA.

Telser, L. G. (1987) *A Theory of Efficient Cooperation and Competition*. Cambridge University Press, Cambridge.

Thomsen, S. and S. Woolcock (1993) *Direct Investment and European Integration: Competition among Firms and Governments*. RIIA/Pinter, London.

Thornhill, D. J. (1988) 'The revealed comparative advantage of Irish exports of manufactures 1969–1982'. *Journal of the Social and Statistical Enquiry Society of Ireland*, vol. 25, no. 5, pp. 91–146.

Tobin, J. (1969) 'A general equilibrium approach to monetary theory'. *Journal of Money, Credit and Banking*, vol. 1. February, pp. 15–29.

Tobin, J. and W. Brainard (1977) 'Asset markets and the cost of capital'. In B. Ballassa and R. Nelson (eds), *Economic Progress, Private Values and Public Policies: Essays in Honour of William Fellner*. North-Holland, Amsterdam.

Tomlinson, J. (1993) 'Is successful regulation possible? Some theoretical issues'. In R. Sugden (ed.), *Industrial Economic Regulation*. Routledge, London.

Trigilia, C. (1990) 'Work and politics in the Third Italy's industrial districts'. In F. Pyke, G. Becattini and W. Sengenberger (eds), *Industrial Districts and Inter-Firm Co-operation in Italy*. International Institute for Labour Studies, Geneva.

Truel, J. L. (1983) 'Structuration en filière et politique industrielle dans l'electronique: un comparaison internationale'. *Revue d'Economie Industrielle*, no. 23, 1st trimester, pp. 293–303.

Tsoukalis, L. (1991) *The New European Economy: The Politics and Economics of Integration*. Oxford University Press, Oxford.

Turpin, E. (1989) 'Le commerce extérieur français: une spécialisation industrielle fragile'. *Economie et Statistique*, nos 217–18, January–February, pp. 51–61.

UNCTC (1991) *Foreign Direct Investment in the Triad*. United Nations, New York.

UNICE (Union of Industrial and Employers' Confederations of Europe) (1994) *Making Europe More Competitive: Towards World Class Performance*. UNICE, Brussels.

US Congress (1982) *Technology, Innovation, and Regional Economic Development*. Office of Technology Assessment, 9 Sept.

Utton, M. (1971) 'The effects of mergers on concentration. UK manufacturing industry, 1954–1965'. *Journal of Industrial Economics*, vol. 20, no. 1, pp. 42–58.

Utton, M. (1974) 'On measuring the effects of industrial mergers'. *Scottish Journal of Political Economy*, vol. 21, no. 1, pp. 13–27.

Vernon, J. M. and D. A. Graham (1971) 'Profitability of monopolization by vertical integration'. *Journal of Political Economy*, vol. 79, no. 4, pp. 924–5.

Vernon, R. (1966) 'International investment and international trade in the product cycle'. *Quarterly Journal of Economics*, vol. 80, May, pp. 190–207.

Vernon, R. (1992) 'Transnational corporations: where are they coming from, where are they headed?' *Transnational Corporations*, vol. 1, no. 2, August, pp. 7–36.

Viner, J. (1950) *The Customs Union Issue*. Stevens & Sons, New York.

Vipond, P. A. (1994) 'The financial environment'. In N. Nugent and R. O'Donnell (eds), *The European Business Environment*. Macmillan, London.

Vives, X. (1991) 'Banking competition and European integration'. In A. Giovannini and C. P. Mayer (eds), *European Financial Integration*. Cambridge University Press, Cambridge.

von Fürstenburg, G. M. (1977) 'Corporate investment: does market valuation matter in the aggregate?' *Brookings Papers on Economic Activity*, vol. 2, pp. 347–97.

von Neuman, J. and O. Morgenstern (1944) *Theory of Games and Economic Behavior*. Princeton University Press, Princeton, NJ.

von Stackelberg, H. (1934) *Marktform und Gleichgewicht*. Julius Springer, Vienna.

Wade, R. (1988) 'The role of government in overcoming market failure: Taiwan, Republic of Korea and Japan'. In H. Hughes (ed.), *Achieving Industrialization in Asia*. Cambridge University Press, Cambridge.

Wade, R. (1990) *Governing the Market: Economic Theory and the Role of Government in East Asian Industrialization*. Princeton University Press, Princeton, NJ.

Waelbroeck, J. (1962) 'La demande extérieure et l'évolution des exportations belges'. *Cahiers Européens*, Bruxelles, no. 15, July.

Walker, W. (1979) *Industrial Innovation and International Trading Performance*. JAI Press, Greenwich, Conn.

Walker, W. (1991) 'Defence'. In C. Freeman, M. Sharp and W. Walker (eds), *Technology and the Future of Europe*. Pinter, London.

Walker, W. (1993) 'National innovation systems: Britain'. In R. R. Nelson (ed.), *National Innovation Systems: A Comparative Analysis*. Oxford University Press, Oxford.

Warner, M. (1994) 'Innovation and Training'. In M. Dodgson and R. Rothwell (eds), *The Handbook of Industrial Innovation*. Edward Elgar, Aldershot.

Waterson, M. (1982) 'Vertical integration, variable proportions and oligopoly'. *Economic Journal*, vol. 92, March, pp. 129–44.

Waterson, M. (1992) 'International advertising expenditure statistics'. *International Journal of Advertising*, vol. 11, no. 1, pp. 14–68.

Waterson, M. (1993) 'Allocative inefficiency and monopoly as a basis for regulation'. In Sugden (ed.), *Industrial Economic Regulation*. Routledge, London.

Weiss, L. W. (1974) 'The concentration–profits relationship and anti-trust'. In H. Goldschmid *et al.* (eds), *Industrial Concentration: The New Learning*. Little, Brown, Boston, pp. 184–232.

Welford, R. and K. Prescott (1994) *European Business: An Issue-Based Approach*. Pitman, London.

Werlauff, E. (1992) 'The development of Community company law'. *European Law Review*, vol. 17, no. 3, pp. 207–31.

Weston, J. F. (1973) 'The nature and significance of conglomerate firms'. *St John's Law Review*, vol. 44. Reprinted in B. Yamey (1973).

Whalley, J. (1985) *Trade Liberalization among Major World Trading Areas*. MIT Press, Cambridge, MA.

Williams, R. (1989) 'The EC's technological policy as an engine for integration'. *Government and Opposition*, vol. 24, no. 2, pp. 158–76.

Williamson, O. E. (1967) 'Hierarchical control and optimum firm size'. *Journal of Political Economy*, vol. 75, pp. 123–38. Reprinted in B. Yamey (1973).

Williamson, O. E. (1977) 'Predatory pricing: a strategic and welfare analysis. *Yale Law Journal*, vol. 87, no. 2, December, pp. 284–340.

Williamson, O. E. (1979) 'Transaction–cost economics: the governance of contractual relations'. *Journal of Law and Economics*, vol. 22, October, pp. 233–61.

Williamson, O. E. (1985) *The Economic Institutions of Capitalism*. Free Press, New York.

Williamson, O. E. (1992) 'Some issues in the transformation of ownership institutions in Poland: comment'. *Journal of Institutional and Theoretical Economics*, vol. 148, no. 1, pp. 69–71.

Woods, S. (1987) *Western Europe: Technology and the Future*. Paper no. 63, The Atlantic Institute for International Affairs, Croom Helm, London.

Woolcock, S. (1982) 'The international politics of trade and production in the steel industry'. In J. Pinder (ed.), *National Industrial Strategies and the World Economy*. Croom Helm, London.

Woolcock, S. (1984) 'Information technology: the challenge to Europe'. *Journal of Common Market Studies*, vol. 22, no. 4.

Woolcock, S. and H. Wallace (1995) 'European Community regulation and national enterprise'. In J. Hayward (ed.), *Industrial Enterprise and European Integration*. Oxford University Press, Oxford.

World Competitiveness Report (1993) IMD International, Lausanne.

Yamey, B. S. (ed.) (1973) *Economics of Industrial Structure*. Penguin, Harmondsworth.

Yannopoulos, G. N. (1992) 'Multinational corporations and the Single European Market'. In J. Cantwell (ed.), *Multinational Investment in Modern Europe*. Edward Elgar, Aldershot.

Young, S. and S. Dunlop (1992) 'Competitive dynamics in the world machine tool industry: battleground UK'. In S. Young and J. Hamill (eds), *Europe and the Multinationals*. Edward Elgar, Aldershot.

Young, S. and J. Hamill (eds) (1992) *Europe and the Multinationals: Issues and Responses for the 1990s*. Edward Elgar, Aldershot.

Young, S. and N. Hood (1992) 'Transnational corporations and policy dilemmas: the problems of the machine-tool industry in the United Kingdom'. *Transnational Corporations*, vol. 1, no. 3.

Zaphirious, G. A. (1970) *European Business Law*. Sweet & Maxwell, London.

Zysman, J. (1990) 'Trade, technology and national competition'. Paper for OECD Conference, Paris, June.

Index